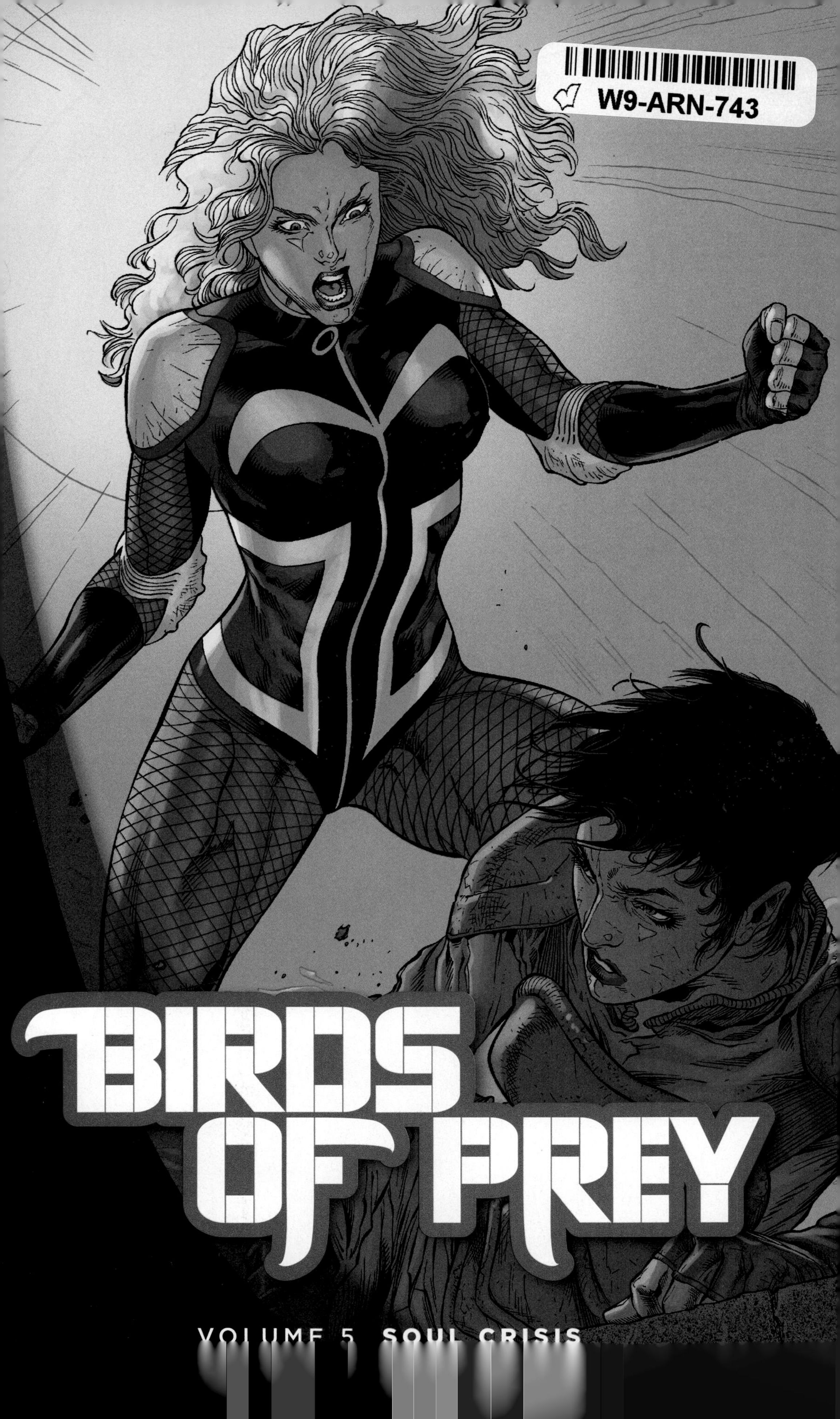
BIRDS OF PREY
VOLUME 5 SOUL CRISIS

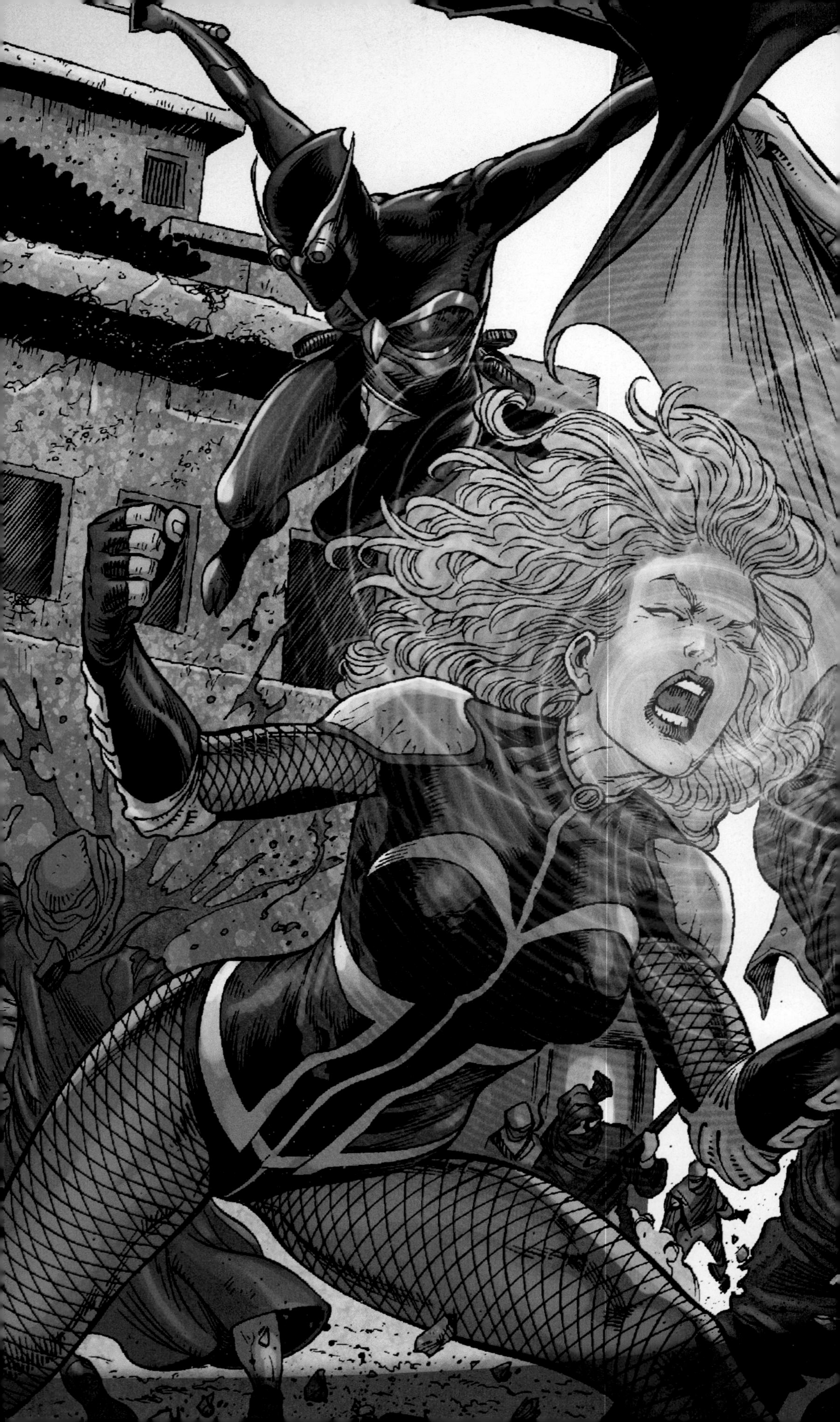

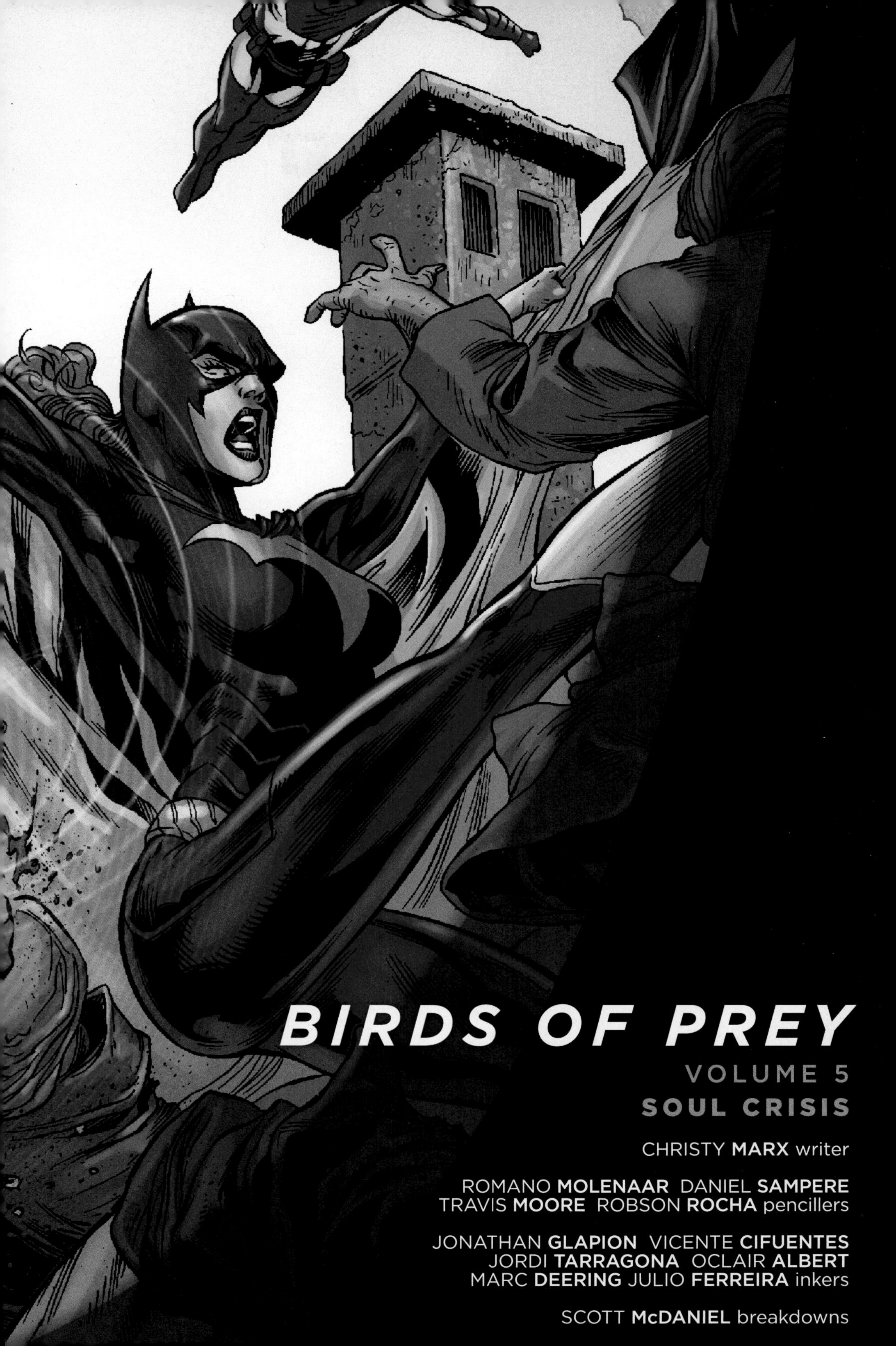

BIRDS OF PREY

VOLUME 5

SOUL CRISIS

CHRISTY **MARX** writer

ROMANO **MOLENAAR** DANIEL **SAMPERE**
TRAVIS **MOORE** ROBSON **ROCHA** pencillers

JONATHAN **GLAPION** VICENTE **CIFUENTES**
JORDI **TARRAGONA** OCLAIR **ALBERT**
MARC **DEERING** JULIO **FERREIRA** inkers

SCOTT **McDANIEL** breakdowns

RACHEL GLUCKSTERN Editor – Original Series DARREN SHAN Associate Editor – Original Series
MATT HUMPHREYS DAVE WIELGOSZ Assistant Editors – Original Series PETER HAMBOUSSI Editor
ROBBIN BROSTERMAN Design Director – Books ROBBIE BIEDERMAN Publication Design

BOB HARRAS Senior VP – Editor-in-Chief, DC Comics

DIANE NELSON President DAN DIDIO and JIM LEE Co-Publishers GEOFF JOHNS Chief Creative Officer
AMIT DESAI Senior VP – Marketing & Franchise Management AMY GENKINS Senior VP – Business & Legal Affairs
NAIRI GARDINER Senior VP – Finance JEFF BOISON VP – Publishing Planning MARK CHIARELLO VP – Art Direction & Design
JOHN CUNNINGHAM VP – Marketing TERRI CUNNINGHAM VP – Editorial Administration LARRY GANEM VP – Talent Relations & Serv
ALISON GILL Senior VP – Manufacturing & Operations HANK KANALZ Senior VP – Vertigo & Integrated Publishing
JAY KOGAN VP – Business & Legal Affairs, Publishing JACK MAHAN VP – Business Affairs, Talent
NICK NAPOLITANO VP – Manufacturing Administration SUE POHJA VP – Book Sales
FRED RUIZ VP – Manufacturing Operations COURTNEY SIMMONS Senior VP – Publicity BOB WAYNE Senior VP – Sales

BIRDS OF PREY VOLUME 5: SOUL CRISIS

DC Comics, 1700 Broadway, New York, NY 10019
A Warner Bros. Entertainment Company.
Printed by RR Donnelley, Owensville, MO, USA. 12/19/14. First Printing.
ISBN: 978-1-4012-5083-6

SUSTAINABLE
FORESTRY
INITIATIVE

Certified Chain of Custody
20% Certified Forest Content,
80% Certified Sourcing
www.sfiprogram.org
SFI-01042
APPLIES TO TEXT STOCK ONLY

Library of Congress Cataloging-in-Publication Data

Marx, Christy, author.
Birds of Prey. Volume 5, Soul Crisis / Christy Marx, writer ; Robson Rocha, Jonathan Glapion, artists.
pages cm. — (The New 52!)
ISBN 978-1-4012-5083-6 (paperback)
1. Graphic novels. I. Rocha, Robson, illustrator. II. Glapion, Jonathan, illustrator. III. Title. IV. Title: Soul Crisis

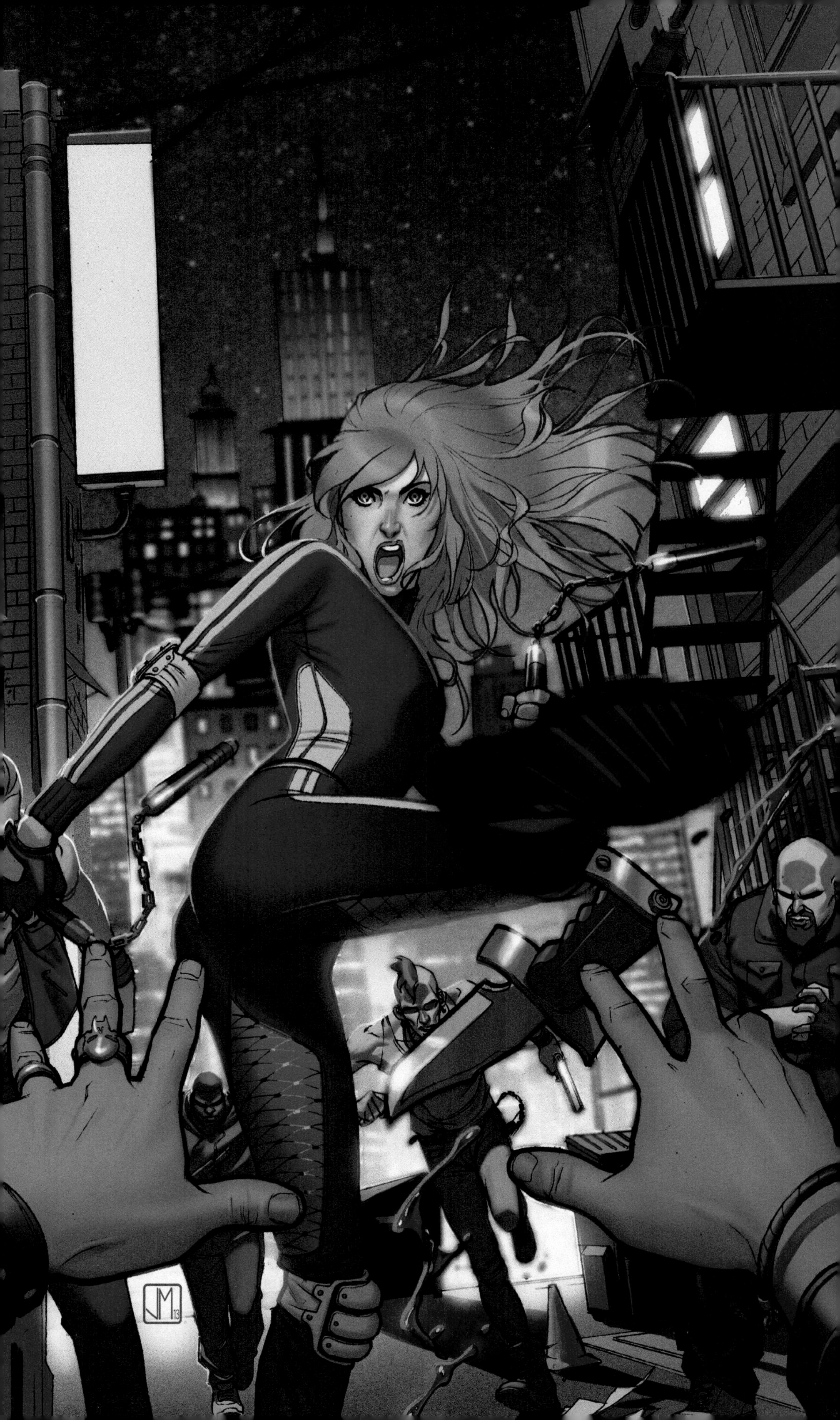

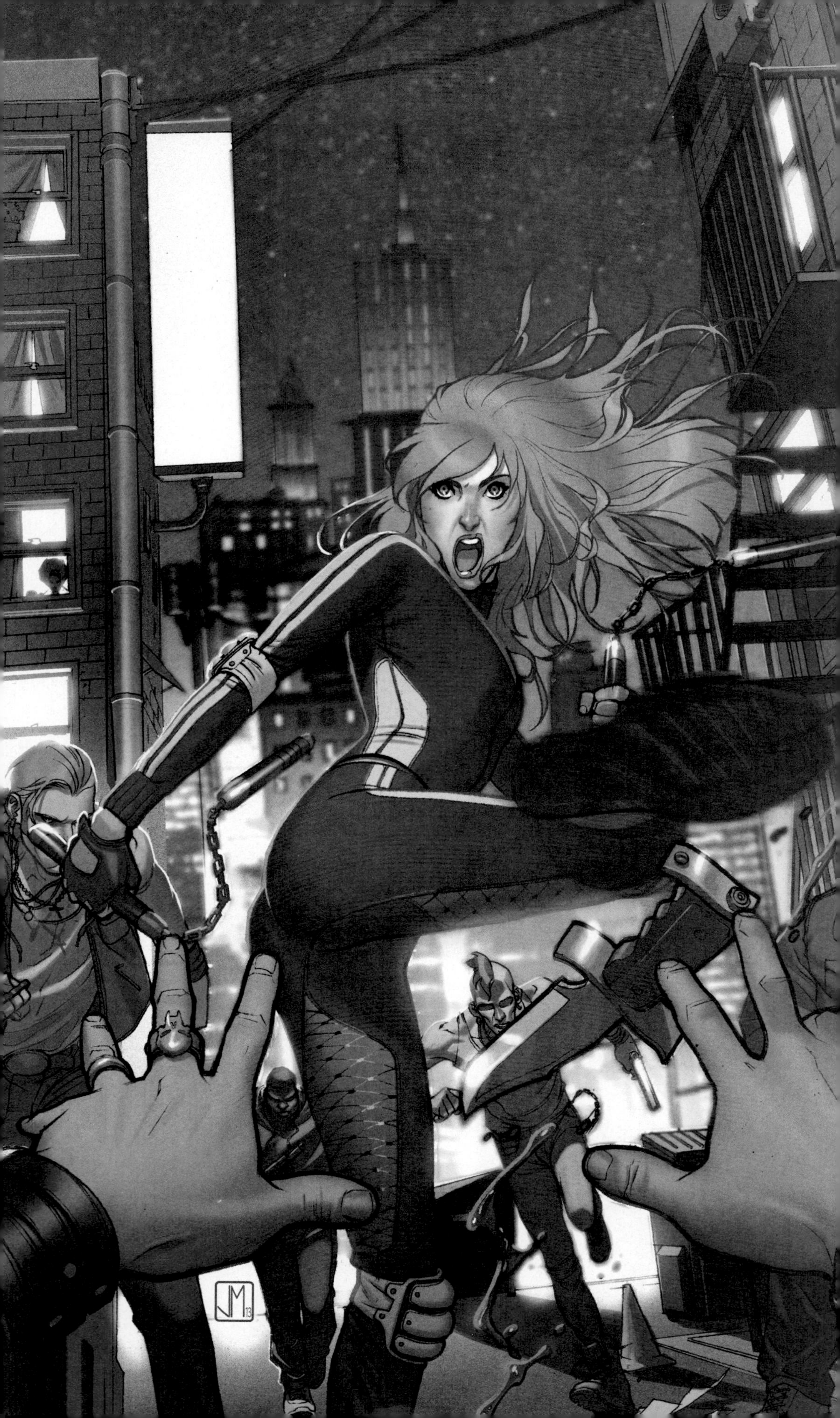

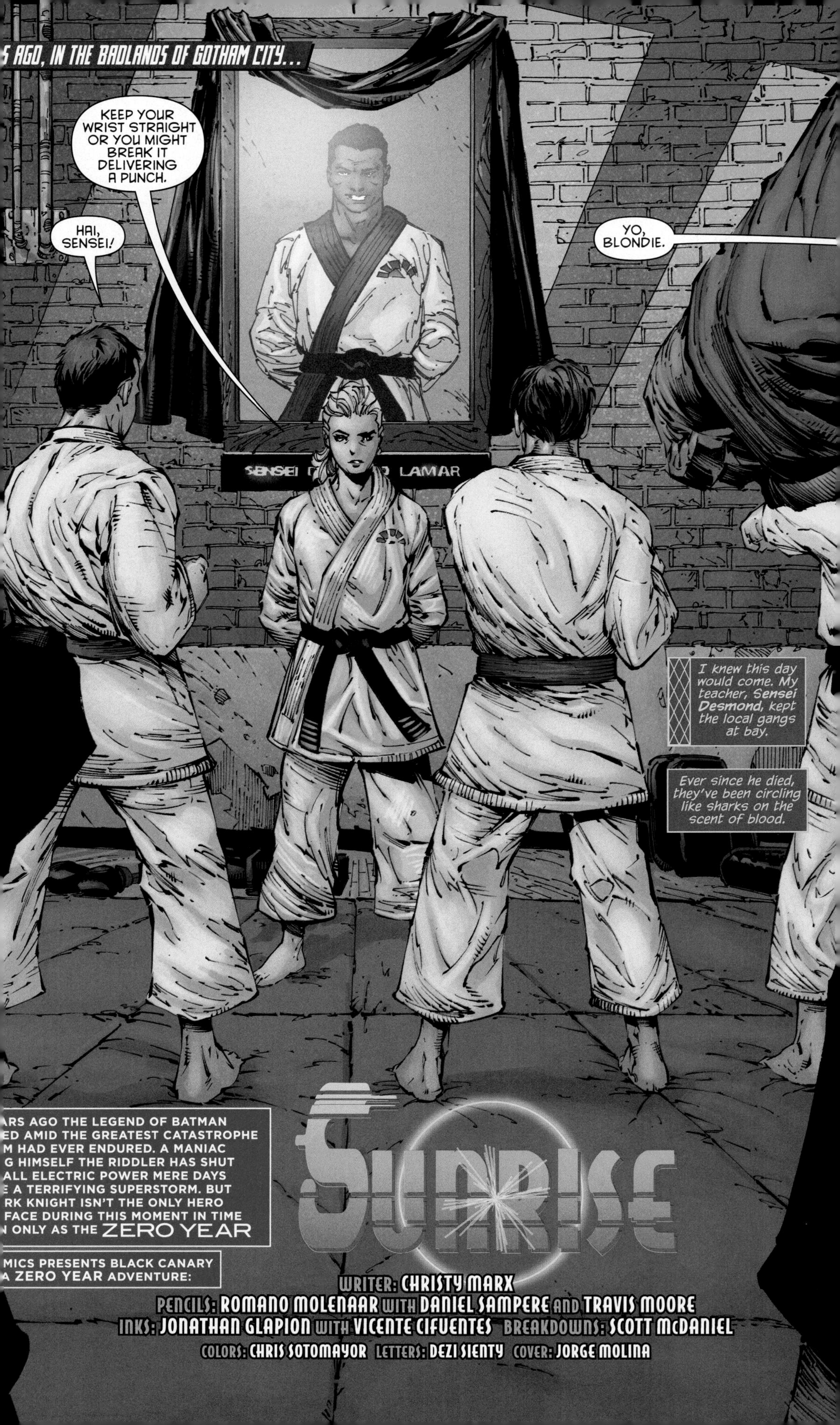
S AGO, IN THE BADLANDS OF GOTHAM CITY...
HAI, SENSEI!
KEEP YOUR WRIST STRAIGHT OR YOU MIGHT BREAK IT DELIVERING A PUNCH.
YO, BLONDIE.
I knew this day would come. My teacher, Sensei Desmond, kept the local gangs at bay.
Ever since he died, they've been circling like sharks on the scent of blood.
ARS AGO THE LEGEND OF BATMAN
ED AMID THE GREATEST CATASTROPHE
M HAD EVER ENDURED. A MANIAC
G HIMSELF THE RIDDLER HAS SHUT
ALL ELECTRIC POWER MERE DAYS
E A TERRIFYING SUPERSTORM. BUT
RK KNIGHT ISN'T THE ONLY HERO
FACE DURING THIS MOMENT IN TIME
N ONLY AS THE ZERO YEAR
MICS PRESENTS BLACK CANARY
A ZERO YEAR ADVENTURE:
SUNRISE
WRITER: CHRISTY MARX
PENCILS: ROMANO MOLENAAR WITH DANIEL SAMPERE AND TRAVIS MOORE
INKS: JONATHAN GLAPION WITH VICENTE CIFUENTES BREAKDOWNS: SCOTT McDANIEL
COLORS: CHRIS SOTOMAYOR LETTERS: DEZI SIENTY COVER: JORGE MOLINA

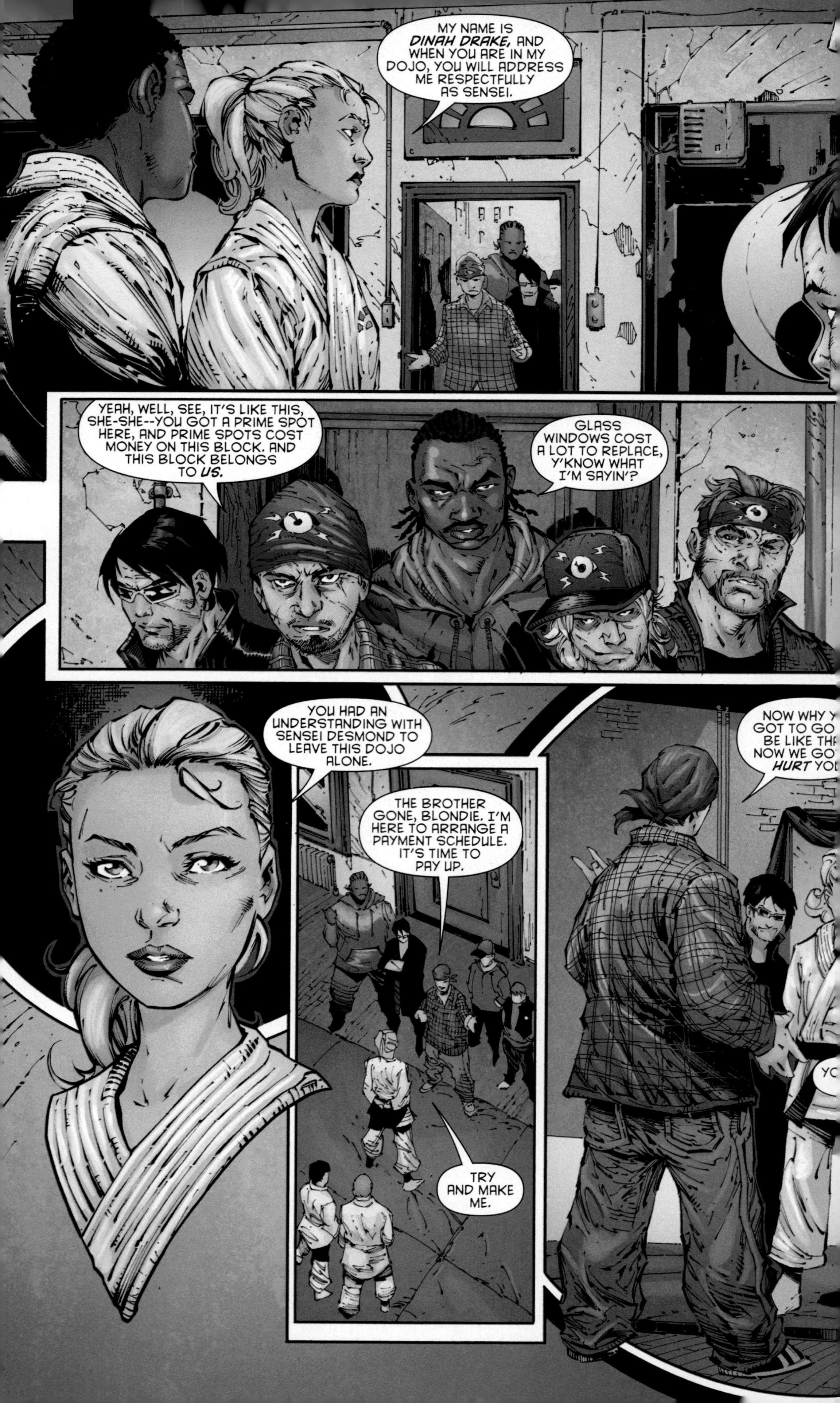
MY NAME IS *DINAH DRAKE,* AND WHEN YOU ARE IN MY DOJO, YOU WILL ADDRESS ME RESPECTFULLY AS SENSEI.
YEAH, WELL, SEE, IT'S LIKE THIS, SHE-SHE--YOU GOT A PRIME SPOT HERE, AND PRIME SPOTS COST MONEY ON THIS BLOCK. AND THIS BLOCK BELONGS TO *US.*
GLASS WINDOWS COST A LOT TO REPLACE, Y'KNOW WHAT I'M SAYIN'?
YOU HAD AN UNDERSTANDING WITH SENSEI DESMOND TO LEAVE THIS DOJO ALONE.
THE BROTHER GONE, BLONDIE. I'M HERE TO ARRANGE A PAYMENT SCHEDULE. IT'S TIME TO PAY UP.
TRY AND MAKE ME.

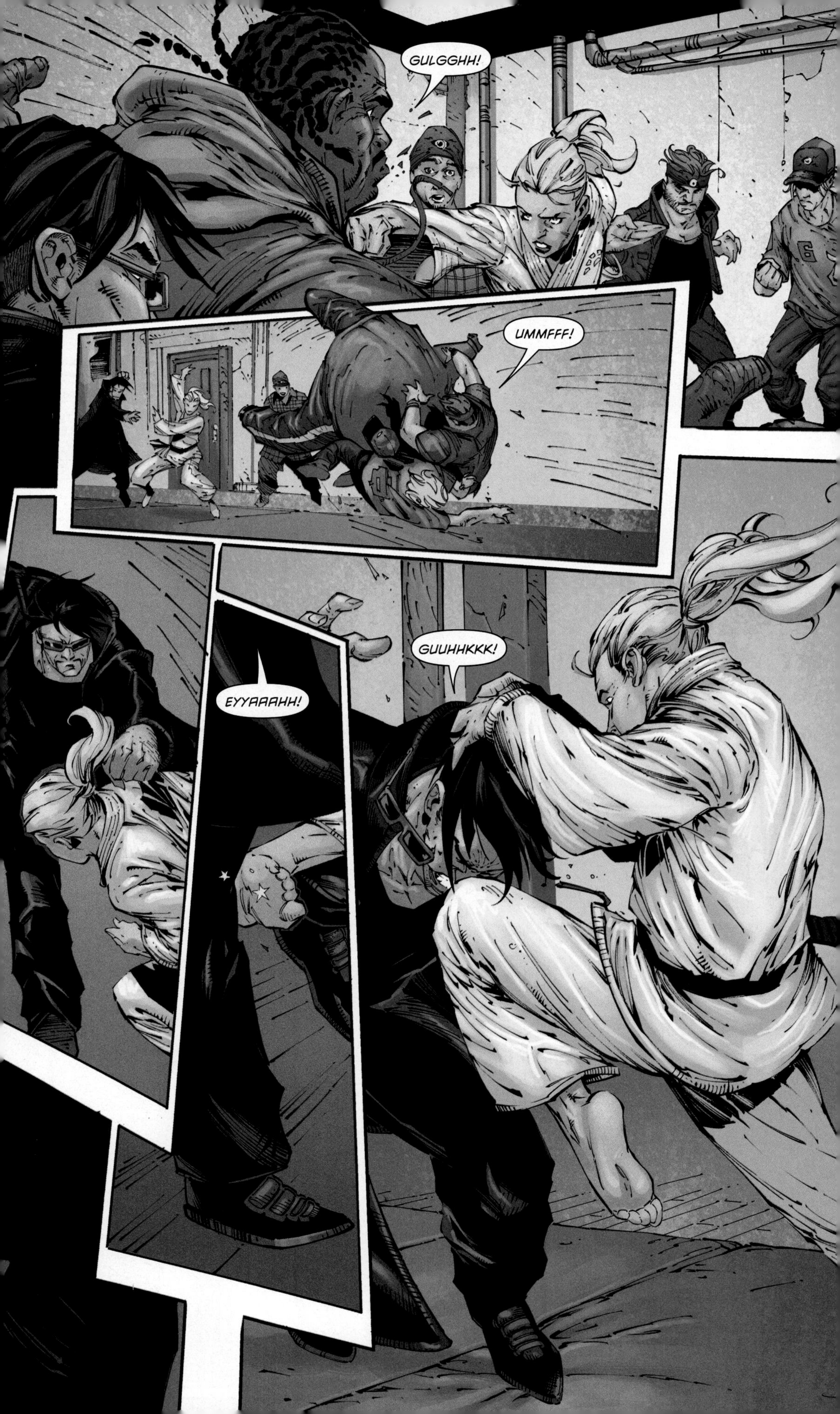
GULGGHH!
UMMFFF!
EYYAAAHH!
GUUHHKKK!

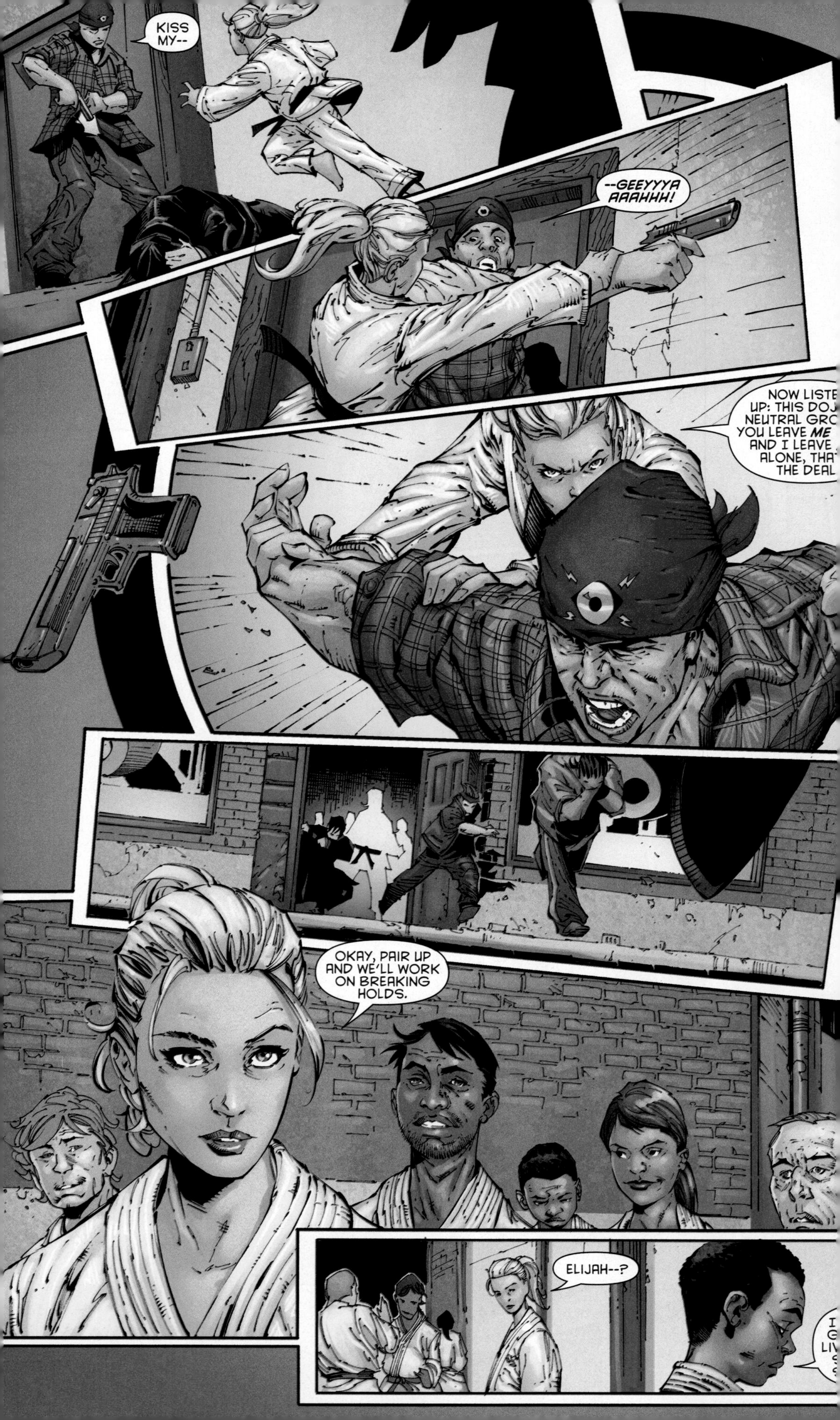
KISS MY--
--GEEYYYA AAAHHH!
NOW LISTE UP: THIS DOJ NEUTRAL GRO YOU LEAVE *ME* AND I LEAVE ALONE, THA THE DEAL
OKAY, PAIR UP AND WE'LL WORK ON BREAKING HOLDS.
ELIJAH--?

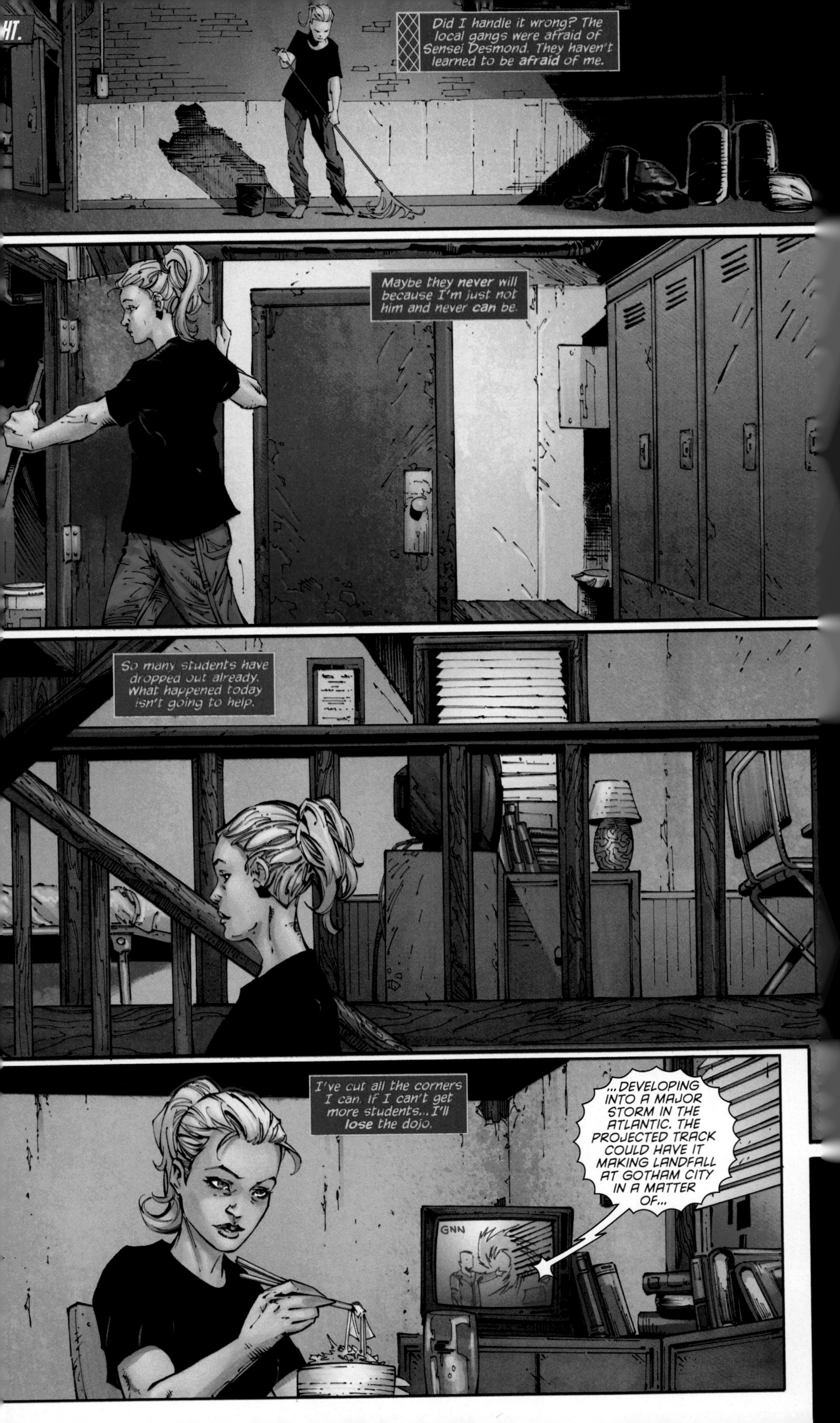
HT.
Did I handle it wrong? The local gangs were afraid of Sensei Desmond. They haven't learned to be afraid of me.
Maybe they never will because I'm just not him and never can be.
So many students have dropped out already. What happened today isn't going to help.
I've cut all the corners I can. If I can't get more students... I'll lose the dojo.
...DEVELOPING INTO A MAJOR STORM IN THE ATLANTIC. THE PROJECTED TRACK COULD HAVE IT MAKING LANDFALL AT GOTHAM CITY IN A MATTER OF...
GNN

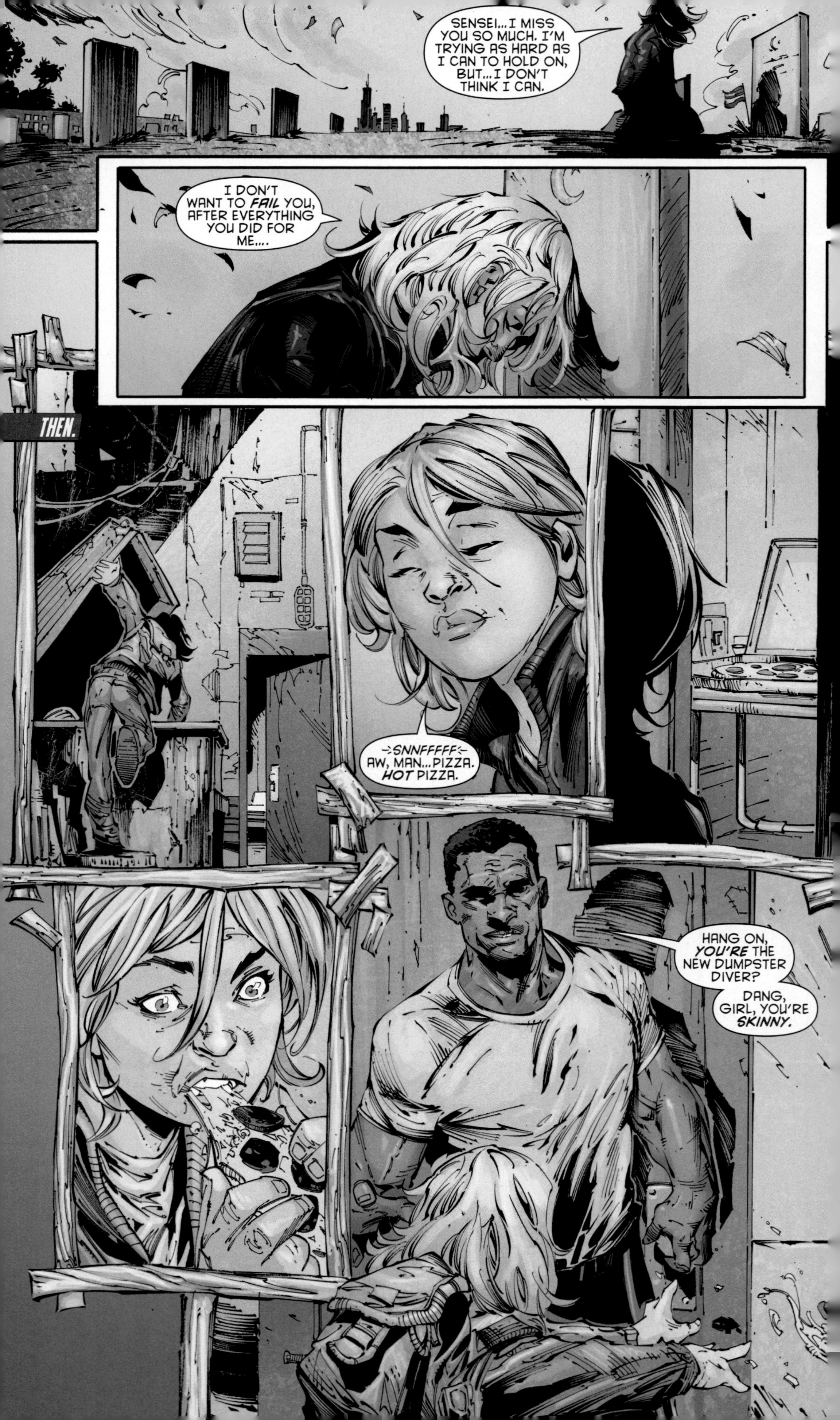
SENSEI...I MISS YOU SO MUCH. I'M TRYING AS HARD AS I CAN TO HOLD ON, BUT...I DON'T THINK I CAN.
I DON'T WANT TO FAIL YOU, AFTER EVERYTHING YOU DID FOR ME....
THEN.
-SNNFFFFF- AW, MAN...PIZZA. HOT PIZZA.
HANG ON, YOU'RE THE NEW DUMPSTER DIVER?
DANG, GIRL, YOU'RE SKINNY.

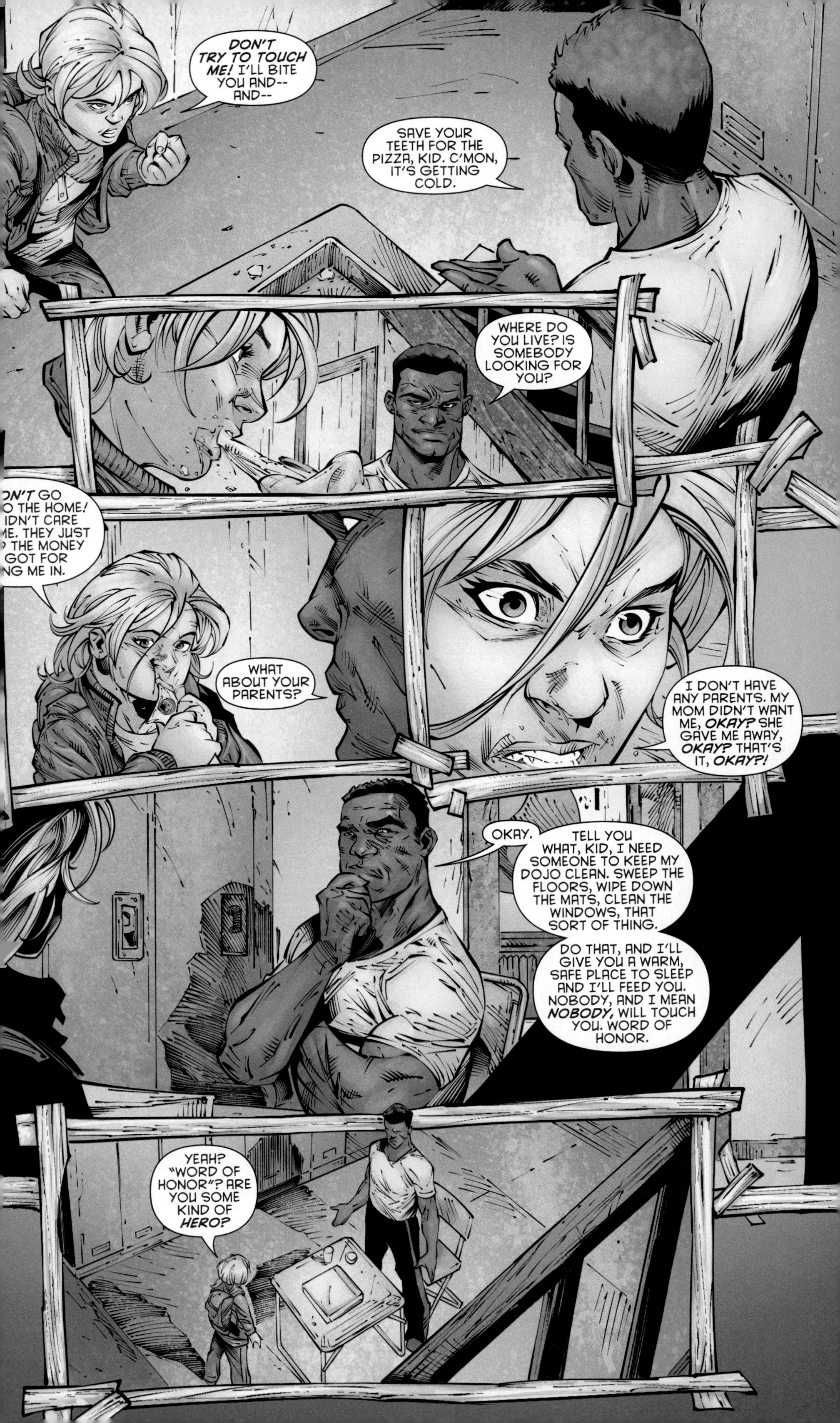
DON'T TRY TO TOUCH ME! I'LL BITE YOU AND-- AND--
SAVE YOUR TEETH FOR THE PIZZA, KID. C'MON, IT'S GETTING COLD.
WHERE DO YOU LIVE? IS SOMEBODY LOOKING FOR YOU?
ON'T GO O THE HOME! IDN'T CARE ME. THEY JUST THE MONEY GOT FOR NG ME IN.
WHAT ABOUT YOUR PARENTS?
I DON'T HAVE ANY PARENTS. MY MOM DIDN'T WANT ME, OKAY? SHE GAVE ME AWAY, OKAY? THAT'S IT, OKAY?!
OKAY.
TELL YOU WHAT, KID, I NEED SOMEONE TO KEEP MY DOJO CLEAN. SWEEP THE FLOORS, WIPE DOWN THE MATS, CLEAN THE WINDOWS, THAT SORT OF THING.
DO THAT, AND I'LL GIVE YOU A WARM, SAFE PLACE TO SLEEP AND I'LL FEED YOU. NOBODY, AND I MEAN NOBODY, WILL TOUCH YOU. WORD OF HONOR.
YEAH? "WORD OF HONOR"? ARE YOU SOME KIND OF HERO?

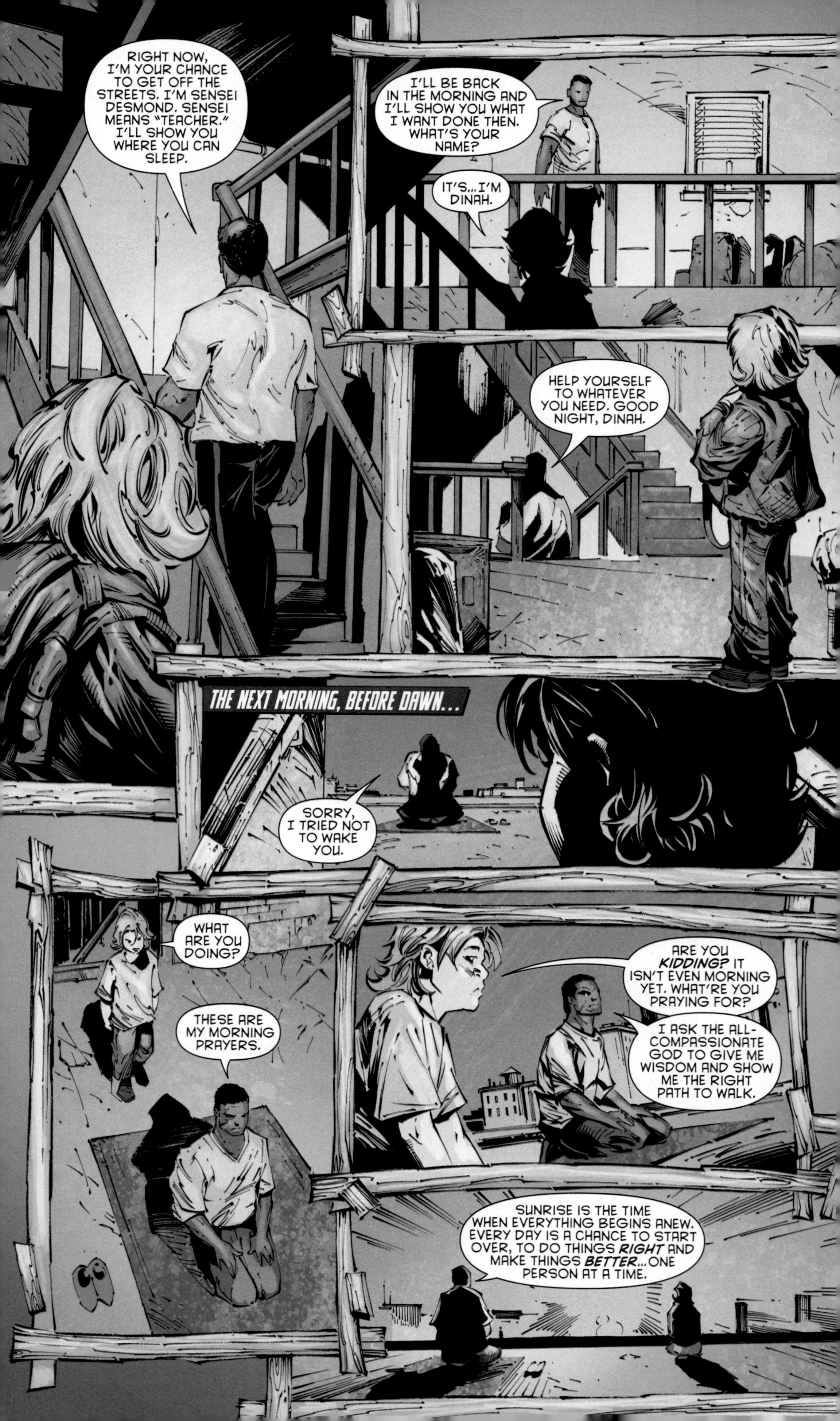
RIGHT NOW, I'M YOUR CHANCE TO GET OFF THE STREETS. I'M SENSEI DESMOND. SENSEI MEANS "TEACHER." I'LL SHOW YOU WHERE YOU CAN SLEEP.
I'LL BE BACK IN THE MORNING AND I'LL SHOW YOU WHAT I WANT DONE THEN. WHAT'S YOUR NAME?
IT'S...I'M DINAH.
HELP YOURSELF TO WHATEVER YOU NEED. GOOD NIGHT, DINAH.
THE NEXT MORNING, BEFORE DAWN...
SORRY, I TRIED NOT TO WAKE YOU.
WHAT ARE YOU DOING?
THESE ARE MY MORNING PRAYERS.
ARE YOU KIDDING? IT ISN'T EVEN MORNING YET. WHAT'RE YOU PRAYING FOR?
I ASK THE ALL-COMPASSIONATE GOD TO GIVE ME WISDOM AND SHOW ME THE RIGHT PATH TO WALK.
SUNRISE IS THE TIME WHEN EVERYTHING BEGINS ANEW. EVERY DAY IS A CHANCE TO START OVER, TO DO THINGS RIGHT AND MAKE THINGS BETTER...ONE PERSON AT A TIME.

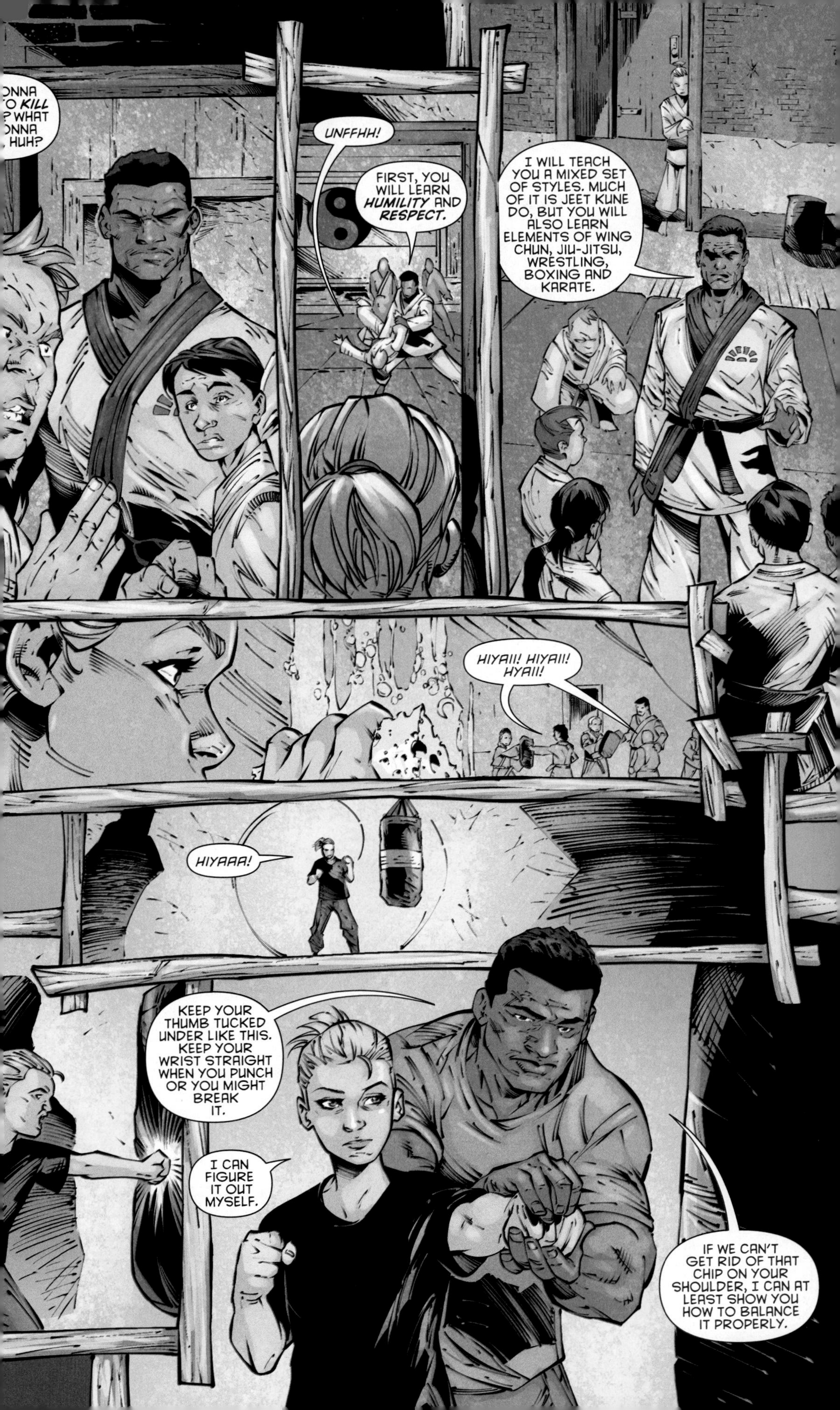
ONNA
TO *KILL*
? WHAT
ONNA
, HUH?
UNFFHH!
FIRST, YOU WILL LEARN *HUMILITY* AND *RESPECT.*
I WILL TEACH YOU A MIXED SET OF STYLES. MUCH OF IT IS JEET KUNE DO, BUT YOU WILL ALSO LEARN ELEMENTS OF WING CHUN, JIU-JITSU, WRESTLING, BOXING AND KARATE.
HIYAII! HIYAII! HYAII!
HIYAAA!
KEEP YOUR THUMB TUCKED UNDER LIKE THIS. KEEP YOUR WRIST STRAIGHT WHEN YOU PUNCH OR YOU MIGHT BREAK IT.
I CAN FIGURE IT OUT MYSELF.
IF WE CAN'T GET RID OF THAT CHIP ON YOUR SHOULDER, I CAN AT LEAST SHOW YOU HOW TO BALANCE IT PROPERLY.

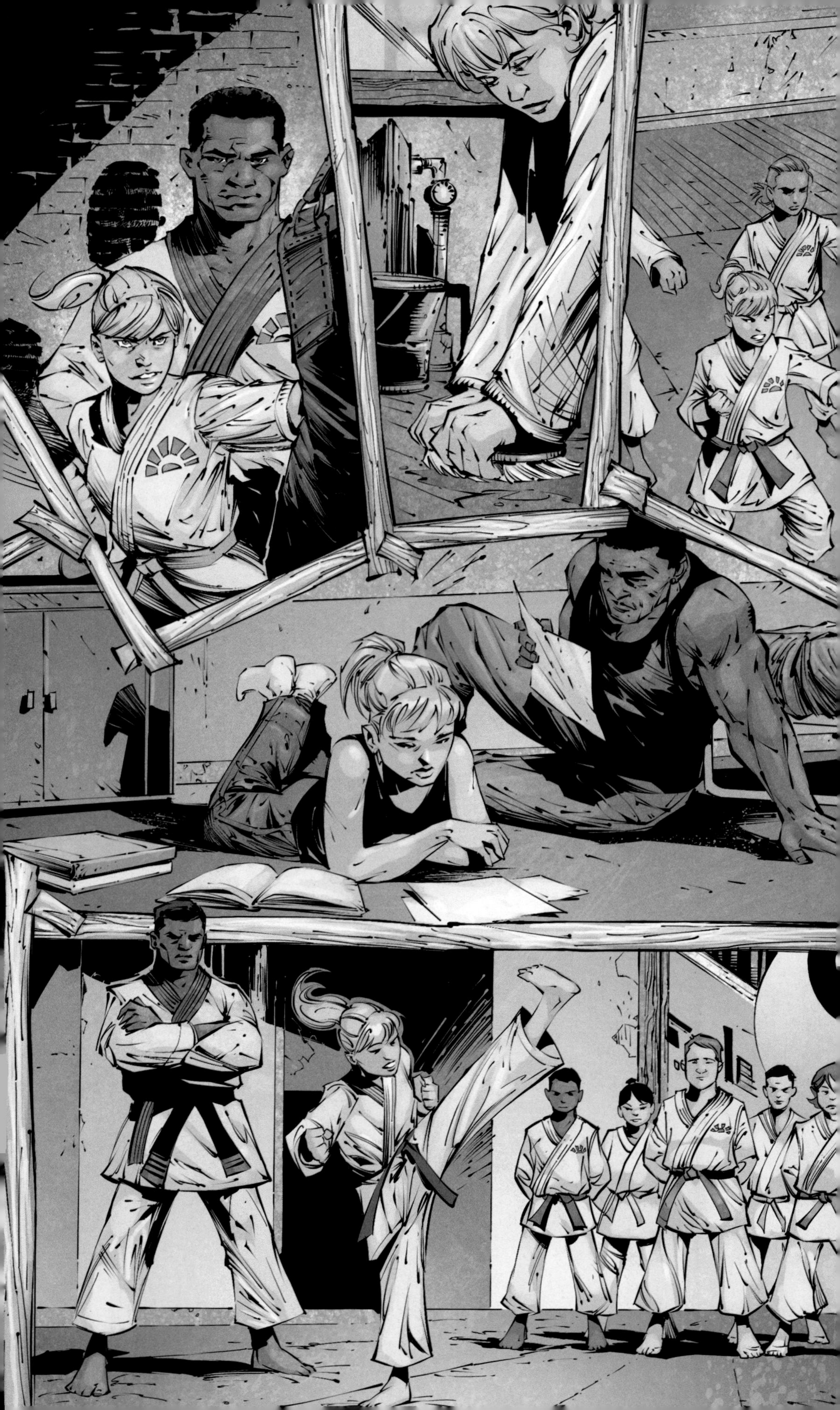

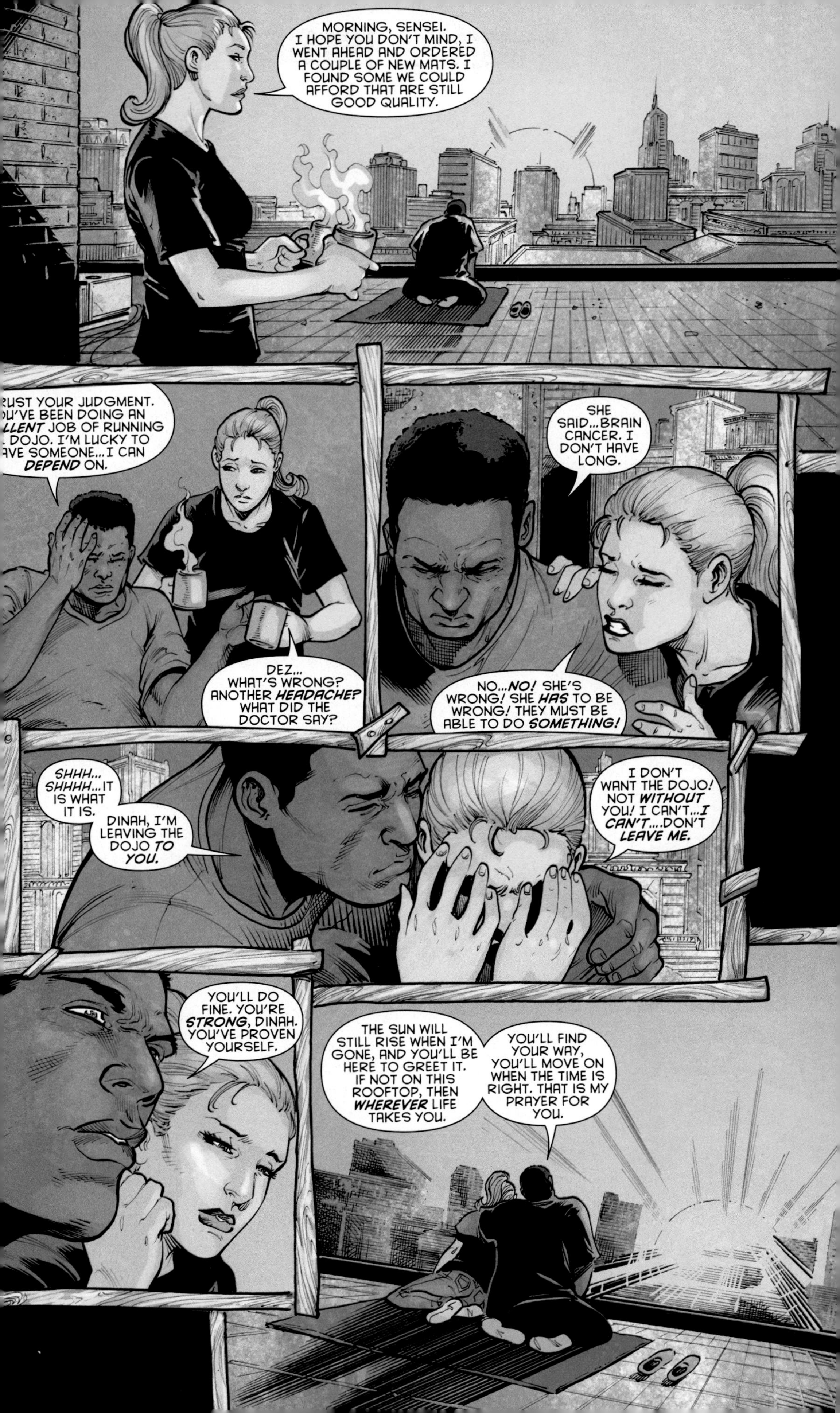
MORNING, SENSEI. I HOPE YOU DON'T MIND, I WENT AHEAD AND ORDERED A COUPLE OF NEW MATS. I FOUND SOME WE COULD AFFORD THAT ARE STILL GOOD QUALITY.
RUST YOUR JUDGMENT. OU'VE BEEN DOING AN LLENT JOB OF RUNNING DOJO. I'M LUCKY TO AVE SOMEONE...I CAN DEPEND ON.
DEZ... WHAT'S WRONG? ANOTHER HEADACHE? WHAT DID THE DOCTOR SAY?
SHE SAID...BRAIN CANCER. I DON'T HAVE LONG.
NO...NO! SHE'S WRONG! SHE HAS TO BE WRONG! THEY MUST BE ABLE TO DO SOMETHING!
SHHH... SHHHH...IT IS WHAT IT IS.
DINAH, I'M LEAVING THE DOJO TO YOU.
I DON'T WANT THE DOJO! NOT WITHOUT YOU! I CAN'T...I CAN'T....DON'T LEAVE ME.
YOU'LL DO FINE. YOU'RE STRONG, DINAH. YOU'VE PROVEN YOURSELF.
THE SUN WILL STILL RISE WHEN I'M GONE, AND YOU'LL BE HERE TO GREET IT. IF NOT ON THIS ROOFTOP, THEN WHEREVER LIFE TAKES YOU.
YOU'LL FIND YOUR WAY, YOU'LL MOVE ON WHEN THE TIME IS RIGHT. THAT IS MY PRAYER FOR YOU.

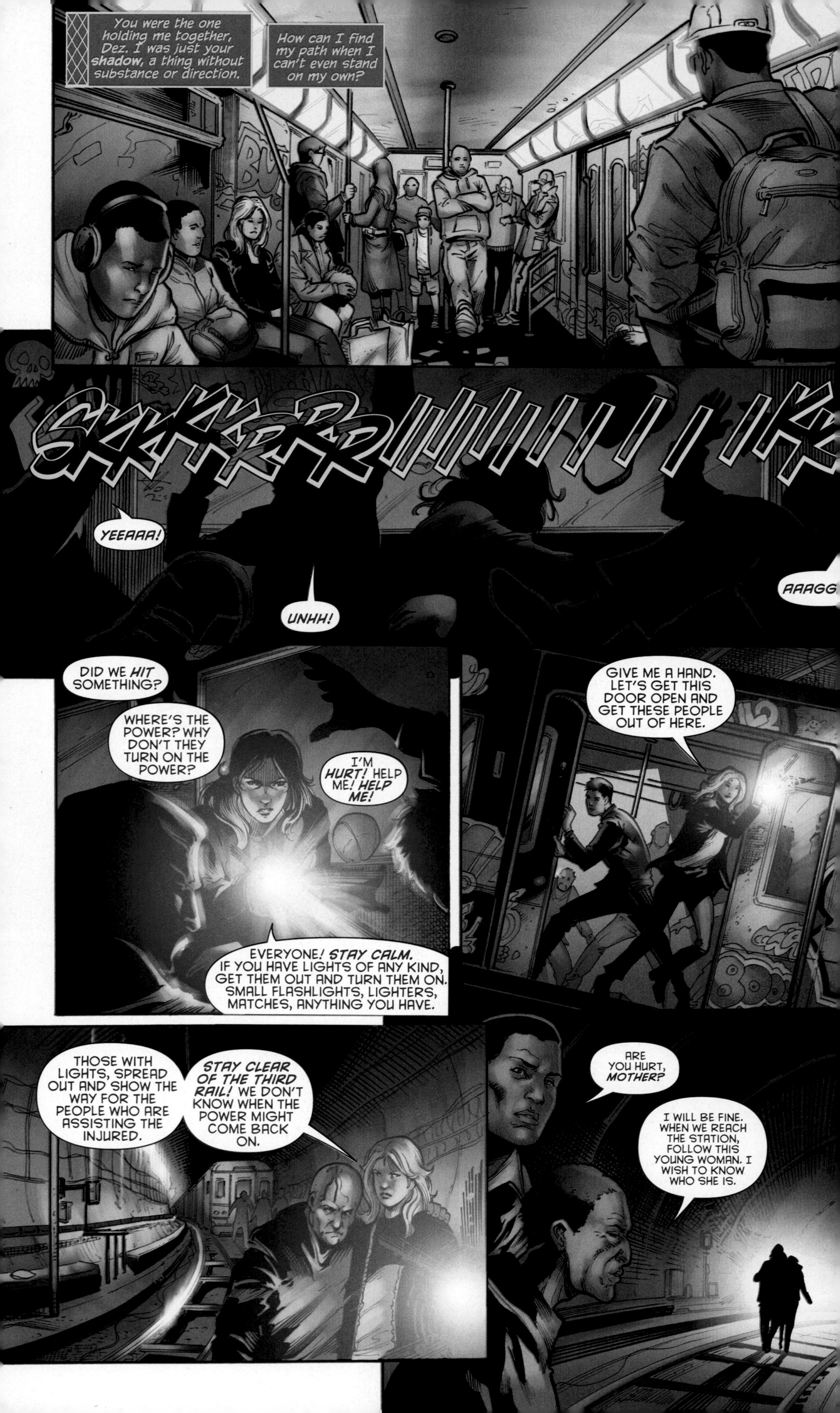

You were the one holding me together, Dez. I was just your shadow, a thing without substance or direction.
How can I find my path when I can't even stand on my own?
SKKKRRRIIIIIIIIK
YEEAAA!
UNHH!
AAAGG
DID WE HIT SOMETHING?
WHERE'S THE POWER? WHY DON'T THEY TURN ON THE POWER?
I'M HURT! HELP ME! HELP ME!
EVERYONE! STAY CALM. IF YOU HAVE LIGHTS OF ANY KIND, GET THEM OUT AND TURN THEM ON. SMALL FLASHLIGHTS, LIGHTERS, MATCHES, ANYTHING YOU HAVE.
GIVE ME A HAND. LET'S GET THIS DOOR OPEN AND GET THESE PEOPLE OUT OF HERE.
THOSE WITH LIGHTS, SPREAD OUT AND SHOW THE WAY FOR THE PEOPLE WHO ARE ASSISTING THE INJURED.
STAY CLEAR OF THE THIRD RAIL! WE DON'T KNOW WHEN THE POWER MIGHT COME BACK ON.
ARE YOU HURT, MOTHER?
I WILL BE FINE. WHEN WE REACH THE STATION, FOLLOW THIS YOUNG WOMAN. I WISH TO KNOW WHO SHE IS.

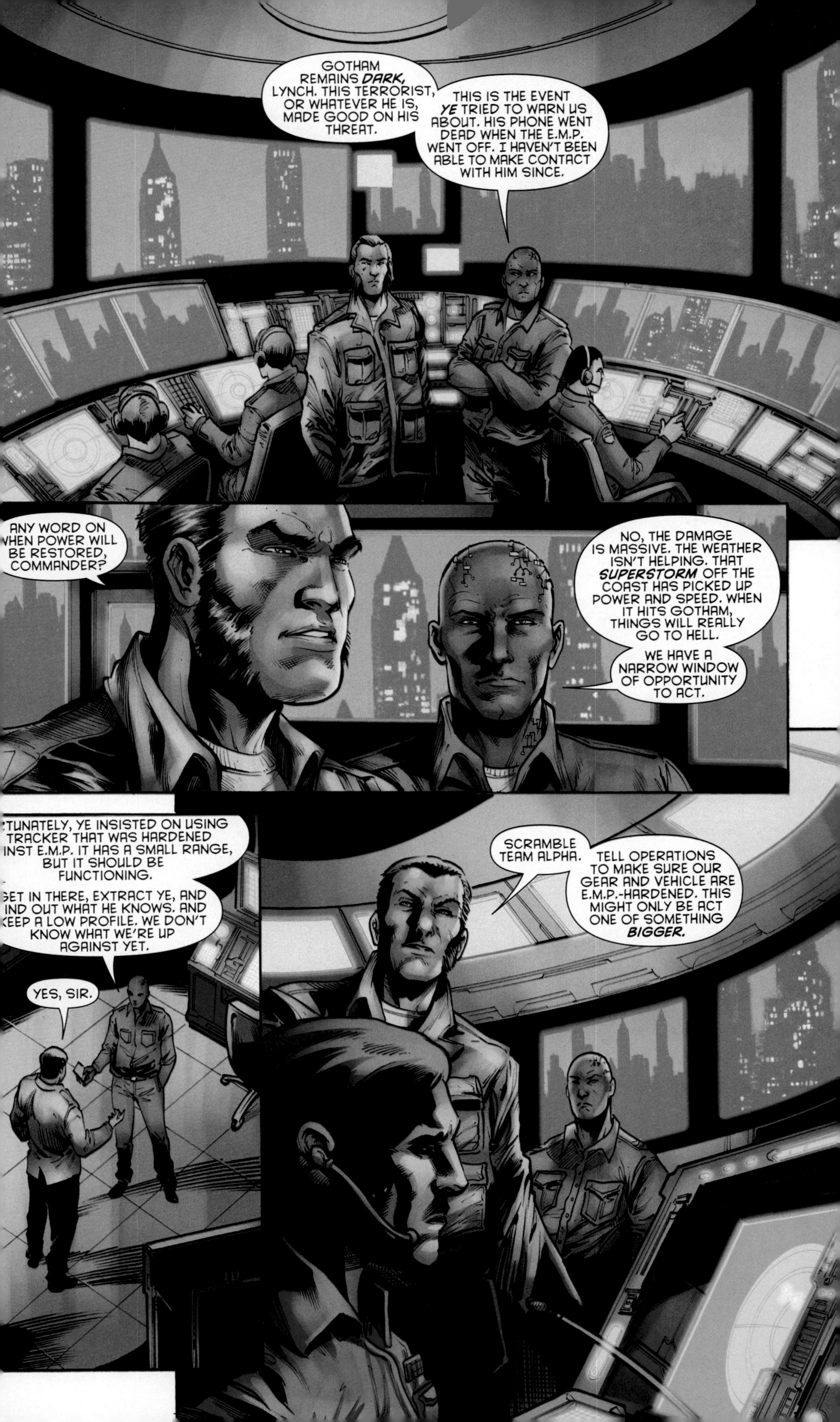
GOTHAM REMAINS DARK, LYNCH. THIS TERRORIST, OR WHATEVER HE IS, MADE GOOD ON HIS THREAT.
THIS IS THE EVENT YE TRIED TO WARN US ABOUT. HIS PHONE WENT DEAD WHEN THE E.M.P. WENT OFF. I HAVEN'T BEEN ABLE TO MAKE CONTACT WITH HIM SINCE.
ANY WORD ON WHEN POWER WILL BE RESTORED, COMMANDER?
NO, THE DAMAGE IS MASSIVE. THE WEATHER ISN'T HELPING. THAT SUPERSTORM OFF THE COAST HAS PICKED UP POWER AND SPEED. WHEN IT HITS GOTHAM, THINGS WILL REALLY GO TO HELL.
WE HAVE A NARROW WINDOW OF OPPORTUNITY TO ACT.
TUNATELY, YE INSISTED ON USING TRACKER THAT WAS HARDENED INST E.M.P. IT HAS A SMALL RANGE, BUT IT SHOULD BE FUNCTIONING.
GET IN THERE, EXTRACT YE, AND IND OUT WHAT HE KNOWS. AND KEEP A LOW PROFILE. WE DON'T KNOW WHAT WE'RE UP AGAINST YET.
YES, SIR.
SCRAMBLE TEAM ALPHA.
TELL OPERATIONS TO MAKE SURE OUR GEAR AND VEHICLE ARE E.M.P.-HARDENED. THIS MIGHT ONLY BE ACT ONE OF SOMETHING BIGGER.

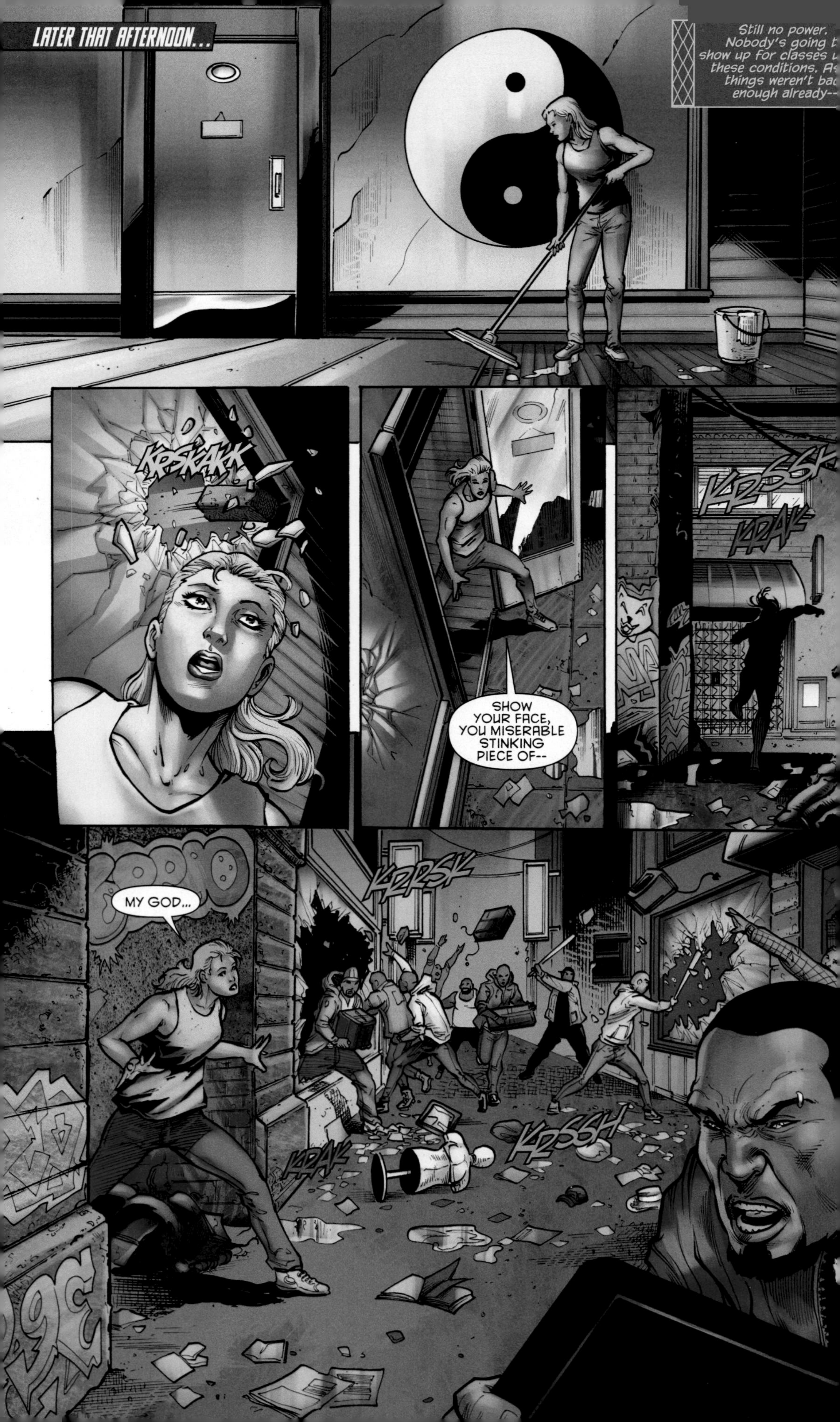
LATER THAT AFTERNOON...
Still no power. Nobody's going t show up for classes u these conditions. As things weren't bad enough already--
KRSKAKK
SHOW YOUR FACE, YOU MISERABLE STINKING PIECE OF--
KRSSSK
KRAK
MY GOD...
KRRSK
KRAK
KRSSSH

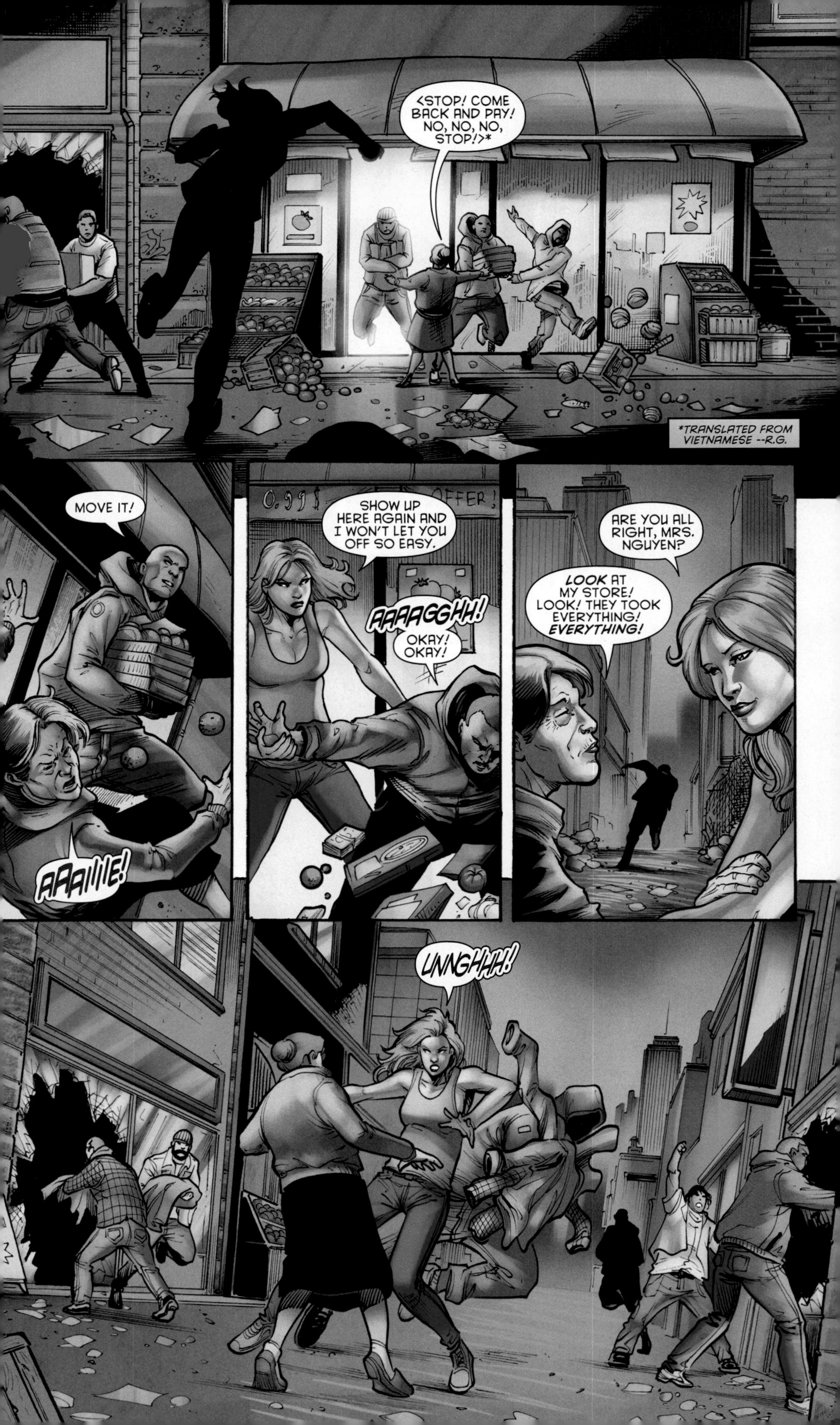
<STOP! COME BACK AND PAY! NO, NO, NO, STOP!>*
*TRANSLATED FROM VIETNAMESE --R.G.
MOVE IT!
AAAIIIIE!
SHOW UP HERE AGAIN AND I WON'T LET YOU OFF SO EASY.
AAAAGGHH!
OKAY! OKAY!
0.99$
OFFER!
ARE YOU ALL RIGHT, MRS. NGUYEN?
LOOK AT MY STORE! LOOK! THEY TOOK EVERYTHING! EVERYTHING!
UNNGHHH!

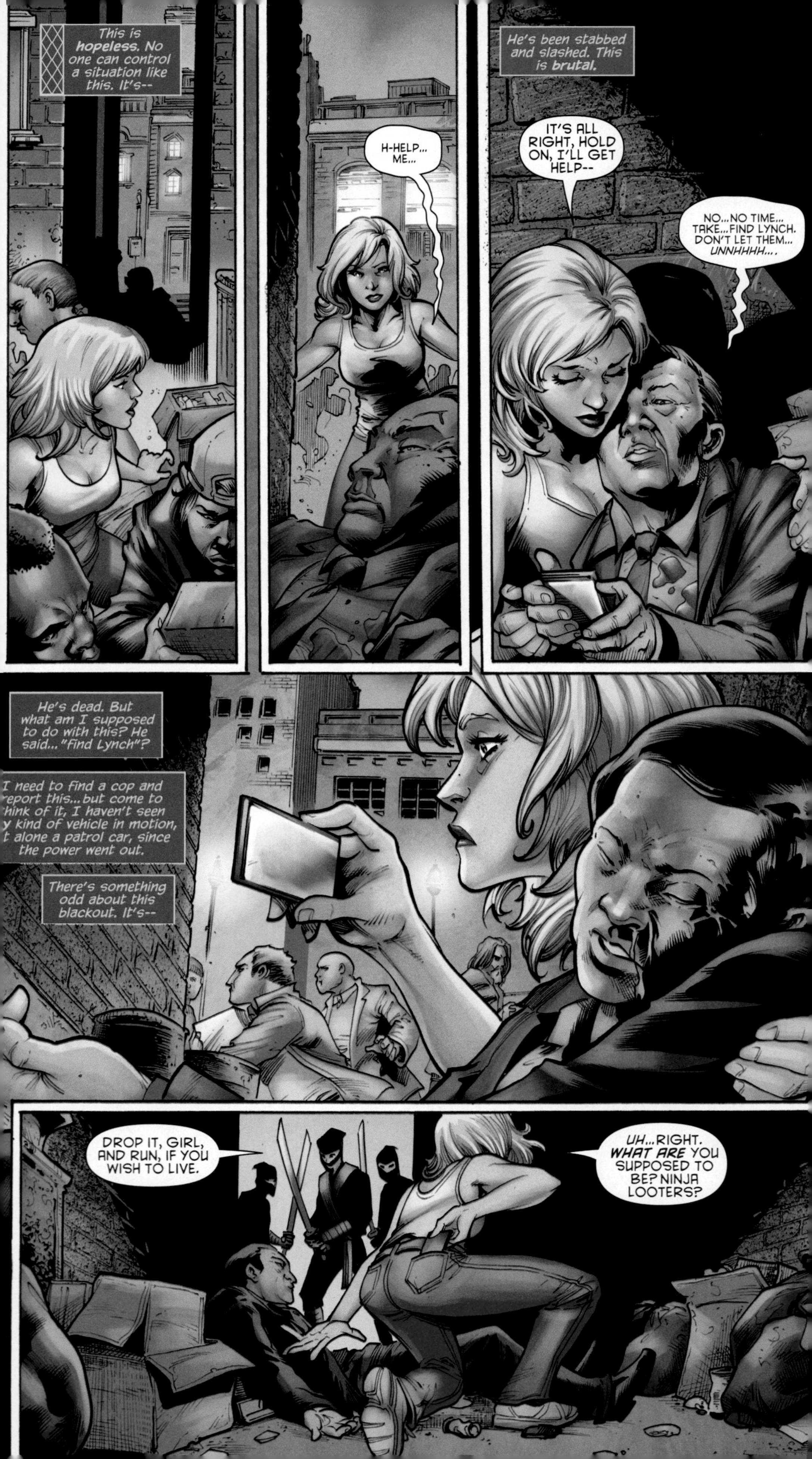
This is hopeless. No one can control a situation like this. It's--
H-HELP... ME...
He's been stabbed and slashed. This is brutal.
IT'S ALL RIGHT, HOLD ON, I'LL GET HELP--
NO...NO TIME... TAKE...FIND LYNCH. DON'T LET THEM... UNNHHHH....
He's dead. But what am I supposed to do with this? He said..."Find Lynch"?
I need to find a cop and report this...but come to think of it, I haven't seen any kind of vehicle in motion, let alone a patrol car, since the power went out.
There's something odd about this blackout. It's--
DROP IT, GIRL, AND RUN, IF YOU WISH TO LIVE.
UH...RIGHT. WHAT ARE YOU SUPPOSED TO BE? NINJA LOOTERS?

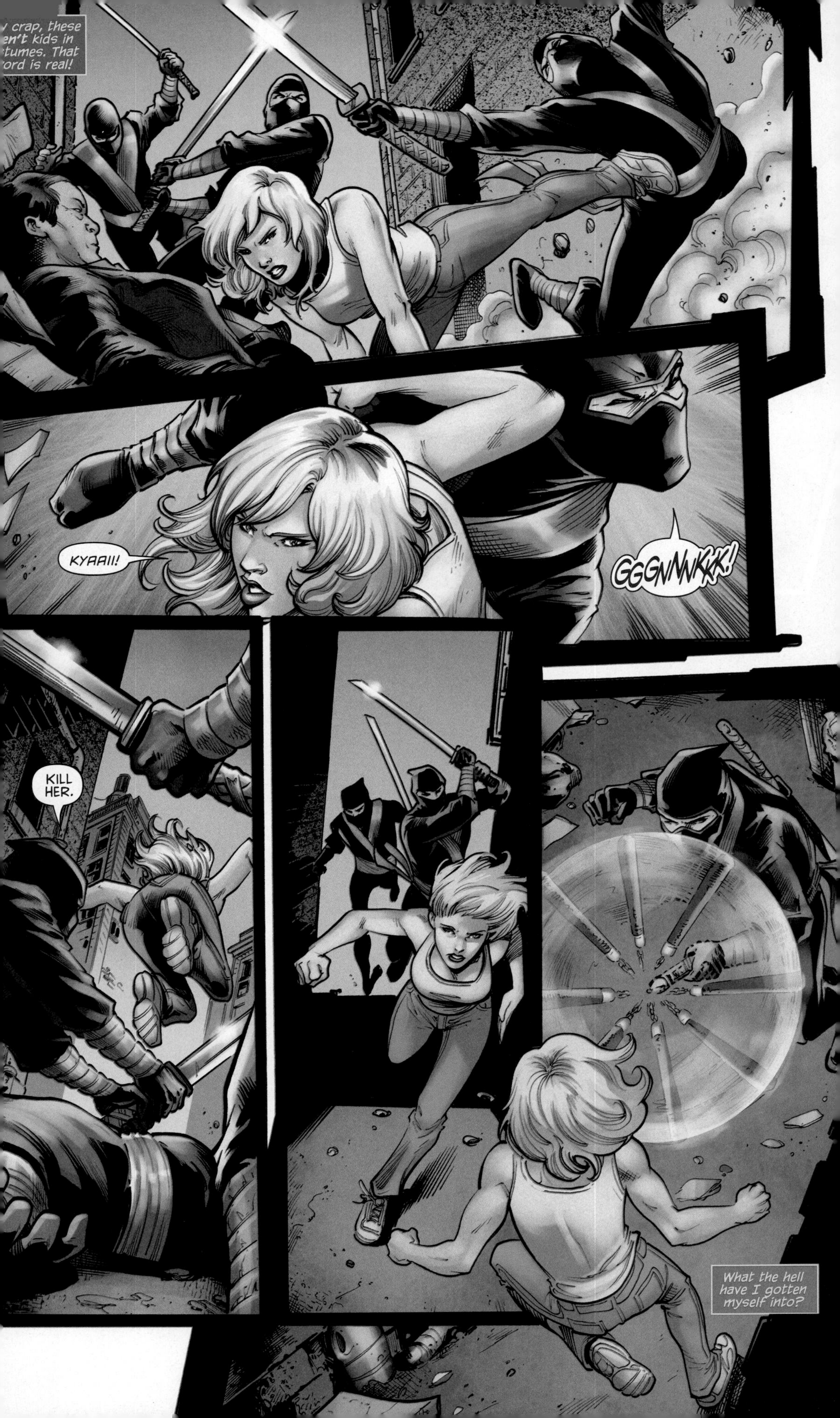
crap, these
n't kids in
tumes. That
ord is real!
KYAAII!
GGGNNNKKK!
KILL HER.
What the hell have I gotten myself into?

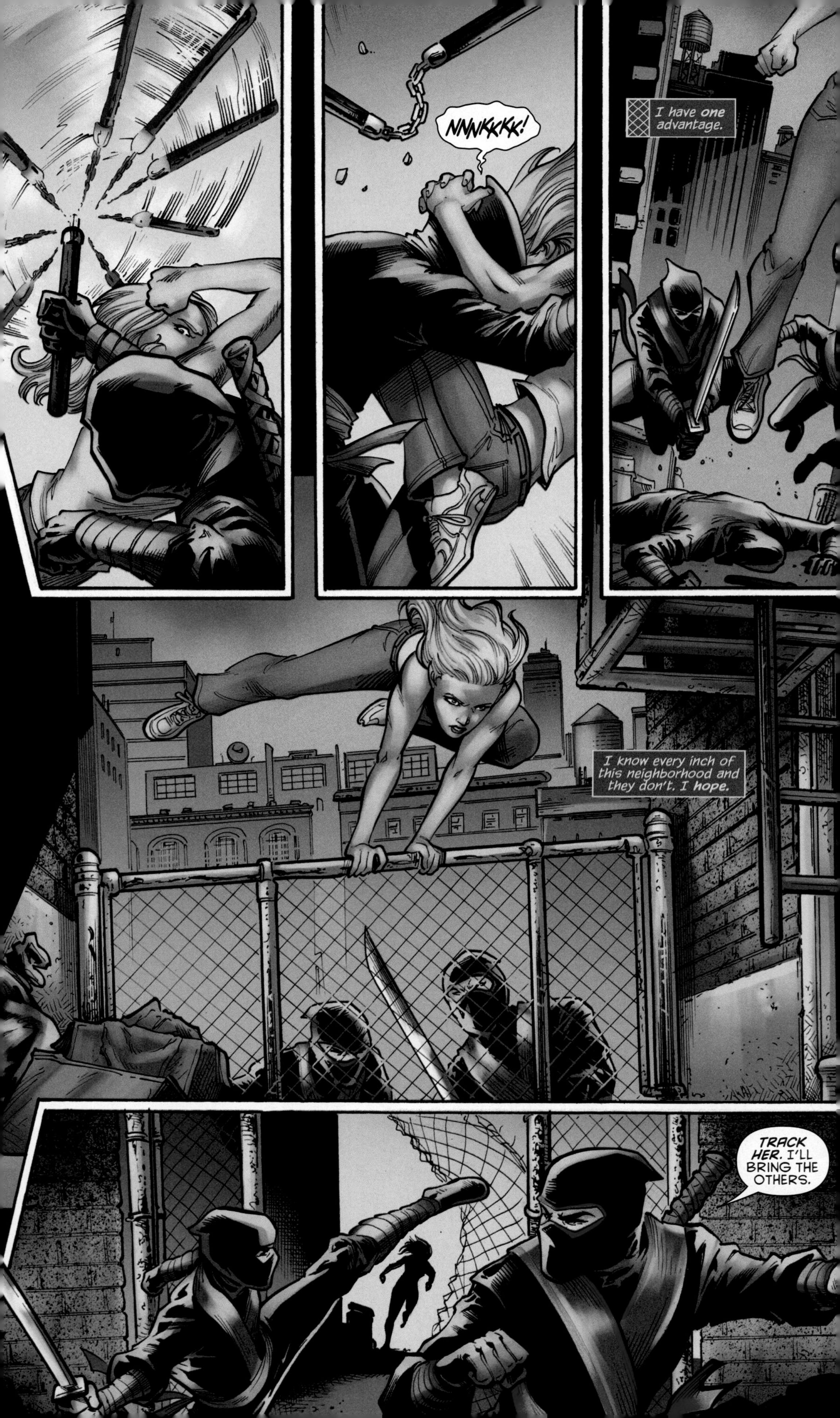
NNNKKKK!
I have one advantage.
I know every inch of this neighborhood and they don't. I hope.
TRACK HER. I'LL BRING THE OTHERS.

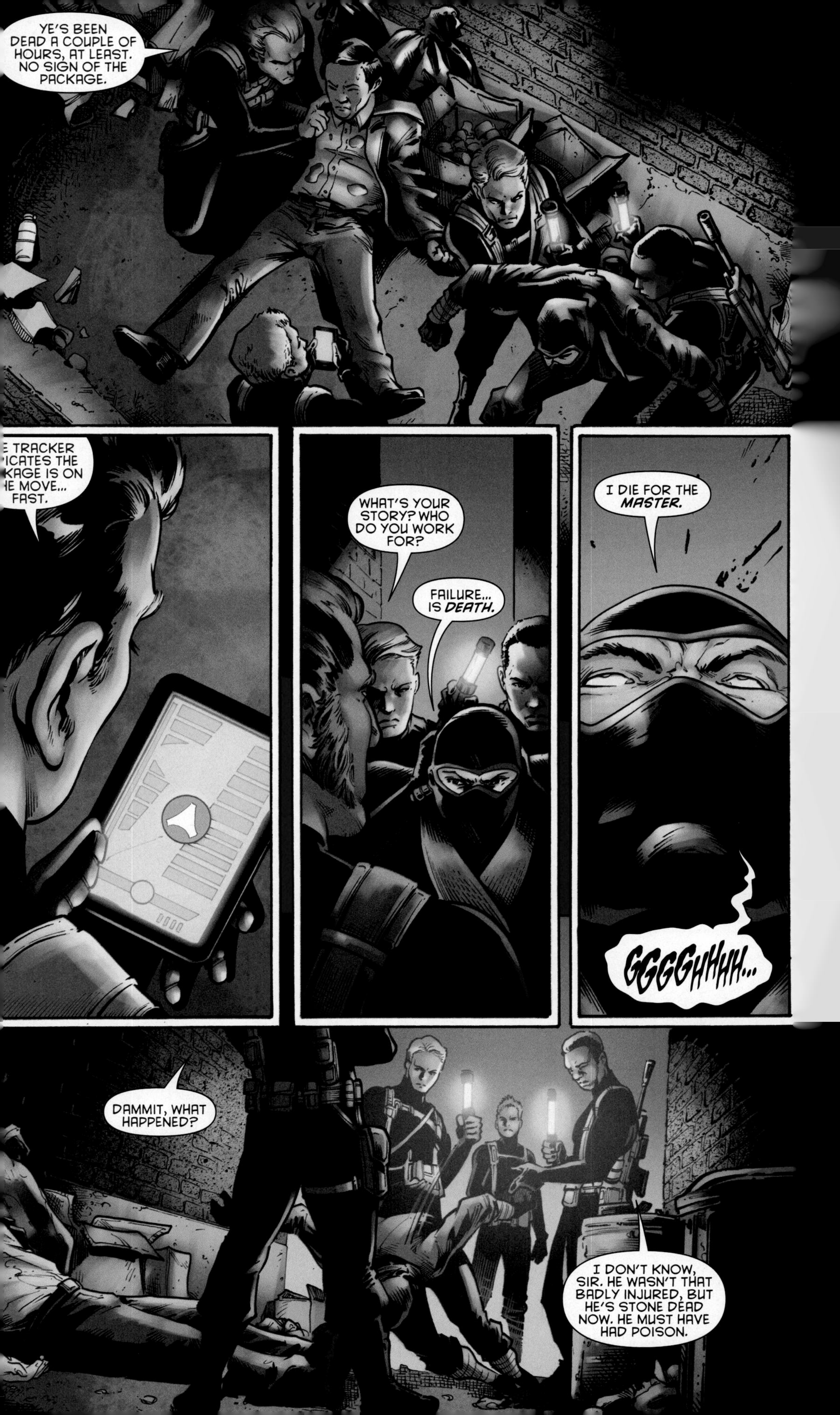
YE'S BEEN DEAD A COUPLE OF HOURS, AT LEAST. NO SIGN OF THE PACKAGE.
E TRACKER ICATES THE KAGE IS ON E MOVE... FAST.
WHAT'S YOUR STORY? WHO DO YOU WORK FOR?
FAILURE... IS DEATH.
I DIE FOR THE MASTER.
GGGGHHHH...
DAMMIT, WHAT HAPPENED?
I DON'T KNOW, SIR. HE WASN'T THAT BADLY INJURED, BUT HE'S STONE DEAD NOW. HE MUST HAVE HAD POISON.

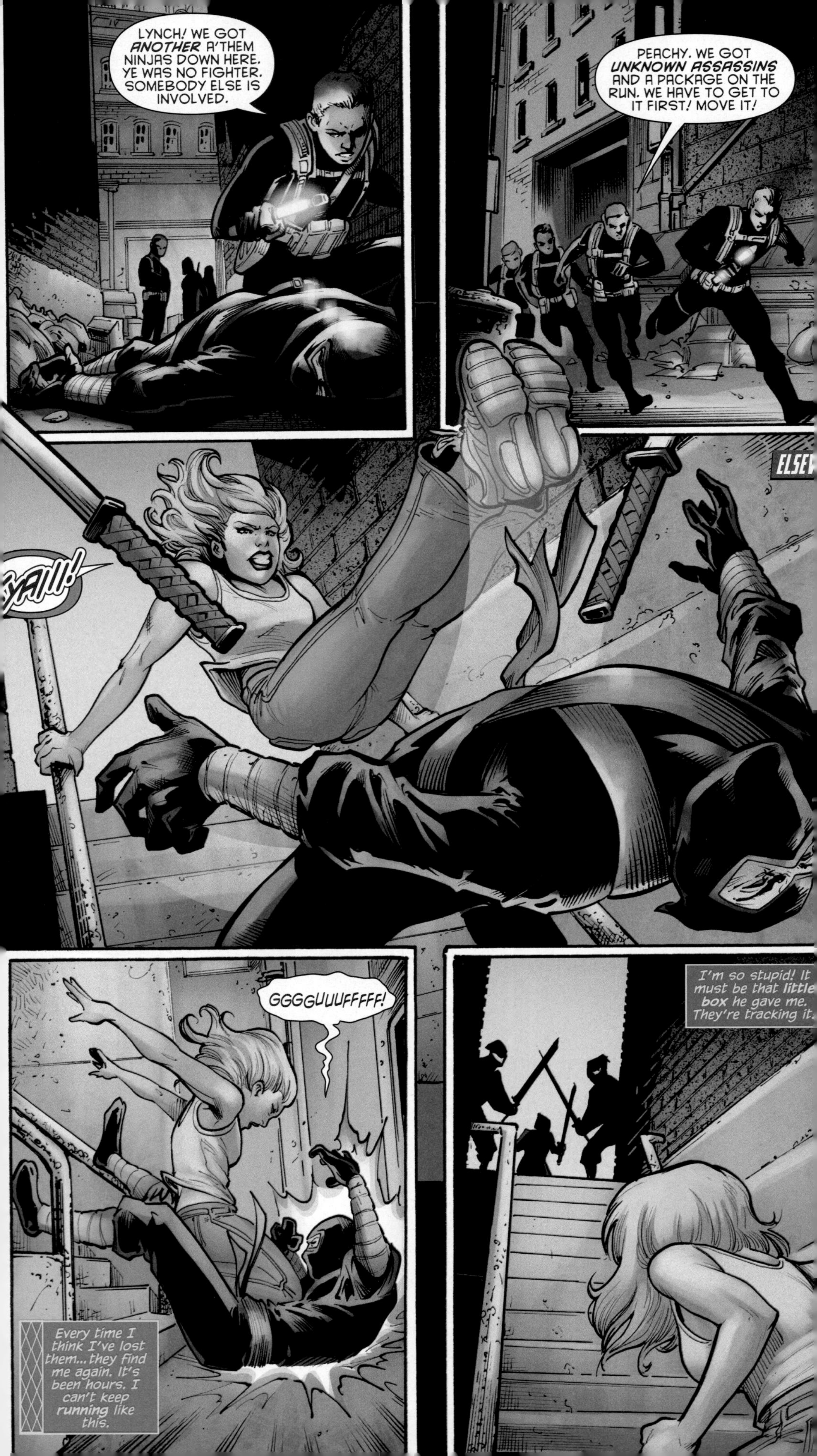
LYNCH! WE GOT ANOTHER A'THEM NINJAS DOWN HERE. YE WAS NO FIGHTER. SOMEBODY ELSE IS INVOLVED.
PEACHY. WE GOT UNKNOWN ASSASSINS AND A PACKAGE ON THE RUN. WE HAVE TO GET TO IT FIRST! MOVE IT!
ELSEW
YAIII!
GGGGUUUFFFFF!
Every time I think I've lost them...they find me again. It's been hours. I can't keep running like this.
I'm so stupid! It must be that little box he gave me. They're tracking it.

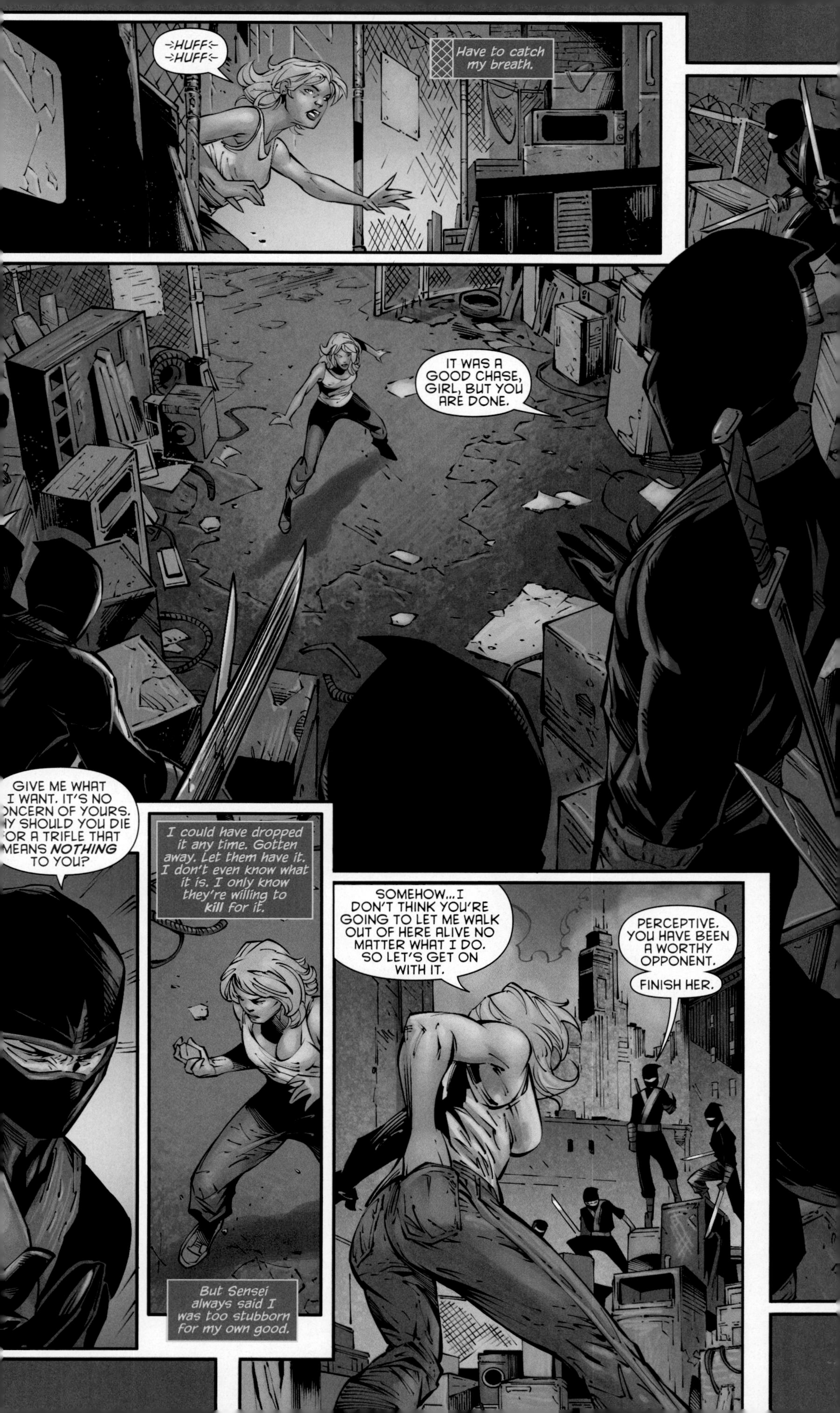

HUFF HUFF
Have to catch my breath.
IT WAS A GOOD CHASE, GIRL, BUT YOU ARE DONE.
GIVE ME WHAT I WANT. IT'S NO ONCERN OF YOURS. HY SHOULD YOU DIE OR A TRIFLE THAT MEANS NOTHING TO YOU?
I could have dropped it any time. Gotten away. Let them have it. I don't even know what it is. I only know they're willing to kill for it.
But Sensei always said I was too stubborn for my own good.
SOMEHOW...I DON'T THINK YOU'RE GOING TO LET ME WALK OUT OF HERE ALIVE NO MATTER WHAT I DO. SO LET'S GET ON WITH IT.
PERCEPTIVE. YOU HAVE BEEN A WORTHY OPPONENT.
FINISH HER.

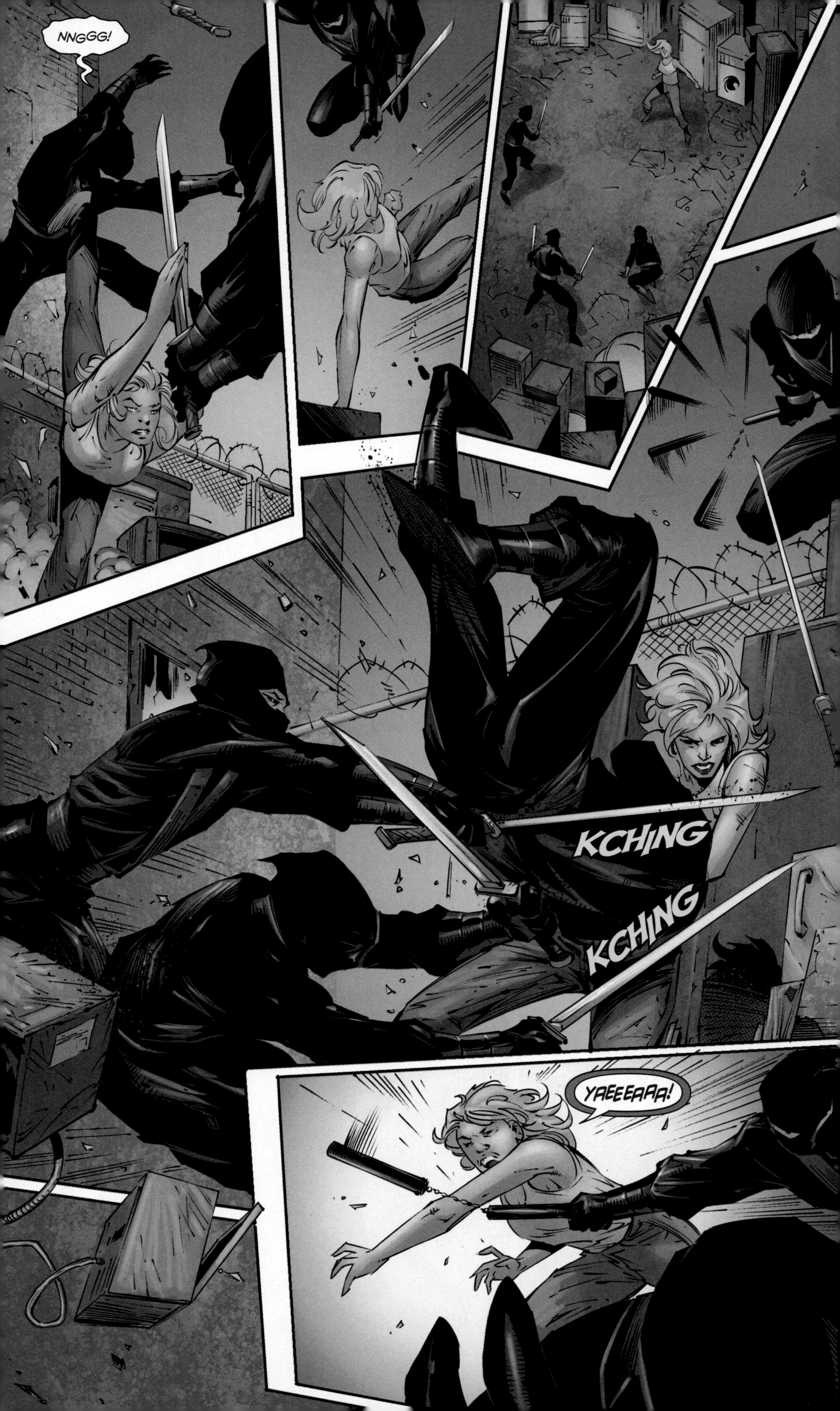
NNGGG!
KCHING
KCHING
YAEEEAAA!

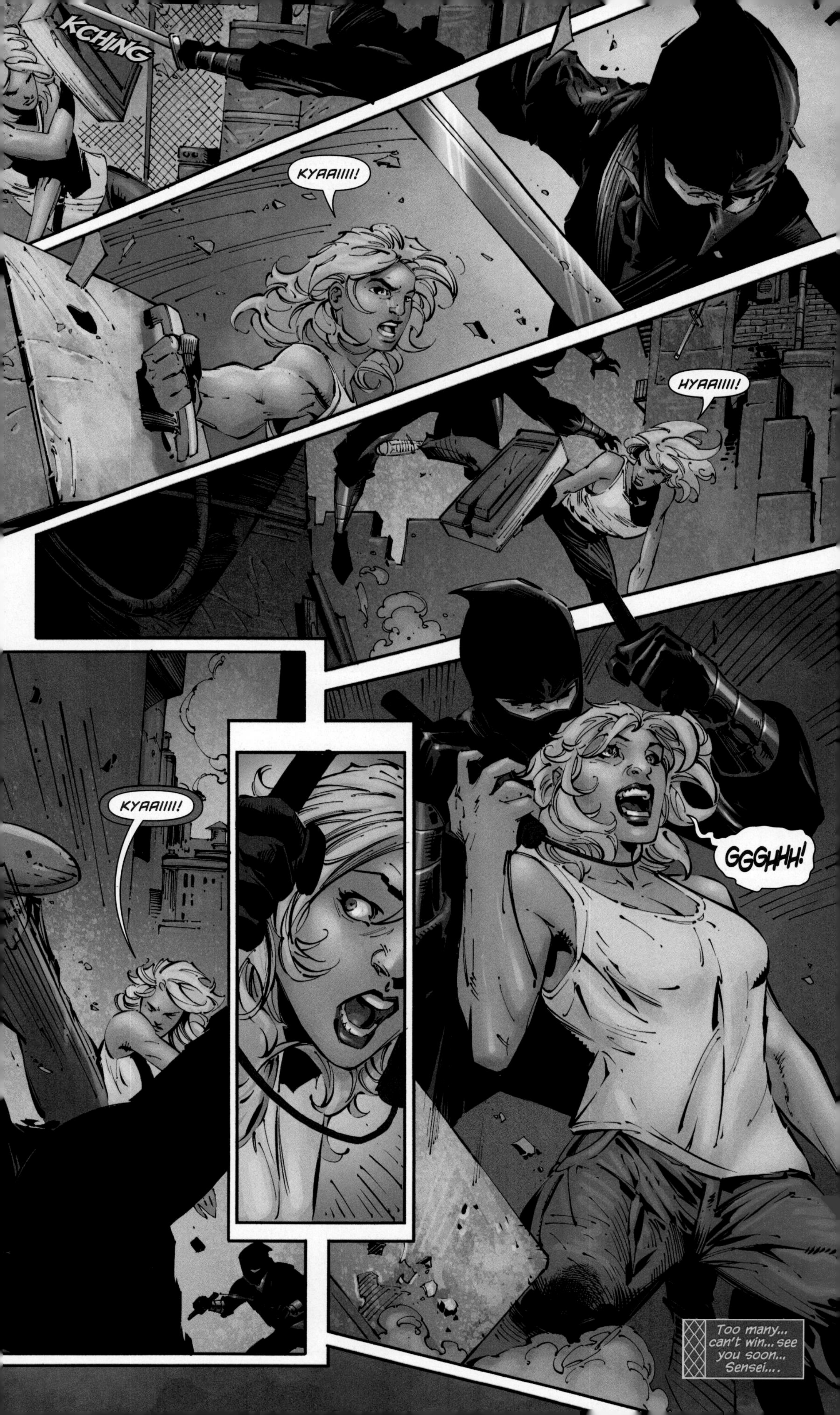

KCHING
KYAAIIII!
HYAAIIII!
KYAAIIII!
GGGHHH!
Too many... can't win... see you soon... Sensei...

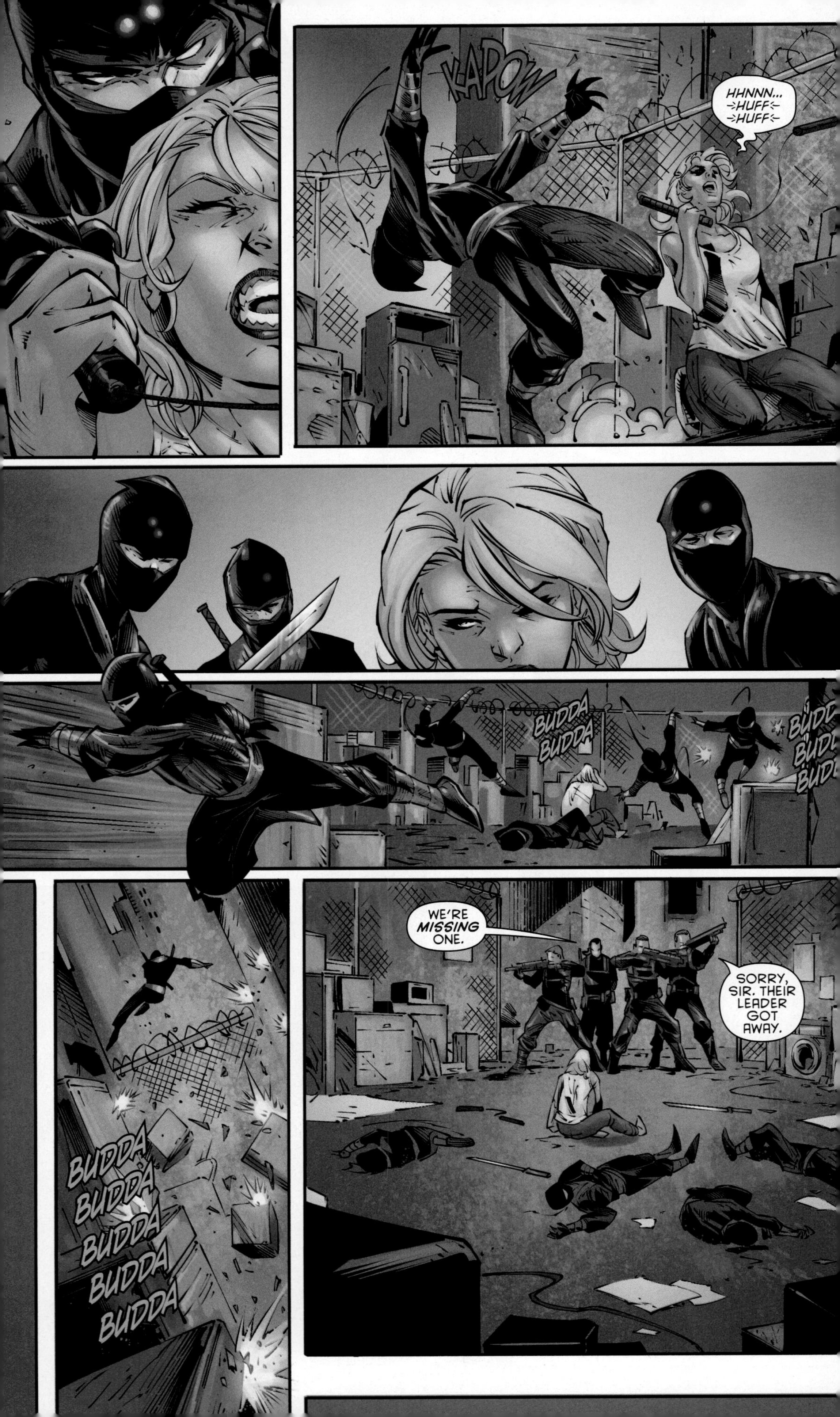
KAPOW
HHNNN... HUFF HUFF
BUDDA BUDDA
BUDDA BUDDA BUDDA
BUDDA BUDDA BUDDA BUDDA BUDDA
WE'RE MISSING ONE.
SORRY, SIR. THEIR LEADER GOT AWAY.

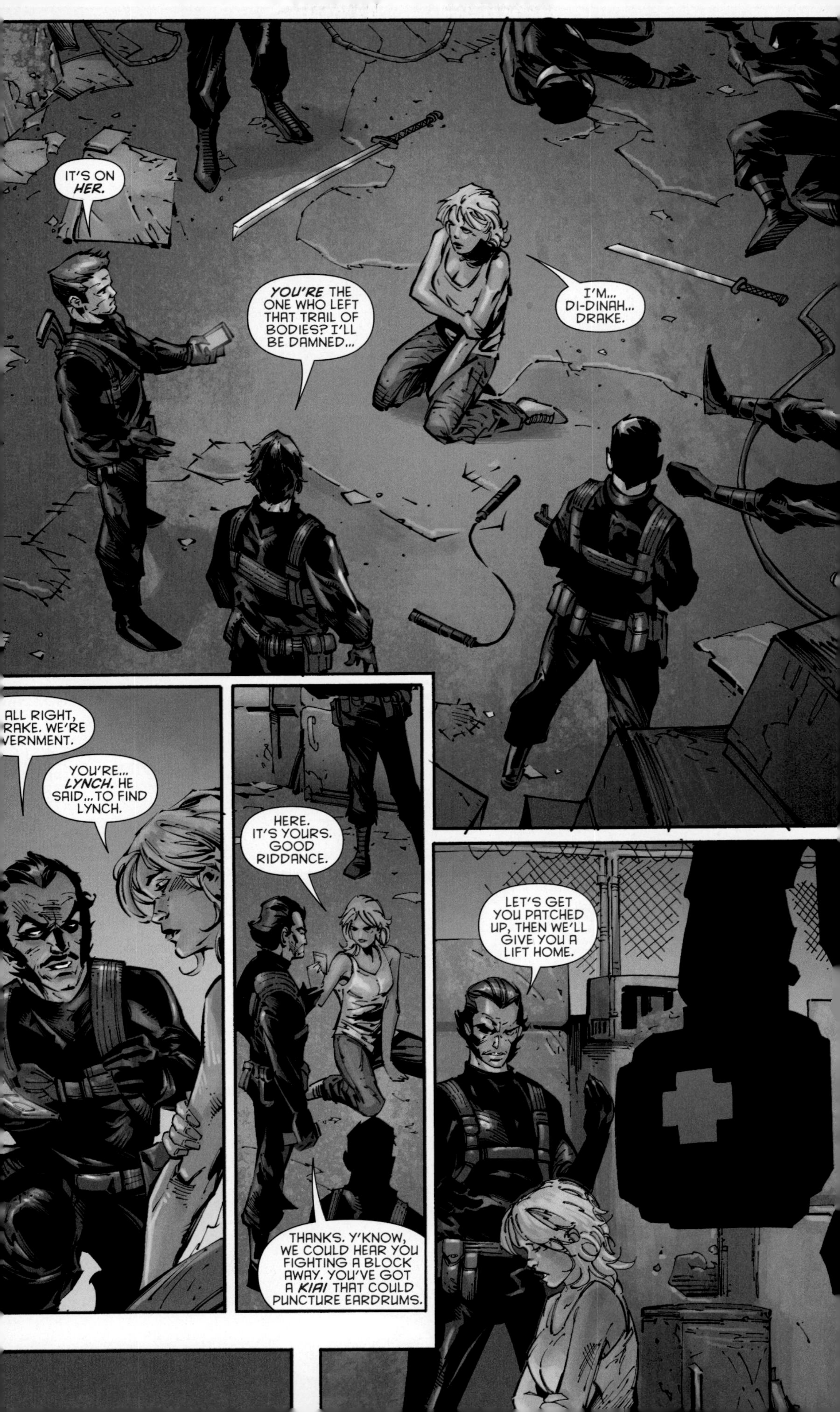

IT'S ON HER.
YOU'RE THE ONE WHO LEFT THAT TRAIL OF BODIES? I'LL BE DAMNED...
I'M... DI-DINAH... DRAKE.
ALL RIGHT, RAKE. WE'RE VERNMENT.
YOU'RE... LYNCH. HE SAID...TO FIND LYNCH.
HERE. IT'S YOURS. GOOD RIDDANCE.
THANKS. Y'KNOW, WE COULD HEAR YOU FIGHTING A BLOCK AWAY. YOU'VE GOT A KIAI THAT COULD PUNCTURE EARDRUMS.
LET'S GET YOU PATCHED UP, THEN WE'LL GIVE YOU A LIFT HOME.

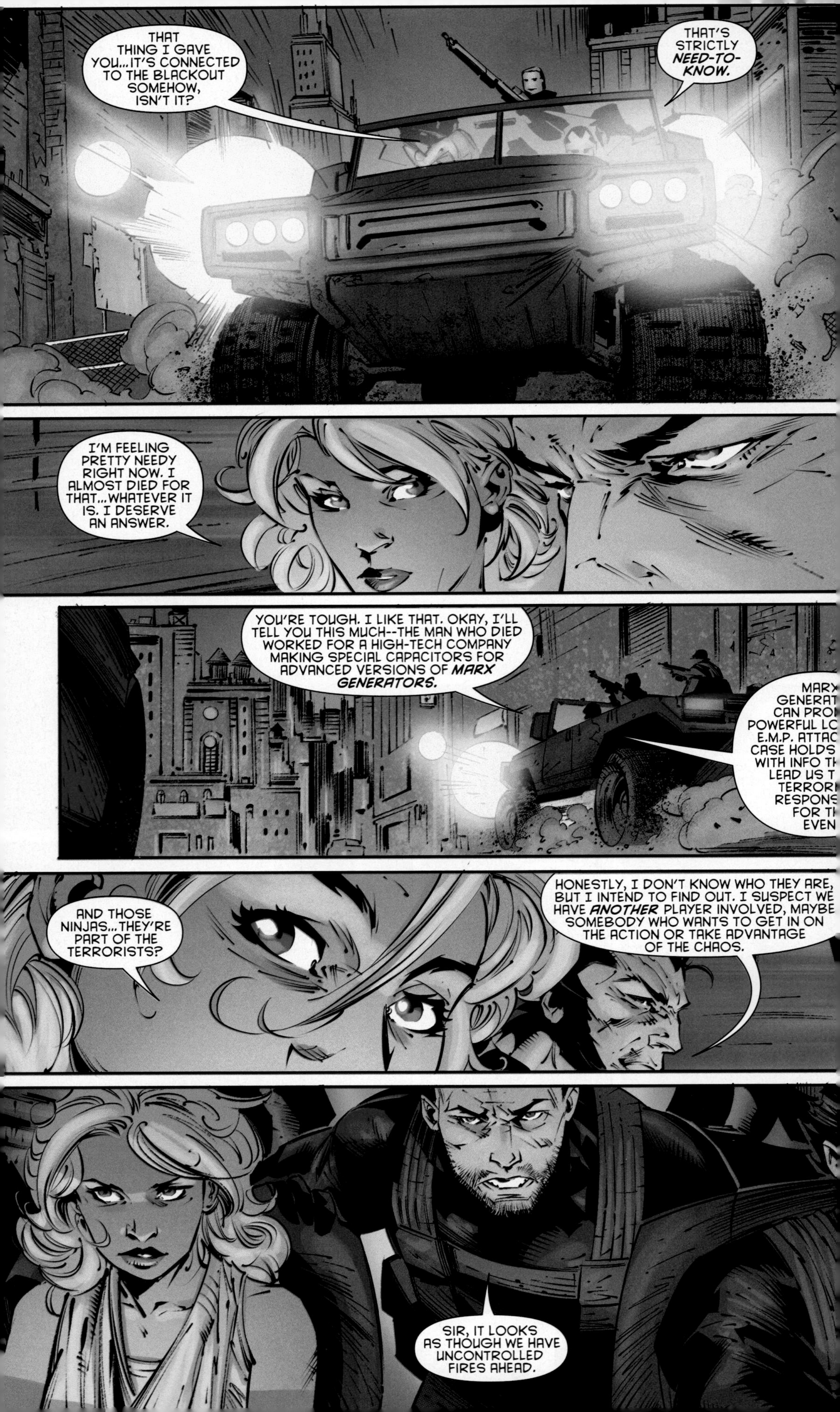
THAT THING I GAVE YOU...IT'S CONNECTED TO THE BLACKOUT SOMEHOW, ISN'T IT?
THAT'S STRICTLY NEED-TO-KNOW.
I'M FEELING PRETTY NEEDY RIGHT NOW. I ALMOST DIED FOR THAT...WHATEVER IT IS. I DESERVE AN ANSWER.
YOU'RE TOUGH. I LIKE THAT. OKAY, I'LL TELL YOU THIS MUCH--THE MAN WHO DIED WORKED FOR A HIGH-TECH COMPANY MAKING SPECIAL CAPACITORS FOR ADVANCED VERSIONS OF MARX GENERATORS.
AND THOSE NINJAS...THEY'RE PART OF THE TERRORISTS?
HONESTLY, I DON'T KNOW WHO THEY ARE, BUT I INTEND TO FIND OUT. I SUSPECT WE HAVE ANOTHER PLAYER INVOLVED, MAYBE SOMEBODY WHO WANTS TO GET IN ON THE ACTION OR TAKE ADVANTAGE OF THE CHAOS.
SIR, IT LOOKS AS THOUGH WE HAVE UNCONTROLLED FIRES AHEAD.

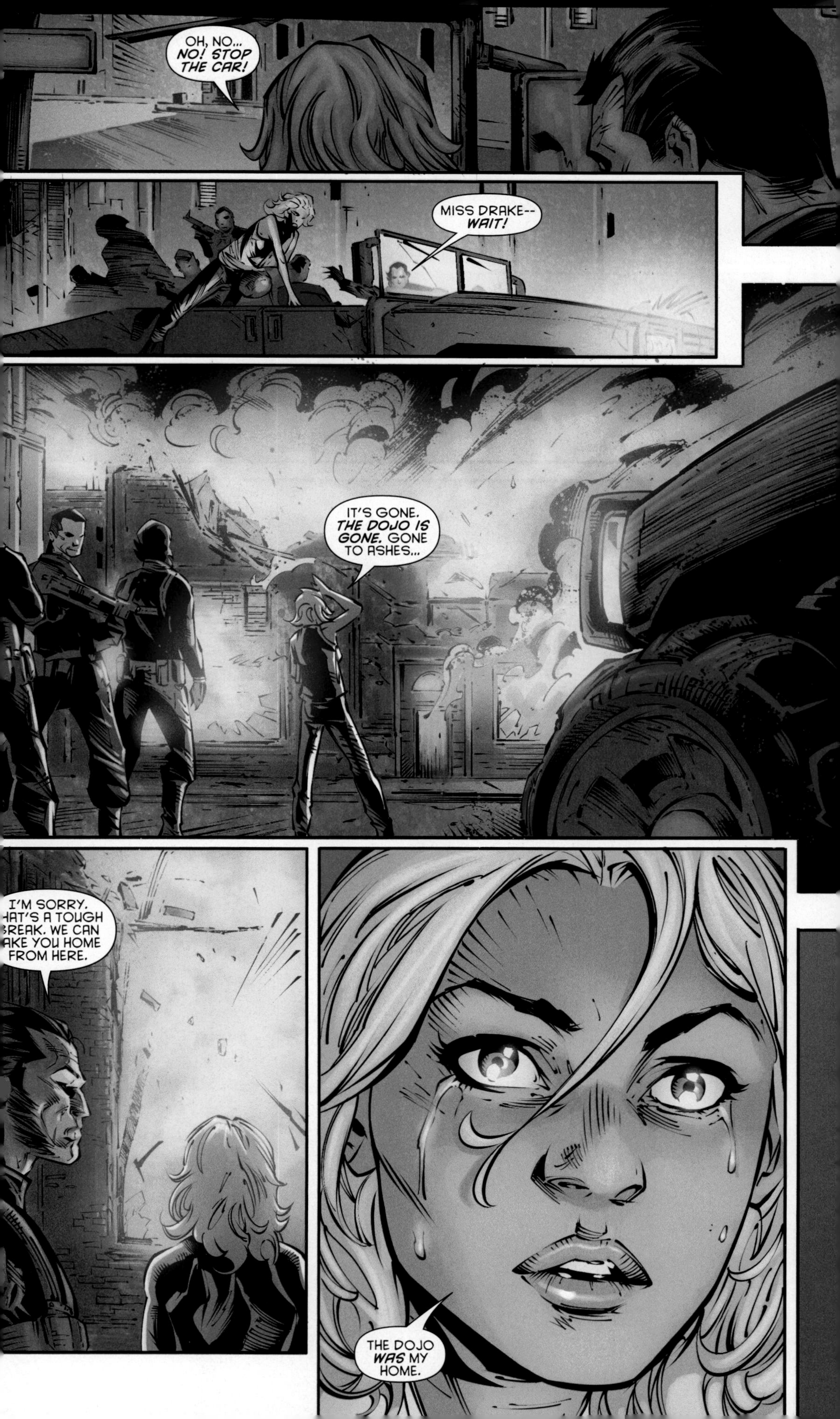
OH, NO... NO! STOP THE CAR!
MISS DRAKE-- WAIT!
IT'S GONE. THE DOJO IS GONE. GONE TO ASHES...
I'M SORRY. HAT'S A TOUGH REAK. WE CAN AKE YOU HOME FROM HERE.
THE DOJO WAS MY HOME.

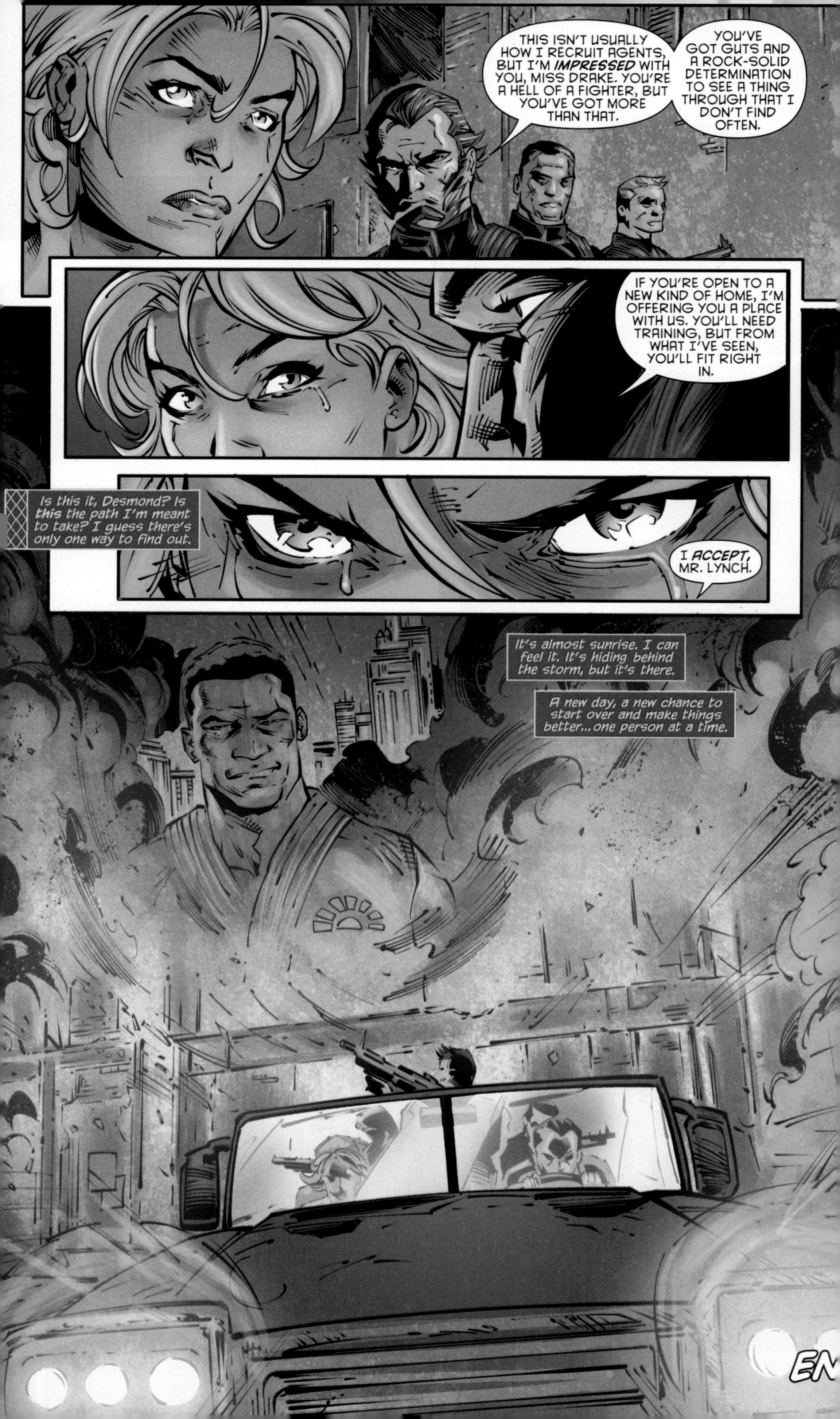
THIS ISN'T USUALLY HOW I RECRUIT AGENTS, BUT I'M IMPRESSED WITH YOU, MISS DRAKE. YOU'RE A HELL OF A FIGHTER, BUT YOU'VE GOT MORE THAN THAT.
YOU'VE GOT GUTS AND A ROCK-SOLID DETERMINATION TO SEE A THING THROUGH THAT I DON'T FIND OFTEN.
IF YOU'RE OPEN TO A NEW KIND OF HOME, I'M OFFERING YOU A PLACE WITH US. YOU'LL NEED TRAINING, BUT FROM WHAT I'VE SEEN, YOU'LL FIT RIGHT IN.
Is this it, Desmond? Is this the path I'm meant to take? I guess there's only one way to find out.
I ACCEPT, MR. LYNCH.
It's almost sunrise. I can feel it. It's hiding behind the storm, but it's there.
A new day, a new chance to start over and make things better...one person at a time.
EN

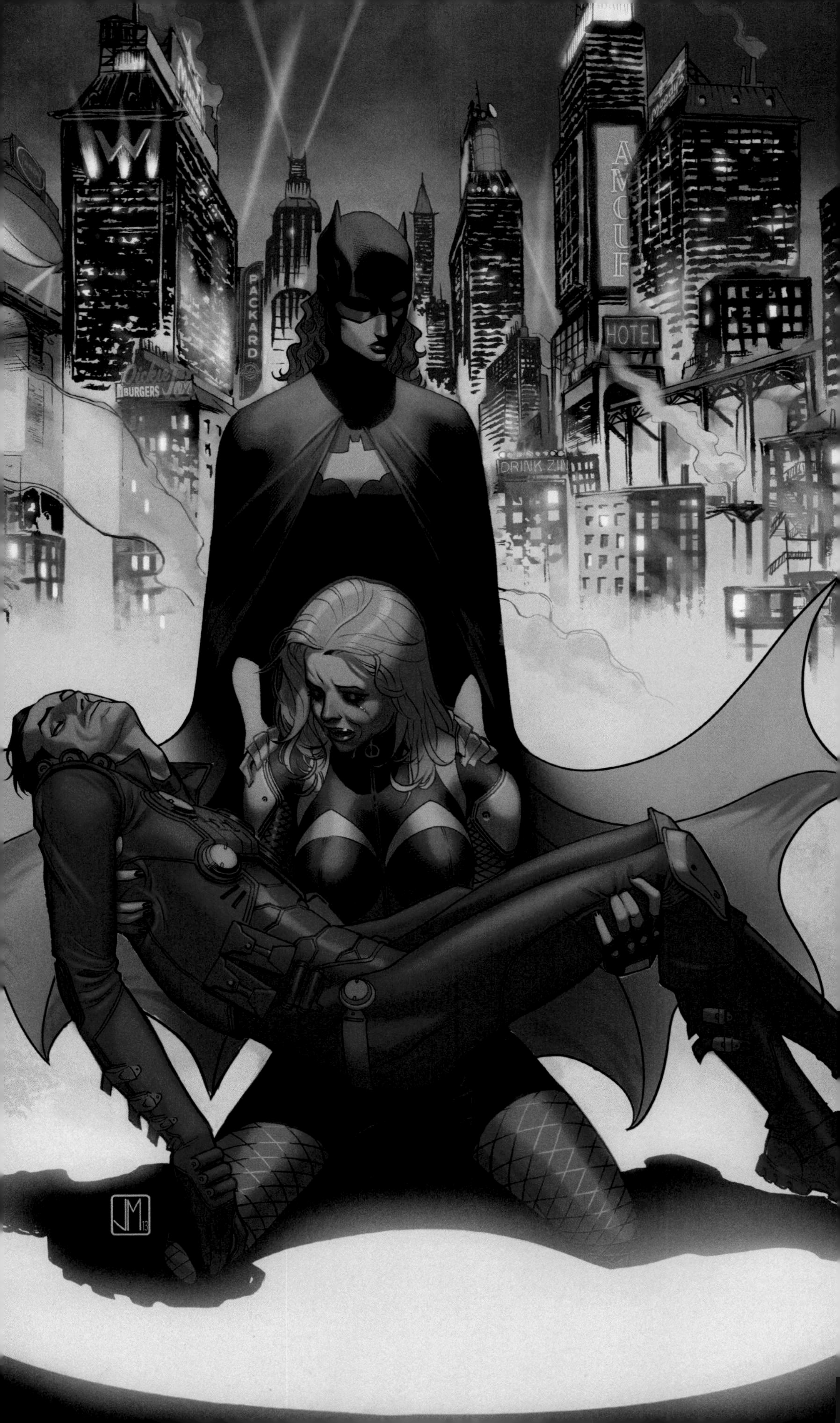
PACKARD
AMOUR
HOTEL
BURGERS
DRINK ZIN

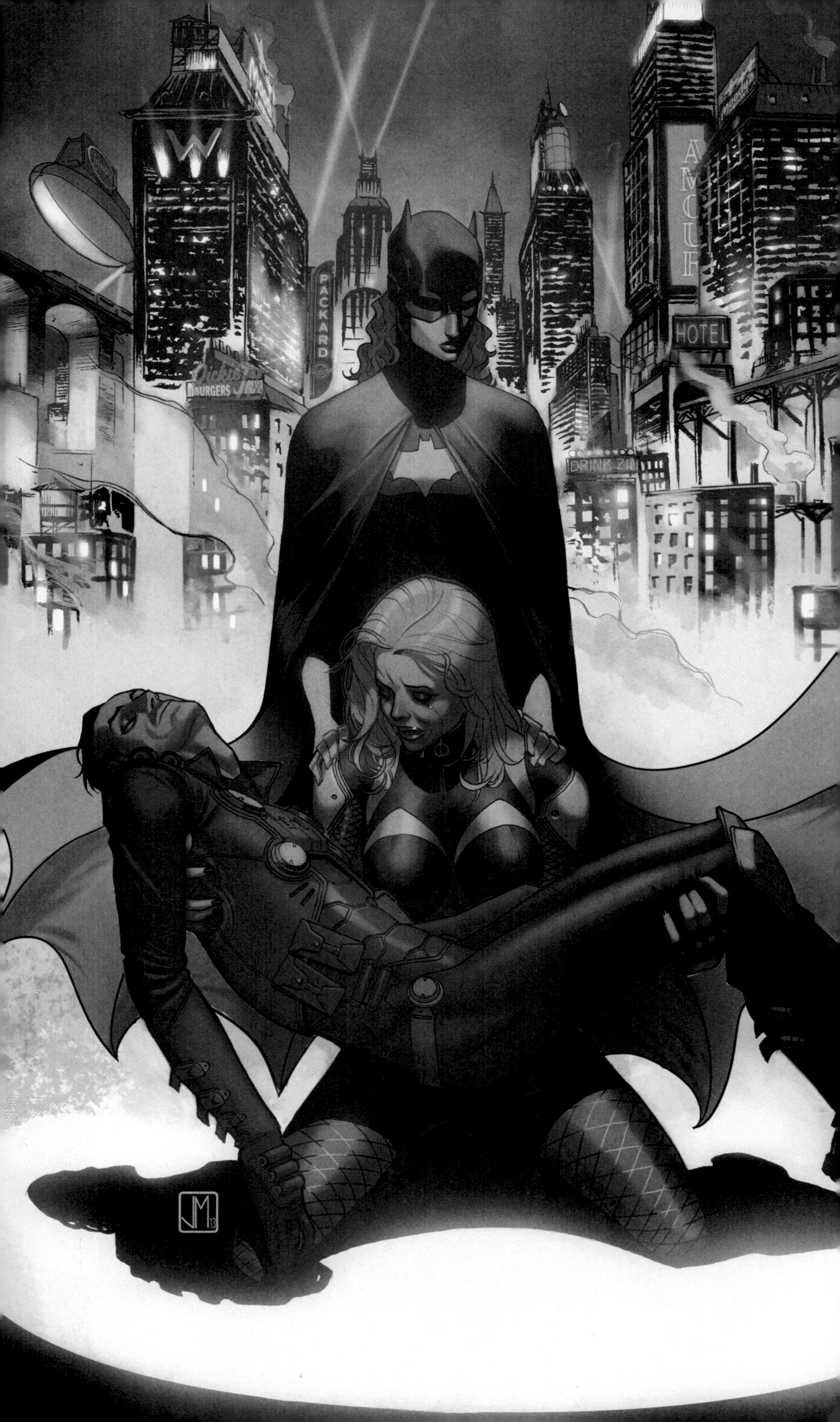
PACKARD
AMOUR
HOTEL
BURGERS
DRINK ZIN

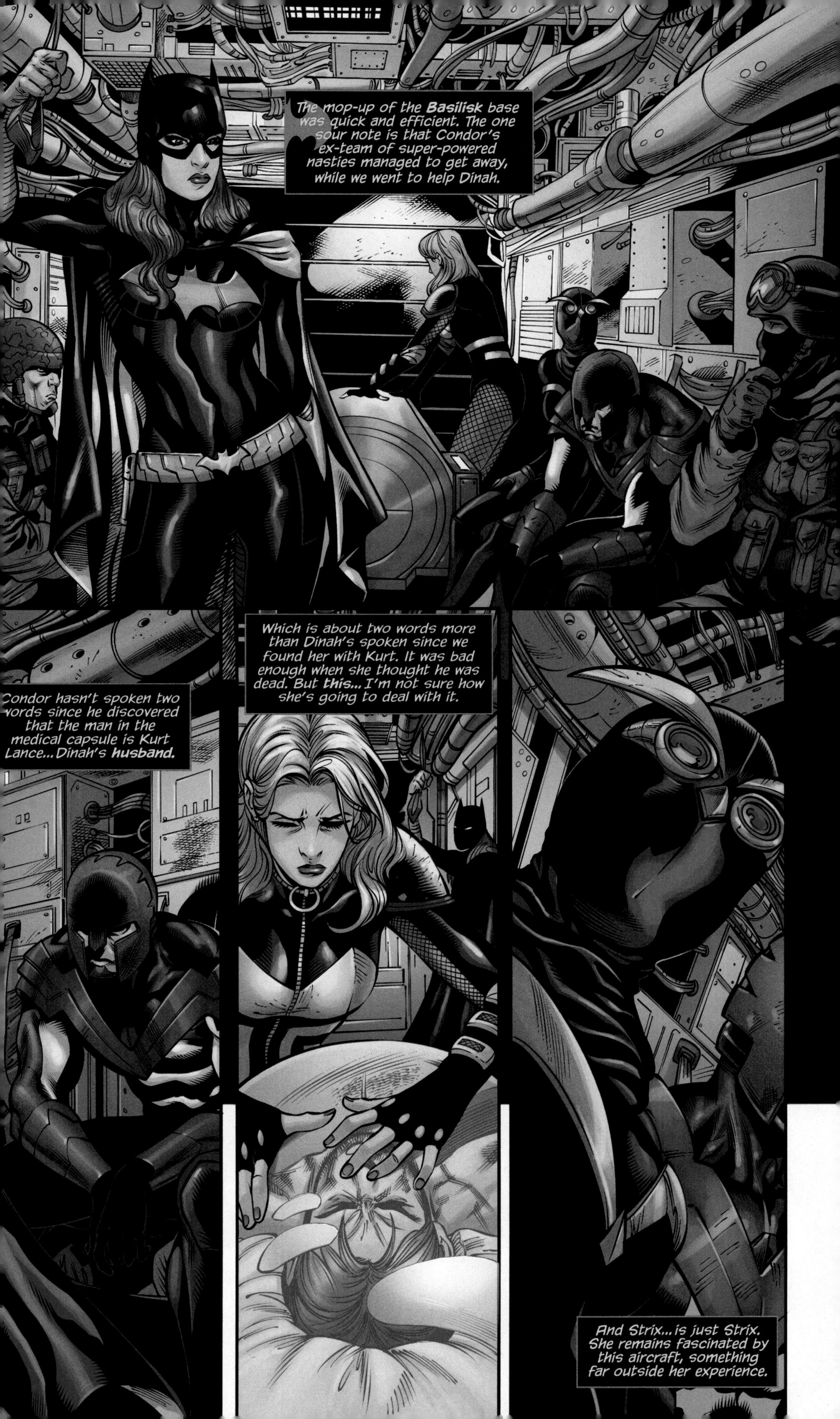
The mop-up of the **Basilisk** base was quick and efficient. The one sour note is that Condor's ex-team of super-powered nasties managed to get away, while we went to help Dinah.
Condor hasn't spoken two words since he discovered that the man in the medical capsule is Kurt Lance...Dinah's **husband.**
Which is about two words more than Dinah's spoken since we found her with Kurt. It was bad enough when she thought he was dead. But **this...** I'm not sure how she's going to deal with it.
And Strix...is just Strix. She remains fascinated by this aircraft, something far outside her experience.

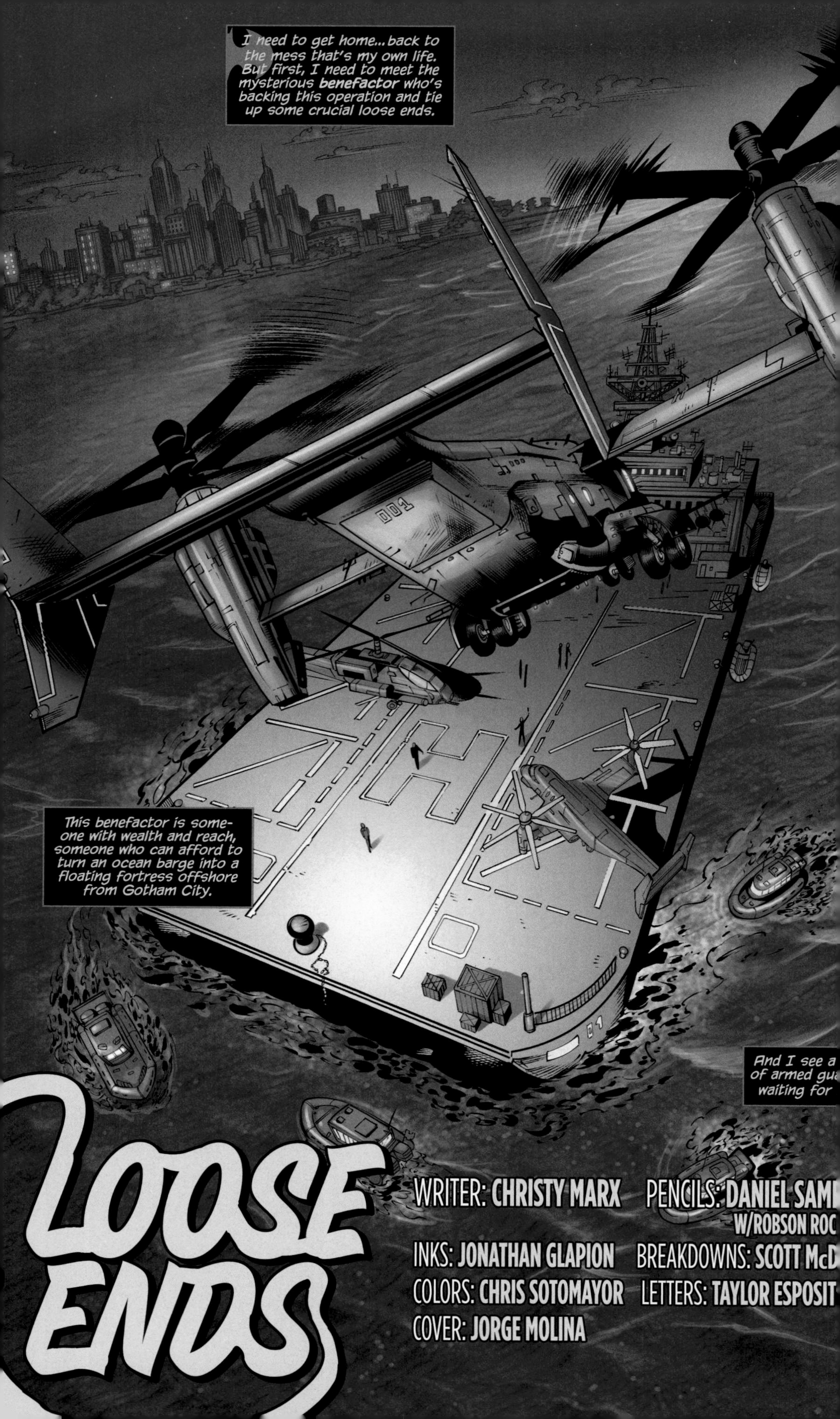
I need to get home... back to the mess that's my own life. But first, I need to meet the mysterious benefactor who's backing this operation and tie up some crucial loose ends.
This benefactor is someone with wealth and reach, someone who can afford to turn an ocean barge into a floating fortress offshore from Gotham City.
And I see a of armed gu waiting for
LOOSE ENDS
WRITER: CHRISTY MARX
PENCILS: DANIEL SAM
W/ROBSON ROC
INKS: JONATHAN GLAPION
BREAKDOWNS: SCOTT McD
COLORS: CHRIS SOTOMAYOR
LETTERS: TAYLOR ESPOSIT
COVER: JORGE MOLINA

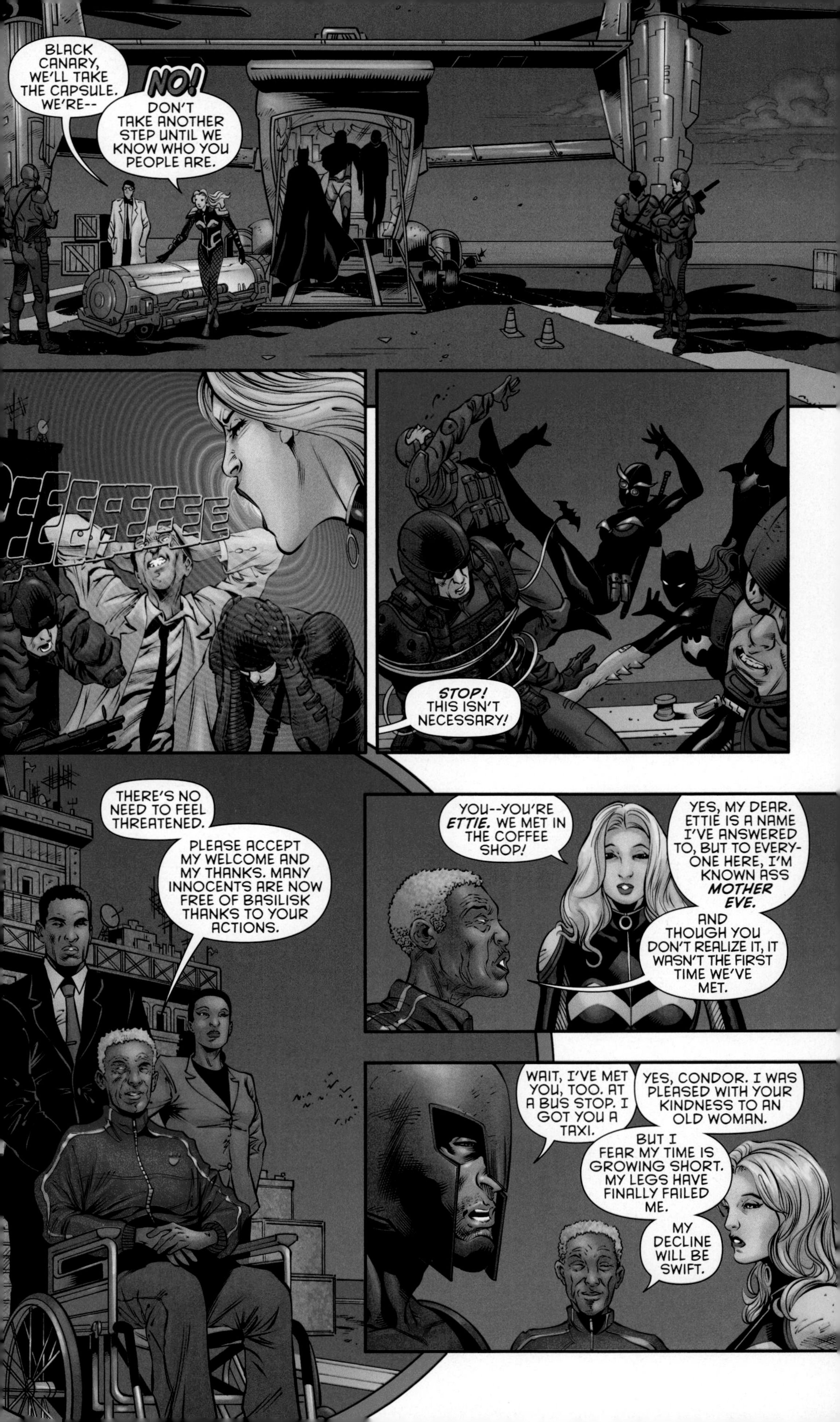
BLACK CANARY, WE'LL TAKE THE CAPSULE. WE'RE--
NO! DON'T TAKE ANOTHER STEP UNTIL WE KNOW WHO YOU PEOPLE ARE.
EEEEEEEE
STOP! THIS ISN'T NECESSARY!
THERE'S NO NEED TO FEEL THREATENED.
PLEASE ACCEPT MY WELCOME AND MY THANKS. MANY INNOCENTS ARE NOW FREE OF BASILISK THANKS TO YOUR ACTIONS.
YOU--YOU'RE ETTIE. WE MET IN THE COFFEE SHOP!
YES, MY DEAR. ETTIE IS A NAME I'VE ANSWERED TO, BUT TO EVERYONE HERE, I'M KNOWN ASS MOTHER EVE.
AND THOUGH YOU DON'T REALIZE IT, IT WASN'T THE FIRST TIME WE'VE MET.
WAIT, I'VE MET YOU, TOO. AT A BUS STOP. I GOT YOU A TAXI.
YES, CONDOR. I WAS PLEASED WITH YOUR KINDNESS TO AN OLD WOMAN.
BUT I FEAR MY TIME IS GROWING SHORT. MY LEGS HAVE FINALLY FAILED ME.
MY DECLINE WILL BE SWIFT.

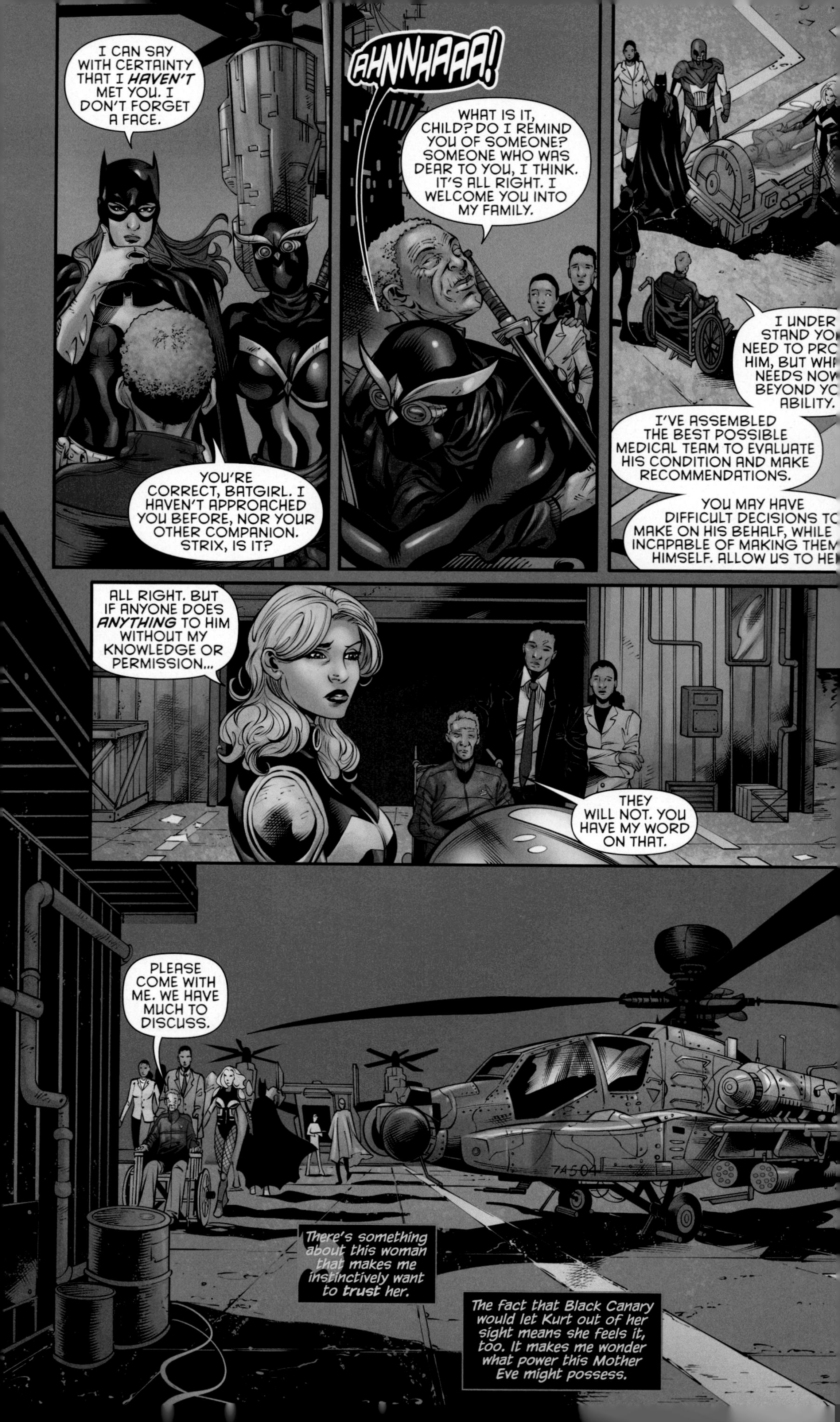

I CAN SAY WITH CERTAINTY THAT I *HAVEN'T* MET YOU. I DON'T FORGET A FACE.
YOU'RE CORRECT, BATGIRL. I HAVEN'T APPROACHED YOU BEFORE, NOR YOUR OTHER COMPANION. STRIX, IS IT?
AHNNHAAA!
WHAT IS IT, CHILD? DO I REMIND YOU OF SOMEONE? SOMEONE WHO WAS DEAR TO YOU, I THINK. IT'S ALL RIGHT. I WELCOME YOU INTO MY FAMILY.
I UNDER STAND YO NEED TO PRO HIM, BUT WH NEEDS NOW BEYOND YO ABILITY.
I'VE ASSEMBLED THE BEST POSSIBLE MEDICAL TEAM TO EVALUATE HIS CONDITION AND MAKE RECOMMENDATIONS.
YOU MAY HAVE DIFFICULT DECISIONS TO MAKE ON HIS BEHALF, WHILE INCAPABLE OF MAKING THEM HIMSELF. ALLOW US TO HE
ALL RIGHT. BUT IF ANYONE DOES *ANYTHING* TO HIM WITHOUT MY KNOWLEDGE OR PERMISSION...
THEY WILL NOT. YOU HAVE MY WORD ON THAT.
PLEASE COME WITH ME. WE HAVE MUCH TO DISCUSS.
74504
*There's something about this woman that makes me instinctively want to **trust** her.*
The fact that Black Canary would let Kurt out of her sight means she feels it, too. It makes me wonder what power this Mother Eve might possess.

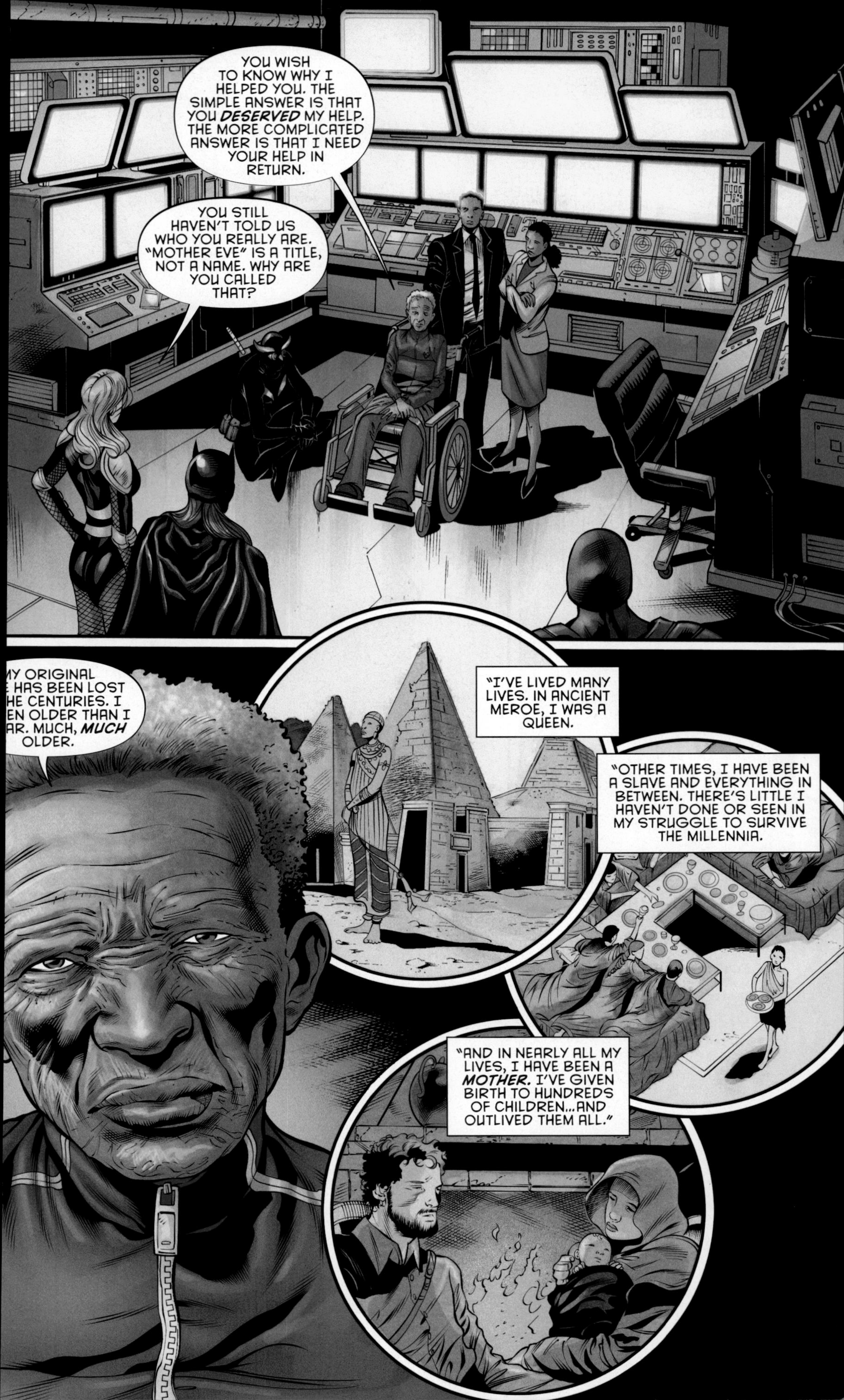

YOU WISH TO KNOW WHY I HELPED YOU. THE SIMPLE ANSWER IS THAT YOU *DESERVED* MY HELP. THE MORE COMPLICATED ANSWER IS THAT I NEED YOUR HELP IN RETURN.
YOU STILL HAVEN'T TOLD US WHO YOU REALLY ARE. "MOTHER EVE" IS A TITLE, NOT A NAME. WHY ARE YOU CALLED THAT?
MY ORIGINAL E HAS BEEN LOST HE CENTURIES. I EN OLDER THAN I AR. MUCH, *MUCH* OLDER.
"I'VE LIVED MANY LIVES. IN ANCIENT MEROE, I WAS A QUEEN.
"OTHER TIMES, I HAVE BEEN A SLAVE AND EVERYTHING IN BETWEEN. THERE'S LITTLE I HAVEN'T DONE OR SEEN IN MY STRUGGLE TO SURVIVE THE MILLENNIA.
"AND IN NEARLY ALL MY LIVES, I HAVE BEEN A *MOTHER.* I'VE GIVEN BIRTH TO HUNDREDS OF CHILDREN...AND OUTLIVED THEM ALL."

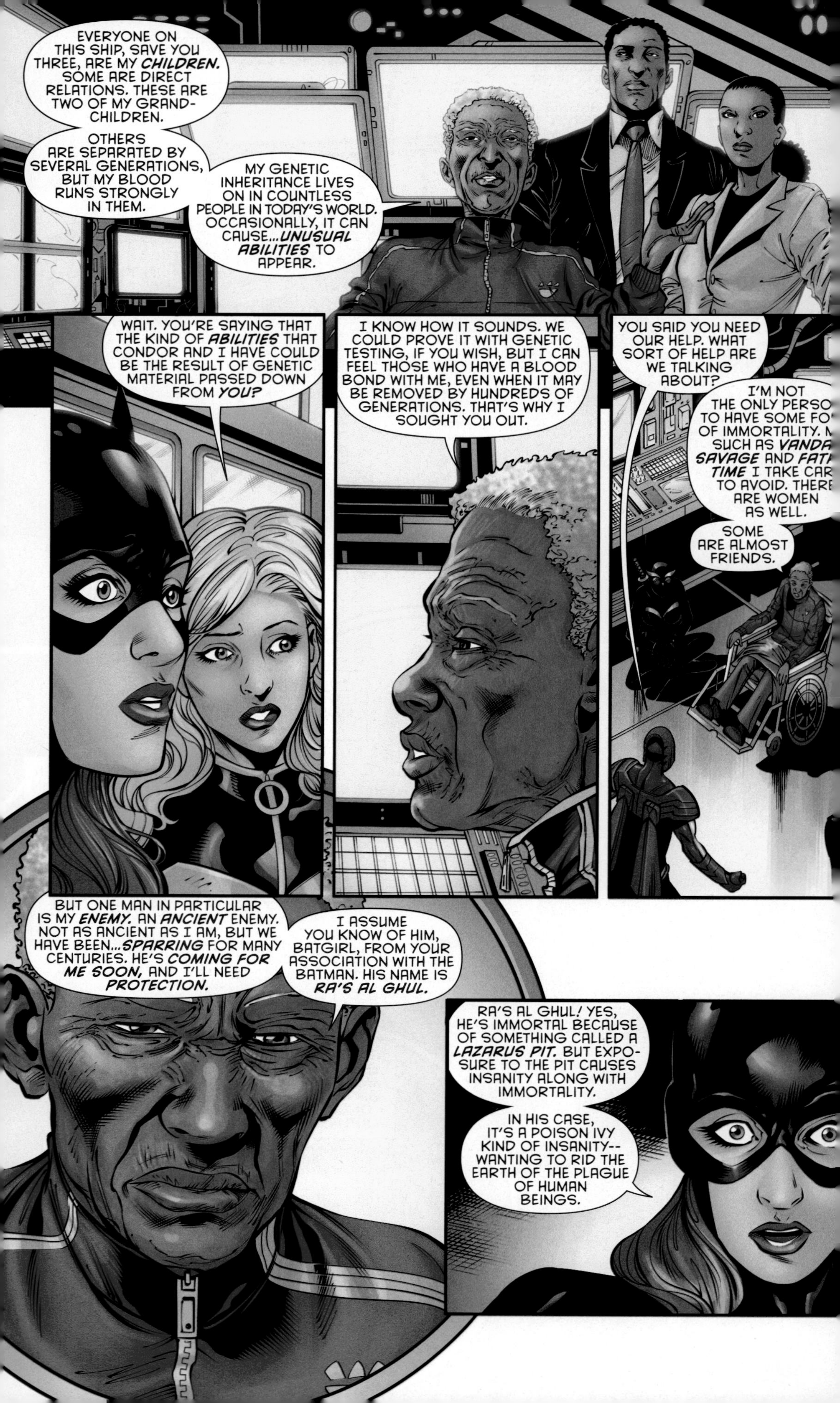

EVERYONE ON THIS SHIP, SAVE YOU THREE, ARE MY CHILDREN. SOME ARE DIRECT RELATIONS. THESE ARE TWO OF MY GRAND-CHILDREN.
OTHERS ARE SEPARATED BY SEVERAL GENERATIONS, BUT MY BLOOD RUNS STRONGLY IN THEM.
MY GENETIC INHERITANCE LIVES ON IN COUNTLESS PEOPLE IN TODAY'S WORLD. OCCASIONALLY, IT CAN CAUSE...UNUSUAL ABILITIES TO APPEAR.
WAIT. YOU'RE SAYING THAT THE KIND OF ABILITIES THAT CONDOR AND I HAVE COULD BE THE RESULT OF GENETIC MATERIAL PASSED DOWN FROM YOU?
I KNOW HOW IT SOUNDS. WE COULD PROVE IT WITH GENETIC TESTING, IF YOU WISH, BUT I CAN FEEL THOSE WHO HAVE A BLOOD BOND WITH ME, EVEN WHEN IT MAY BE REMOVED BY HUNDREDS OF GENERATIONS. THAT'S WHY I SOUGHT YOU OUT.
YOU SAID YOU NEED OUR HELP. WHAT SORT OF HELP ARE WE TALKING ABOUT?
I'M NOT THE ONLY PERSO TO HAVE SOME FO OF IMMORTALITY. M SUCH AS VANDA SAVAGE AND FATH TIME I TAKE CAR TO AVOID. THERE ARE WOMEN AS WELL.
SOME ARE ALMOST FRIENDS.
BUT ONE MAN IN PARTICULAR IS MY ENEMY. AN ANCIENT ENEMY. NOT AS ANCIENT AS I AM, BUT WE HAVE BEEN...SPARRING FOR MANY CENTURIES. HE'S COMING FOR ME SOON, AND I'LL NEED PROTECTION.
I ASSUME YOU KNOW OF HIM, BATGIRL, FROM YOUR ASSOCIATION WITH THE BATMAN. HIS NAME IS RA'S AL GHUL.
RA'S AL GHUL! YES, HE'S IMMORTAL BECAUSE OF SOMETHING CALLED A LAZARUS PIT. BUT EXPO-SURE TO THE PIT CAUSES INSANITY ALONG WITH IMMORTALITY.
IN HIS CASE, IT'S A POISON IVY KIND OF INSANITY-- WANTING TO RID THE EARTH OF THE PLAGUE OF HUMAN BEINGS.

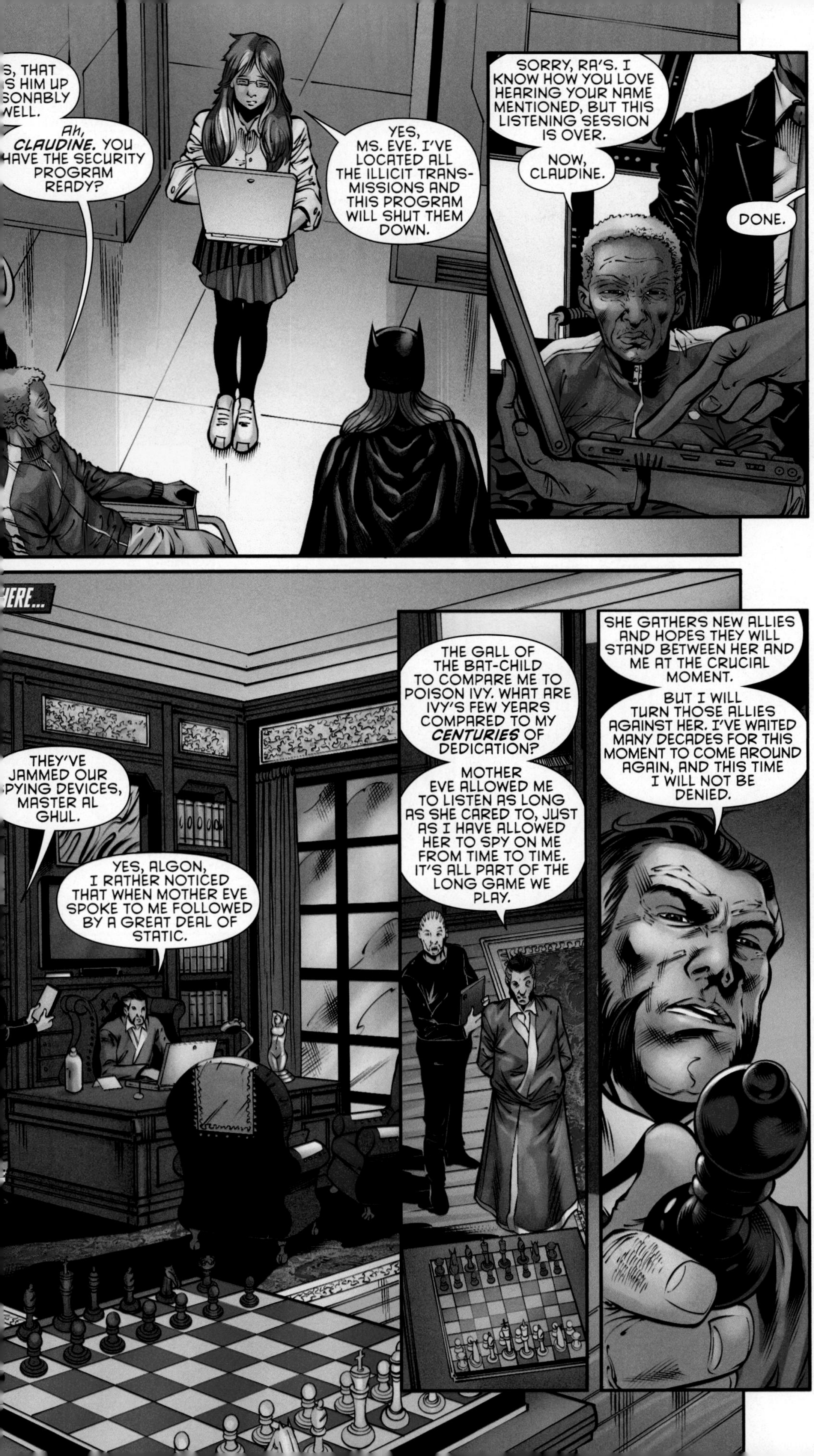
S, THAT
S HIM UP
SONABLY
WELL.
Ah, CLAUDINE. YOU HAVE THE SECURITY PROGRAM READY?
YES, MS. EVE. I'VE LOCATED ALL THE ILLICIT TRANSMISSIONS AND THIS PROGRAM WILL SHUT THEM DOWN.
SORRY, RA'S. I KNOW HOW YOU LOVE HEARING YOUR NAME MENTIONED, BUT THIS LISTENING SESSION IS OVER.
NOW, CLAUDINE.
DONE.
HERE...
THEY'VE JAMMED OUR SPYING DEVICES, MASTER AL GHUL.
YES, ALGON, I RATHER NOTICED THAT WHEN MOTHER EVE SPOKE TO ME FOLLOWED BY A GREAT DEAL OF STATIC.
THE GALL OF THE BAT-CHILD TO COMPARE ME TO POISON IVY. WHAT ARE IVY'S FEW YEARS COMPARED TO MY CENTURIES OF DEDICATION?
MOTHER EVE ALLOWED ME TO LISTEN AS LONG AS SHE CARED TO, JUST AS I HAVE ALLOWED HER TO SPY ON ME FROM TIME TO TIME. IT'S ALL PART OF THE LONG GAME WE PLAY.
SHE GATHERS NEW ALLIES AND HOPES THEY WILL STAND BETWEEN HER AND ME AT THE CRUCIAL MOMENT.
BUT I WILL TURN THOSE ALLIES AGAINST HER. I'VE WAITED MANY DECADES FOR THIS MOMENT TO COME AROUND AGAIN, AND THIS TIME I WILL NOT BE DENIED.

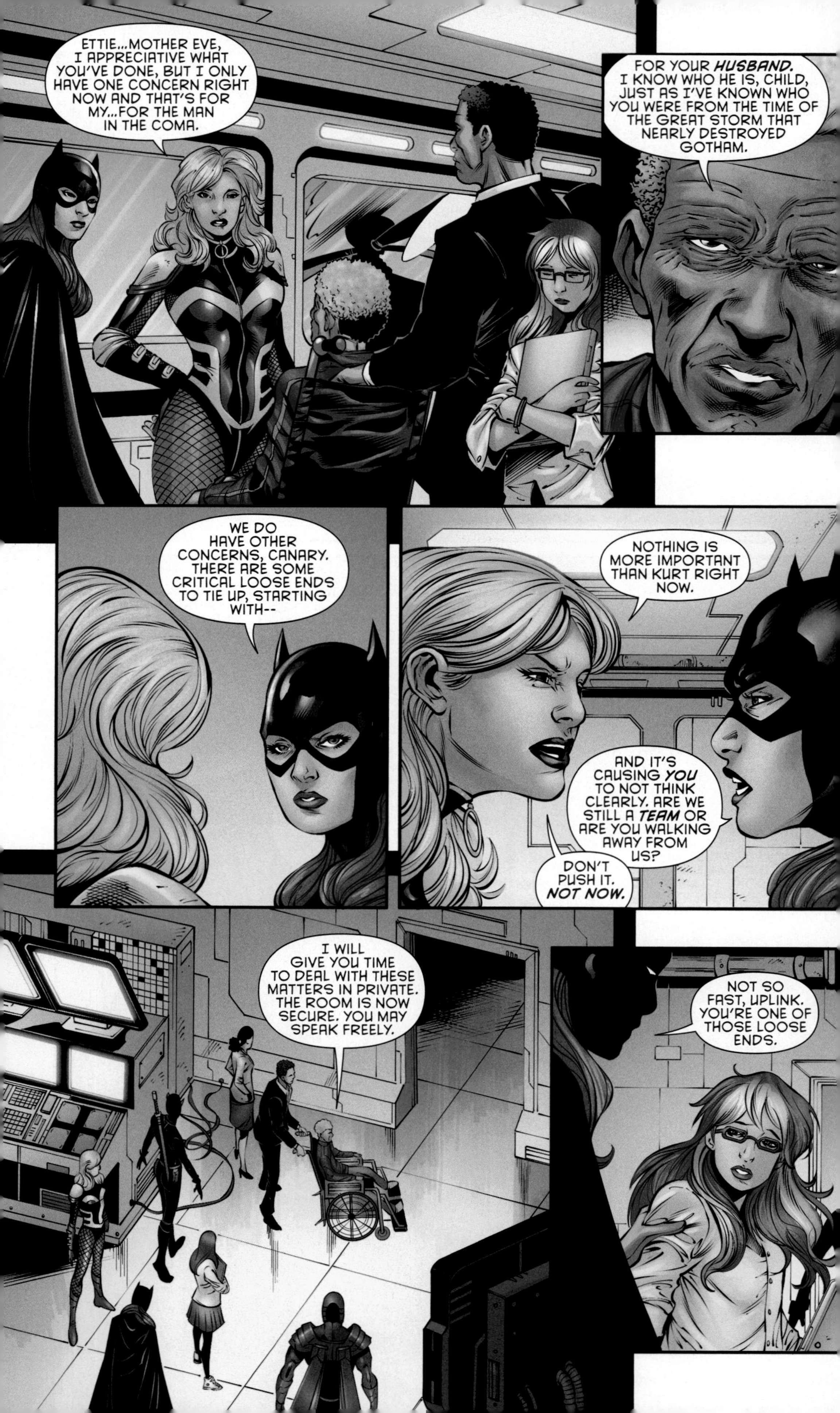
ETTIE...MOTHER EVE, I APPRECIATIVE WHAT YOU'VE DONE, BUT I ONLY HAVE ONE CONCERN RIGHT NOW AND THAT'S FOR MY...FOR THE MAN IN THE COMA.
FOR YOUR *HUSBAND.* I KNOW WHO HE IS, CHILD, JUST AS I'VE KNOWN WHO YOU WERE FROM THE TIME OF THE GREAT STORM THAT NEARLY DESTROYED GOTHAM.
WE DO HAVE OTHER CONCERNS, CANARY. THERE ARE SOME CRITICAL LOOSE ENDS TO TIE UP, STARTING WITH--
NOTHING IS MORE IMPORTANT THAN KURT RIGHT NOW.
AND IT'S CAUSING *YOU* TO NOT THINK CLEARLY. ARE WE STILL A *TEAM* OR ARE YOU WALKING AWAY FROM US?
DON'T PUSH IT. ***NOT NOW.***
I WILL GIVE YOU TIME TO DEAL WITH THESE MATTERS IN PRIVATE. THE ROOM IS NOW SECURE. YOU MAY SPEAK FREELY.
NOT SO FAST, UPLINK. YOU'RE ONE OF THOSE LOOSE ENDS.

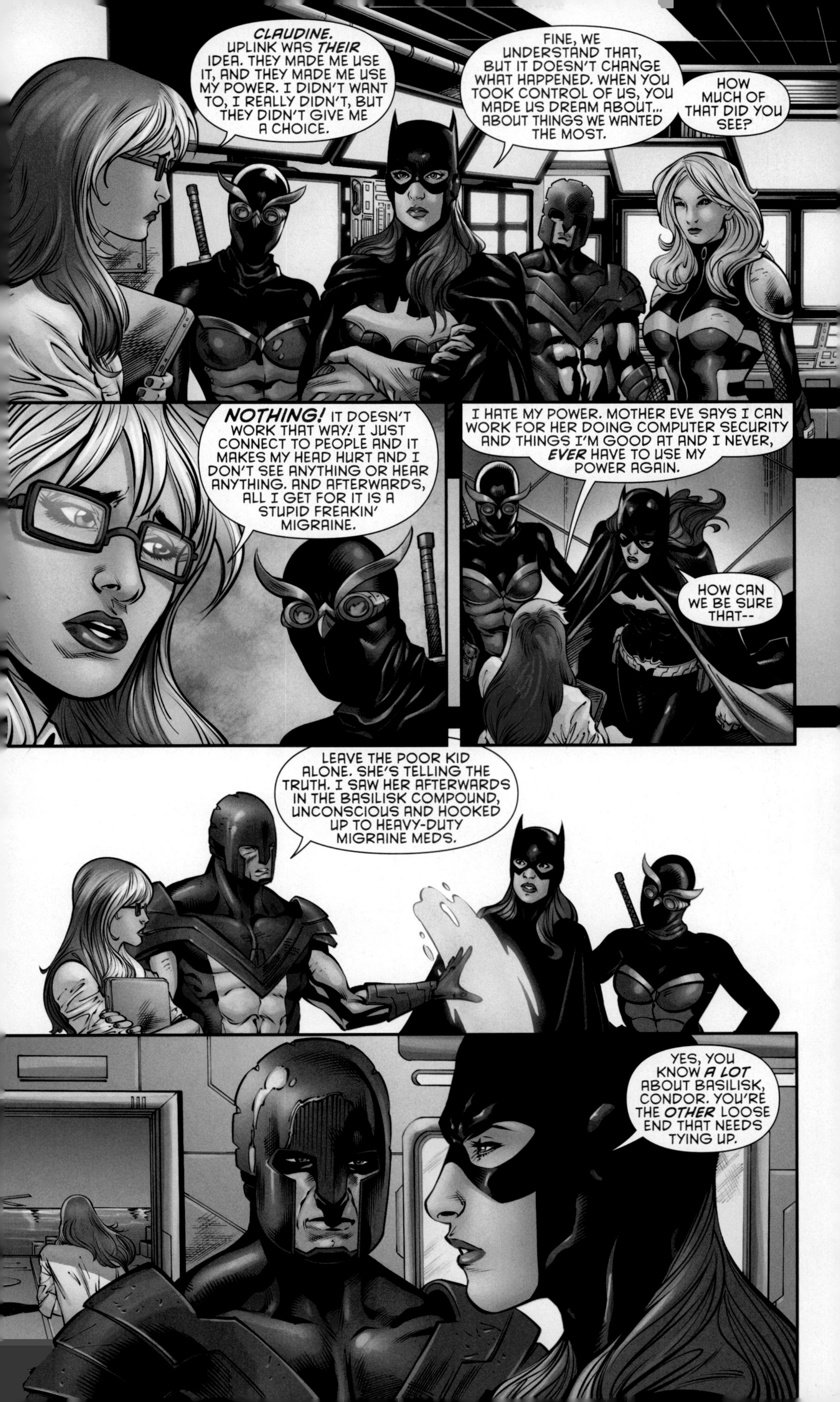
CLAUDINE. UPLINK WAS THEIR IDEA. THEY MADE ME USE IT, AND THEY MADE ME USE MY POWER. I DIDN'T WANT TO, I REALLY DIDN'T, BUT THEY DIDN'T GIVE ME A CHOICE.
FINE, WE UNDERSTAND THAT, BUT IT DOESN'T CHANGE WHAT HAPPENED. WHEN YOU TOOK CONTROL OF US, YOU MADE US DREAM ABOUT... ABOUT THINGS WE WANTED THE MOST.
HOW MUCH OF THAT DID YOU SEE?
NOTHING! IT DOESN'T WORK THAT WAY! I JUST CONNECT TO PEOPLE AND IT MAKES MY HEAD HURT AND I DON'T SEE ANYTHING OR HEAR ANYTHING. AND AFTERWARDS, ALL I GET FOR IT IS A STUPID FREAKIN' MIGRAINE.
I HATE MY POWER. MOTHER EVE SAYS I CAN WORK FOR HER DOING COMPUTER SECURITY AND THINGS I'M GOOD AT AND I NEVER, EVER HAVE TO USE MY POWER AGAIN.
HOW CAN WE BE SURE THAT--
LEAVE THE POOR KID ALONE. SHE'S TELLING THE TRUTH. I SAW HER AFTERWARDS IN THE BASILISK COMPOUND, UNCONSCIOUS AND HOOKED UP TO HEAVY-DUTY MIGRAINE MEDS.
YES, YOU KNOW A LOT ABOUT BASILISK, CONDOR. YOU'RE THE OTHER LOOSE END THAT NEEDS TYING UP.

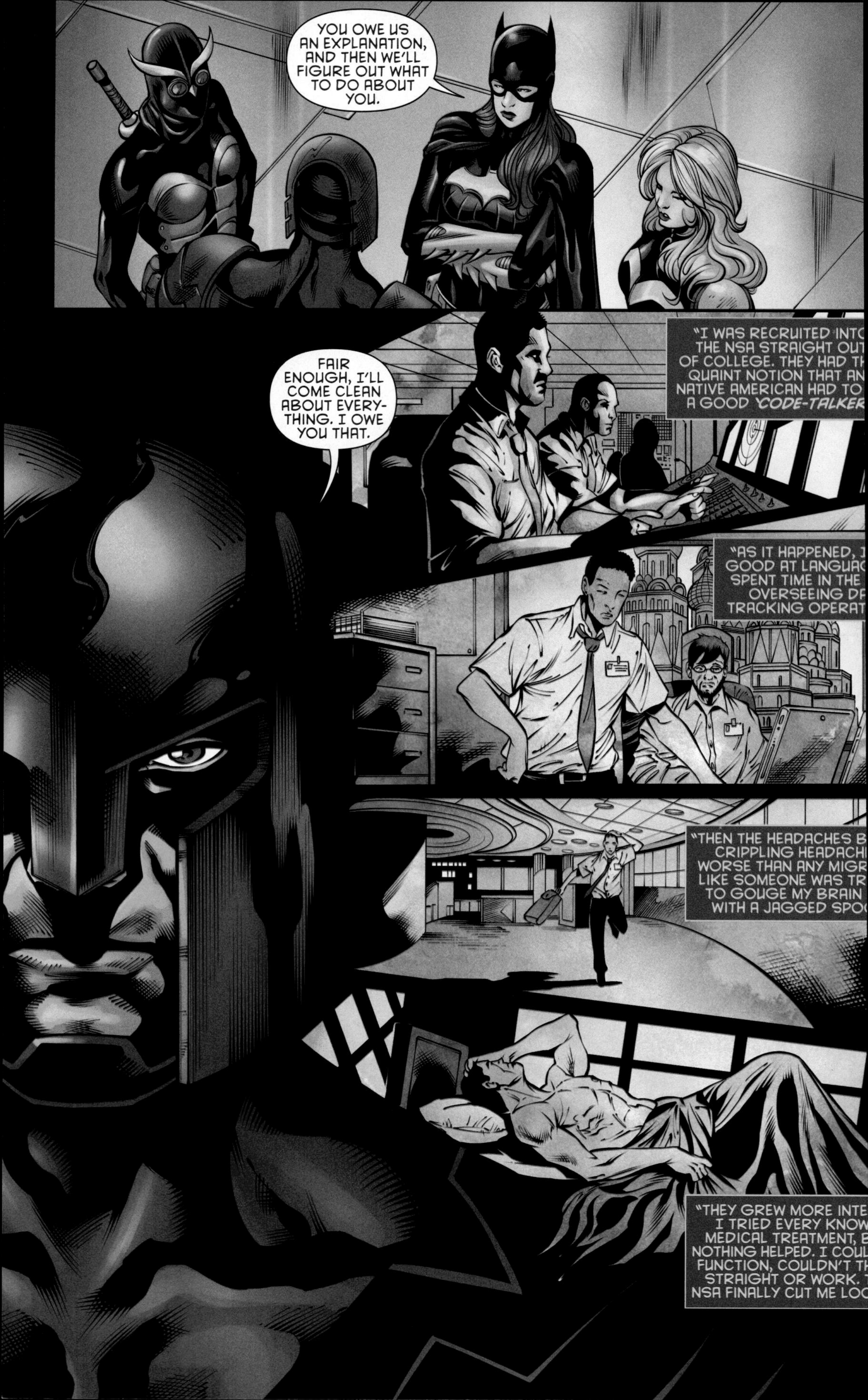
YOU OWE US AN EXPLANATION, AND THEN WE'LL FIGURE OUT WHAT TO DO ABOUT YOU.
FAIR ENOUGH, I'LL COME CLEAN ABOUT EVERY-THING. I OWE YOU THAT.
"I WAS RECRUITED INTO THE NSA STRAIGHT OUT OF COLLEGE. THEY HAD TH QUAINT NOTION THAT AN NATIVE AMERICAN HAD TO A GOOD 'CODE-TALKER
"AS IT HAPPENED, I GOOD AT LANGUAG SPENT TIME IN THE OVERSEEING DA TRACKING OPERAT
"THEN THE HEADACHES B CRIPPLING HEADACH WORSE THAN ANY MIGR LIKE SOMEONE WAS TR TO GOUGE MY BRAIN WITH A JAGGED SPOO
"THEY GREW MORE INTE I TRIED EVERY KNOW MEDICAL TREATMENT, B NOTHING HELPED. I COUL FUNCTION, COULDN'T TH STRAIGHT OR WORK. T NSA FINALLY CUT ME LOO

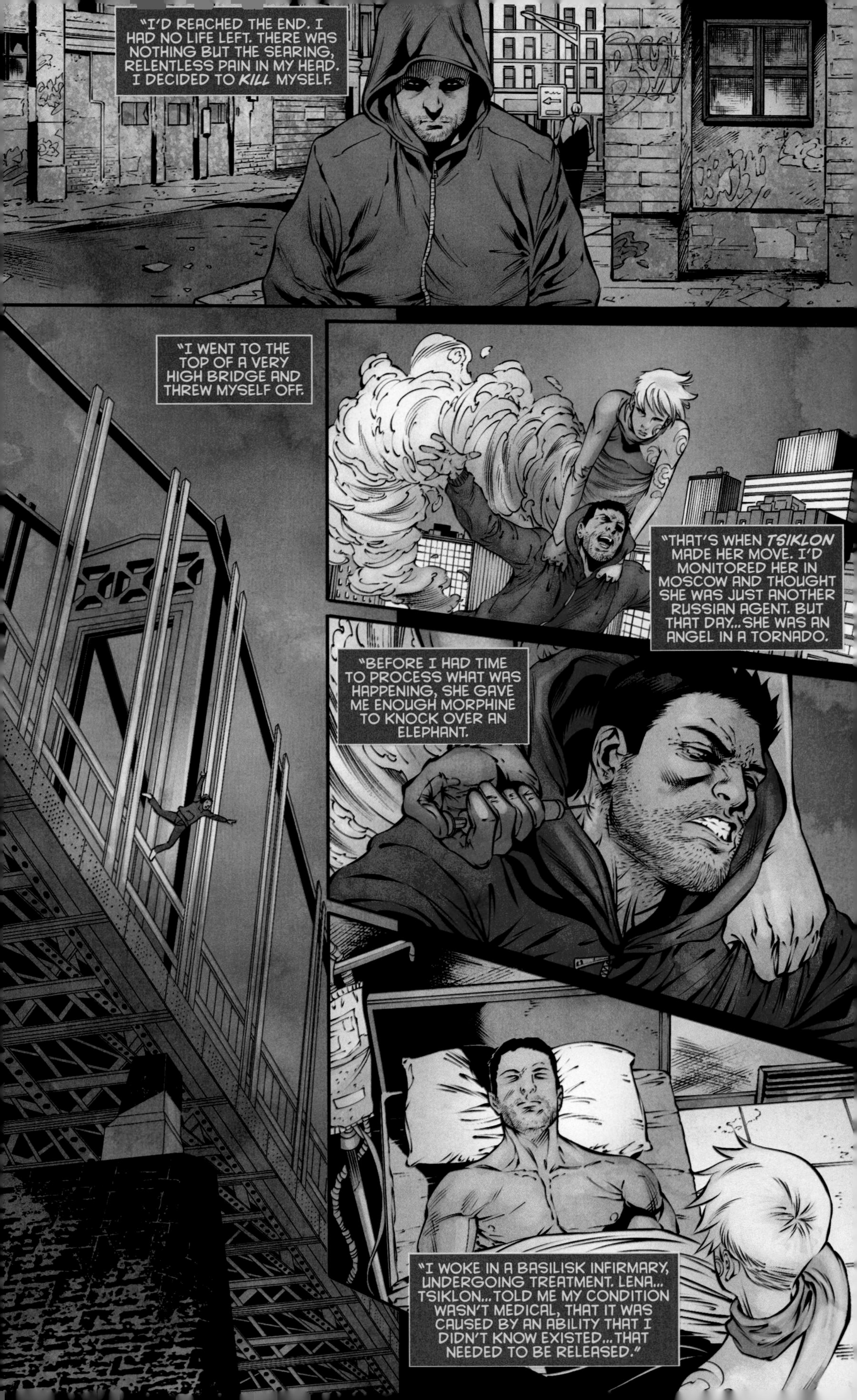
"I'D REACHED THE END. I HAD NO LIFE LEFT. THERE WAS NOTHING BUT THE SEARING, RELENTLESS PAIN IN MY HEAD. I DECIDED TO KILL MYSELF.
"I WENT TO THE TOP OF A VERY HIGH BRIDGE AND THREW MYSELF OFF.
"THAT'S WHEN TSIKLON MADE HER MOVE. I'D MONITORED HER IN MOSCOW AND THOUGHT SHE WAS JUST ANOTHER RUSSIAN AGENT. BUT THAT DAY... SHE WAS AN ANGEL IN A TORNADO.
"BEFORE I HAD TIME TO PROCESS WHAT WAS HAPPENING, SHE GAVE ME ENOUGH MORPHINE TO KNOCK OVER AN ELEPHANT.
"I WOKE IN A BASILISK INFIRMARY, UNDERGOING TREATMENT. LENA... TSIKLON... TOLD ME MY CONDITION WASN'T MEDICAL, THAT IT WAS CAUSED BY AN ABILITY THAT I DIDN'T KNOW EXISTED... THAT NEEDED TO BE RELEASED."

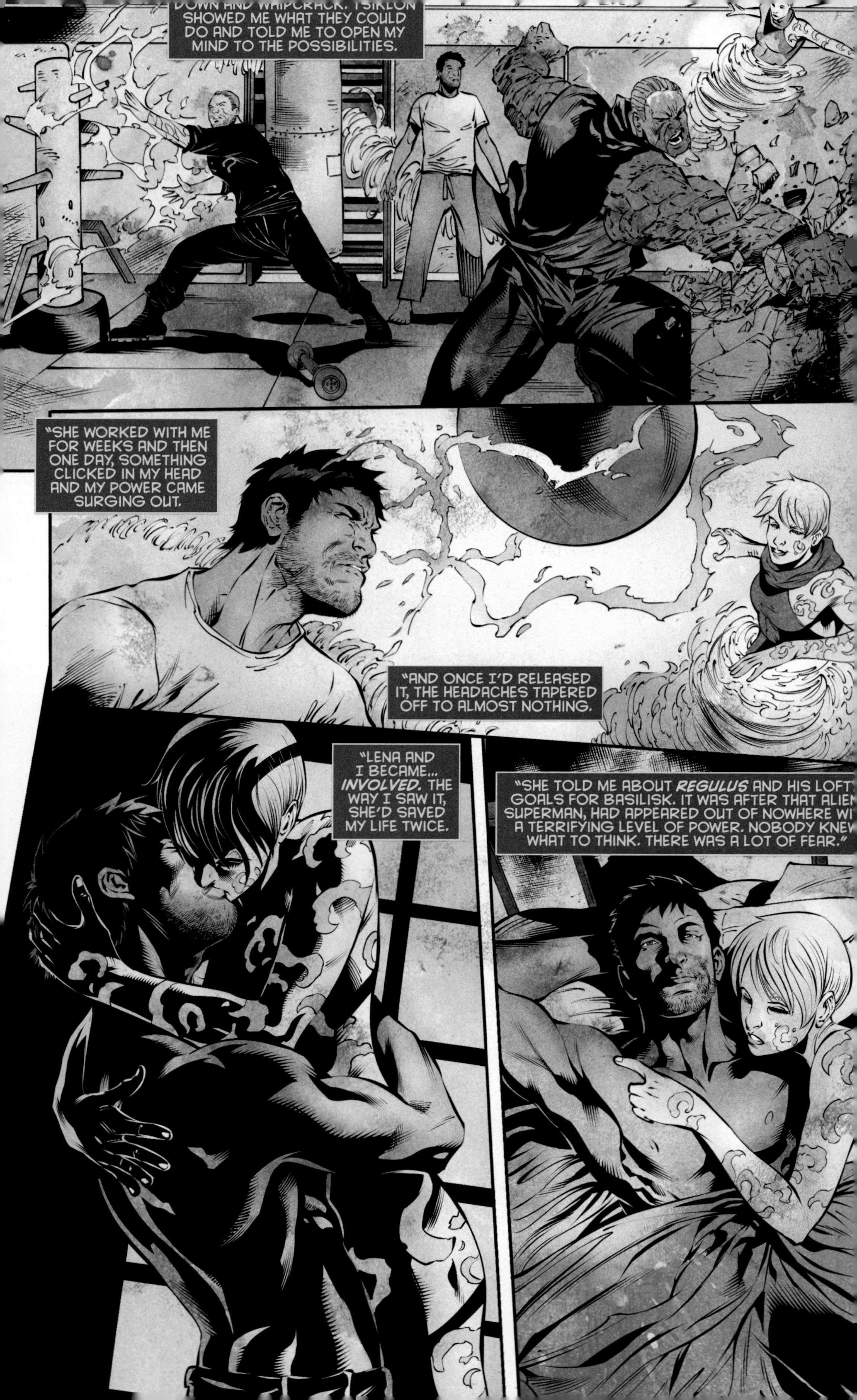
DOWN AND WHIPCRACK. TSIKLON SHOWED ME WHAT THEY COULD DO AND TOLD ME TO OPEN MY MIND TO THE POSSIBILITIES.
"SHE WORKED WITH ME FOR WEEKS AND THEN ONE DAY, SOMETHING CLICKED IN MY HEAD AND MY POWER CAME SURGING OUT.
"AND ONCE I'D RELEASED IT, THE HEADACHES TAPERED OFF TO ALMOST NOTHING.
"LENA AND I BECAME... *INVOLVED.* THE WAY I SAW IT, SHE'D SAVED MY LIFE TWICE.
"SHE TOLD ME ABOUT *REGULUS* AND HIS LOFT GOALS FOR BASILISK. IT WAS AFTER THAT ALIE SUPERMAN, HAD APPEARED OUT OF NOWHERE WI A TERRIFYING LEVEL OF POWER. NOBODY KNEW WHAT TO THINK. THERE WAS A LOT OF FEAR."

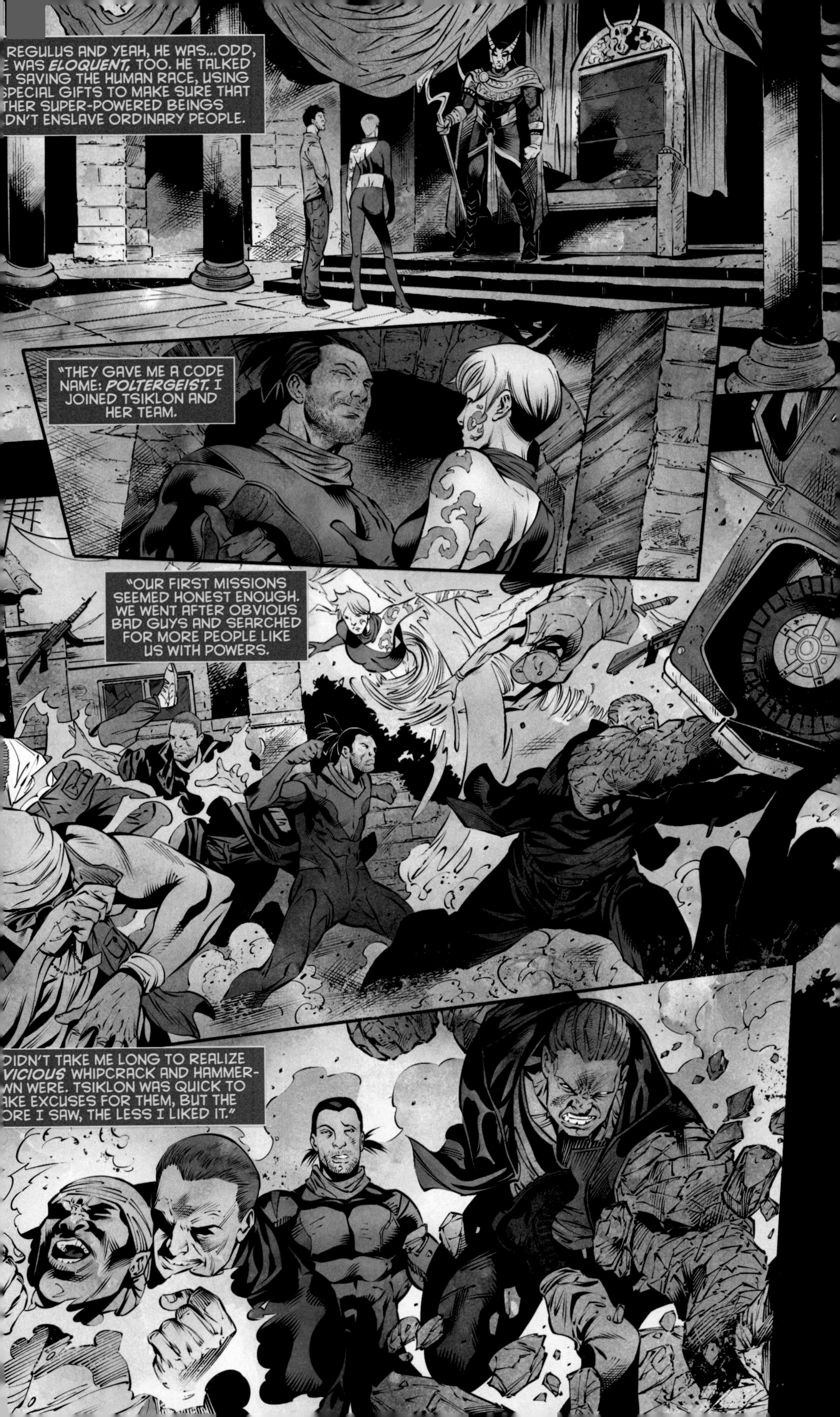
REGULUS AND YEAH, HE WAS...ODD, E WAS ELOQUENT, TOO. HE TALKED T SAVING THE HUMAN RACE, USING SPECIAL GIFTS TO MAKE SURE THAT THER SUPER-POWERED BEINGS DN'T ENSLAVE ORDINARY PEOPLE.
"THEY GAVE ME A CODE NAME: POLTERGEIST. I JOINED TSIKLON AND HER TEAM.
"OUR FIRST MISSIONS SEEMED HONEST ENOUGH. WE WENT AFTER OBVIOUS BAD GUYS AND SEARCHED FOR MORE PEOPLE LIKE US WITH POWERS.
DIDN'T TAKE ME LONG TO REALIZE VICIOUS WHIPCRACK AND HAMMER- WN WERE. TSIKLON WAS QUICK TO AKE EXCUSES FOR THEM, BUT THE ORE I SAW, THE LESS I LIKED IT."

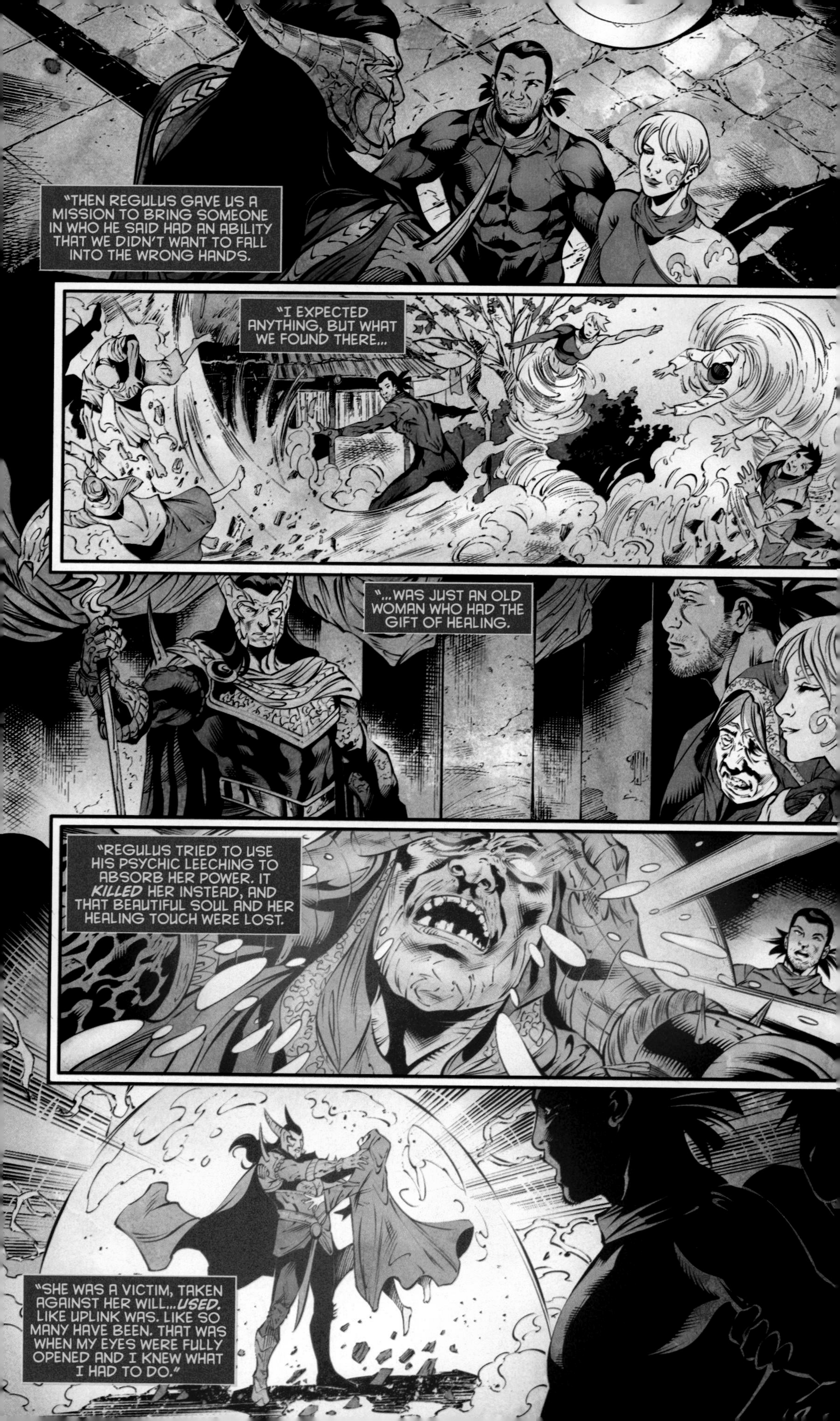
"THEN REGULUS GAVE US A MISSION TO BRING SOMEONE IN WHO HE SAID HAD AN ABILITY THAT WE DIDN'T WANT TO FALL INTO THE WRONG HANDS.
"I EXPECTED ANYTHING, BUT WHAT WE FOUND THERE...
"...WAS JUST AN OLD WOMAN WHO HAD THE GIFT OF HEALING.
"REGULUS TRIED TO USE HIS PSYCHIC LEECHING TO ABSORB HER POWER. IT *KILLED* HER INSTEAD, AND THAT BEAUTIFUL SOUL AND HER HEALING TOUCH WERE LOST.
"SHE WAS A VICTIM, TAKEN AGAINST HER WILL...*USED*. LIKE UPLINK WAS. LIKE SO MANY HAVE BEEN. THAT WAS WHEN MY EYES WERE FULLY OPENED AND I KNEW WHAT I HAD TO DO."

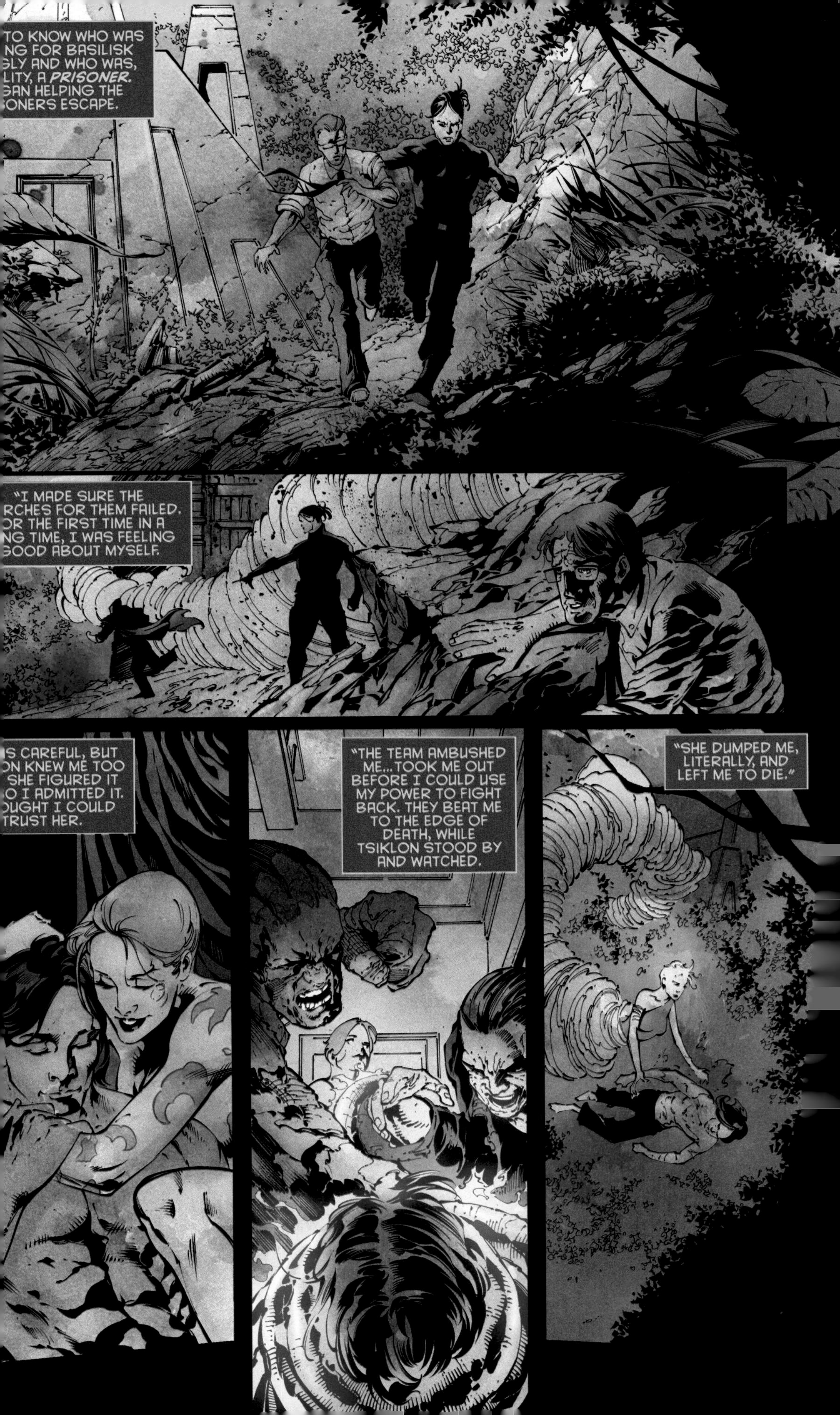
TO KNOW WHO WAS
NG FOR BASILISK
GLY AND WHO WAS,
LITY, A *PRISONER*.
GAN HELPING THE
ONERS ESCAPE.
"I MADE SURE THE
RCHES FOR THEM FAILED.
OR THE FIRST TIME IN A
NG TIME, I WAS FEELING
GOOD ABOUT MYSELF.
S CAREFUL, BUT
ON KNEW ME TOO
SHE FIGURED IT
O I ADMITTED IT.
OUGHT I COULD
TRUST HER.
"THE TEAM AMBUSHED ME...TOOK ME OUT BEFORE I COULD USE MY POWER TO FIGHT BACK. THEY BEAT ME TO THE EDGE OF DEATH, WHILE TSIKLON STOOD BY AND WATCHED.
"SHE DUMPED ME, LITERALLY, AND LEFT ME TO DIE."

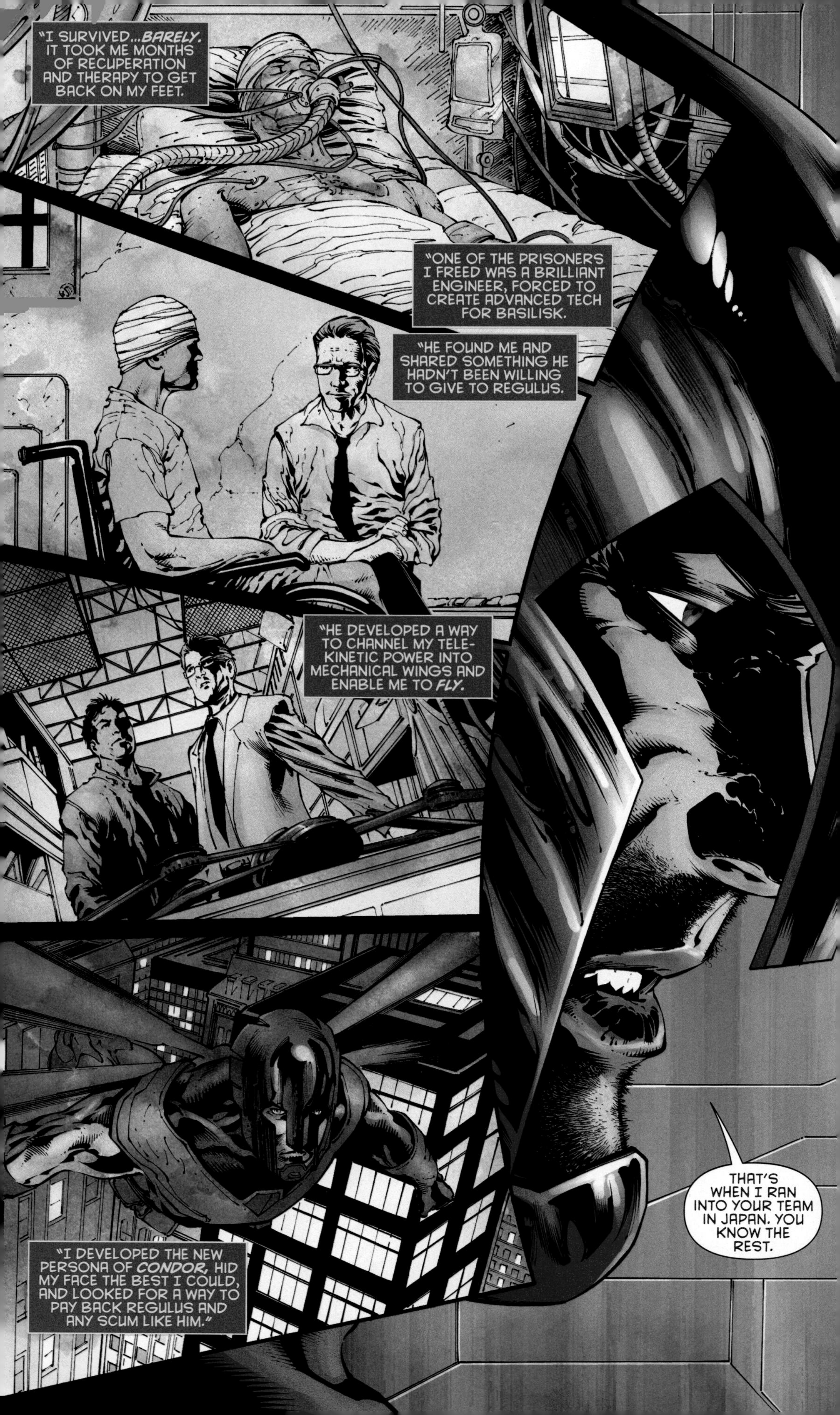
"I SURVIVED...*BARELY.* IT TOOK ME MONTHS OF RECUPERATION AND THERAPY TO GET BACK ON MY FEET.
"ONE OF THE PRISONERS I FREED WAS A BRILLIANT ENGINEER, FORCED TO CREATE ADVANCED TECH FOR BASILISK.
"HE FOUND ME AND SHARED SOMETHING HE HADN'T BEEN WILLING TO GIVE TO REGULUS.
"HE DEVELOPED A WAY TO CHANNEL MY TELE-KINETIC POWER INTO MECHANICAL WINGS AND ENABLE ME TO *FLY.*
"I DEVELOPED THE NEW PERSONA OF *CONDOR,* HID MY FACE THE BEST I COULD, AND LOOKED FOR A WAY TO PAY BACK REGULUS AND ANY SCUM LIKE HIM."
THAT'S WHEN I RAN INTO YOUR TEAM IN JAPAN. YOU KNOW THE REST.

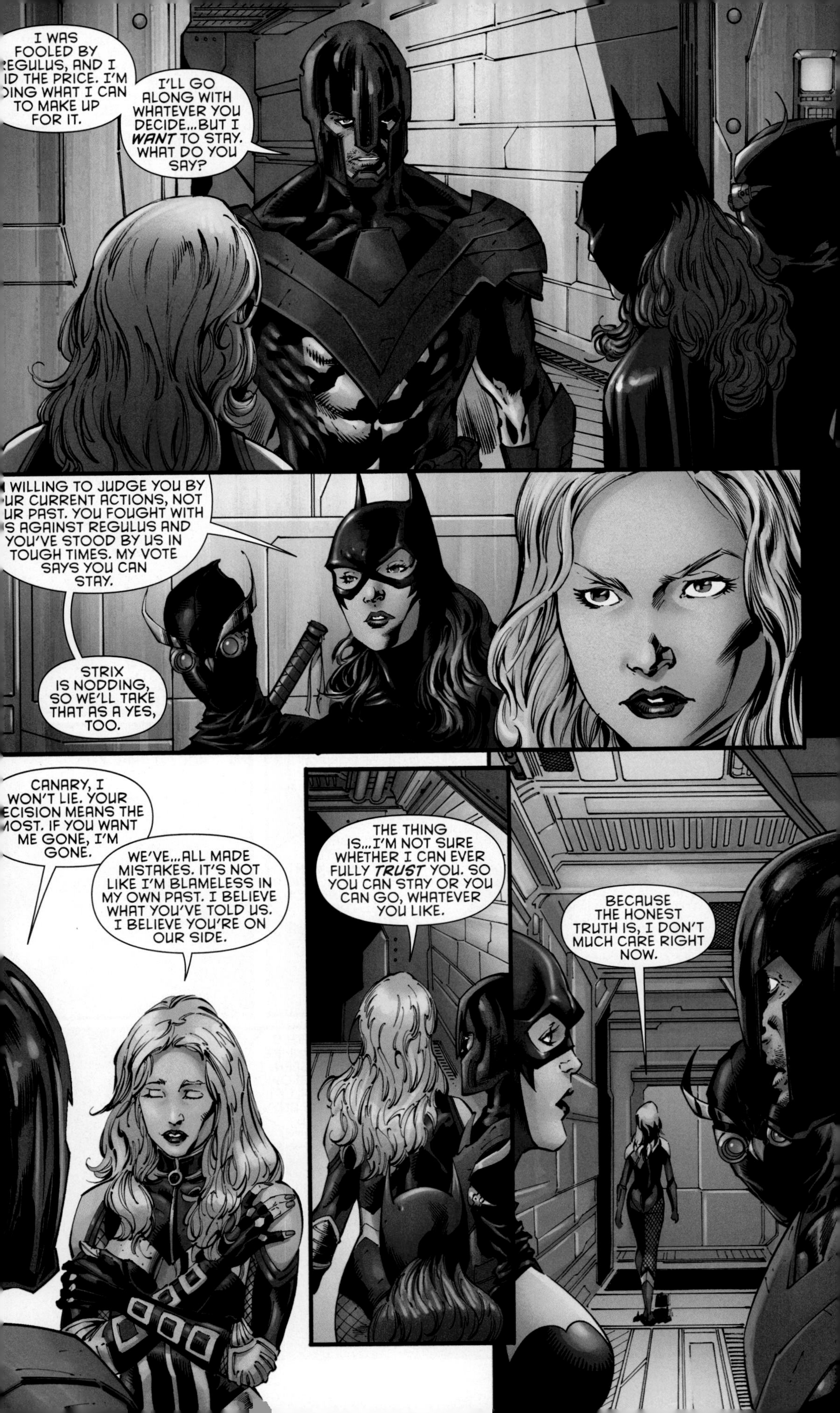
I WAS FOOLED BY REGULUS, AND I ID THE PRICE. I'M OING WHAT I CAN TO MAKE UP FOR IT.
I'LL GO ALONG WITH WHATEVER YOU DECIDE...BUT I *WANT* TO STAY. WHAT DO YOU SAY?
WILLING TO JUDGE YOU BY UR CURRENT ACTIONS, NOT UR PAST. YOU FOUGHT WITH S AGAINST REGULUS AND YOU'VE STOOD BY US IN TOUGH TIMES. MY VOTE SAYS YOU CAN STAY.
STRIX IS NODDING, SO WE'LL TAKE THAT AS A YES, TOO.
CANARY, I WON'T LIE. YOUR ECISION MEANS THE MOST. IF YOU WANT ME GONE, I'M GONE.
WE'VE...ALL MADE MISTAKES. IT'S NOT LIKE I'M BLAMELESS IN MY OWN PAST. I BELIEVE WHAT YOU'VE TOLD US. I BELIEVE YOU'RE ON OUR SIDE.
THE THING IS...I'M NOT SURE WHETHER I CAN EVER FULLY *TRUST* YOU. SO YOU CAN STAY OR YOU CAN GO, WHATEVER YOU LIKE.
BECAUSE THE HONEST TRUTH IS, I DON'T MUCH CARE RIGHT NOW.

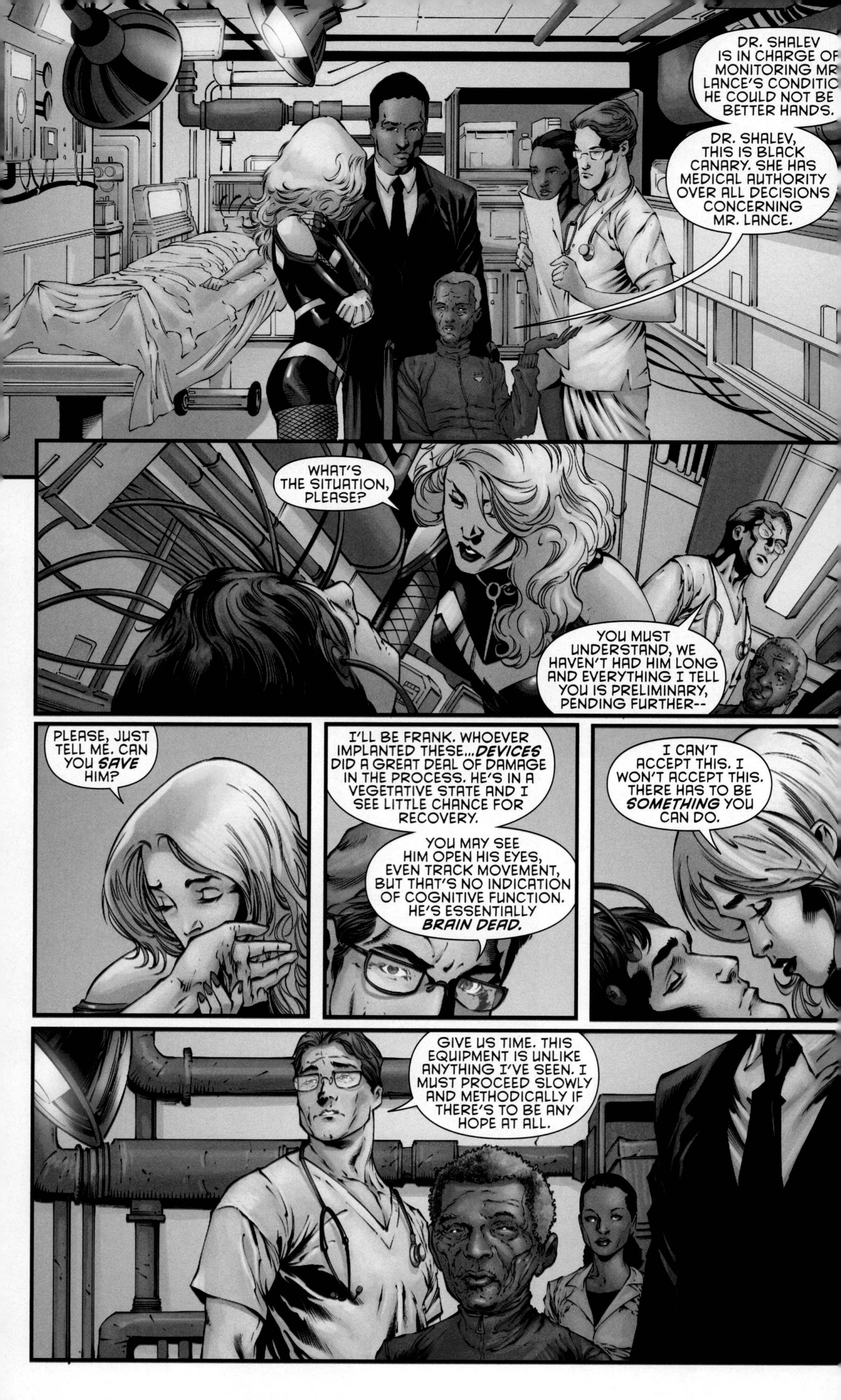

DR. SHALEV IS IN CHARGE OF MONITORING MR LANCE'S CONDITIO HE COULD NOT BE BETTER HANDS.
DR. SHALEV, THIS IS BLACK CANARY. SHE HAS MEDICAL AUTHORITY OVER ALL DECISIONS CONCERNING MR. LANCE.
WHAT'S THE SITUATION, PLEASE?
YOU MUST UNDERSTAND, WE HAVEN'T HAD HIM LONG AND EVERYTHING I TELL YOU IS PRELIMINARY, PENDING FURTHER--
PLEASE, JUST TELL ME. CAN YOU SAVE HIM?
I'LL BE FRANK. WHOEVER IMPLANTED THESE...DEVICES DID A GREAT DEAL OF DAMAGE IN THE PROCESS. HE'S IN A VEGETATIVE STATE AND I SEE LITTLE CHANCE FOR RECOVERY.
YOU MAY SEE HIM OPEN HIS EYES, EVEN TRACK MOVEMENT, BUT THAT'S NO INDICATION OF COGNITIVE FUNCTION. HE'S ESSENTIALLY BRAIN DEAD.
I CAN'T ACCEPT THIS. I WON'T ACCEPT THIS. THERE HAS TO BE SOMETHING YOU CAN DO.
GIVE US TIME. THIS EQUIPMENT IS UNLIKE ANYTHING I'VE SEEN. I MUST PROCEED SLOWLY AND METHODICALLY IF THERE'S TO BE ANY HOPE AT ALL.

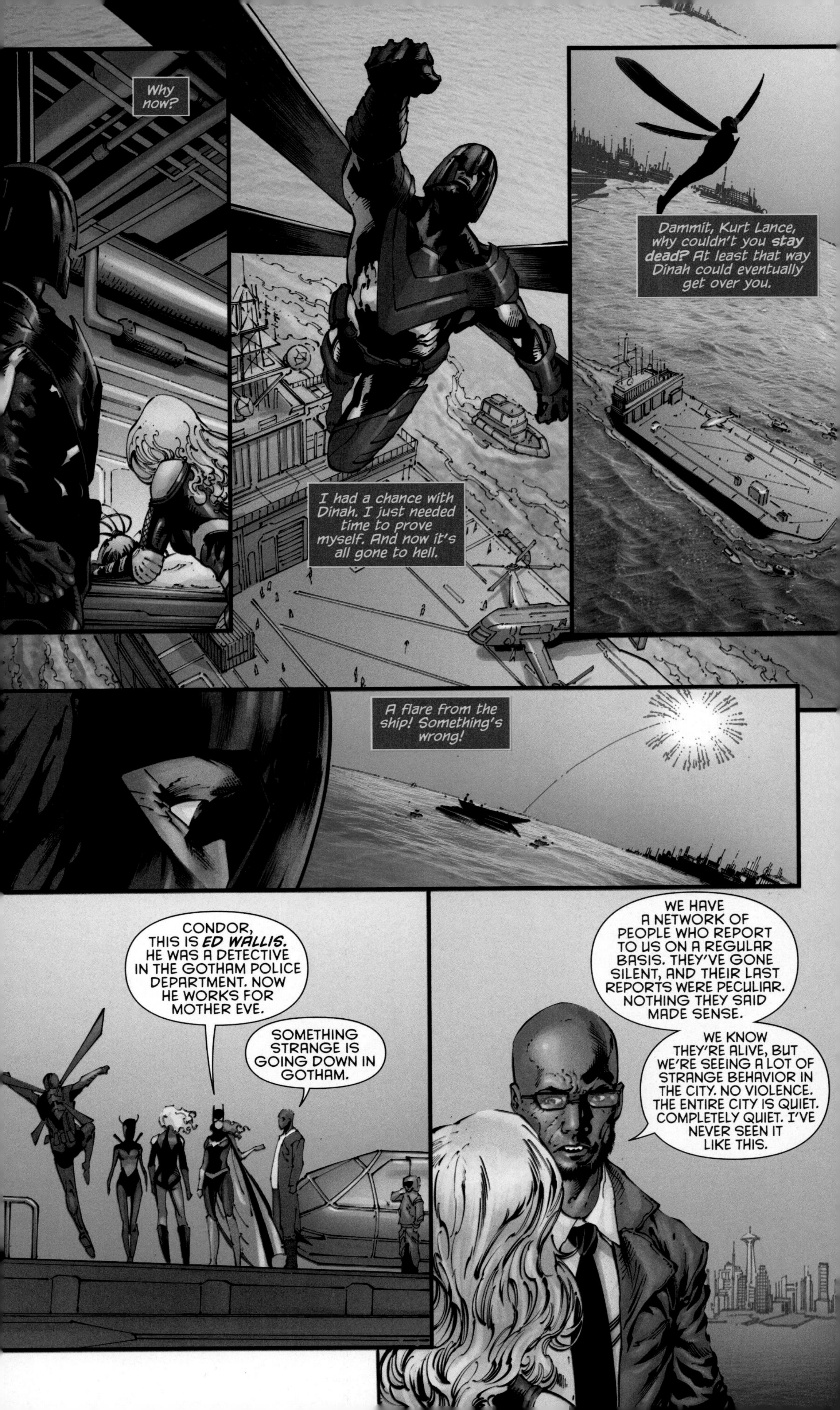

Why now?
I had a chance with Dinah. I just needed time to prove myself. And now it's all gone to hell.
Dammit, Kurt Lance, why couldn't you **stay dead?** At least that way Dinah could eventually get over you.
A flare from the ship! Something's wrong!
CONDOR, THIS IS ***ED WALLIS.*** HE WAS A DETECTIVE IN THE GOTHAM POLICE DEPARTMENT. NOW HE WORKS FOR MOTHER EVE.
SOMETHING STRANGE IS GOING DOWN IN GOTHAM.
WE HAVE A NETWORK OF PEOPLE WHO REPORT TO US ON A REGULAR BASIS. THEY'VE GONE SILENT, AND THEIR LAST REPORTS WERE PECULIAR. NOTHING THEY SAID MADE SENSE.
WE KNOW THEY'RE ALIVE, BUT WE'RE SEEING A LOT OF STRANGE BEHAVIOR IN THE CITY. NO VIOLENCE. THE ENTIRE CITY IS QUIET. COMPLETELY QUIET. I'VE NEVER SEEN IT LIKE THIS.

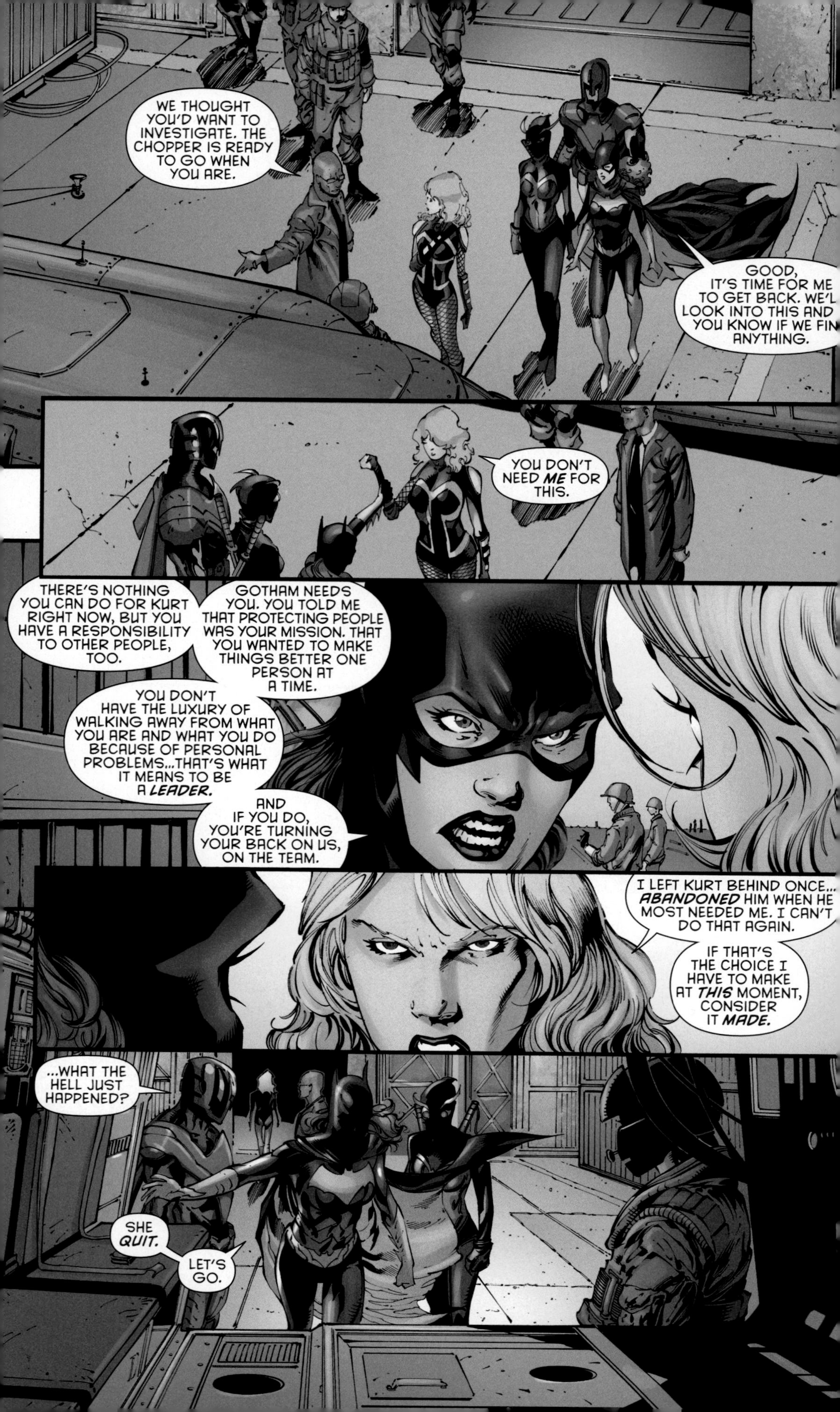
WE THOUGHT YOU'D WANT TO INVESTIGATE. THE CHOPPER IS READY TO GO WHEN YOU ARE.
GOOD, IT'S TIME FOR ME TO GET BACK. WE'L LOOK INTO THIS AND YOU KNOW IF WE FIN ANYTHING.
YOU DON'T NEED *ME* FOR THIS.
THERE'S NOTHING YOU CAN DO FOR KURT RIGHT NOW, BUT YOU HAVE A RESPONSIBILITY TO OTHER PEOPLE, TOO.
GOTHAM NEEDS YOU. YOU TOLD ME THAT PROTECTING PEOPLE WAS YOUR MISSION. THAT YOU WANTED TO MAKE THINGS BETTER ONE PERSON AT A TIME.
YOU DON'T HAVE THE LUXURY OF WALKING AWAY FROM WHAT YOU ARE AND WHAT YOU DO BECAUSE OF PERSONAL PROBLEMS...THAT'S WHAT IT MEANS TO BE A *LEADER.*
AND IF YOU DO, YOU'RE TURNING YOUR BACK ON US, ON THE TEAM.
I LEFT KURT BEHIND ONCE... *ABANDONED* HIM WHEN HE MOST NEEDED ME. I CAN'T DO THAT AGAIN.
IF THAT'S THE CHOICE I HAVE TO MAKE AT *THIS* MOMENT, CONSIDER IT *MADE.*
...WHAT THE HELL JUST HAPPENED?
SHE *QUIT.*
LET'S GO.

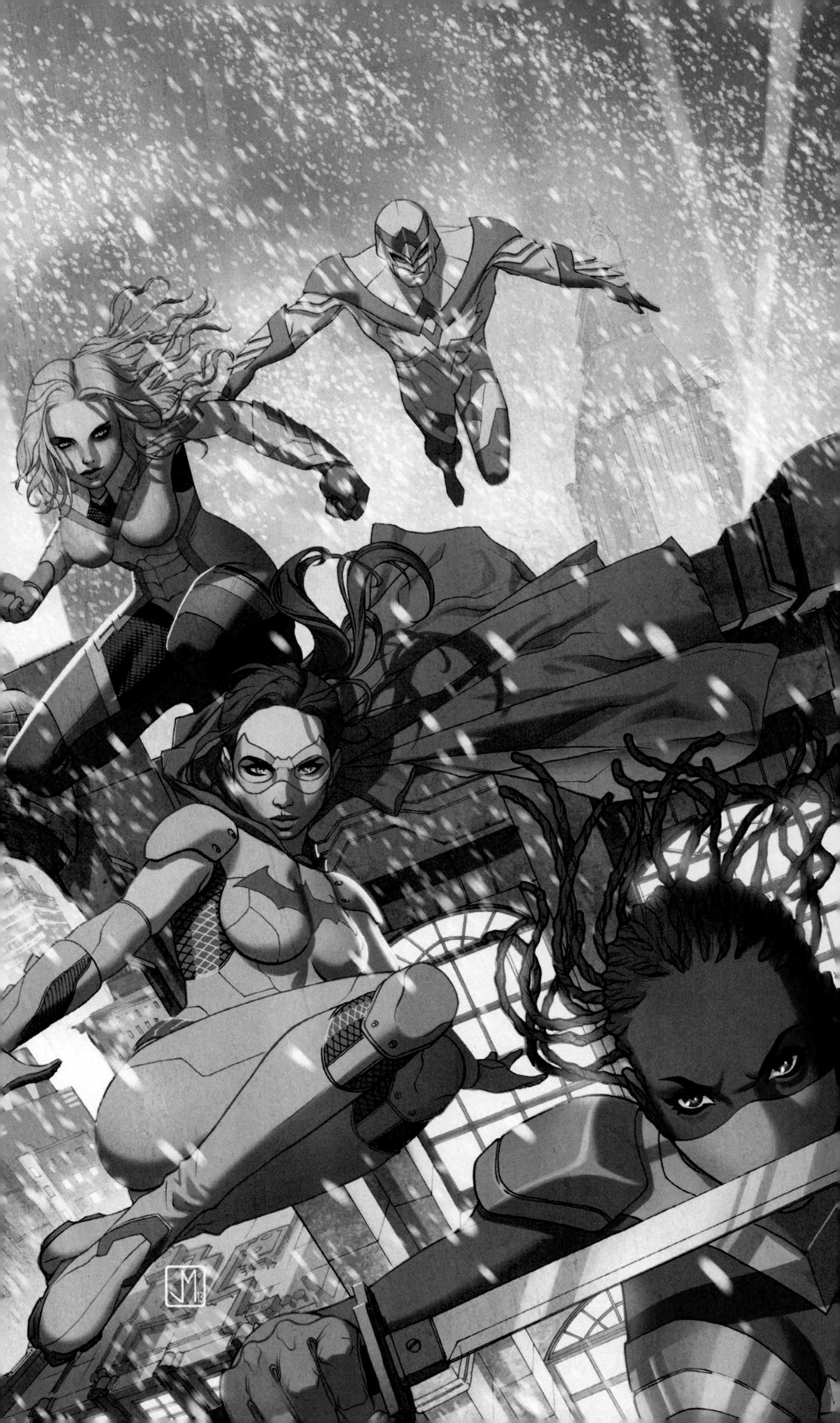

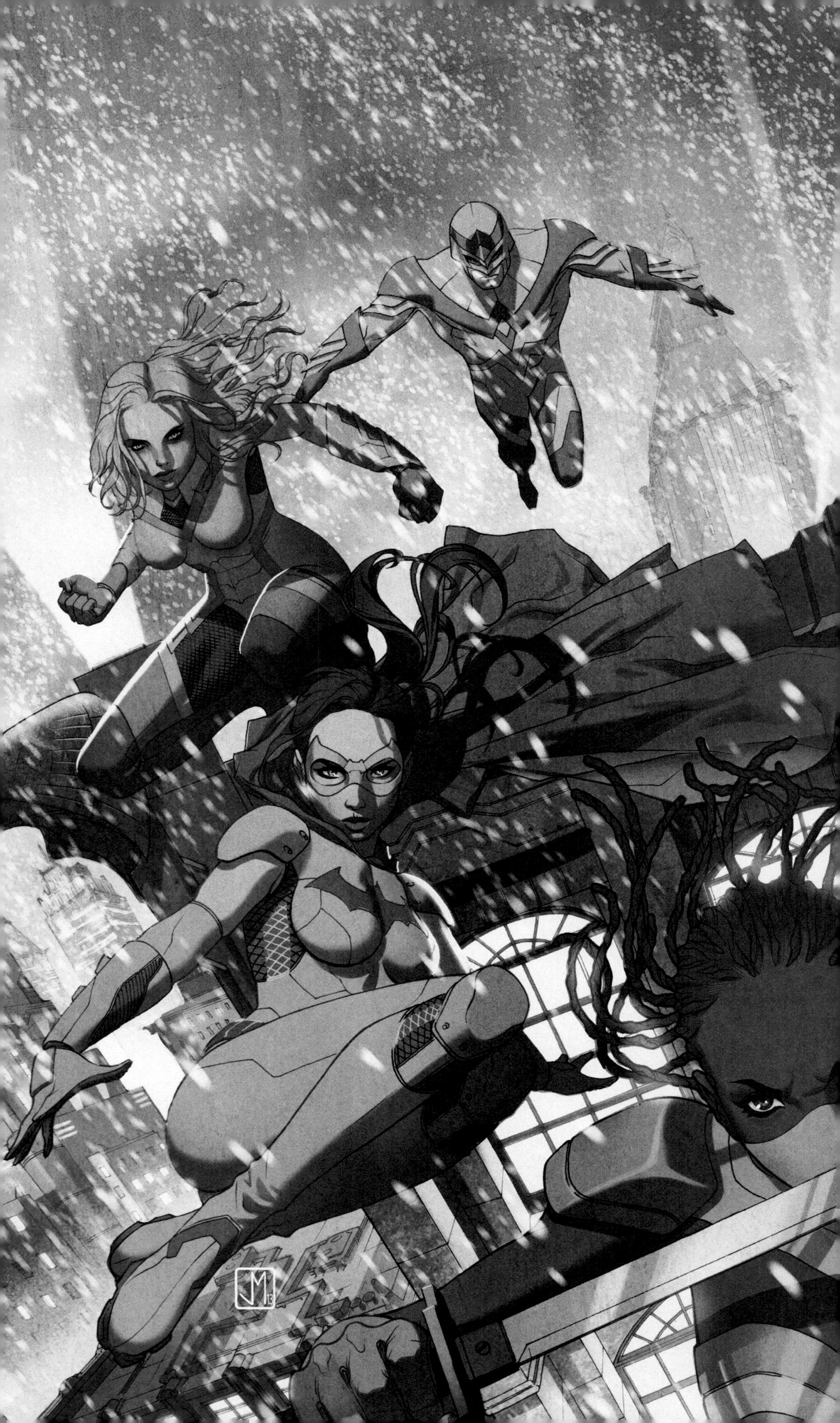

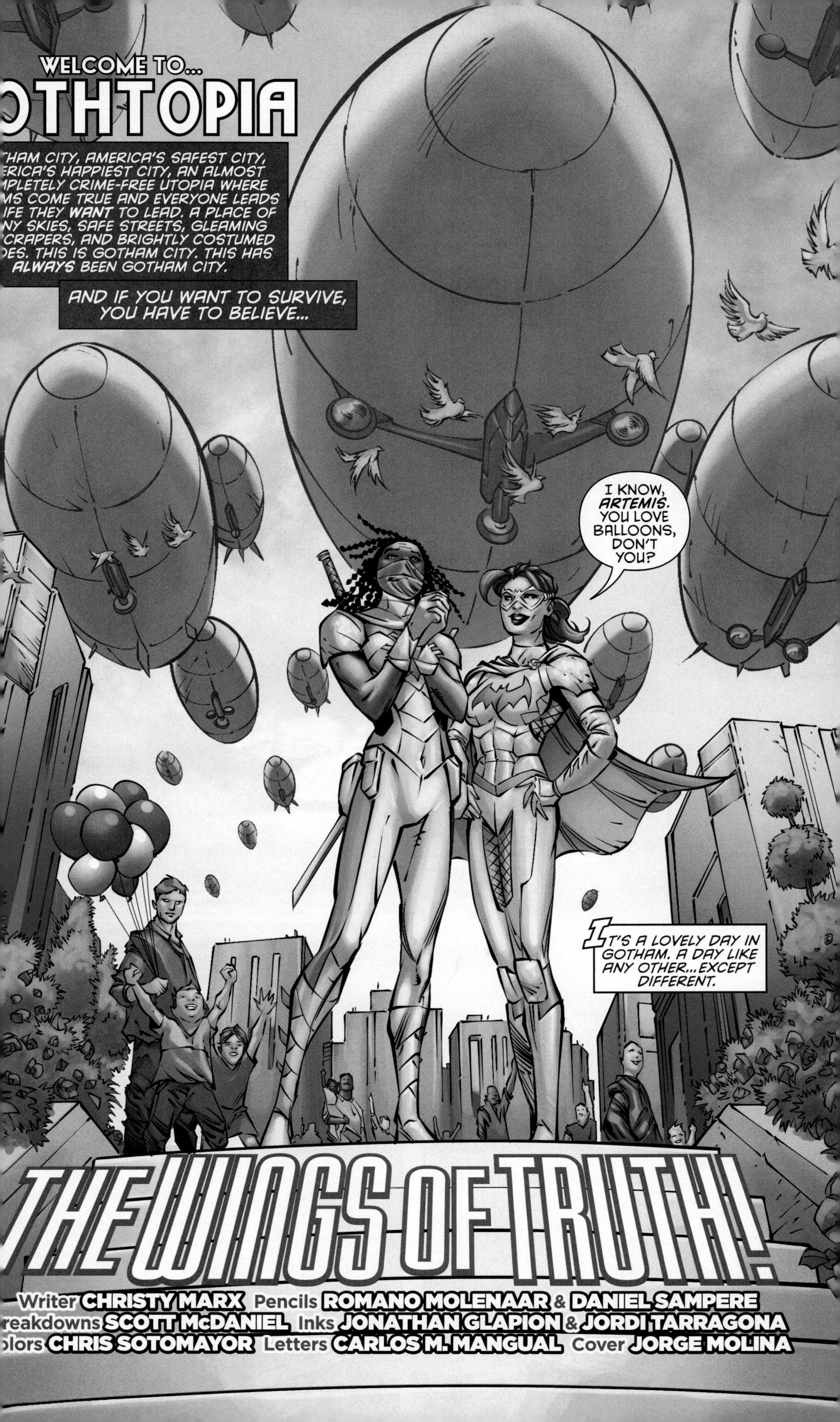
WELCOME TO...
OTHTOPIA
THAM CITY, AMERICA'S SAFEST CITY, ERICA'S HAPPIEST CITY, AN ALMOST MPLETELY CRIME-FREE UTOPIA WHERE MS COME TRUE AND EVERYONE LEADS IFE THEY WANT TO LEAD. A PLACE OF NY SKIES, SAFE STREETS, GLEAMING CRAPERS, AND BRIGHTLY COSTUMED DES. THIS IS GOTHAM CITY. THIS HAS ALWAYS BEEN GOTHAM CITY.
AND IF YOU WANT TO SURVIVE, YOU HAVE TO BELIEVE...
I KNOW, ARTEMIS. YOU LOVE BALLOONS, DON'T YOU?
IT'S A LOVELY DAY IN GOTHAM. A DAY LIKE ANY OTHER... EXCEPT DIFFERENT.
THE WINGS OF TRUTH!
Writer CHRISTY MARX Pencils ROMANO MOLENAAR & DANIEL SAMPERE
reakdowns SCOTT McDANIEL Inks JONATHAN GLAPION & JORDI TARRAGONA
olors CHRIS SOTOMAYOR Letters CARLOS M. MANGUAL Cover JORGE MOLINA

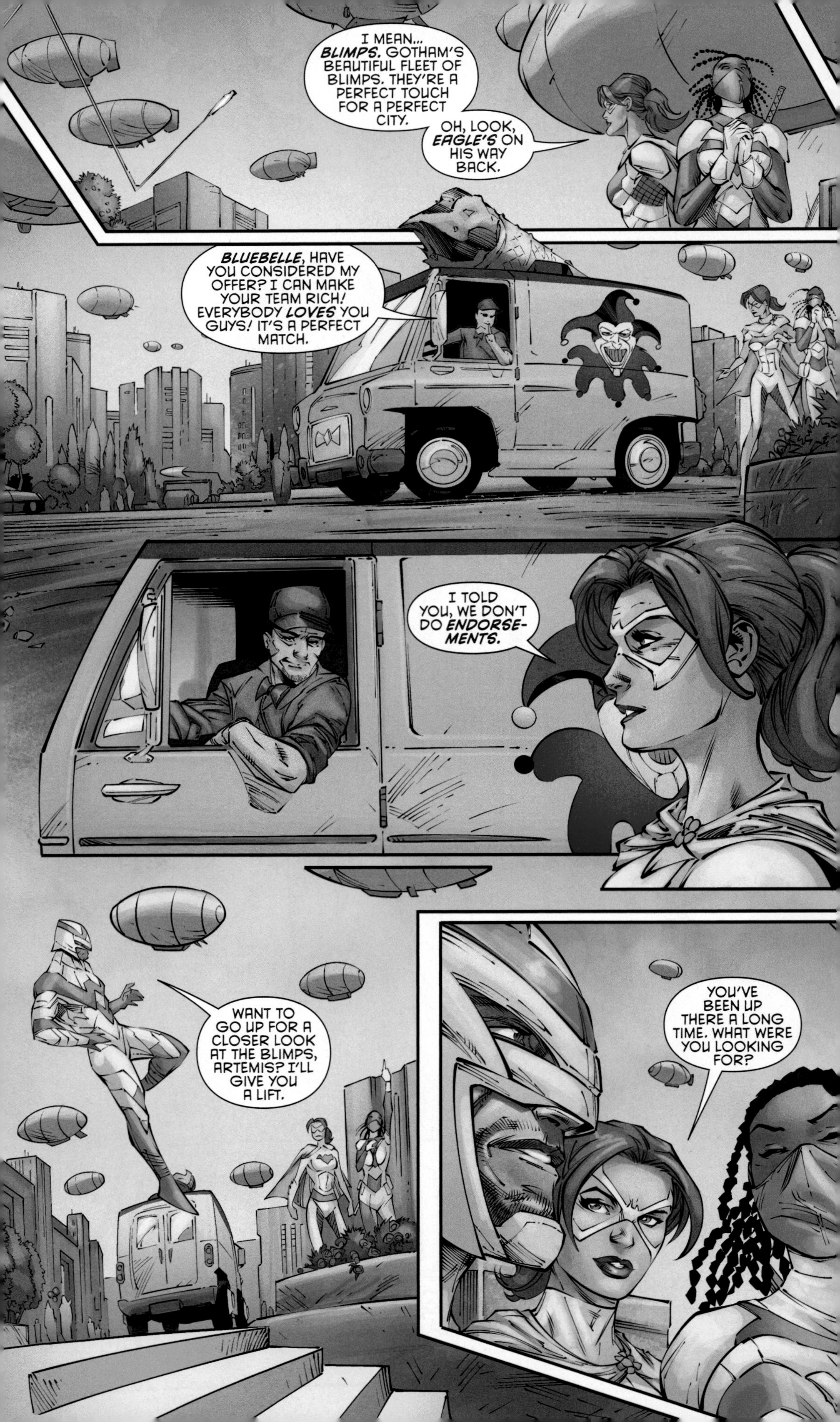
I MEAN... BLIMPS. GOTHAM'S BEAUTIFUL FLEET OF BLIMPS. THEY'RE A PERFECT TOUCH FOR A PERFECT CITY.
OH, LOOK, EAGLE'S ON HIS WAY BACK.
BLUEBELLE, HAVE YOU CONSIDERED MY OFFER? I CAN MAKE YOUR TEAM RICH! EVERYBODY LOVES YOU GUYS! IT'S A PERFECT MATCH.
I TOLD YOU, WE DON'T DO ENDORSE-MENTS.
WANT TO GO UP FOR A CLOSER LOOK AT THE BLIMPS, ARTEMIS? I'LL GIVE YOU A LIFT.
YOU'VE BEEN UP THERE A LONG TIME. WHAT WERE YOU LOOKING FOR?

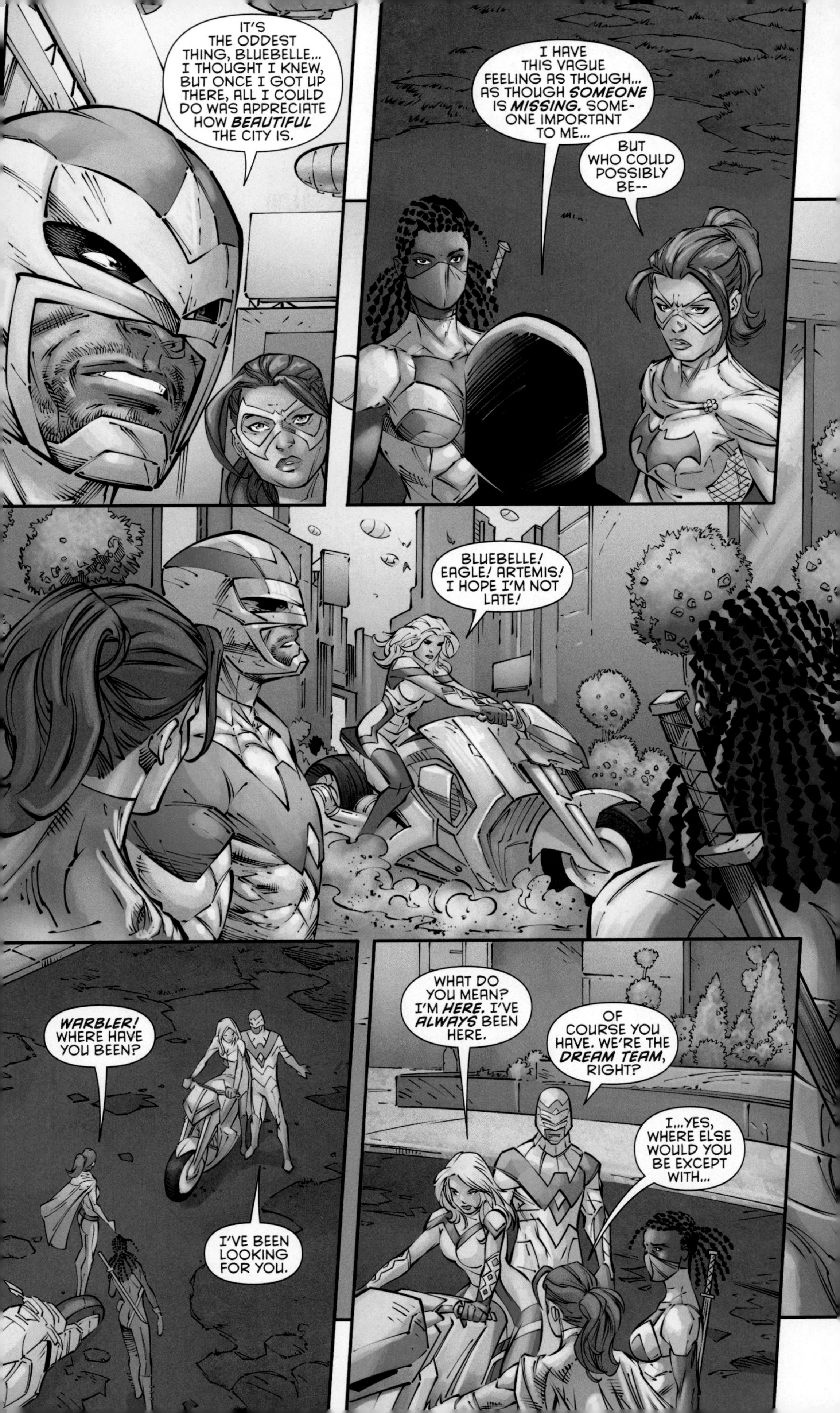
IT'S THE ODDEST THING, BLUEBELLE... I THOUGHT I KNEW, BUT ONCE I GOT UP THERE, ALL I COULD DO WAS APPRECIATE HOW BEAUTIFUL THE CITY IS.
I HAVE THIS VAGUE FEELING AS THOUGH... AS THOUGH SOMEONE IS MISSING. SOME-ONE IMPORTANT TO ME...
BUT WHO COULD POSSIBLY BE--
BLUEBELLE! EAGLE! ARTEMIS! I HOPE I'M NOT LATE!
WARBLER! WHERE HAVE YOU BEEN?
I'VE BEEN LOOKING FOR YOU.
WHAT DO YOU MEAN? I'M HERE. I'VE ALWAYS BEEN HERE.
OF COURSE YOU HAVE. WE'RE THE DREAM TEAM, RIGHT?
I...YES, WHERE ELSE WOULD YOU BE EXCEPT WITH...

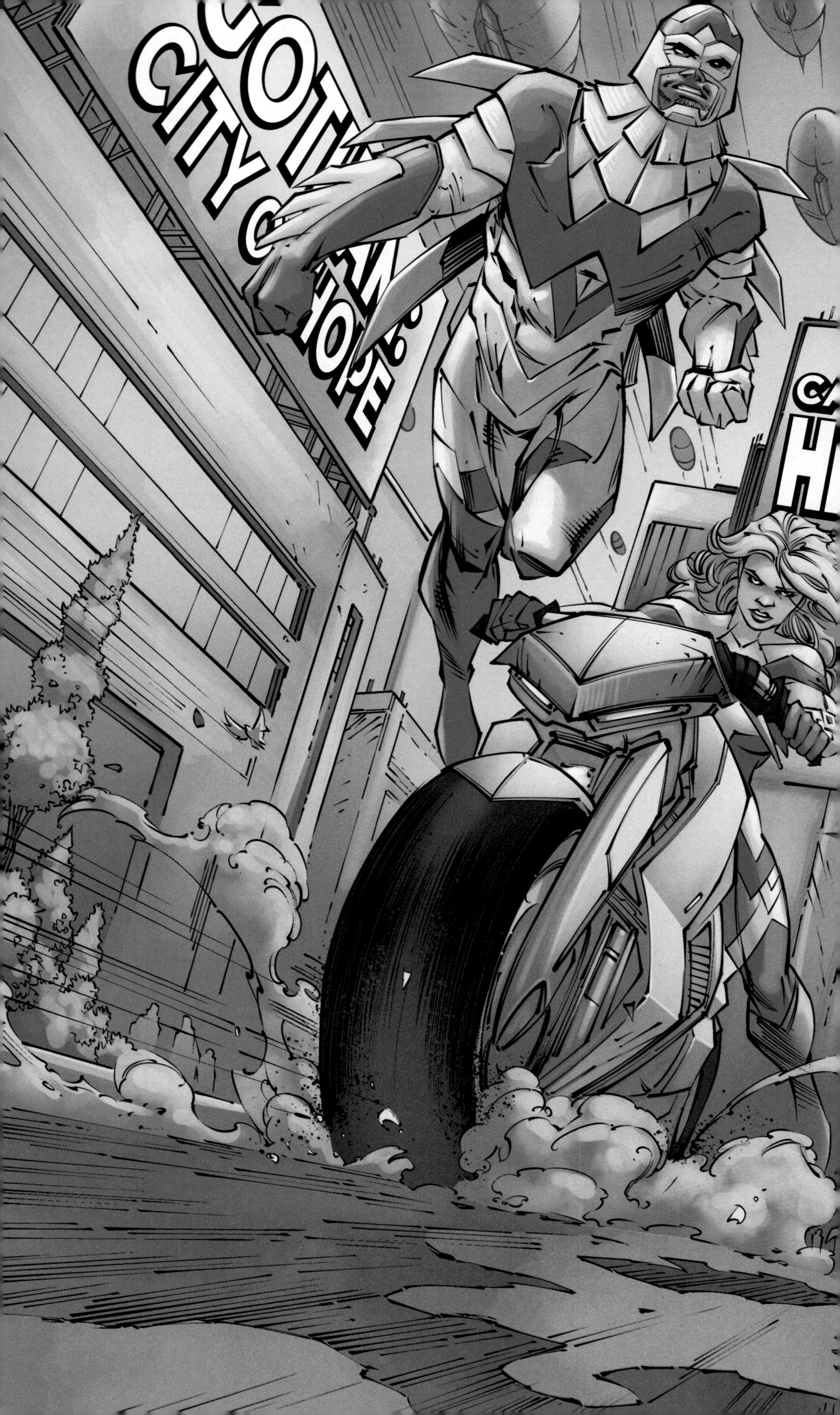
CITY

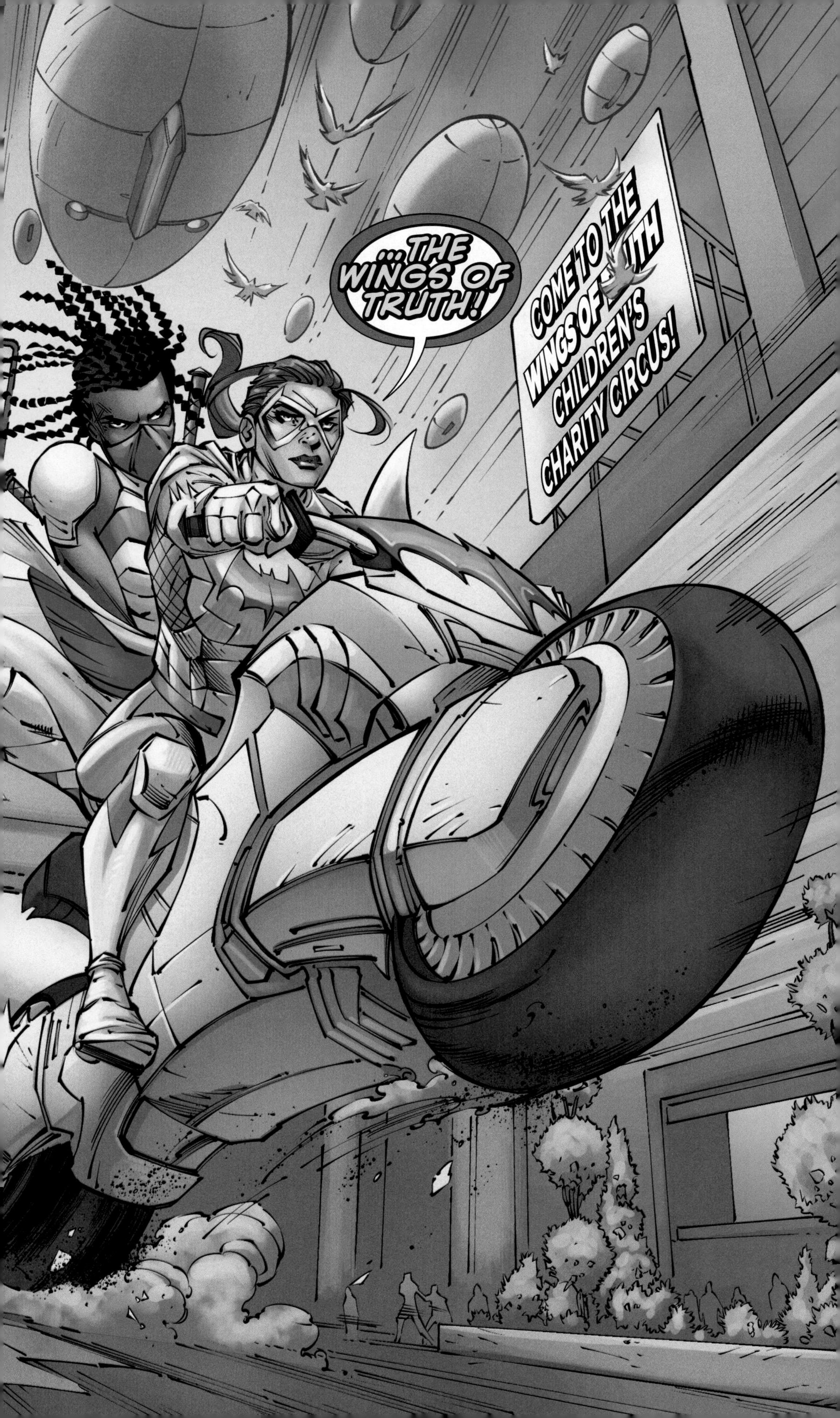
...THE WINGS OF TRUTH!
COME TO THE WINGS OF UTH CHILDREN'S CHARITY CIRCUS!

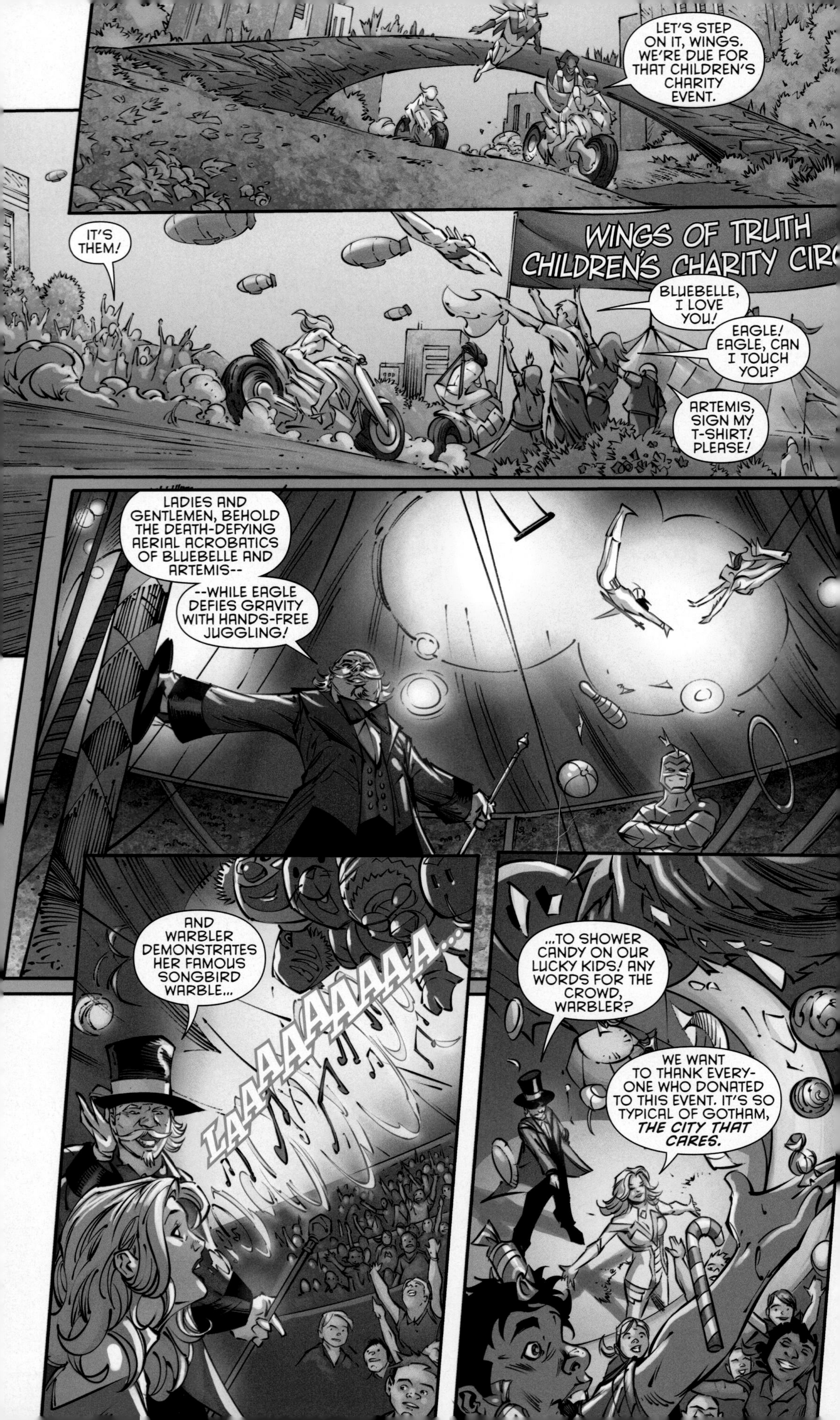
LET'S STEP ON IT, WINGS. WE'RE DUE FOR THAT CHILDREN'S CHARITY EVENT.
IT'S THEM!
WINGS OF TRUTH CHILDREN'S CHARITY CIRC
BLUEBELLE, I LOVE YOU!
EAGLE! EAGLE, CAN I TOUCH YOU?
ARTEMIS, SIGN MY T-SHIRT! PLEASE!
LADIES AND GENTLEMEN, BEHOLD THE DEATH-DEFYING AERIAL ACROBATICS OF BLUEBELLE AND ARTEMIS--
--WHILE EAGLE DEFIES GRAVITY WITH HANDS-FREE JUGGLING!
AND WARBLER DEMONSTRATES HER FAMOUS SONGBIRD WARBLE...
LAAAAAAAAA...
...TO SHOWER CANDY ON OUR LUCKY KIDS! ANY WORDS FOR THE CROWD, WARBLER?
WE WANT TO THANK EVERY-ONE WHO DONATED TO THIS EVENT. IT'S SO TYPICAL OF GOTHAM, *THE CITY THAT CARES.*

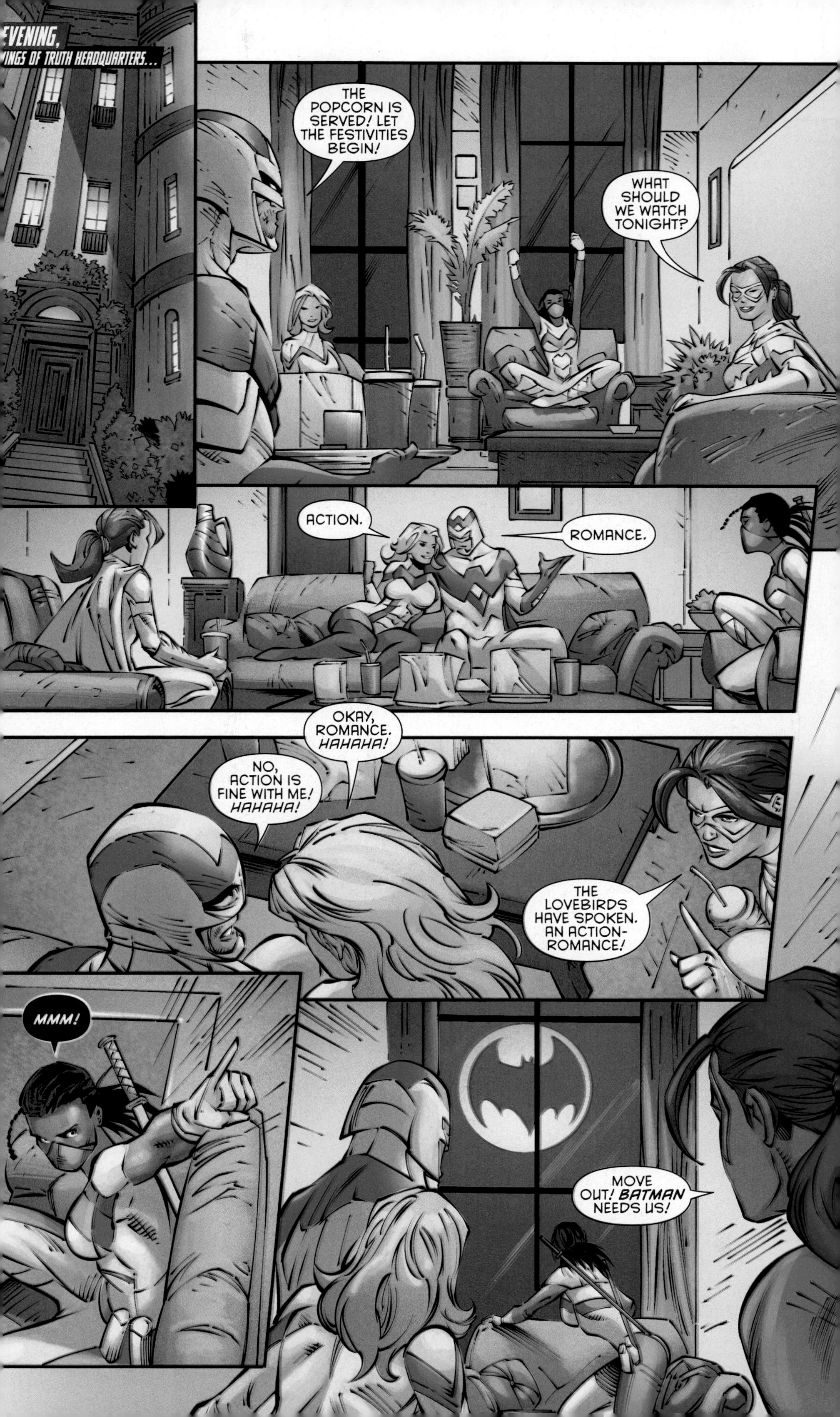
EVENING,
WINGS OF TRUTH HEADQUARTERS...
THE POPCORN IS SERVED! LET THE FESTIVITIES BEGIN!
WHAT SHOULD WE WATCH TONIGHT?
ACTION.
ROMANCE.
OKAY, ROMANCE. HAHAHA!
NO, ACTION IS FINE WITH ME! HAHAHA!
THE LOVEBIRDS HAVE SPOKEN. AN ACTION-ROMANCE!
MMM!
MOVE OUT! BATMAN NEEDS US!

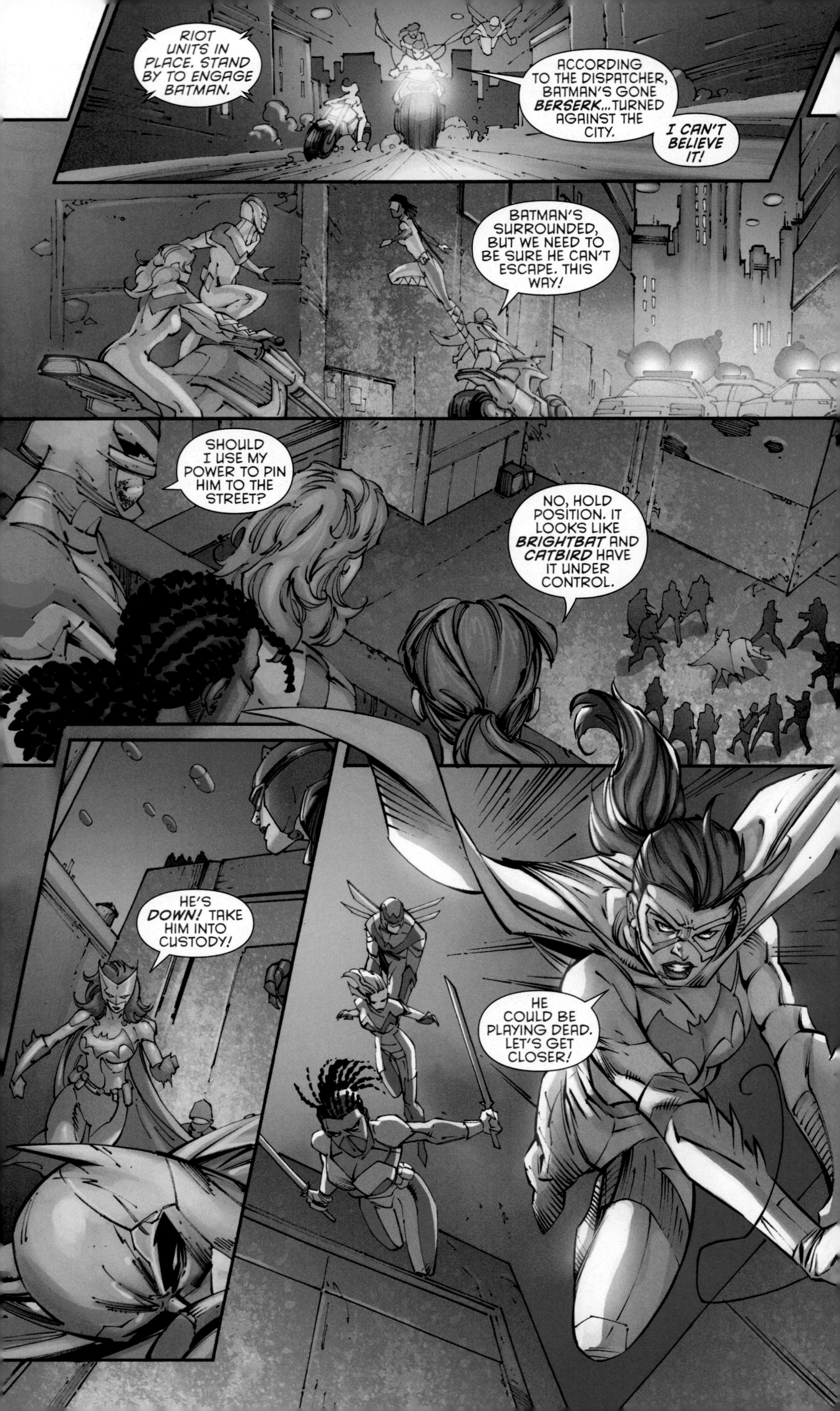
RIOT UNITS IN PLACE. STAND BY TO ENGAGE BATMAN.
ACCORDING TO THE DISPATCHER, BATMAN'S GONE BERSERK...TURNED AGAINST THE CITY.
I CAN'T BELIEVE IT!
BATMAN'S SURROUNDED, BUT WE NEED TO BE SURE HE CAN'T ESCAPE. THIS WAY!
SHOULD I USE MY POWER TO PIN HIM TO THE STREET?
NO, HOLD POSITION. IT LOOKS LIKE BRIGHTBAT AND CATBIRD HAVE IT UNDER CONTROL.
HE'S DOWN! TAKE HIM INTO CUSTODY!
HE COULD BE PLAYING DEAD. LET'S GET CLOSER!

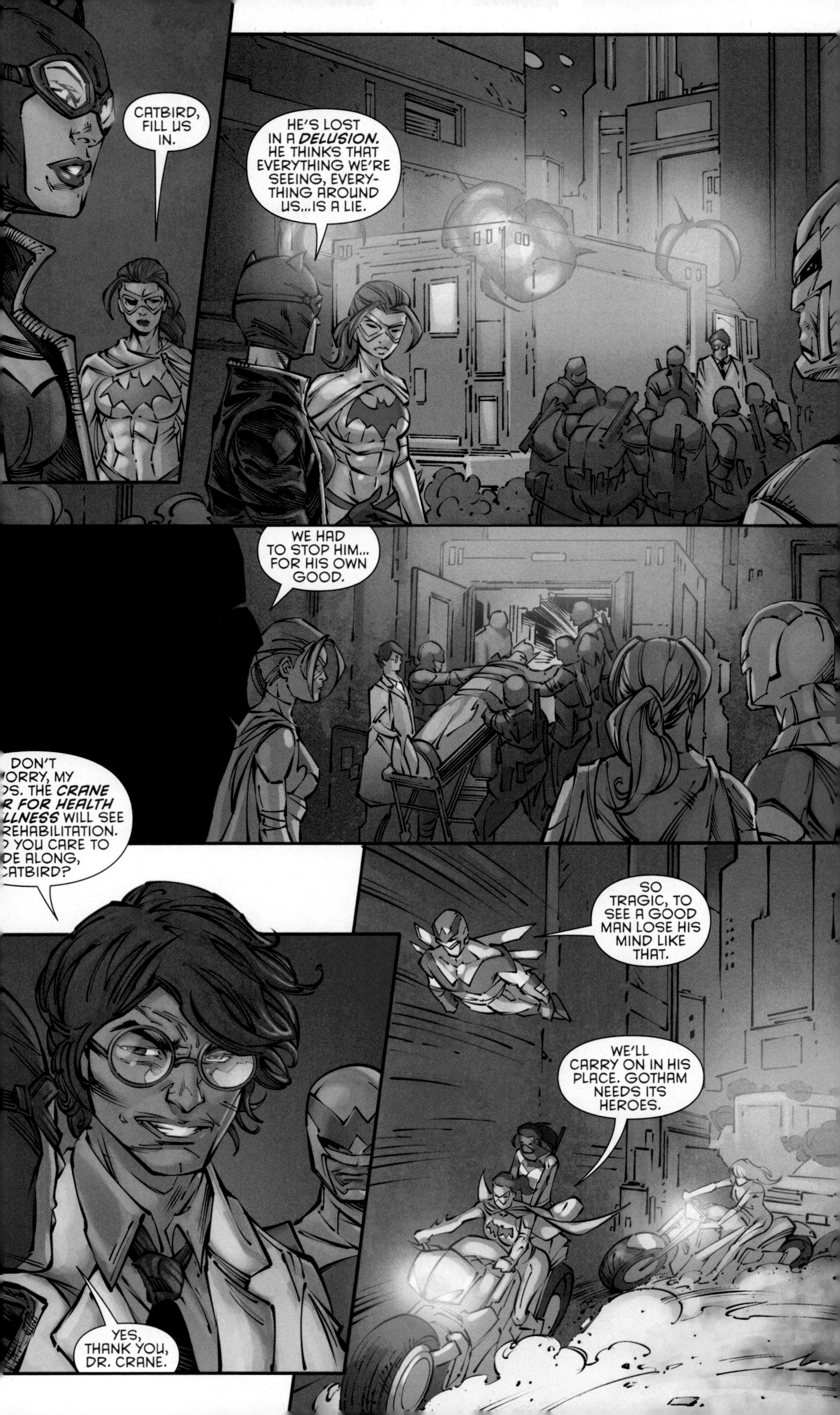
CATBIRD, FILL US IN.
HE'S LOST IN A *DELUSION.* HE THINKS THAT EVERYTHING WE'RE SEEING, EVERY-THING AROUND US...IS A LIE.
WE HAD TO STOP HIM... FOR HIS OWN GOOD.
DON'T ORRY, MY DS. THE *CRANE* *R FOR HEALTH* *LLNESS* WILL SEE REHABILITATION. D YOU CARE TO DE ALONG, ATBIRD?
YES, THANK YOU, DR. CRANE.
SO TRAGIC, TO SEE A GOOD MAN LOSE HIS MIND LIKE THAT.
WE'LL CARRY ON IN HIS PLACE. GOTHAM NEEDS ITS HEROES.

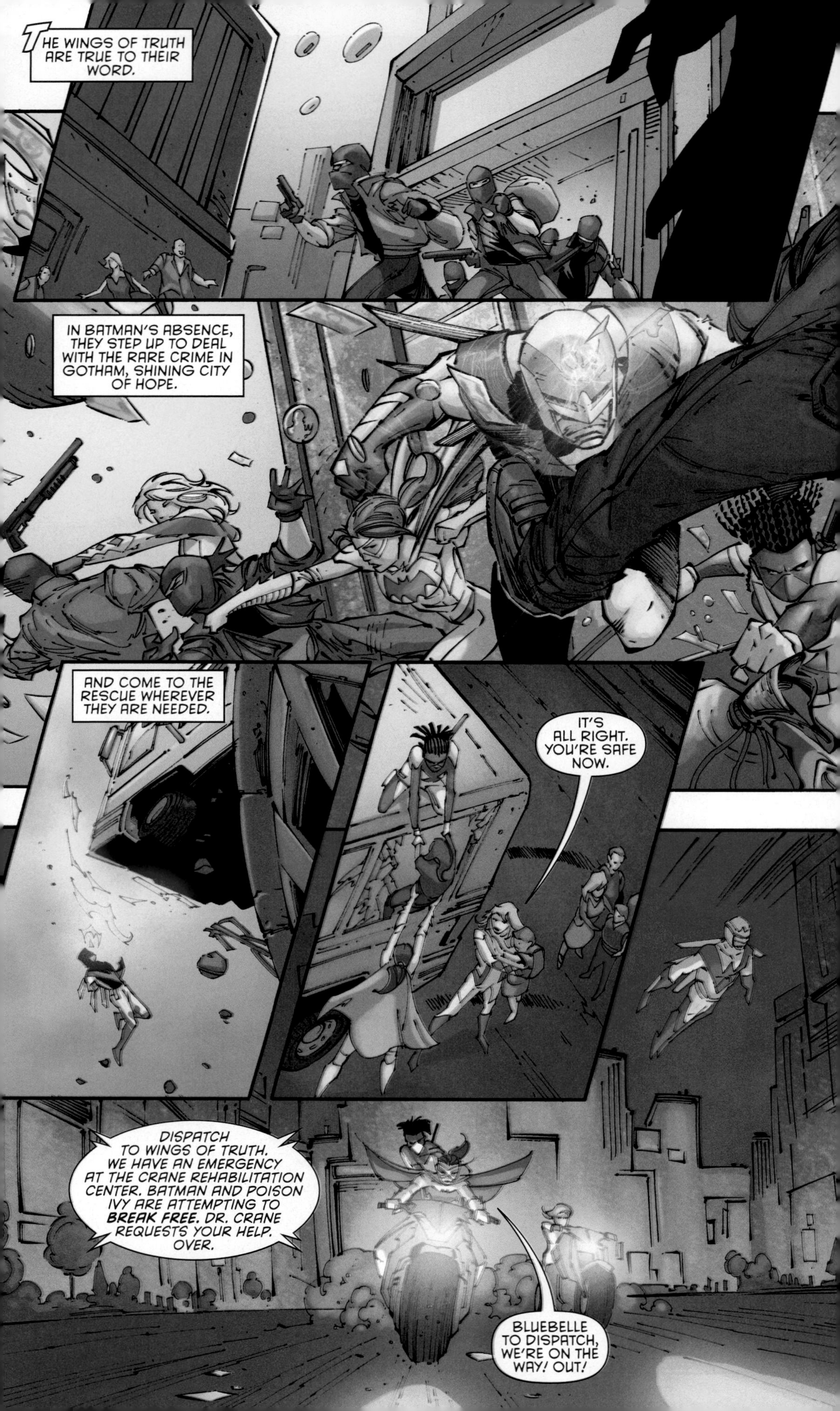
THE WINGS OF TRUTH ARE TRUE TO THEIR WORD.
IN BATMAN'S ABSENCE, THEY STEP UP TO DEAL WITH THE RARE CRIME IN GOTHAM, SHINING CITY OF HOPE.
AND COME TO THE RESCUE WHEREVER THEY ARE NEEDED.
IT'S ALL RIGHT. YOU'RE SAFE NOW.
DISPATCH TO WINGS OF TRUTH. WE HAVE AN EMERGENCY AT THE CRANE REHABILITATION CENTER. BATMAN AND POISON IVY ARE ATTEMPTING TO BREAK FREE. DR. CRANE REQUESTS YOUR HELP. OVER.
BLUEBELLE TO DISPATCH, WE'RE ON THE WAY! OUT!

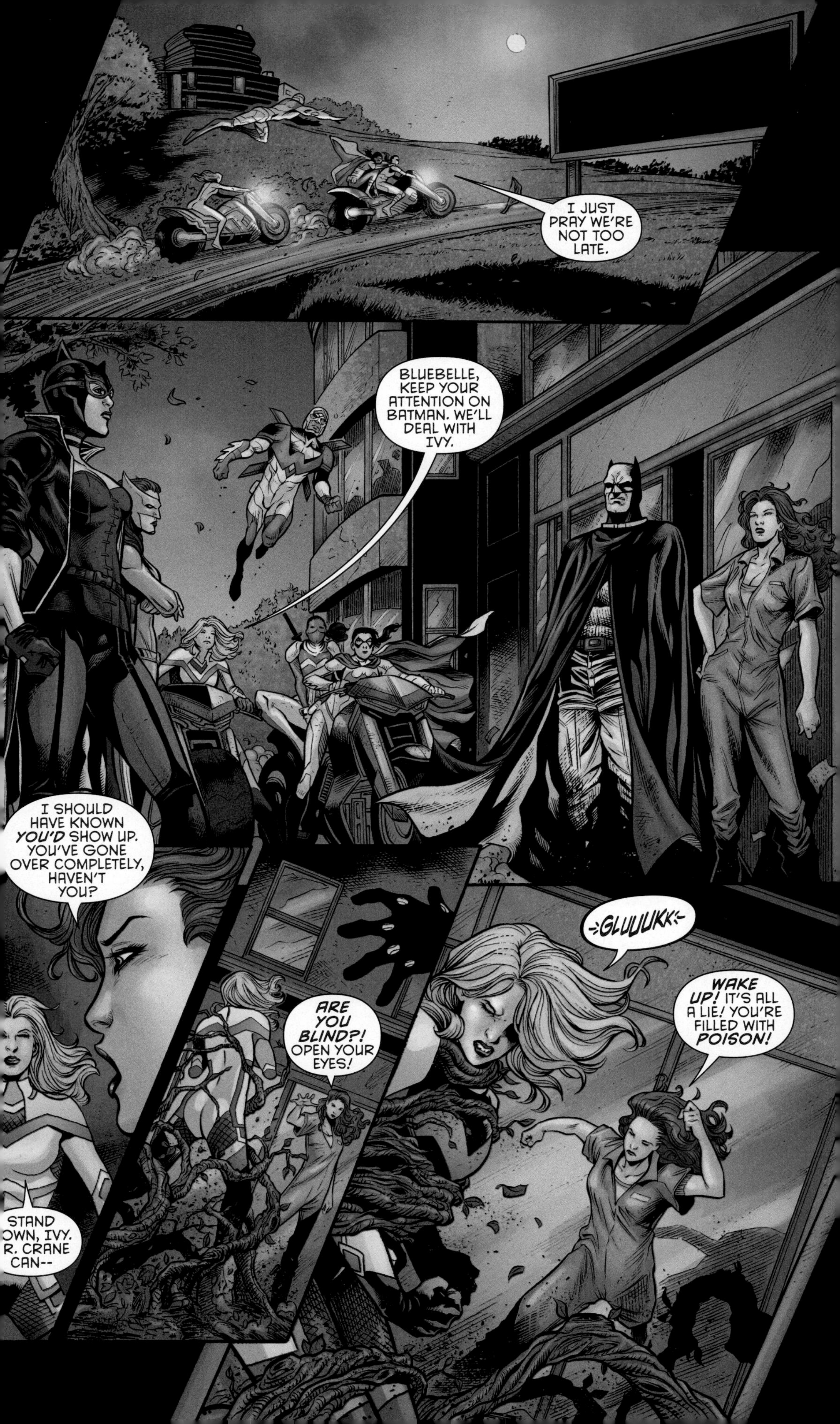

I JUST PRAY WE'RE NOT TOO LATE.
BLUEBELLE, KEEP YOUR ATTENTION ON BATMAN. WE'LL DEAL WITH IVY.
I SHOULD HAVE KNOWN YOU'D SHOW UP. YOU'VE GONE OVER COMPLETELY, HAVEN'T YOU?
STAND OWN, IVY. R. CRANE CAN--
ARE YOU BLIND?! OPEN YOUR EYES!
GLUUUKK
WAKE UP! IT'S ALL A LIE! YOU'RE FILLED WITH POISON!

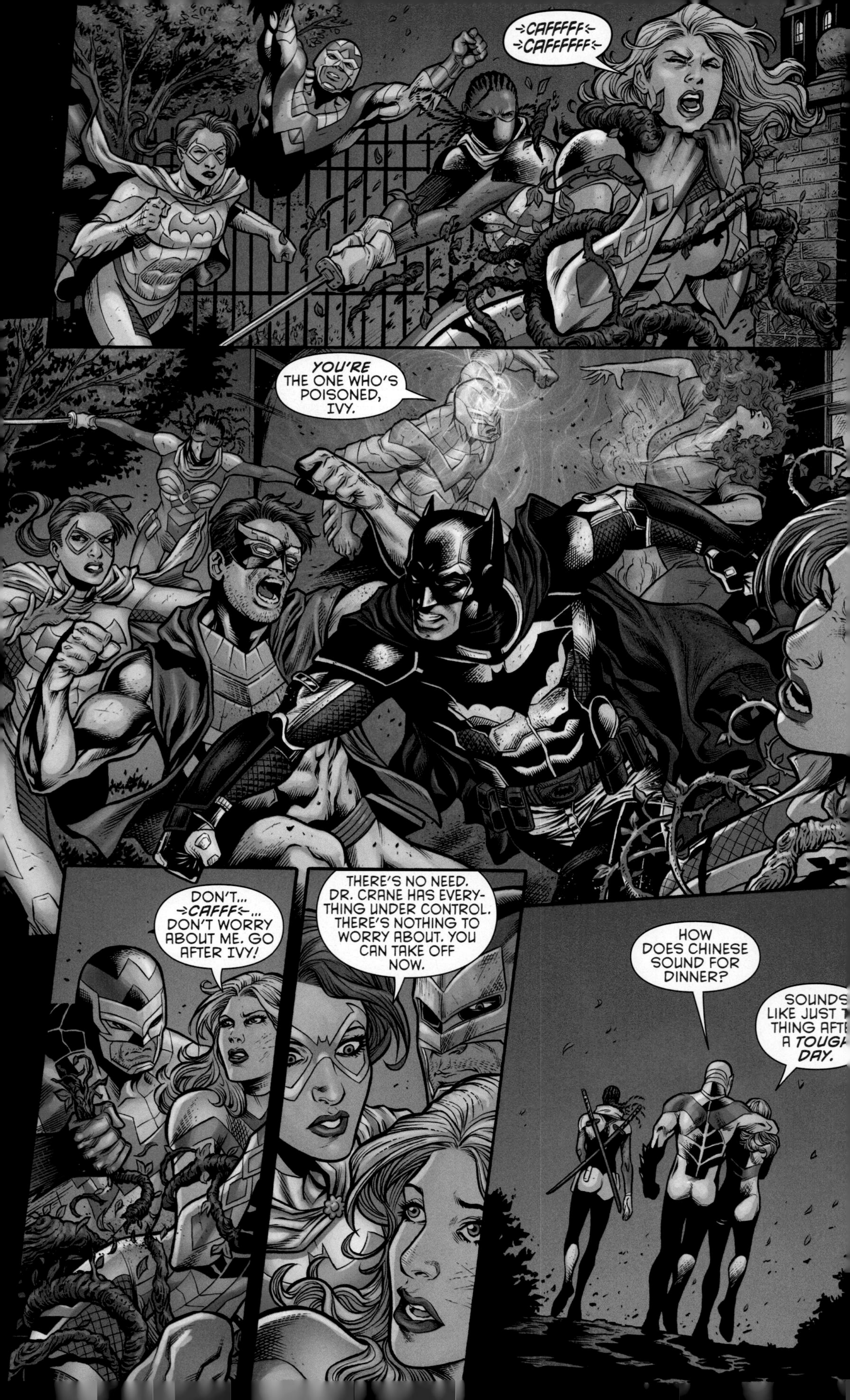

-CAFFFFF-
-CAFFFFFF-
YOU'RE THE ONE WHO'S POISONED, IVY.
DON'T... -*CAFFF*-... DON'T WORRY ABOUT ME. GO AFTER IVY!
THERE'S NO NEED. DR. CRANE HAS EVERYTHING UNDER CONTROL. THERE'S NOTHING TO WORRY ABOUT. YOU CAN TAKE OFF NOW.
HOW DOES CHINESE SOUND FOR DINNER?
SOUNDS LIKE JUST THING AFTE A *TOUGH* DAY.

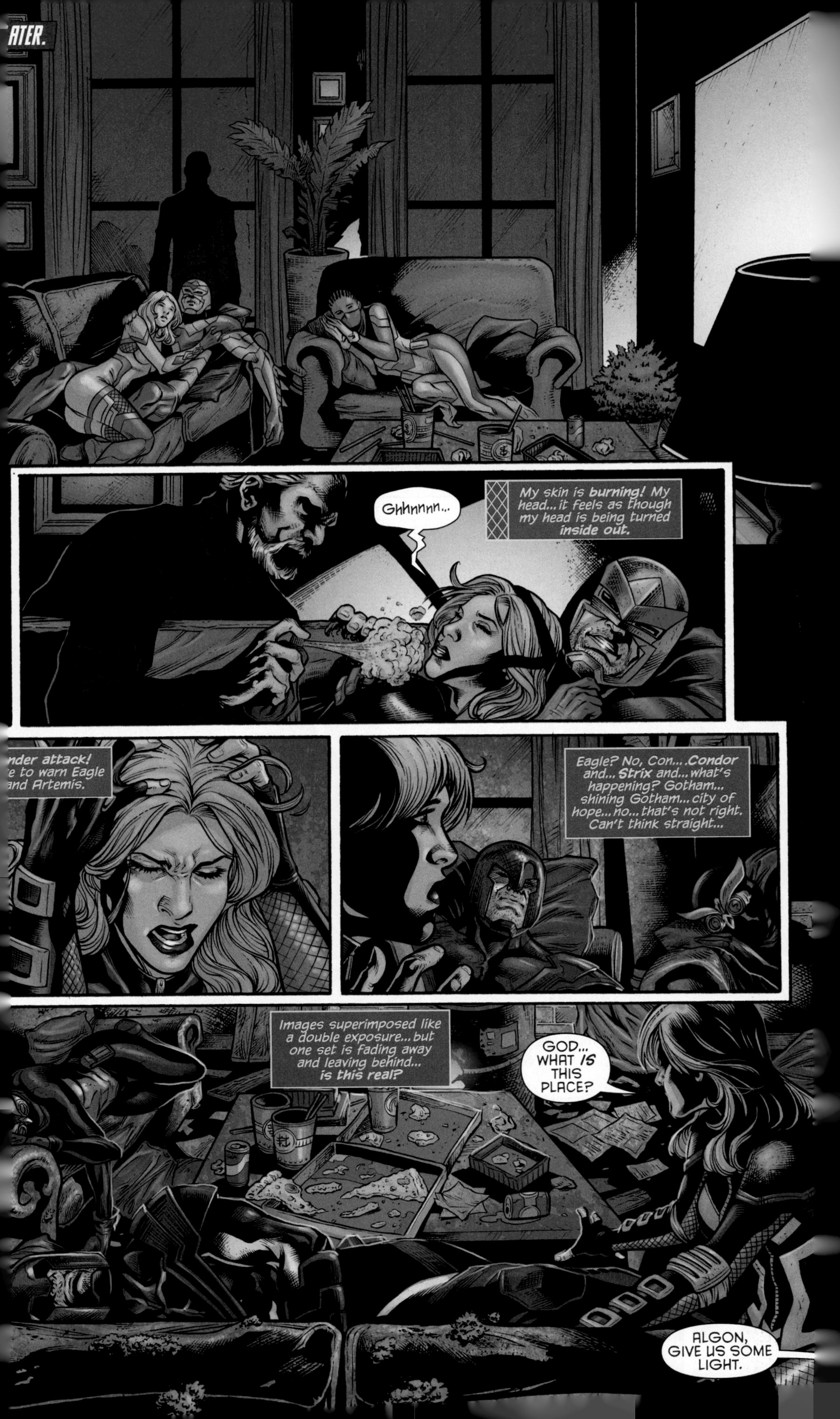

ATER.
Ghhnnnn...
My skin is burning! My head...it feels as though my head is being turned inside out.
nder attack! e to warn Eagle and Artemis.
Eagle? No, Con....Condor and... Strix and...what's happening? Gotham... shining Gotham...city of hope...no...that's not right. Can't think straight...
Images superimposed like a double exposure...but one set is fading away and leaving behind... is this real?
GOD... WHAT IS THIS PLACE?
ALGON, GIVE US SOME LIGHT.

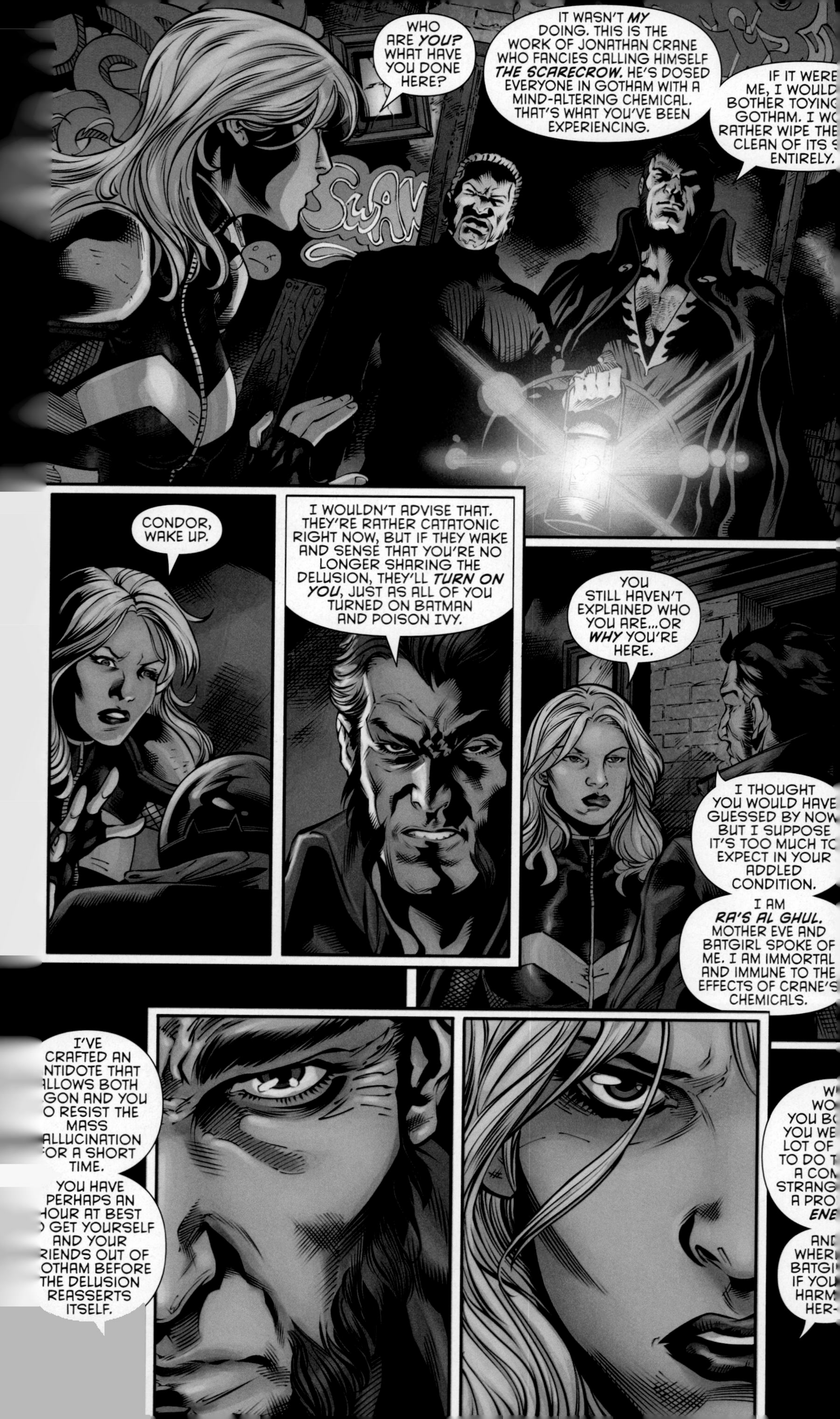
WHO ARE YOU? WHAT HAVE YOU DONE HERE?
IT WASN'T MY DOING. THIS IS THE WORK OF JONATHAN CRANE WHO FANCIES CALLING HIMSELF THE SCARECROW. HE'S DOSED EVERYONE IN GOTHAM WITH A MIND-ALTERING CHEMICAL. THAT'S WHAT YOU'VE BEEN EXPERIENCING.
IF IT WERE ME, I WOULD BOTHER TOYING GOTHAM. I WO RATHER WIPE THE CLEAN OF ITS ENTIRELY.
SWAM
CONDOR, WAKE UP.
I WOULDN'T ADVISE THAT. THEY'RE RATHER CATATONIC RIGHT NOW, BUT IF THEY WAKE AND SENSE THAT YOU'RE NO LONGER SHARING THE DELUSION, THEY'LL TURN ON YOU, JUST AS ALL OF YOU TURNED ON BATMAN AND POISON IVY.
YOU STILL HAVEN'T EXPLAINED WHO YOU ARE...OR WHY YOU'RE HERE.
I THOUGHT YOU WOULD HAVE GUESSED BY NOW BUT I SUPPOSE IT'S TOO MUCH TO EXPECT IN YOUR ADDLED CONDITION.
I AM RA'S AL GHUL. MOTHER EVE AND BATGIRL SPOKE OF ME. I AM IMMORTAL AND IMMUNE TO THE EFFECTS OF CRANE'S CHEMICALS.
I'VE CRAFTED AN NTIDOTE THAT LLOWS BOTH GON AND YOU O RESIST THE MASS ALLUCINATION FOR A SHORT TIME.
YOU HAVE PERHAPS AN HOUR AT BEST O GET YOURSELF AND YOUR RIENDS OUT OF OTHAM BEFORE THE DELUSION REASSERTS ITSELF.

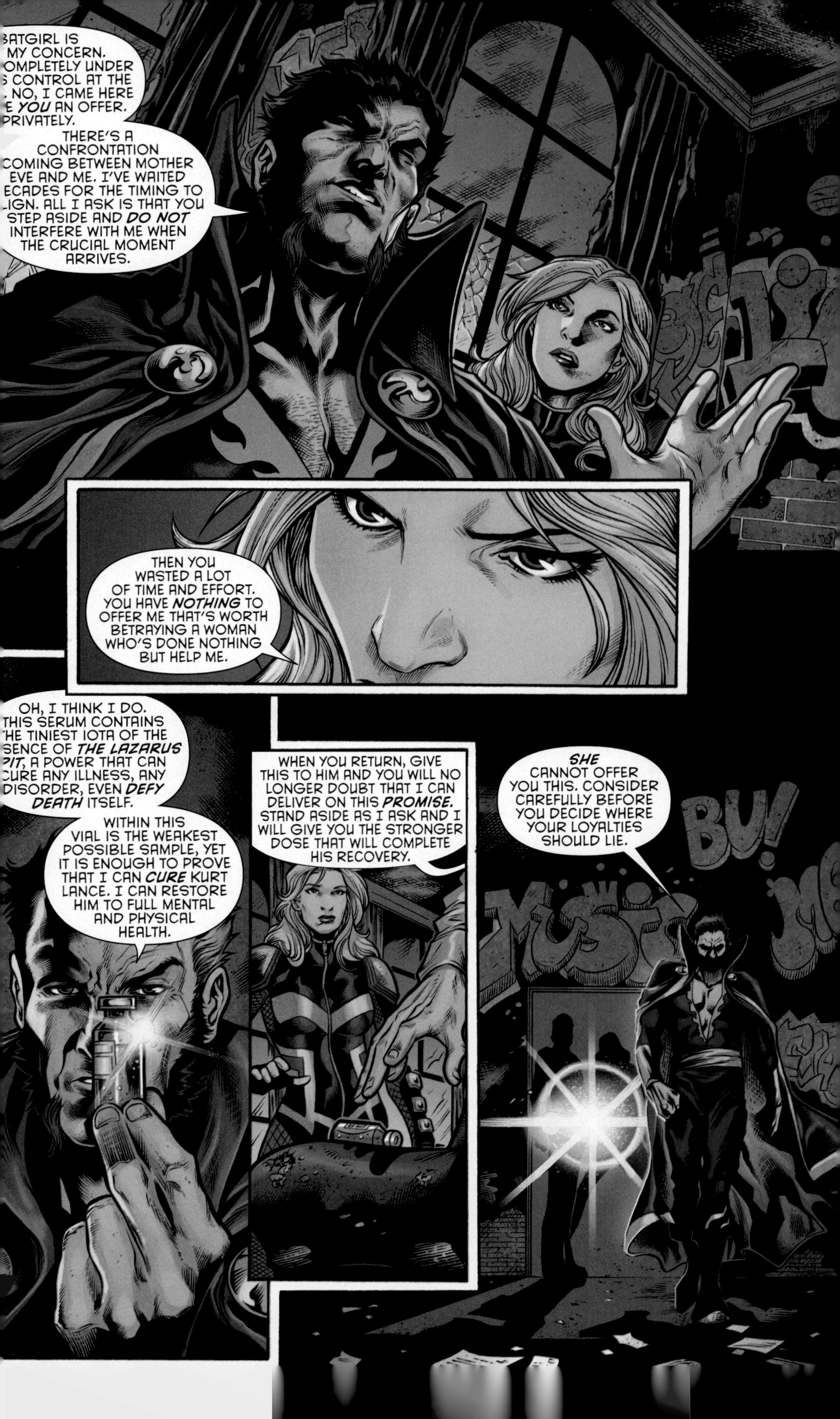

BATGIRL IS MY CONCERN. OMPLETELY UNDER S CONTROL AT THE . NO, I CAME HERE E YOU AN OFFER. PRIVATELY.
THERE'S A CONFRONTATION COMING BETWEEN MOTHER EVE AND ME. I'VE WAITED ECADES FOR THE TIMING TO LIGN. ALL I ASK IS THAT YOU STEP ASIDE AND DO NOT INTERFERE WITH ME WHEN THE CRUCIAL MOMENT ARRIVES.
THEN YOU WASTED A LOT OF TIME AND EFFORT. YOU HAVE NOTHING TO OFFER ME THAT'S WORTH BETRAYING A WOMAN WHO'S DONE NOTHING BUT HELP ME.
OH, I THINK I DO. THIS SERUM CONTAINS HE TINIEST IOTA OF THE SENCE OF THE LAZARUS PIT, A POWER THAT CAN CURE ANY ILLNESS, ANY DISORDER, EVEN DEFY DEATH ITSELF.
WITHIN THIS VIAL IS THE WEAKEST POSSIBLE SAMPLE, YET IT IS ENOUGH TO PROVE THAT I CAN CURE KURT LANCE. I CAN RESTORE HIM TO FULL MENTAL AND PHYSICAL HEALTH.
WHEN YOU RETURN, GIVE THIS TO HIM AND YOU WILL NO LONGER DOUBT THAT I CAN DELIVER ON THIS PROMISE. STAND ASIDE AS I ASK AND I WILL GIVE YOU THE STRONGER DOSE THAT WILL COMPLETE HIS RECOVERY.
SHE CANNOT OFFER YOU THIS. CONSIDER CAREFULLY BEFORE YOU DECIDE WHERE YOUR LOYALTIES SHOULD LIE.

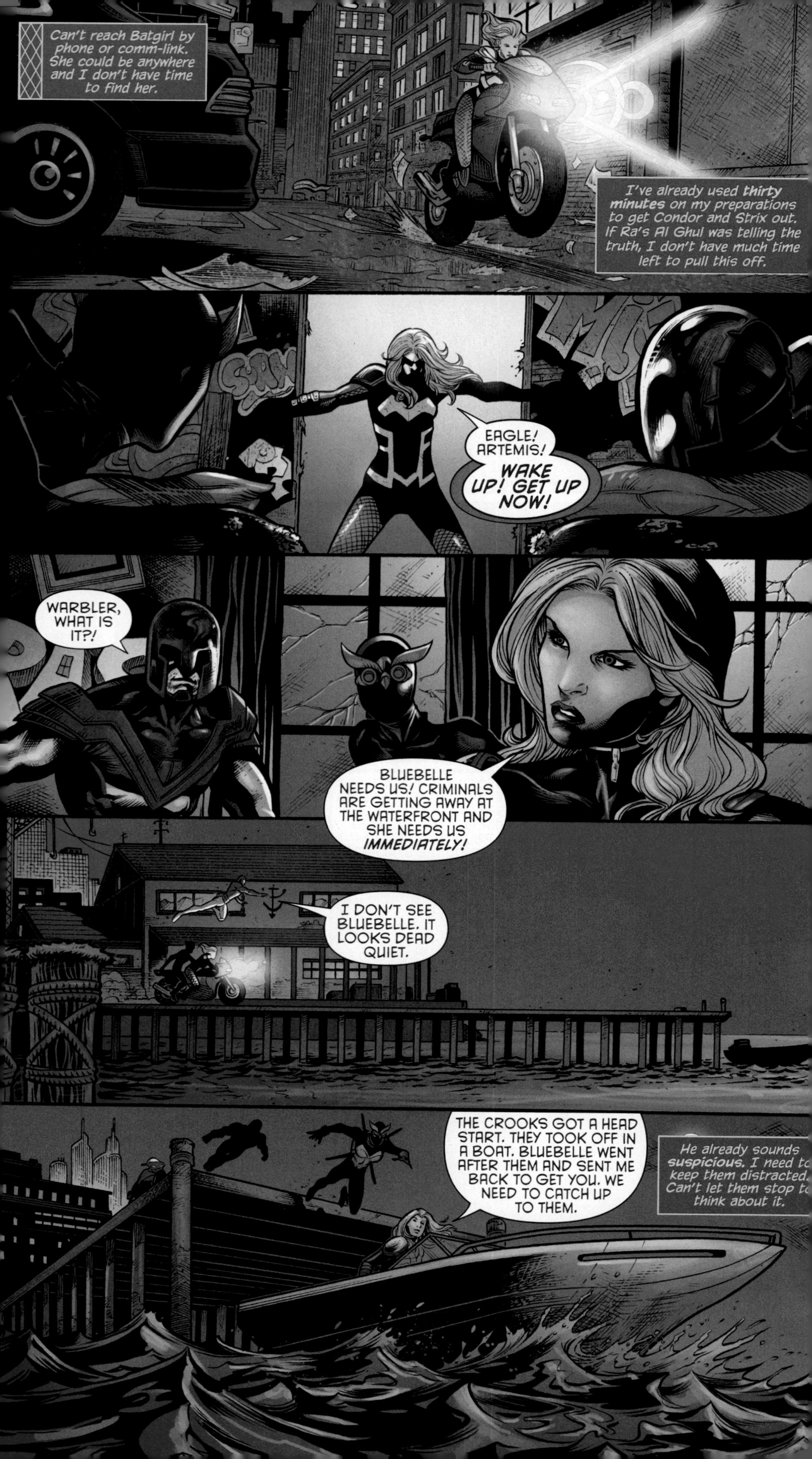
Can't reach Batgirl by phone or comm-link. She could be anywhere and I don't have time to find her.
I've already used **thirty minutes** on my preparations to get Condor and Strix out. If Ra's Al Ghul was telling the truth, I don't have much time left to pull this off.
EAGLE! ARTEMIS! ***WAKE UP! GET UP NOW!***
WARBLER, WHAT IS IT?!
BLUEBELLE NEEDS US! CRIMINALS ARE GETTING AWAY AT THE WATERFRONT AND SHE NEEDS US *IMMEDIATELY!*
I DON'T SEE BLUEBELLE. IT LOOKS DEAD QUIET.
THE CROOKS GOT A HEAD START. THEY TOOK OFF IN A BOAT. BLUEBELLE WENT AFTER THEM AND SENT ME BACK TO GET YOU. WE NEED TO CATCH UP TO THEM.
He already sounds **suspicious.** I need to keep them distracted. Can't let them stop to think about it.

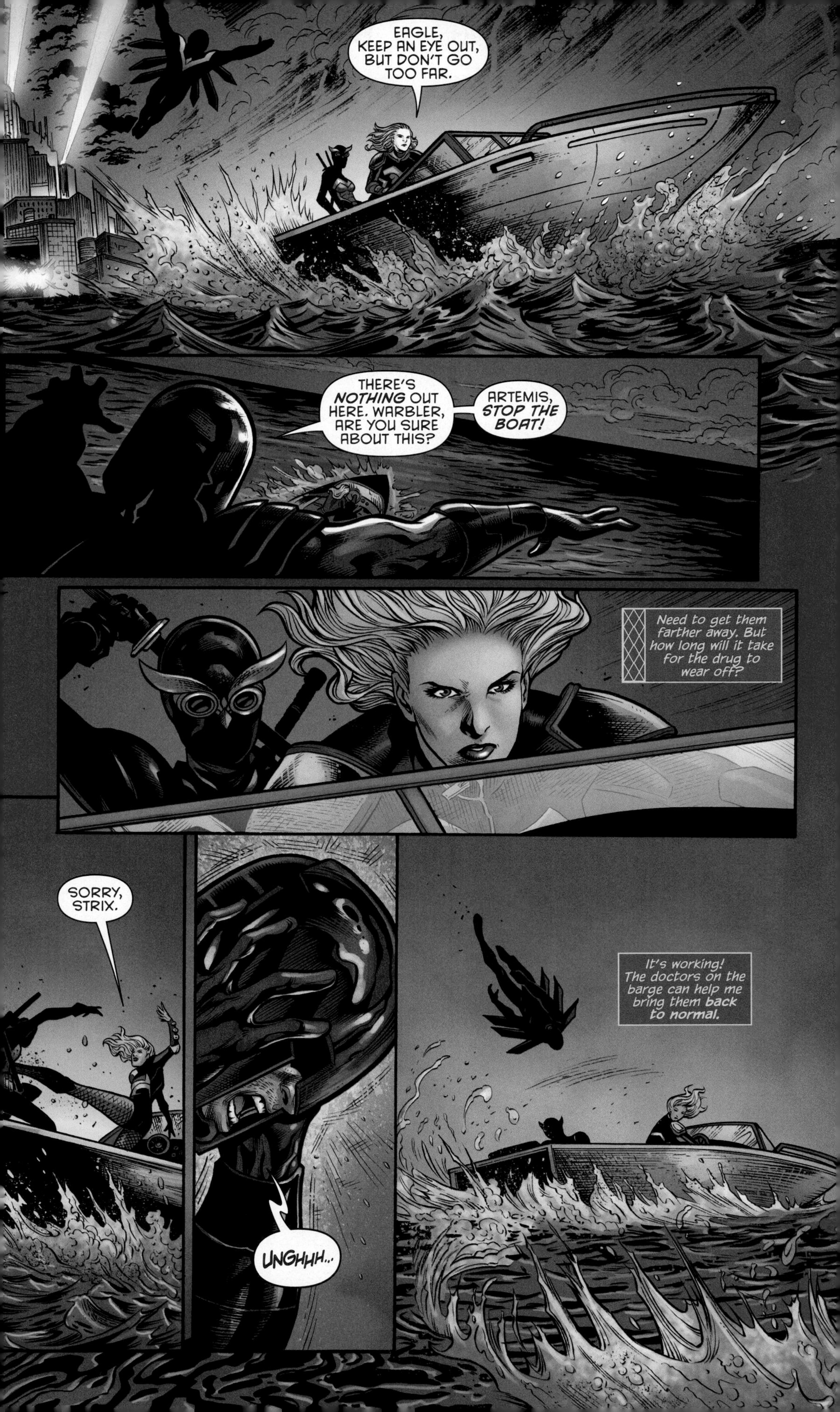
EAGLE, KEEP AN EYE OUT, BUT DON'T GO TOO FAR.
THERE'S NOTHING OUT HERE. WARBLER, ARE YOU SURE ABOUT THIS?
ARTEMIS, STOP THE BOAT!
Need to get them farther away. But how long will it take for the drug to wear off?
SORRY, STRIX.
UNGHHH...
It's working! The doctors on the barge can help me bring them back to normal.

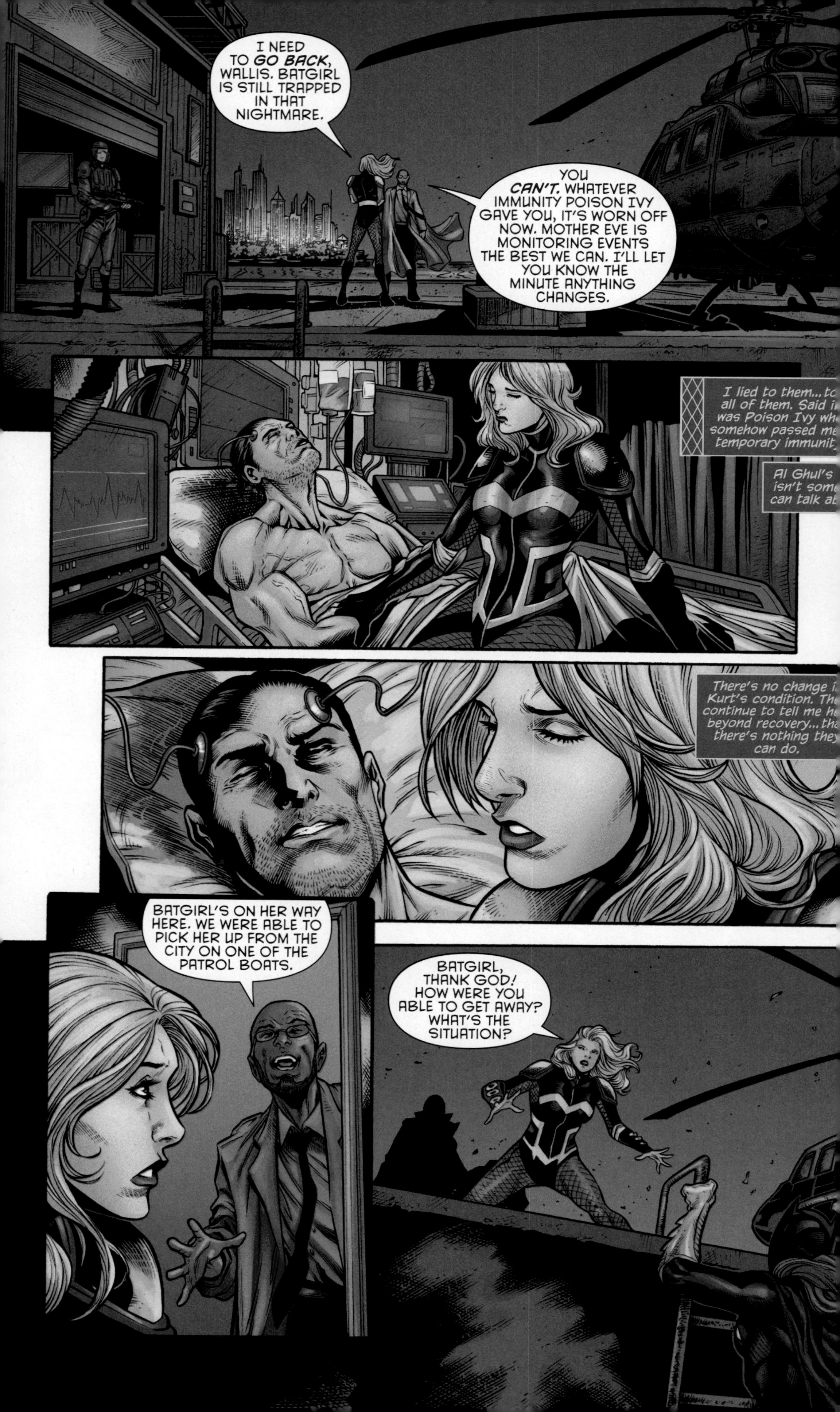

I NEED TO *GO BACK*, WALLIS. BATGIRL IS STILL TRAPPED IN THAT NIGHTMARE.
YOU *CAN'T.* WHATEVER IMMUNITY POISON IVY GAVE YOU, IT'S WORN OFF NOW. MOTHER EVE IS MONITORING EVENTS THE BEST WE CAN. I'LL LET YOU KNOW THE MINUTE ANYTHING CHANGES.
I lied to them...t all of them. Said i was Poison Ivy wh somehow passed m temporary immunit
Al Ghul's isn't som can talk a
There's no change i Kurt's condition. Th continue to tell me h beyond recovery...th there's nothing the can do.
BATGIRL'S ON HER WAY HERE. WE WERE ABLE TO PICK HER UP FROM THE CITY ON ONE OF THE PATROL BOATS.
BATGIRL, THANK GOD! HOW WERE YOU ABLE TO GET AWAY? WHAT'S THE SITUATION?

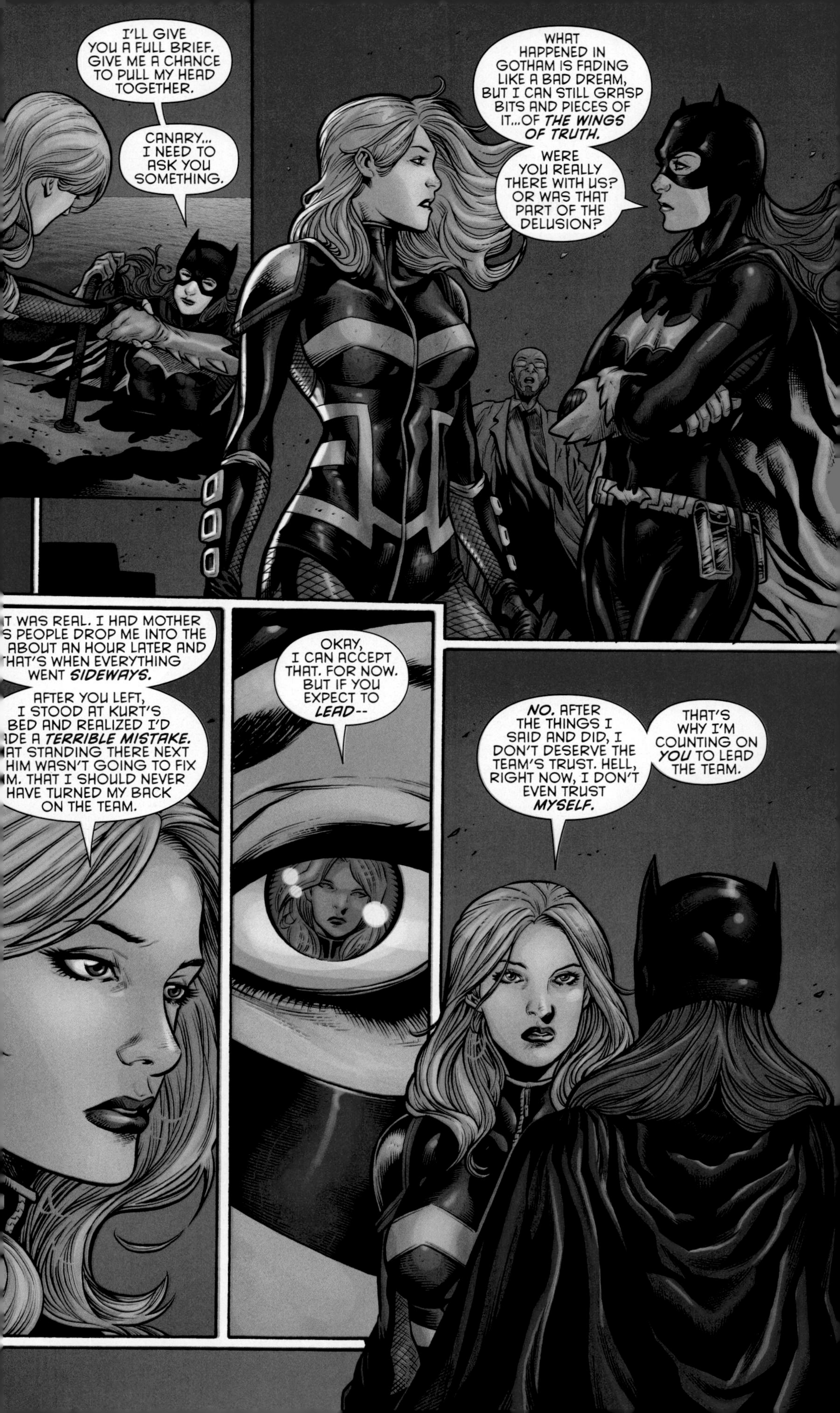
I'LL GIVE YOU A FULL BRIEF. GIVE ME A CHANCE TO PULL MY HEAD TOGETHER.
CANARY... I NEED TO ASK YOU SOMETHING.
WHAT HAPPENED IN GOTHAM IS FADING LIKE A BAD DREAM, BUT I CAN STILL GRASP BITS AND PIECES OF IT...OF THE WINGS OF TRUTH.
WERE YOU REALLY THERE WITH US? OR WAS THAT PART OF THE DELUSION?
WENT SIDEWAYS.
AFTER YOU LEFT, I STOOD AT KURT'S BED AND REALIZED I'D
HAVE TURNED MY BACK ON THE TEAM.
OKAY, I CAN ACCEPT THAT. FOR NOW. BUT IF YOU EXPECT TO LEAD--
NO. AFTER THE THINGS I SAID AND DID, I DON'T DESERVE THE TEAM'S TRUST. HELL, RIGHT NOW, I DON'T EVEN TRUST MYSELF.
THAT'S WHY I'M COUNTING ON YOU TO LEAD THE TEAM.

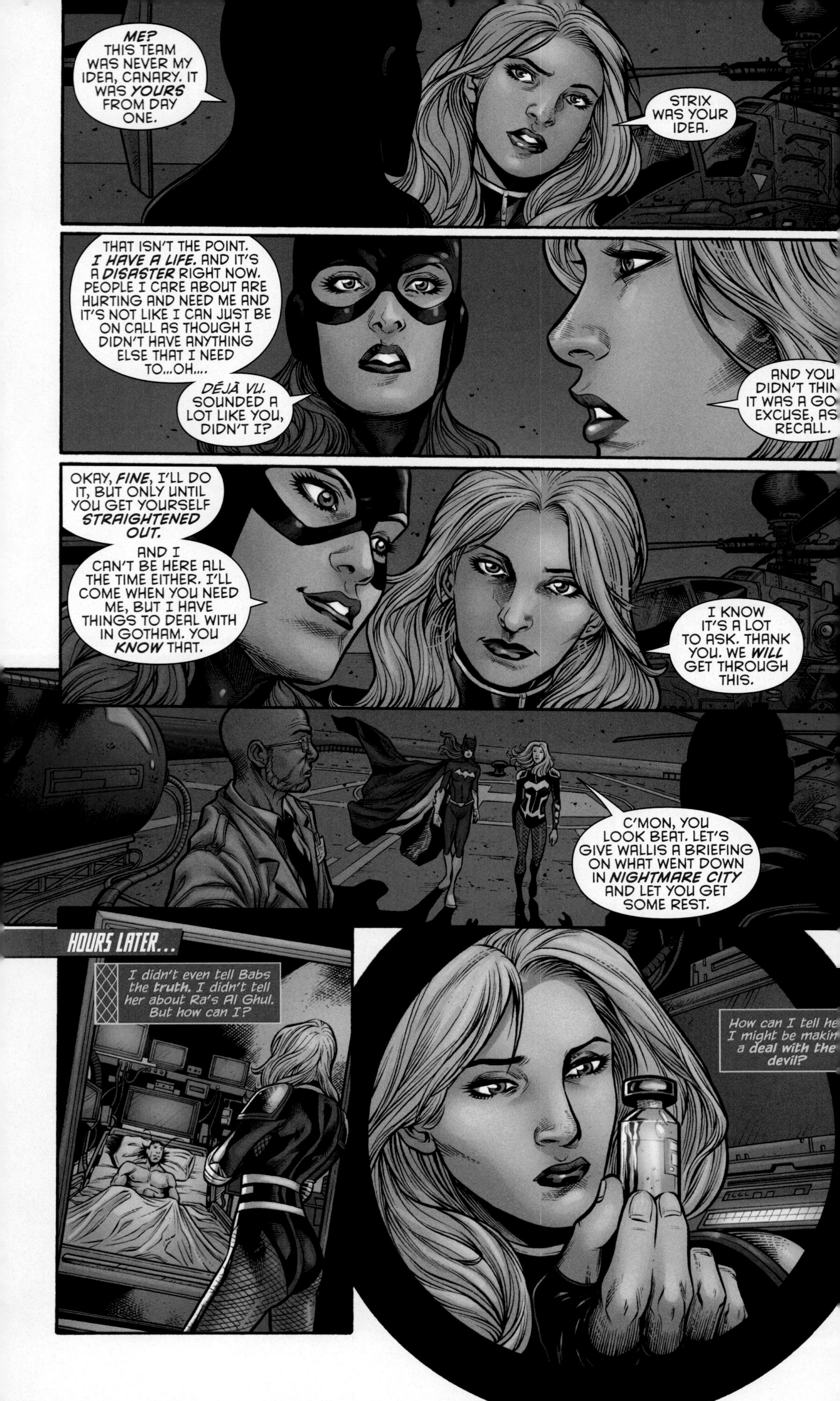
ME? THIS TEAM WAS NEVER MY IDEA, CANARY. IT WAS YOURS FROM DAY ONE.
STRIX WAS YOUR IDEA.
THAT ISN'T THE POINT. I HAVE A LIFE. AND IT'S A DISASTER RIGHT NOW. PEOPLE I CARE ABOUT ARE HURTING AND NEED ME AND IT'S NOT LIKE I CAN JUST BE ON CALL AS THOUGH I DIDN'T HAVE ANYTHING ELSE THAT I NEED TO...OH....
DÉJÀ VU. SOUNDED A LOT LIKE YOU, DIDN'T I?
AND YOU DIDN'T THIN IT WAS A GO EXCUSE, AS RECALL.
OKAY, FINE, I'LL DO IT, BUT ONLY UNTIL YOU GET YOURSELF STRAIGHTENED OUT.
AND I CAN'T BE HERE ALL THE TIME EITHER. I'LL COME WHEN YOU NEED ME, BUT I HAVE THINGS TO DEAL WITH IN GOTHAM. YOU KNOW THAT.
I KNOW IT'S A LOT TO ASK. THANK YOU. WE WILL GET THROUGH THIS.
C'MON, YOU LOOK BEAT. LET'S GIVE WALLIS A BRIEFING ON WHAT WENT DOWN IN NIGHTMARE CITY AND LET YOU GET SOME REST.
HOURS LATER...
I didn't even tell Babs the truth. I didn't tell her about Ra's Al Ghul. But how can I?
How can I tell he I might be makin a deal with the devil?

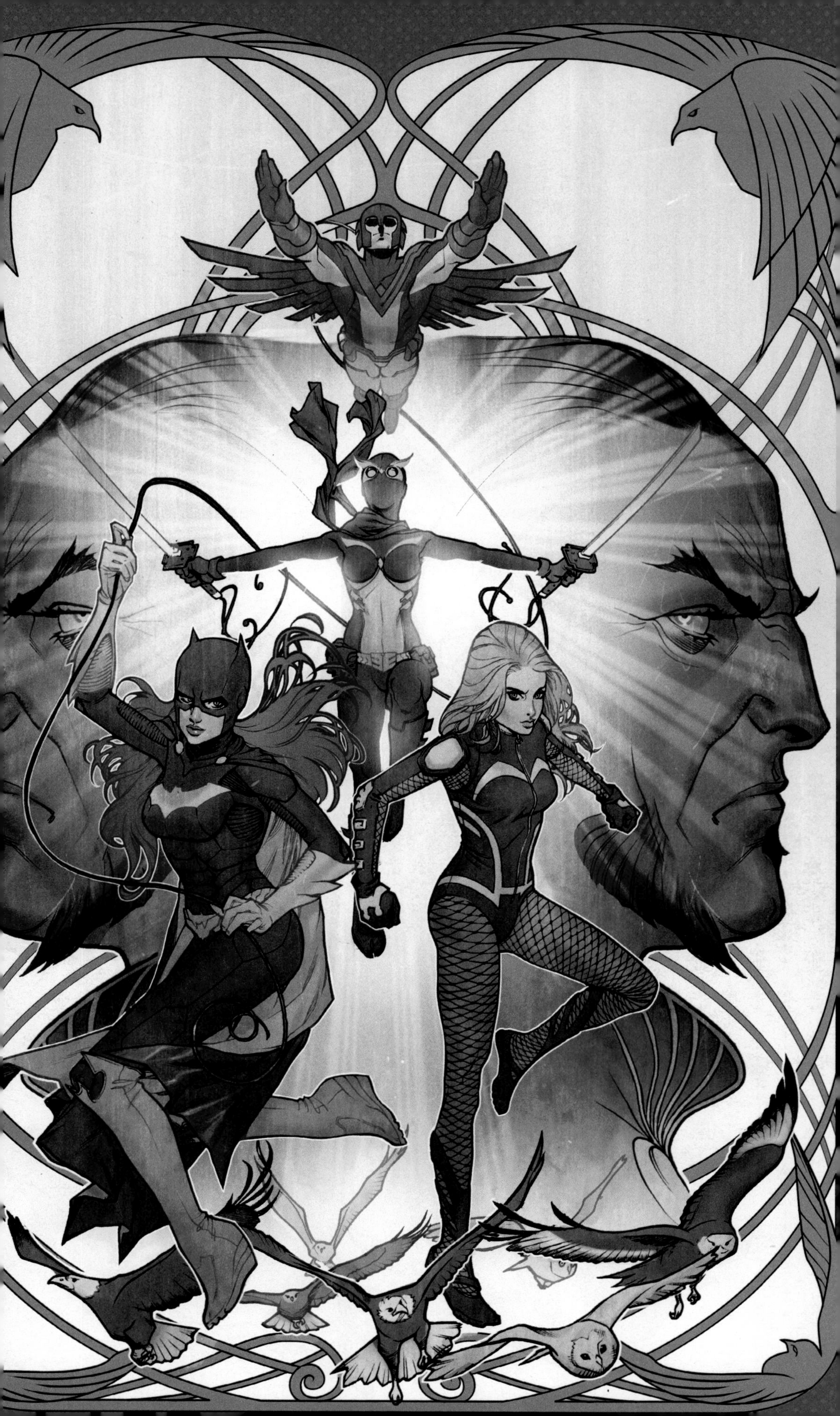

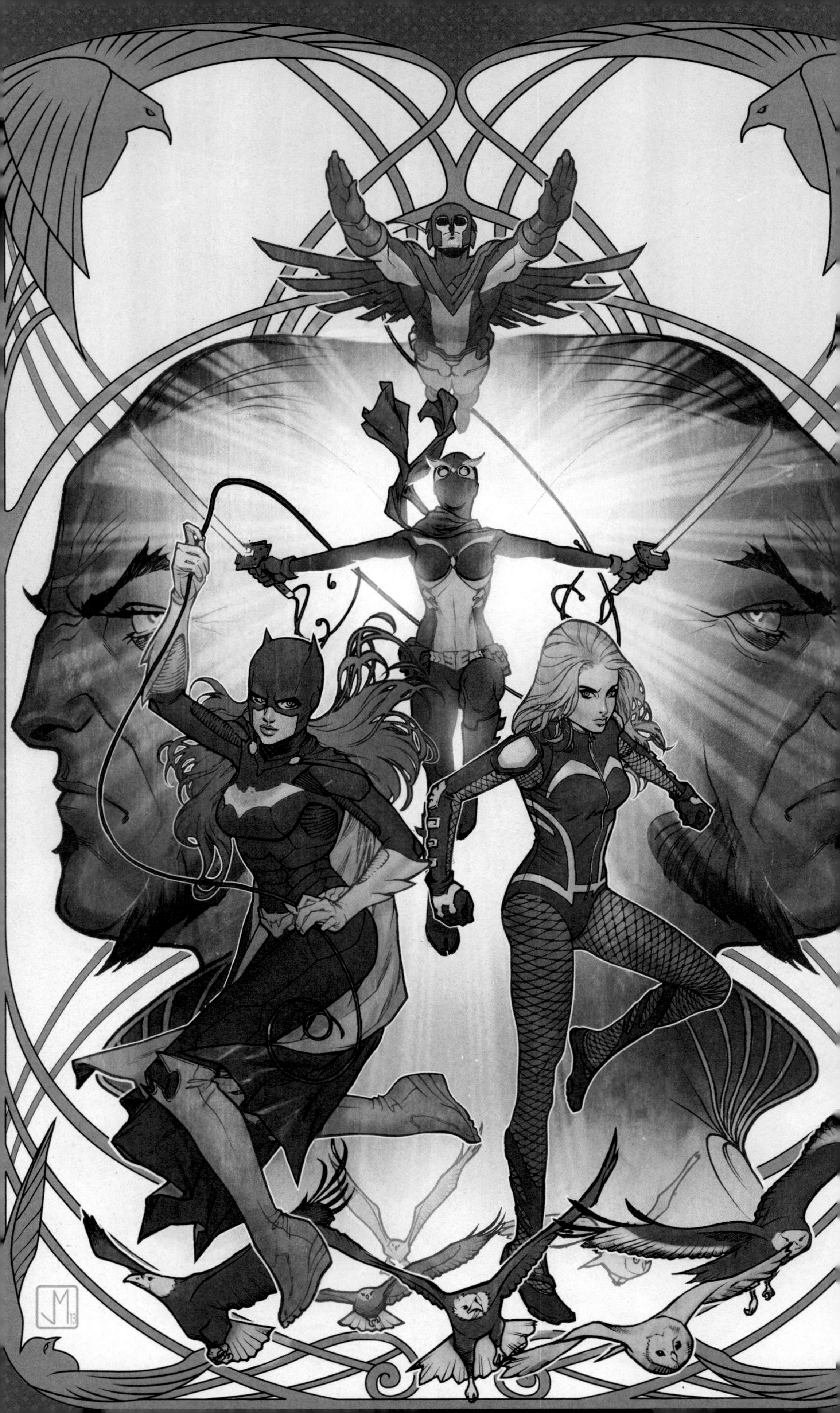

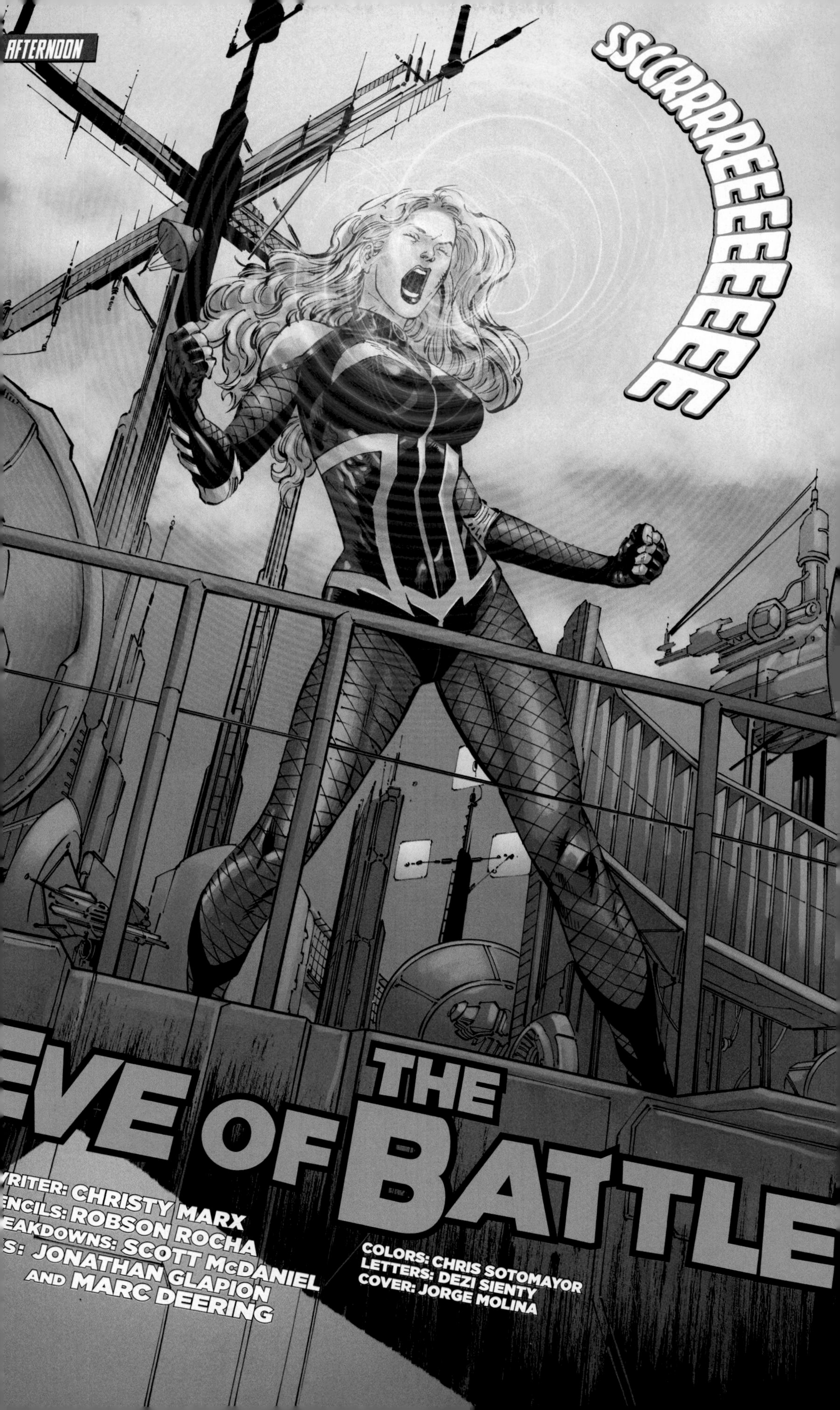

AFTERNOON
SSCRRREEEEEEEE
EVE OF THE BATTLE
RITER: CHRISTY MARX
ENCILS: ROBSON ROCHA
EAKDOWNS: SCOTT McDANIEL
S: JONATHAN GLAPION
AND MARC DEERING
COLORS: CHRIS SOTOMAYOR
LETTERS: DEZI SIENTY
COVER: JORGE MOLINA

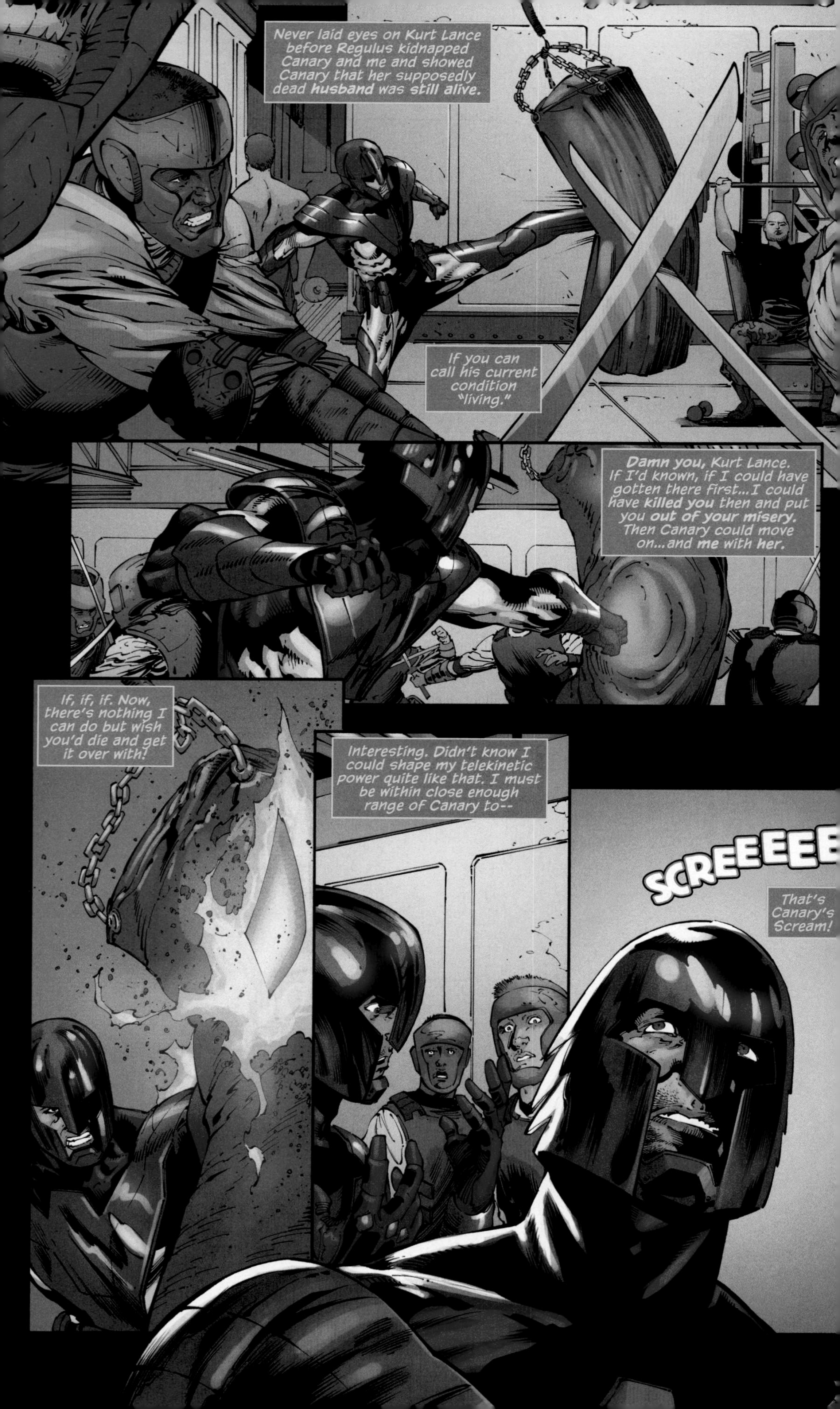
Never laid eyes on Kurt Lance before Regulus kidnapped Canary and me and showed Canary that her supposedly dead **husband** was **still alive.**
If you can call his current condition "living."
Damn you, Kurt Lance. If I'd known, if I could have gotten there first...I could have **killed you** then and put you **out of your misery.** Then Canary could move on...and **me** with **her.**
If, if, if. Now, there's nothing I can do but wish you'd die and get it over with!
Interesting. Didn't know I could shape my telekinetic power quite like that. I must be within close enough range of Canary to--
SCREEEEE
That's Canary's Scream!

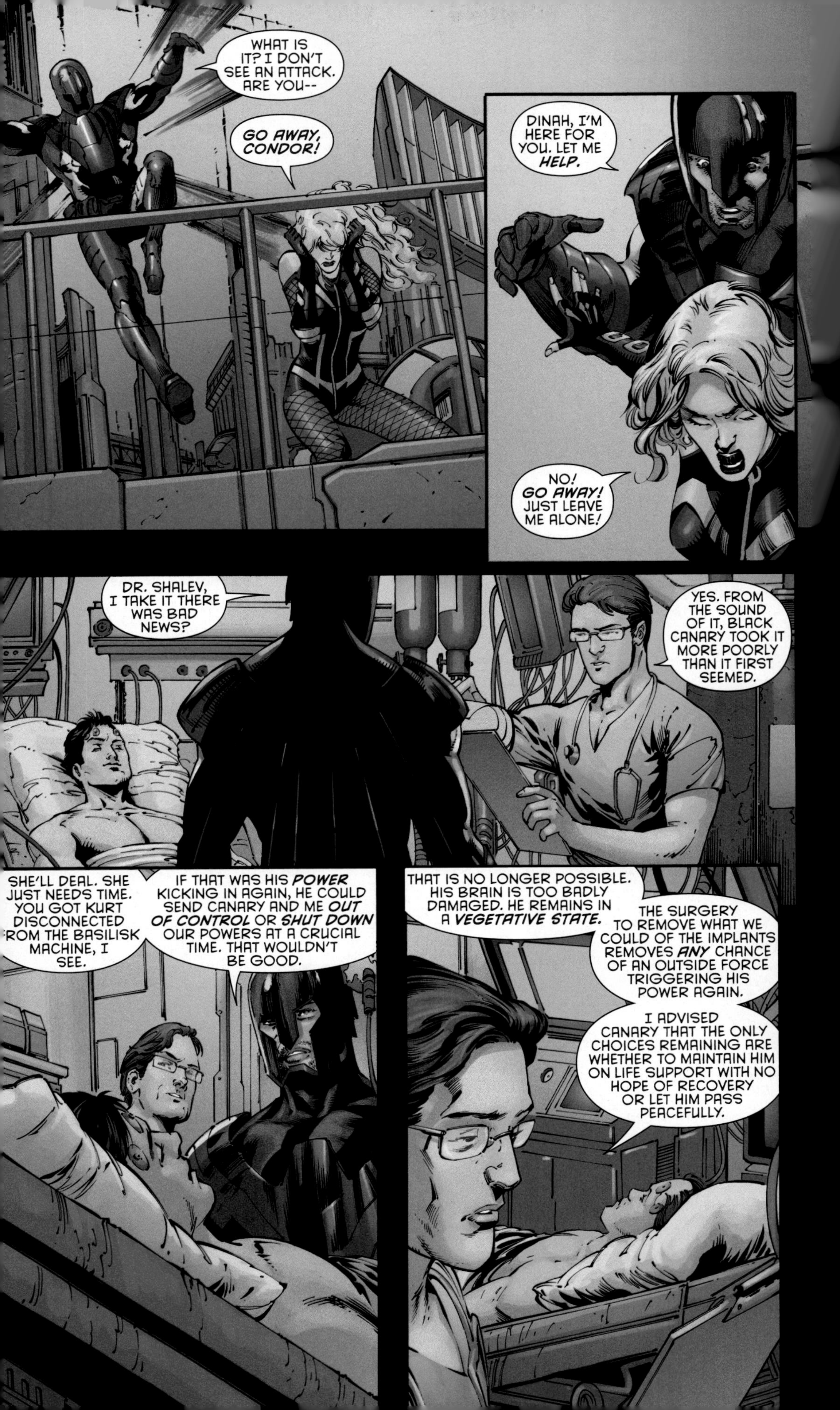
WHAT IS IT? I DON'T SEE AN ATTACK. ARE YOU--
GO AWAY, CONDOR!
DINAH, I'M HERE FOR YOU. LET ME HELP.
NO! GO AWAY! JUST LEAVE ME ALONE!
DR. SHALEV, I TAKE IT THERE WAS BAD NEWS?
YES. FROM THE SOUND OF IT, BLACK CANARY TOOK IT MORE POORLY THAN IT FIRST SEEMED.
SHE'LL DEAL. SHE JUST NEEDS TIME. YOU GOT KURT DISCONNECTED FROM THE BASILISK MACHINE, I SEE.
IF THAT WAS HIS POWER KICKING IN AGAIN, HE COULD SEND CANARY AND ME OUT OF CONTROL OR SHUT DOWN OUR POWERS AT A CRUCIAL TIME. THAT WOULDN'T BE GOOD.
THAT IS NO LONGER POSSIBLE. HIS BRAIN IS TOO BADLY DAMAGED. HE REMAINS IN A VEGETATIVE STATE.
THE SURGERY TO REMOVE WHAT WE COULD OF THE IMPLANTS REMOVES ANY CHANCE OF AN OUTSIDE FORCE TRIGGERING HIS POWER AGAIN.
I ADVISED CANARY THAT THE ONLY CHOICES REMAINING ARE WHETHER TO MAINTAIN HIM ON LIFE SUPPORT WITH NO HOPE OF RECOVERY OR LET HIM PASS PEACEFULLY.

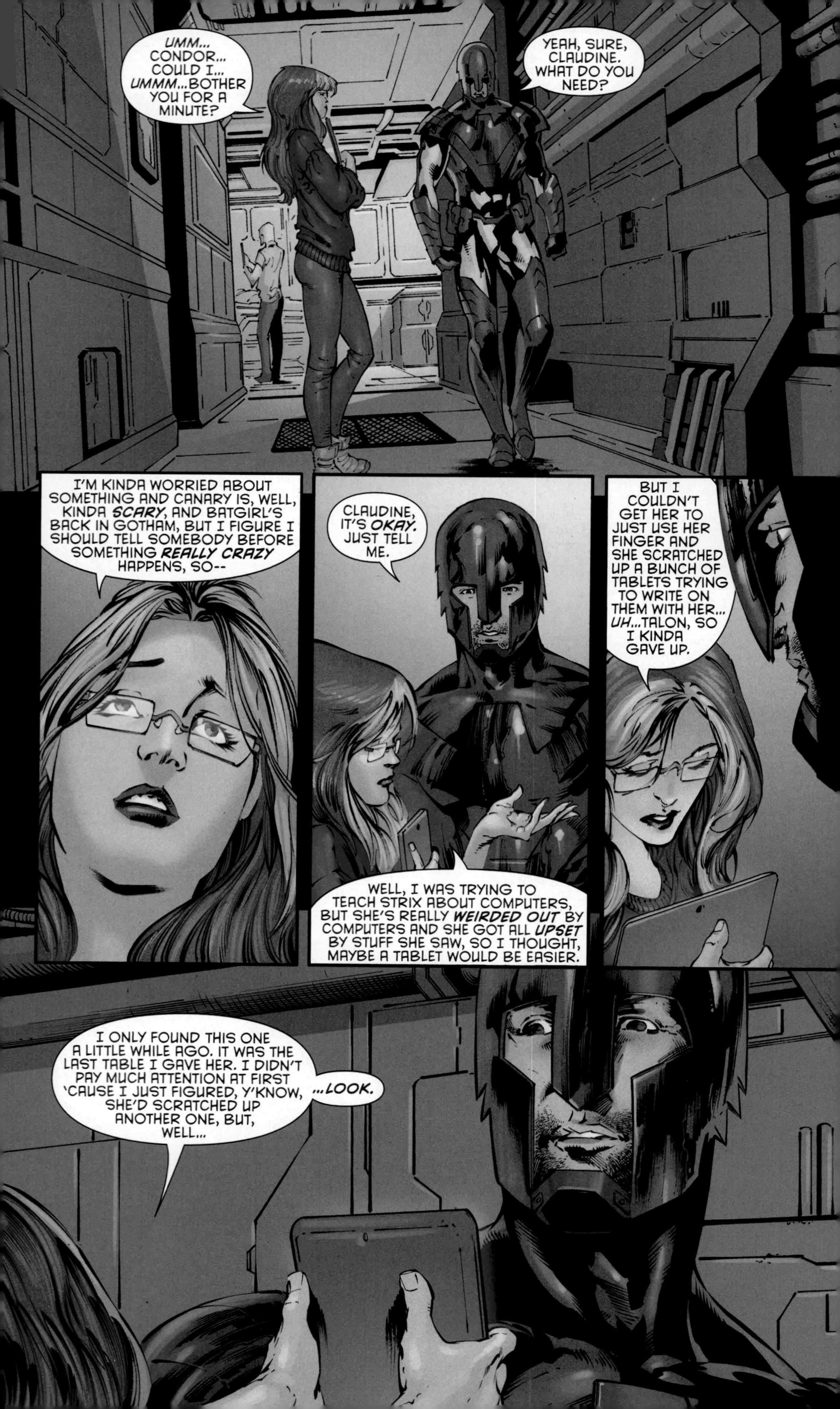

UMM... CONDOR... COULD I... UMMM...BOTHER YOU FOR A MINUTE?
YEAH, SURE, CLAUDINE. WHAT DO YOU NEED?
I'M KINDA WORRIED ABOUT SOMETHING AND CANARY IS, WELL, KINDA SCARY, AND BATGIRL'S BACK IN GOTHAM, BUT I FIGURE I SHOULD TELL SOMEBODY BEFORE SOMETHING REALLY CRAZY HAPPENS, SO--
CLAUDINE, IT'S OKAY. JUST TELL ME.
WELL, I WAS TRYING TO TEACH STRIX ABOUT COMPUTERS, BUT SHE'S REALLY WEIRDED OUT BY COMPUTERS AND SHE GOT ALL UPSET BY STUFF SHE SAW, SO I THOUGHT, MAYBE A TABLET WOULD BE EASIER.
BUT I COULDN'T GET HER TO JUST USE HER FINGER AND SHE SCRATCHED UP A BUNCH OF TABLETS TRYING TO WRITE ON THEM WITH HER... UH...TALON, SO I KINDA GAVE UP.
I ONLY FOUND THIS ONE A LITTLE WHILE AGO. IT WAS THE LAST TABLE I GAVE HER. I DIDN'T PAY MUCH ATTENTION AT FIRST 'CAUSE I JUST FIGURED, Y'KNOW, SHE'D SCRATCHED UP ANOTHER ONE, BUT, WELL...
...LOOK.

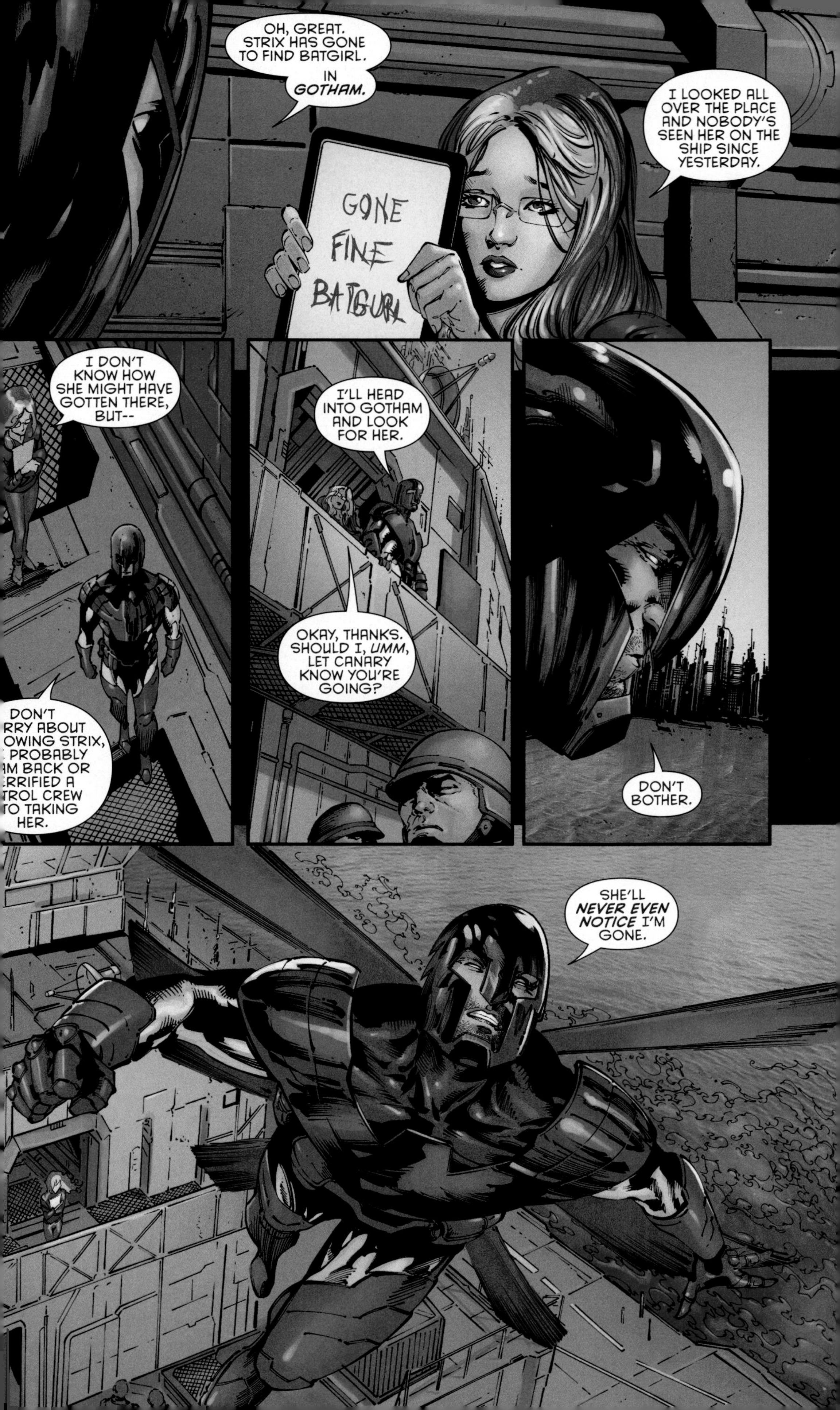
OH, GREAT. STRIX HAS GONE TO FIND BATGIRL. IN *GOTHAM.*
GONE FINE BATGURL
I LOOKED ALL OVER THE PLACE AND NOBODY'S SEEN HER ON THE SHIP SINCE YESTERDAY.
I DON'T KNOW HOW SHE MIGHT HAVE GOTTEN THERE, BUT--
DON'T RRY ABOUT OWING STRIX, PROBABLY M BACK OR RRIFIED A TROL CREW O TAKING HER.
I'LL HEAD INTO GOTHAM AND LOOK FOR HER.
OKAY, THANKS. SHOULD I, *UMM,* LET CANARY KNOW YOU'RE GOING?
DON'T BOTHER.
SHE'LL ***NEVER EVEN NOTICE*** I'M GONE.

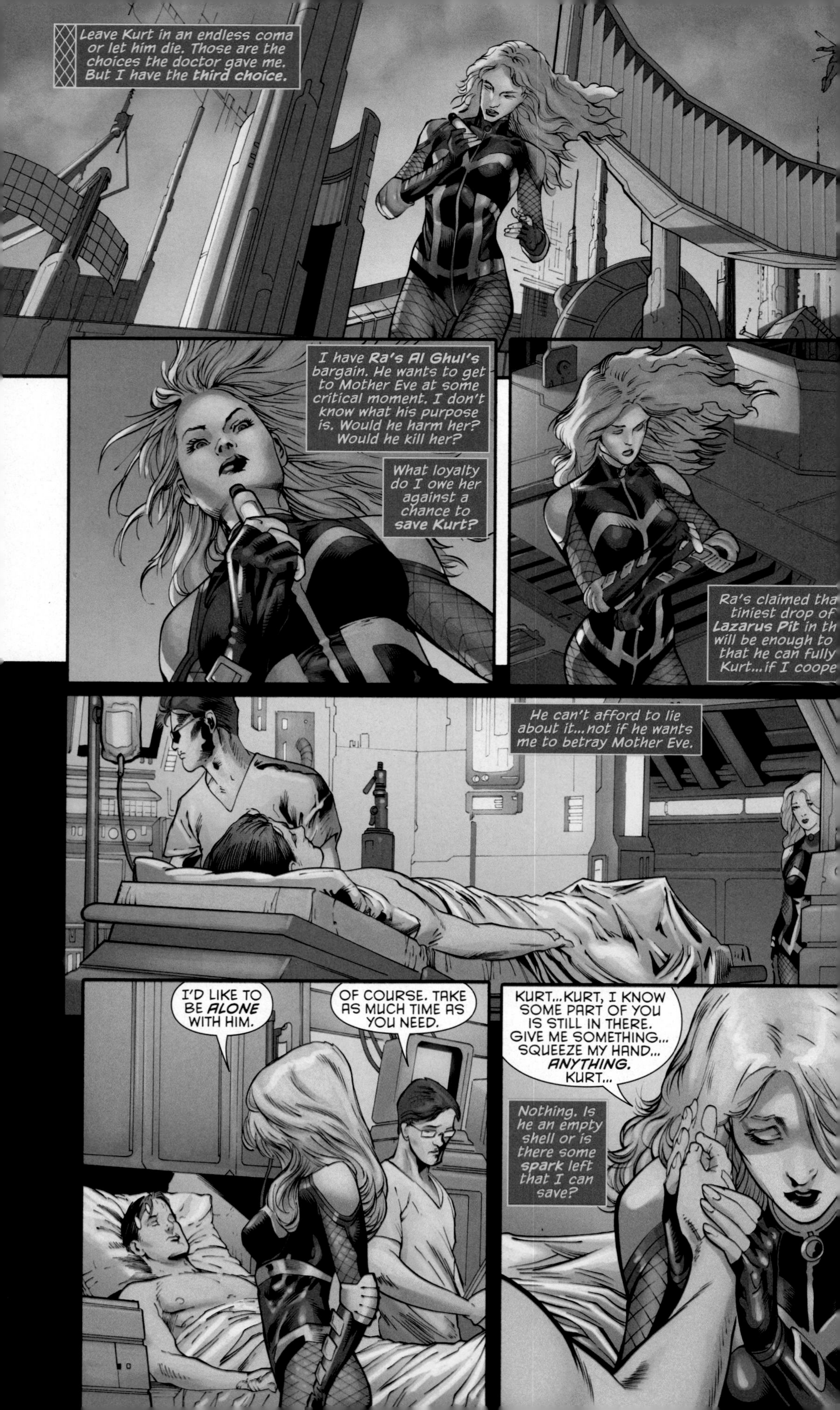
Leave Kurt in an endless coma or let him die. Those are the choices the doctor gave me. But I have the third choice.
I have Ra's Al Ghul's bargain. He wants to get to Mother Eve at some critical moment. I don't know what his purpose is. Would he harm her? Would he kill her?
What loyalty do I owe her against a chance to save Kurt?
Ra's claimed tha tiniest drop of Lazarus Pit in th will be enough to that he can fully Kurt...if I coope
He can't afford to lie about it...not if he wants me to betray Mother Eve.
I'D LIKE TO BE ALONE WITH HIM.
OF COURSE. TAKE AS MUCH TIME AS YOU NEED.
KURT...KURT, I KNOW SOME PART OF YOU IS STILL IN THERE. GIVE ME SOMETHING... SQUEEZE MY HAND... ANYTHING. KURT...
Nothing. Is he an empty shell or is there some spark left that I can save?

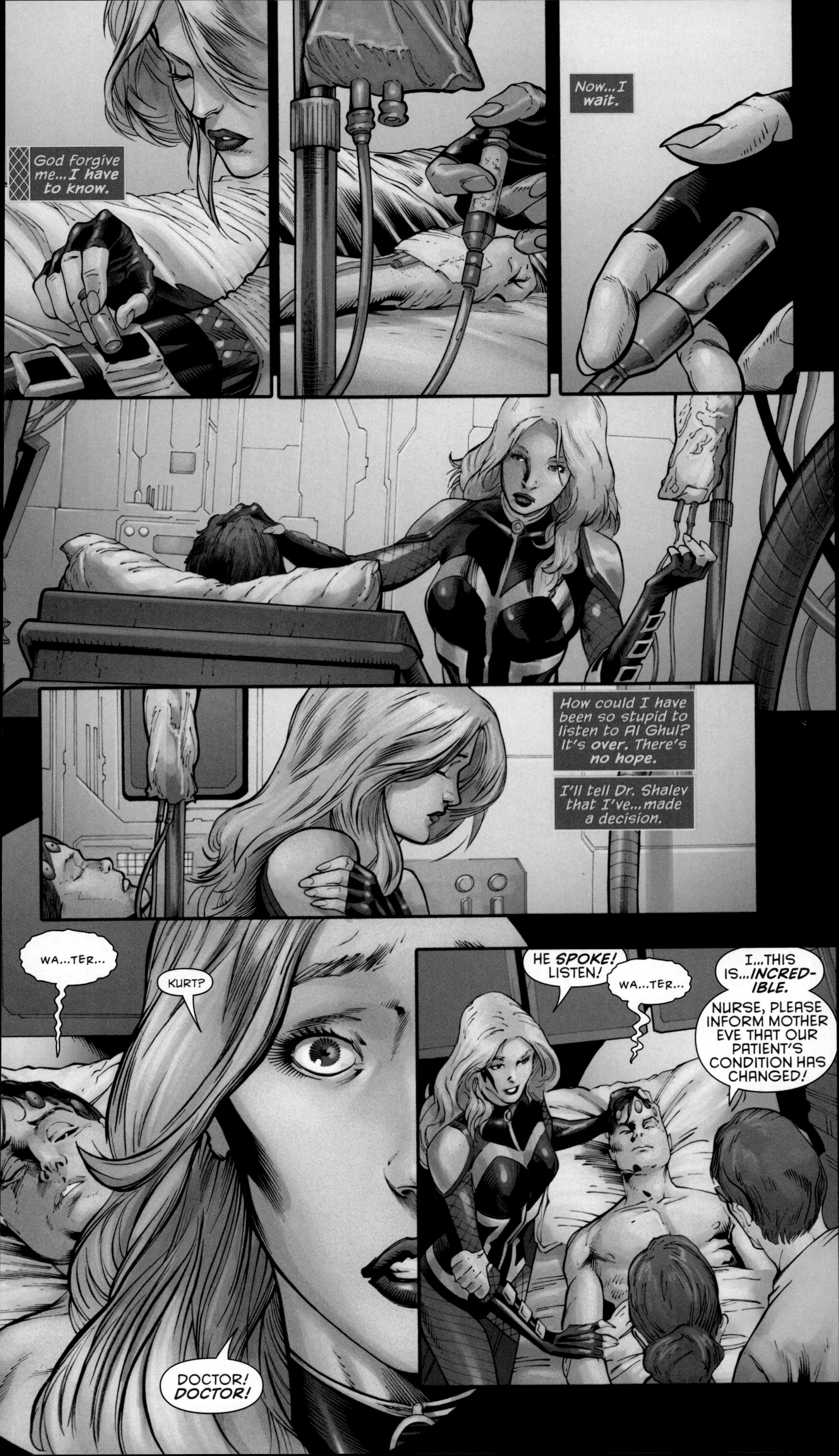
God forgive me...I have to know.
Now...I wait.
How could I have been so stupid to listen to Al Ghul? It's over. There's no hope.
I'll tell Dr. Shalev that I've...made a decision.
WA...TER...
KURT?
DOCTOR! DOCTOR!
HE SPOKE! LISTEN!
WA...TER...
I...THIS IS...INCREDIBLE.
NURSE, PLEASE INFORM MOTHER EVE THAT OUR PATIENT'S CONDITION HAS CHANGED!

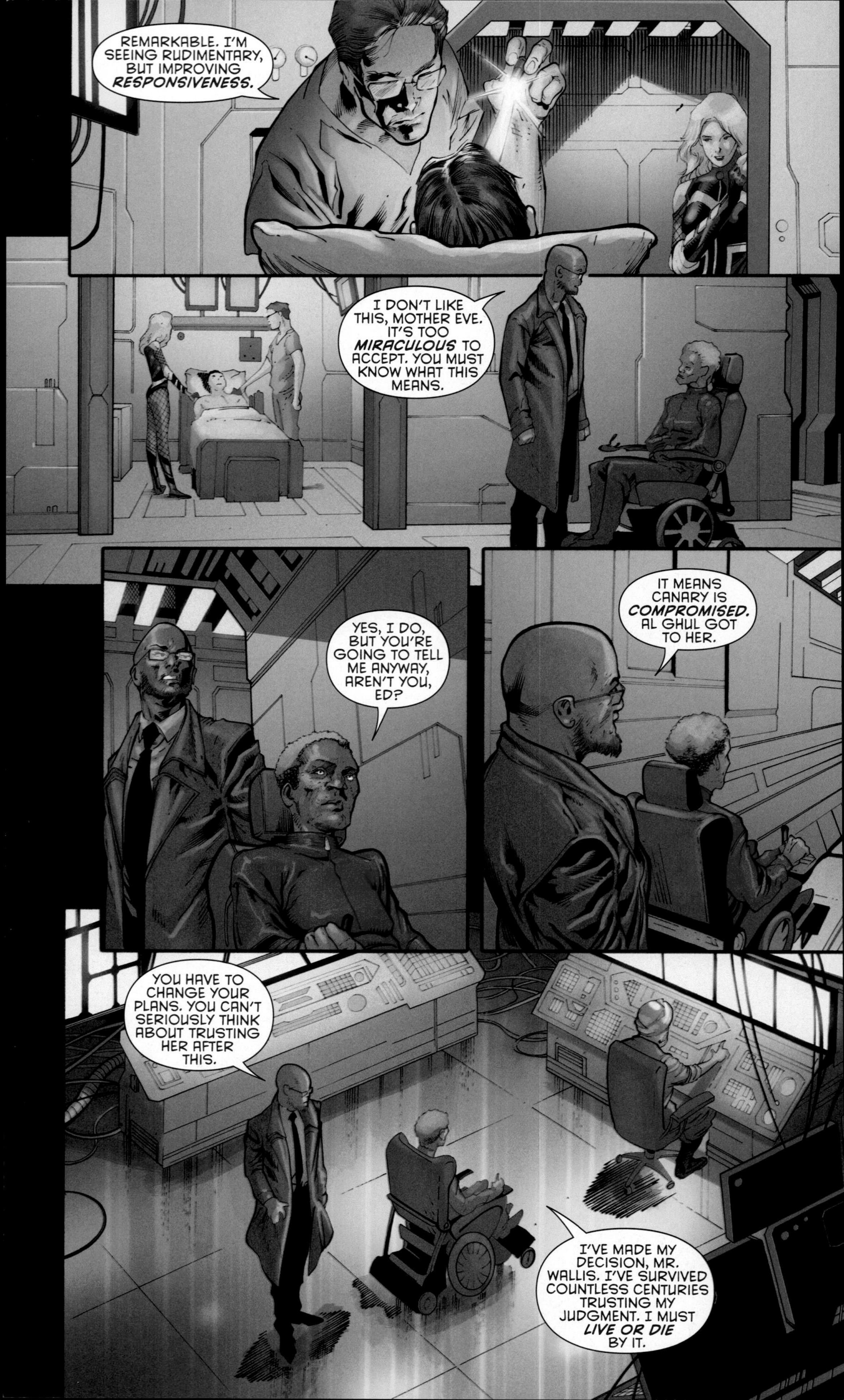
REMARKABLE. I'M SEEING RUDIMENTARY, BUT IMPROVING RESPONSIVENESS.
I DON'T LIKE THIS, MOTHER EVE. IT'S TOO MIRACULOUS TO ACCEPT. YOU MUST KNOW WHAT THIS MEANS.
YES, I DO, BUT YOU'RE GOING TO TELL ME ANYWAY, AREN'T YOU, ED?
IT MEANS CANARY IS COMPROMISED. AL GHUL GOT TO HER.
YOU HAVE TO CHANGE YOUR PLANS. YOU CAN'T SERIOUSLY THINK ABOUT TRUSTING HER AFTER THIS.
I'VE MADE MY DECISION, MR. WALLIS. I'VE SURVIVED COUNTLESS CENTURIES TRUSTING MY JUDGMENT. I MUST LIVE OR DIE BY IT.

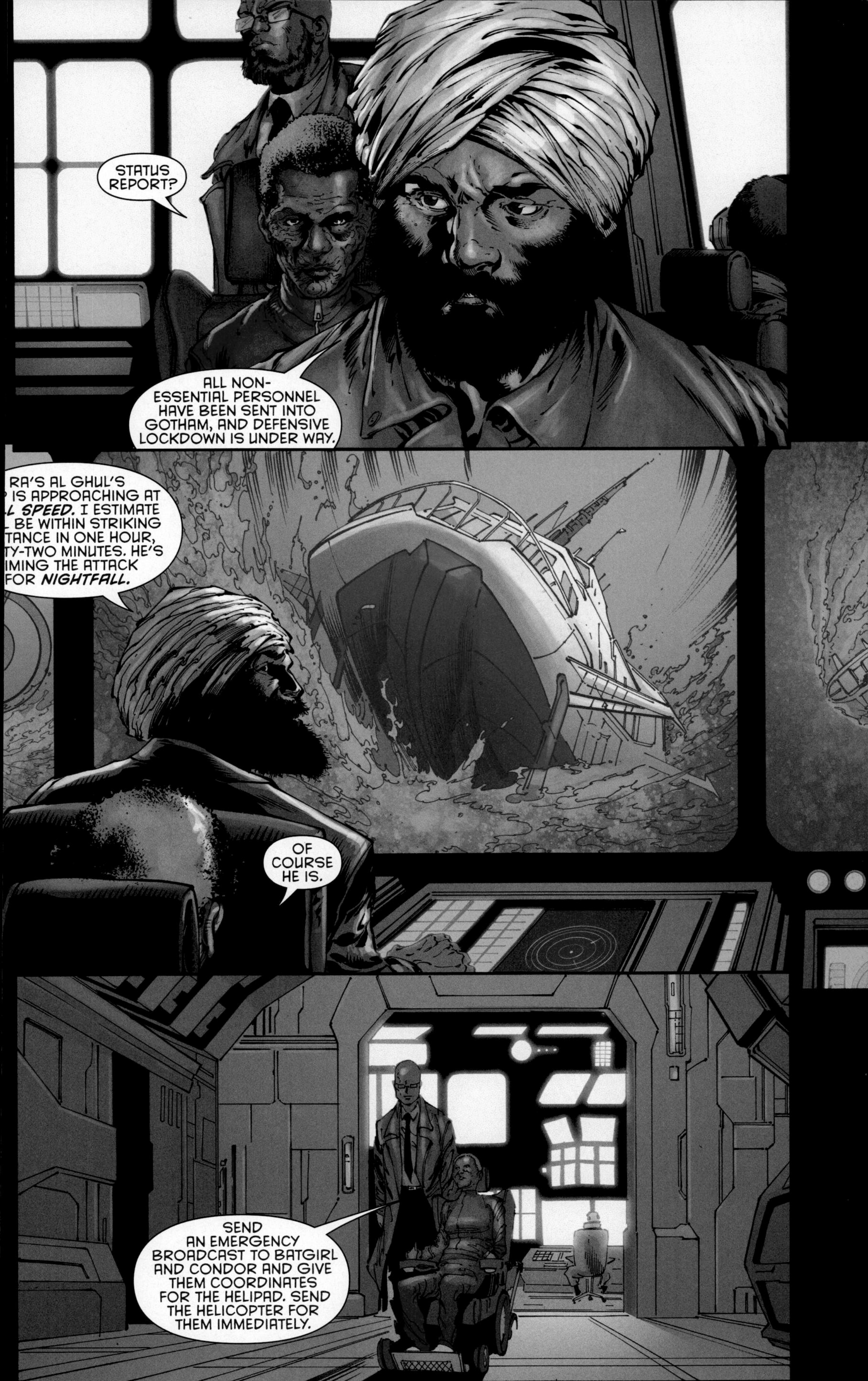
STATUS REPORT?
ALL NON-ESSENTIAL PERSONNEL HAVE BEEN SENT INTO GOTHAM, AND DEFENSIVE LOCKDOWN IS UNDER WAY.
RA'S AL GHUL'S
IS APPROACHING AT
L SPEED. I ESTIMATE
L BE WITHIN STRIKING
TANCE IN ONE HOUR,
TY-TWO MINUTES. HE'S
IMING THE ATTACK
FOR NIGHTFALL.
OF COURSE HE IS.
SEND AN EMERGENCY BROADCAST TO BATGIRL AND CONDOR AND GIVE THEM COORDINATES FOR THE HELIPAD. SEND THE HELICOPTER FOR THEM IMMEDIATELY.

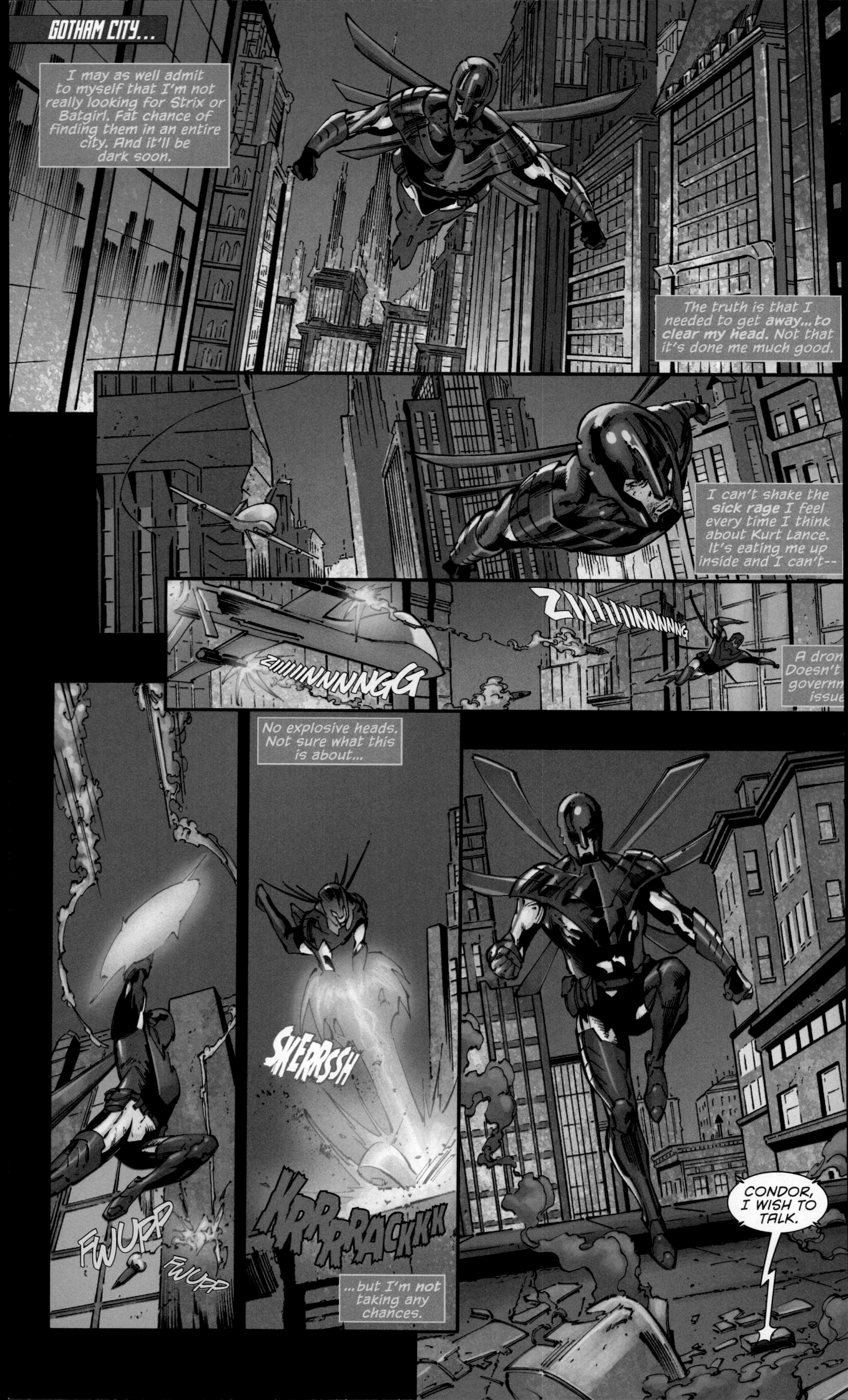

GOTHAM CITY...
I may as well admit to myself that I'm not really looking for Strix or Batgirl. Fat chance of finding them in an entire city. And it'll be dark soon.
The truth is that I needed to get away...to clear my head. Not that it's done me much good.
I can't shake the sick rage I feel every time I think about Kurt Lance. It's eating me up inside and I can't--
ZIIIIIINNNNNG
ZIIIIINNNNGG
No explosive heads. Not sure what this is about...
SKERRSSH
FWUPP
FWUPP
KRRRRACKKK
...but I'm not taking any chances.
CONDOR, I WISH TO TALK.

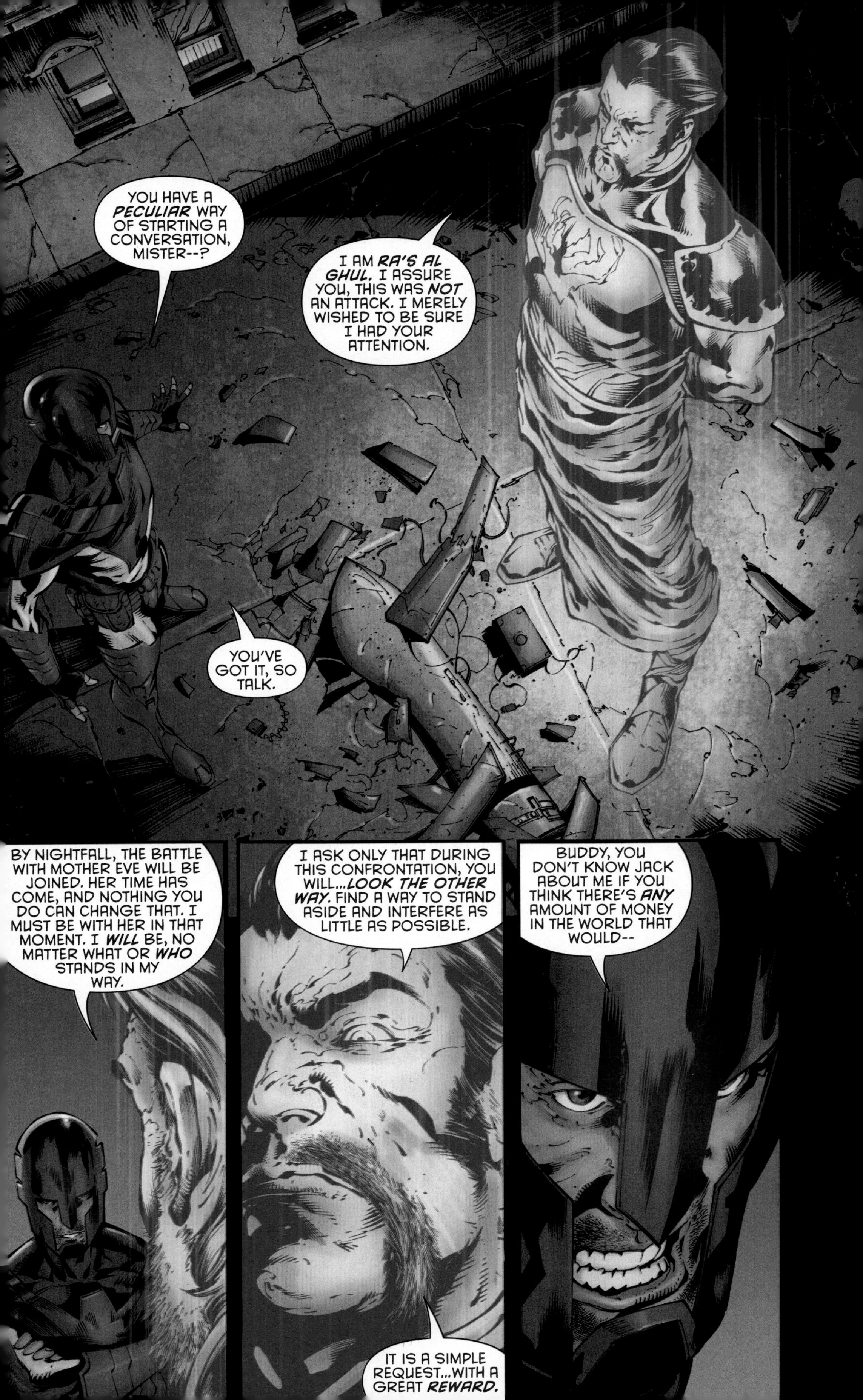
YOU HAVE A *PECULIAR* WAY OF STARTING A CONVERSATION, MISTER--?
I AM *RA'S AL GHUL.* I ASSURE YOU, THIS WAS *NOT* AN ATTACK. I MERELY WISHED TO BE SURE I HAD YOUR ATTENTION.
YOU'VE GOT IT, SO TALK.
BY NIGHTFALL, THE BATTLE WITH MOTHER EVE WILL BE JOINED. HER TIME HAS COME, AND NOTHING YOU DO CAN CHANGE THAT. I MUST BE WITH HER IN THAT MOMENT. I *WILL* BE, NO MATTER WHAT OR *WHO* STANDS IN MY WAY.
I ASK ONLY THAT DURING THIS CONFRONTATION, YOU WILL...*LOOK THE OTHER WAY.* FIND A WAY TO STAND ASIDE AND INTERFERE AS LITTLE AS POSSIBLE.
IT IS A SIMPLE REQUEST...WITH A GREAT *REWARD.*
BUDDY, YOU DON'T KNOW JACK ABOUT ME IF YOU THINK THERE'S *ANY* AMOUNT OF MONEY IN THE WORLD THAT WOULD--

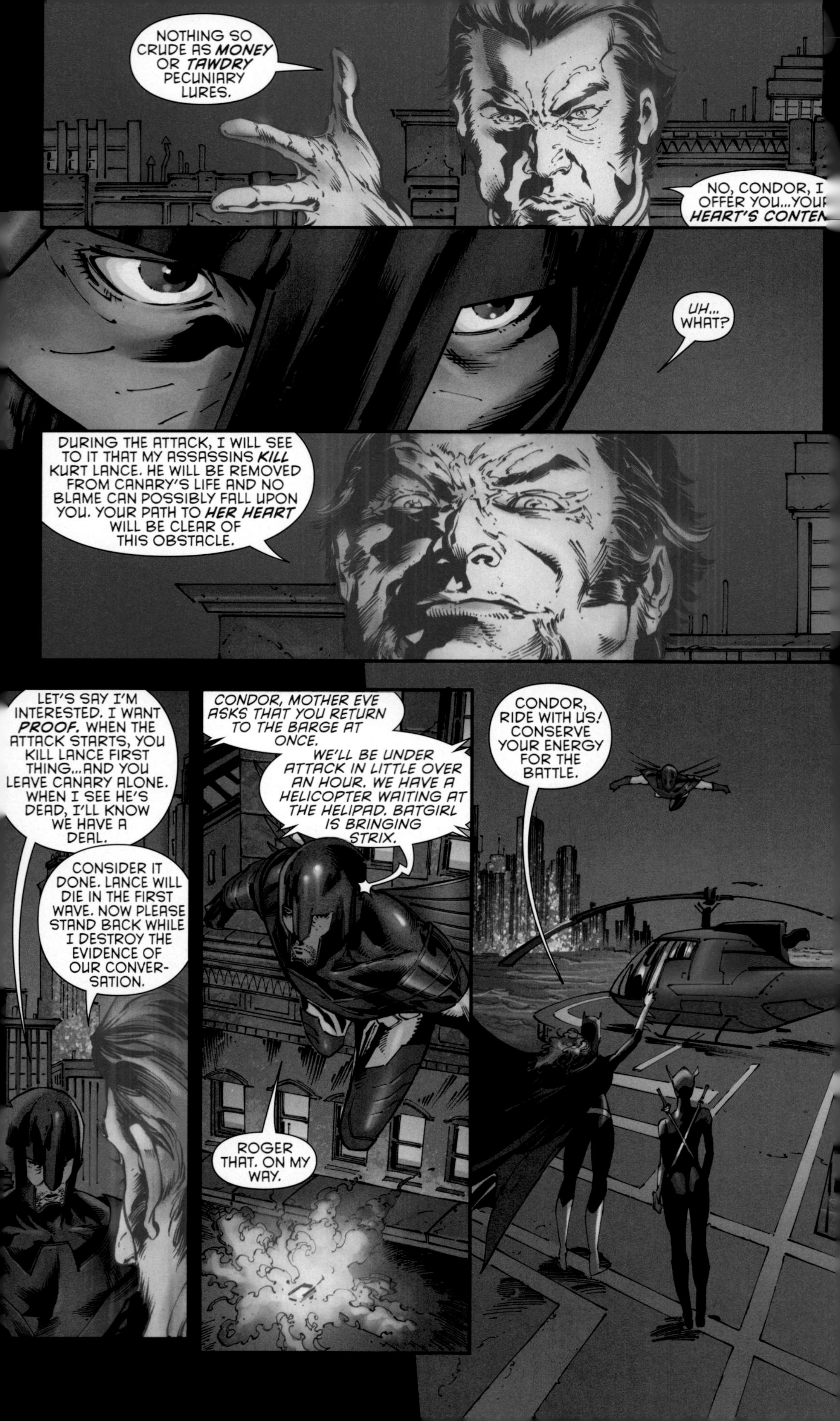
NOTHING SO CRUDE AS MONEY OR TAWDRY PECUNIARY LURES.
NO, CONDOR, I OFFER YOU...YOUR HEART'S CONTEN
UH... WHAT?
DURING THE ATTACK, I WILL SEE TO IT THAT MY ASSASSINS KILL KURT LANCE. HE WILL BE REMOVED FROM CANARY'S LIFE AND NO BLAME CAN POSSIBLY FALL UPON YOU. YOUR PATH TO HER HEART WILL BE CLEAR OF THIS OBSTACLE.
LET'S SAY I'M INTERESTED. I WANT PROOF. WHEN THE ATTACK STARTS, YOU KILL LANCE FIRST THING...AND YOU LEAVE CANARY ALONE. WHEN I SEE HE'S DEAD, I'LL KNOW WE HAVE A DEAL.
CONSIDER IT DONE. LANCE WILL DIE IN THE FIRST WAVE. NOW PLEASE STAND BACK WHILE I DESTROY THE EVIDENCE OF OUR CONVERSATION.
CONDOR, MOTHER EVE ASKS THAT YOU RETURN TO THE BARGE AT ONCE.
WE'LL BE UNDER ATTACK IN LITTLE OVER AN HOUR. WE HAVE A HELICOPTER WAITING AT THE HELIPAD. BATGIRL IS BRINGING STRIX.
ROGER THAT. ON MY WAY.
CONDOR, RIDE WITH US! CONSERVE YOUR ENERGY FOR THE BATTLE.

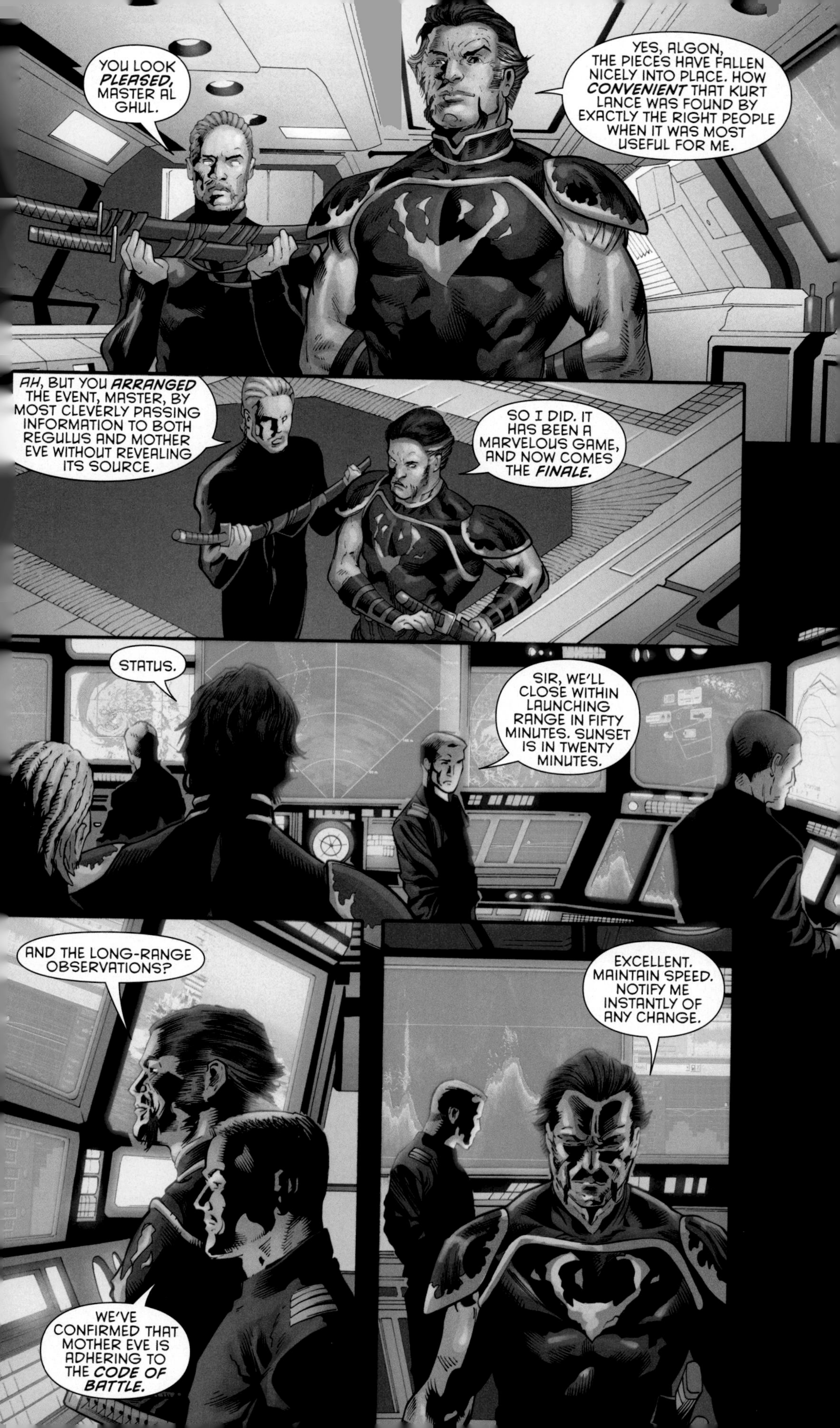
YOU LOOK *PLEASED,* MASTER AL GHUL.
YES, ALGON, THE PIECES HAVE FALLEN NICELY INTO PLACE. HOW *CONVENIENT* THAT KURT LANCE WAS FOUND BY EXACTLY THE RIGHT PEOPLE WHEN IT WAS MOST USEFUL FOR ME.
AH, BUT YOU *ARRANGED* THE EVENT, MASTER, BY MOST CLEVERLY PASSING INFORMATION TO BOTH REGULUS AND MOTHER EVE WITHOUT REVEALING ITS SOURCE.
SO I DID. IT HAS BEEN A MARVELOUS GAME, AND NOW COMES THE *FINALE.*
STATUS.
SIR, WE'LL CLOSE WITHIN LAUNCHING RANGE IN FIFTY MINUTES. SUNSET IS IN TWENTY MINUTES.
AND THE LONG-RANGE OBSERVATIONS?
WE'VE CONFIRMED THAT MOTHER EVE IS ADHERING TO THE *CODE OF BATTLE.*
EXCELLENT. MAINTAIN SPEED. NOTIFY ME INSTANTLY OF ANY CHANGE.

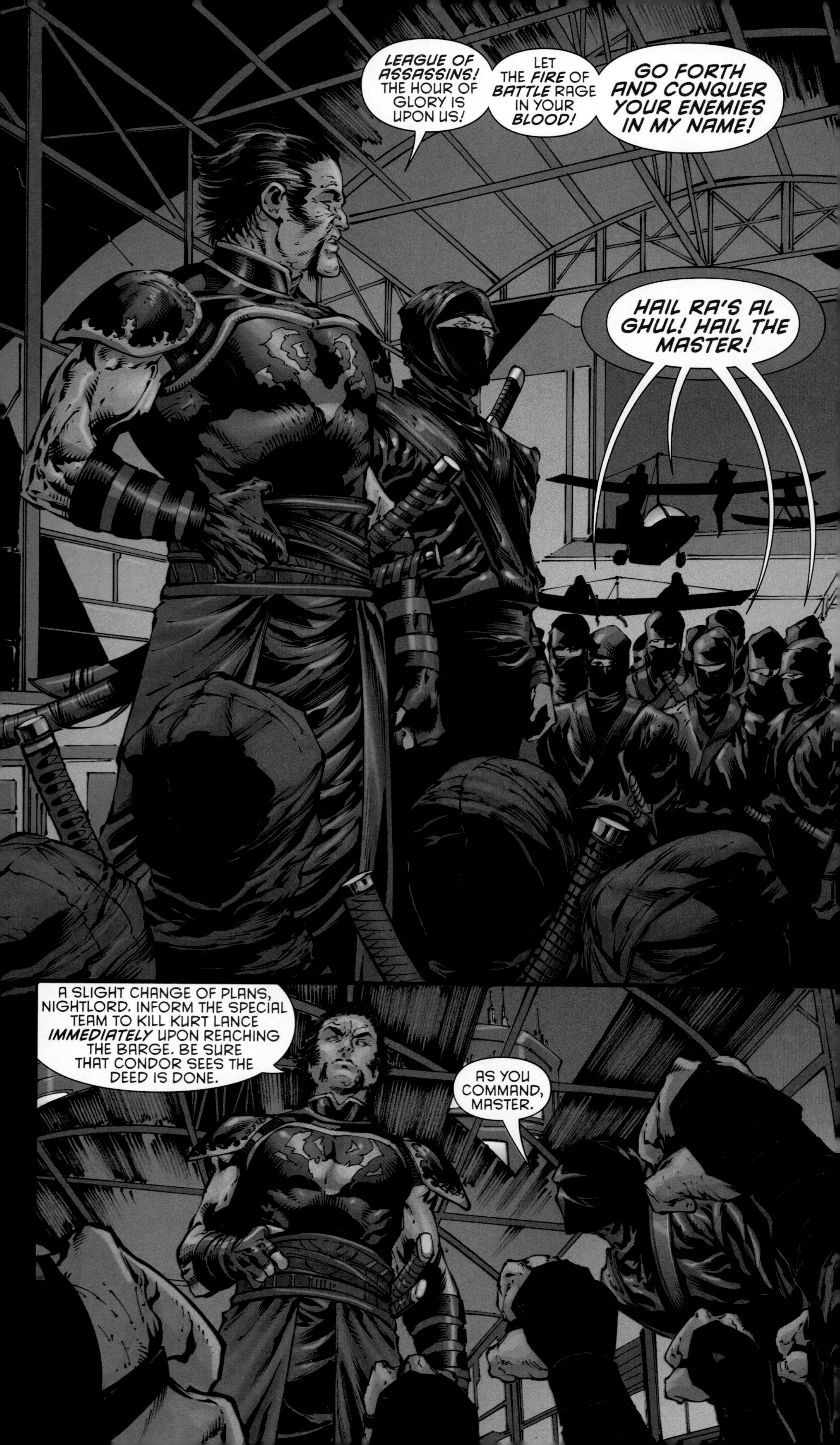
LEAGUE OF ASSASSINS! THE HOUR OF GLORY IS UPON US!
LET THE FIRE OF BATTLE RAGE IN YOUR BLOOD!
GO FORTH AND CONQUER YOUR ENEMIES IN MY NAME!
HAIL RA'S AL GHUL! HAIL THE MASTER!
A SLIGHT CHANGE OF PLANS, NIGHTLORD. INFORM THE SPECIAL TEAM TO KILL KURT LANCE IMMEDIATELY UPON REACHING THE BARGE. BE SURE THAT CONDOR SEES THE DEED IS DONE.
AS YOU COMMAND, MASTER.

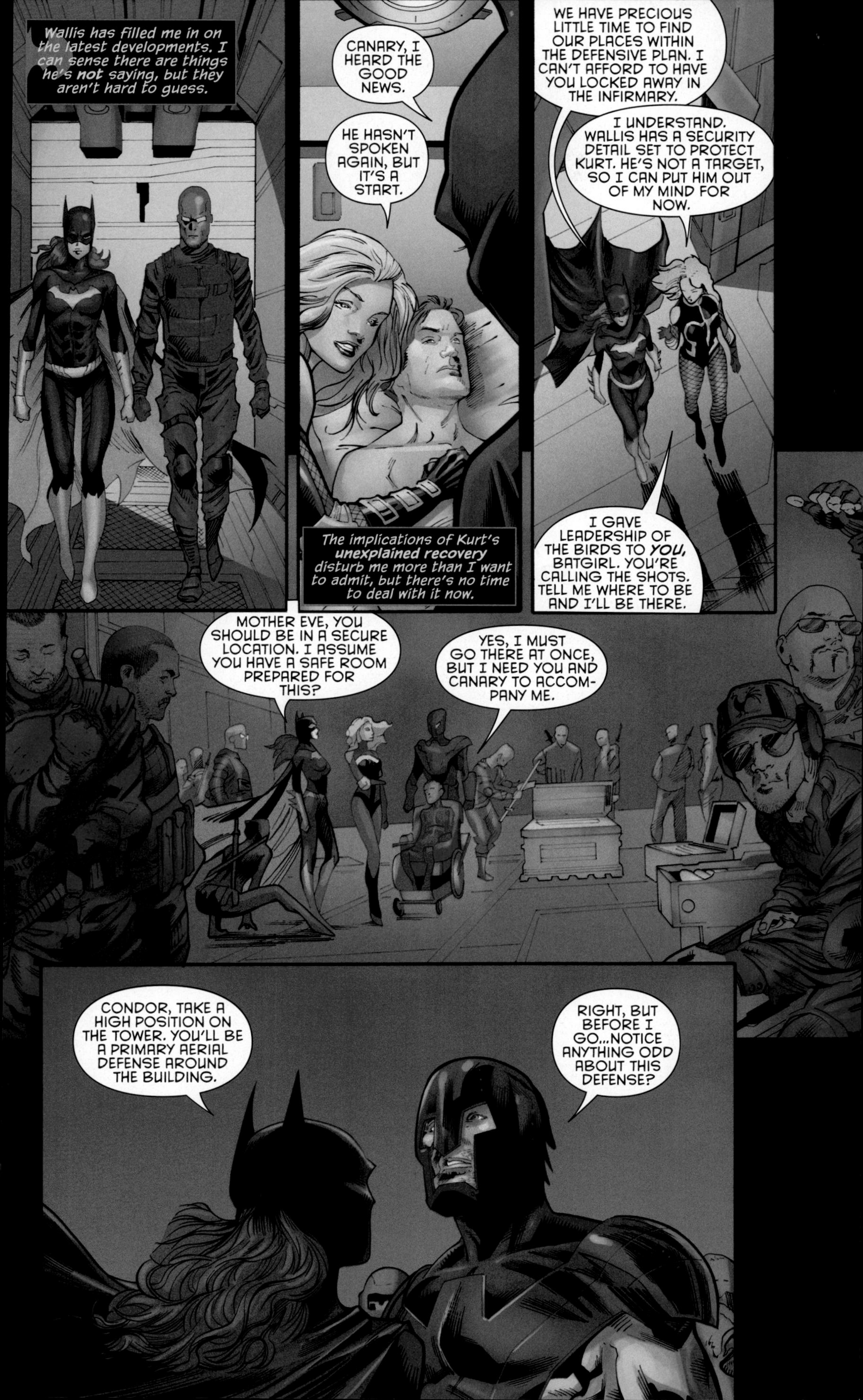
Wallis has filled me in on the latest developments. I can sense there are things he's **not** saying, but they aren't hard to guess.
CANARY, I HEARD THE GOOD NEWS.
HE HASN'T SPOKEN AGAIN, BUT IT'S A START.
The implications of Kurt's **unexplained recovery** disturb me more than I want to admit, but there's no time to deal with it now.
WE HAVE PRECIOUS LITTLE TIME TO FIND OUR PLACES WITHIN THE DEFENSIVE PLAN. I CAN'T AFFORD TO HAVE YOU LOCKED AWAY IN THE INFIRMARY.
I UNDERSTAND. WALLIS HAS A SECURITY DETAIL SET TO PROTECT KURT. HE'S NOT A TARGET, SO I CAN PUT HIM OUT OF MY MIND FOR NOW.
I GAVE LEADERSHIP OF THE BIRDS TO *YOU*, BATGIRL. YOU'RE CALLING THE SHOTS. TELL ME WHERE TO BE AND I'LL BE THERE.
MOTHER EVE, YOU SHOULD BE IN A SECURE LOCATION. I ASSUME YOU HAVE A SAFE ROOM PREPARED FOR THIS?
YES, I MUST GO THERE AT ONCE, BUT I NEED YOU AND CANARY TO ACCOM-PANY ME.
CONDOR, TAKE A HIGH POSITION ON THE TOWER. YOU'LL BE A PRIMARY AERIAL DEFENSE AROUND THE BUILDING.
RIGHT, BUT BEFORE I GO...NOTICE ANYTHING ODD ABOUT THIS DEFENSE?

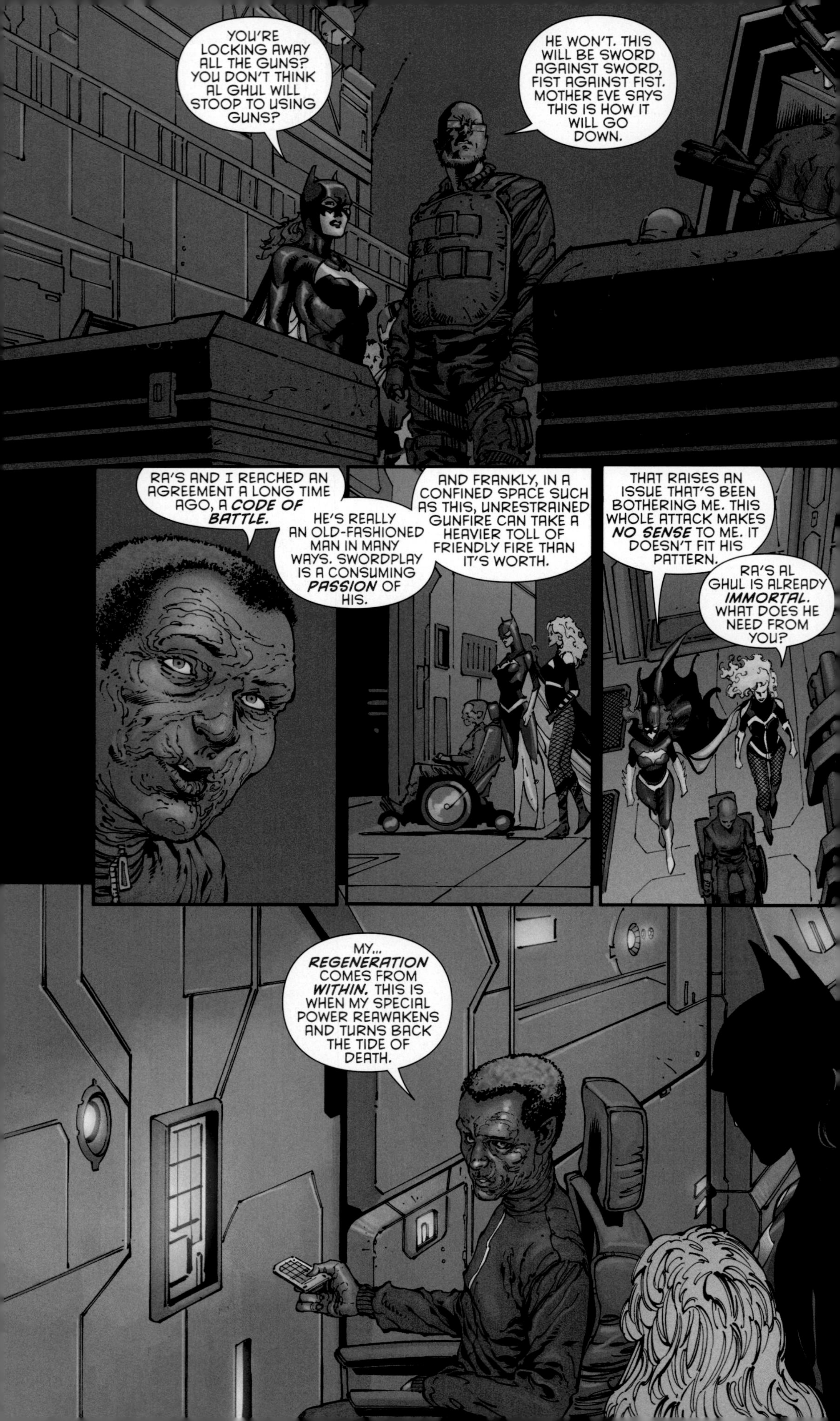
YOU'RE LOCKING AWAY ALL THE GUNS? YOU DON'T THINK AL GHUL WILL STOOP TO USING GUNS?
HE WON'T. THIS WILL BE SWORD AGAINST SWORD, FIST AGAINST FIST. MOTHER EVE SAYS THIS IS HOW IT WILL GO DOWN.
RA'S AND I REACHED AN AGREEMENT A LONG TIME AGO, A CODE OF BATTLE.
HE'S REALLY AN OLD-FASHIONED MAN IN MANY WAYS. SWORDPLAY IS A CONSUMING PASSION OF HIS.
AND FRANKLY, IN A CONFINED SPACE SUCH AS THIS, UNRESTRAINED GUNFIRE CAN TAKE A HEAVIER TOLL OF FRIENDLY FIRE THAN IT'S WORTH.
THAT RAISES AN ISSUE THAT'S BEEN BOTHERING ME. THIS WHOLE ATTACK MAKES NO SENSE TO ME. IT DOESN'T FIT HIS PATTERN.
RA'S AL GHUL IS ALREADY IMMORTAL. WHAT DOES HE NEED FROM YOU?
MY... REGENERATION COMES FROM WITHIN. THIS IS WHEN MY SPECIAL POWER REAWAKENS AND TURNS BACK THE TIDE OF DEATH.

...RA'S IMMORTALITY / COMES FROM THE *LAZARUS PIT,* / OUTSIDE SOURCE, ONE THAT / COULD BE DESTROYED, LOST / OR TAKEN FROM HIM.

HE SEEKS WHAT I'VE / KEPT *HIDDEN* FROM HIM-- / HOW MY POWER WORKS. HE / WANTS TO LEARN HOW HE / CAN *DUPLICATE* IT WITHIN / HIMSELF. I WILL *NOT* / ALLOW THAT TO / HAPPEN.

THERE ARE THREE BULKHEADS BETWEEN THE SURFACE OF THE BARGE AND MY REGENERATION ROOM.

BUT MAKE NO MISTAKE, I ONLY EXPECT THEM TO *SLOW* RA'S, NOT STOP HIM.

THIS IS WHERE I'LL BE. DURING THE REGENERATION, I WILL BE *COMPLETELY HELPLESS,* UNABLE TO RESPOND IN ANY WAY.

HOW LONG DOES THIS PROCESS TAKE?

ROUGHLY TWO TO THREE HOURS. IT IS INTENSE, BUT *BRIEF.* THAT'S WHAT DRIVES RA'S WITH SUCH URGENCY.

IF YOU COULD KINDLY HELP ME INTO THE POD...

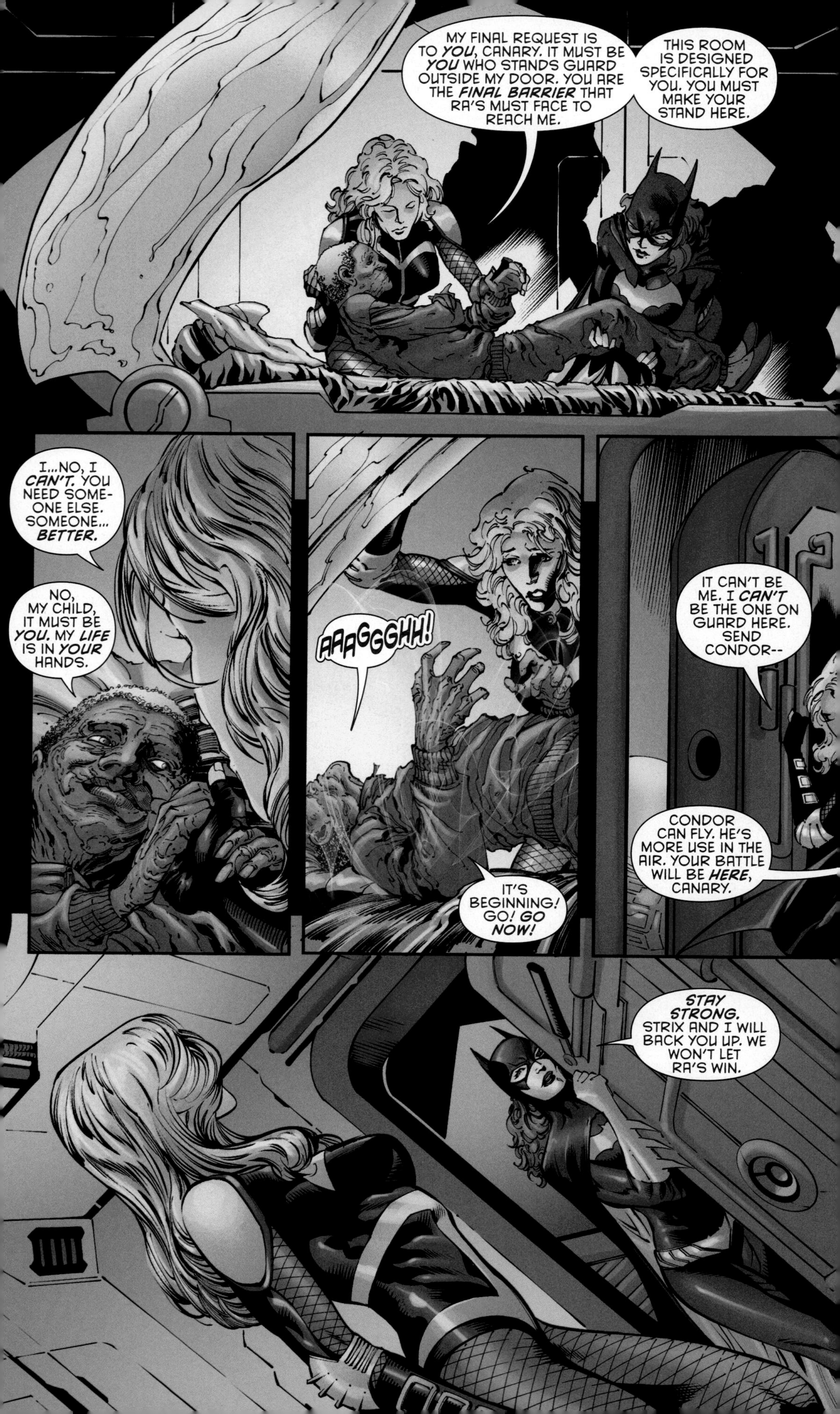
MY FINAL REQUEST IS TO YOU, CANARY. IT MUST BE YOU WHO STANDS GUARD OUTSIDE MY DOOR. YOU ARE THE FINAL BARRIER THAT RA'S MUST FACE TO REACH ME.
THIS ROOM IS DESIGNED SPECIFICALLY FOR YOU. YOU MUST MAKE YOUR STAND HERE.
I...NO, I CAN'T. YOU NEED SOME-ONE ELSE. SOMEONE... BETTER.
NO, MY CHILD, IT MUST BE YOU. MY LIFE IS IN YOUR HANDS.
AAAGGGHH!
IT'S BEGINNING! GO! GO NOW!
IT CAN'T BE ME. I CAN'T BE THE ONE ON GUARD HERE. SEND CONDOR--
CONDOR CAN FLY. HE'S MORE USE IN THE AIR. YOUR BATTLE WILL BE HERE, CANARY.
STAY STRONG. STRIX AND I WILL BACK YOU UP. WE WON'T LET RA'S WIN.

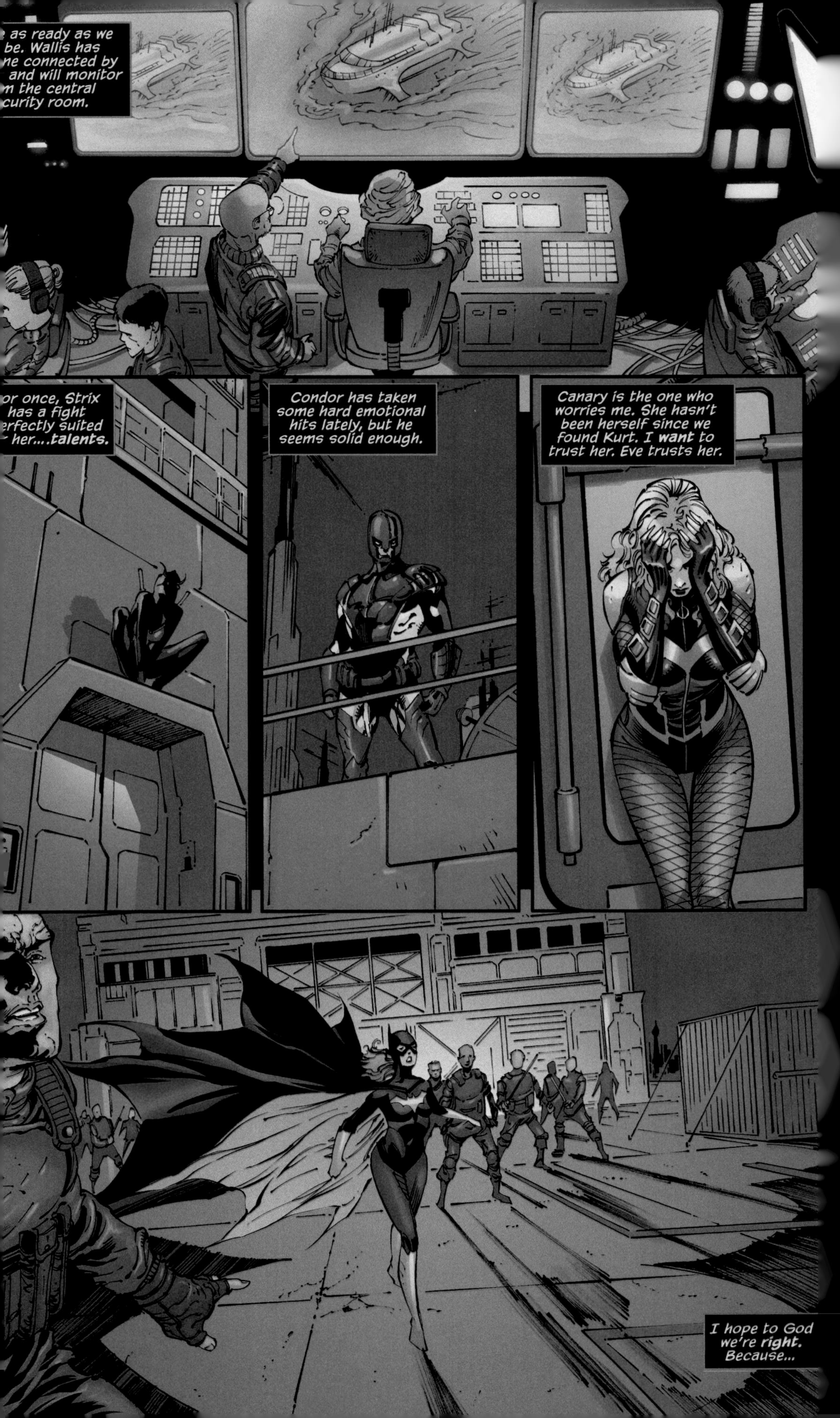
as ready as we be. Wallis has ne connected by and will monitor m the central curity room.
or once, Strix has a fight erfectly suited her....talents.
Condor has taken some hard emotional hits lately, but he seems solid enough.
Canary is the one who worries me. She hasn't been herself since we found Kurt. I want to trust her. Eve trusts her.
I hope to God we're right. Because...

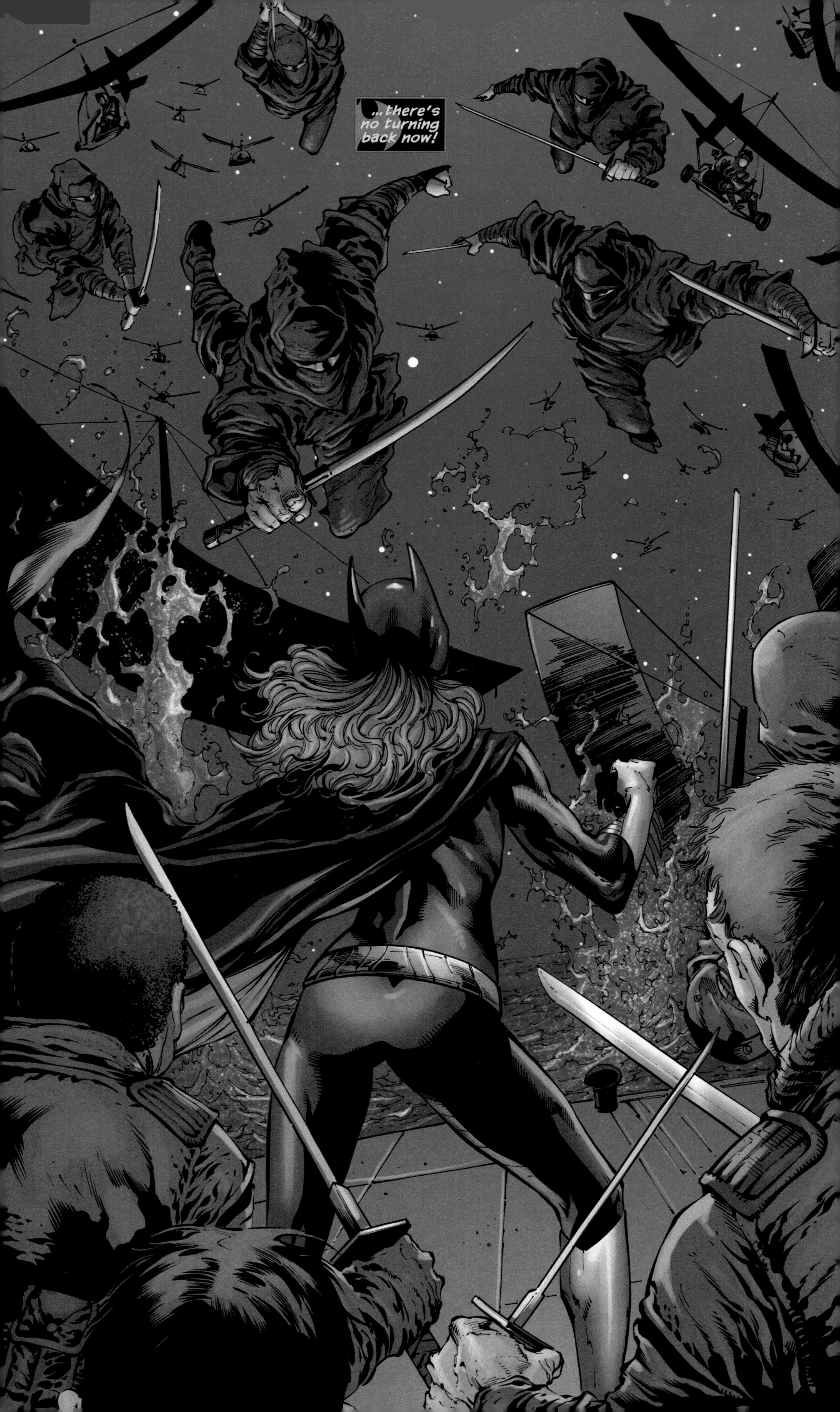
...there's no turning back now!

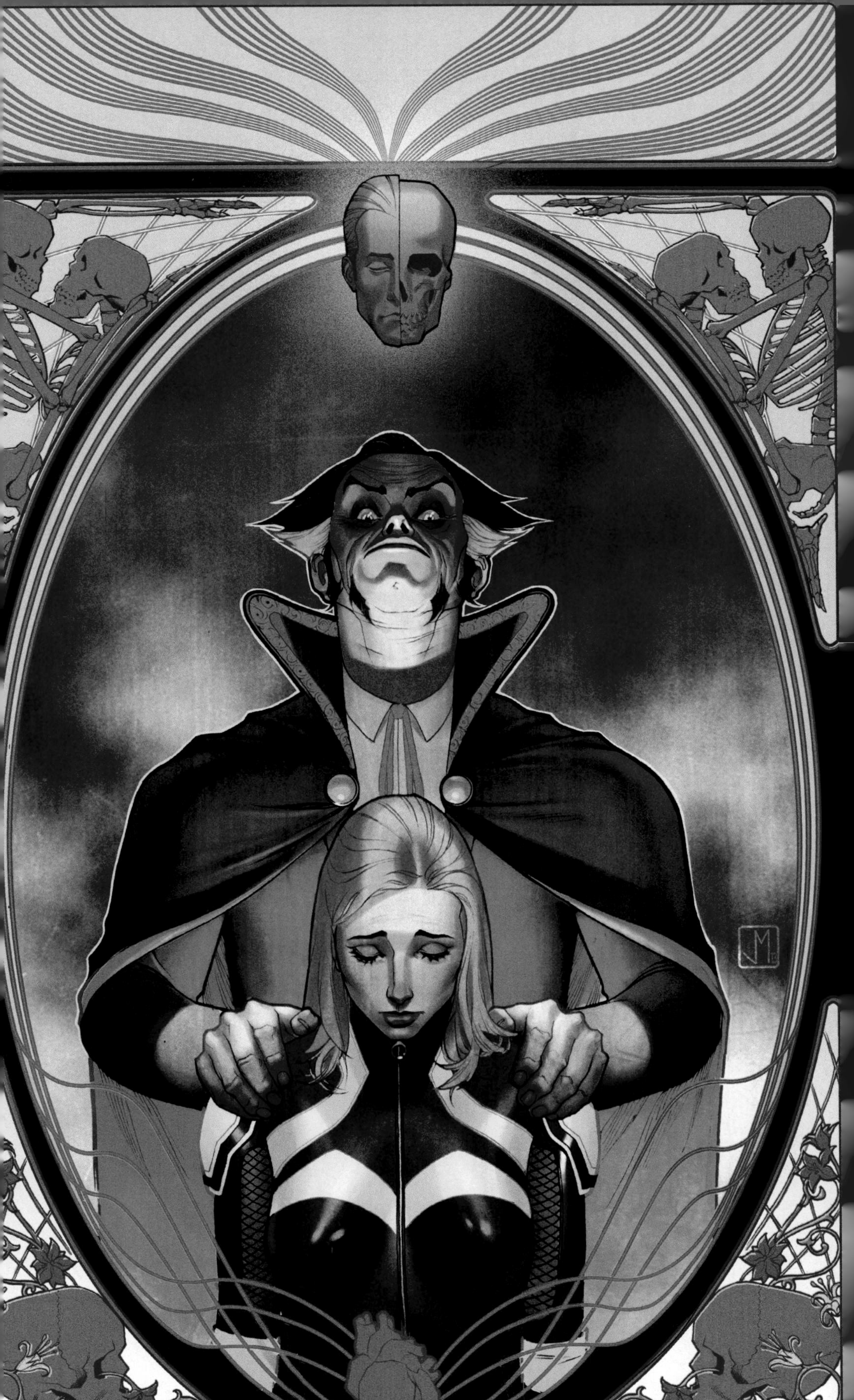

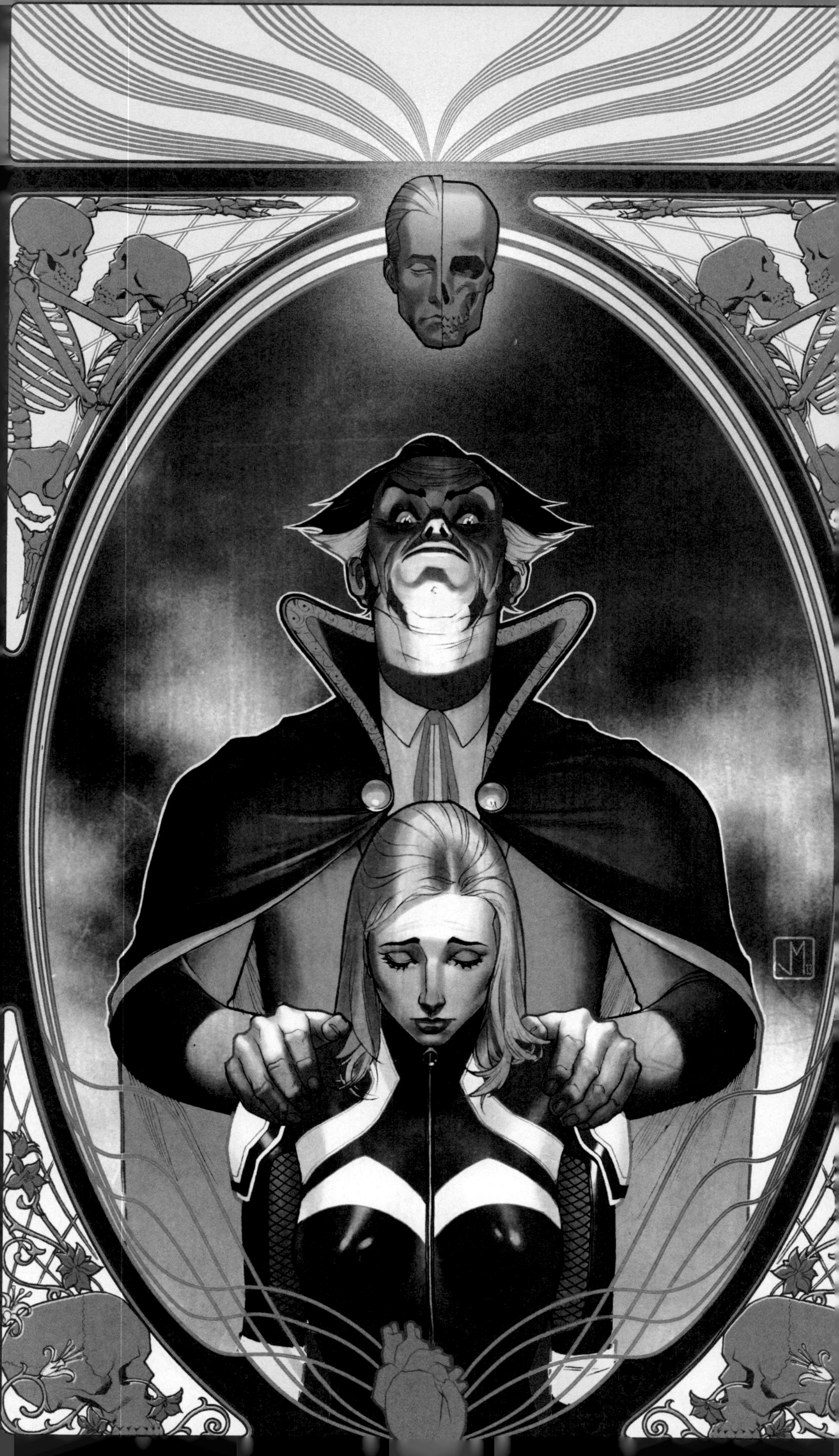

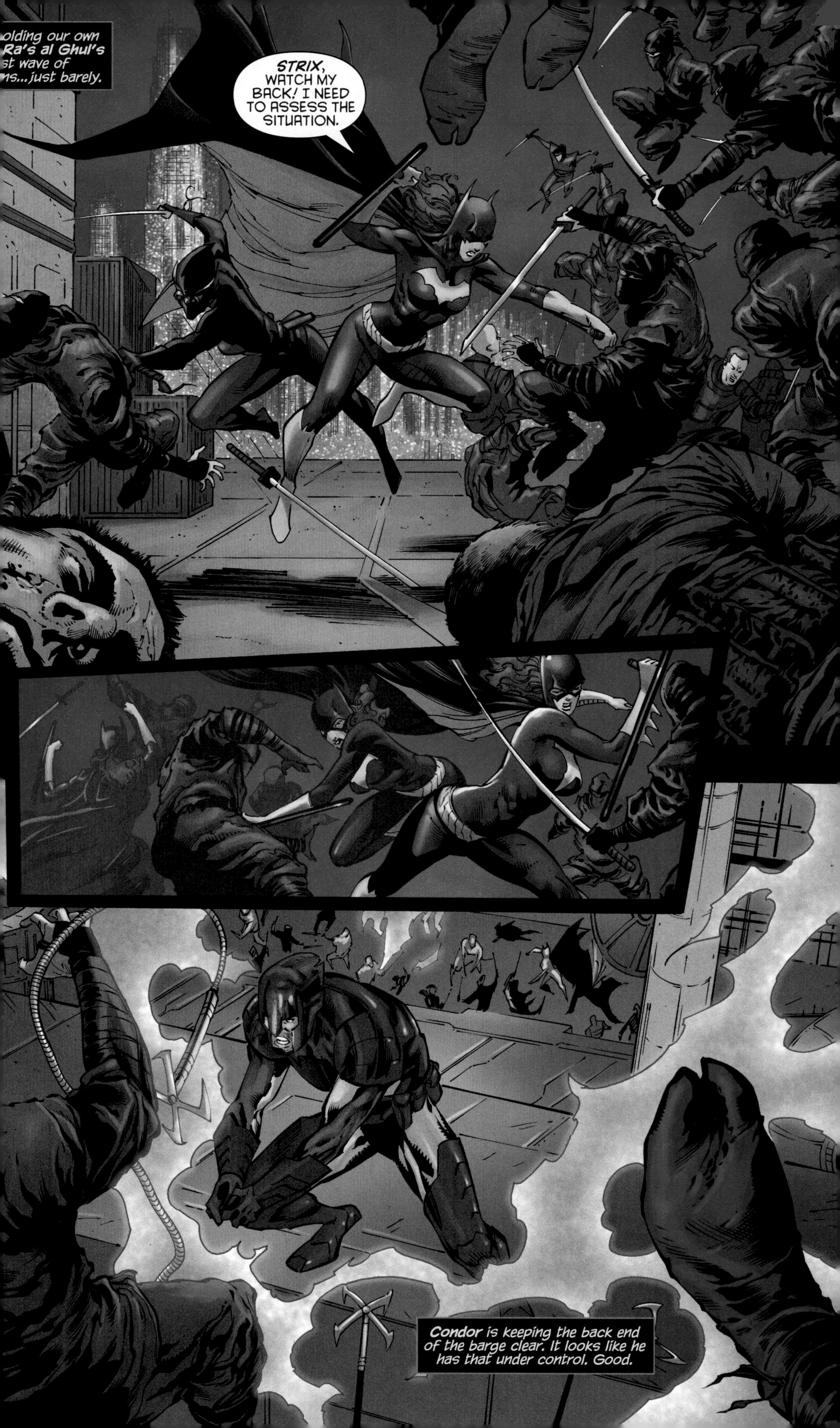
olding our own
Ra's al Ghul's
st wave of
ns...just barely.
STRIX, WATCH MY BACK! I NEED TO ASSESS THE SITUATION.
Condor is keeping the back end of the barge clear. It looks like he has that under control. Good.

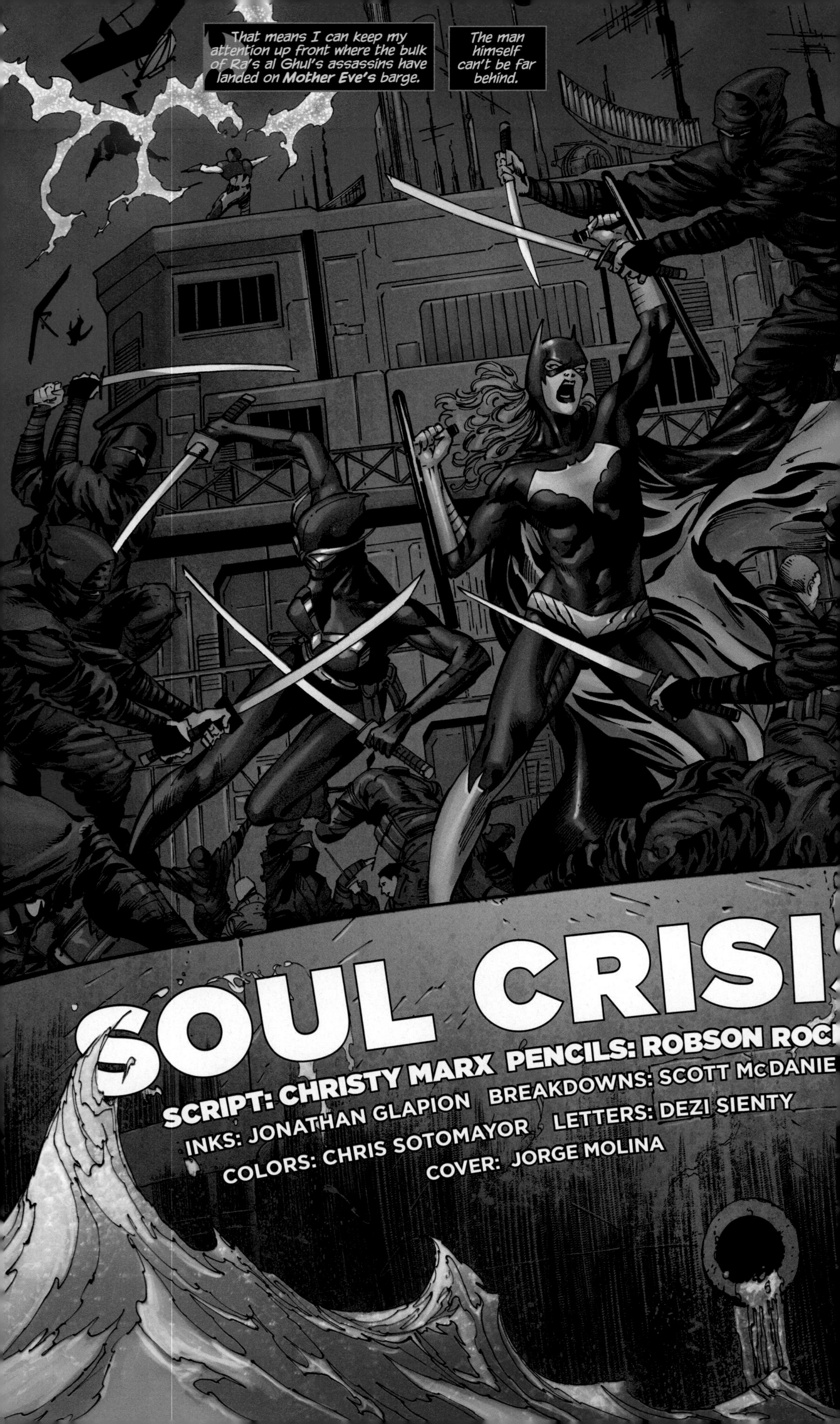
That means I can keep my attention up front where the bulk of Ra's al Ghul's assassins have landed on Mother Eve's barge.
The man himself can't be far behind.
SOUL CRISI
SCRIPT: CHRISTY MARX PENCILS: ROBSON ROC
INKS: JONATHAN GLAPION BREAKDOWNS: SCOTT McDANIE
COLORS: CHRIS SOTOMAYOR LETTERS: DEZI SIENTY
COVER: JORGE MOLINA

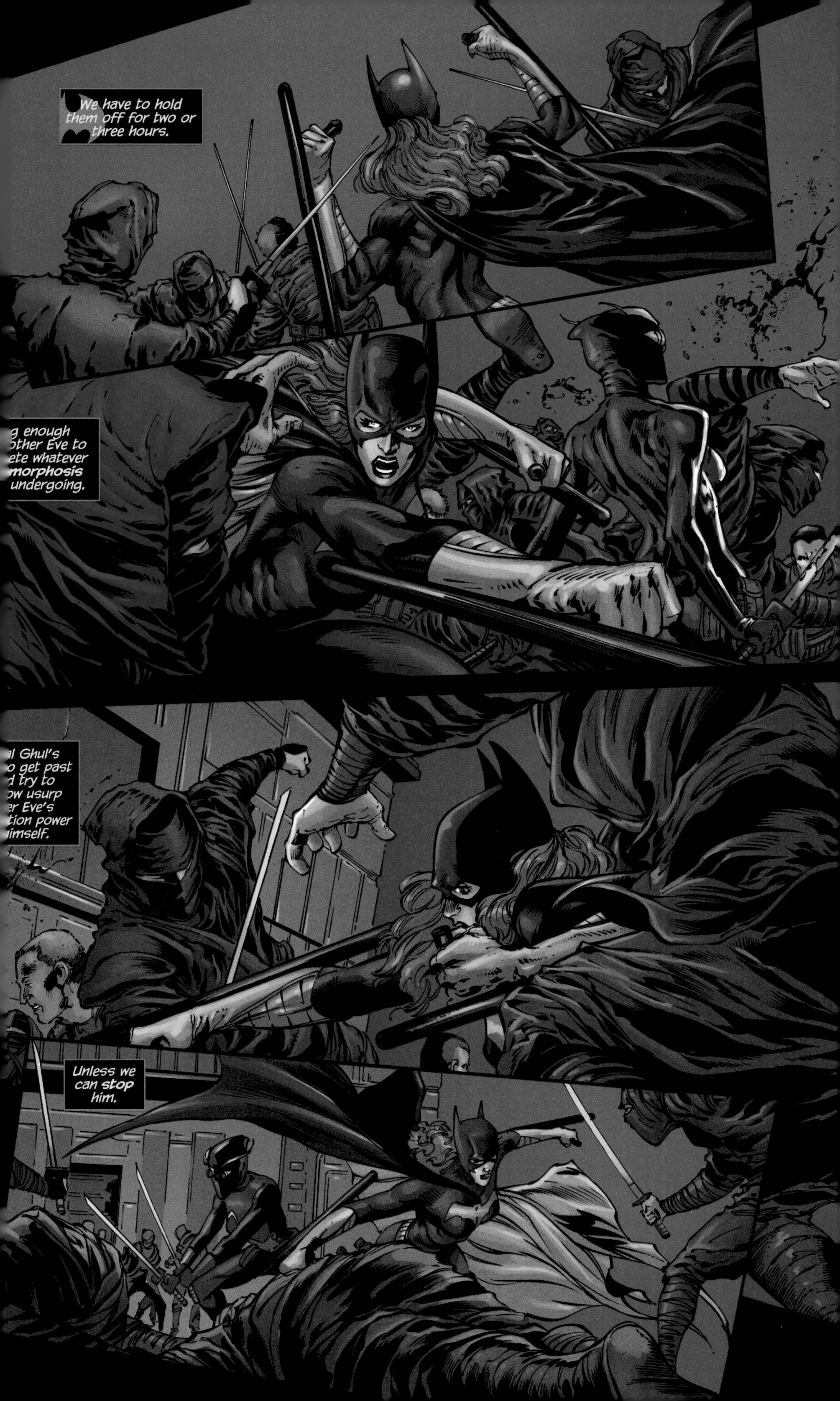

We have to hold them off for two or three hours.
g enough other Eve to ete whatever morphosis undergoing.
l Ghul's o get past d try to ow usurp er Eve's tion power imself.
Unless we can stop him.

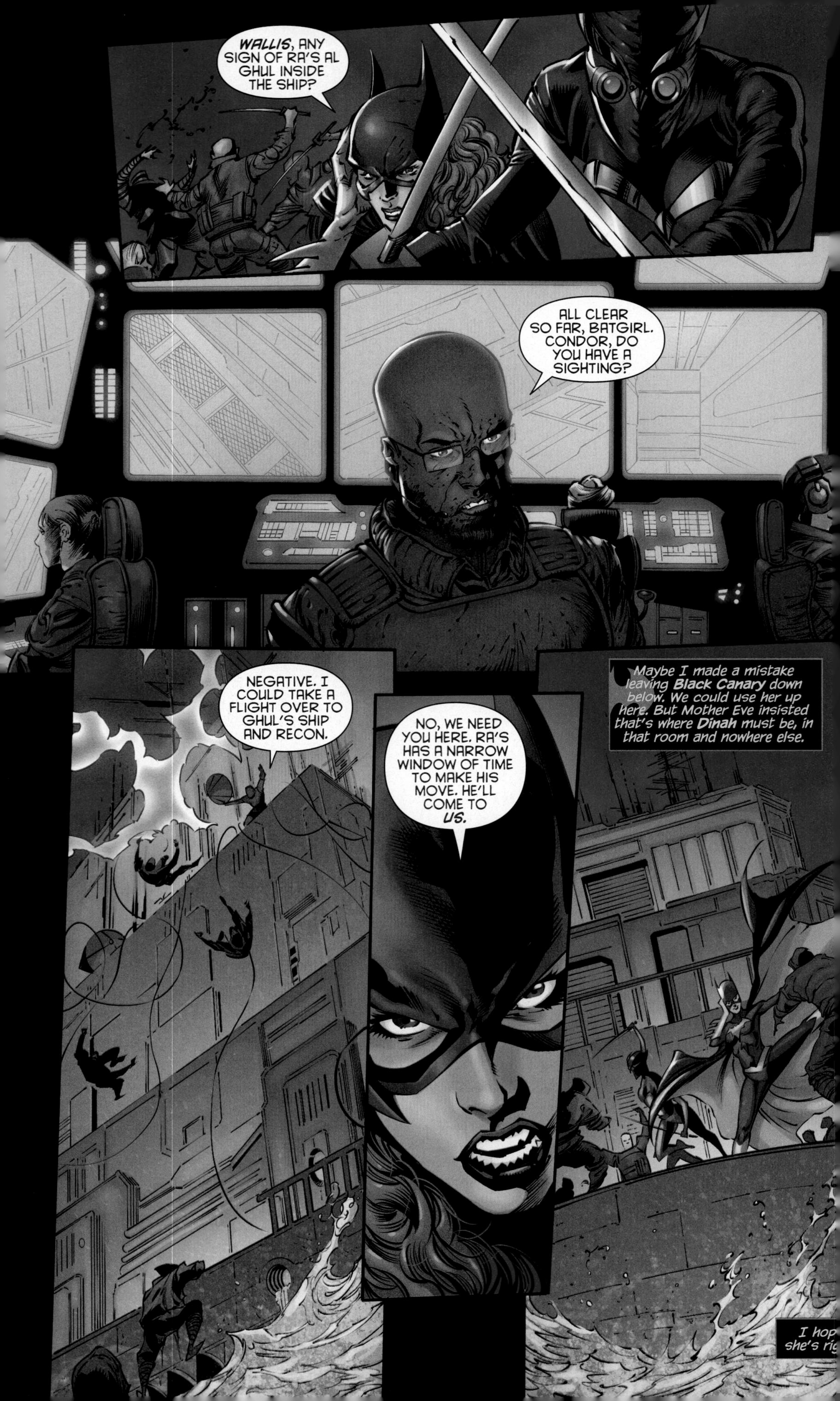

WALLIS, ANY SIGN OF RA'S AL GHUL INSIDE THE SHIP?
ALL CLEAR SO FAR, BATGIRL. CONDOR, DO YOU HAVE A SIGHTING?
NEGATIVE. I COULD TAKE A FLIGHT OVER TO GHUL'S SHIP AND RECON.
NO, WE NEED YOU HERE. RA'S HAS A NARROW WINDOW OF TIME TO MAKE HIS MOVE. HE'LL COME TO US.
Maybe I made a mistake leaving Black Canary down below. We could use her up here. But Mother Eve insisted that's where Dinah must be, in that room and nowhere else.
I hop
she's ri

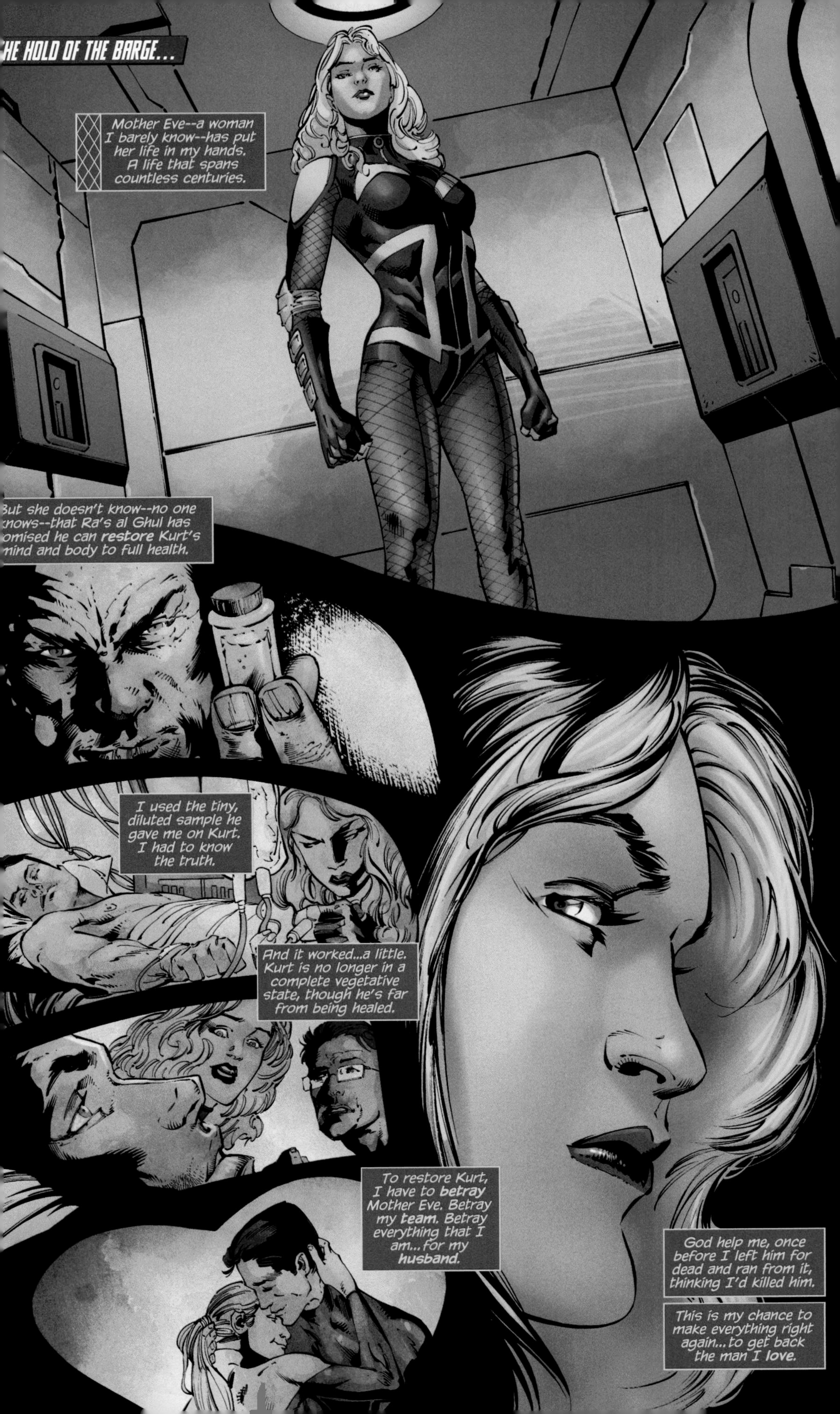
HE HOLD OF THE BARGE...
Mother Eve--a woman I barely know--has put her life in my hands. A life that spans countless centuries.
But she doesn't know--no one knows--that Ra's al Ghul has omised he can restore Kurt's mind and body to full health.
I used the tiny, diluted sample he gave me on Kurt. I had to know the truth.
And it worked...a little. Kurt is no longer in a complete vegetative state, though he's far from being healed.
To restore Kurt, I have to betray Mother Eve. Betray my team. Betray everything that I am...for my husband.
God help me, once before I left him for dead and ran from it, thinking I'd killed him.
This is my chance to make everything right again...to get back the man I love.

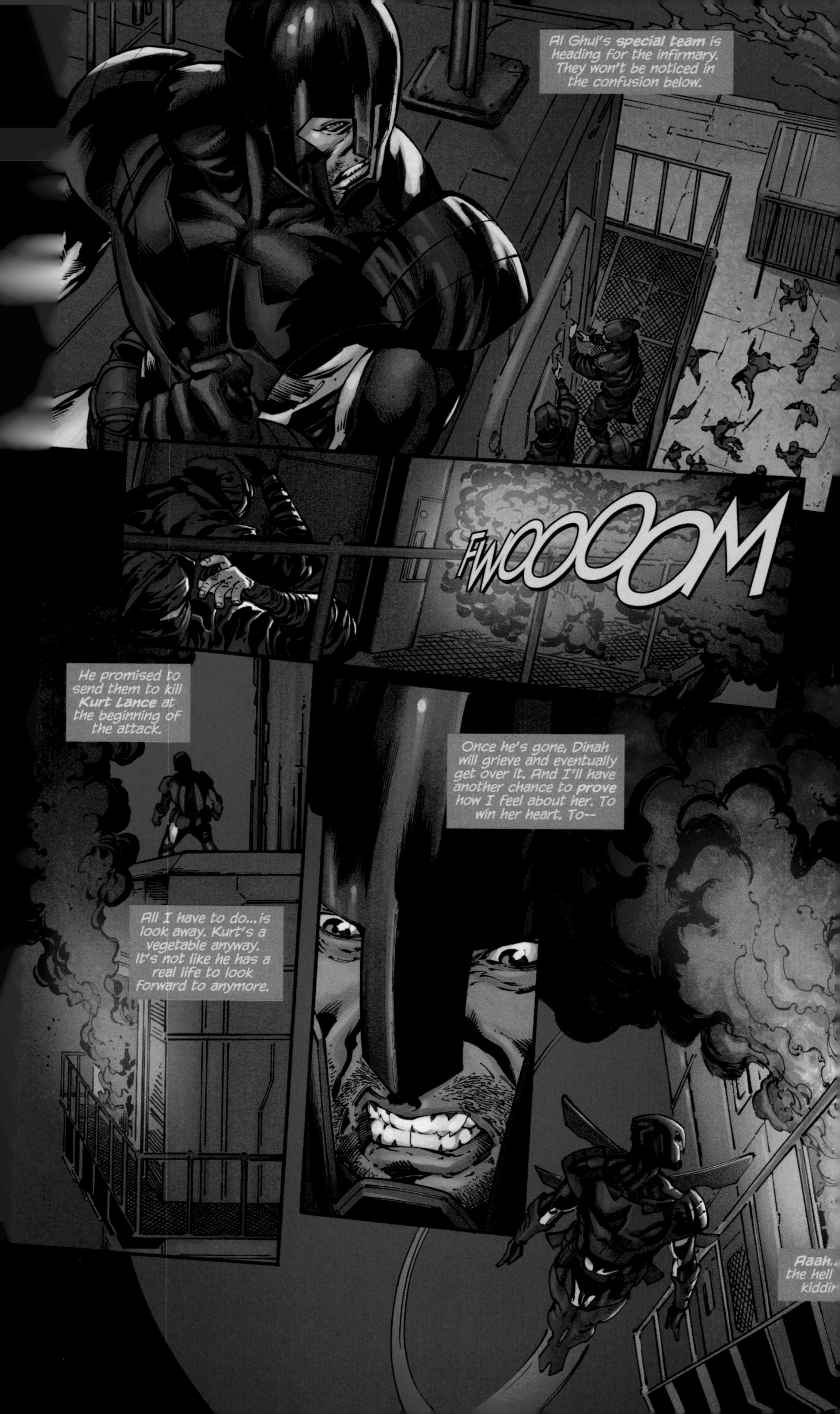

Al Ghul's **special team** is heading for the infirmary. They won't be noticed in the confusion below.
FWOOOOM
He promised to send them to kill **Kurt Lance** at the beginning of the attack.
Once he's gone, Dinah will grieve and eventually get over it. And I'll have another chance to **prove** how I feel about her. To win her heart. To--
All I have to do...is look away. Kurt's a vegetable anyway. It's not like he has a real life to look forward to anymore.

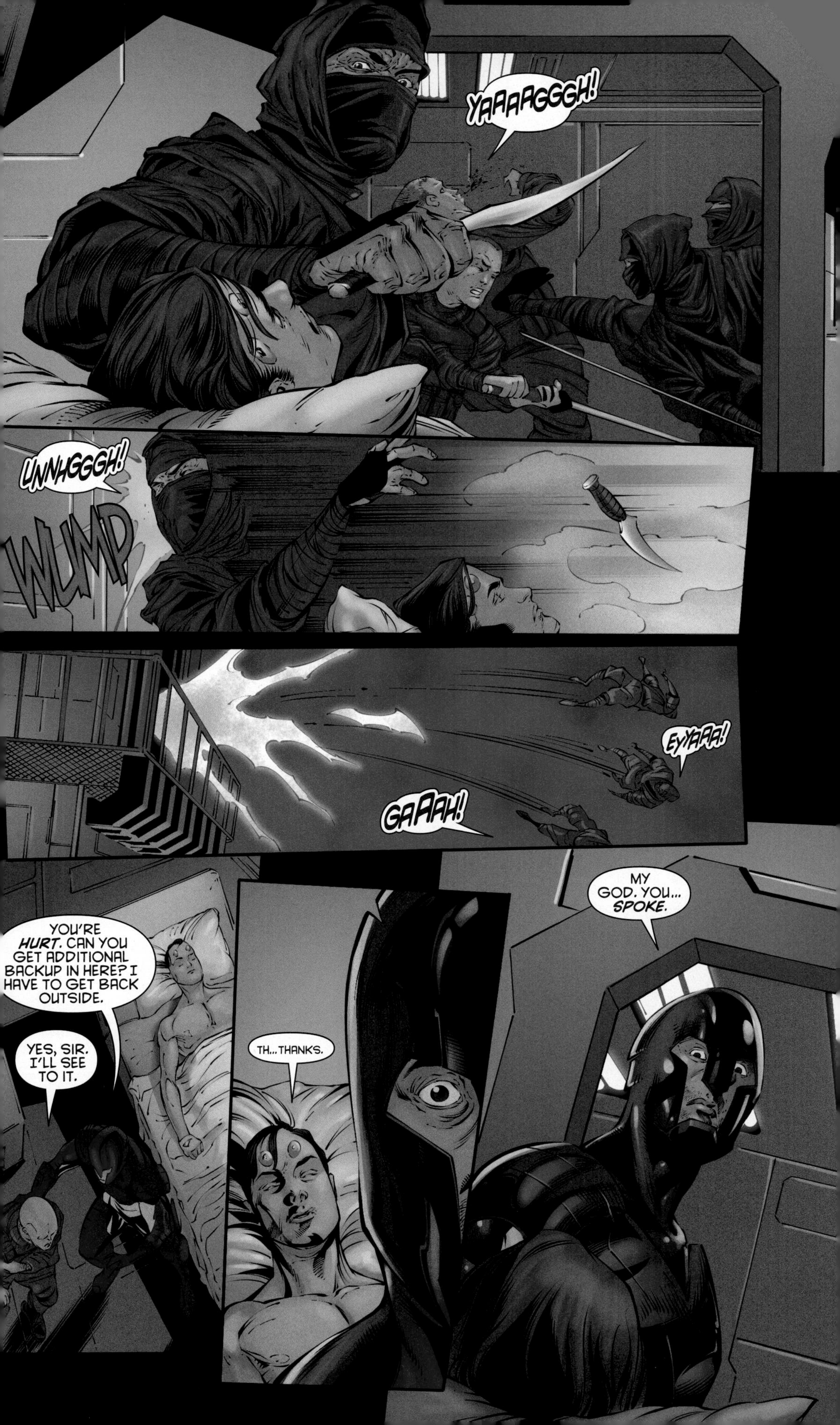
YAAAAGGGH!
UNNHGGGH!
WUMP
EYYAAA!
GAAAH!
YOU'RE HURT. CAN YOU GET ADDITIONAL BACKUP IN HERE? I HAVE TO GET BACK OUTSIDE.
YES, SIR. I'LL SEE TO IT.
TH...THANKS.
MY GOD. YOU... SPOKE.

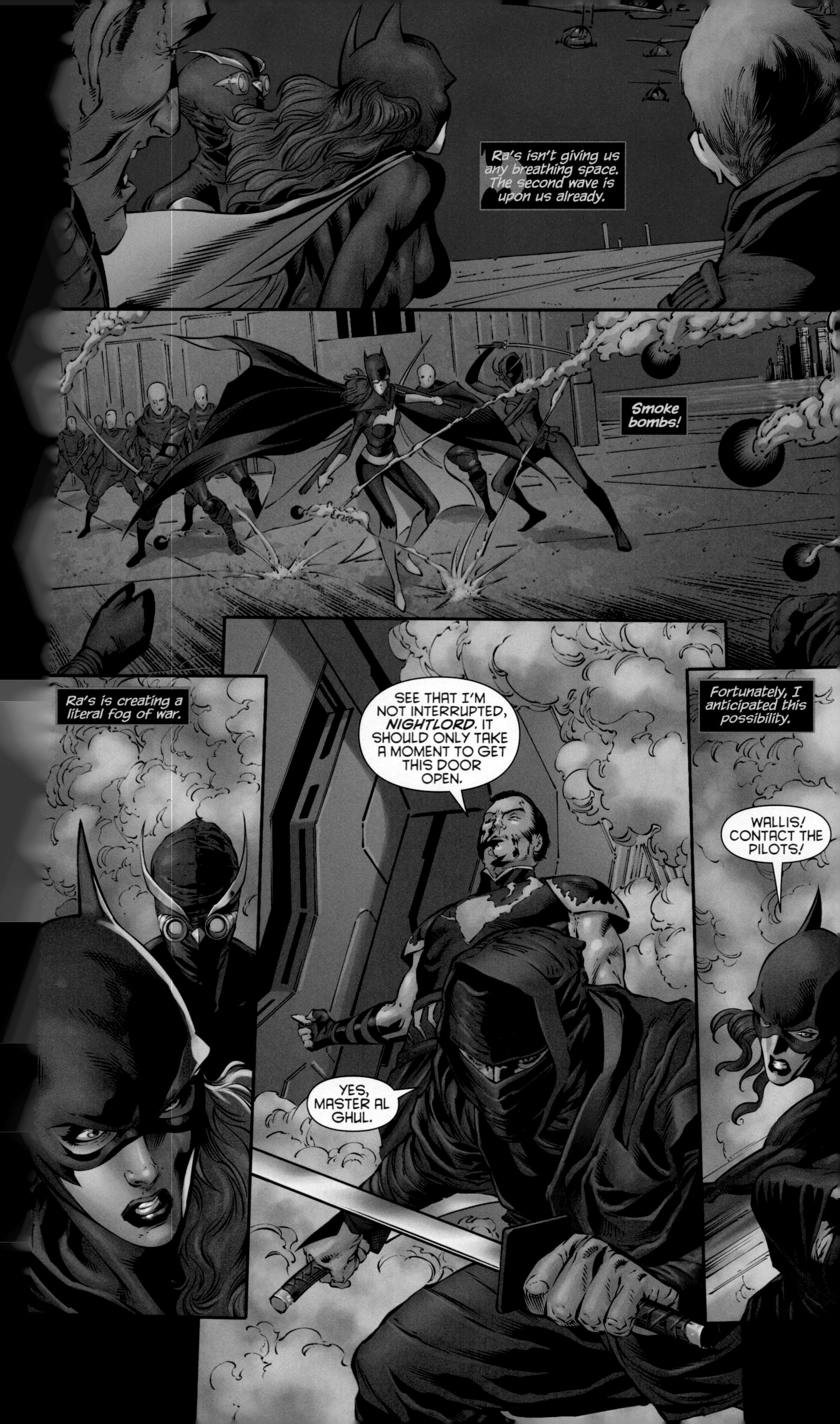
Ra's isn't giving us any breathing space. The second wave is upon us already.
Smoke bombs!
Ra's is creating a literal fog of war.
SEE THAT I'M NOT INTERRUPTED, NIGHTLORD. IT SHOULD ONLY TAKE A MOMENT TO GET THIS DOOR OPEN.
YES, MASTER AL GHUL.
Fortunately, I anticipated this possibility.
WALLIS! CONTACT THE PILOTS!

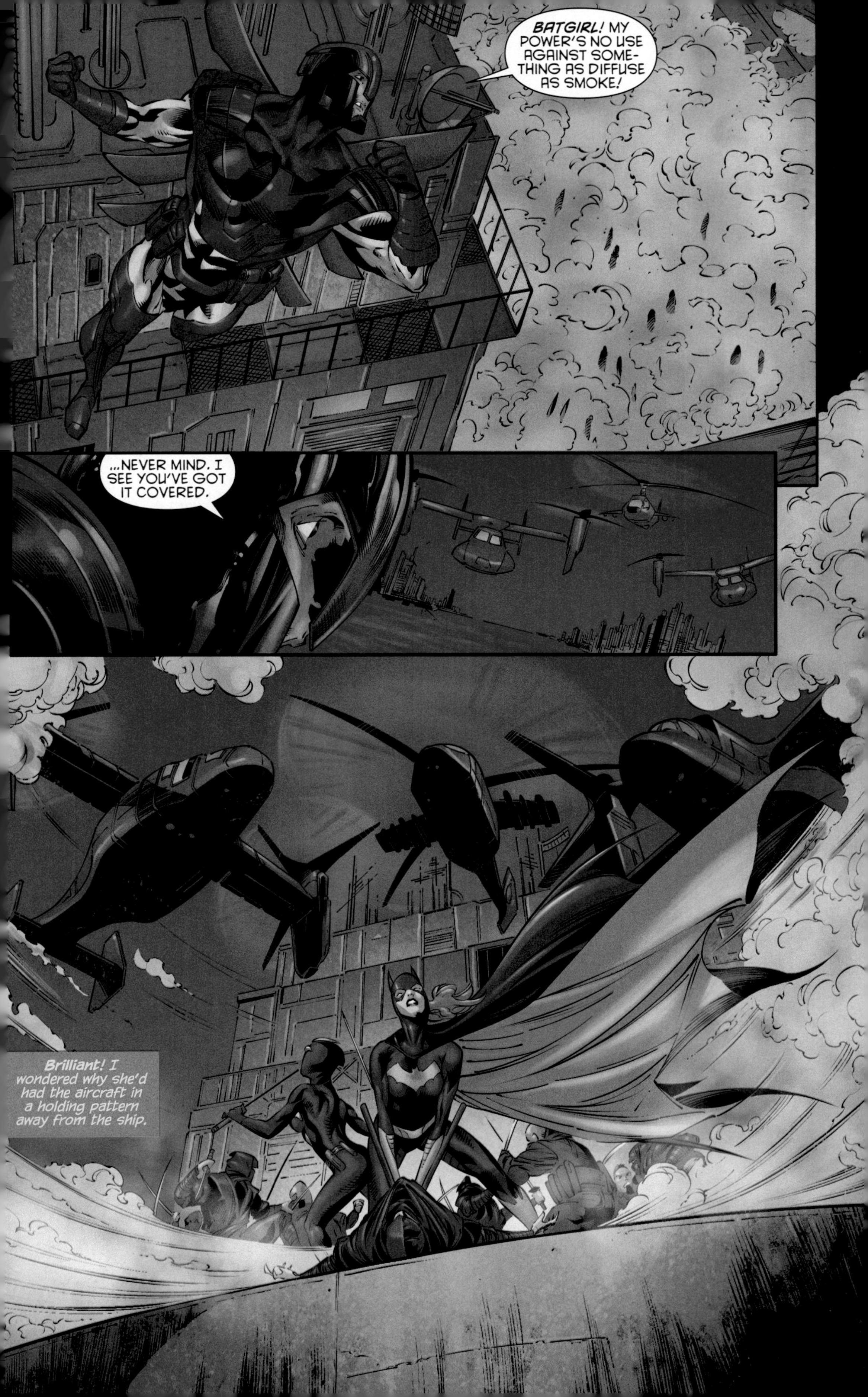
BATGIRL! MY POWER'S NO USE AGAINST SOME-THING AS DIFFUSE AS SMOKE!
...NEVER MIND. I SEE YOU'VE GOT IT COVERED.
Brilliant! I wondered why she'd had the aircraft in a holding pattern away from the ship.

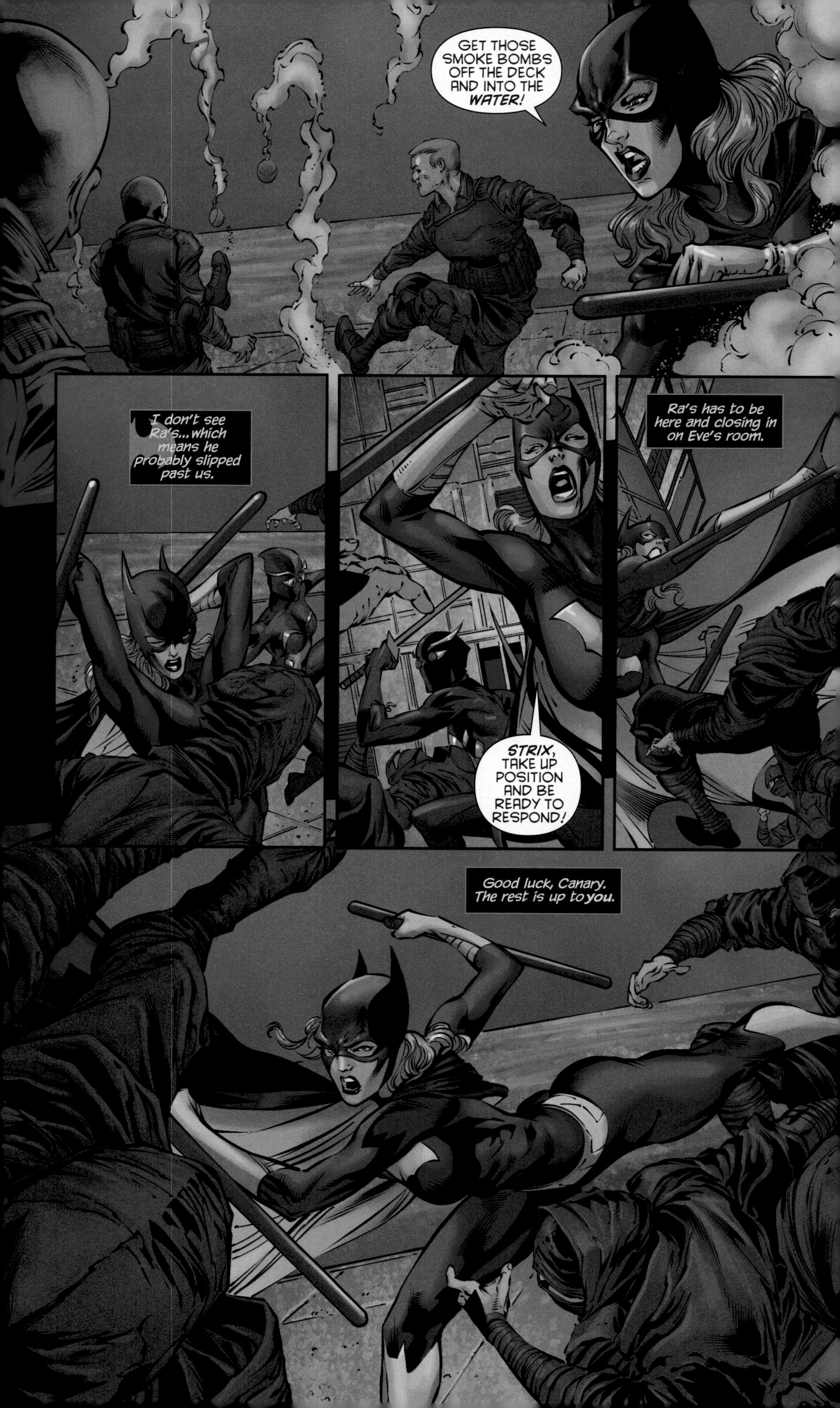
GET THOSE SMOKE BOMBS OFF THE DECK AND INTO THE WATER!
I don't see Ra's...which means he probably slipped past us.
STRIX, TAKE UP POSITION AND BE READY TO RESPOND!
Ra's has to be here and closing in on Eve's room.
Good luck, Canary. The rest is up to you.

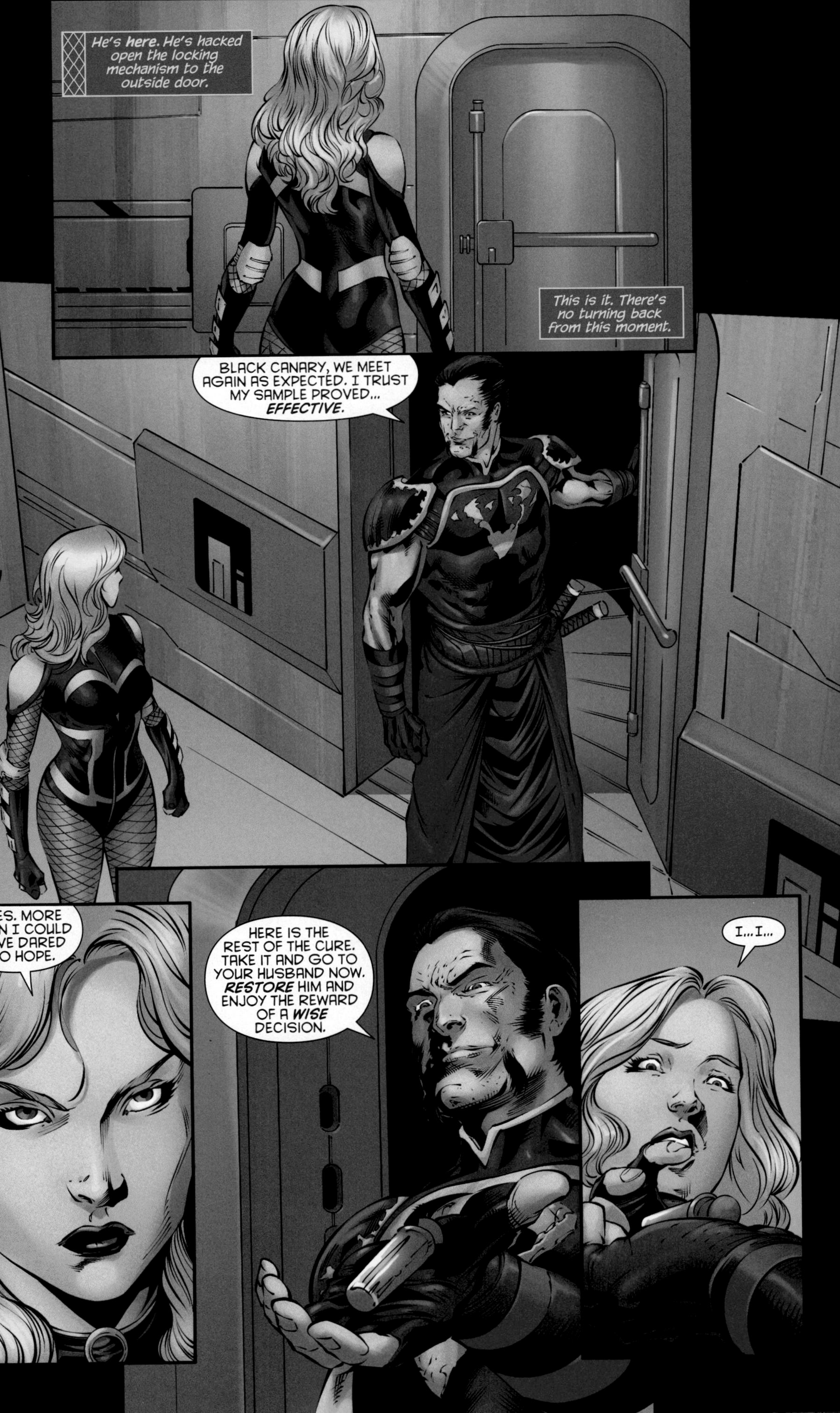
He's here. He's hacked open the locking mechanism to the outside door.
This is it. There's no turning back from this moment.
BLACK CANARY, WE MEET AGAIN AS EXPECTED. I TRUST MY SAMPLE PROVED... EFFECTIVE.
ES. MORE N I COULD VE DARED O HOPE.
HERE IS THE REST OF THE CURE. TAKE IT AND GO TO YOUR HUSBAND NOW. RESTORE HIM AND ENJOY THE REWARD OF A WISE DECISION.
I... I...

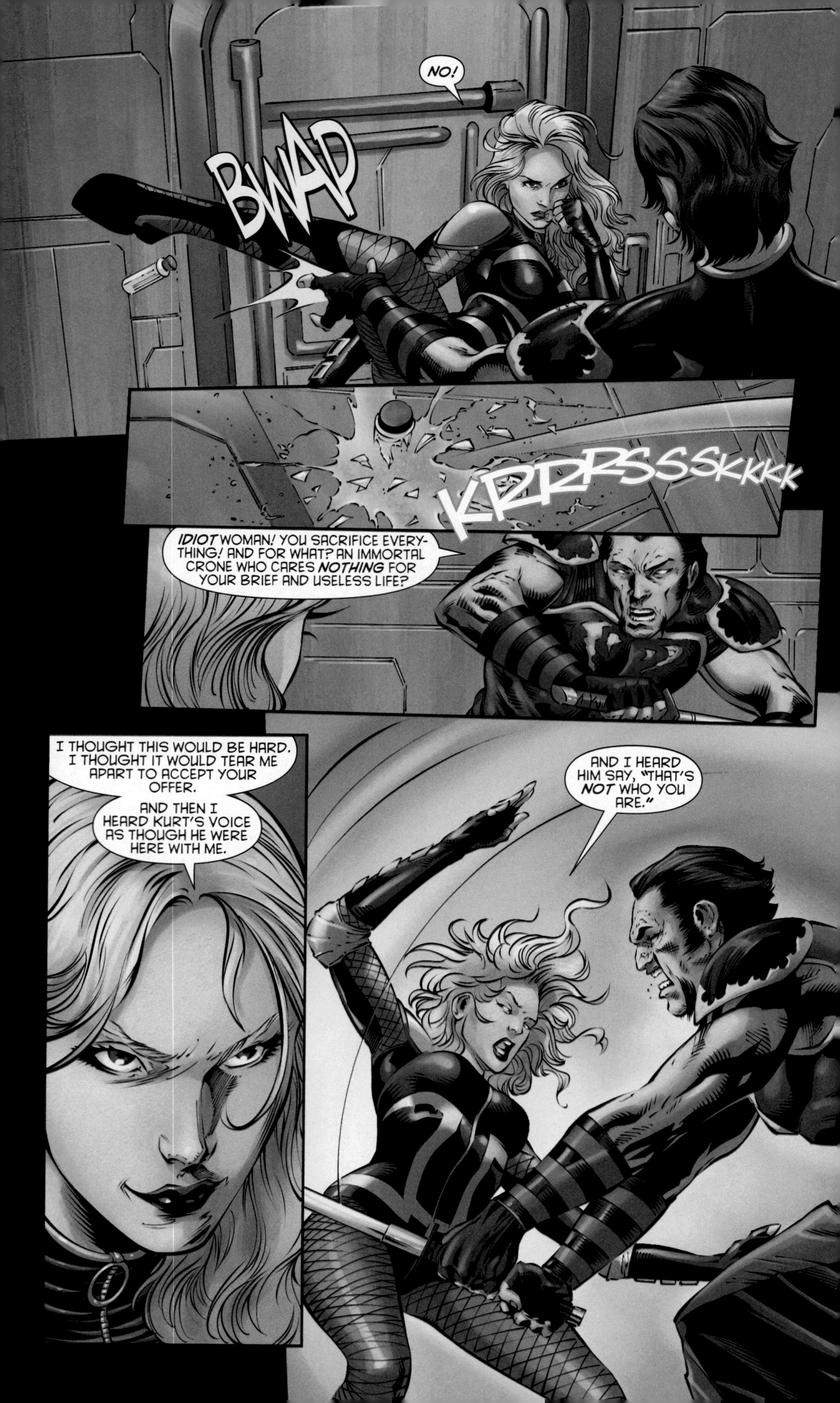
NO!
BWAP
KRRRSSSKKKK
IDIOT WOMAN! YOU SACRIFICE EVERYTHING! AND FOR WHAT? AN IMMORTAL CRONE WHO CARES NOTHING FOR YOUR BRIEF AND USELESS LIFE?
I THOUGHT THIS WOULD BE HARD. I THOUGHT IT WOULD TEAR ME APART TO ACCEPT YOUR OFFER.
AND THEN I HEARD KURT'S VOICE AS THOUGH HE WERE HERE WITH ME.
AND I HEARD HIM SAY, "THAT'S NOT WHO YOU ARE."

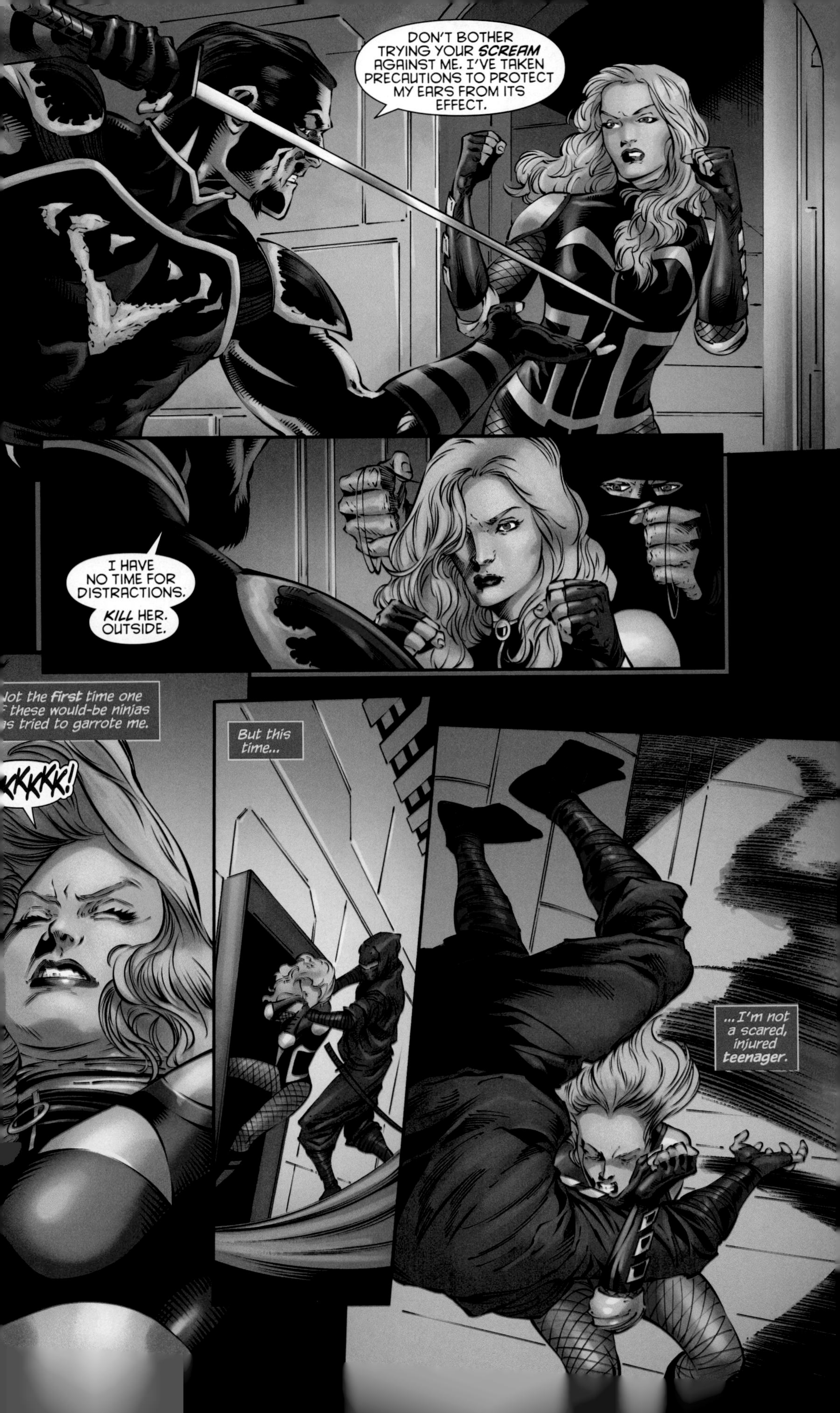

DON'T BOTHER TRYING YOUR SCREAM AGAINST ME. I'VE TAKEN PRECAUTIONS TO PROTECT MY EARS FROM ITS EFFECT.
I HAVE NO TIME FOR DISTRACTIONS.
KILL HER. OUTSIDE.
ot the first time one f these would-be ninjas s tried to garrote me.
KKKKK!
But this time...
...I'm not a scared, injured teenager.

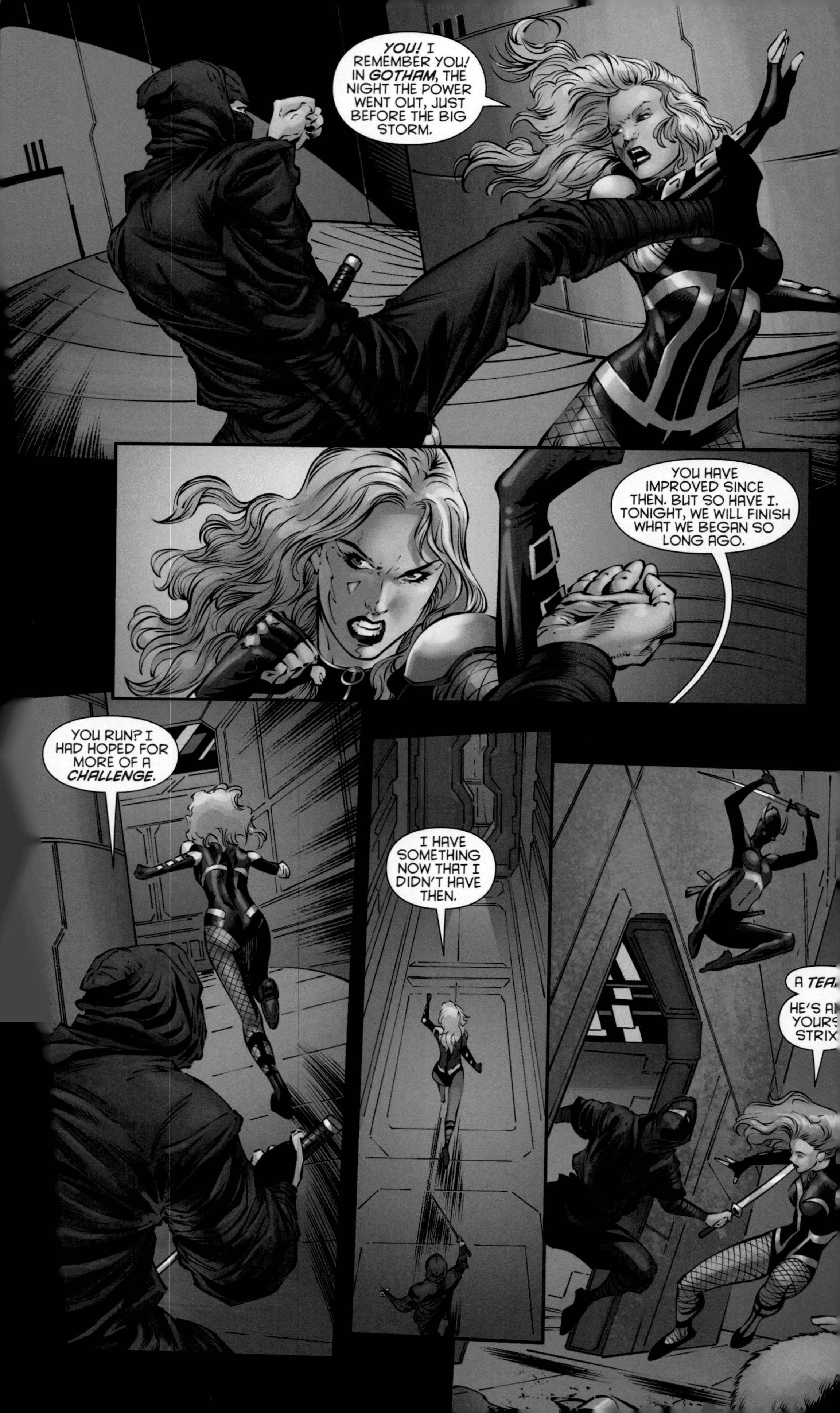
YOU! I REMEMBER YOU! IN GOTHAM, THE NIGHT THE POWER WENT OUT, JUST BEFORE THE BIG STORM.
YOU HAVE IMPROVED SINCE THEN. BUT SO HAVE I. TONIGHT, WE WILL FINISH WHAT WE BEGAN SO LONG AGO.
YOU RUN? I HAD HOPED FOR MORE OF A CHALLENGE.
I HAVE SOMETHING NOW THAT I DIDN'T HAVE THEN.

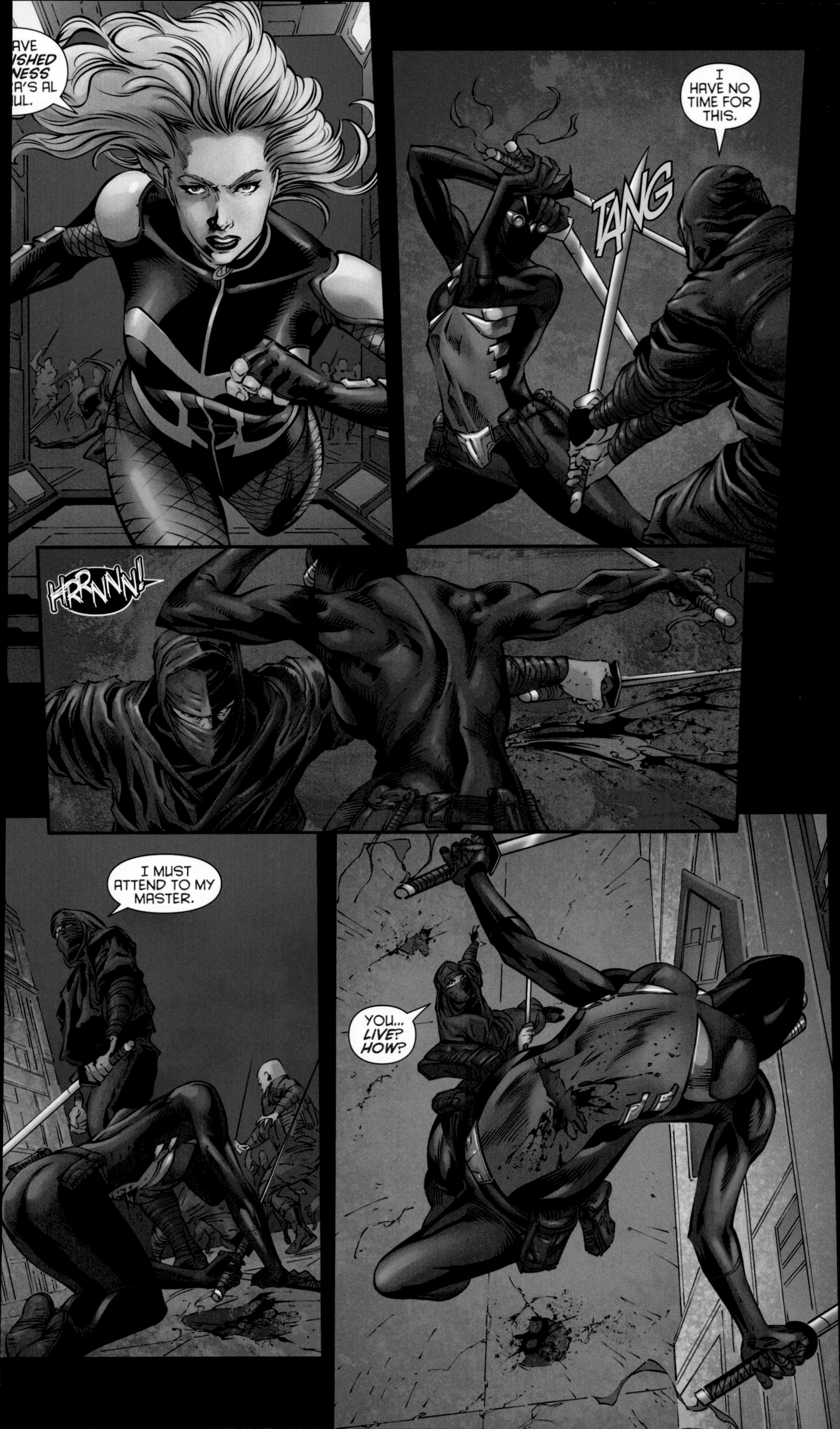

I HAVE NO TIME FOR THIS.
TANG
HRRNNN!
I MUST ATTEND TO MY MASTER.
YOU... *LIVE? HOW?*

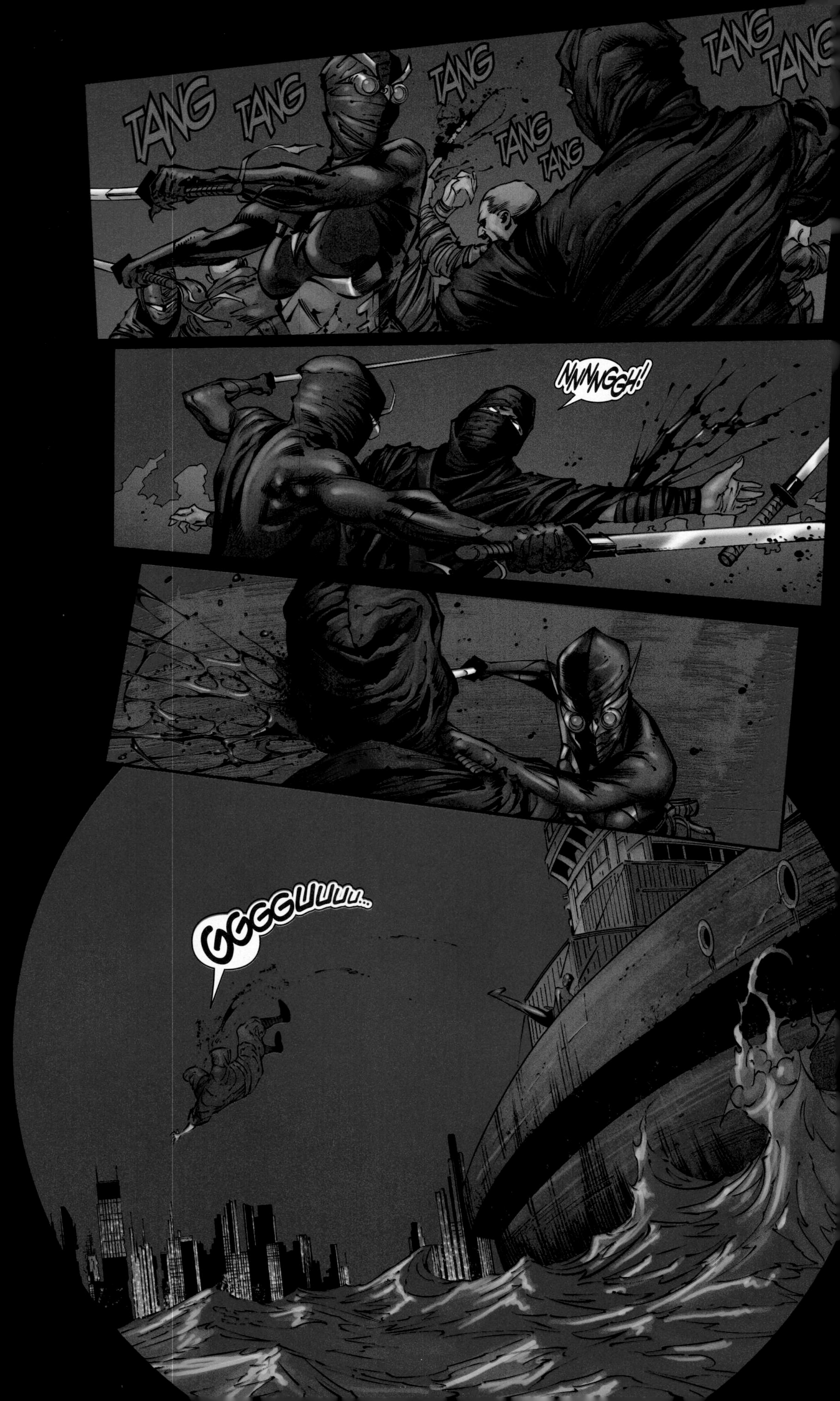
TANG
TANG
TANG
TANG
TANG
TANG
TANG
NNNNGGH!
GGGGUUUU...

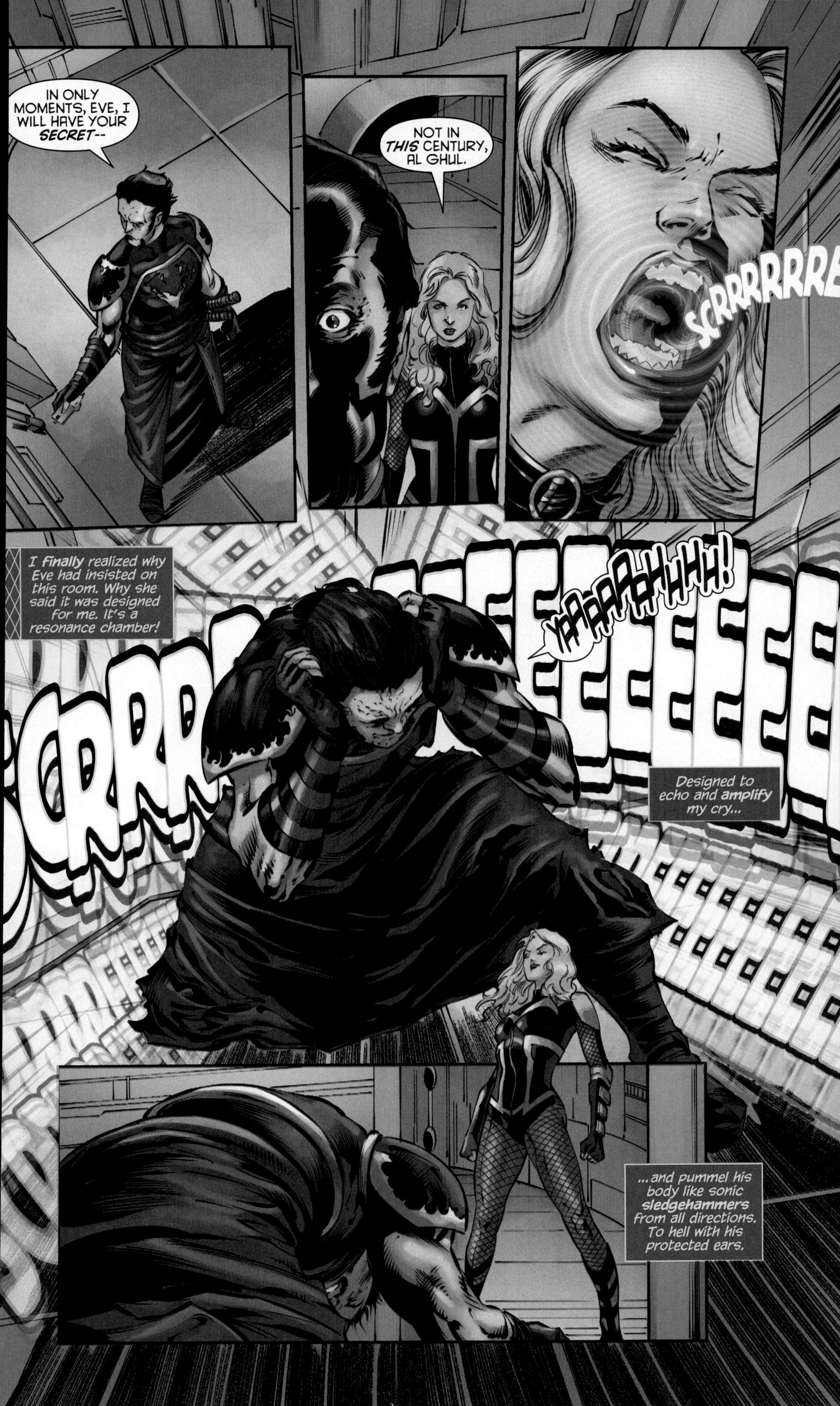

IN ONLY MOMENTS, EVE, I WILL HAVE YOUR SECRET--
NOT IN THIS CENTURY, AL GHUL.
SCRRRRRRE
I finally realized why Eve had insisted on this room. Why she said it was designed for me. It's a resonance chamber!
YAAAAAHHHHH!
Designed to echo and amplify my cry...
...and pummel his body like sonic sledgehammers from all directions. To hell with his protected ears.

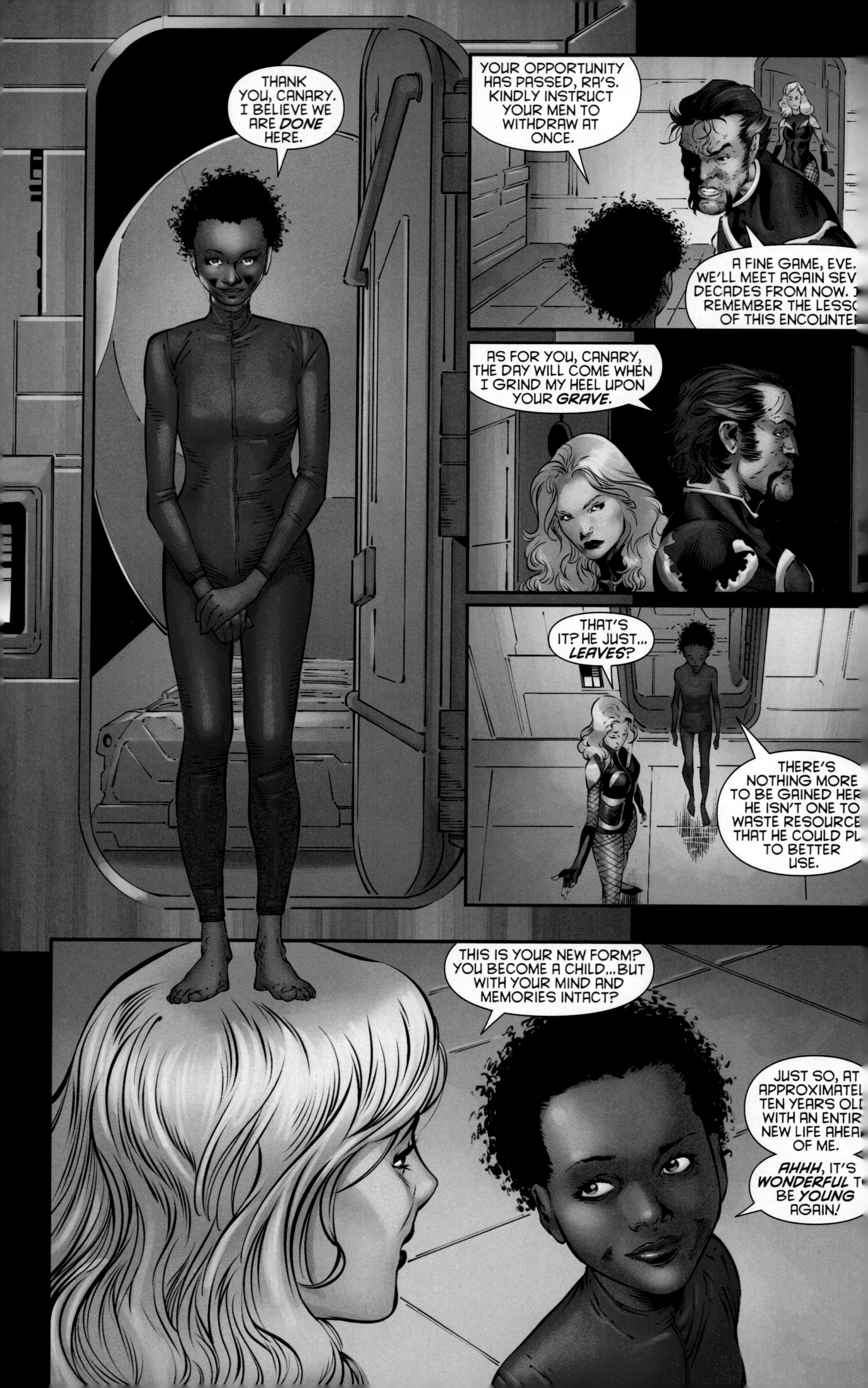
THANK YOU, CANARY. I BELIEVE WE ARE *DONE* HERE.
YOUR OPPORTUNITY HAS PASSED, RA'S. KINDLY INSTRUCT YOUR MEN TO WITHDRAW AT ONCE.
A FINE GAME, EVE. WE'LL MEET AGAIN SEV DECADES FROM NOW. REMEMBER THE LESS OF THIS ENCOUNTE
AS FOR YOU, CANARY, THE DAY WILL COME WHEN I GRIND MY HEEL UPON YOUR *GRAVE*.
THAT'S IT? HE JUST... *LEAVES*?
THERE'S NOTHING MORE TO BE GAINED HER HE ISN'T ONE TO WASTE RESOURCE THAT HE COULD PL TO BETTER USE.
THIS IS YOUR NEW FORM? YOU BECOME A CHILD...BUT WITH YOUR MIND AND MEMORIES INTACT?
JUST SO, AT APPROXIMATEL TEN YEARS OL WITH AN ENTIR NEW LIFE AHEA OF ME.
AHHH, IT'S *WONDERFUL* T BE *YOUNG* AGAIN!

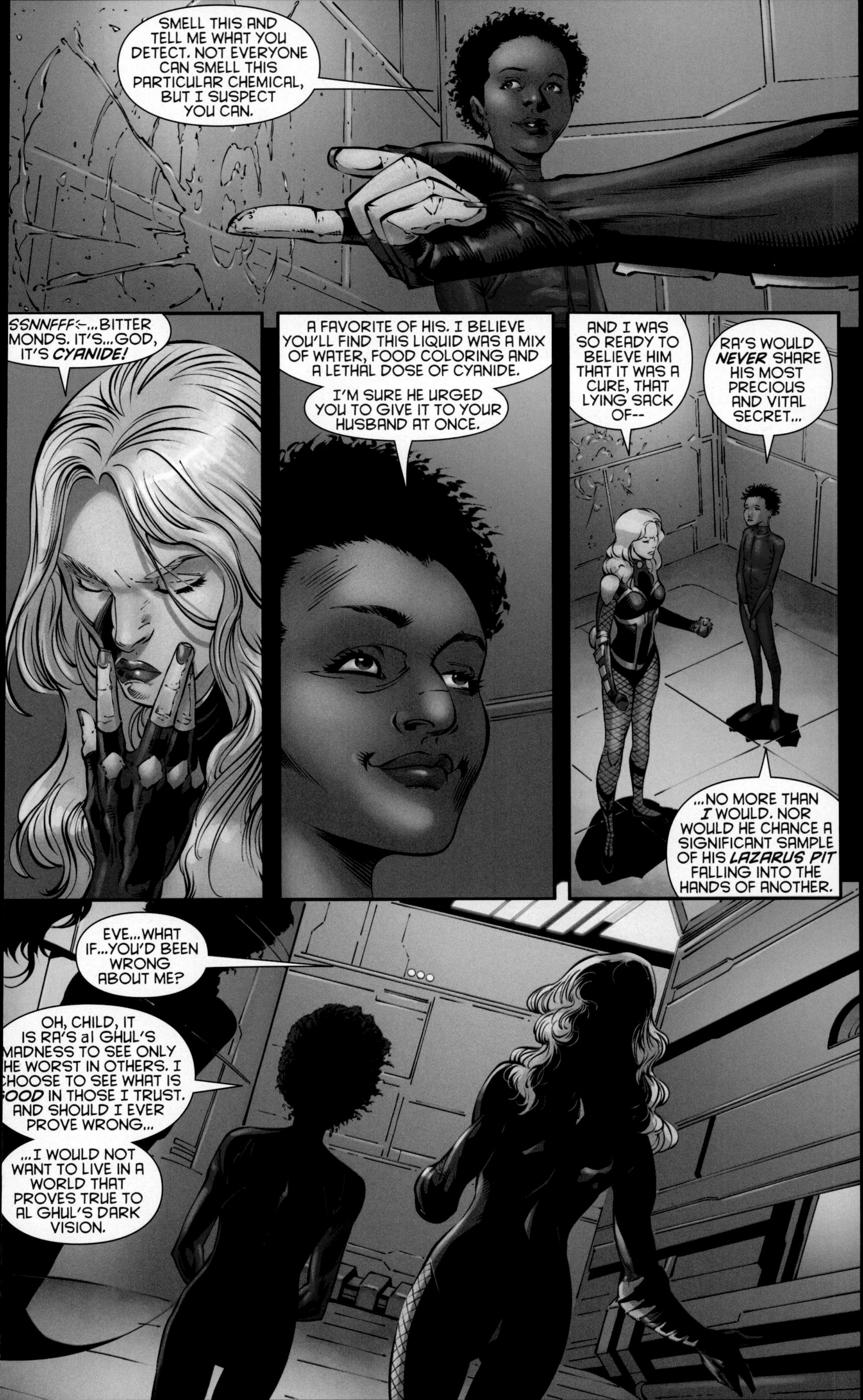
SMELL THIS AND TELL ME WHAT YOU DETECT. NOT EVERYONE CAN SMELL THIS PARTICULAR CHEMICAL, BUT I SUSPECT YOU CAN.
SSNNFFF--...BITTER MONDS. IT'S...GOD, IT'S CYANIDE!
A FAVORITE OF HIS. I BELIEVE YOU'LL FIND THIS LIQUID WAS A MIX OF WATER, FOOD COLORING AND A LETHAL DOSE OF CYANIDE.
I'M SURE HE URGED YOU TO GIVE IT TO YOUR HUSBAND AT ONCE.
AND I WAS SO READY TO BELIEVE HIM THAT IT WAS A CURE, THAT LYING SACK OF--
RA'S WOULD NEVER SHARE HIS MOST PRECIOUS AND VITAL SECRET...
...NO MORE THAN I WOULD. NOR WOULD HE CHANCE A SIGNIFICANT SAMPLE OF HIS LAZARUS PIT FALLING INTO THE HANDS OF ANOTHER.
EVE...WHAT IF...YOU'D BEEN WRONG ABOUT ME?
OH, CHILD, IT IS RA'S al GHUL'S MADNESS TO SEE ONLY HE WORST IN OTHERS. I CHOOSE TO SEE WHAT IS OOD IN THOSE I TRUST. AND SHOULD I EVER PROVE WRONG...
...I WOULD NOT WANT TO LIVE IN A WORLD THAT PROVES TRUE TO AL GHUL'S DARK VISION.

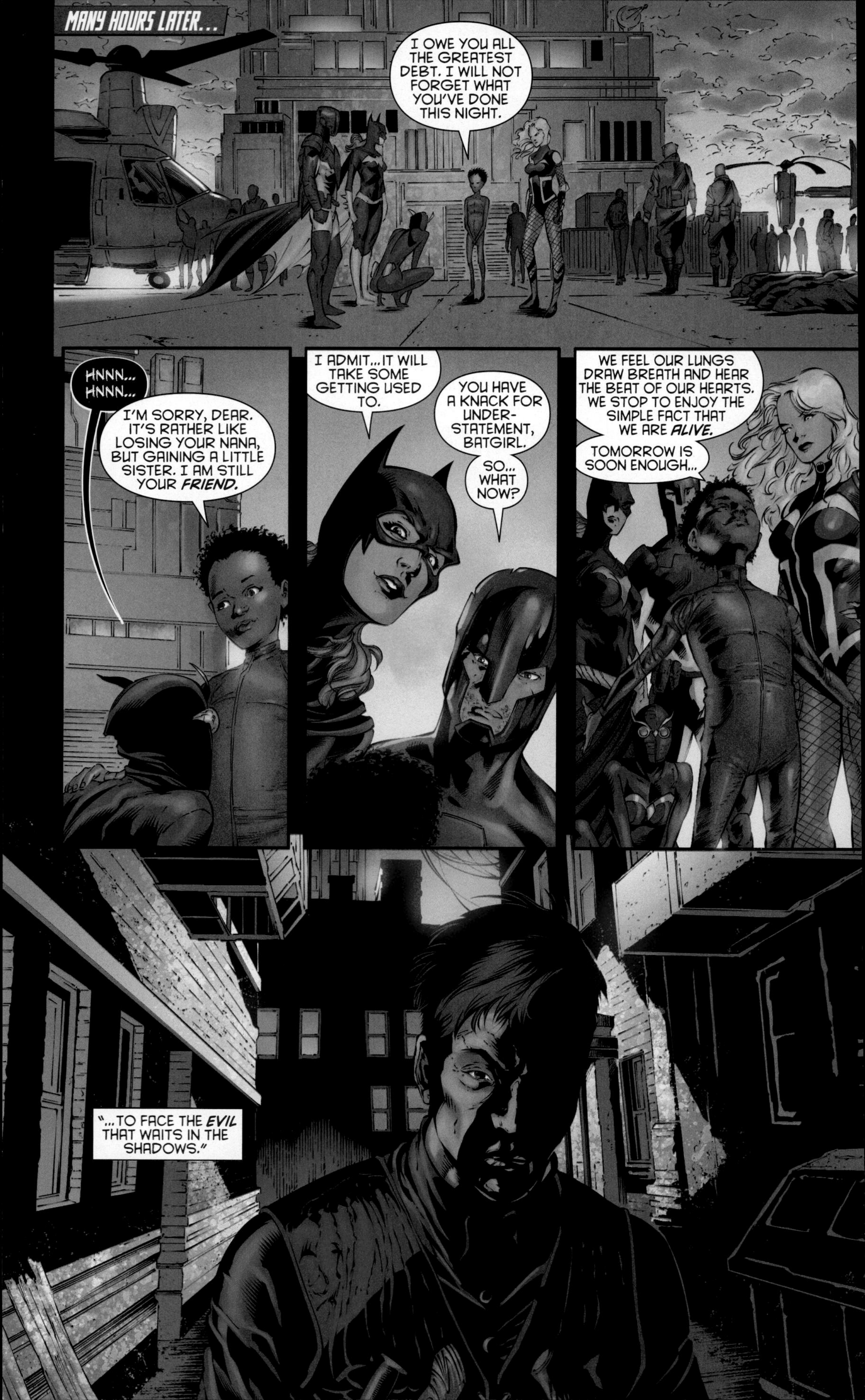
MANY HOURS LATER...
I OWE YOU ALL THE GREATEST DEBT. I WILL NOT FORGET WHAT YOU'VE DONE THIS NIGHT.
HNNN... HNNN...
I'M SORRY, DEAR. IT'S RATHER LIKE LOSING YOUR NANA, BUT GAINING A LITTLE SISTER. I AM STILL YOUR FRIEND.
I ADMIT...IT WILL TAKE SOME GETTING USED TO.
YOU HAVE A KNACK FOR UNDER-STATEMENT, BATGIRL.
SO... WHAT NOW?
WE FEEL OUR LUNGS DRAW BREATH AND HEAR THE BEAT OF OUR HEARTS. WE STOP TO ENJOY THE SIMPLE FACT THAT WE ARE ALIVE.
TOMORROW IS SOON ENOUGH...
"...TO FACE THE EVIL THAT WAITS IN THE SHADOWS."

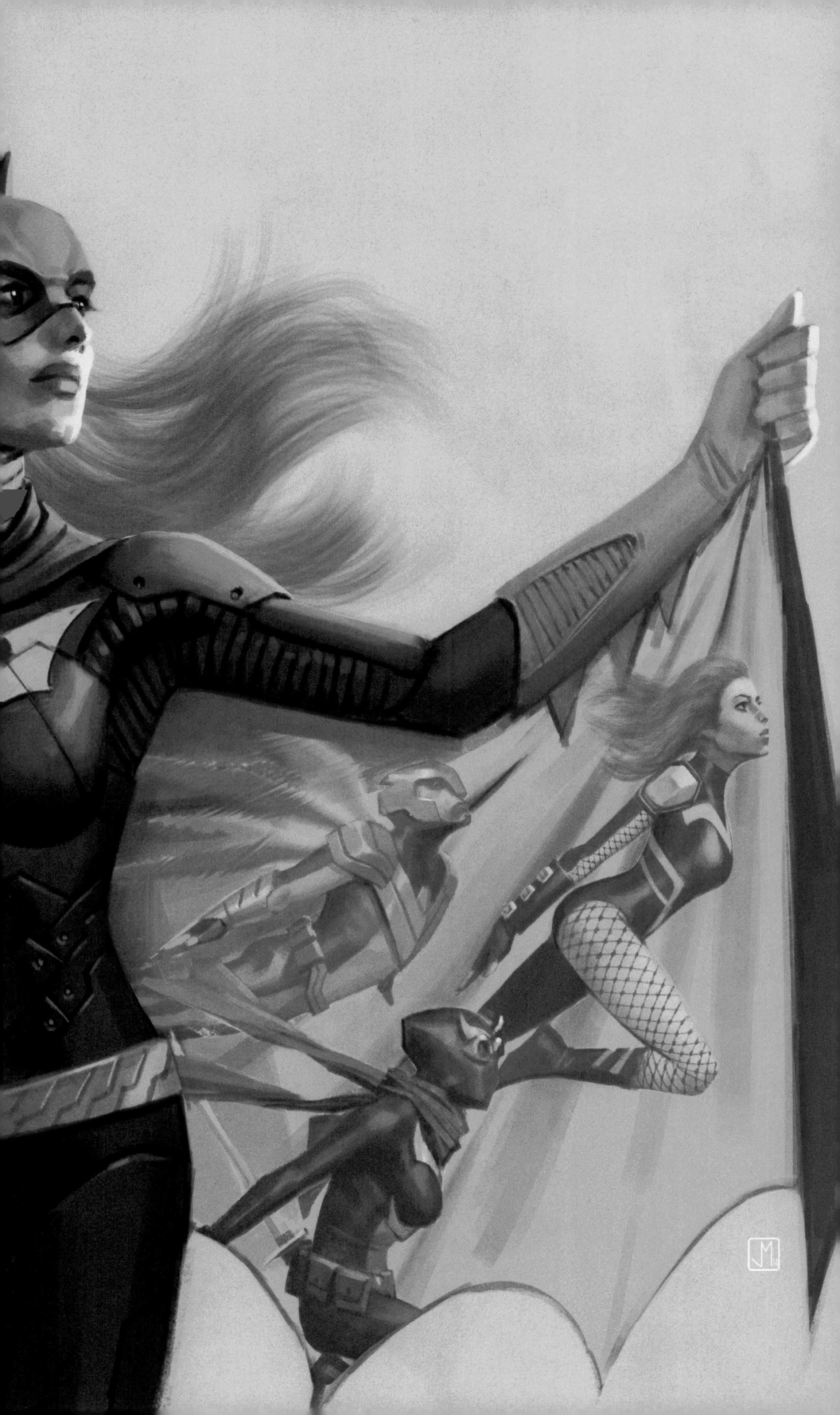

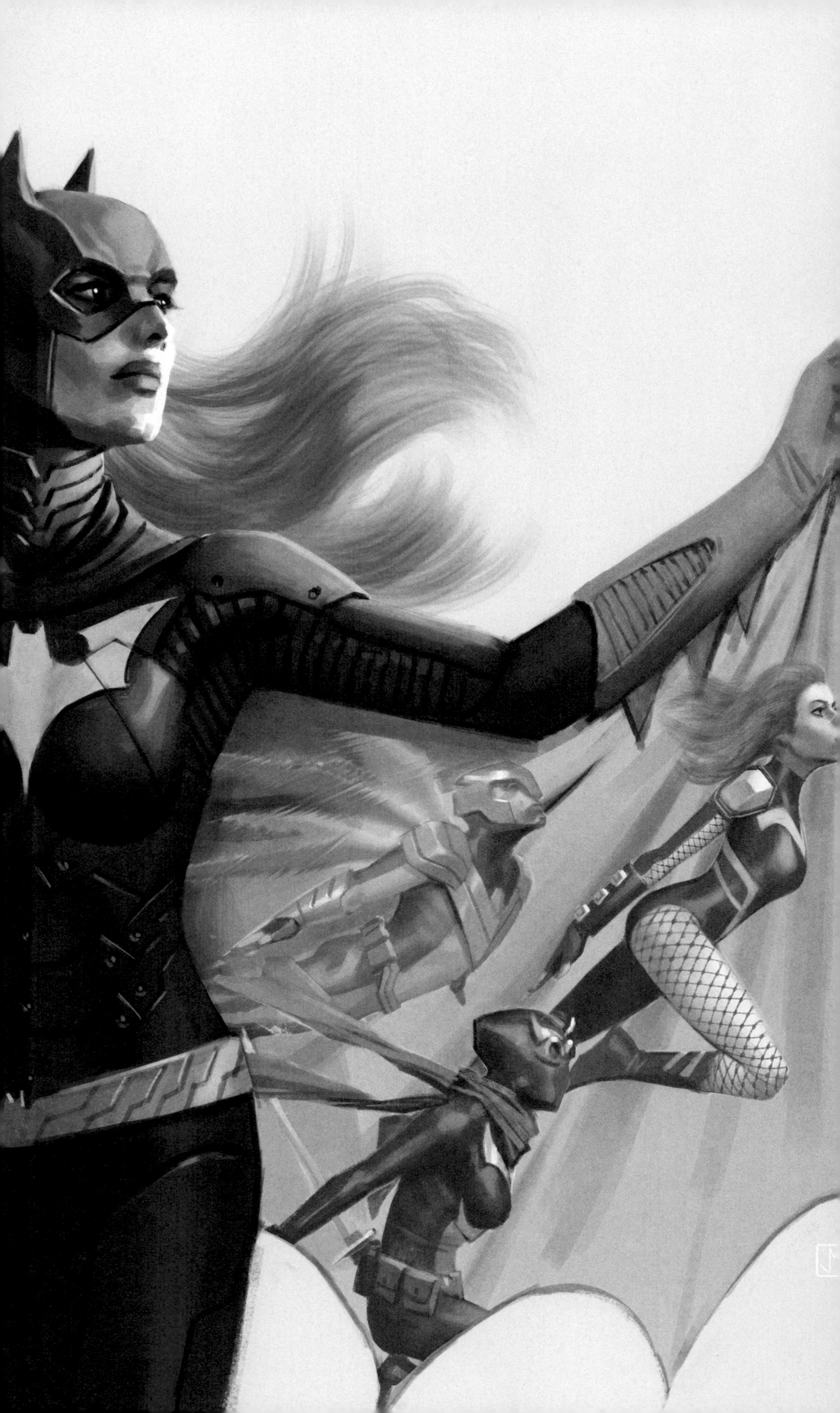

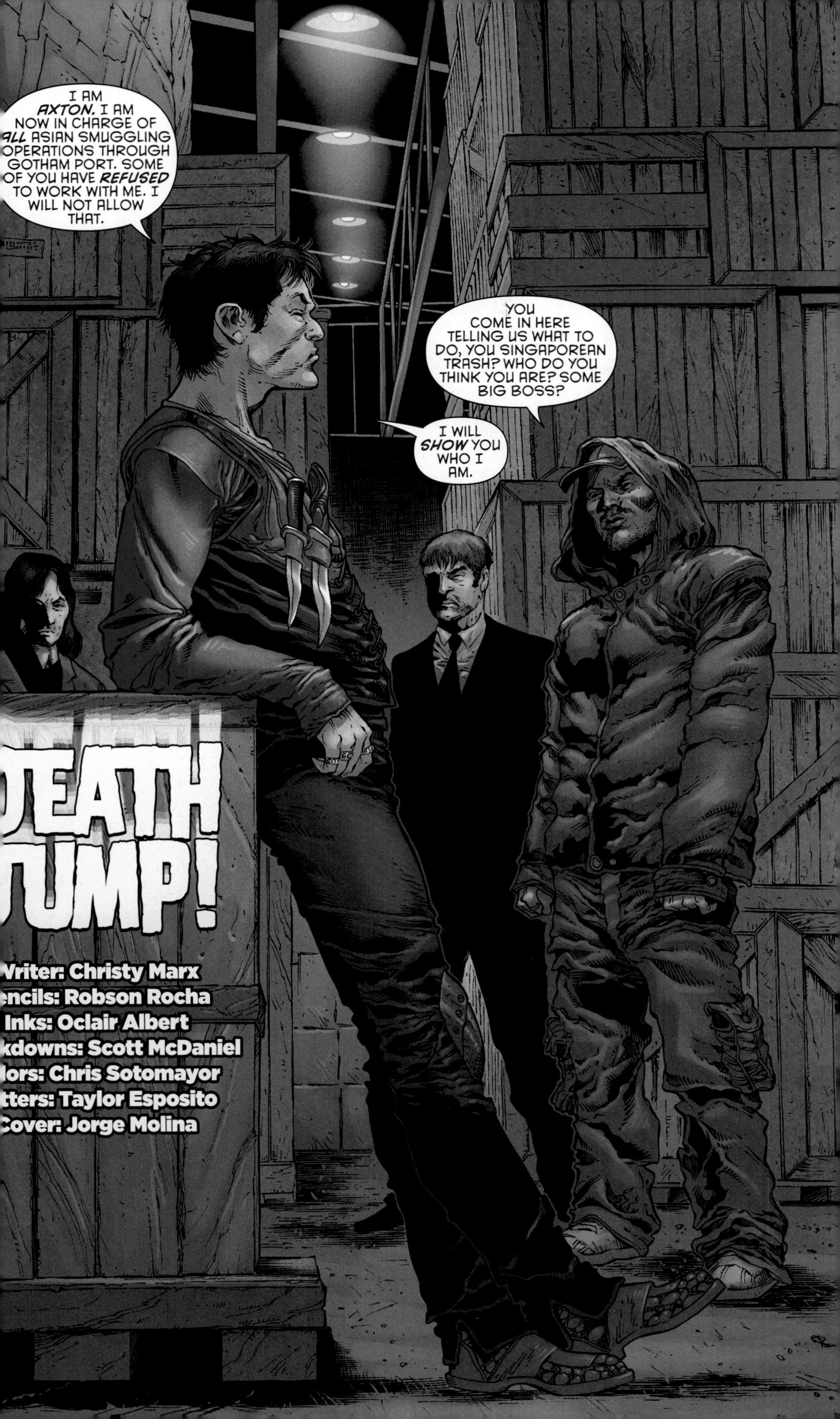
I AM AXTON. I AM NOW IN CHARGE OF ALL ASIAN SMUGGLING OPERATIONS THROUGH GOTHAM PORT. SOME OF YOU HAVE REFUSED TO WORK WITH ME. I WILL NOT ALLOW THAT.
YOU COME IN HERE TELLING US WHAT TO DO, YOU SINGAPOREAN TRASH? WHO DO YOU THINK YOU ARE? SOME BIG BOSS?
I WILL SHOW YOU WHO I AM.
DEATH
JUMP!
Writer: Christy Marx
encils: Robson Rocha
Inks: Oclair Albert
kdowns: Scott McDaniel
lors: Chris Sotomayor
tters: Taylor Esposito
Cover: Jorge Molina

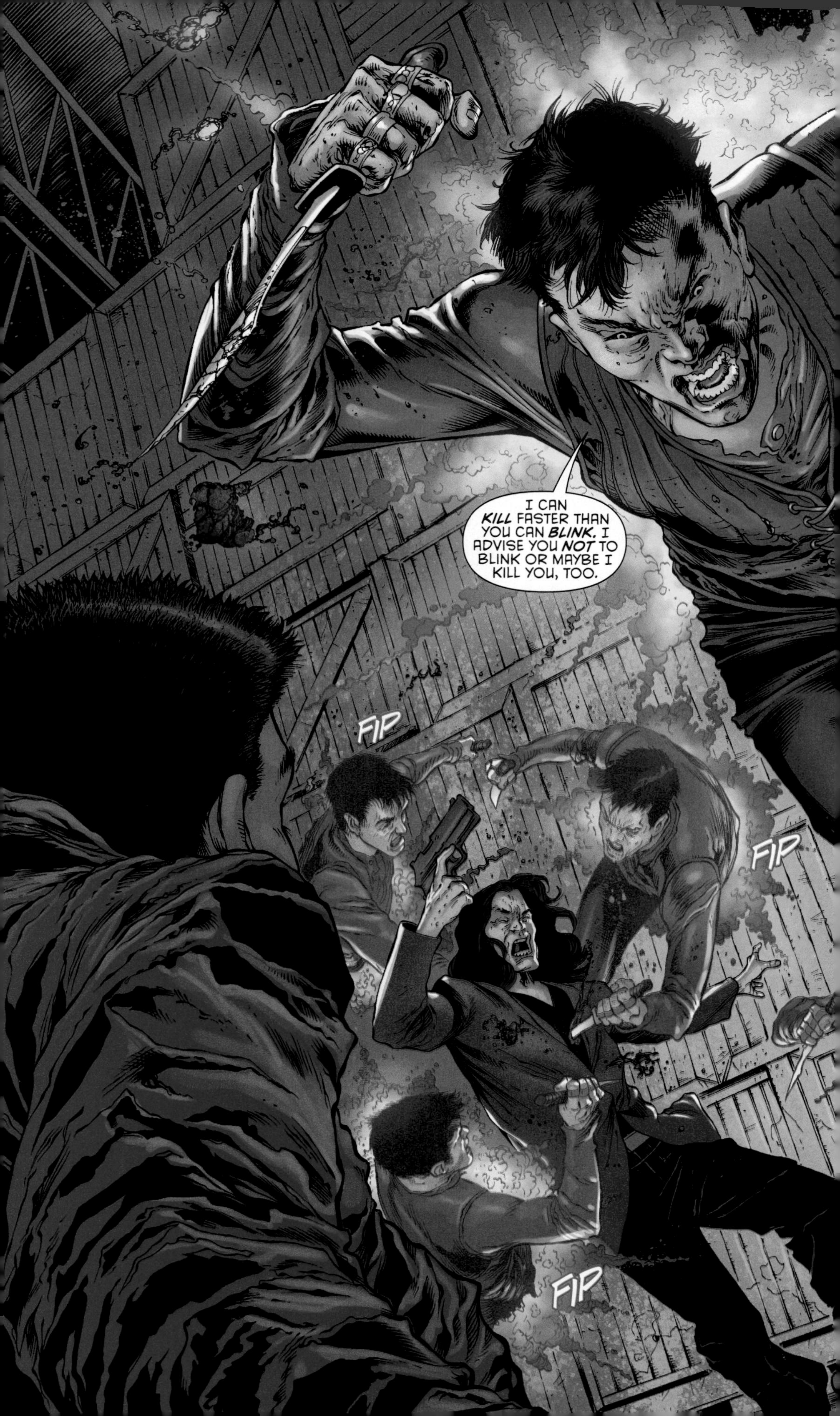
I CAN KILL FASTER THAN YOU CAN BLINK. I ADVISE YOU NOT TO BLINK OR MAYBE I KILL YOU, TOO.
FIP
FIP
FIP

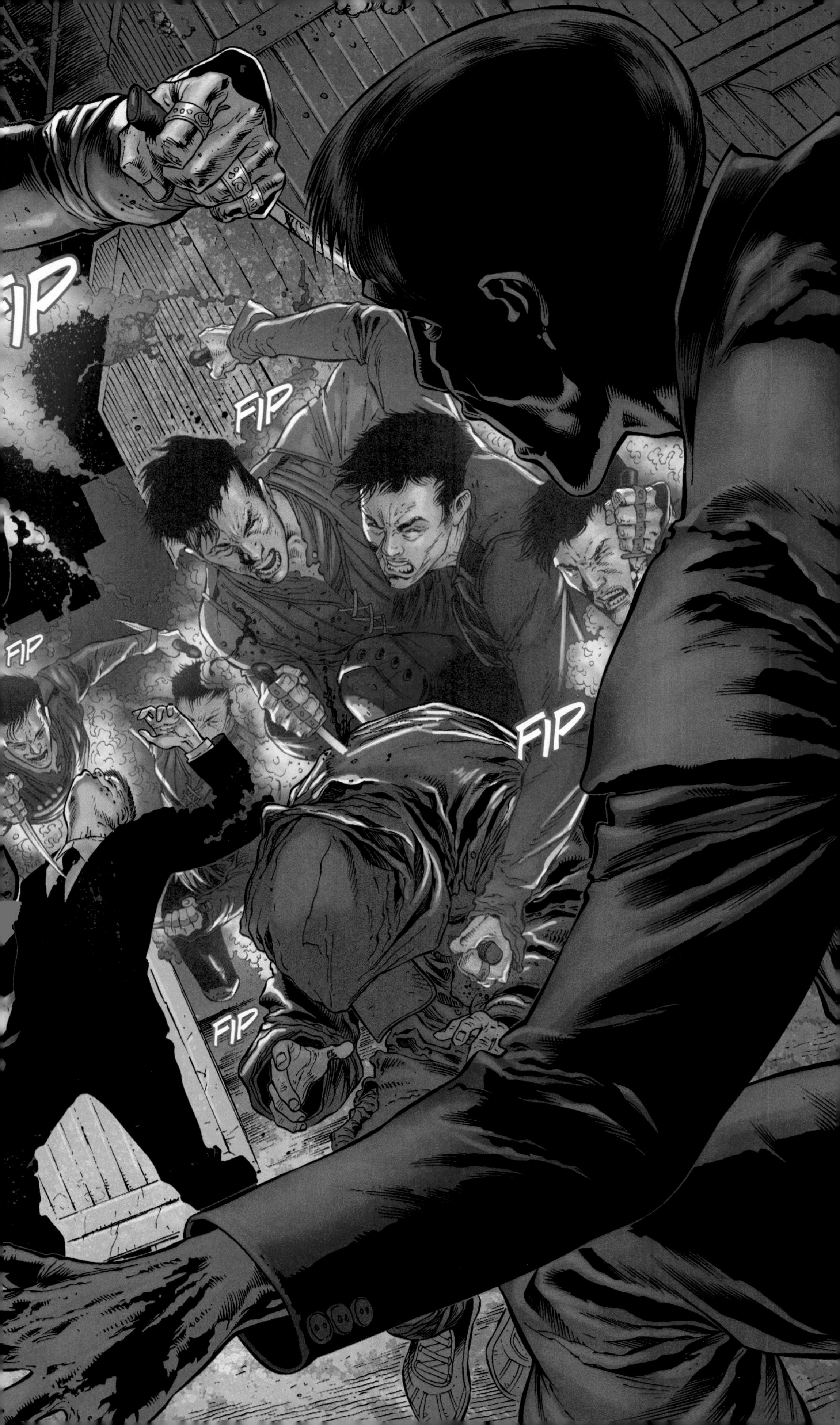
FIP
FIP
FIP
FIP
FIP

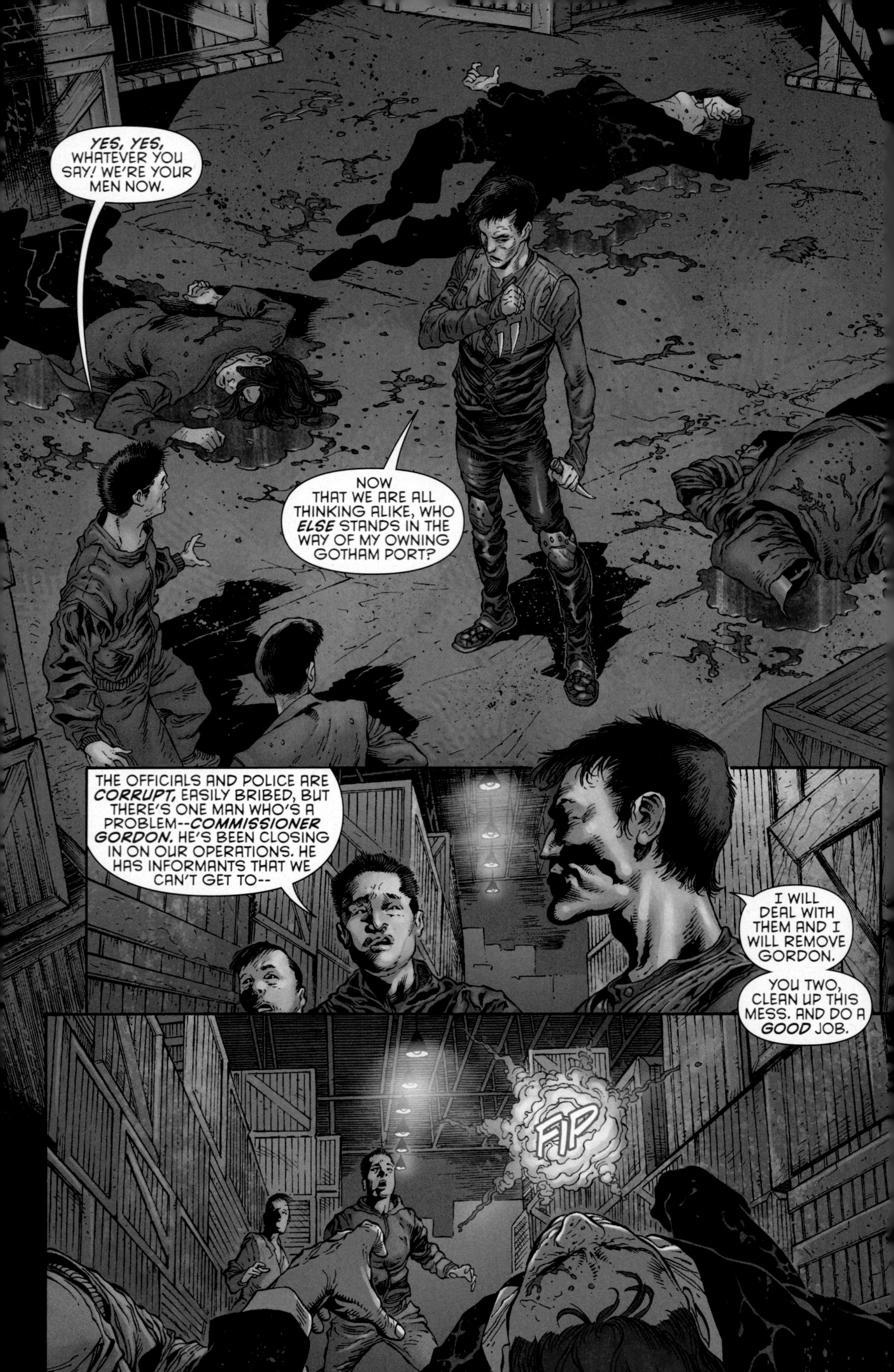
YES, YES, WHATEVER YOU SAY! WE'RE YOUR MEN NOW.
NOW THAT WE ARE ALL THINKING ALIKE, WHO ELSE STANDS IN THE WAY OF MY OWNING GOTHAM PORT?
THE OFFICIALS AND POLICE ARE CORRUPT, EASILY BRIBED, BUT THERE'S ONE MAN WHO'S A PROBLEM--COMMISSIONER GORDON. HE'S BEEN CLOSING IN ON OUR OPERATIONS. HE HAS INFORMANTS THAT WE CAN'T GET TO--
I WILL DEAL WITH THEM AND I WILL REMOVE GORDON.
YOU TWO, CLEAN UP THIS MESS. AND DO A GOOD JOB.
FTP

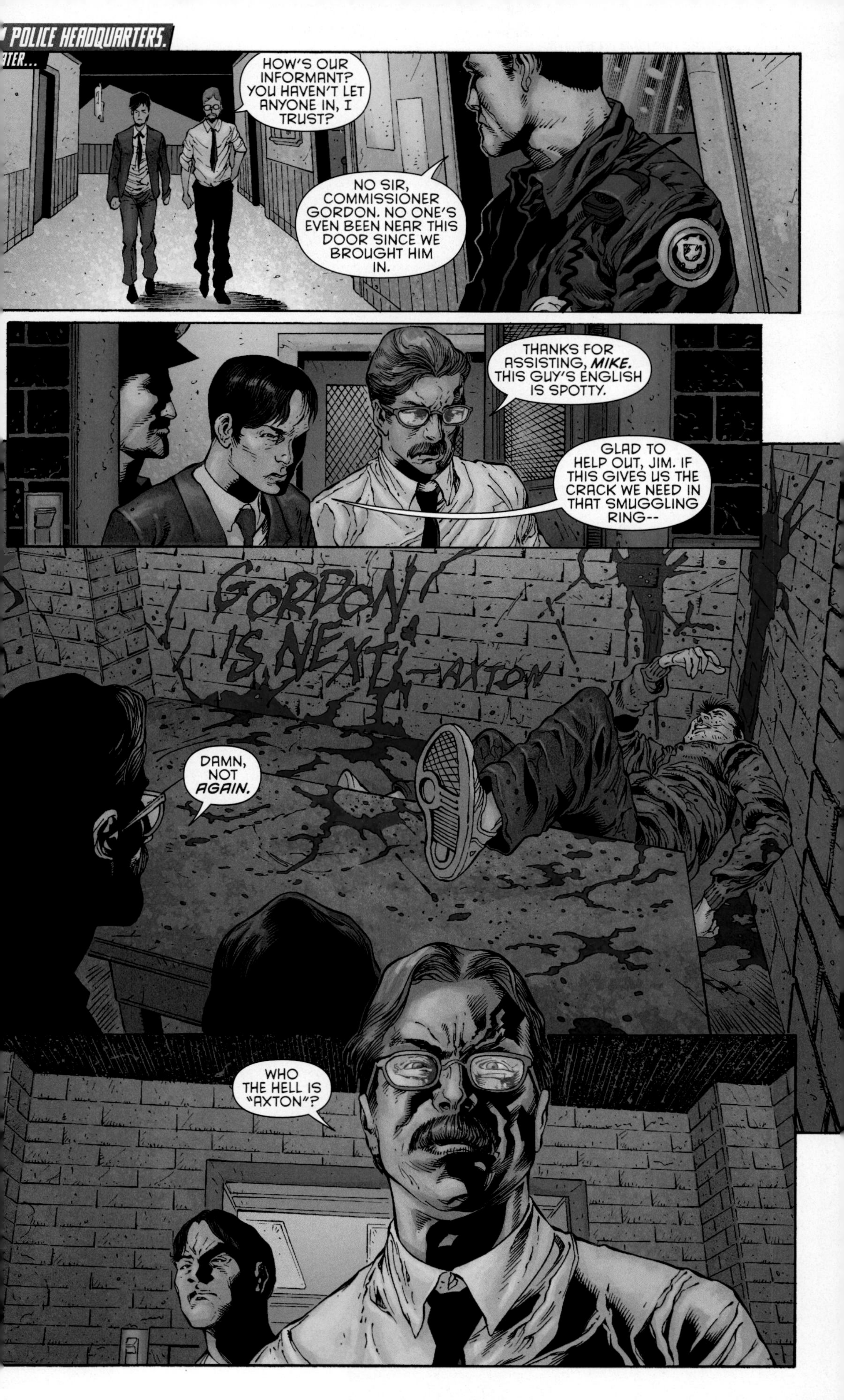
POLICE HEADQUARTERS.
ATER...
HOW'S OUR INFORMANT? YOU HAVEN'T LET ANYONE IN, I TRUST?
NO SIR, COMMISSIONER GORDON. NO ONE'S EVEN BEEN NEAR THIS DOOR SINCE WE BROUGHT HIM IN.
THANKS FOR ASSISTING, MIKE. THIS GUY'S ENGLISH IS SPOTTY.
GLAD TO HELP OUT, JIM. IF THIS GIVES US THE CRACK WE NEED IN THAT SMUGGLING RING--
GORDON IS NEXT -AXTON
DAMN, NOT AGAIN.
WHO THE HELL IS "AXTON"?

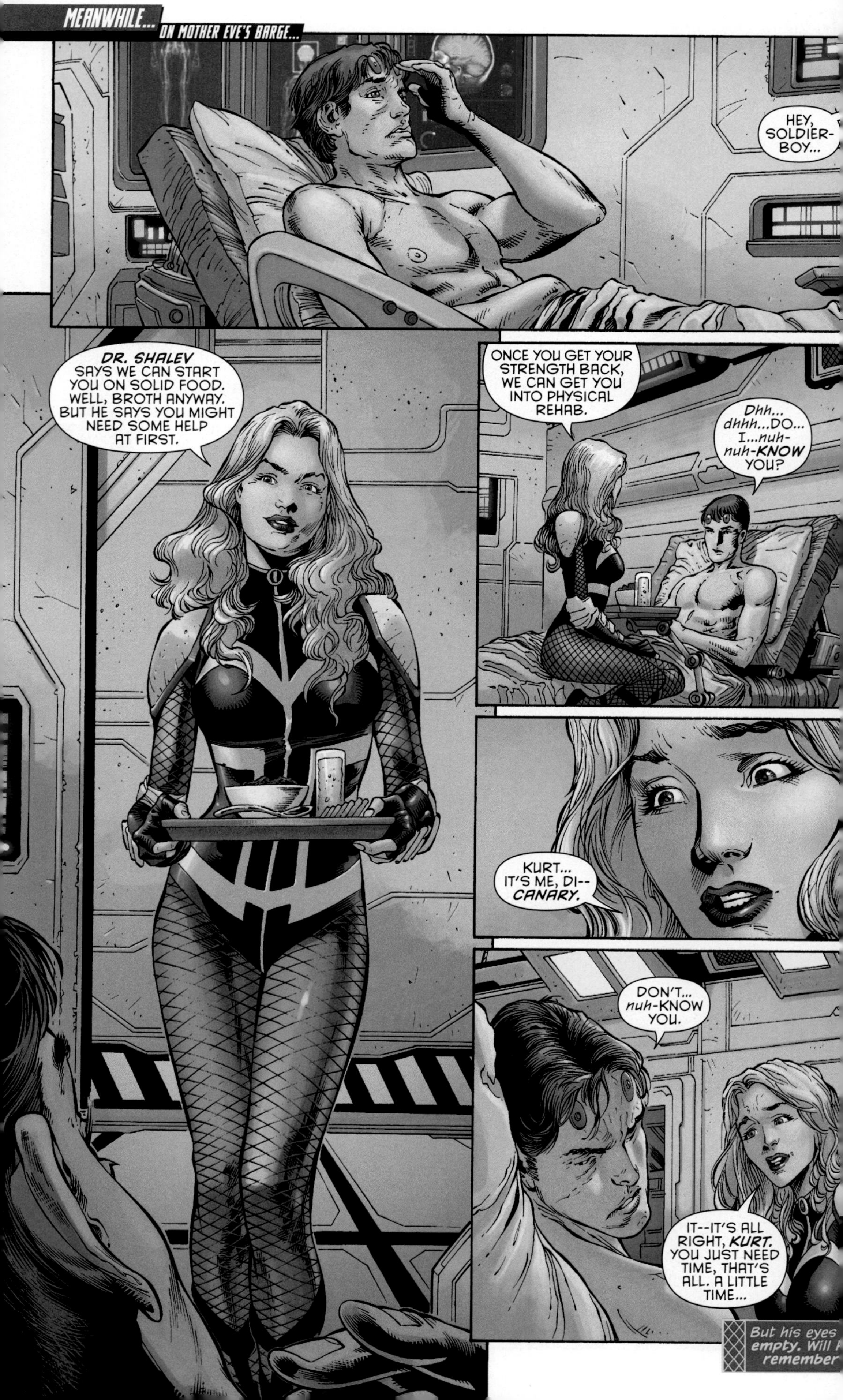
MEANWHILE...
ON MOTHER EVE'S BARGE...
HEY, SOLDIER-BOY...
DR. SHALEV SAYS WE CAN START YOU ON SOLID FOOD. WELL, BROTH ANYWAY. BUT HE SAYS YOU MIGHT NEED SOME HELP AT FIRST.
ONCE YOU GET YOUR STRENGTH BACK, WE CAN GET YOU INTO PHYSICAL REHAB.
Dhh... dhhh...DO... I...nuh-nuh-KNOW YOU?
KURT... IT'S ME, DI-- CANARY.
DON'T... nuh-KNOW YOU.
IT--IT'S ALL RIGHT, KURT. YOU JUST NEED TIME, THAT'S ALL. A LITTLE TIME...
But his eyes
empty. Will
remember

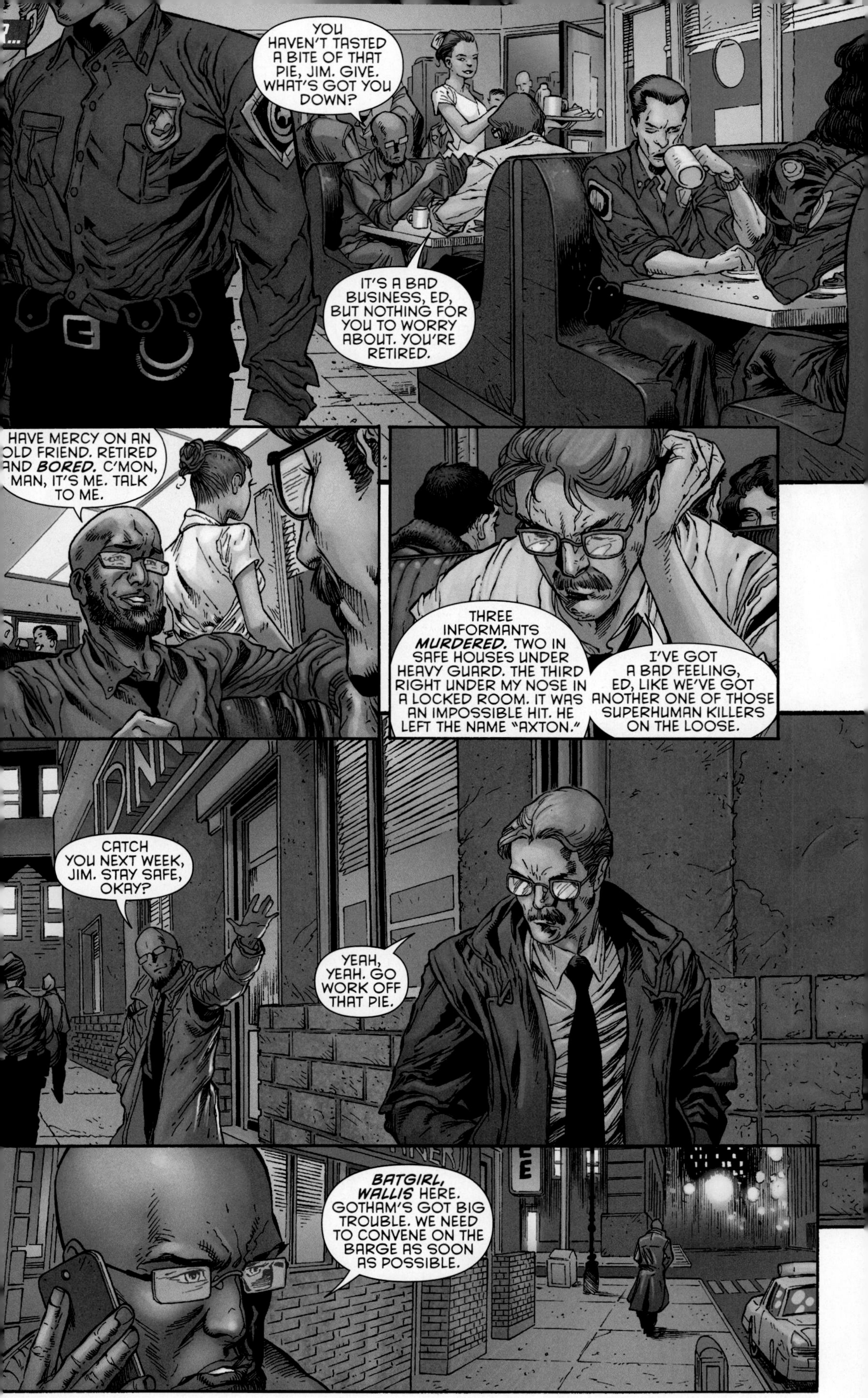

YOU HAVEN'T TASTED A BITE OF THAT PIE, JIM. GIVE. WHAT'S GOT YOU DOWN?
IT'S A BAD BUSINESS, ED, BUT NOTHING FOR YOU TO WORRY ABOUT. YOU'RE RETIRED.
HAVE MERCY ON AN OLD FRIEND. RETIRED AND BORED. C'MON, MAN, IT'S ME. TALK TO ME.
THREE INFORMANTS MURDERED. TWO IN SAFE HOUSES UNDER HEAVY GUARD. THE THIRD RIGHT UNDER MY NOSE IN A LOCKED ROOM. IT WAS AN IMPOSSIBLE HIT. HE LEFT THE NAME "AXTON."
I'VE GOT A BAD FEELING, ED, LIKE WE'VE GOT ANOTHER ONE OF THOSE SUPERHUMAN KILLERS ON THE LOOSE.
CATCH YOU NEXT WEEK, JIM. STAY SAFE, OKAY?
YEAH, YEAH. GO WORK OFF THAT PIE.
BATGIRL, WALLIS HERE. GOTHAM'S GOT BIG TROUBLE. WE NEED TO CONVENE ON THE BARGE AS SOON AS POSSIBLE.

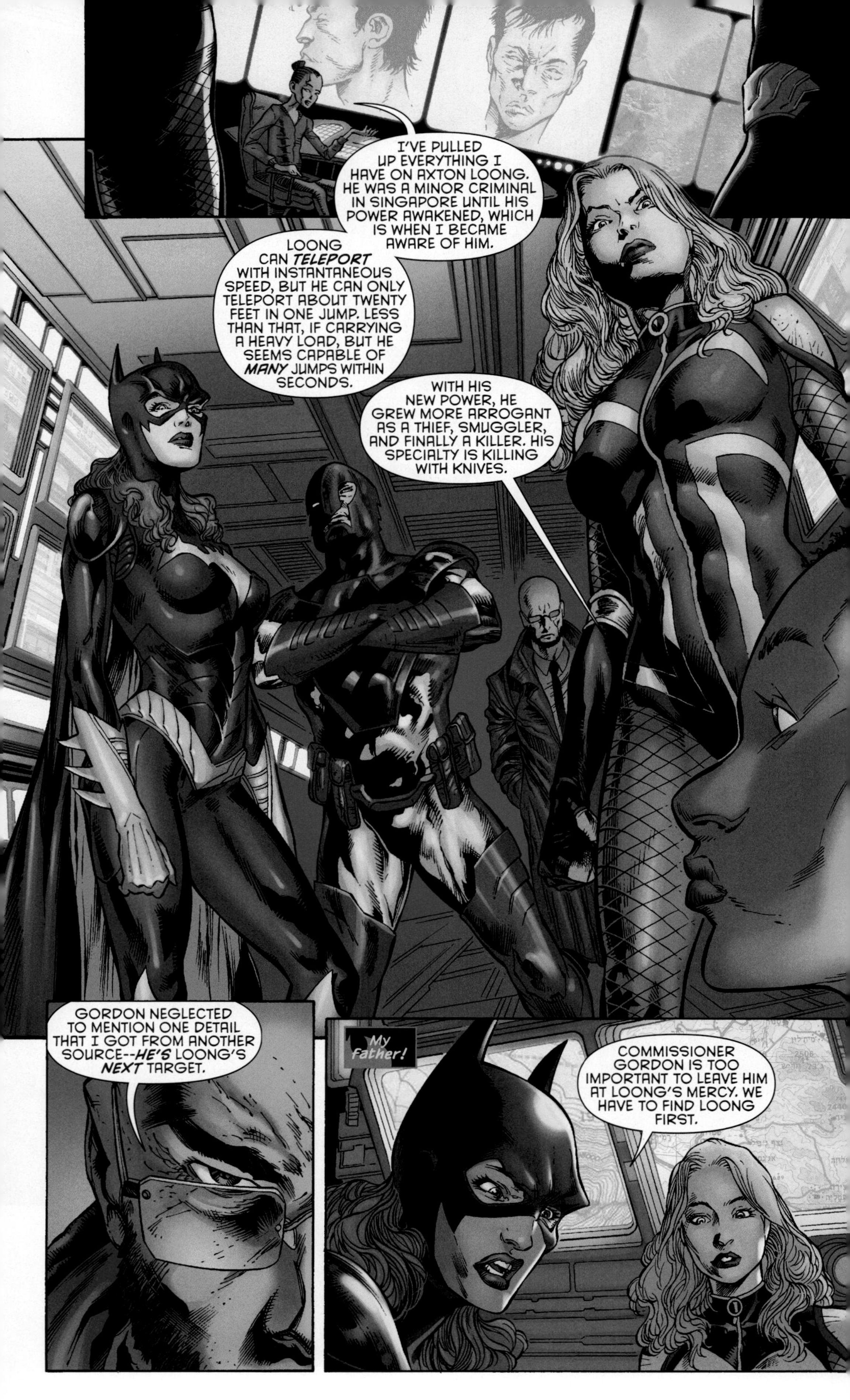
I'VE PULLED UP EVERYTHING I HAVE ON AXTON LOONG. HE WAS A MINOR CRIMINAL IN SINGAPORE UNTIL HIS POWER AWAKENED, WHICH IS WHEN I BECAME AWARE OF HIM.
LOONG CAN *TELEPORT* WITH INSTANTANEOUS SPEED, BUT HE CAN ONLY TELEPORT ABOUT TWENTY FEET IN ONE JUMP. LESS THAN THAT, IF CARRYING A HEAVY LOAD, BUT HE SEEMS CAPABLE OF *MANY* JUMPS WITHIN SECONDS.
WITH HIS NEW POWER, HE GREW MORE ARROGANT AS A THIEF, SMUGGLER, AND FINALLY A KILLER. HIS SPECIALTY IS KILLING WITH KNIVES.
GORDON NEGLECTED TO MENTION ONE DETAIL THAT I GOT FROM ANOTHER SOURCE--*HE'S* LOONG'S *NEXT* TARGET.
My father!
COMMISSIONER GORDON IS TOO IMPORTANT TO LEAVE HIM AT LOONG'S MERCY. WE HAVE TO FIND LOONG FIRST.

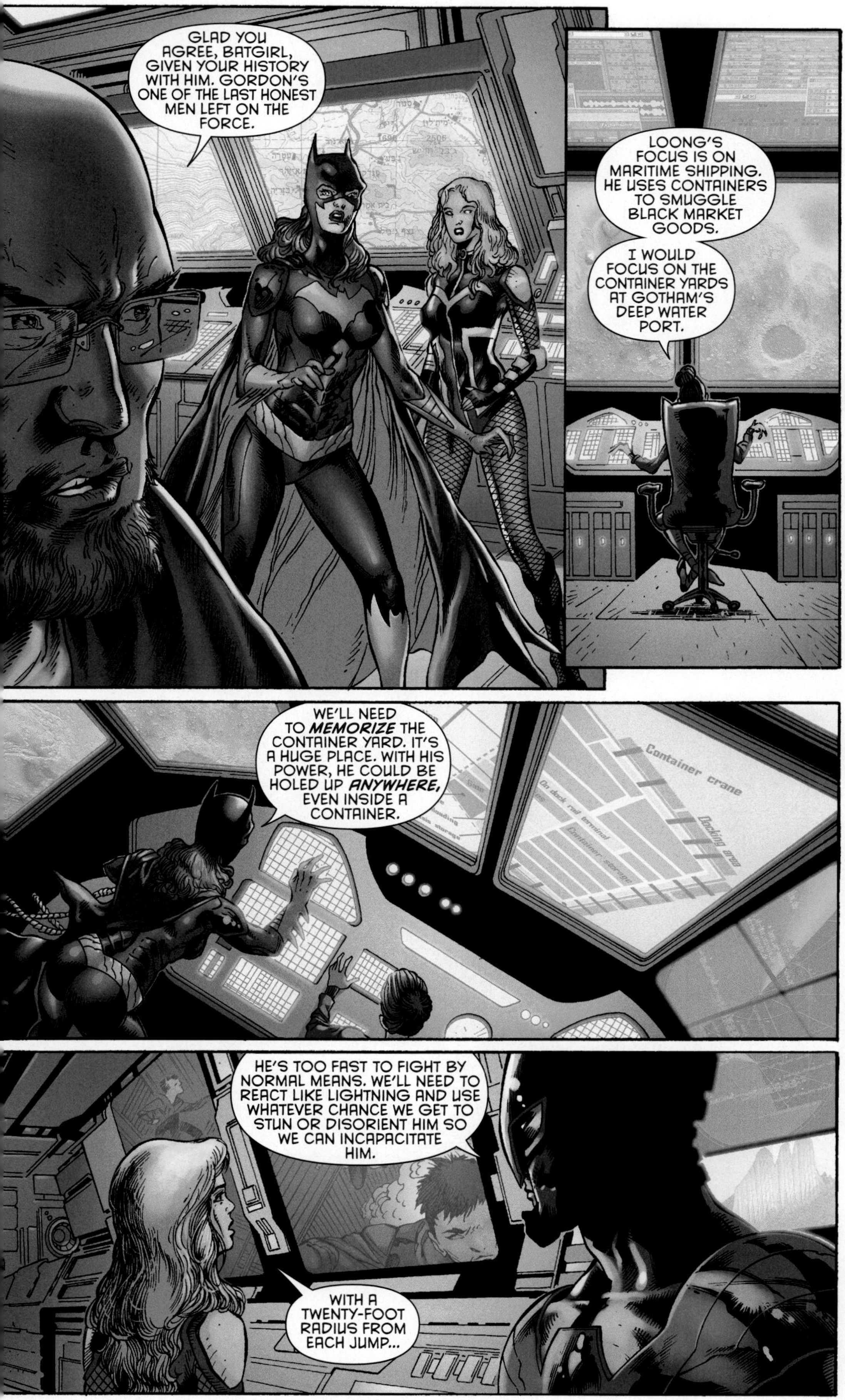
GLAD YOU AGREE, BATGIRL, GIVEN YOUR HISTORY WITH HIM. GORDON'S ONE OF THE LAST HONEST MEN LEFT ON THE FORCE.
LOONG'S FOCUS IS ON MARITIME SHIPPING. HE USES CONTAINERS TO SMUGGLE BLACK MARKET GOODS.
I WOULD FOCUS ON THE CONTAINER YARDS AT GOTHAM'S DEEP WATER PORT.
WE'LL NEED TO ***MEMORIZE*** THE CONTAINER YARD. IT'S A HUGE PLACE. WITH HIS POWER, HE COULD BE HOLED UP ***ANYWHERE,*** EVEN INSIDE A CONTAINER.
Container crane
On dock rail terminal
Container storage
Docking area
HE'S TOO FAST TO FIGHT BY NORMAL MEANS. WE'LL NEED TO REACT LIKE LIGHTNING AND USE WHATEVER CHANCE WE GET TO STUN OR DISORIENT HIM SO WE CAN INCAPACITATE HIM.
WITH A TWENTY-FOOT RADIUS FROM EACH JUMP...

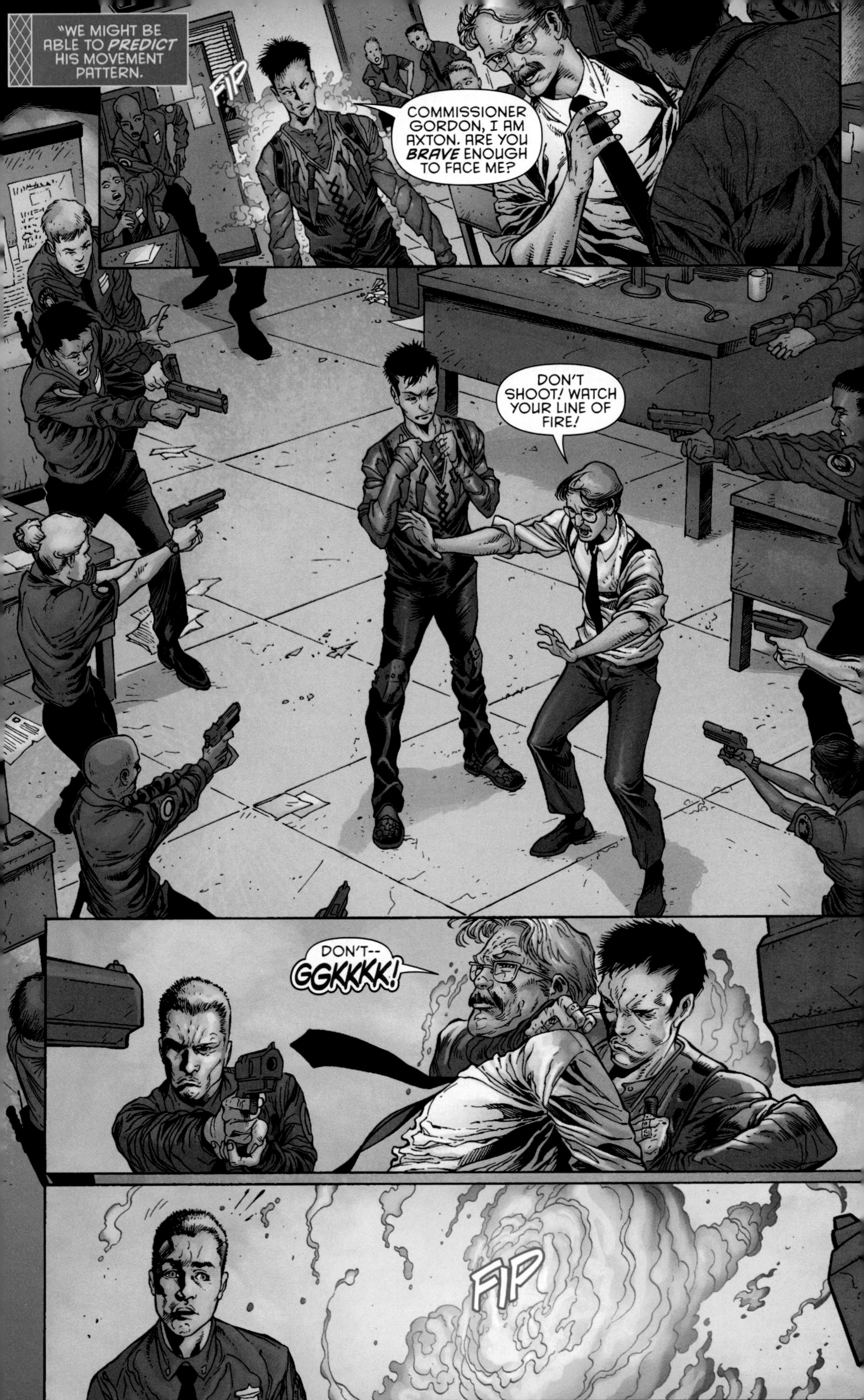
"WE MIGHT BE ABLE TO *PREDICT* HIS MOVEMENT PATTERN.
FIP
COMMISSIONER GORDON, I AM AXTON. ARE YOU *BRAVE* ENOUGH TO FACE ME?
DON'T SHOOT! WATCH YOUR LINE OF FIRE!
DON'T-- GGKKKK!
FIP

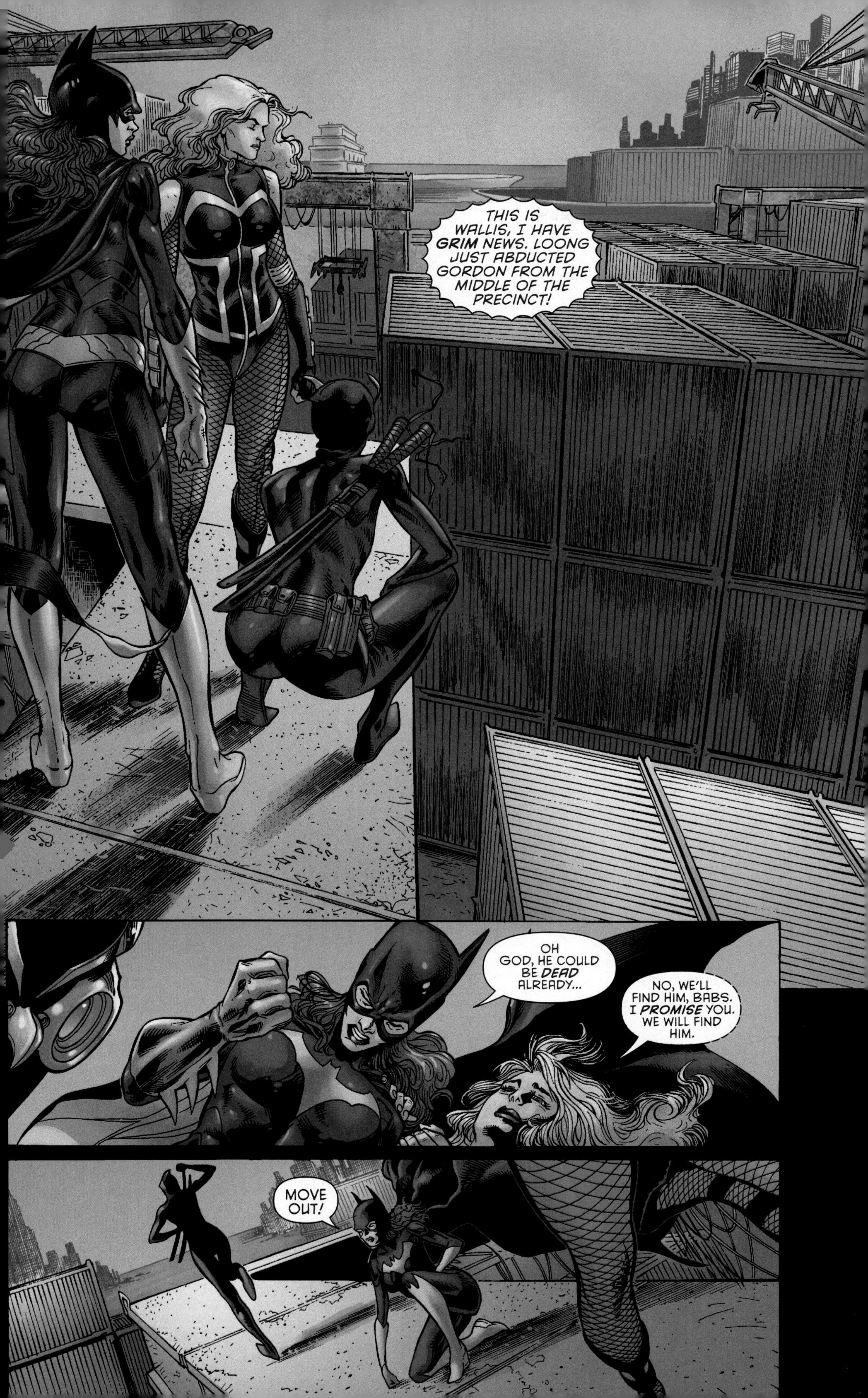
THIS IS WALLIS, I HAVE GRIM NEWS. LOONG JUST ABDUCTED GORDON FROM THE MIDDLE OF THE PRECINCT!
OH GOD, HE COULD BE DEAD ALREADY...
NO, WE'LL FIND HIM, BABS. I PROMISE YOU. WE WILL FIND HIM.
MOVE OUT!

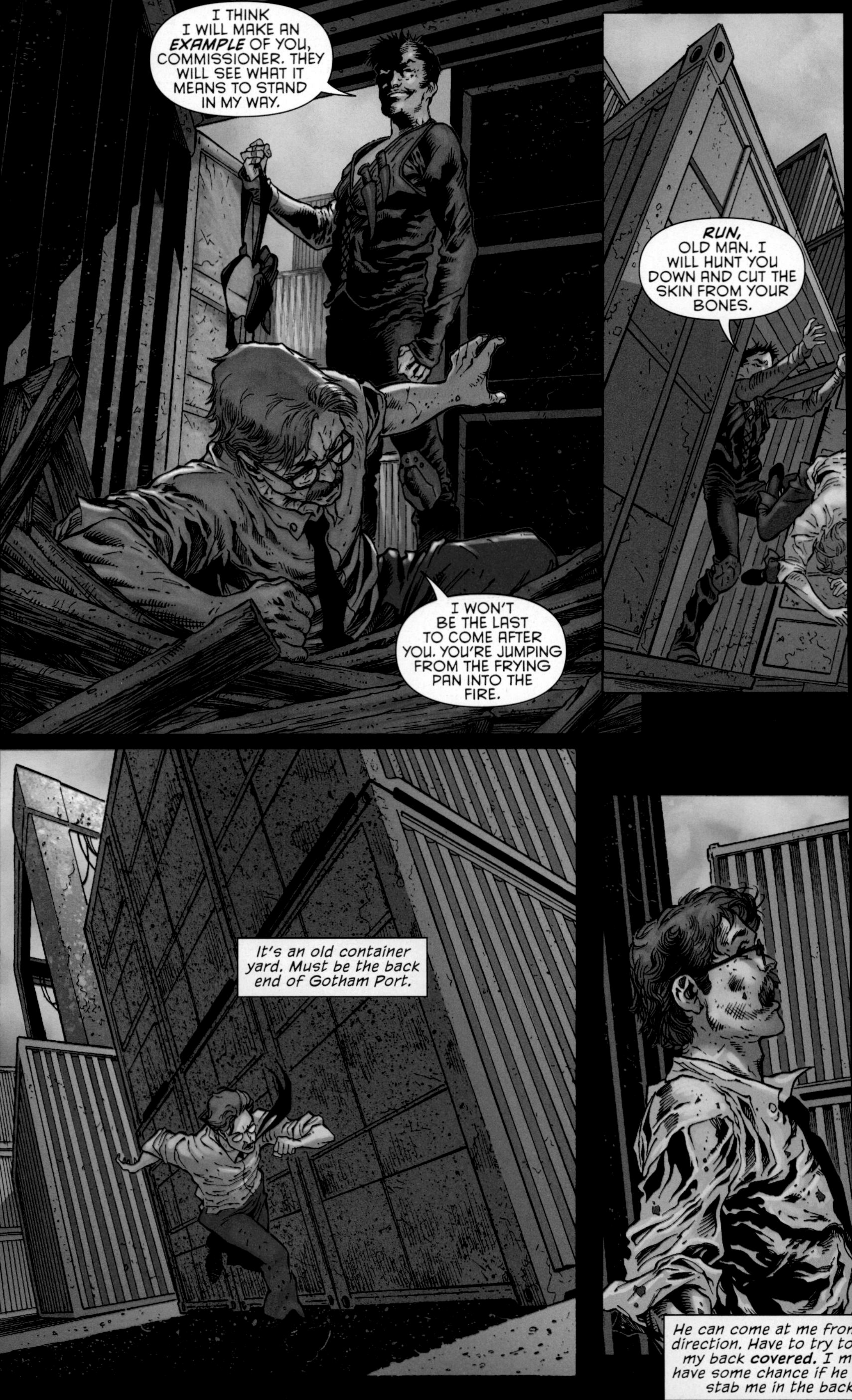

I THINK I WILL MAKE AN *EXAMPLE* OF YOU, COMMISSIONER. THEY WILL SEE WHAT IT MEANS TO STAND IN MY WAY.
I WON'T BE THE LAST TO COME AFTER YOU. YOU'RE JUMPING FROM THE FRYING PAN INTO THE FIRE.
RUN, OLD MAN. I WILL HUNT YOU DOWN AND CUT THE SKIN FROM YOUR BONES.
It's an old container yard. Must be the back end of Gotham Port.
He can come at me fro
direction. Have to try to
my back ***covered.*** *I m*
have some chance if he
stab me in the back

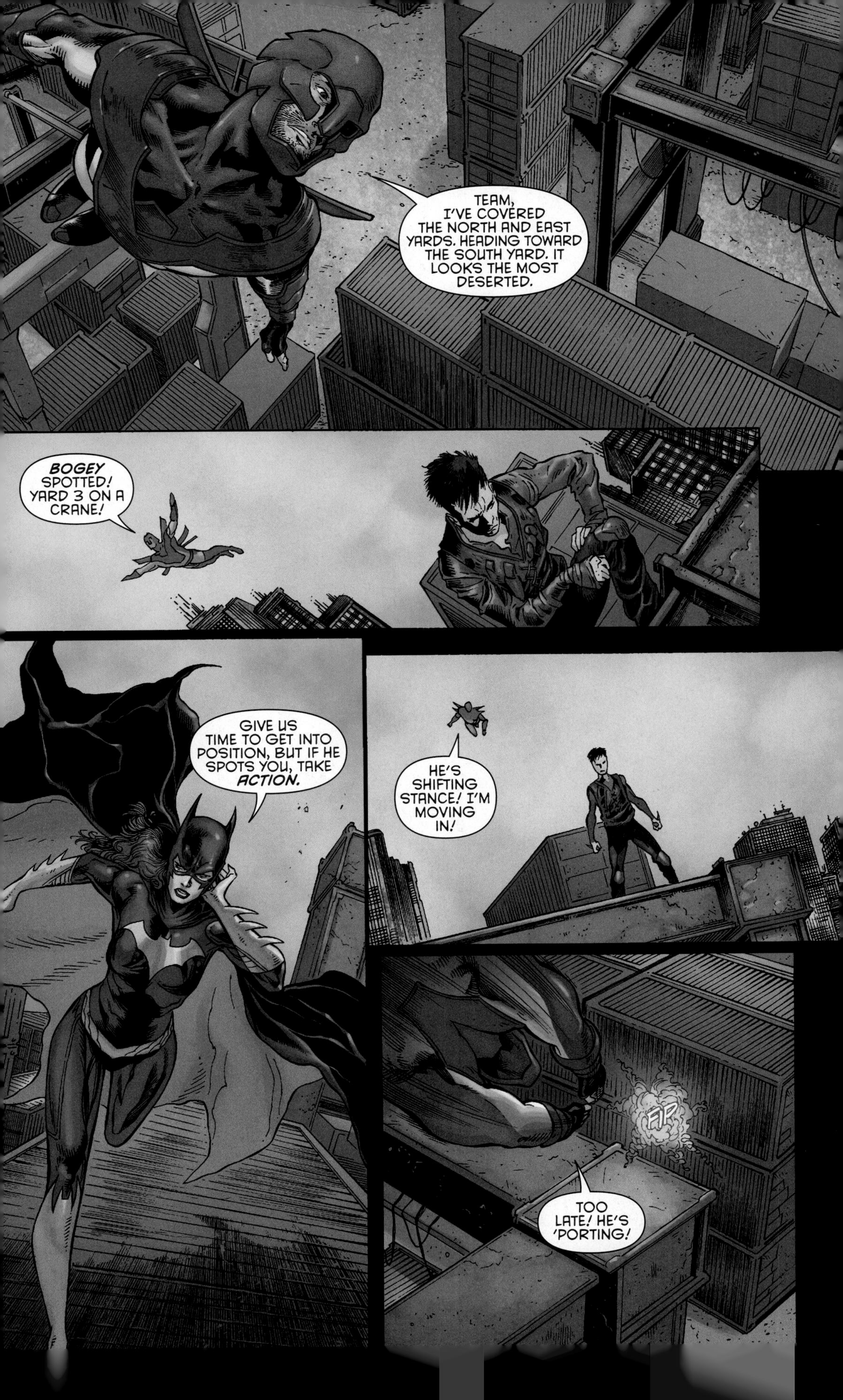
TEAM, I'VE COVERED THE NORTH AND EAST YARDS. HEADING TOWARD THE SOUTH YARD. IT LOOKS THE MOST DESERTED.
BOGEY SPOTTED! YARD 3 ON A CRANE!
GIVE US TIME TO GET INTO POSITION, BUT IF HE SPOTS YOU, TAKE *ACTION.*
HE'S SHIFTING STANCE! I'M MOVING IN!
FIP
TOO LATE! HE'S 'PORTING!

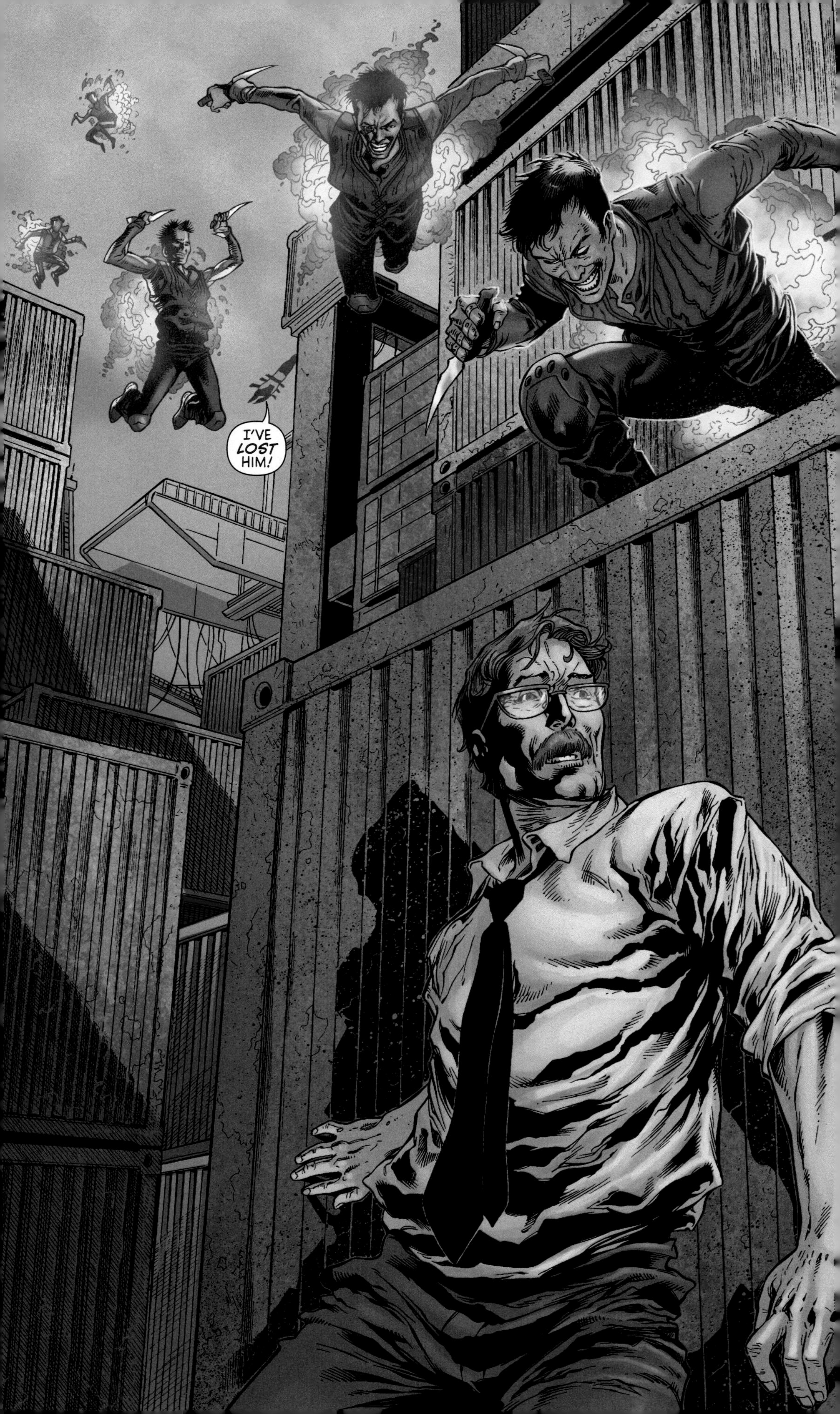
I'VE LOST HIM!

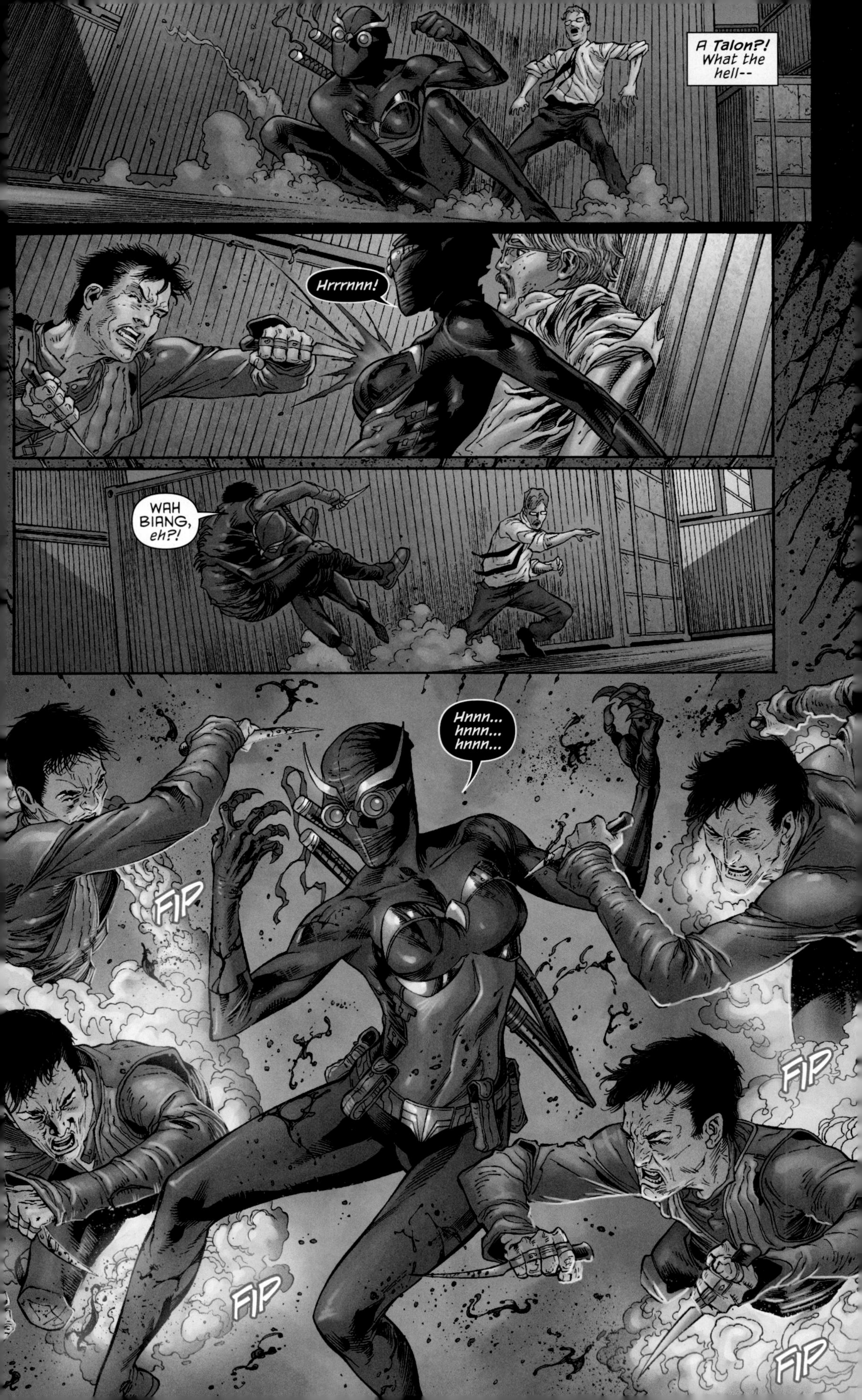
A Talon?! What the hell--
Hrrrnnn!
WAH BIANG, eh?!
Hnnn... hnnn... hnnn...
FIP
FIP
FIP
FIP

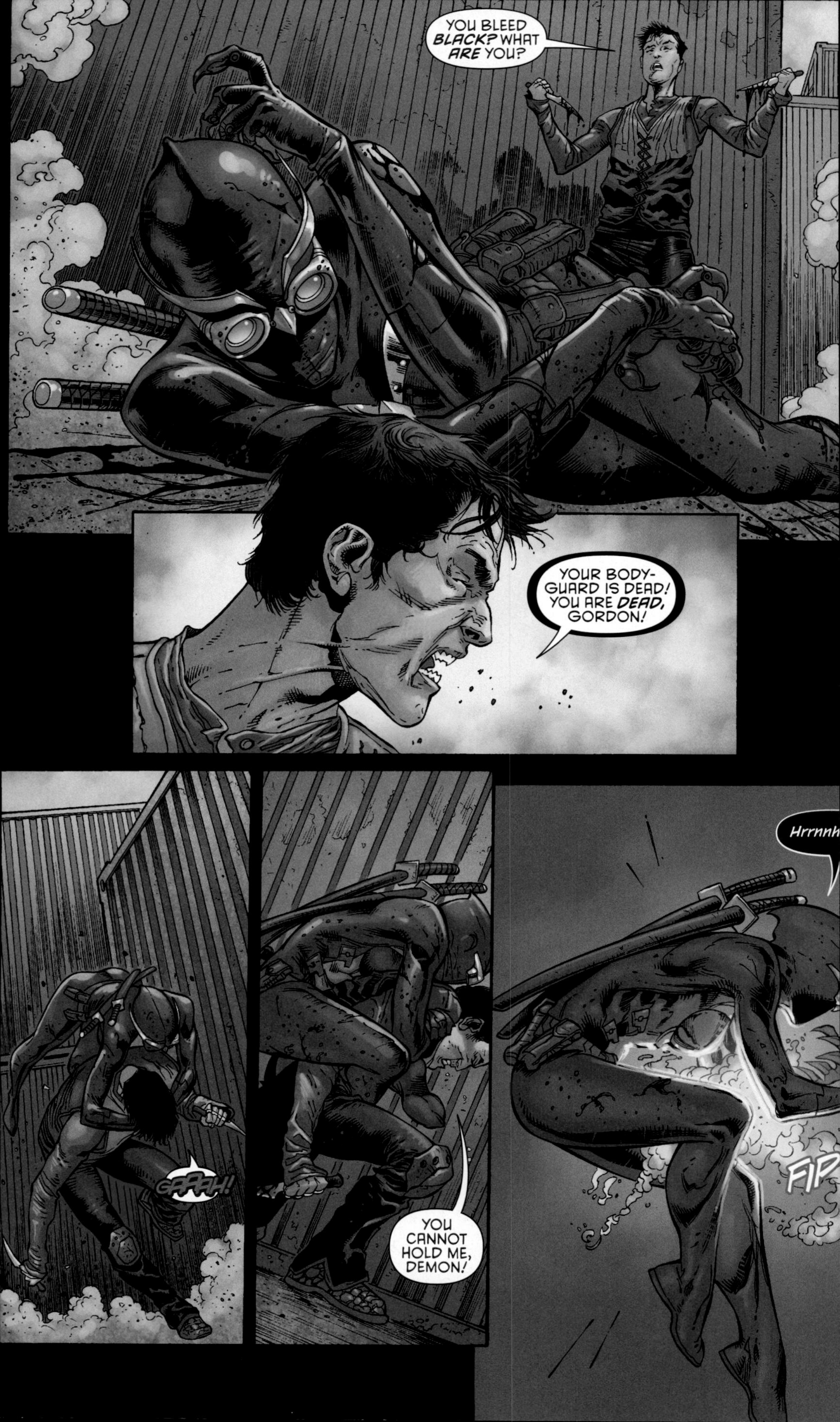
YOU BLEED BLACK? WHAT ARE YOU?
YOUR BODY-GUARD IS DEAD! YOU ARE DEAD, GORDON!
GRAAH!
YOU CANNOT HOLD ME, DEMON!
Hrrnnh
FIP

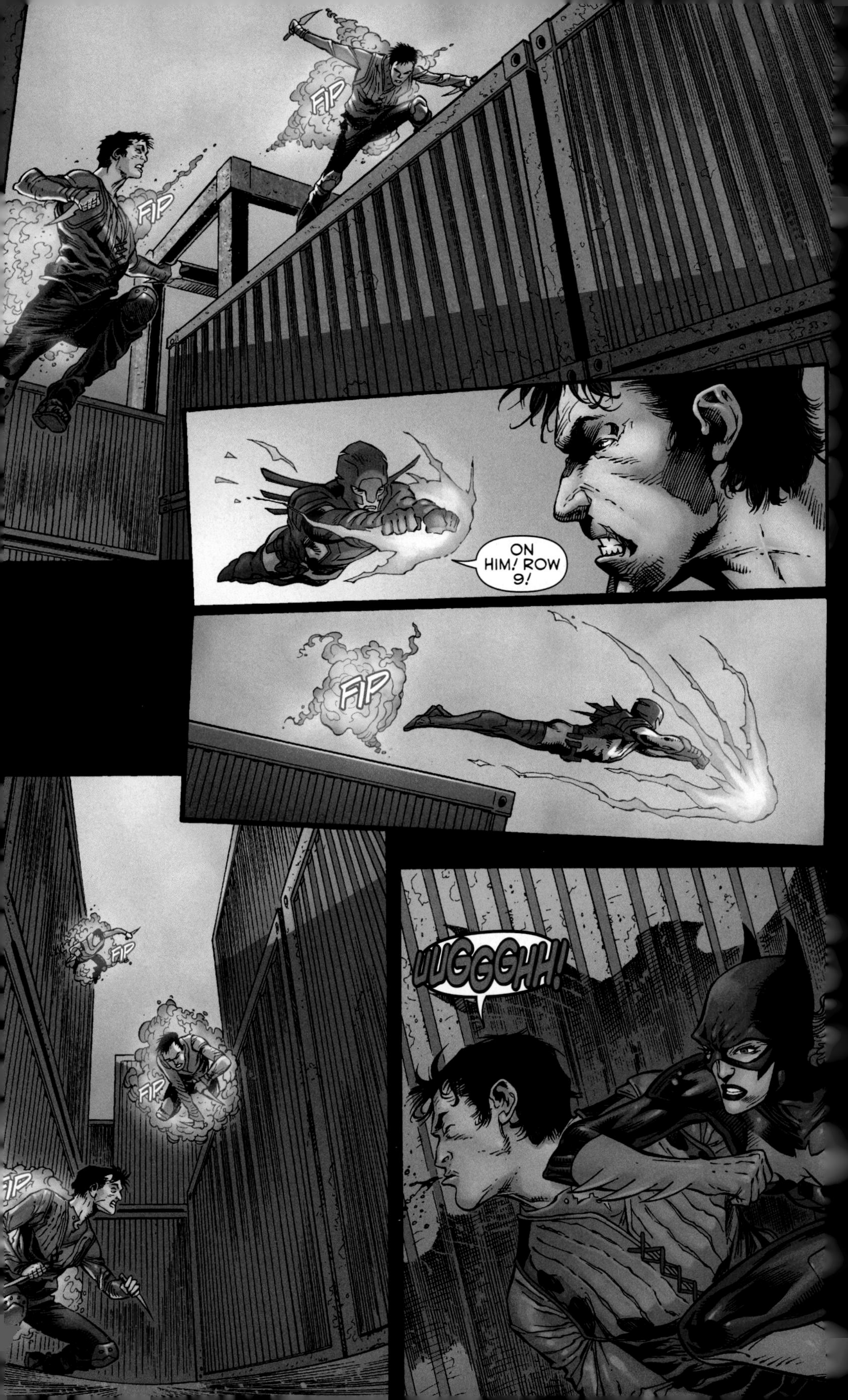
FIP
FIP
ON HIM! ROW 9!
FIP
FIP
FIP
FIP
UUGGGHH!

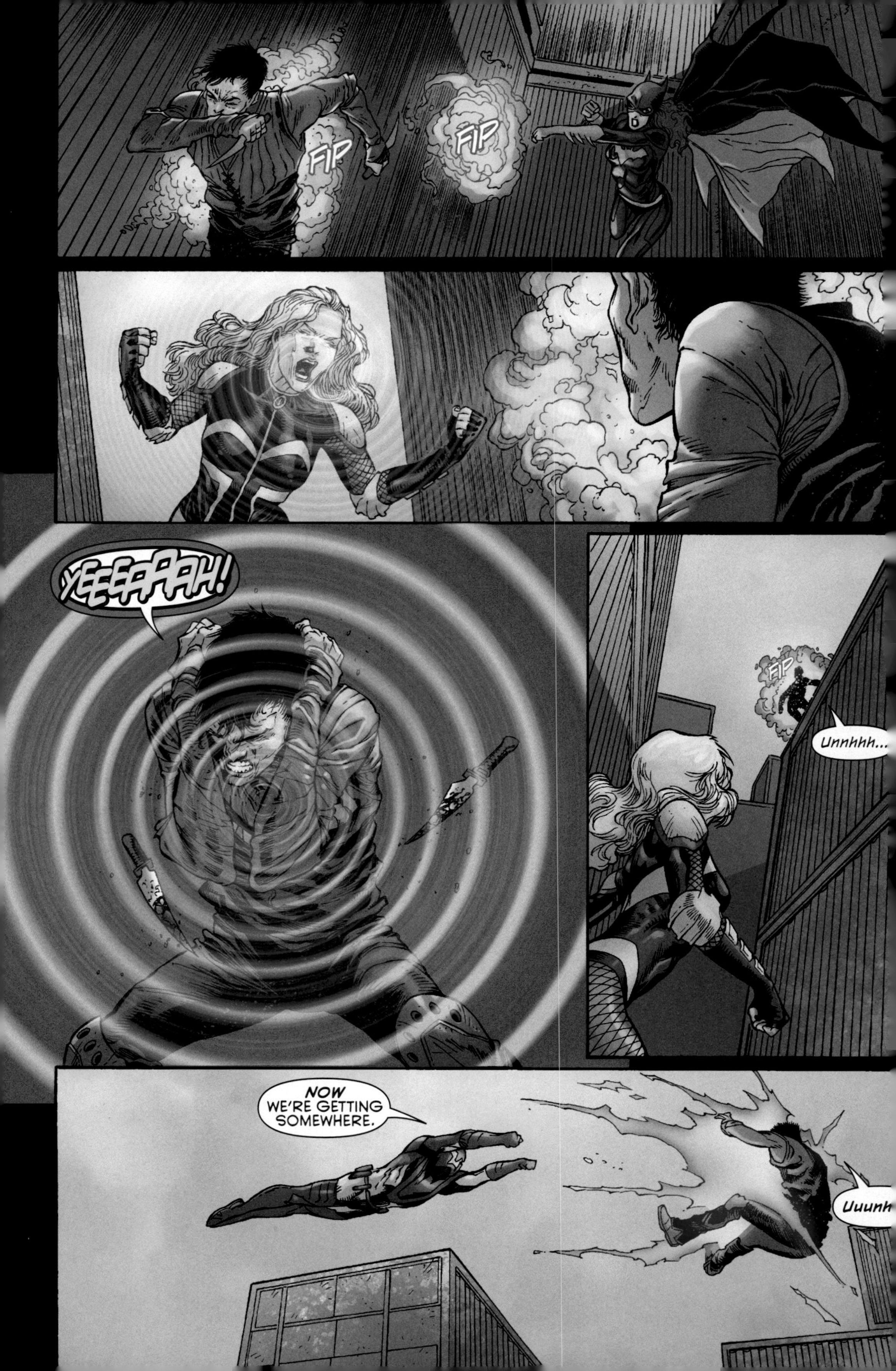
FIP
FIP
YEEEAAAAH!
FIP
Unnhhh...
NOW WE'RE GETTING SOMEWHERE.
Uuunh

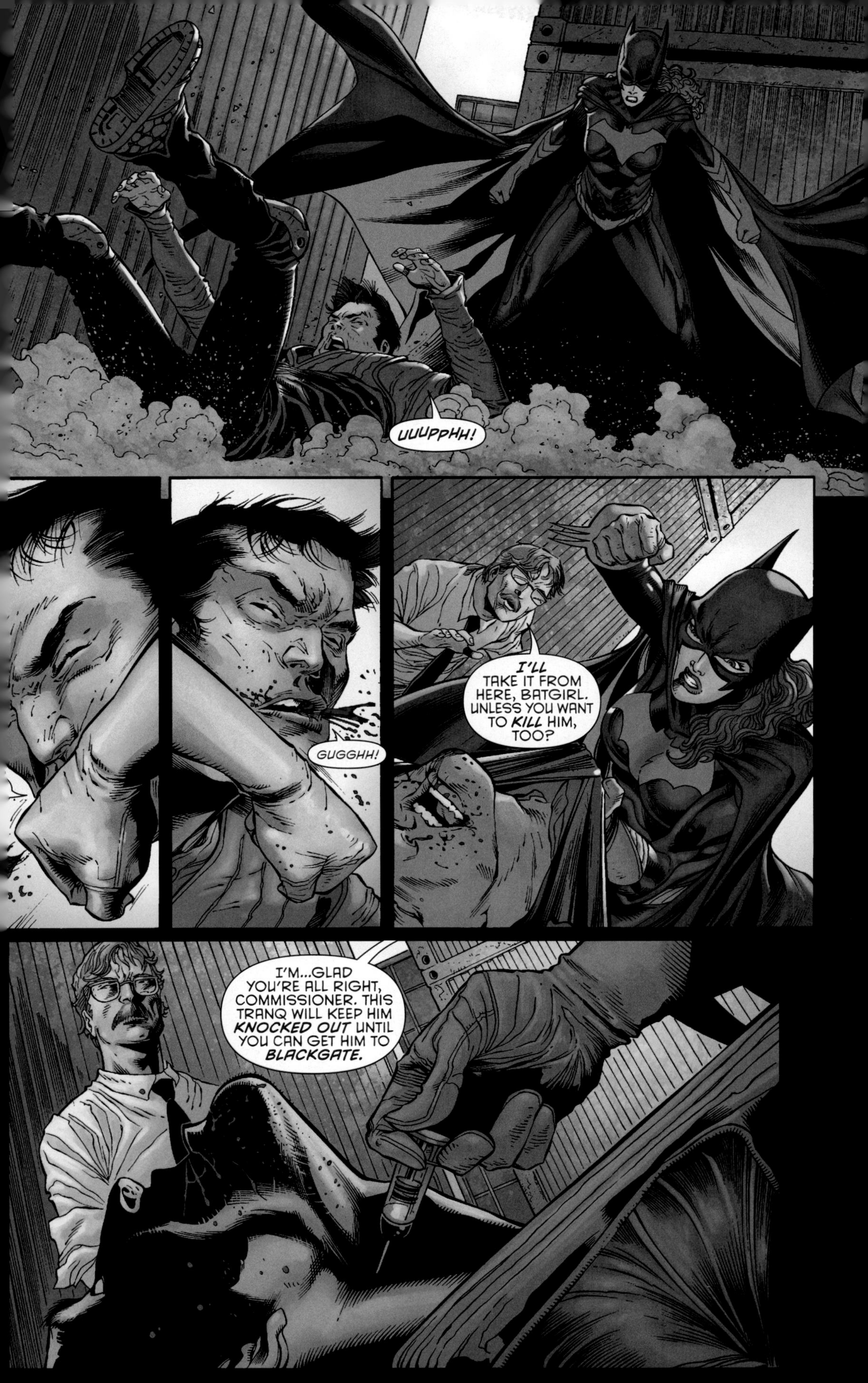
UUUPPHH!
GUGGHH!
I'LL TAKE IT FROM HERE, BATGIRL. UNLESS YOU WANT TO KILL HIM, TOO?
I'M...GLAD YOU'RE ALL RIGHT, COMMISSIONER. THIS TRANQ WILL KEEP HIM KNOCKED OUT UNTIL YOU CAN GET HIM TO BLACKGATE.

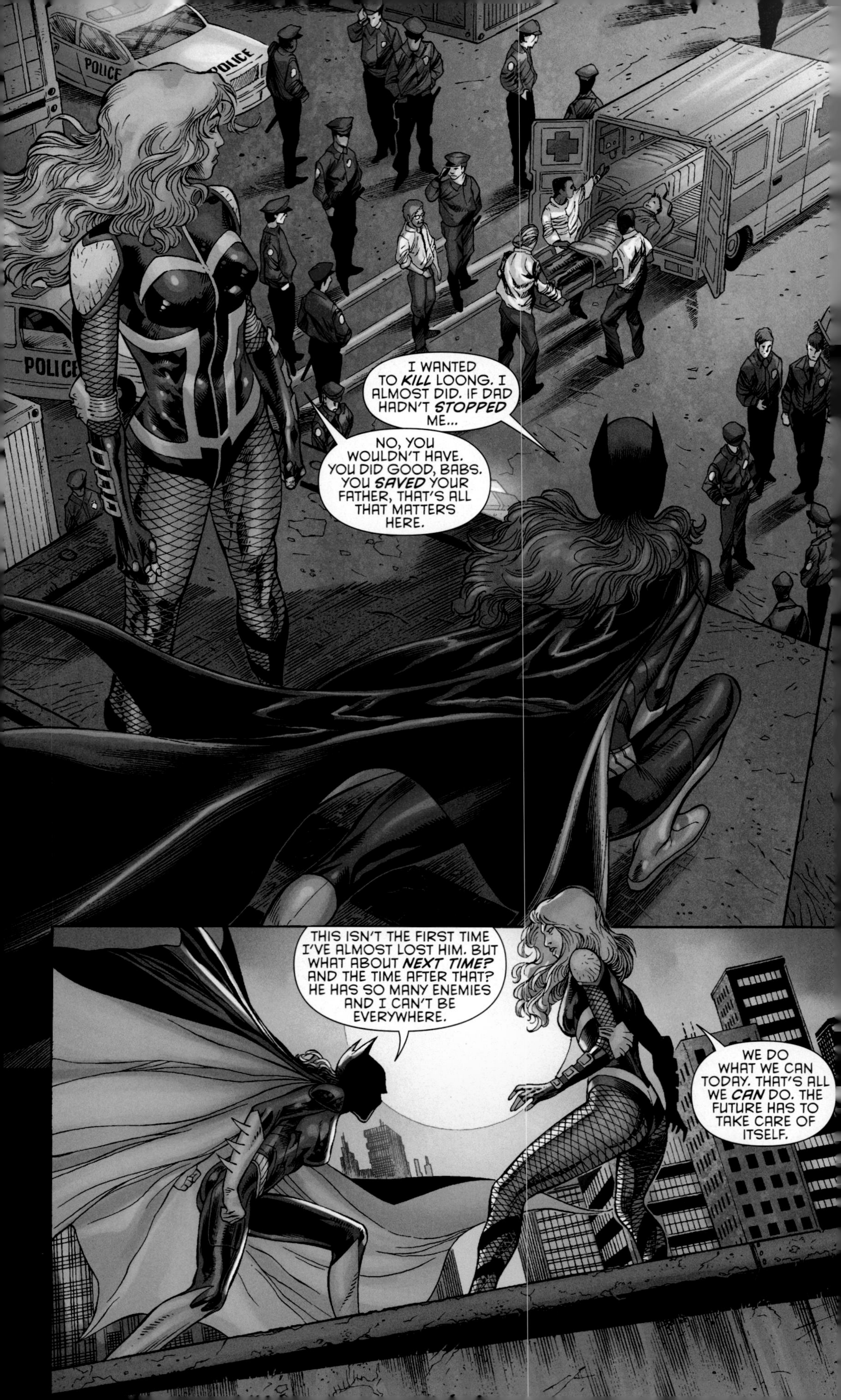
POLICE
POLICE
POLICE
I WANTED TO KILL LOONG. I ALMOST DID. IF DAD HADN'T STOPPED ME...
NO, YOU WOULDN'T HAVE. YOU DID GOOD, BABS. YOU SAVED YOUR FATHER, THAT'S ALL THAT MATTERS HERE.
THIS ISN'T THE FIRST TIME I'VE ALMOST LOST HIM. BUT WHAT ABOUT NEXT TIME? AND THE TIME AFTER THAT? HE HAS SO MANY ENEMIES AND I CAN'T BE EVERYWHERE.
WE DO WHAT WE CAN TODAY. THAT'S ALL WE CAN DO. THE FUTURE HAS TO TAKE CARE OF ITSELF.

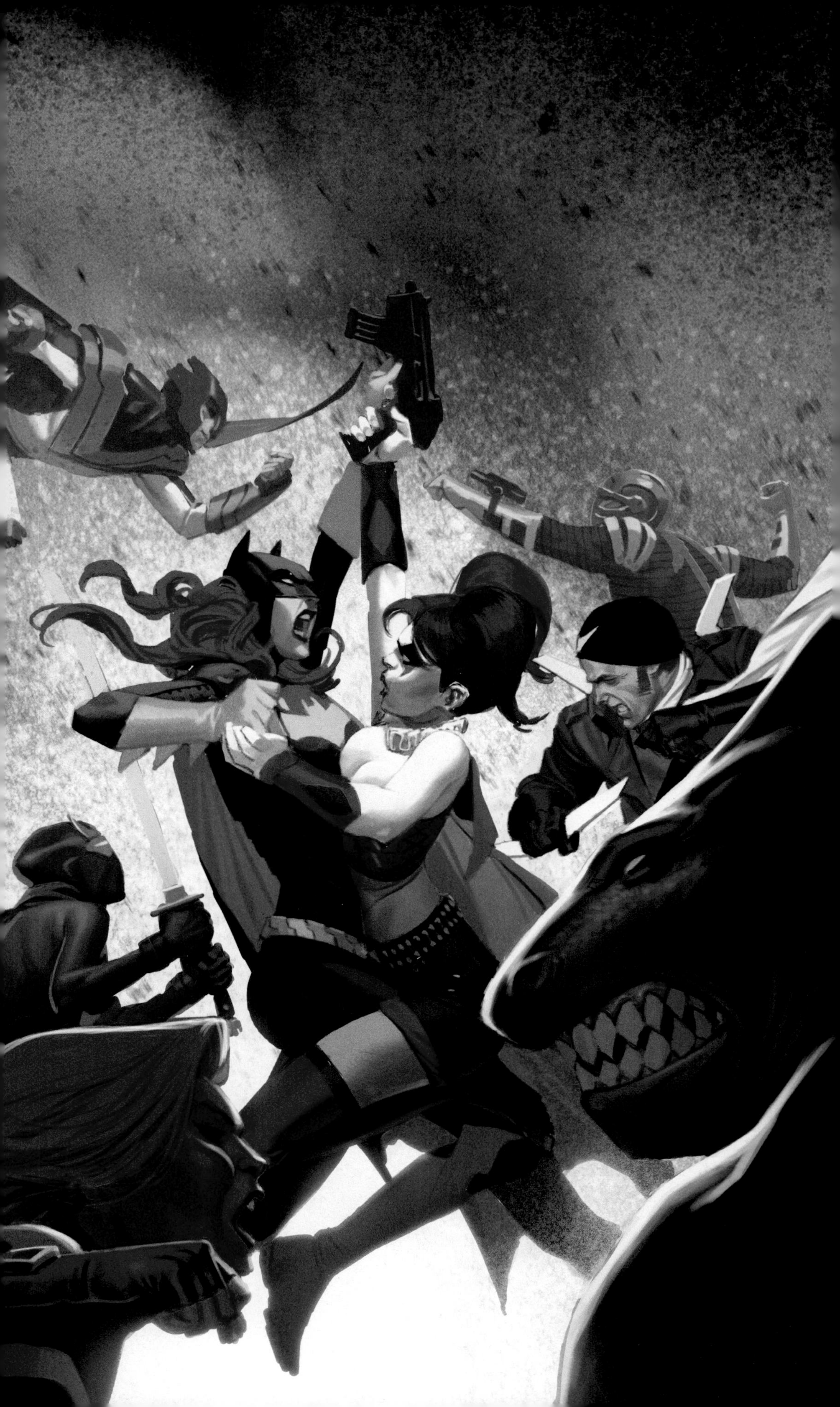

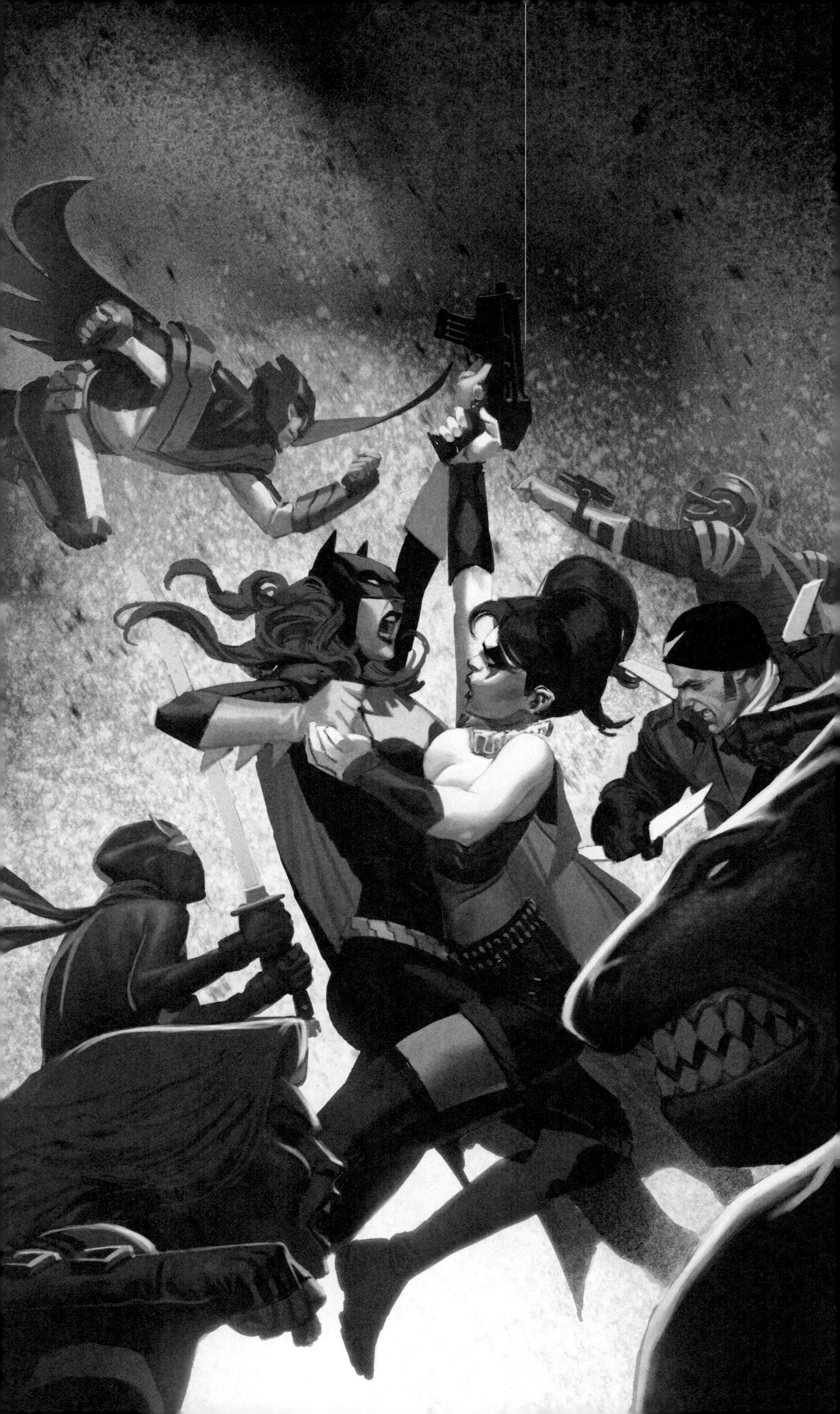

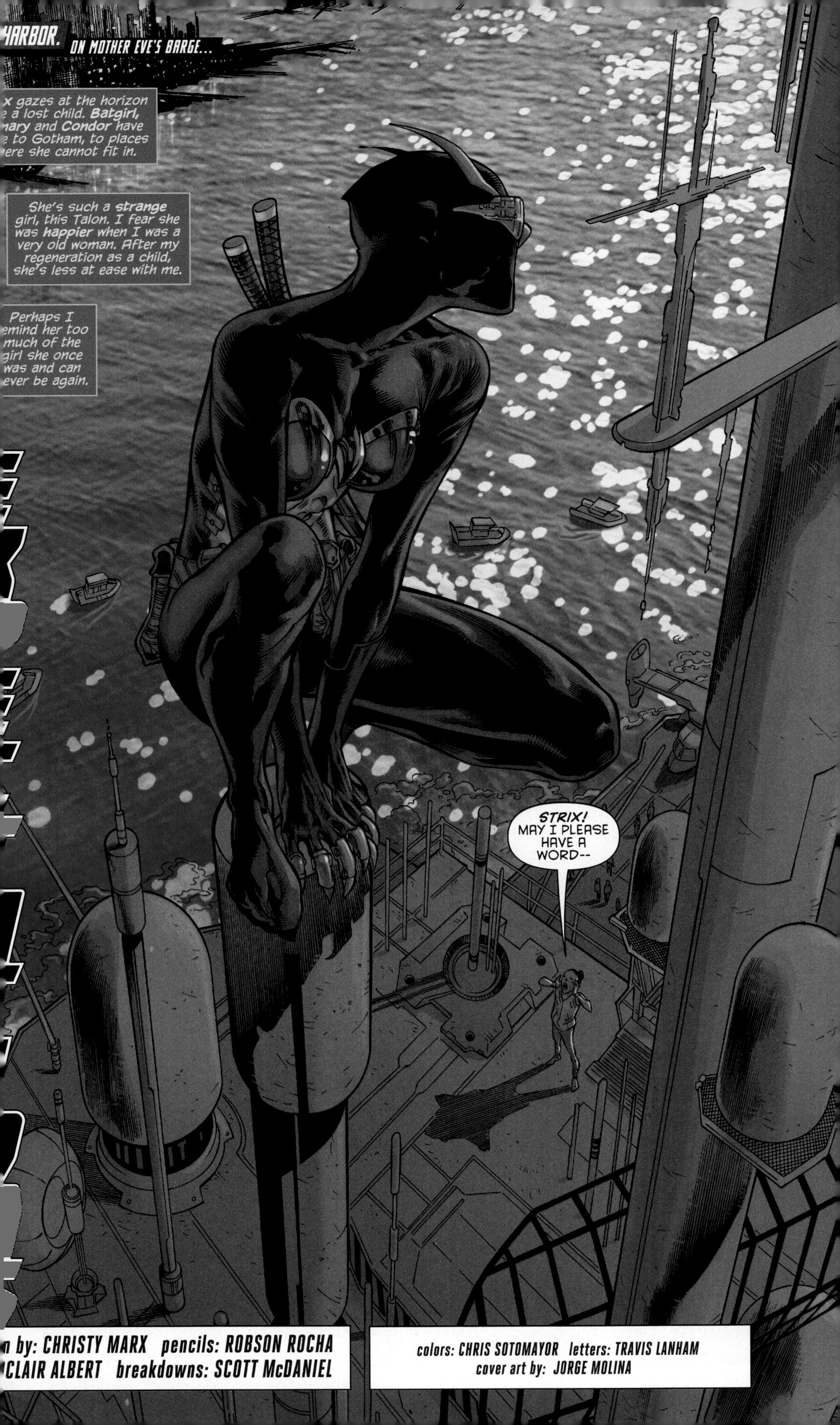

HARBOR. ON MOTHER EVE'S BARGE...
x gazes at the horizon e a lost child. Batgirl, nary and Condor have e to Gotham, to places ere she cannot fit in.
She's such a strange girl, this Talon. I fear she was happier when I was a very old woman. After my regeneration as a child, she's less at ease with me.
Perhaps I emind her too much of the girl she once was and can ever be again.
STRIX! MAY I PLEASE HAVE A WORD--
n by: CHRISTY MARX pencils: ROBSON ROCHA
CLAIR ALBERT breakdowns: SCOTT McDANIEL
colors: CHRIS SOTOMAYOR letters: TRAVIS LANHAM
cover art by: JORGE MOLINA

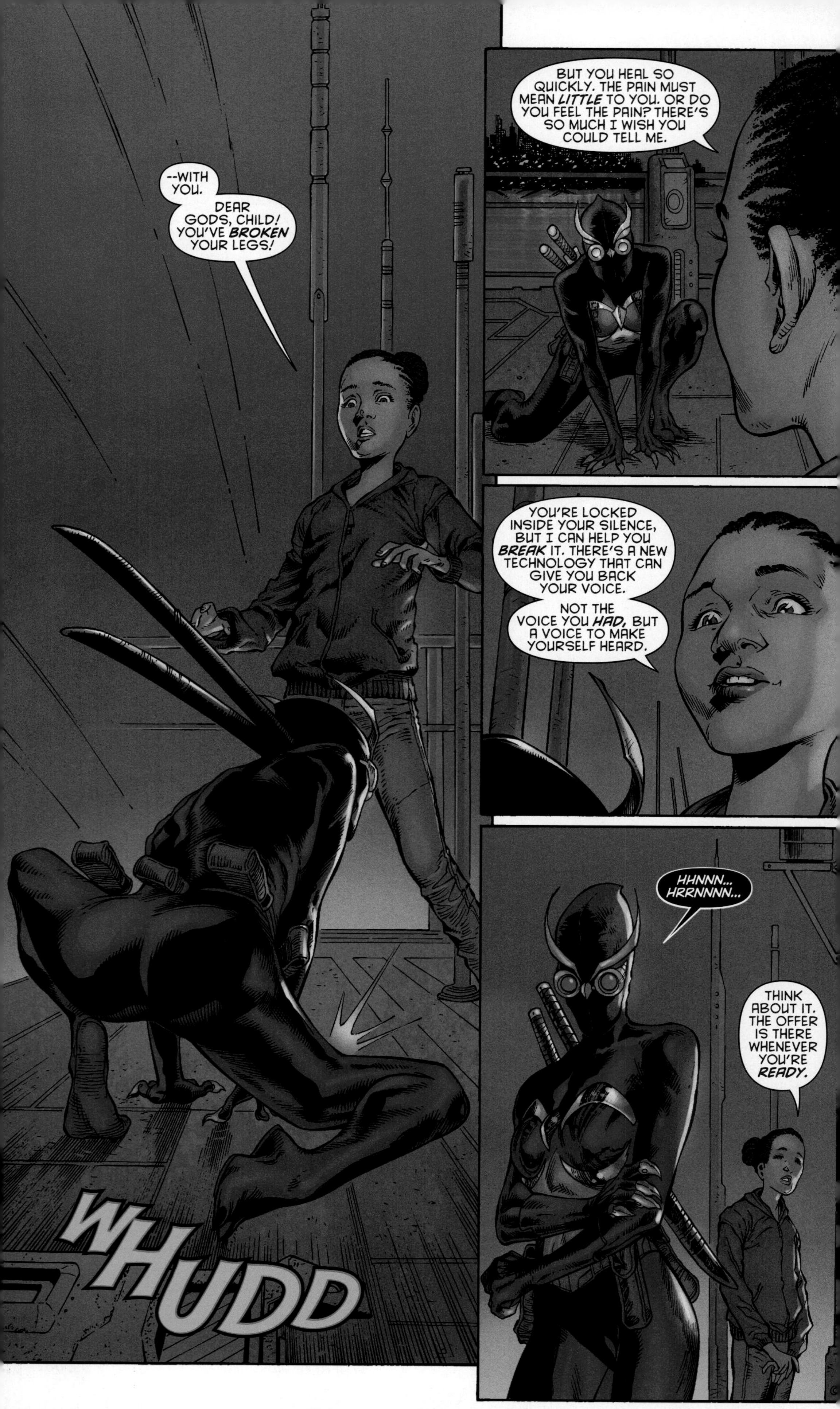
--WITH YOU.
DEAR GODS, CHILD! YOU'VE *BROKEN* YOUR LEGS!
WHUDD
BUT YOU HEAL SO QUICKLY. THE PAIN MUST MEAN *LITTLE* TO YOU. OR DO YOU FEEL THE PAIN? THERE'S SO MUCH I WISH YOU COULD TELL ME.
YOU'RE LOCKED INSIDE YOUR SILENCE, BUT I CAN HELP YOU *BREAK* IT. THERE'S A NEW TECHNOLOGY THAT CAN GIVE YOU BACK YOUR VOICE.
NOT THE VOICE YOU *HAD,* BUT A VOICE TO MAKE YOURSELF HEARD.
HHNNN... HRRNNNN...
THINK ABOUT IT. THE OFFER IS THERE WHENEVER YOU'RE *READY.*

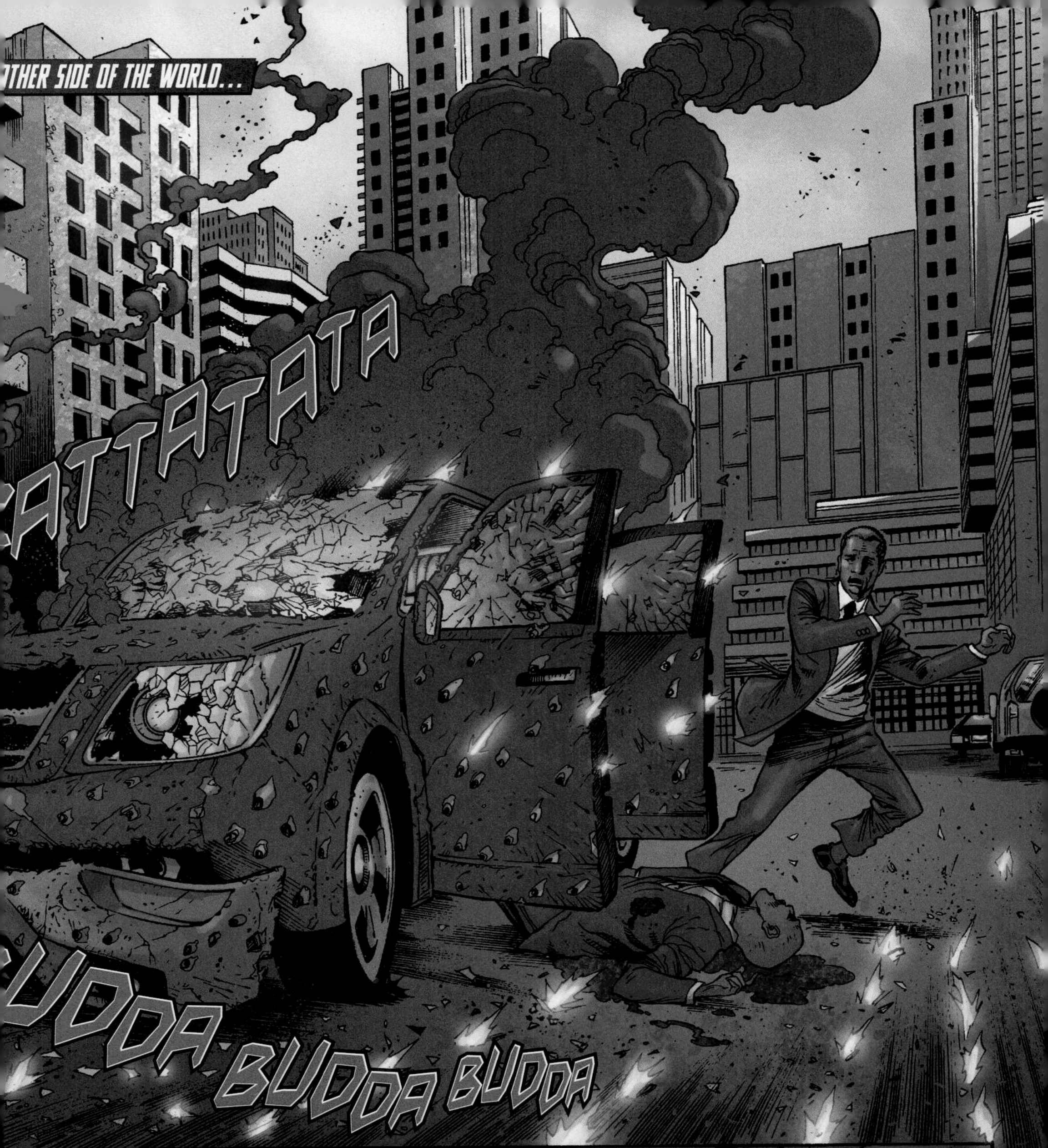
OTHER SIDE OF THE WORLD...
CATTATATA
BUDDA BUDDA BUDDA

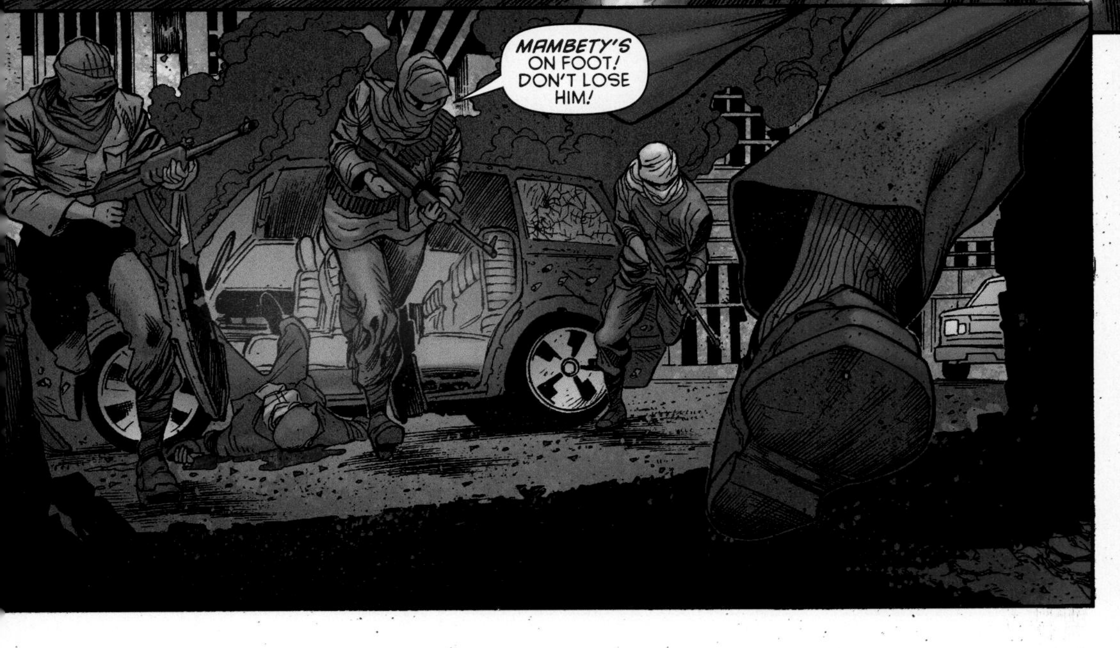
MAMBETY'S ON FOOT! DON'T LOSE HIM!

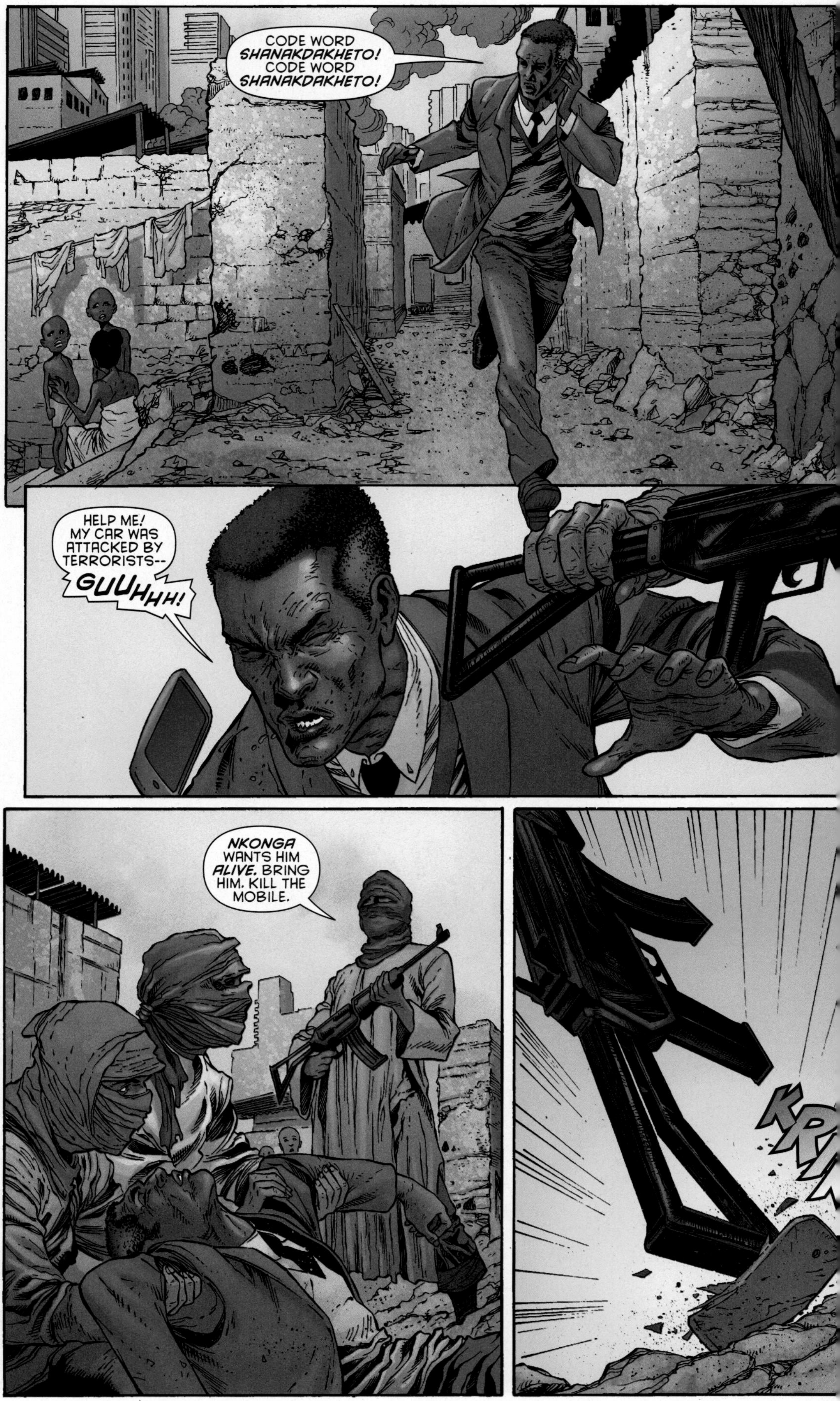
CODE WORD *SHANAKDAKHETO!* CODE WORD *SHANAKDAKHETO!*
HELP ME! MY CAR WAS ATTACKED BY TERRORISTS--
GUUHHH!
NKONGA WANTS HIM *ALIVE.* BRING HIM. KILL THE MOBILE.
KRI

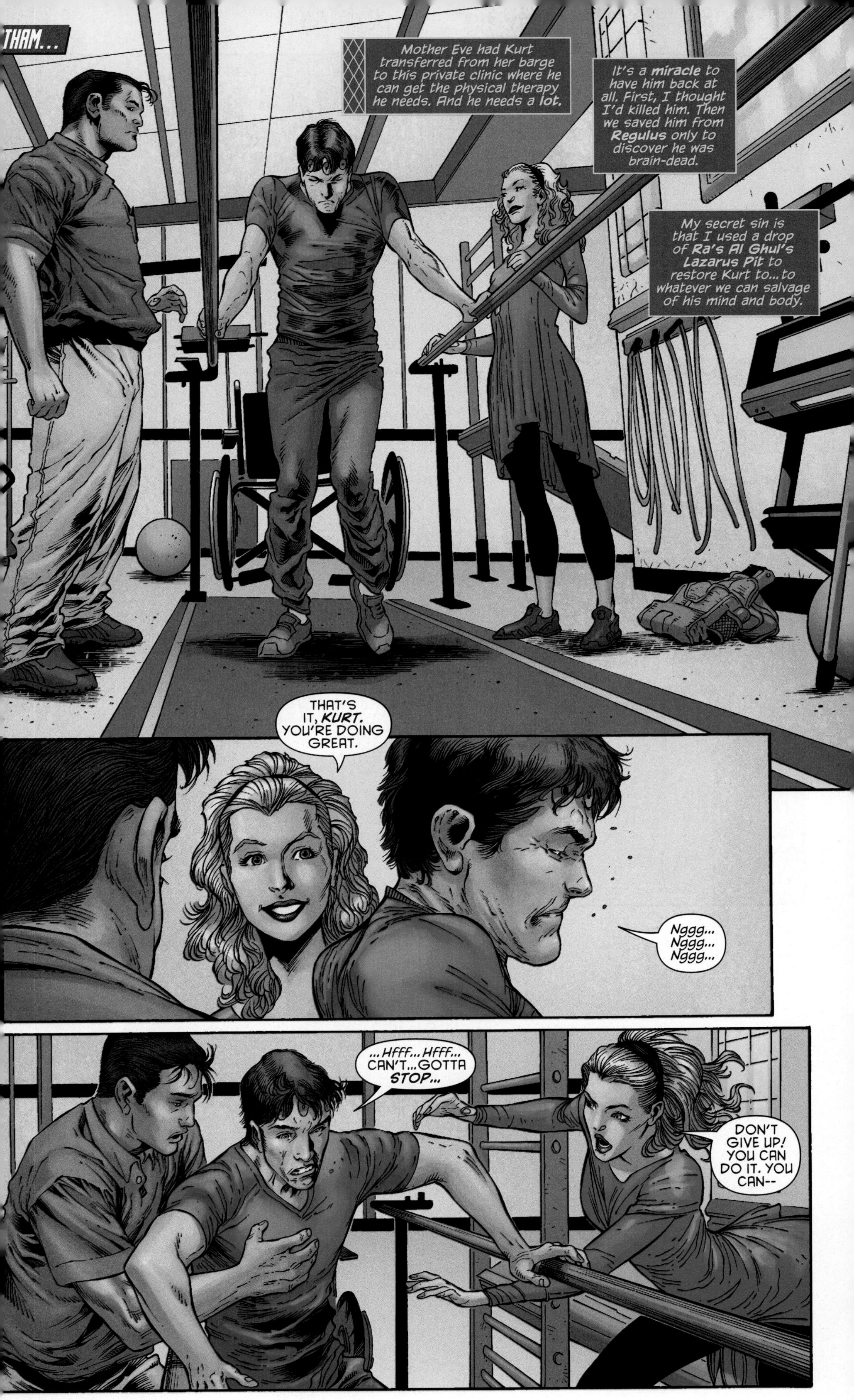

THAM...
Mother Eve had Kurt transferred from her barge to this private clinic where he can get the physical therapy he needs. And he needs a lot.
It's a miracle to have him back at all. First, I thought I'd killed him. Then we saved him from Regulus only to discover he was brain-dead.
My secret sin is that I used a drop of Ra's Al Ghul's Lazarus Pit to restore Kurt to...to whatever we can salvage of his mind and body.
THAT'S IT, KURT. YOU'RE DOING GREAT.
Nggg... Nggg... Nggg...
...HFFF...HFFF... CAN'T...GOTTA STOP...
DON'T GIVE UP! YOU CAN DO IT. YOU CAN--

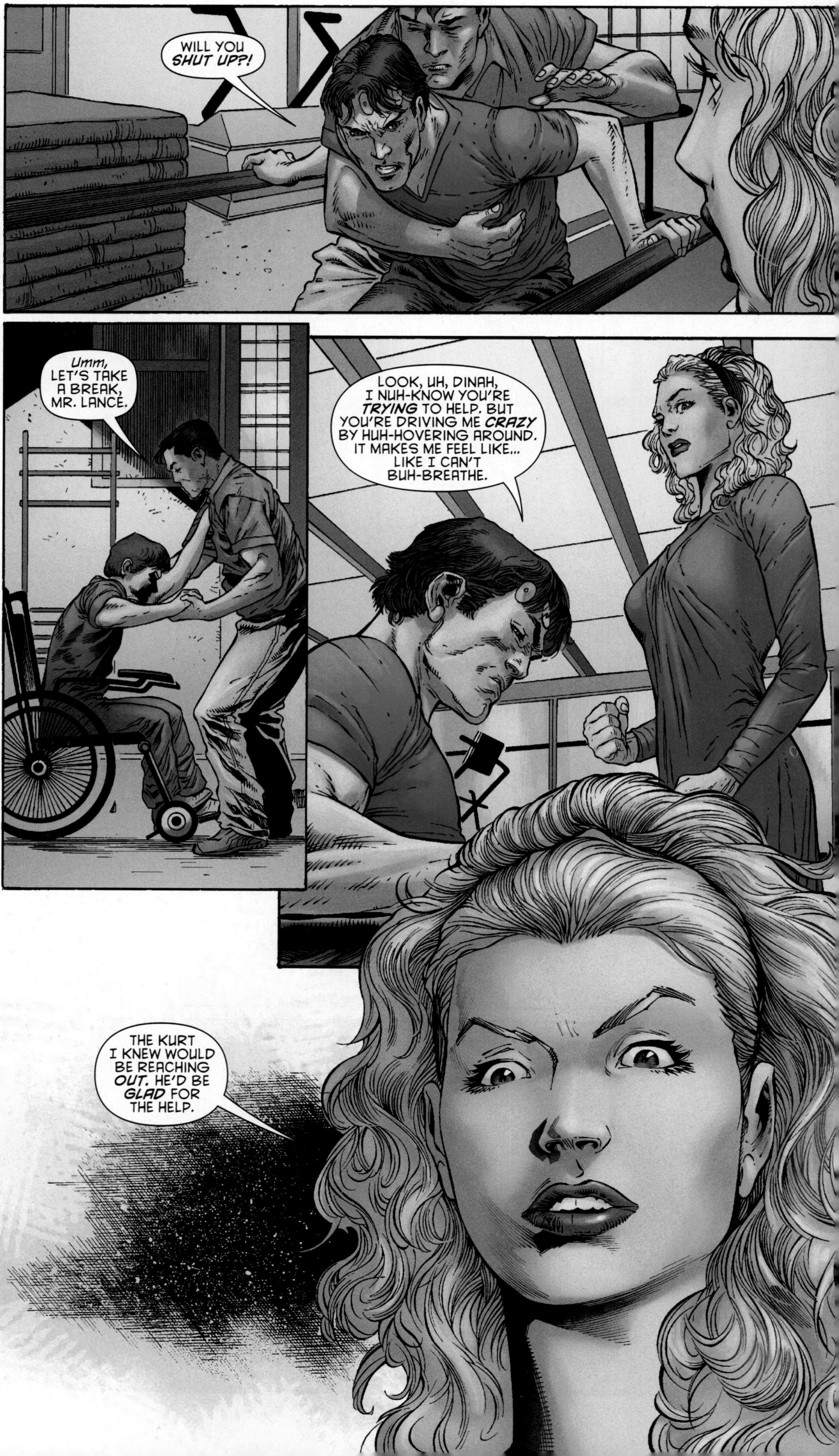
WILL YOU SHUT UP?!
Umm, LET'S TAKE A BREAK, MR. LANCE.
LOOK, UH, DINAH, I NUH-KNOW YOU'RE TRYING TO HELP. BUT YOU'RE DRIVING ME CRAZY BY HUH-HOVERING AROUND. IT MAKES ME FEEL LIKE... LIKE I CAN'T BUH-BREATHE.
THE KURT I KNEW WOULD BE REACHING OUT. HE'D BE GLAD FOR THE HELP.

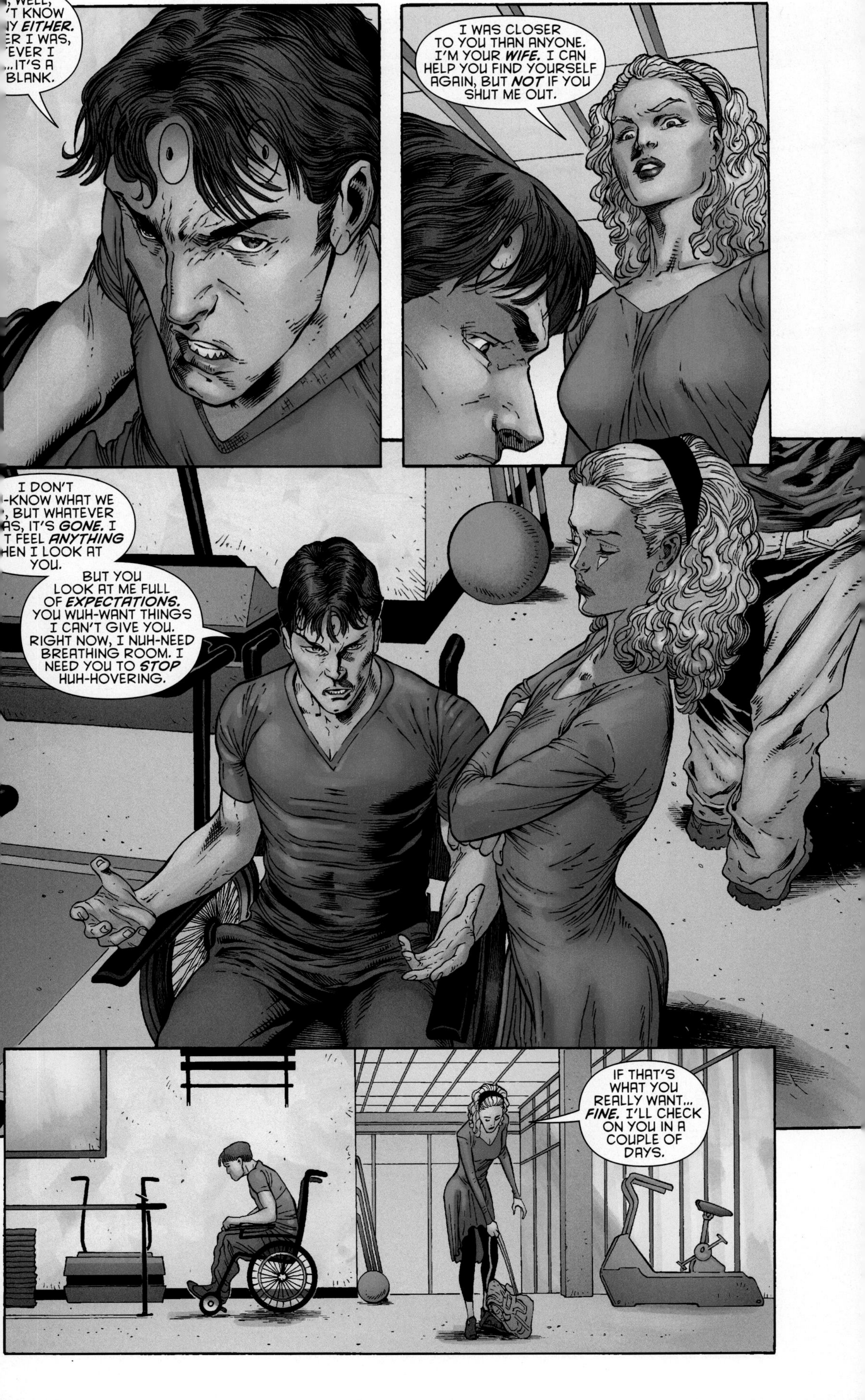

, WELL, 'T KNOW NY EITHER. ER I WAS, TEVER I ...IT'S A BLANK.
I WAS CLOSER TO YOU THAN ANYONE. I'M YOUR WIFE. I CAN HELP YOU FIND YOURSELF AGAIN, BUT NOT IF YOU SHUT ME OUT.
I DON'T -KNOW WHAT WE , BUT WHATEVER AS, IT'S GONE. I T FEEL ANYTHING HEN I LOOK AT YOU.
BUT YOU LOOK AT ME FULL OF EXPECTATIONS. YOU WUH-WANT THINGS I CAN'T GIVE YOU. RIGHT NOW, I NUH-NEED BREATHING ROOM. I NEED YOU TO STOP HUH-HOVERING.
IF THAT'S WHAT YOU REALLY WANT... FINE. I'LL CHECK ON YOU IN A COUPLE OF DAYS.

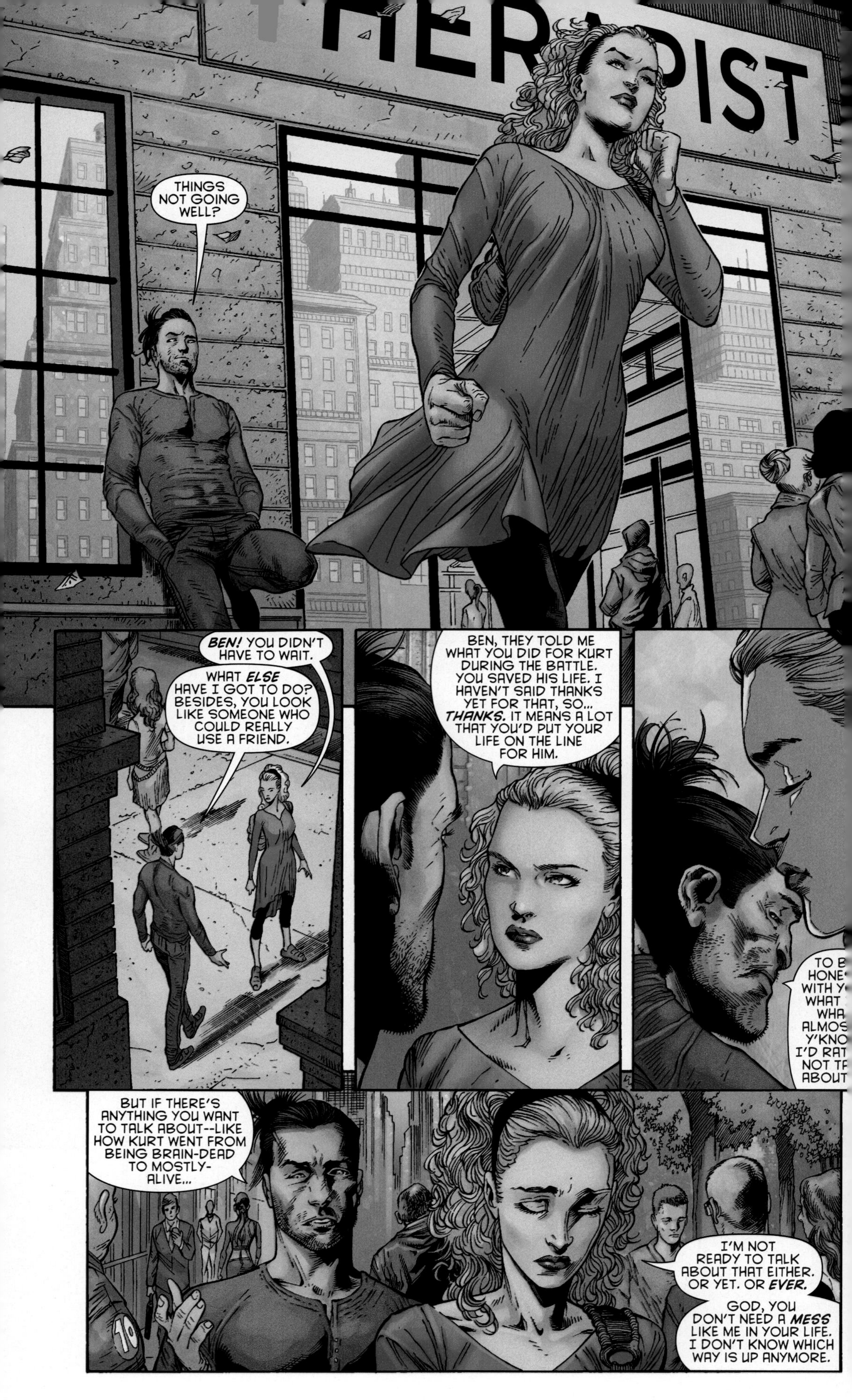
HERAPIST
THINGS NOT GOING WELL?
BEN! YOU DIDN'T HAVE TO WAIT.
WHAT *ELSE* HAVE I GOT TO DO? BESIDES, YOU LOOK LIKE SOMEONE WHO COULD REALLY USE A FRIEND.
BEN, THEY TOLD ME WHAT YOU DID FOR KURT DURING THE BATTLE. YOU SAVED HIS LIFE. I HAVEN'T SAID THANKS YET FOR THAT, SO... ***THANKS.*** IT MEANS A LOT THAT YOU'D PUT YOUR LIFE ON THE LINE FOR HIM.
TO B HONES WITH Y WHAT WHA ALMOS Y'KNO I'D RAT NOT T ABOUT
BUT IF THERE'S ANYTHING YOU WANT TO TALK ABOUT--LIKE HOW KURT WENT FROM BEING BRAIN-DEAD TO MOSTLY-ALIVE...
I'M NOT READY TO TALK ABOUT THAT EITHER. OR YET. OR ***EVER.***
GOD, YOU DON'T NEED A ***MESS*** LIKE ME IN YOUR LIFE. I DON'T KNOW WHICH WAY IS UP ANYMORE.

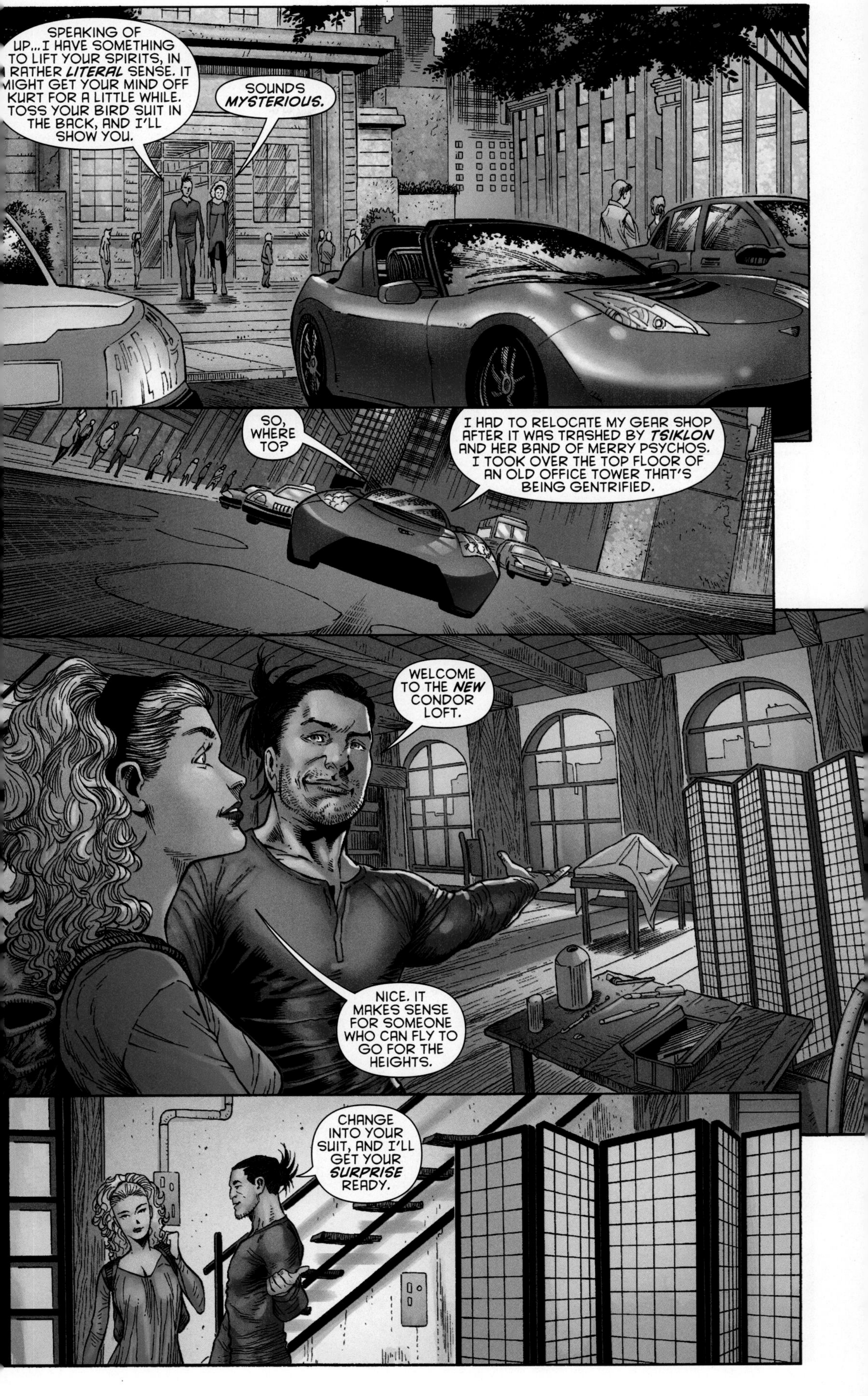
SPEAKING OF UP... I HAVE SOMETHING TO LIFT YOUR SPIRITS, IN RATHER LITERAL SENSE. IT MIGHT GET YOUR MIND OFF KURT FOR A LITTLE WHILE. TOSS YOUR BIRD SUIT IN THE BACK, AND I'LL SHOW YOU.
SOUNDS MYSTERIOUS.
SO, WHERE TO?
I HAD TO RELOCATE MY GEAR SHOP AFTER IT WAS TRASHED BY TSIKLON AND HER BAND OF MERRY PSYCHOS. I TOOK OVER THE TOP FLOOR OF AN OLD OFFICE TOWER THAT'S BEING GENTRIFIED.
WELCOME TO THE NEW CONDOR LOFT.
NICE. IT MAKES SENSE FOR SOMEONE WHO CAN FLY TO GO FOR THE HEIGHTS.
CHANGE INTO YOUR SUIT, AND I'LL GET YOUR SURPRISE READY.

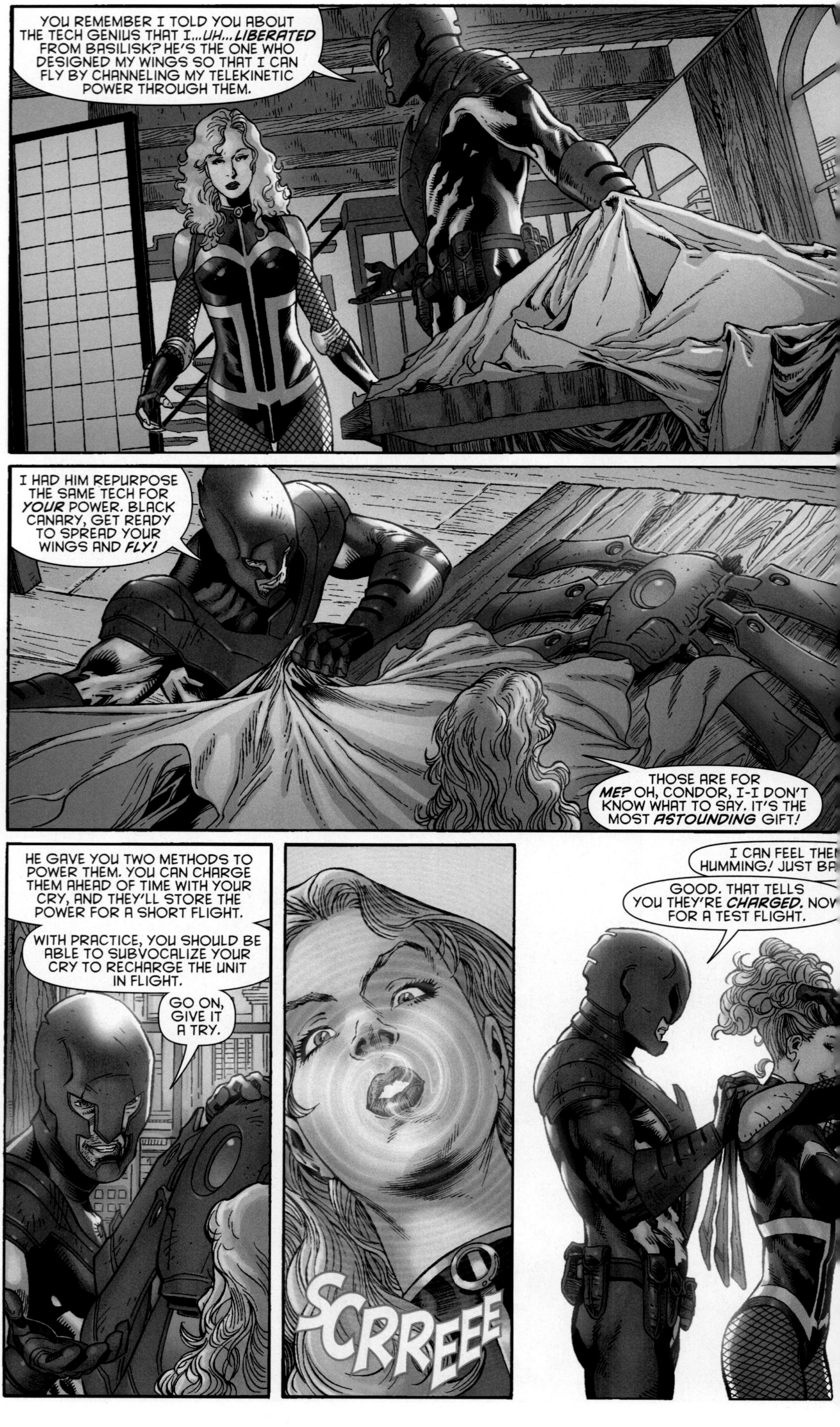
YOU REMEMBER I TOLD YOU ABOUT THE TECH GENIUS THAT I...UH...LIBERATED FROM BASILISK? HE'S THE ONE WHO DESIGNED MY WINGS SO THAT I CAN FLY BY CHANNELING MY TELEKINETIC POWER THROUGH THEM.
I HAD HIM REPURPOSE THE SAME TECH FOR YOUR POWER. BLACK CANARY, GET READY TO SPREAD YOUR WINGS AND FLY!
THOSE ARE FOR ME? OH, CONDOR, I-I DON'T KNOW WHAT TO SAY. IT'S THE MOST ASTOUNDING GIFT!
HE GAVE YOU TWO METHODS TO POWER THEM. YOU CAN CHARGE THEM AHEAD OF TIME WITH YOUR CRY, AND THEY'LL STORE THE POWER FOR A SHORT FLIGHT.
WITH PRACTICE, YOU SHOULD BE ABLE TO SUBVOCALIZE YOUR CRY TO RECHARGE THE UNIT IN FLIGHT.
GO ON, GIVE IT A TRY.
SCRREEE
I CAN FEEL THEM HUMMING! JUST BA
GOOD. THAT TELLS YOU THEY'RE CHARGED. NOV FOR A TEST FLIGHT.

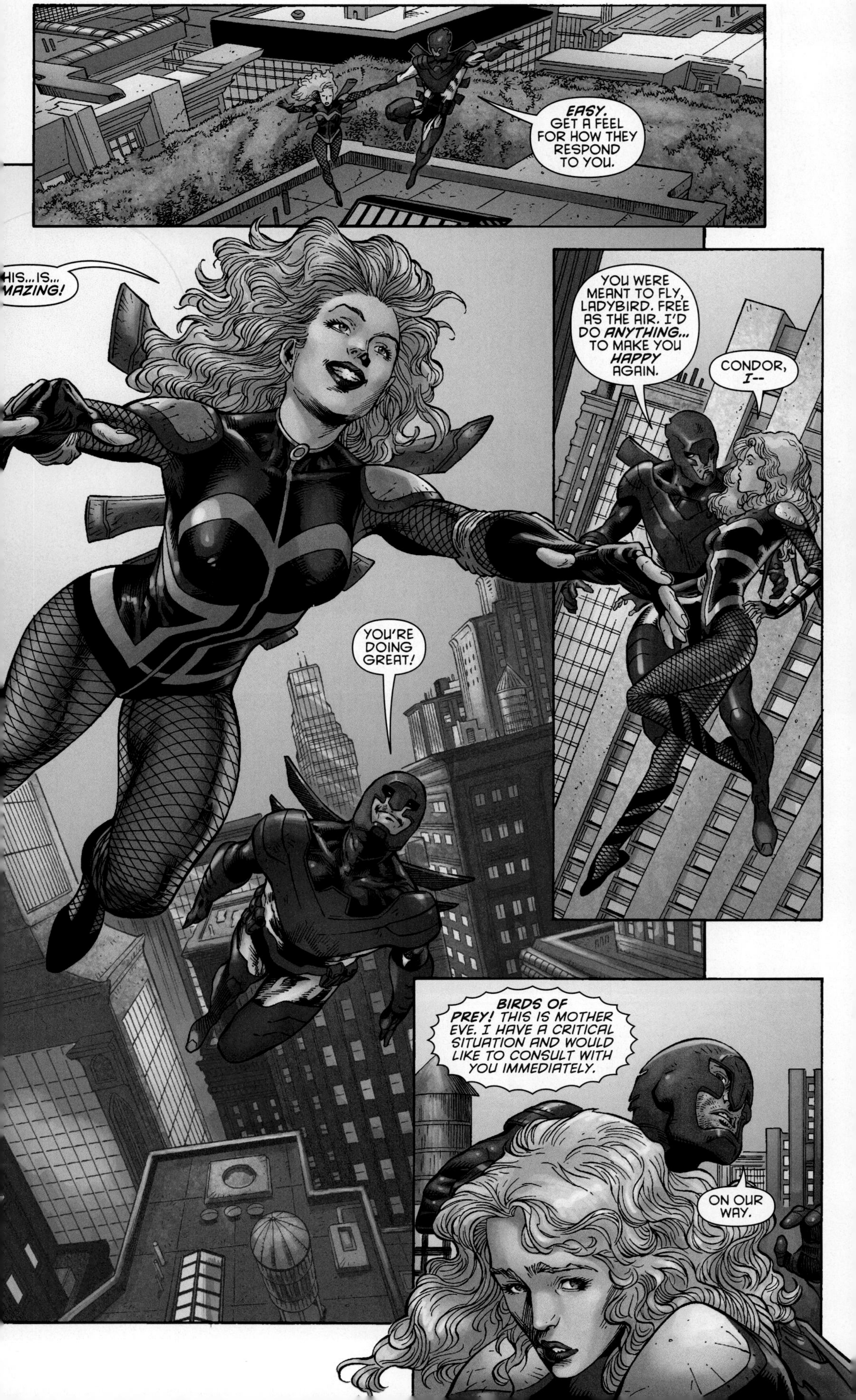
EASY. GET A FEEL FOR HOW THEY RESPOND TO YOU.
HIS...IS... MAZING!
YOU'RE DOING GREAT!
YOU WERE MEANT TO FLY, LADYBIRD. FREE AS THE AIR. I'D DO ANYTHING... TO MAKE YOU HAPPY AGAIN.
CONDOR, I--
BIRDS OF PREY! THIS IS MOTHER EVE. I HAVE A CRITICAL SITUATION AND WOULD LIKE TO CONSULT WITH YOU IMMEDIATELY.
ON OUR WAY.

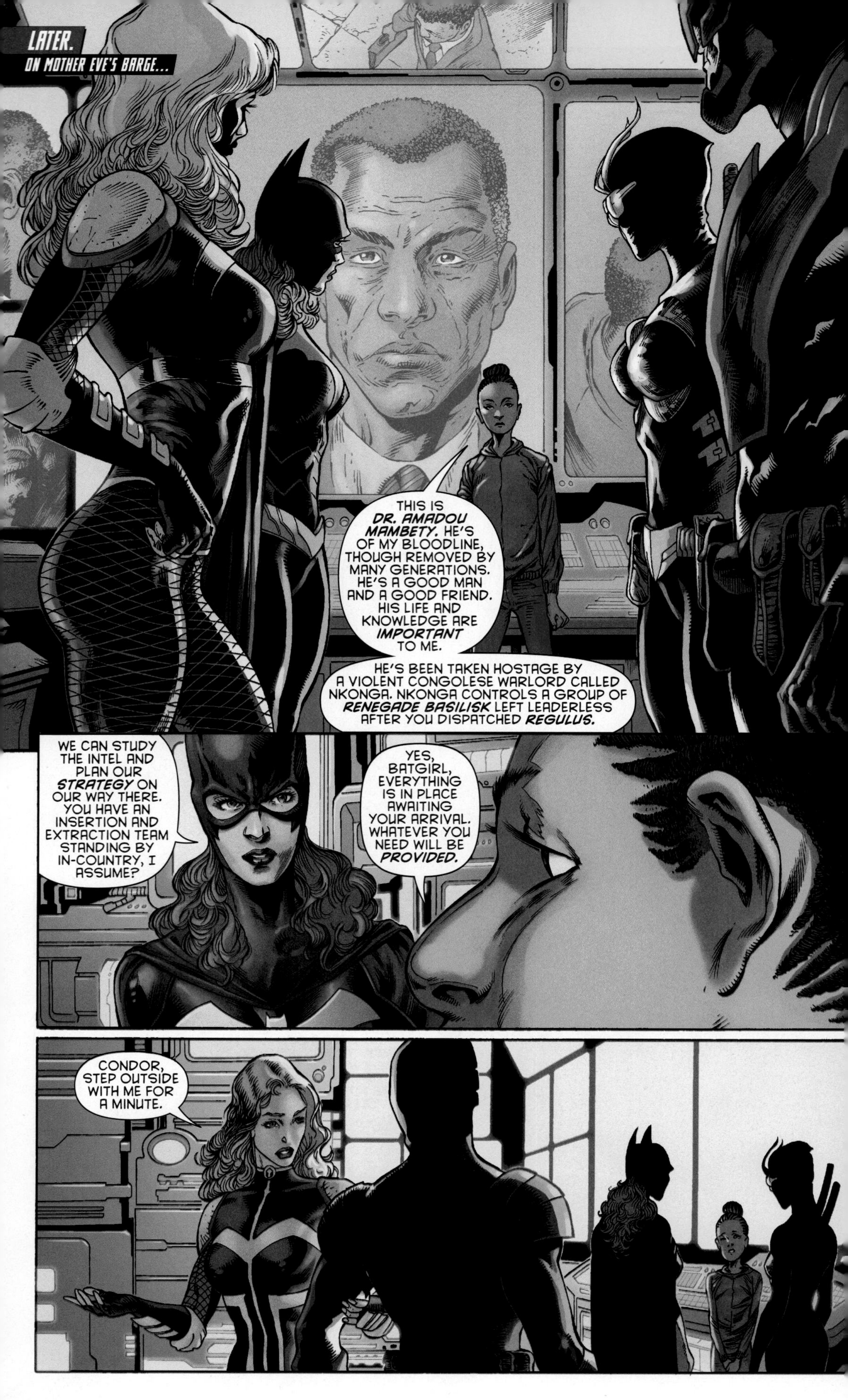
LATER. ON MOTHER EVE'S BARGE...
THIS IS DR. AMADOU MAMBETY. HE'S OF MY BLOODLINE, THOUGH REMOVED BY MANY GENERATIONS. HE'S A GOOD MAN AND A GOOD FRIEND. HIS LIFE AND KNOWLEDGE ARE IMPORTANT TO ME.
HE'S BEEN TAKEN HOSTAGE BY A VIOLENT CONGOLESE WARLORD CALLED NKONGA. NKONGA CONTROLS A GROUP OF RENEGADE BASILISK LEFT LEADERLESS AFTER YOU DISPATCHED REGULUS.
WE CAN STUDY THE INTEL AND PLAN OUR STRATEGY ON OUR WAY THERE. YOU HAVE AN INSERTION AND EXTRACTION TEAM STANDING BY IN-COUNTRY, I ASSUME?
YES, BATGIRL, EVERYTHING IS IN PLACE AWAITING YOUR ARRIVAL. WHATEVER YOU NEED WILL BE PROVIDED.
CONDOR, STEP OUTSIDE WITH ME FOR A MINUTE.

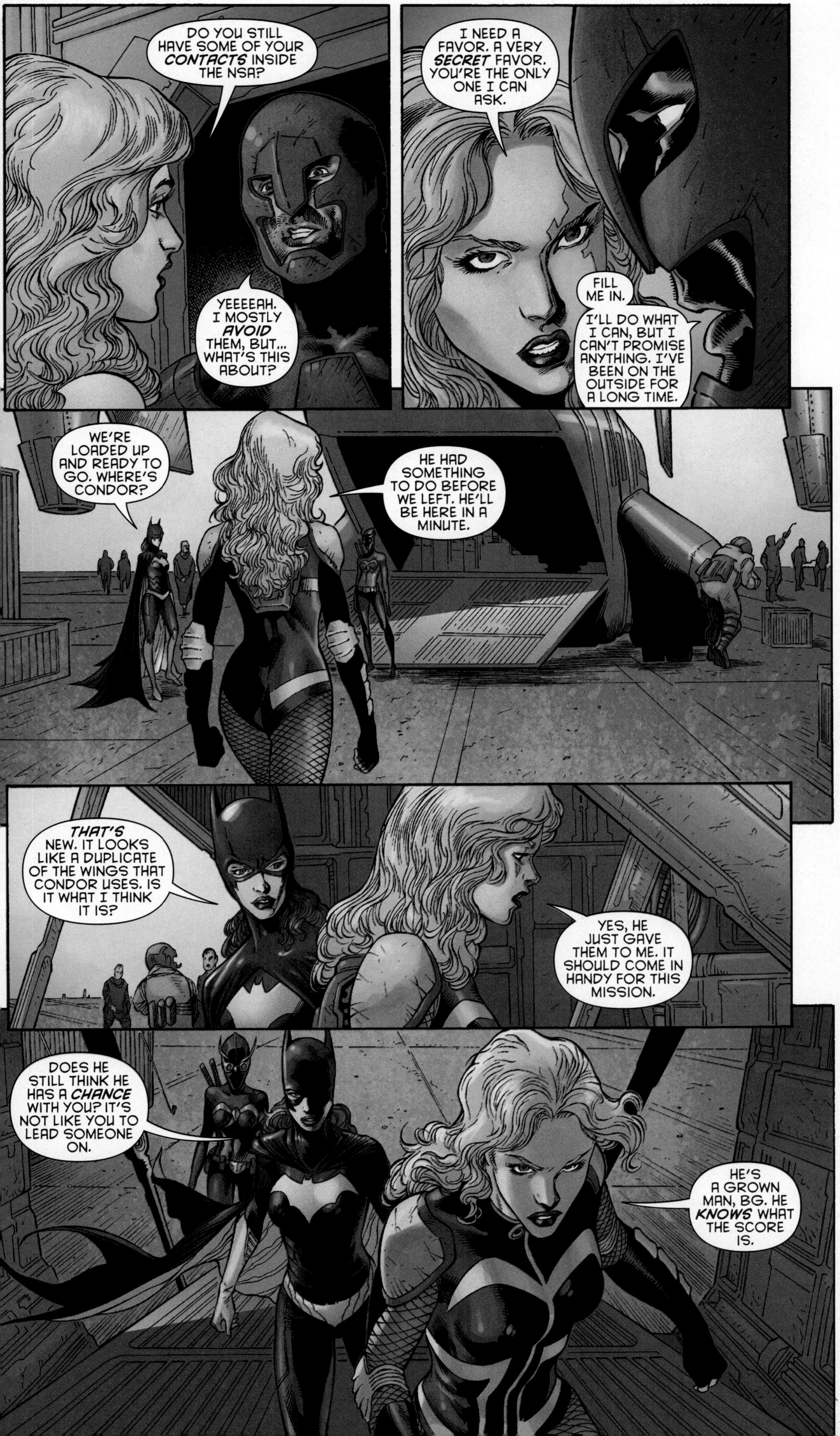
DO YOU STILL HAVE SOME OF YOUR CONTACTS INSIDE THE NSA?
YEEEEAH. I MOSTLY AVOID THEM, BUT... WHAT'S THIS ABOUT?
I NEED A FAVOR. A VERY SECRET FAVOR. YOU'RE THE ONLY ONE I CAN ASK.
FILL ME IN.
I'LL DO WHAT I CAN, BUT I CAN'T PROMISE ANYTHING. I'VE BEEN ON THE OUTSIDE FOR A LONG TIME.
WE'RE LOADED UP AND READY TO GO. WHERE'S CONDOR?
HE HAD SOMETHING TO DO BEFORE WE LEFT. HE'LL BE HERE IN A MINUTE.
THAT'S NEW. IT LOOKS LIKE A DUPLICATE OF THE WINGS THAT CONDOR USES. IS IT WHAT I THINK IT IS?
YES, HE JUST GAVE THEM TO ME. IT SHOULD COME IN HANDY FOR THIS MISSION.
DOES HE STILL THINK HE HAS A CHANCE WITH YOU? IT'S NOT LIKE YOU TO LEAD SOMEONE ON.
HE'S A GROWN MAN, BG. HE KNOWS WHAT THE SCORE IS.

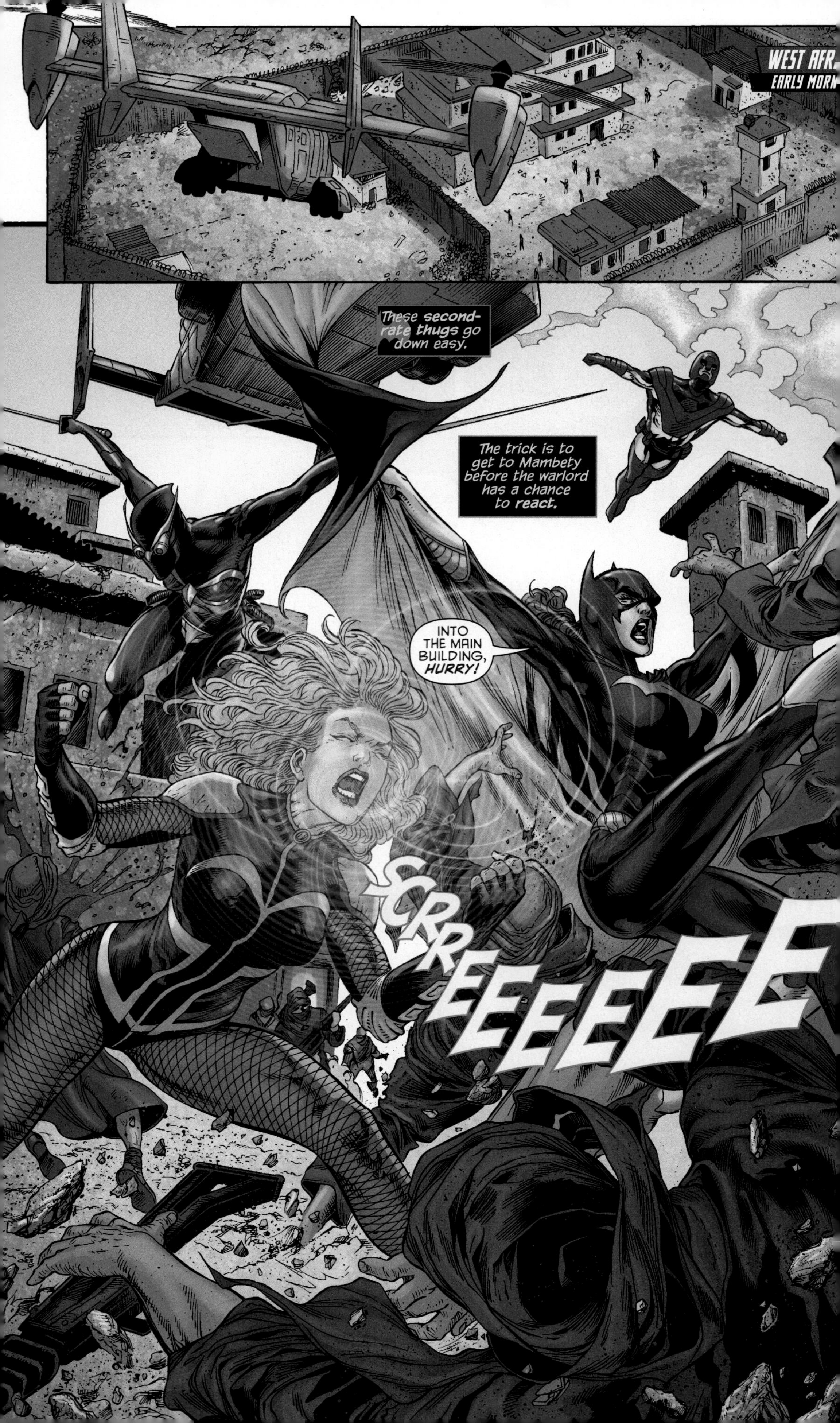
WEST AFR
EARLY MORN
These second-rate thugs go down easy.
The trick is to get to Mambety before the warlord has a chance to react.
INTO THE MAIN BUILDING, HURRY!
SCRREEEEEEE

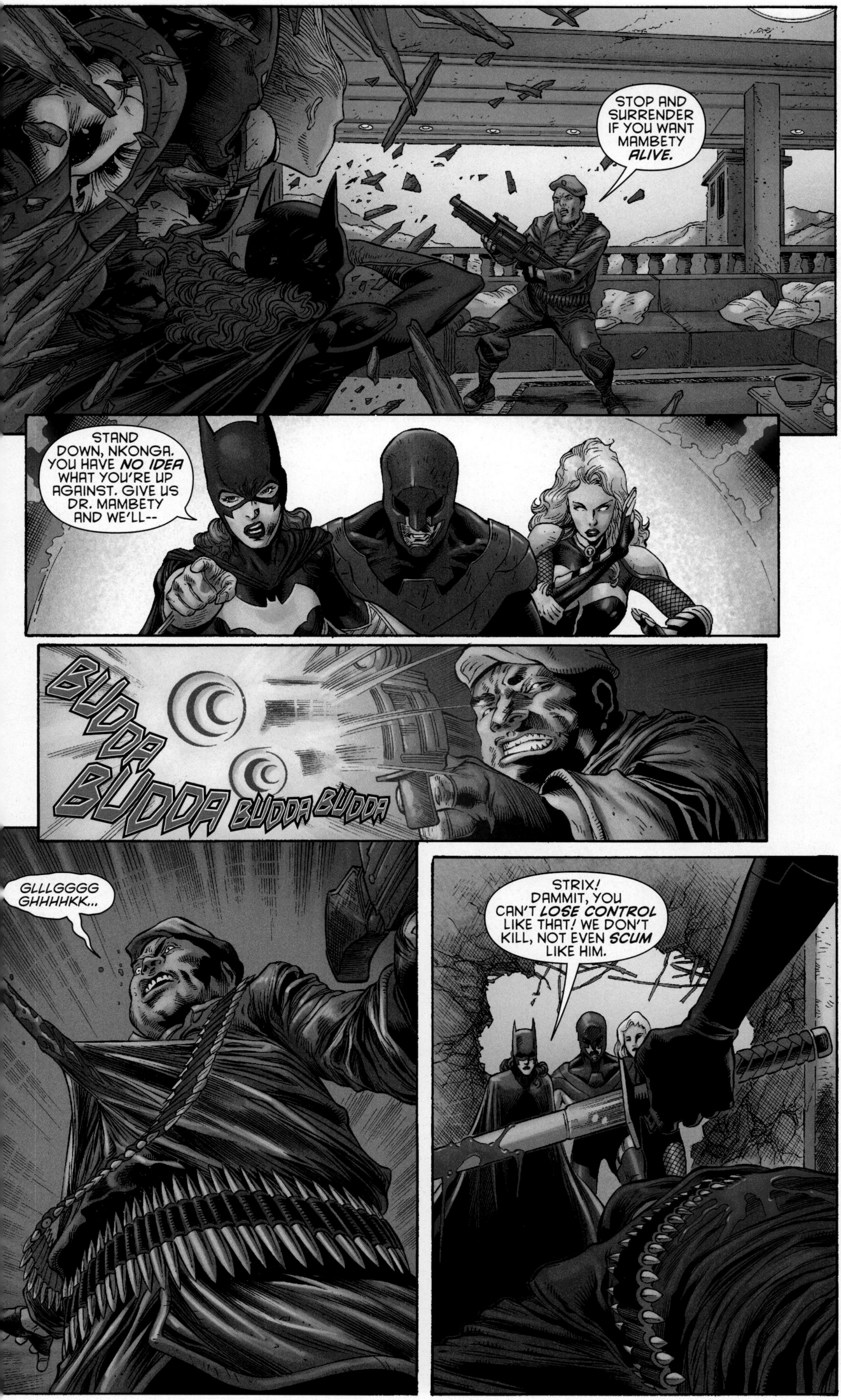
STOP AND SURRENDER IF YOU WANT MAMBETY ALIVE.
STAND DOWN, NKONGA. YOU HAVE NO IDEA WHAT YOU'RE UP AGAINST. GIVE US DR. MAMBETY AND WE'LL--
BUDDA BUDDA BUDDA BUDDA
GLLLGGGG GHHHHKK...
STRIX! DAMMIT, YOU CAN'T LOSE CONTROL LIKE THAT! WE DON'T KILL, NOT EVEN SCUM LIKE HIM.

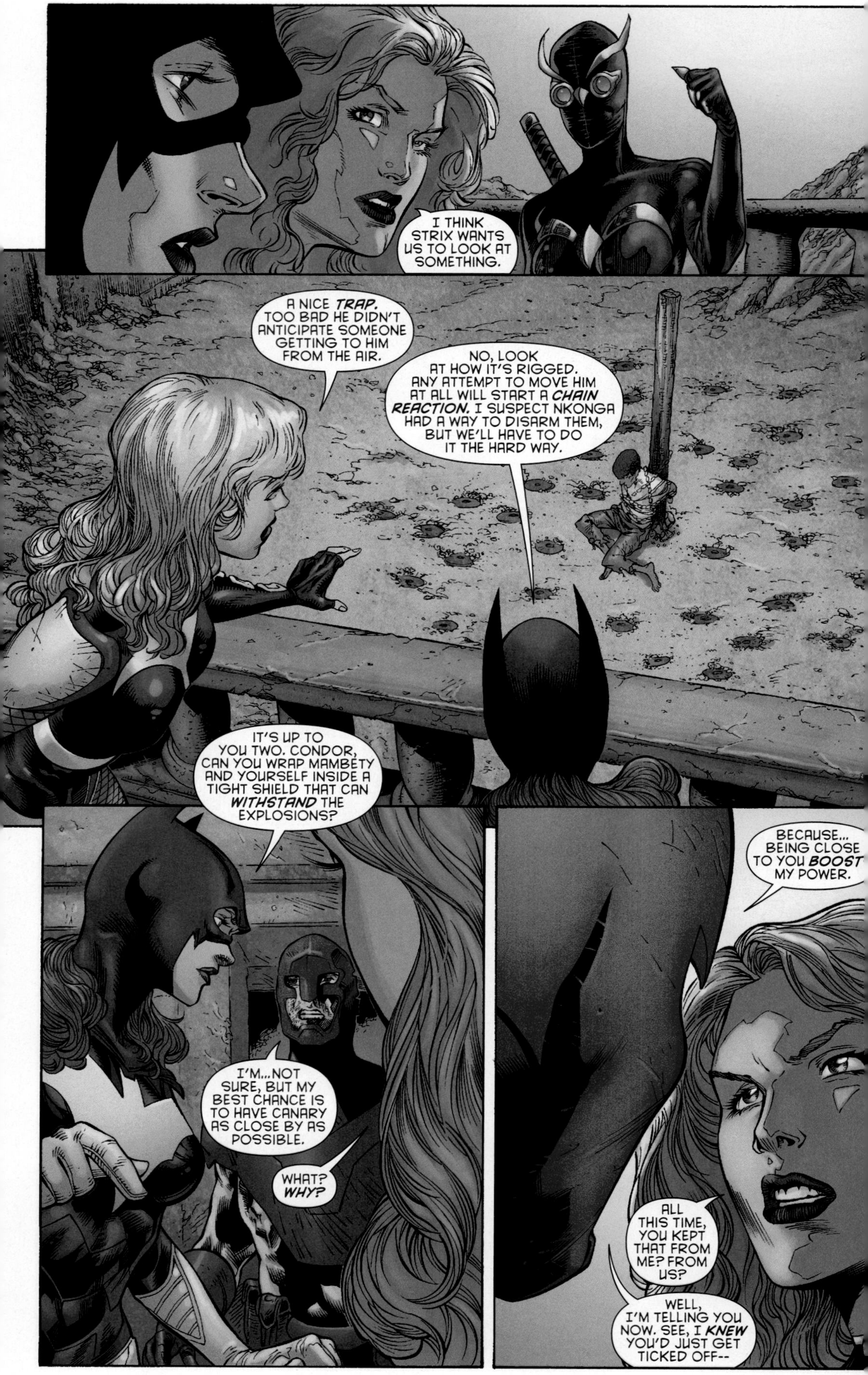
I THINK STRIX WANTS US TO LOOK AT SOMETHING.
A NICE *TRAP.* TOO BAD HE DIDN'T ANTICIPATE SOMEONE GETTING TO HIM FROM THE AIR.
NO, LOOK AT HOW IT'S RIGGED. ANY ATTEMPT TO MOVE HIM AT ALL WILL START A *CHAIN REACTION.* I SUSPECT NKONGA HAD A WAY TO DISARM THEM, BUT WE'LL HAVE TO DO IT THE HARD WAY.
IT'S UP TO YOU TWO. CONDOR, CAN YOU WRAP MAMBÉTY AND YOURSELF INSIDE A TIGHT SHIELD THAT CAN *WITHSTAND* THE EXPLOSIONS?
I'M...NOT SURE, BUT MY BEST CHANCE IS TO HAVE CANARY AS CLOSE BY AS POSSIBLE.
WHAT? *WHY?*
BECAUSE... BEING CLOSE TO YOU *BOOST* MY POWER.
ALL THIS TIME, YOU KEPT THAT FROM ME? FROM US?
WELL, I'M TELLING YOU NOW. SEE, I *KNEW* YOU'D JUST GET TICKED OFF--

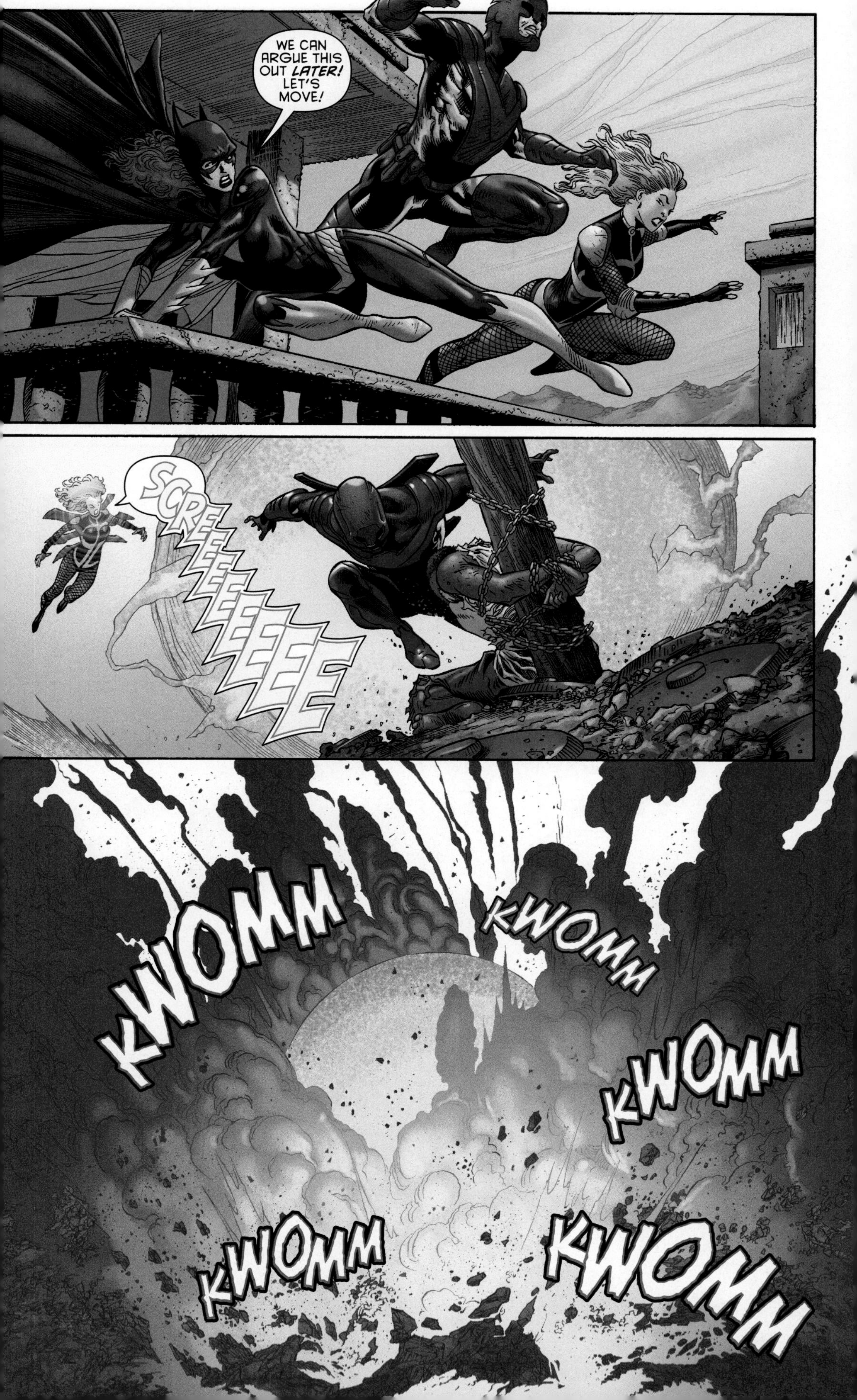
WE CAN ARGUE THIS OUT LATER! LET'S MOVE!
SCREEEEEEEEEEE
KWOMM
KWOMM
KWOMM
KWOMM
KWOMM

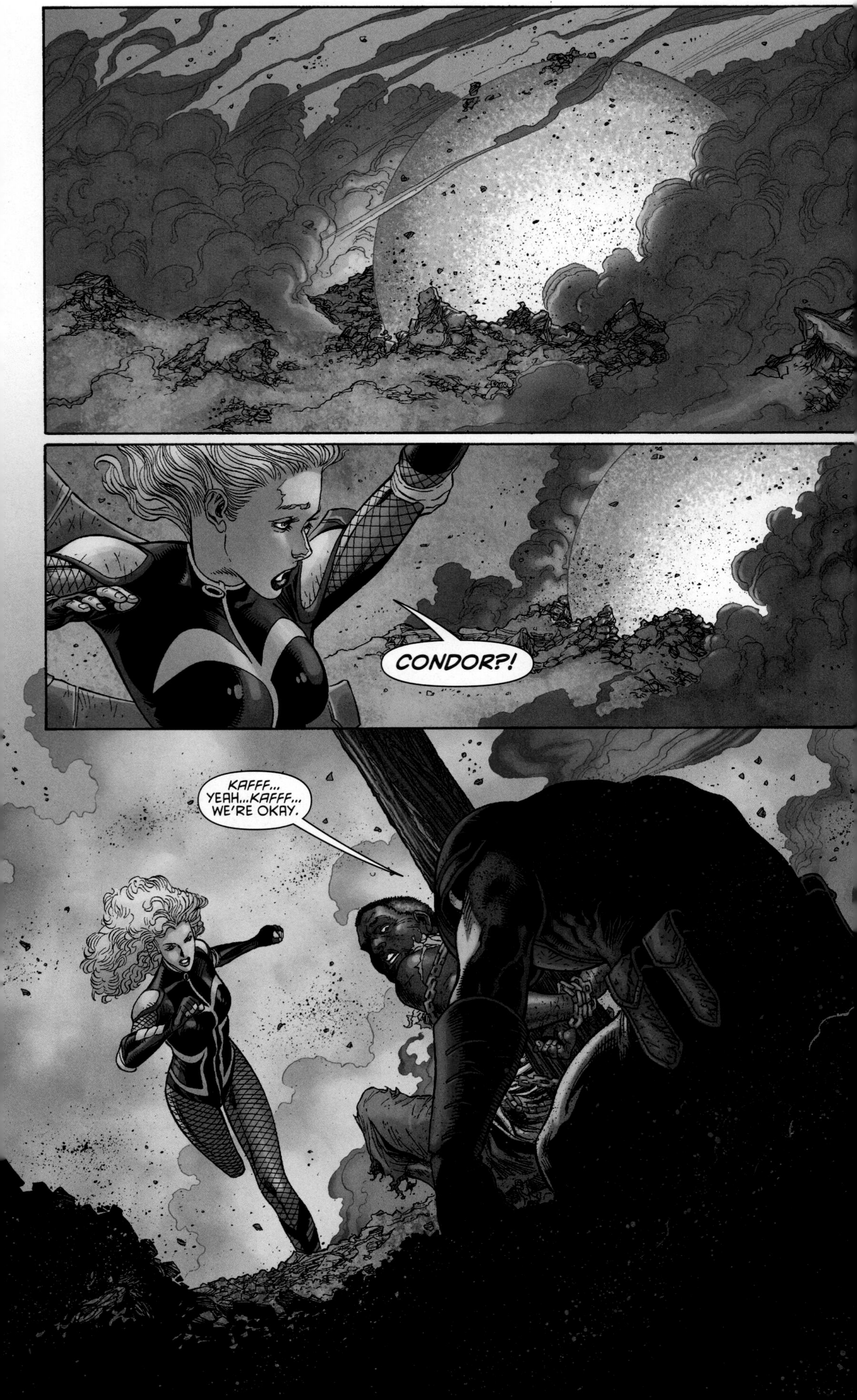
CONDOR?!
KAFFF... YEAH...KAFFF... WE'RE OKAY.

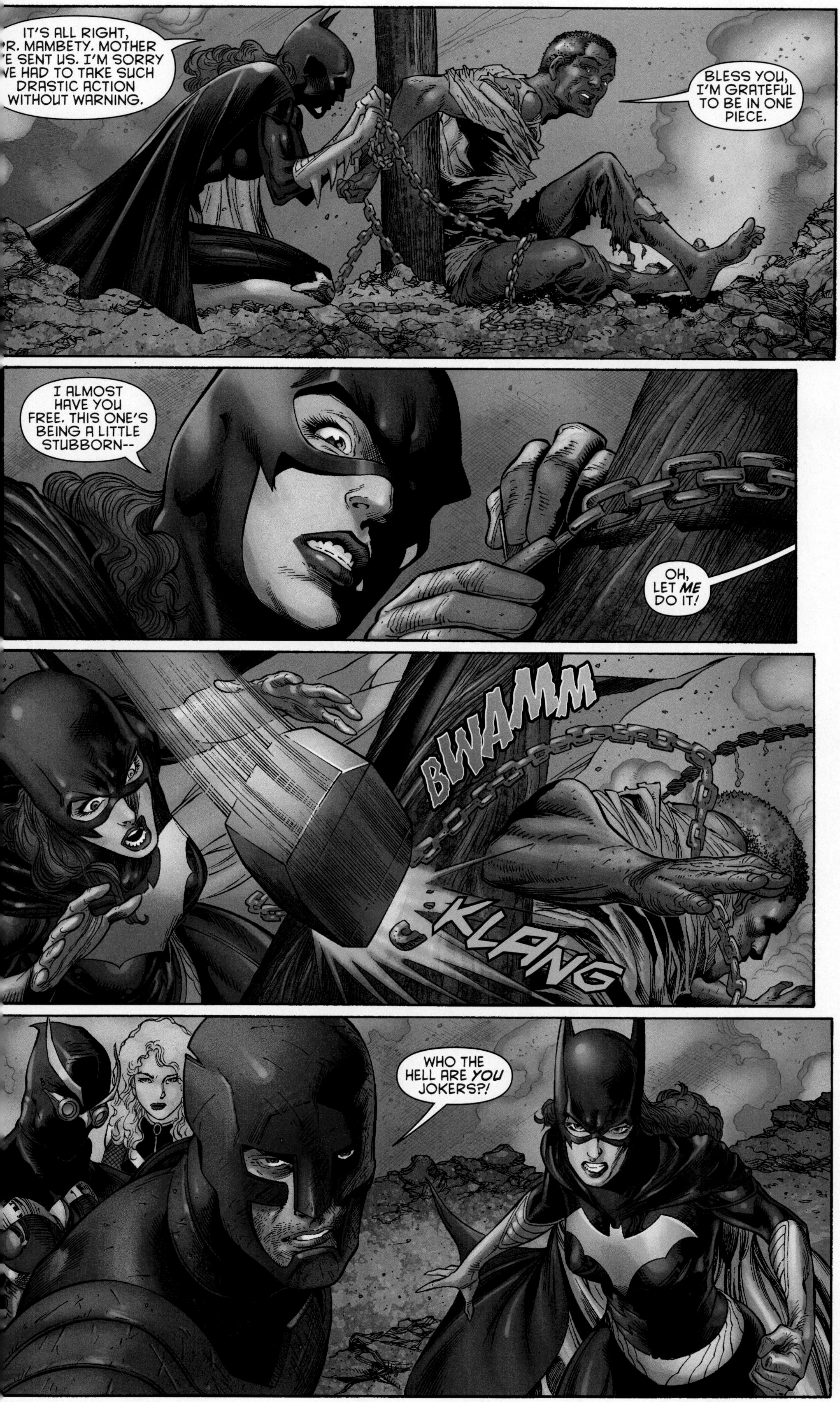
IT'S ALL RIGHT, R. MAMBETY. MOTHER E SENT US. I'M SORRY VE HAD TO TAKE SUCH DRASTIC ACTION WITHOUT WARNING.
BLESS YOU, I'M GRATEFUL TO BE IN ONE PIECE.
I ALMOST HAVE YOU FREE. THIS ONE'S BEING A LITTLE STUBBORN--
OH, LET *ME* DO IT!
BWAMM
KLANG
WHO THE HELL ARE *YOU* JOKERS?!

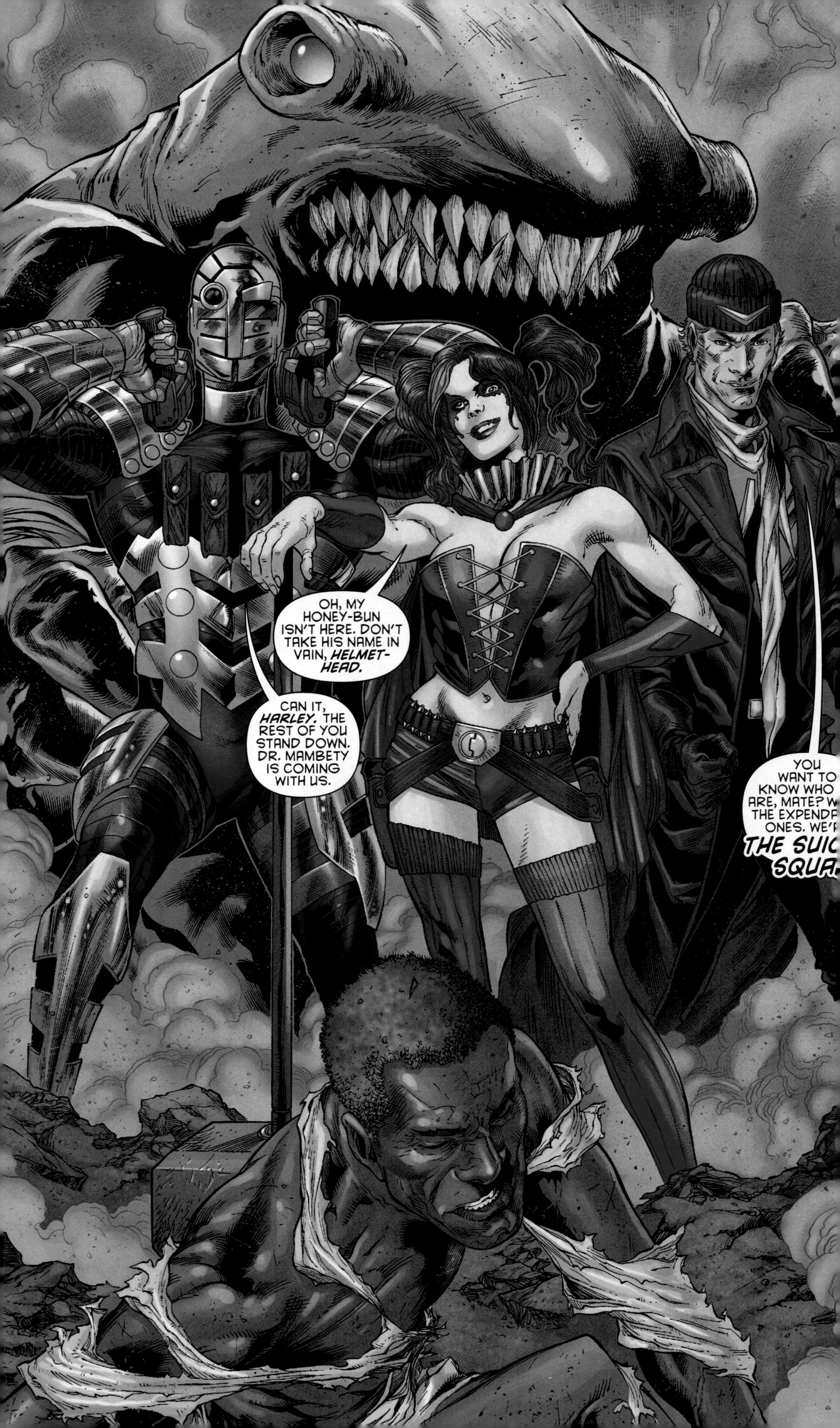
OH, MY HONEY-BUN ISN'T HERE. DON'T TAKE HIS NAME IN VAIN, *HELMET-HEAD.*
CAN IT, *HARLEY.* THE REST OF YOU STAND DOWN. DR. MAMBETY IS COMING WITH US.

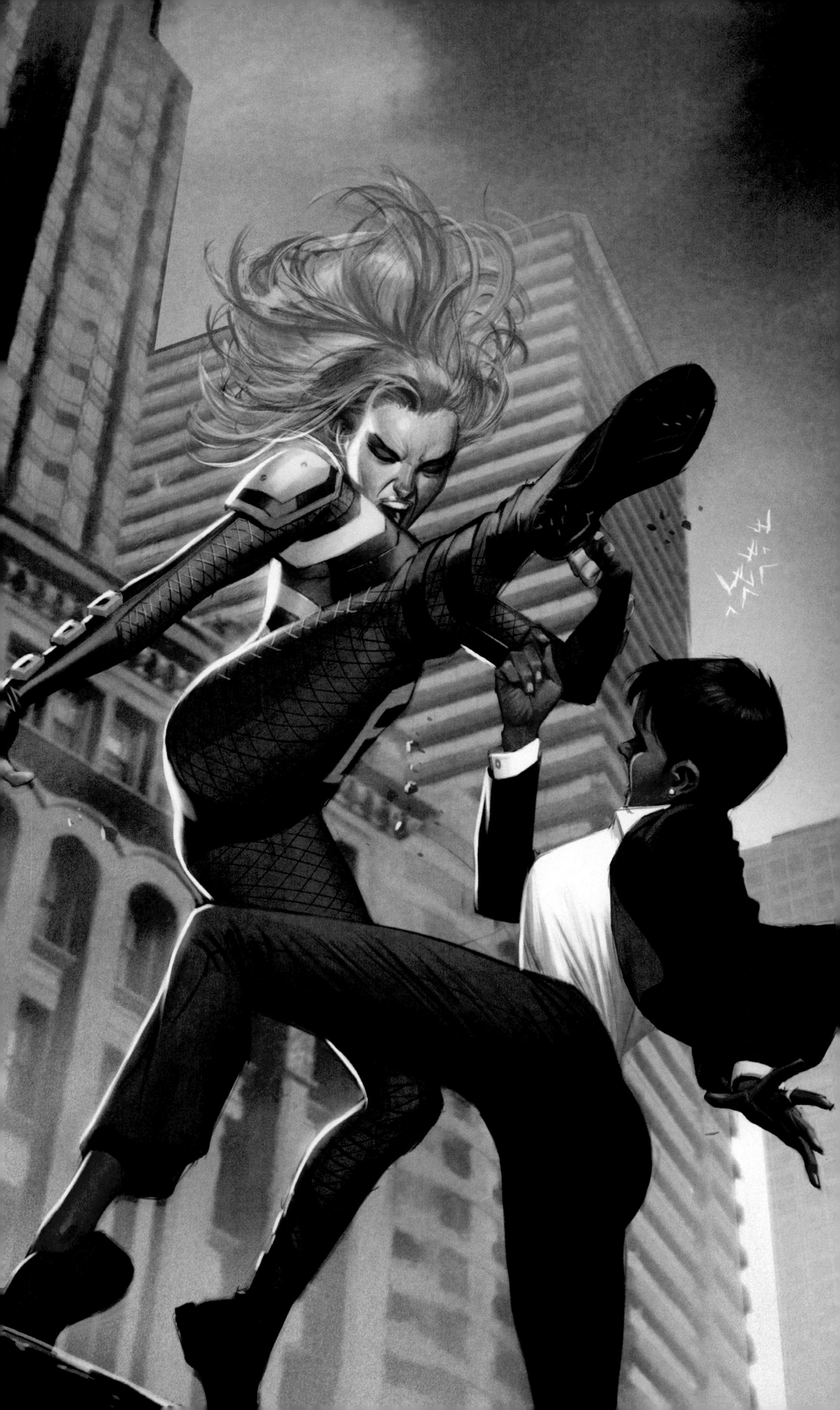

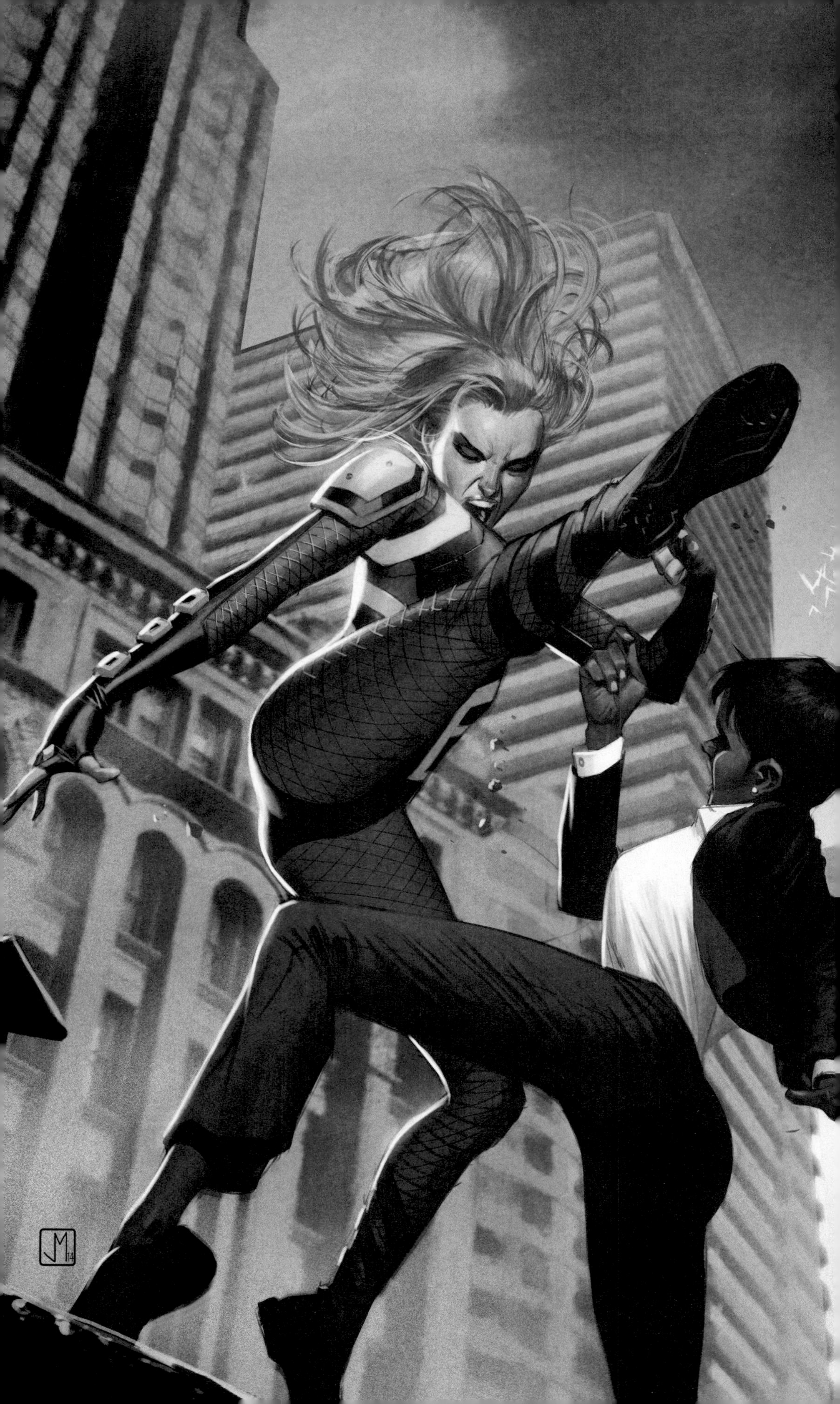

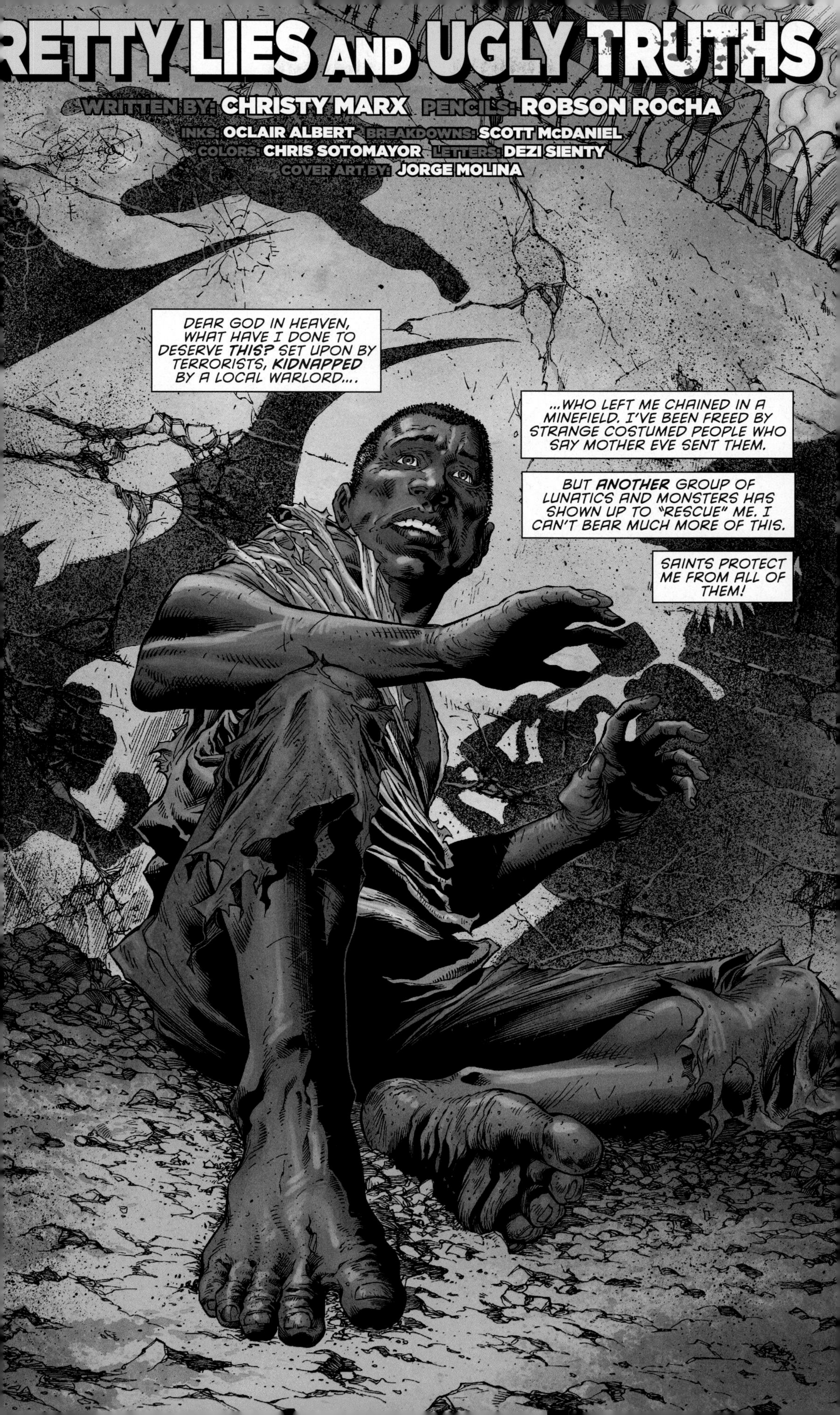
RETTY LIES AND UGLY TRUTHS
WRITTEN BY: CHRISTY MARX PENCILS: ROBSON ROCHA
INKS: OCLAIR ALBERT BREAKDOWNS: SCOTT McDANIEL
COLORS: CHRIS SOTOMAYOR LETTERS: DEZI SIENTY
COVER ART BY: JORGE MOLINA
DEAR GOD IN HEAVEN, WHAT HAVE I DONE TO DESERVE THIS? SET UPON BY TERRORISTS, KIDNAPPED BY A LOCAL WARLORD....
...WHO LEFT ME CHAINED IN A MINEFIELD. I'VE BEEN FREED BY STRANGE COSTUMED PEOPLE WHO SAY MOTHER EVE SENT THEM.
BUT ANOTHER GROUP OF LUNATICS AND MONSTERS HAS SHOWN UP TO "RESCUE" ME. I CAN'T BEAR MUCH MORE OF THIS.
SAINTS PROTECT ME FROM ALL OF THEM!

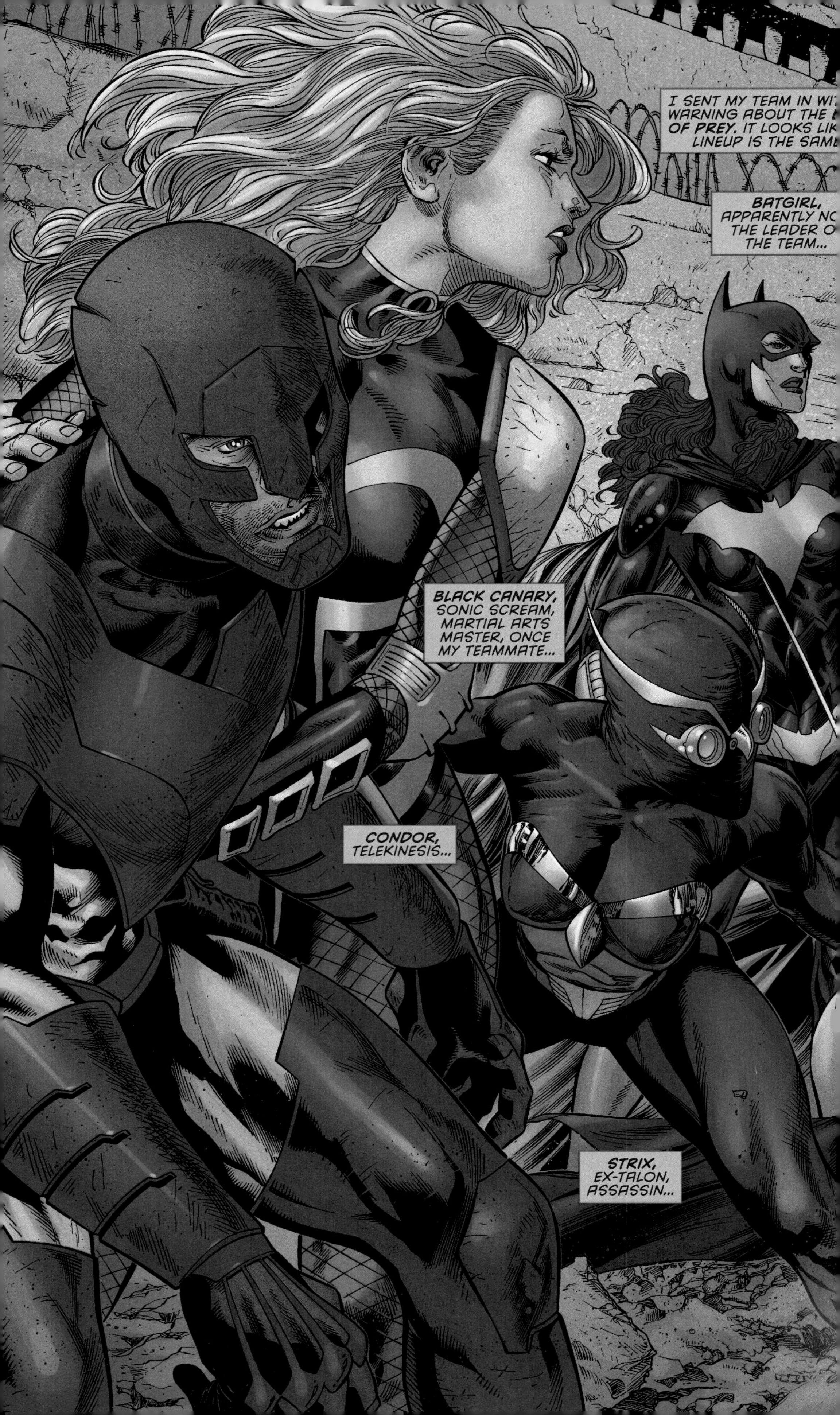
I SENT MY TEAM IN WI
WARNING ABOUT THE
OF PREY. IT LOOKS LIK
LINEUP IS THE SAM
BATGIRL, APPARENTLY NO
THE LEADER O
THE TEAM...
BLACK CANARY, SONIC SCREAM, MARTIAL ARTS MASTER, ONCE MY TEAMMATE...
CONDOR, TELEKINESIS...
STRIX, EX-TALON, ASSASSIN...

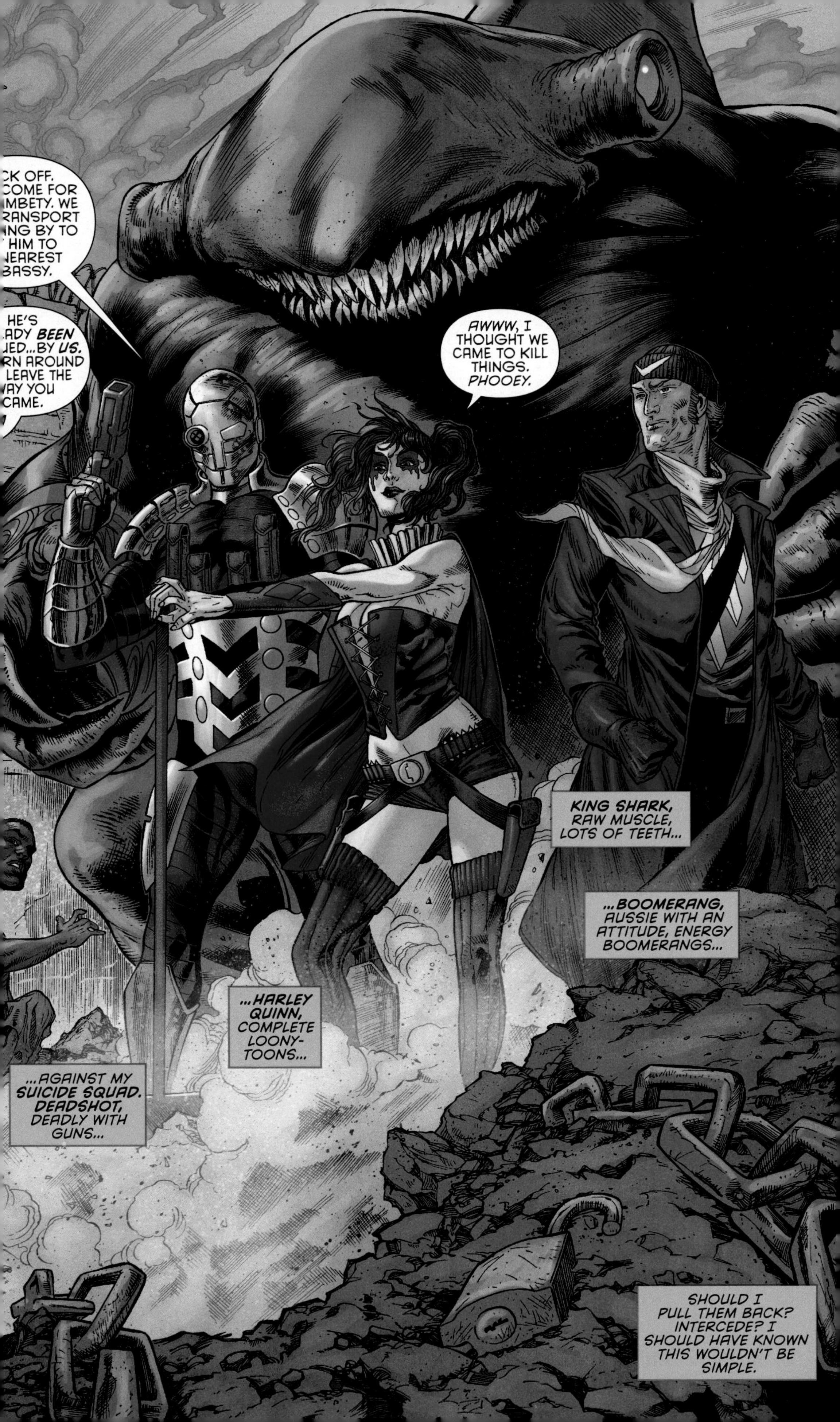
CK OFF. COME FOR MBETY. WE RANSPORT NG BY TO HIM TO NEAREST BASSY.
HE'S ADY **BEEN** ED...BY **US.** RN AROUND LEAVE THE AY YOU CAME.
AWWW, I THOUGHT WE CAME TO KILL THINGS. *PHOOEY.*
...AGAINST MY ***SUICIDE SQUAD. DEADSHOT,*** *DEADLY WITH GUNS...*
...HARLEY QUINN, *COMPLETE LOONY-TOONS...*
KING SHARK, *RAW MUSCLE, LOTS OF TEETH...*
...BOOMERANG, *AUSSIE WITH AN ATTITUDE, ENERGY BOOMERANGS...*
SHOULD I PULL THEM BACK? INTERCEDE? I SHOULD HAVE KNOWN THIS WOULDN'T BE SIMPLE.

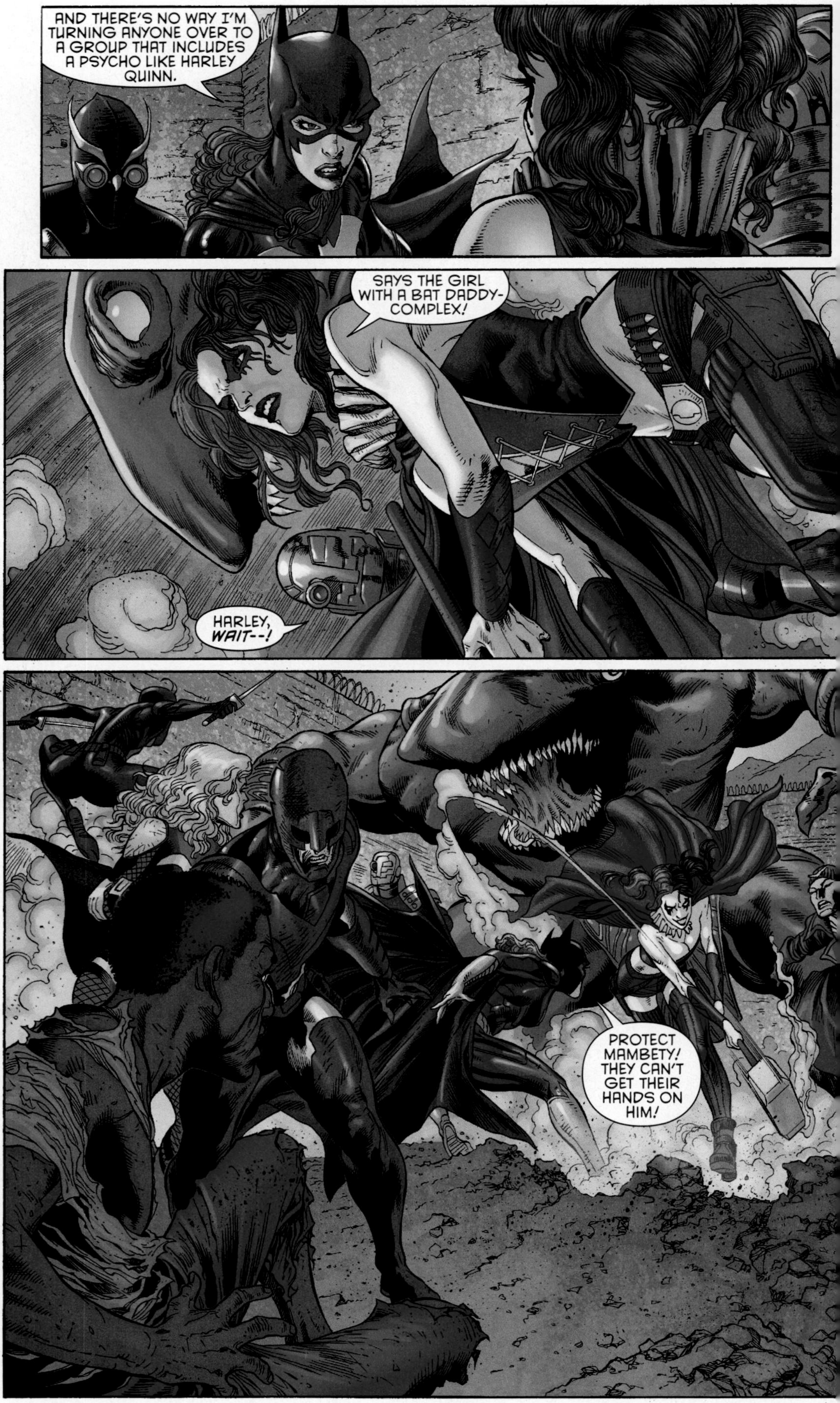
AND THERE'S NO WAY I'M TURNING ANYONE OVER TO A GROUP THAT INCLUDES A PSYCHO LIKE HARLEY QUINN.
SAYS THE GIRL WITH A BAT DADDY-COMPLEX!
HARLEY, WAIT--!
PROTECT MAMBETY! THEY CAN'T GET THEIR HANDS ON HIM!

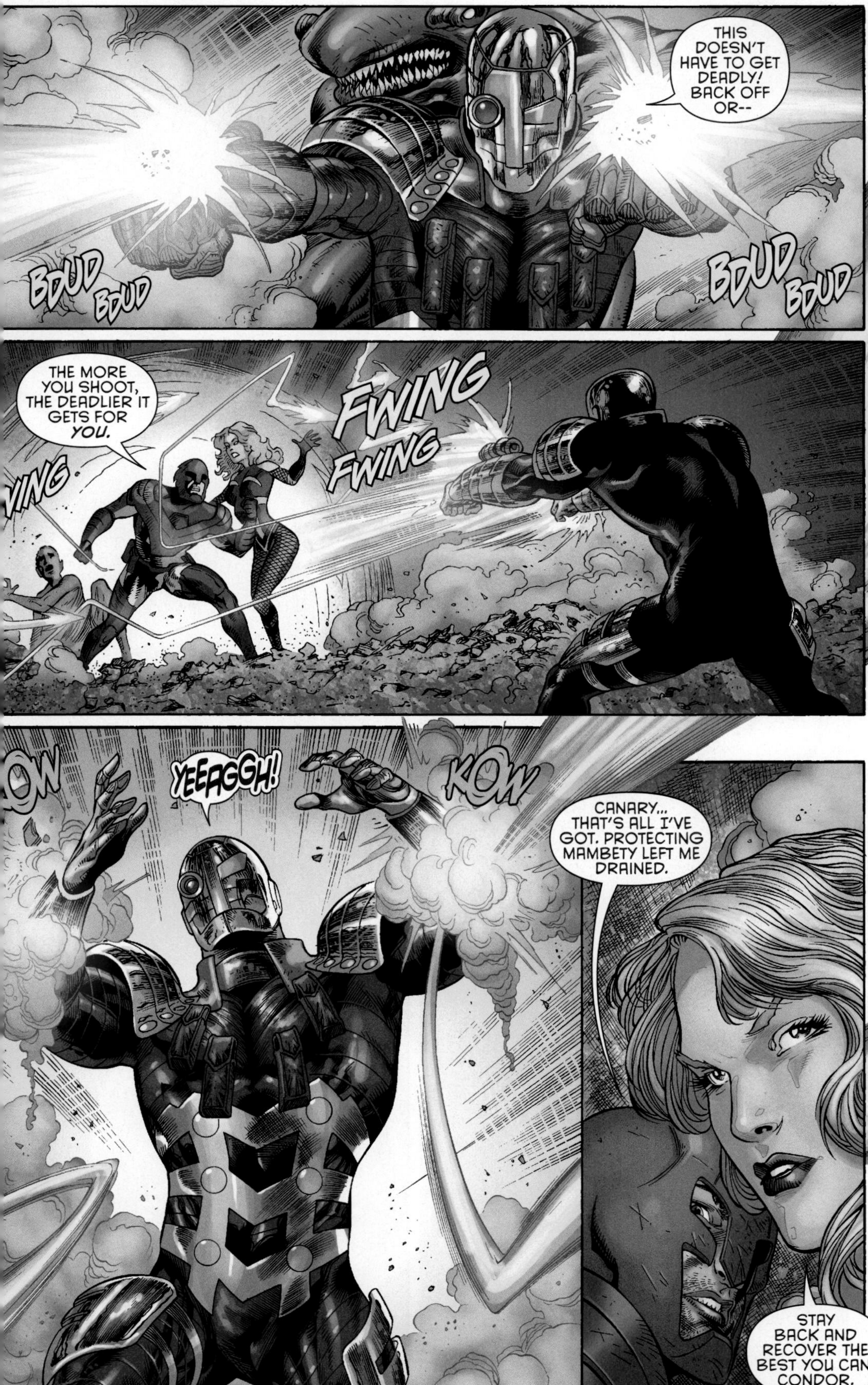
THIS DOESN'T HAVE TO GET DEADLY! BACK OFF OR--
BDUD BDUD
BDUD BDUD
THE MORE YOU SHOOT, THE DEADLIER IT GETS FOR YOU.
VING
FWING FWING
OW
YEEAGGH!
KOW
CANARY... THAT'S ALL I'VE GOT. PROTECTING MAMBETY LEFT ME DRAINED.
STAY BACK AND RECOVER THE BEST YOU CAN, CONDOR.

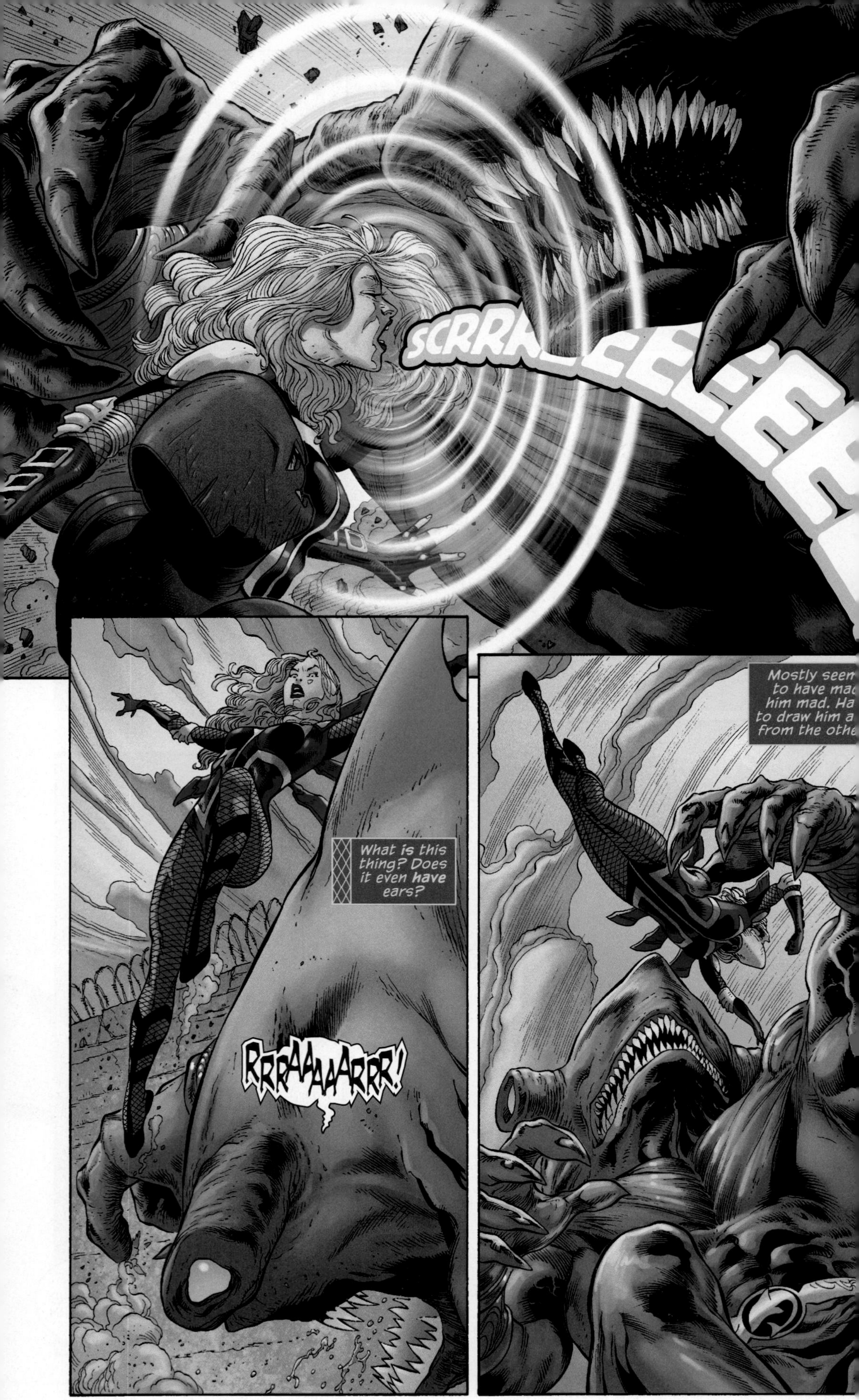
SCRR
What is this thing? Does it even have ears?
RRRAAAAARRR!
Mostly seem to have mad him mad. Ha to draw him a from the othe

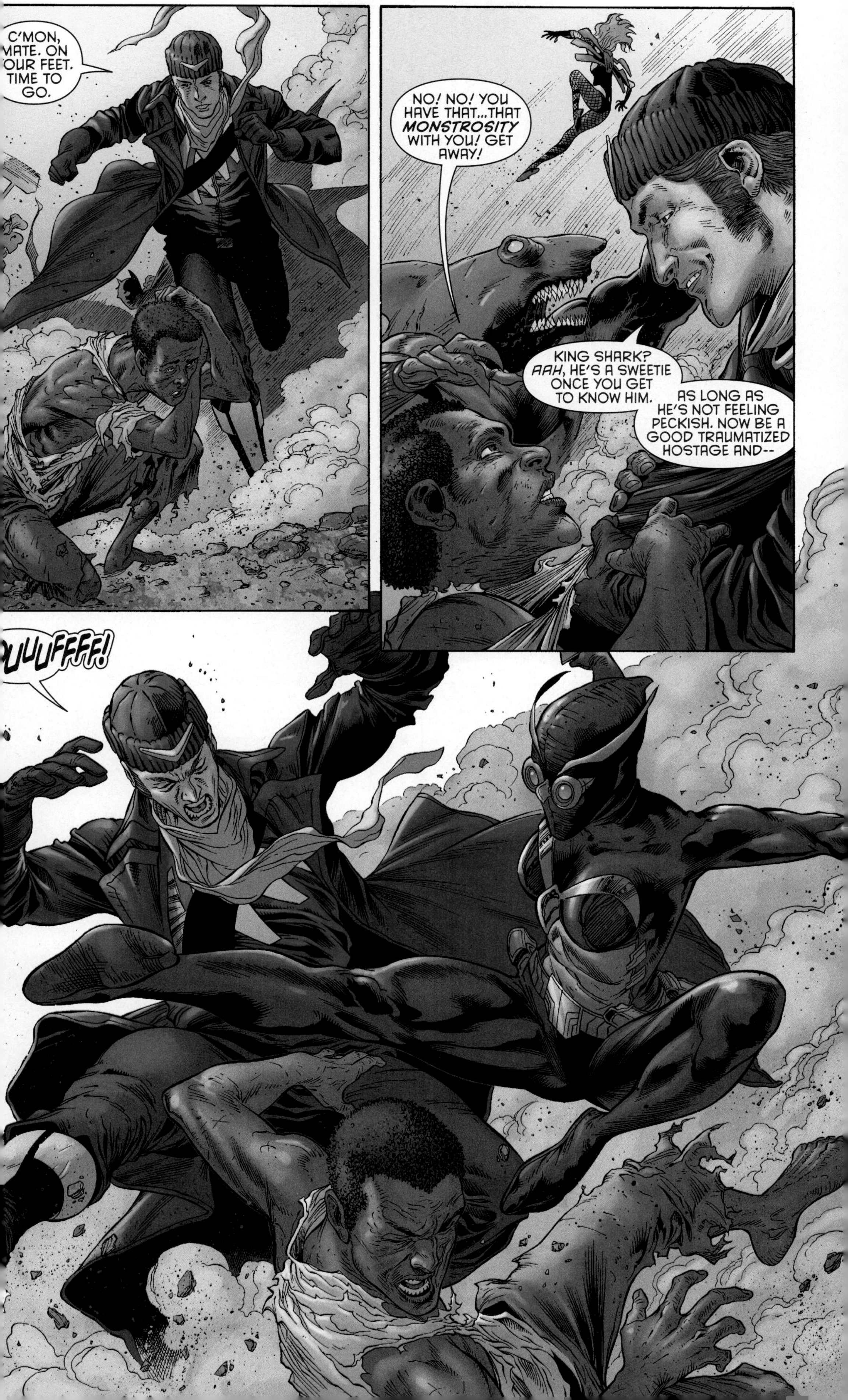
C'MON, MATE. ON OUR FEET. TIME TO GO.
NO! NO! YOU HAVE THAT...THAT MONSTROSITY WITH YOU! GET AWAY!
KING SHARK? AAH, HE'S A SWEETIE ONCE YOU GET TO KNOW HIM.
AS LONG AS HE'S NOT FEELING PECKISH. NOW BE A GOOD TRAUMATIZED HOSTAGE AND--
UUUFFFF!

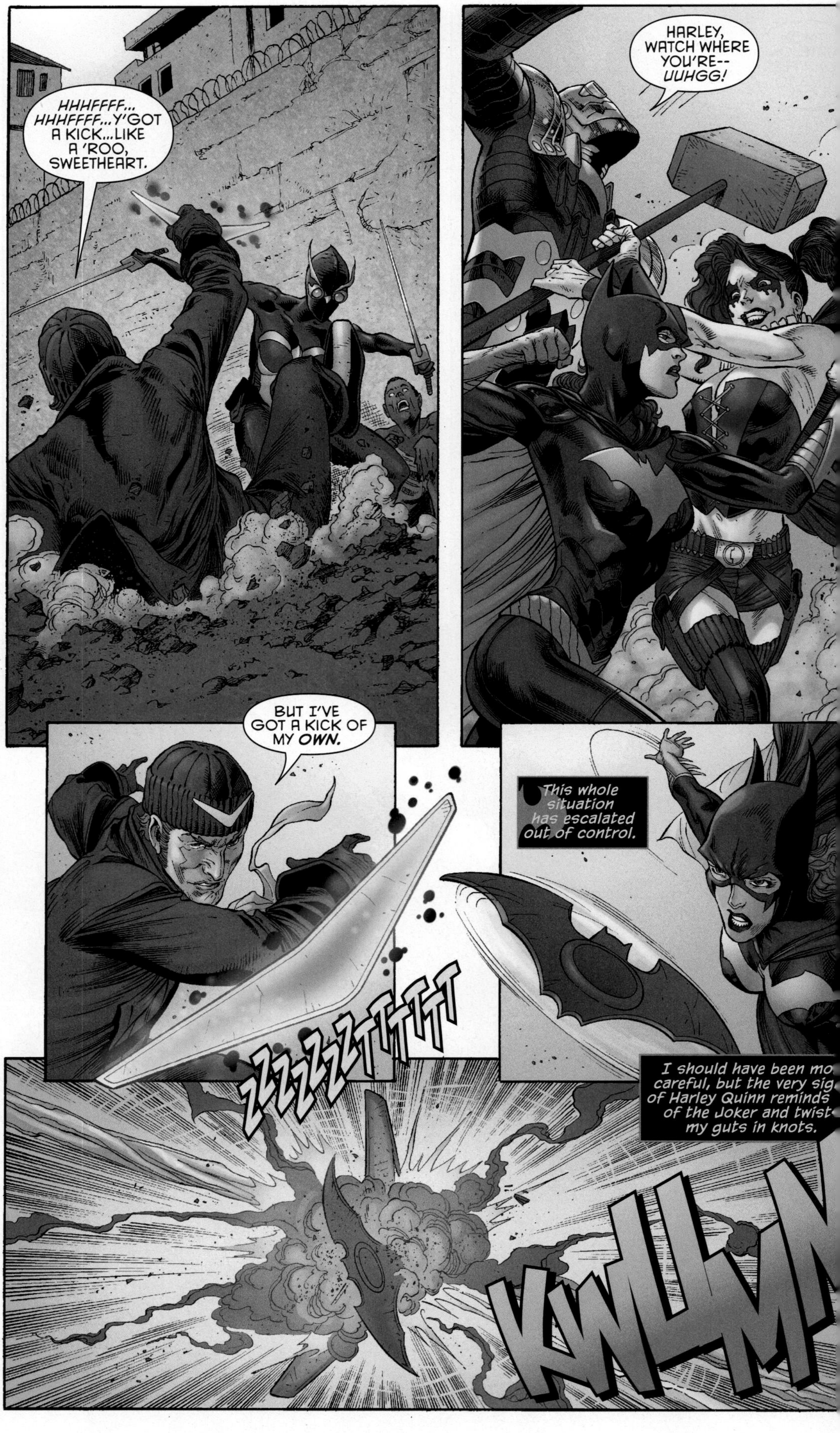
HHHFFFF... HHHFFFF...Y'GOT A KICK...LIKE A 'ROO, SWEETHEART.
HARLEY, WATCH WHERE YOU'RE-- UUHGG!
BUT I'VE GOT A KICK OF MY OWN.
This whole situation has escalated out of control.
ZZZZZZTTTTTT
I should have been mo careful, but the very sig of Harley Quinn reminds of the Joker and twist my guts in knots.
KWUMM

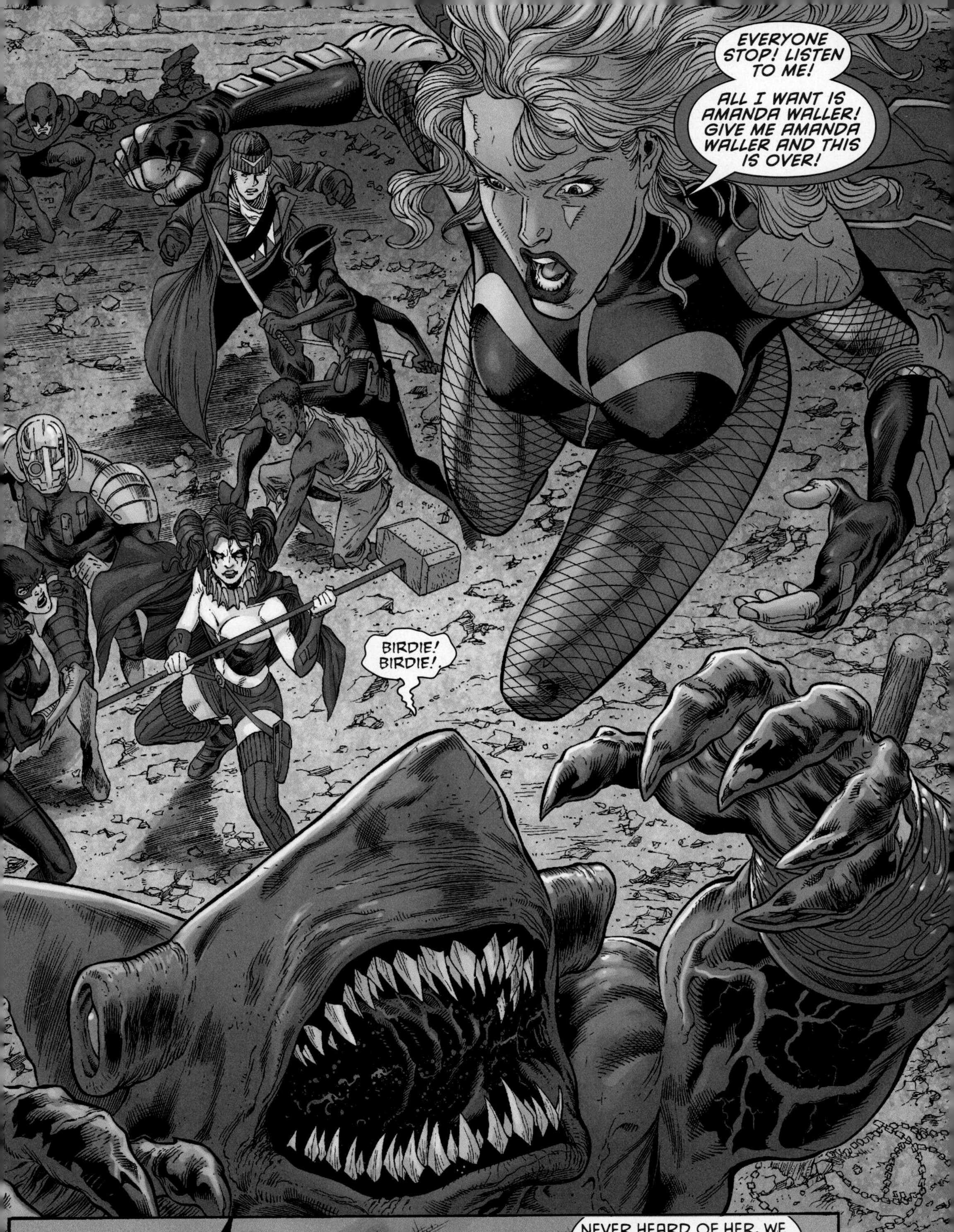
EVERYONE STOP! LISTEN TO ME!
ALL I WANT IS AMANDA WALLER! GIVE ME AMANDA WALLER AND THIS IS OVER!
BIRDIE! BIRDIE!

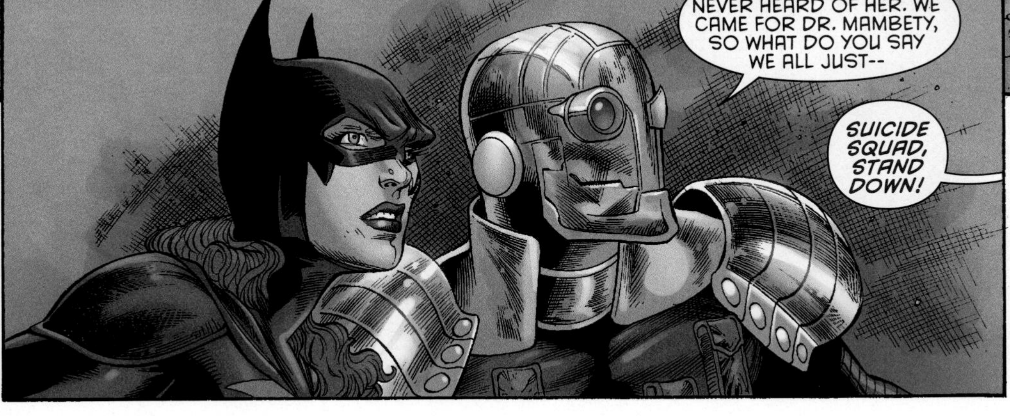
NEVER HEARD OF HER. WE CAME FOR DR. MAMBETY, SO WHAT DO YOU SAY WE ALL JUST--
SUICIDE SQUAD, STAND DOWN!

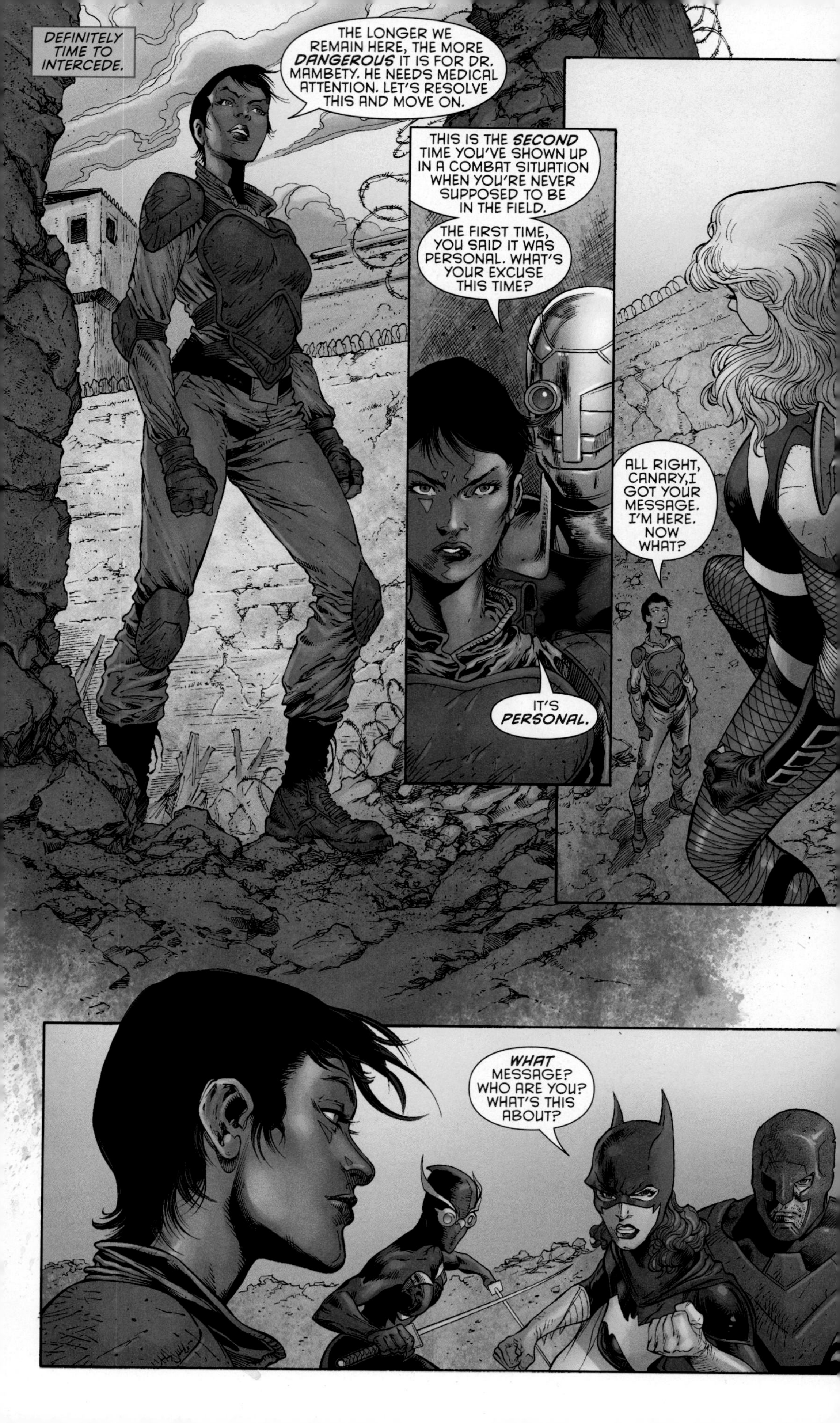
DEFINITELY TIME TO INTERCEDE.
THE LONGER WE REMAIN HERE, THE MORE DANGEROUS IT IS FOR DR. MAMBETY. HE NEEDS MEDICAL ATTENTION. LET'S RESOLVE THIS AND MOVE ON.
THIS IS THE SECOND TIME YOU'VE SHOWN UP IN A COMBAT SITUATION WHEN YOU'RE NEVER SUPPOSED TO BE IN THE FIELD.
THE FIRST TIME, YOU SAID IT WAS PERSONAL. WHAT'S YOUR EXCUSE THIS TIME?
IT'S PERSONAL.
ALL RIGHT, CANARY, I GOT YOUR MESSAGE. I'M HERE. NOW WHAT?
WHAT MESSAGE? WHO ARE YOU? WHAT'S THIS ABOUT?

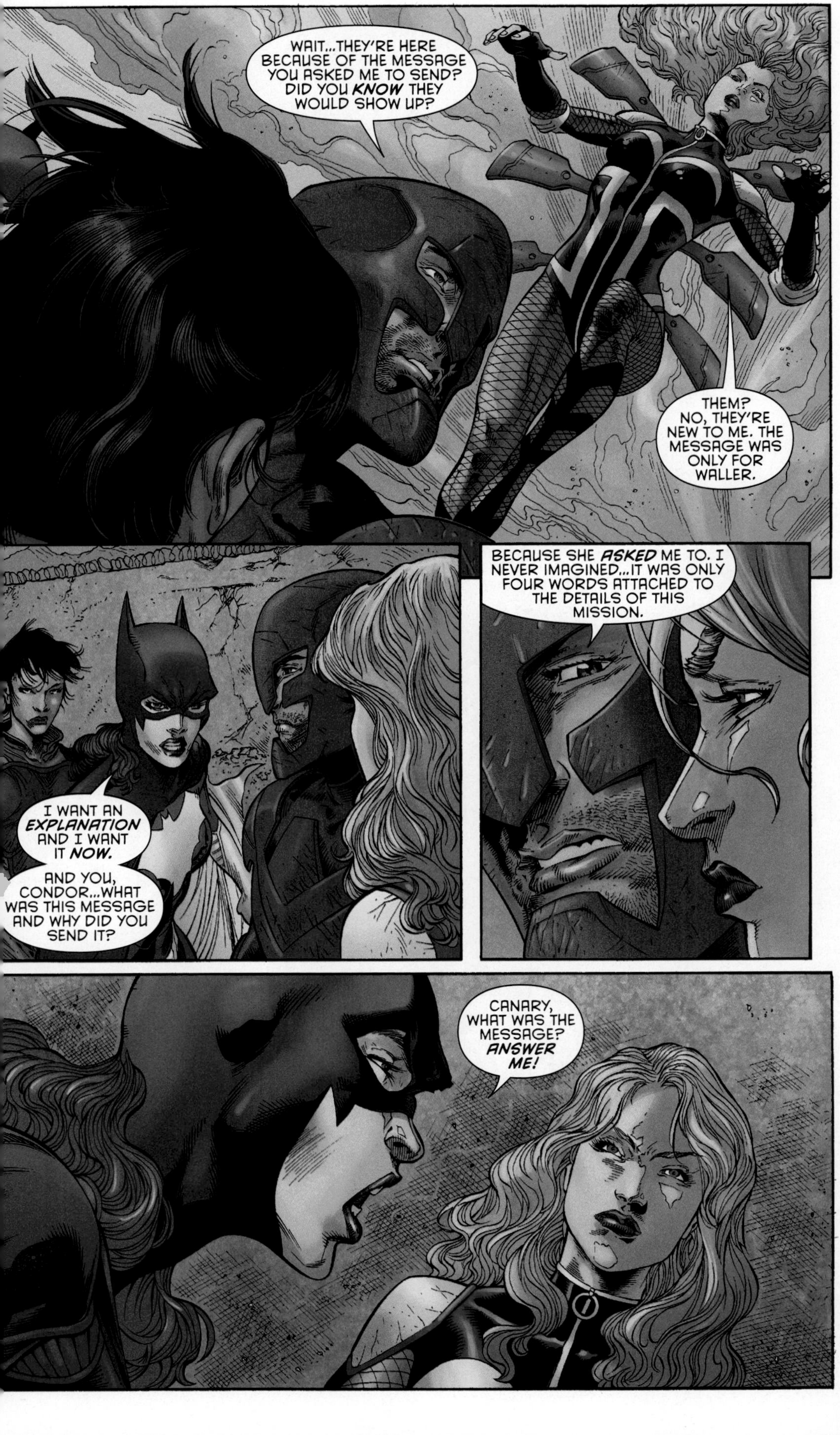
WAIT...THEY'RE HERE BECAUSE OF THE MESSAGE YOU ASKED ME TO SEND? DID YOU *KNOW* THEY WOULD SHOW UP?
THEM? NO, THEY'RE NEW TO ME. THE MESSAGE WAS ONLY FOR WALLER.
I WANT AN *EXPLANATION* AND I WANT IT *NOW.*
AND YOU, CONDOR...WHAT WAS THIS MESSAGE AND WHY DID YOU SEND IT?
BECAUSE SHE *ASKED* ME TO. I NEVER IMAGINED...IT WAS ONLY FOUR WORDS ATTACHED TO THE DETAILS OF THIS MISSION.
CANARY, WHAT WAS THE MESSAGE? *ANSWER ME!*

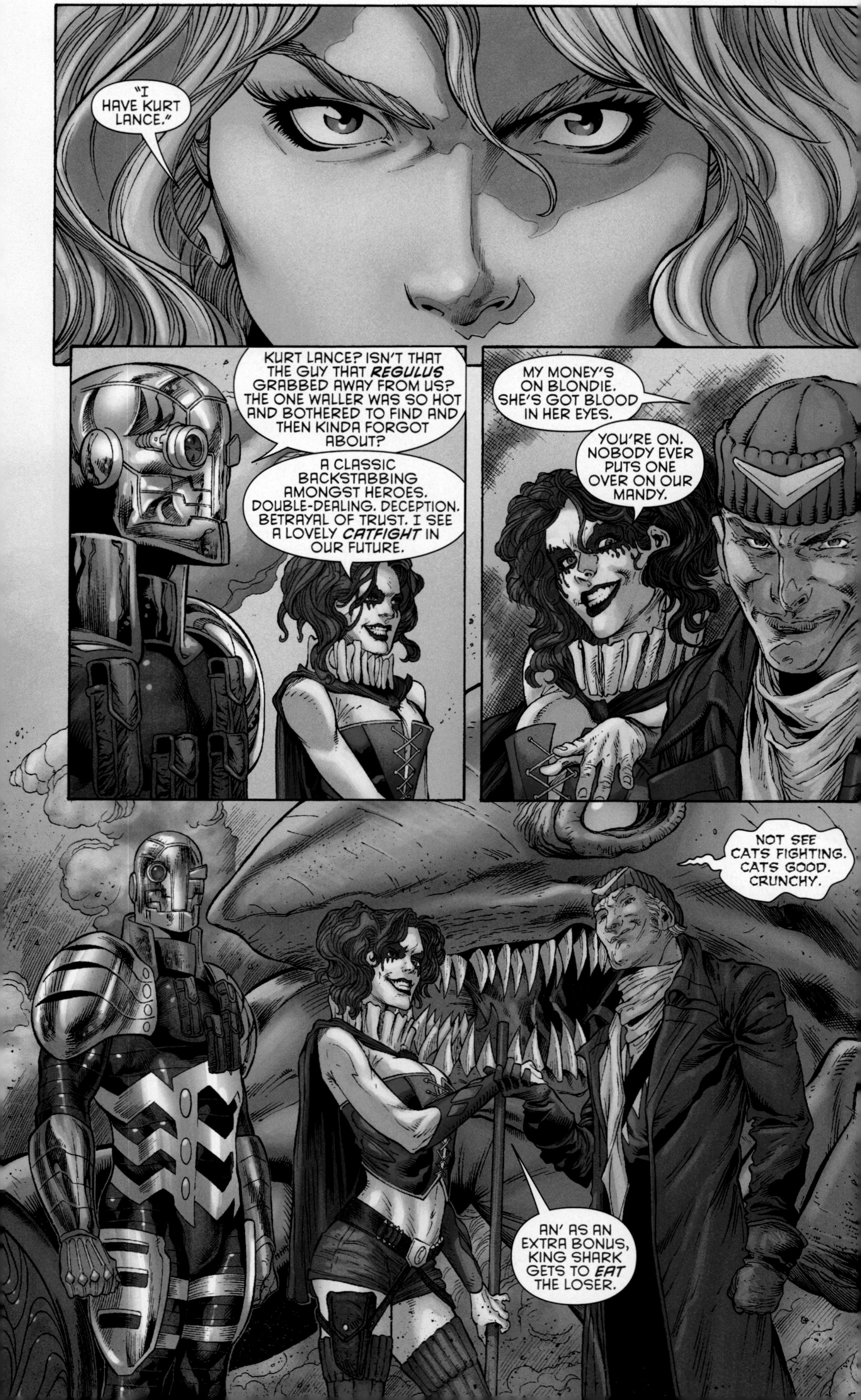
"I HAVE KURT LANCE."
KURT LANCE? ISN'T THAT THE GUY THAT *REGULUS* GRABBED AWAY FROM US? THE ONE WALLER WAS SO HOT AND BOTHERED TO FIND AND THEN KINDA FORGOT ABOUT?
A CLASSIC BACKSTABBING AMONGST HEROES. DOUBLE-DEALING. DECEPTION. BETRAYAL OF TRUST. I SEE A LOVELY *CATFIGHT* IN OUR FUTURE.
MY MONEY'S ON BLONDIE. SHE'S GOT BLOOD IN HER EYES.
YOU'RE ON. NOBODY EVER PUTS ONE OVER ON OUR MANDY.
NOT SEE CATS FIGHTING. CATS GOOD. CRUNCHY.
AN' AS AN EXTRA BONUS, KING SHARK GETS TO *EAT* THE LOSER.

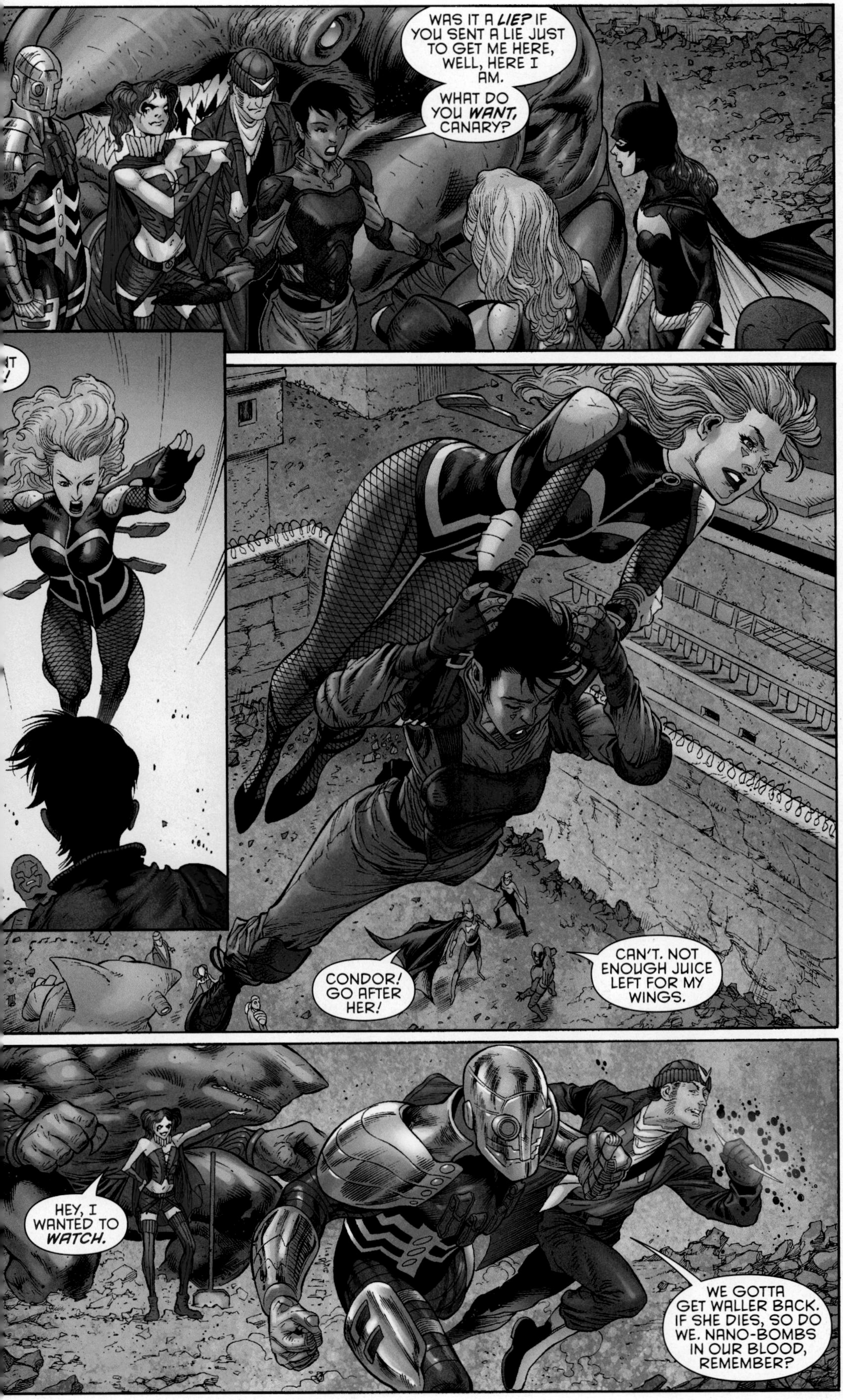
WAS IT A *LIE?* IF YOU SENT A LIE JUST TO GET ME HERE, WELL, HERE I AM.
WHAT DO YOU *WANT,* CANARY?
CONDOR! GO AFTER HER!
CAN'T. NOT ENOUGH JUICE LEFT FOR MY WINGS.
HEY, I WANTED TO *WATCH.*
WE GOTTA GET WALLER BACK. IF SHE DIES, SO DO WE. NANO-BOMBS IN OUR BLOOD, REMEMBER?

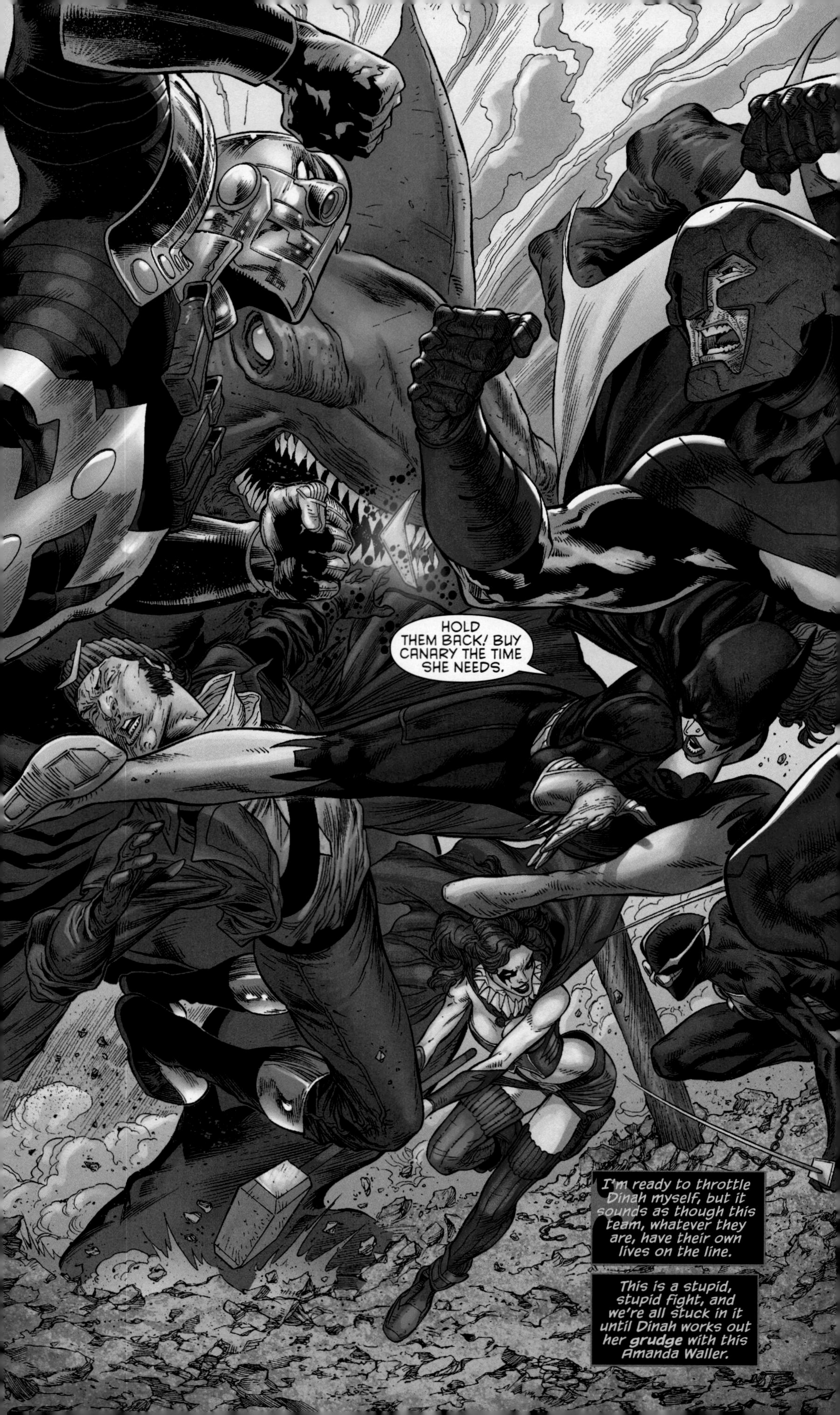
HOLD THEM BACK! BUY CANARY THE TIME SHE NEEDS.
I'm ready to throttle Dinah myself, but it sounds as though this team, whatever they are, have their own lives on the line.
This is a stupid, stupid fight, and we're all stuck in it until Dinah works out her **grudge** with this Amanda Waller.

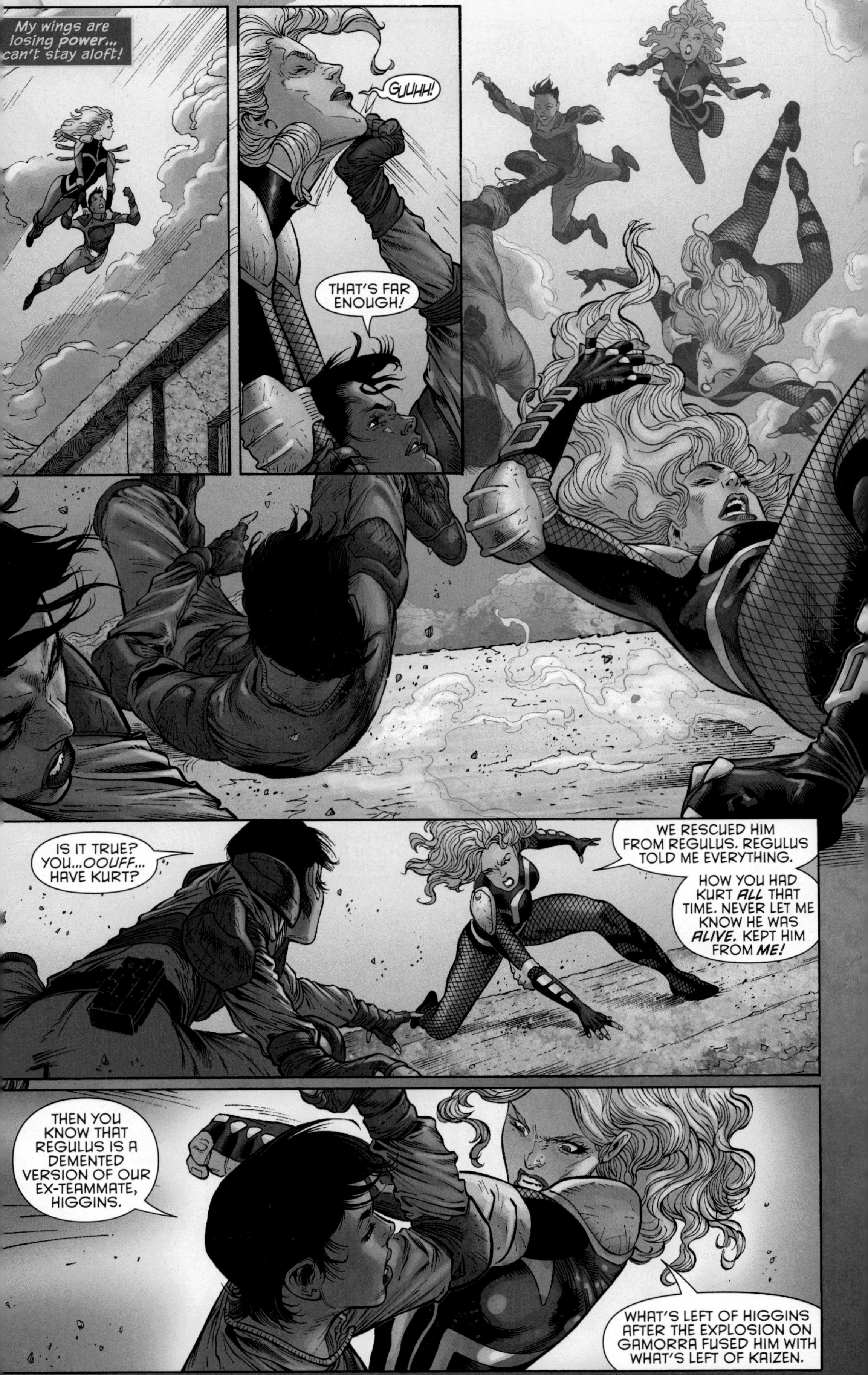
My wings are losing power... can't stay aloft!
GUUHH!
THAT'S FAR ENOUGH!
IS IT TRUE? YOU...OOUFF... HAVE KURT?
WE RESCUED HIM FROM REGULUS. REGULUS TOLD ME EVERYTHING.
HOW YOU HAD KURT ALL THAT TIME. NEVER LET ME KNOW HE WAS ALIVE. KEPT HIM FROM ME!
THEN YOU KNOW THAT REGULUS IS A DEMENTED VERSION OF OUR EX-TEAMMATE, HIGGINS.
WHAT'S LEFT OF HIGGINS AFTER THE EXPLOSION ON GAMORRA FUSED HIM WITH WHAT'S LEFT OF KAIZEN.

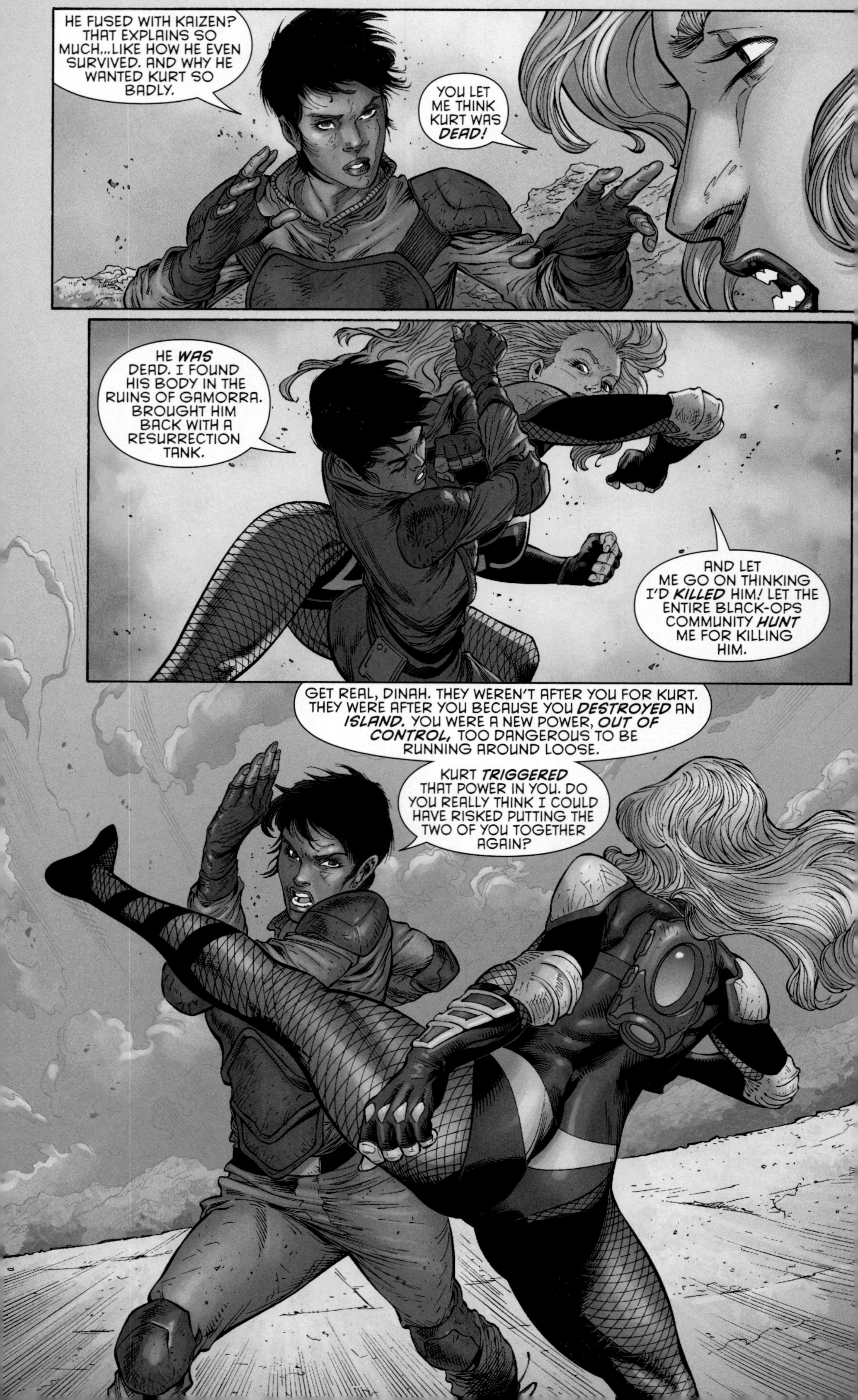
HE FUSED WITH KAIZEN? THAT EXPLAINS SO MUCH...LIKE HOW HE EVEN SURVIVED. AND WHY HE WANTED KURT SO BADLY.
YOU LET ME THINK KURT WAS *DEAD!*
HE *WAS* DEAD. I FOUND HIS BODY IN THE RUINS OF GAMORRA. BROUGHT HIM BACK WITH A RESURRECTION TANK.
AND LET ME GO ON THINKING I'D *KILLED* HIM! LET THE ENTIRE BLACK-OPS COMMUNITY *HUNT* ME FOR KILLING HIM.
GET REAL, DINAH. THEY WEREN'T AFTER YOU FOR KURT. THEY WERE AFTER YOU BECAUSE YOU *DESTROYED* AN *ISLAND.* YOU WERE A NEW POWER, *OUT OF CONTROL,* TOO DANGEROUS TO BE RUNNING AROUND LOOSE.
KURT *TRIGGERED* THAT POWER IN YOU. DO YOU REALLY THINK I COULD HAVE RISKED PUTTING THE TWO OF YOU TOGETHER AGAIN?

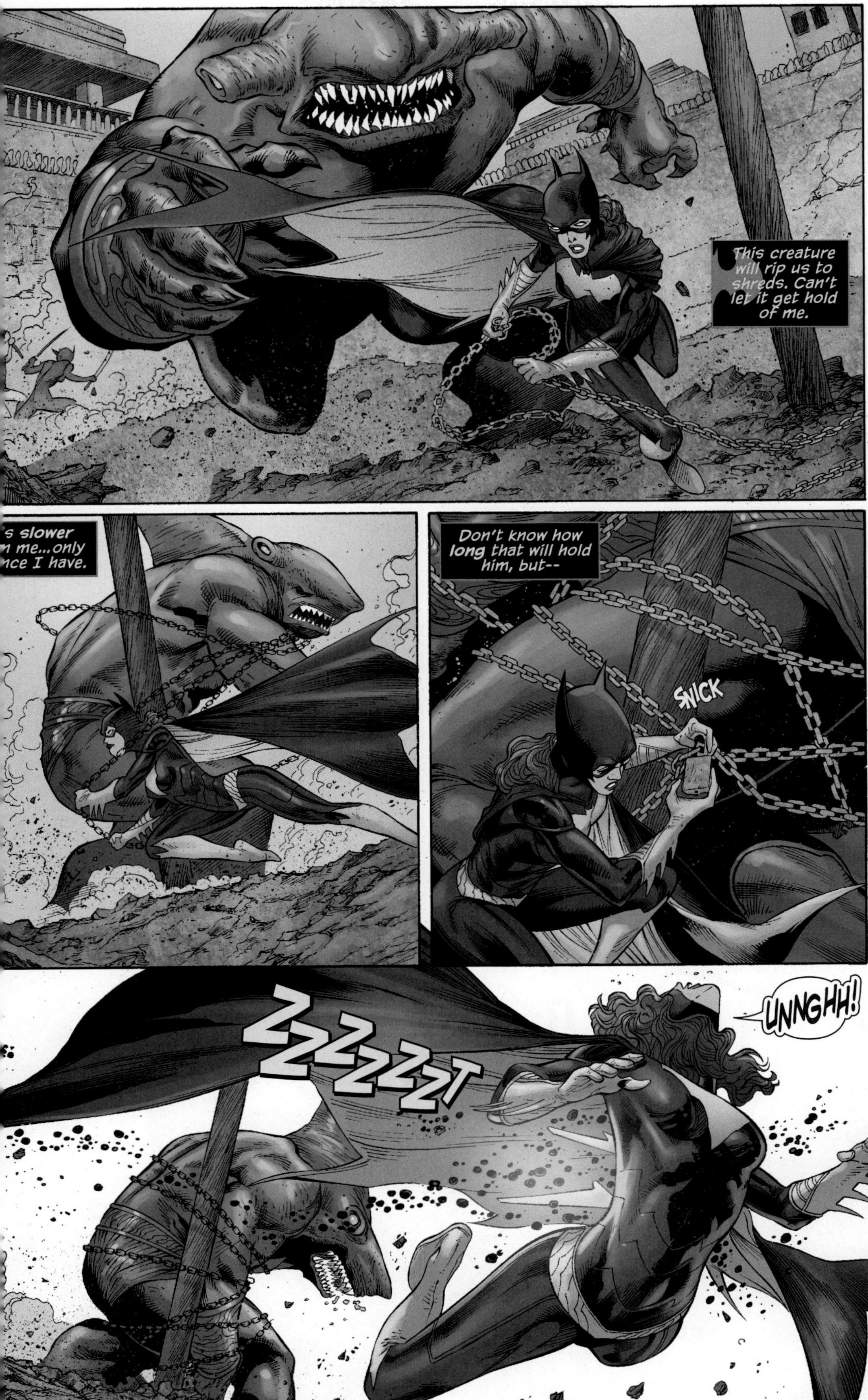
This creature will rip us to shreds. Can't let it get hold of me.
...'s slower ...n me...only ...nce I have.
Don't know how long that will hold him, but--
SNICK
ZZZZZZT
UNNGHH!

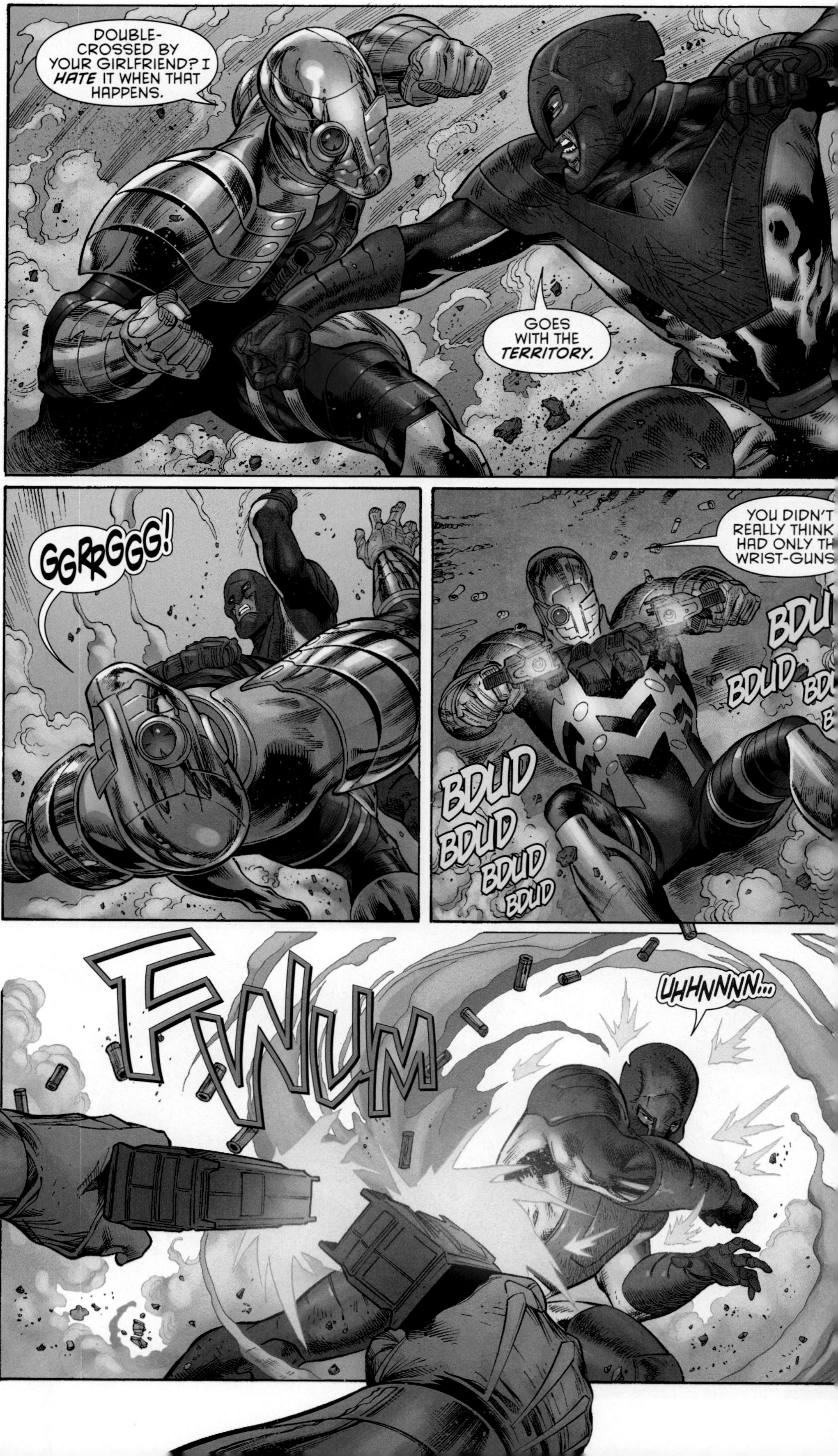
DOUBLE-CROSSED BY YOUR GIRLFRIEND? I *HATE* IT WHEN THAT HAPPENS.
GOES WITH THE *TERRITORY.*
GGRRGGG!
YOU DIDN'T REALLY THINK HAD ONLY TH WRIST-GUNS
BDUD
BDUD BDUD BDUD BDUD
FWNUM
UHHNNNN...

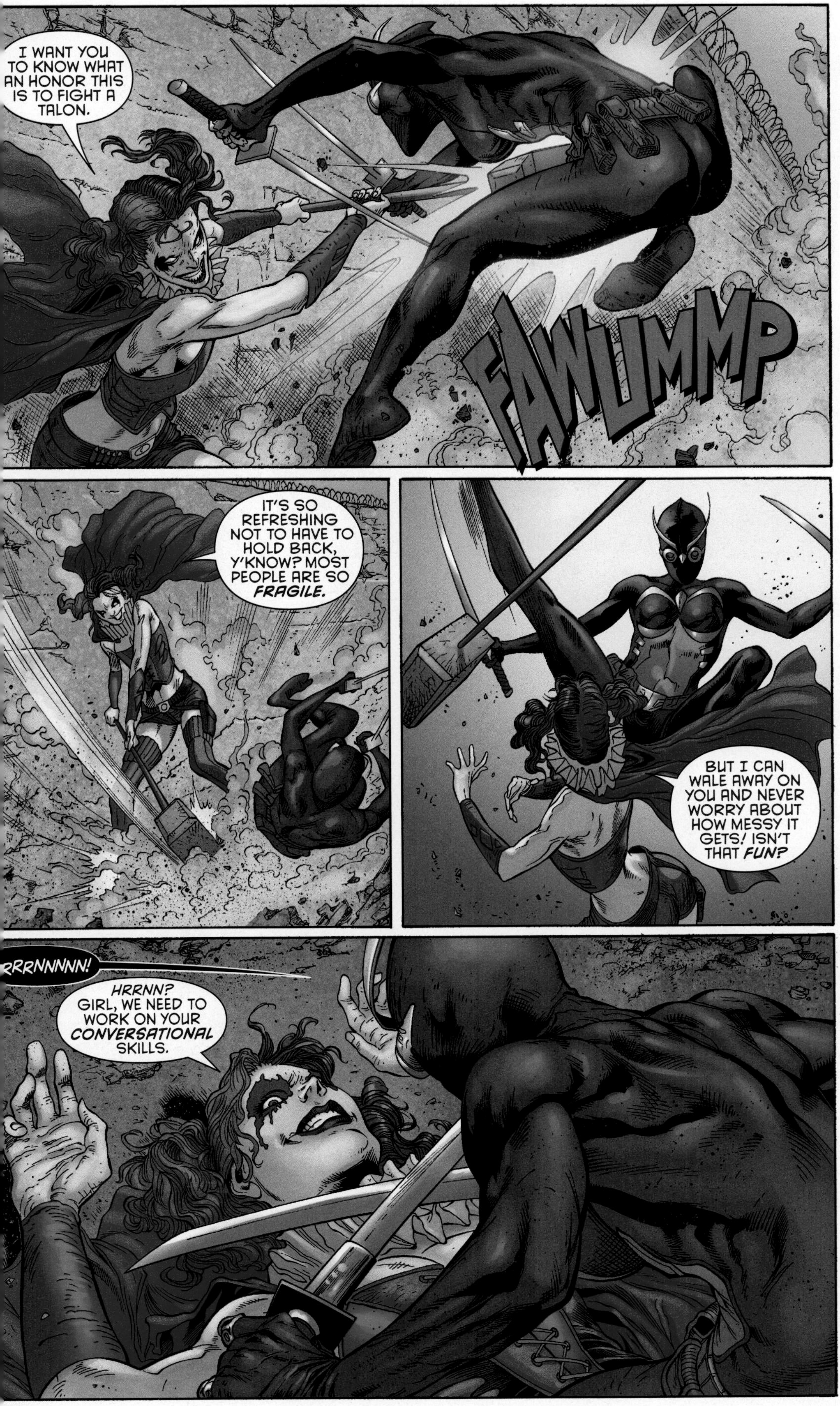
I WANT YOU TO KNOW WHAT AN HONOR THIS IS TO FIGHT A TALON.
FAWUMMP
IT'S SO REFRESHING NOT TO HAVE TO HOLD BACK, Y'KNOW? MOST PEOPLE ARE SO FRAGILE.
BUT I CAN WALE AWAY ON YOU AND NEVER WORRY ABOUT HOW MESSY IT GETS! ISN'T THAT FUN?
RRRNNNNN!
HRRNN? GIRL, WE NEED TO WORK ON YOUR CONVERSATIONAL SKILLS.

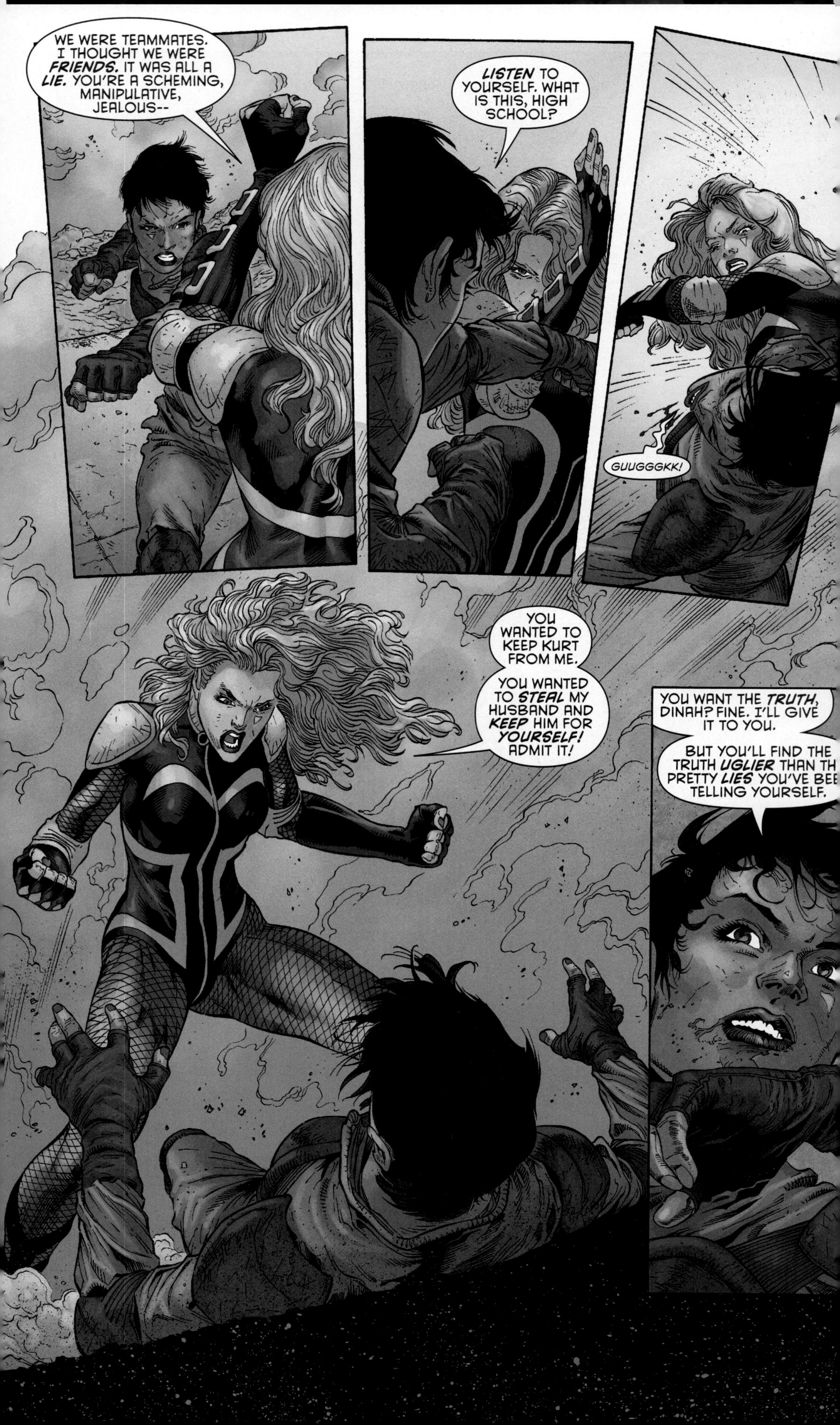
WE WERE TEAMMATES. I THOUGHT WE WERE FRIENDS. IT WAS ALL A LIE. YOU'RE A SCHEMING, MANIPULATIVE, JEALOUS--
LISTEN TO YOURSELF. WHAT IS THIS, HIGH SCHOOL?
GUUGGGKK!
YOU WANTED TO KEEP KURT FROM ME.
YOU WANTED TO STEAL MY HUSBAND AND KEEP HIM FOR YOURSELF! ADMIT IT!
YOU WANT THE TRUTH, DINAH? FINE. I'LL GIVE IT TO YOU.
BUT YOU'LL FIND THE TRUTH UGLIER THAN TH PRETTY LIES YOU'VE BEE TELLING YOURSELF.

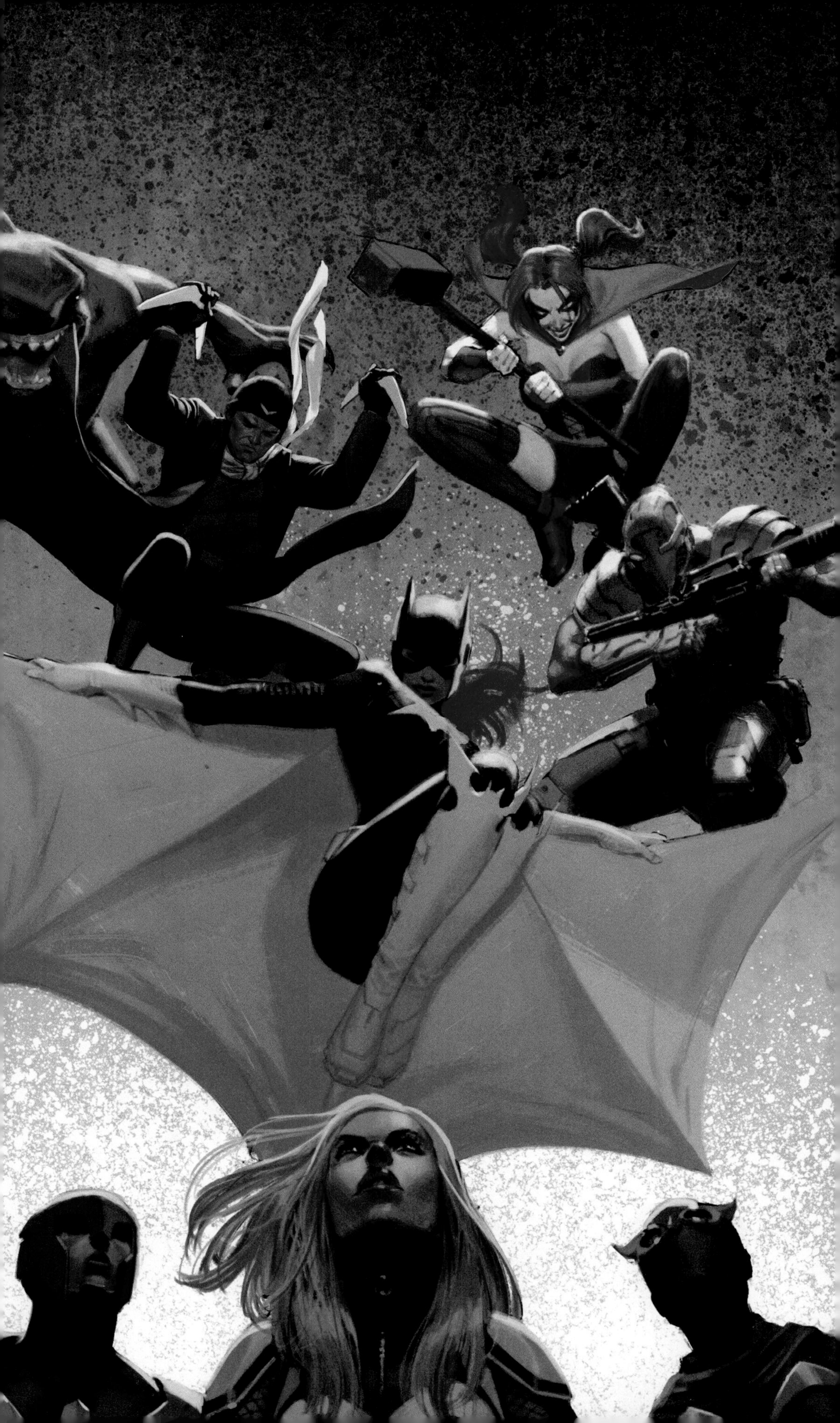

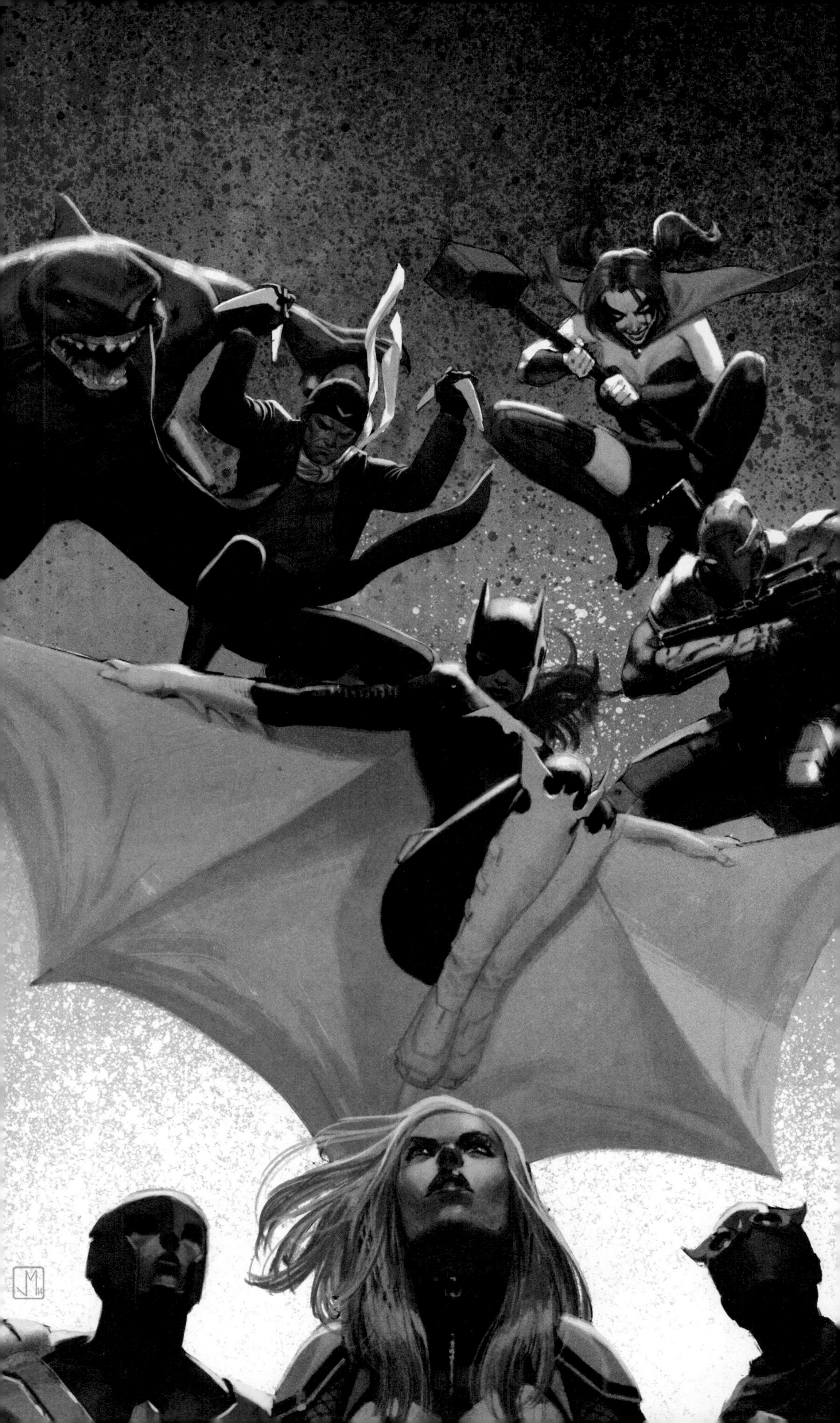

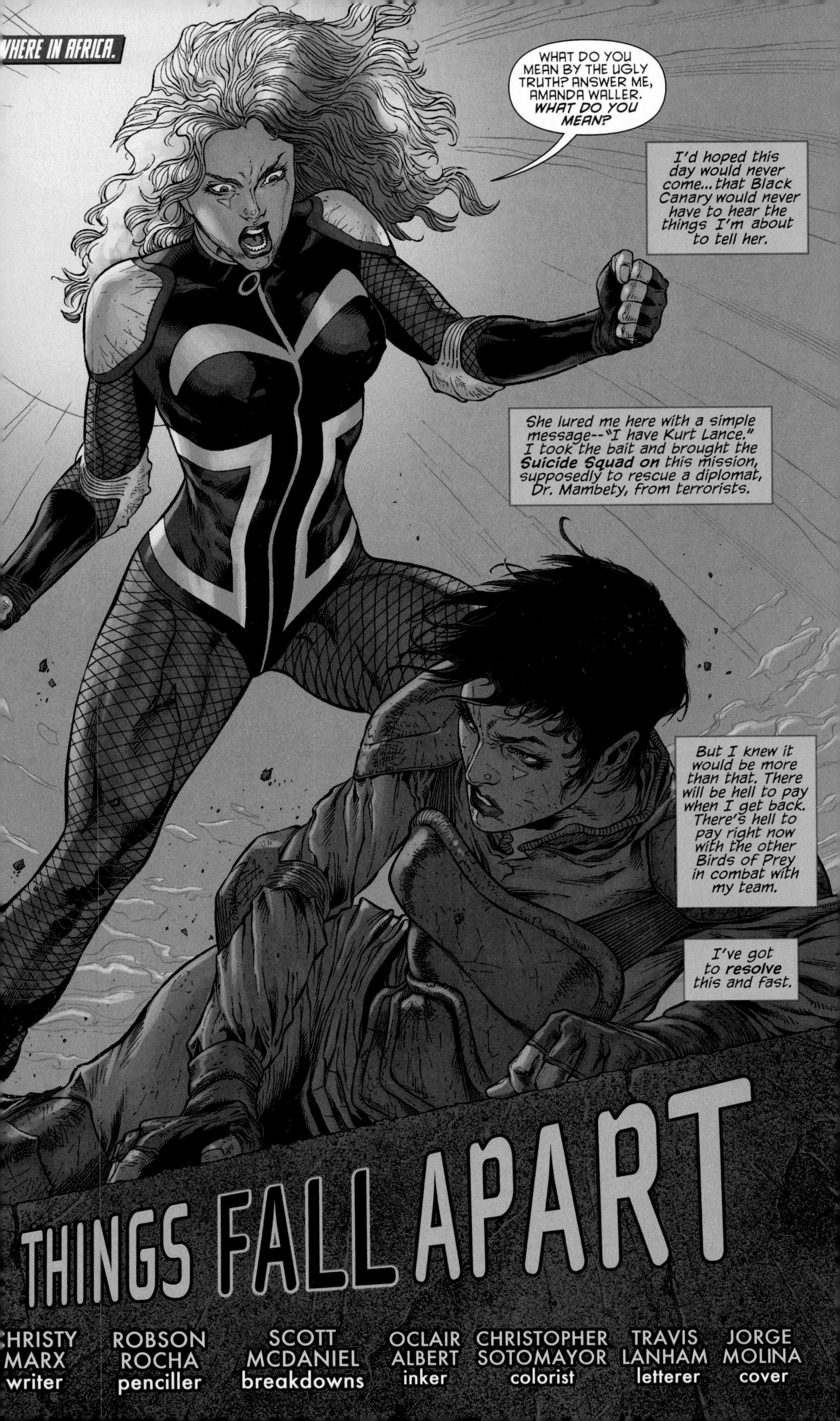

WHERE IN AFRICA.
WHAT DO YOU MEAN BY THE UGLY TRUTH? ANSWER ME, AMANDA WALLER. *WHAT DO YOU MEAN?*
I'd hoped this day would never come...that Black Canary would never have to hear the things I'm about to tell her.
She lured me here with a simple message--"I have Kurt Lance." I took the bait and brought the **Suicide Squad on** this mission, supposedly to rescue a diplomat, Dr. Mambety, from terrorists.
But I knew it would be more than that. There will be hell to pay when I get back. There's hell to pay right now with the other Birds of Prey in combat with my team.
I've got to **resolve** this and fast.
THINGS FALL APART
HRISTY MARX writer
ROBSON ROCHA penciller
SCOTT MCDANIEL breakdowns
OCLAIR ALBERT inker
CHRISTOPHER SOTOMAYOR colorist
TRAVIS LANHAM letterer
JORGE MOLINA cover

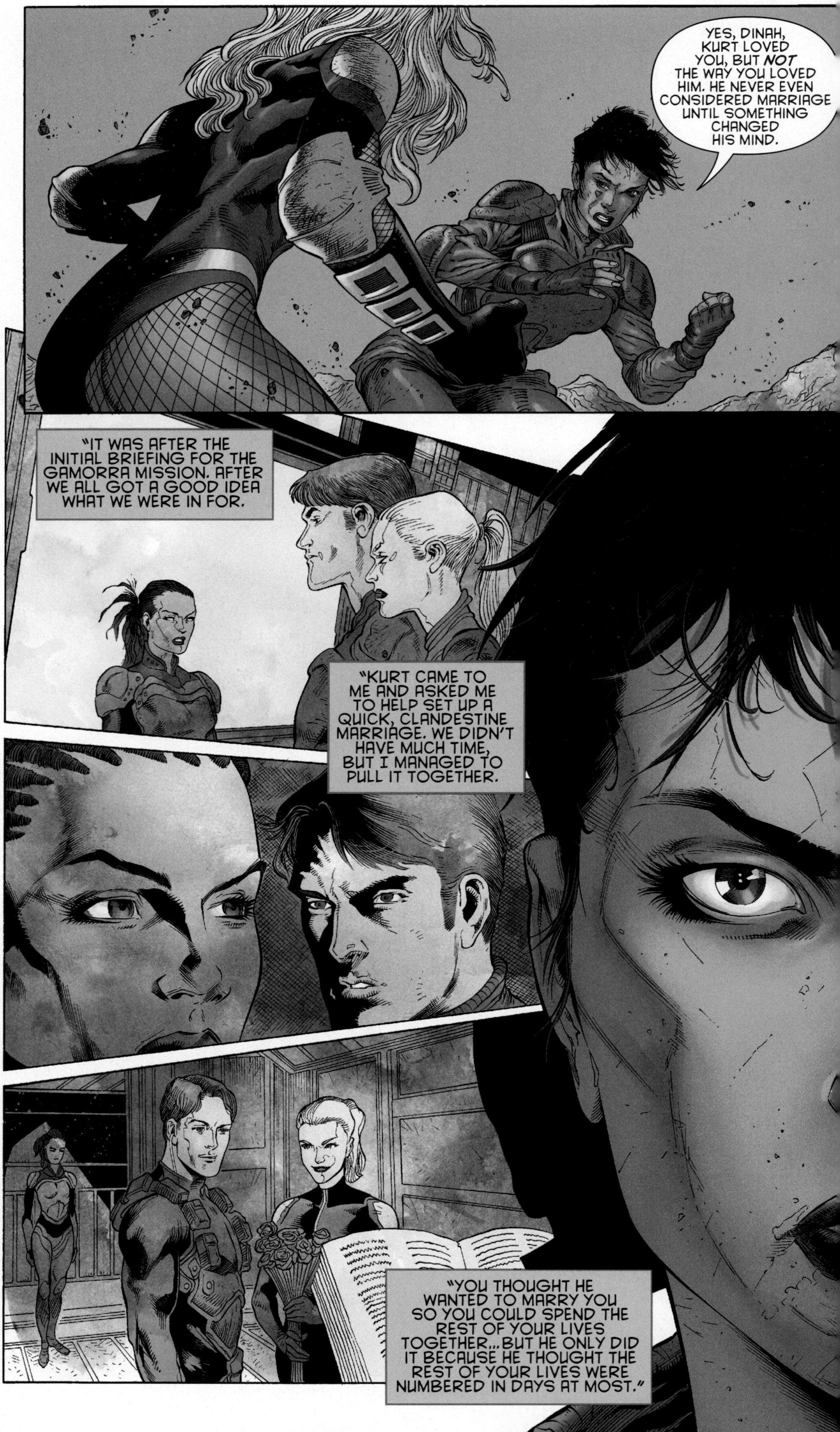
YES, DINAH, KURT LOVED YOU, BUT ***NOT*** THE WAY YOU LOVED HIM. HE NEVER EVEN CONSIDERED MARRIAGE UNTIL SOMETHING CHANGED HIS MIND.
"IT WAS AFTER THE INITIAL BRIEFING FOR THE GAMORRA MISSION. AFTER WE ALL GOT A GOOD IDEA WHAT WE WERE IN FOR.
"KURT CAME TO ME AND ASKED ME TO HELP SET UP A QUICK, CLANDESTINE MARRIAGE. WE DIDN'T HAVE MUCH TIME, BUT I MANAGED TO PULL IT TOGETHER.
"YOU THOUGHT HE WANTED TO MARRY YOU SO YOU COULD SPEND THE REST OF YOUR LIVES TOGETHER...BUT HE ONLY DID IT BECAUSE HE THOUGHT THE REST OF YOUR LIVES WERE NUMBERED IN DAYS AT MOST."

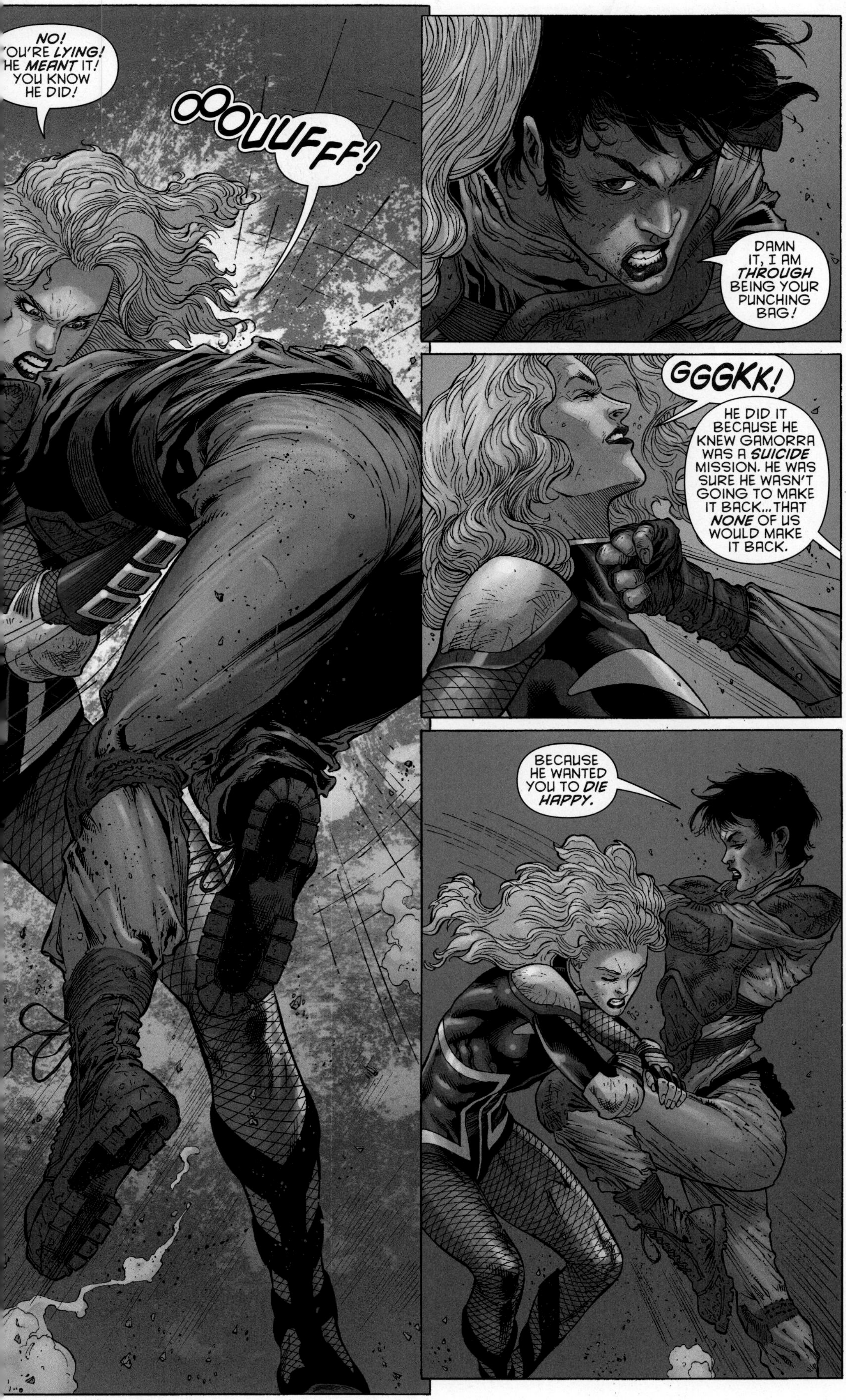

NO! YOU'RE LYING! HE MEANT IT! YOU KNOW HE DID!
OOOUUUFFF!
DAMN IT, I AM THROUGH BEING YOUR PUNCHING BAG!
GGGKK!
HE DID IT BECAUSE HE KNEW GAMORRA WAS A SUICIDE MISSION. HE WAS SURE HE WASN'T GOING TO MAKE IT BACK... THAT NONE OF US WOULD MAKE IT BACK.
BECAUSE HE WANTED YOU TO DIE HAPPY.

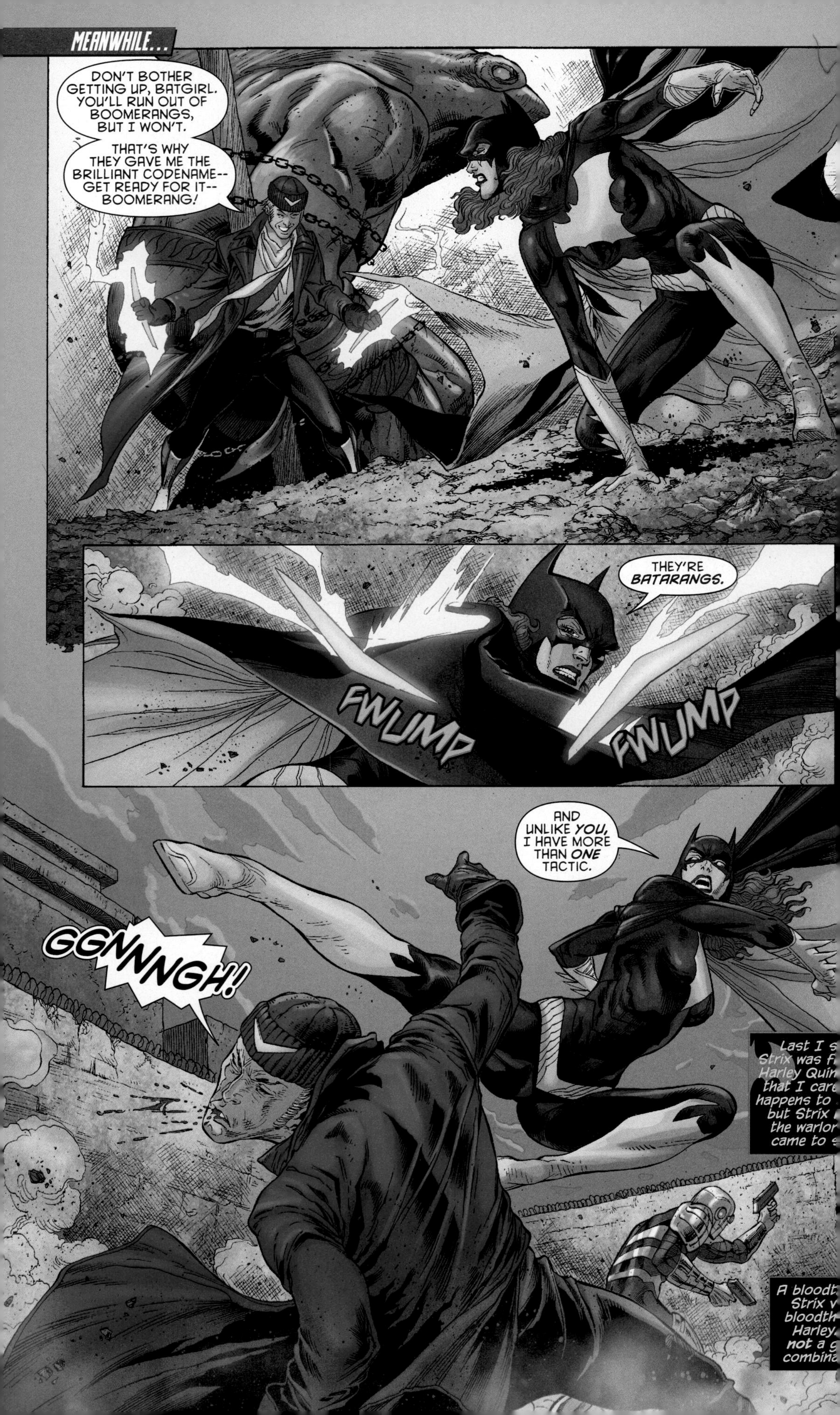

MEANWHILE...
DON'T BOTHER GETTING UP, BATGIRL. YOU'LL RUN OUT OF BOOMERANGS, BUT I WON'T.
THAT'S WHY THEY GAVE ME THE BRILLIANT CODENAME-- GET READY FOR IT-- BOOMERANG!
THEY'RE *BATARANGS.*
FWUMP
FWUMP
AND UNLIKE *YOU,* I HAVE MORE THAN *ONE* TACTIC.
GGNNNGH!
Last I s
Strix was f
Harley Quin
that I car
happens to
but Strix
the warlor
came to s
A bloodt
Strix v
bloodth
Harley,
not a g
combina

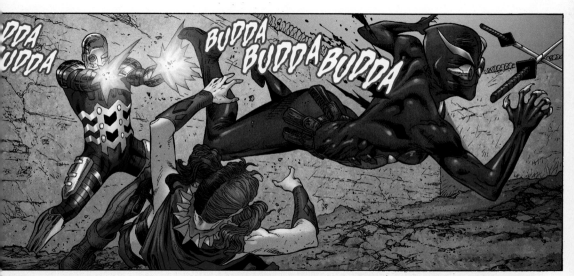

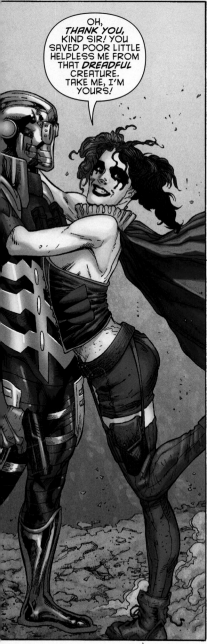

DDA
UDDA
BUDDA
BUDDA BUDDA
OH, THANK YOU, KIND SIR! YOU SAVED POOR LITTLE HELPLESS ME FROM THAT DREADFUL CREATURE. TAKE ME, I'M YOURS!
GIVE IT A REST, HARLEY. IT'S WEIRD THOUGH. SHE DIDN'T EVEN TRY TO DODGE MY BULLETS. SHE WENT DOWN WAY TOO EASILY...
HRRRRNNNNNN!
OR... MAYBE NOT.

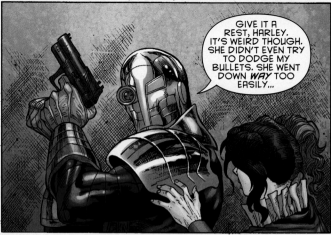

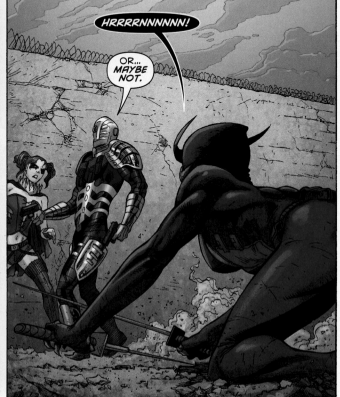

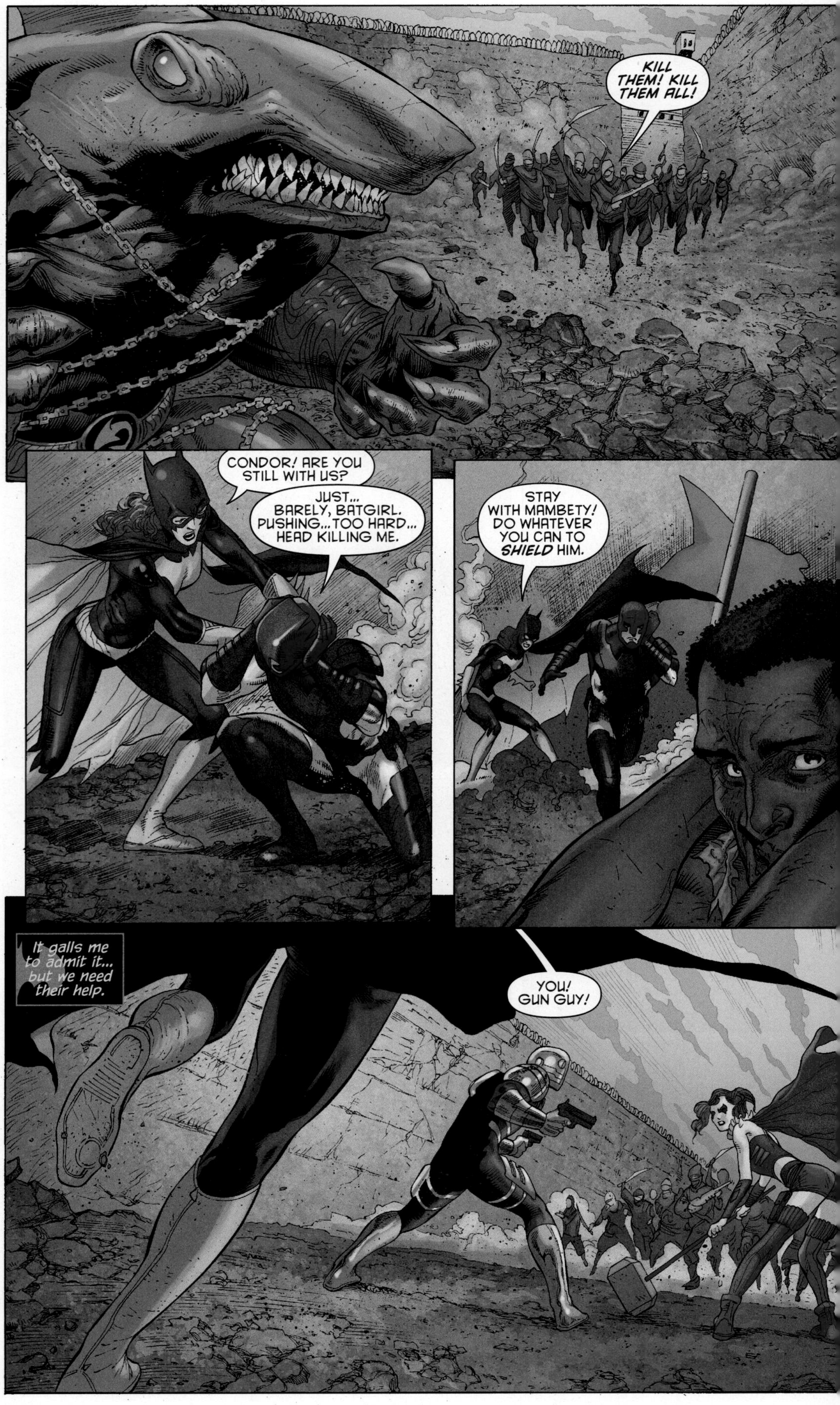
KILL THEM! KILL THEM ALL!
CONDOR! ARE YOU STILL WITH US?
JUST... BARELY, BATGIRL. PUSHING...TOO HARD... HEAD KILLING ME.
STAY WITH MAMBETY! DO WHATEVER YOU CAN TO SHIELD HIM.
It galls me to admit it... but we need their help.
YOU! GUN GUY!

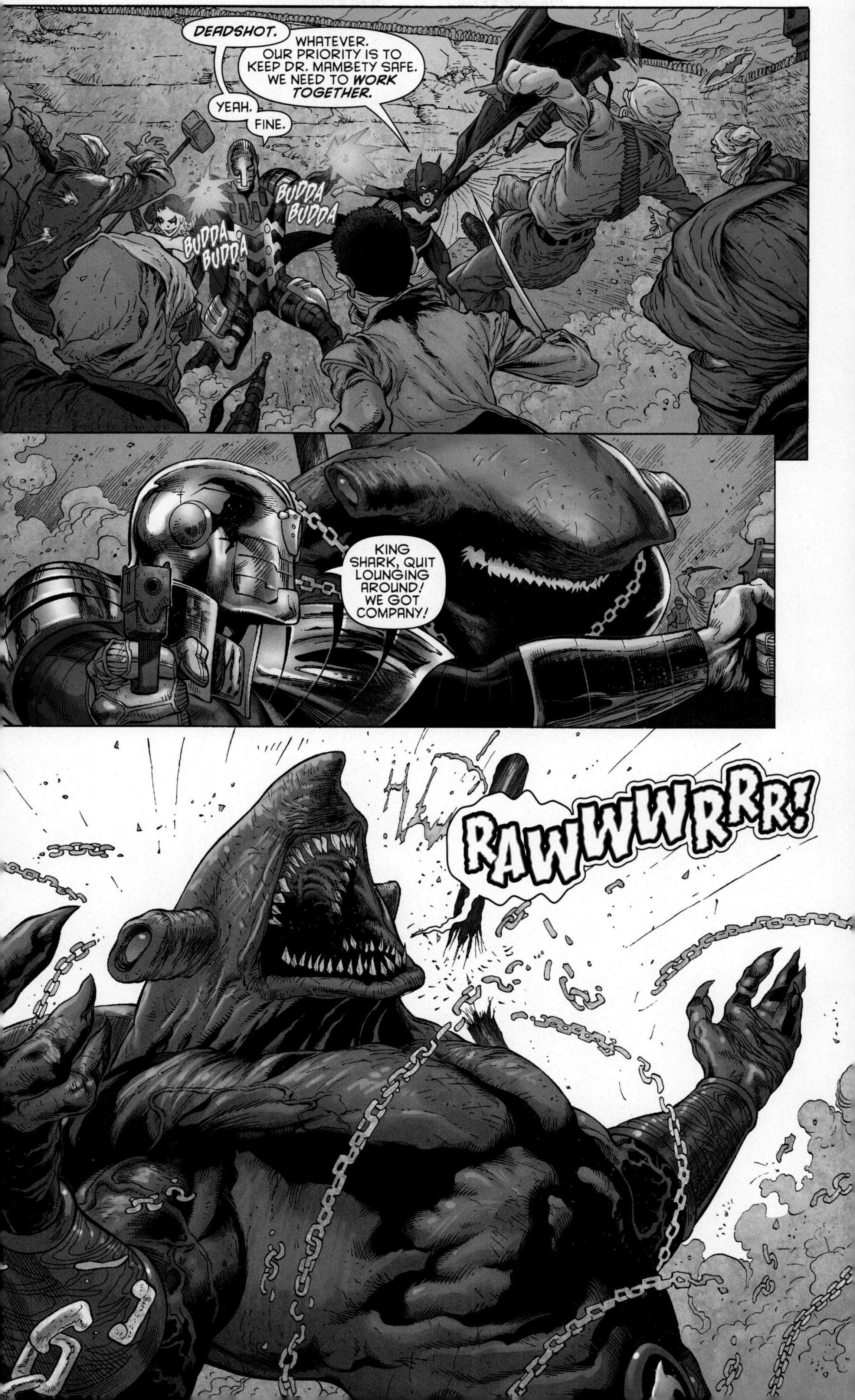
DEADSHOT.
WHATEVER. OUR PRIORITY IS TO KEEP DR. MAMBETY SAFE. WE NEED TO WORK TOGETHER.
YEAH.
FINE.
BUDDA BUDDA
BUDDA BUDDA
KING SHARK, QUIT LOUNGING AROUND! WE GOT COMPANY!
RAWWWRRR!

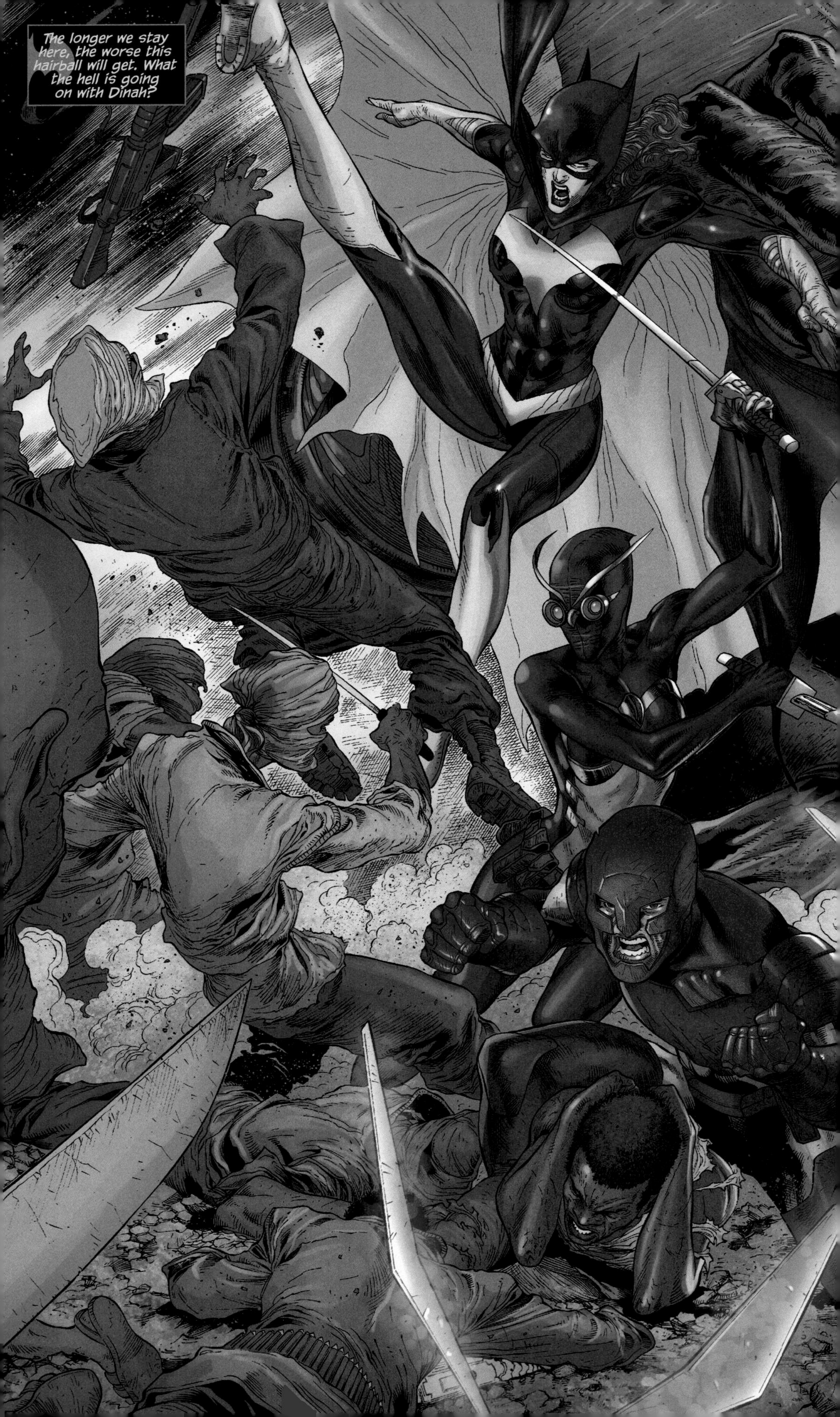
The longer we stay here, the worse this hairball will get. What the hell is going on with Dinah?

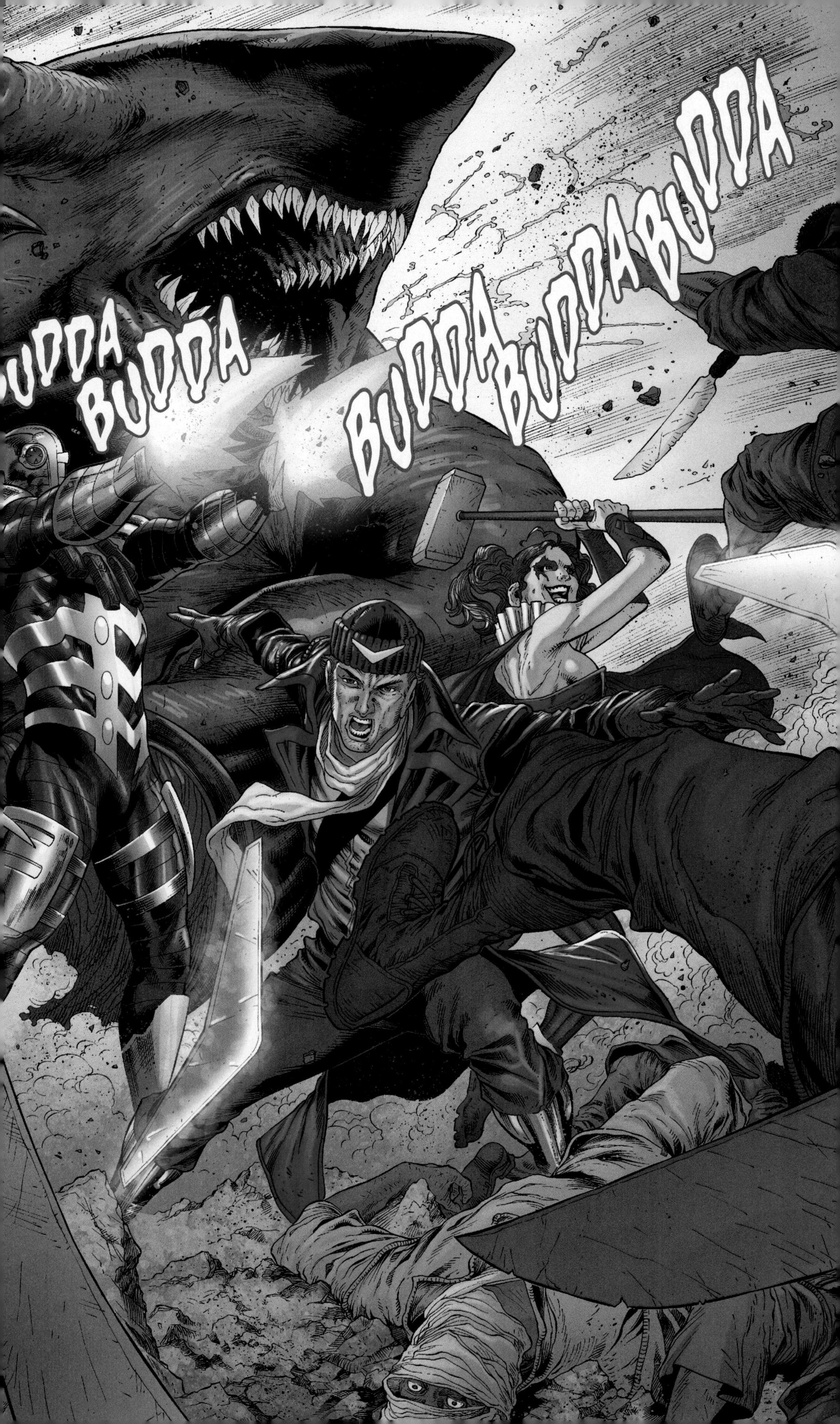

UDDA
BUDDA
BUDDA
BUDDA
BUDDA

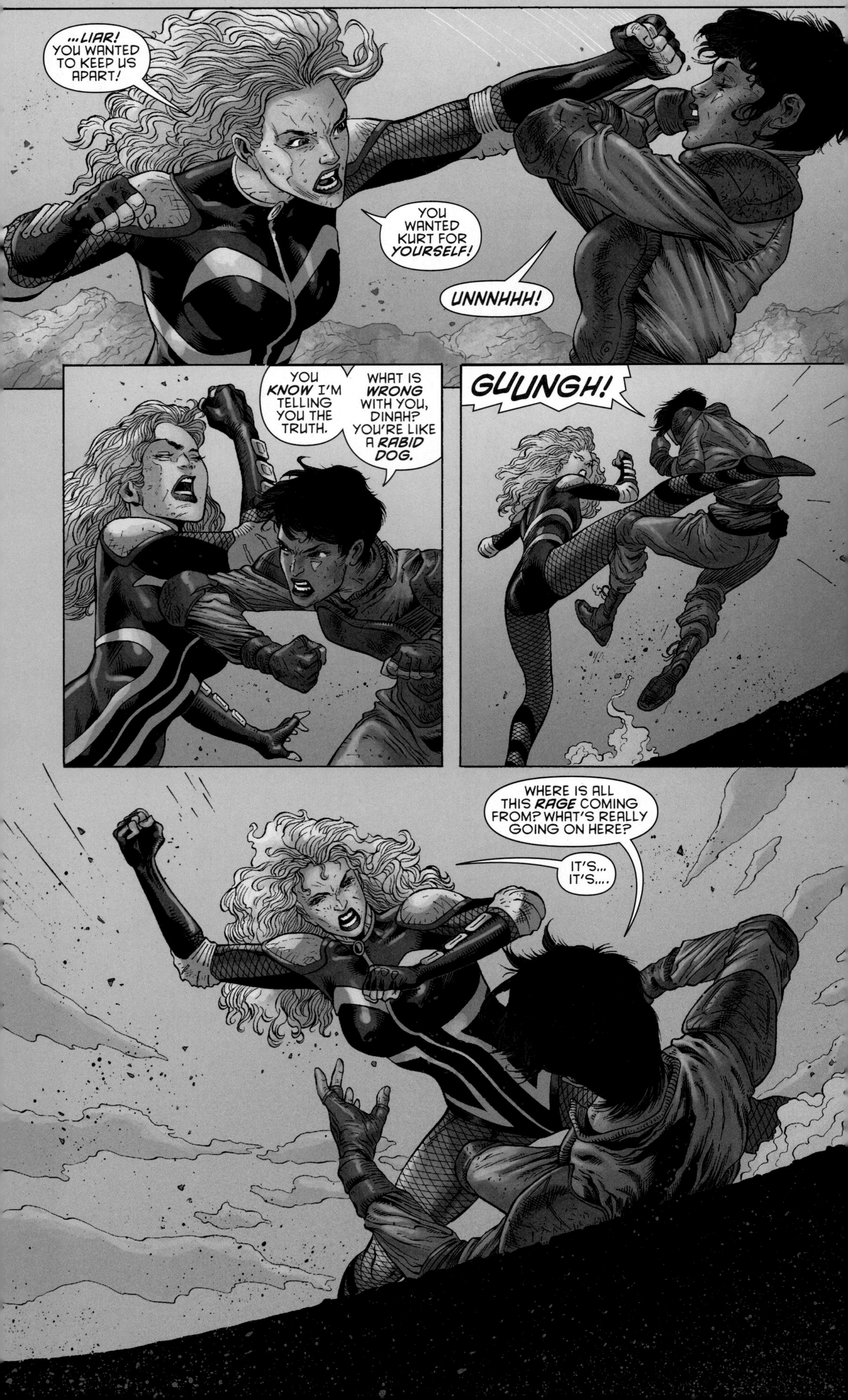

...LIAR! YOU WANTED TO KEEP US APART!
YOU WANTED KURT FOR YOURSELF!
UNNNHHH!
YOU KNOW I'M TELLING YOU THE TRUTH.
WHAT IS WRONG WITH YOU, DINAH? YOU'RE LIKE A RABID DOG.
GUUNGH!
WHERE IS ALL THIS RAGE COMING FROM? WHAT'S REALLY GOING ON HERE?
IT'S... IT'S....

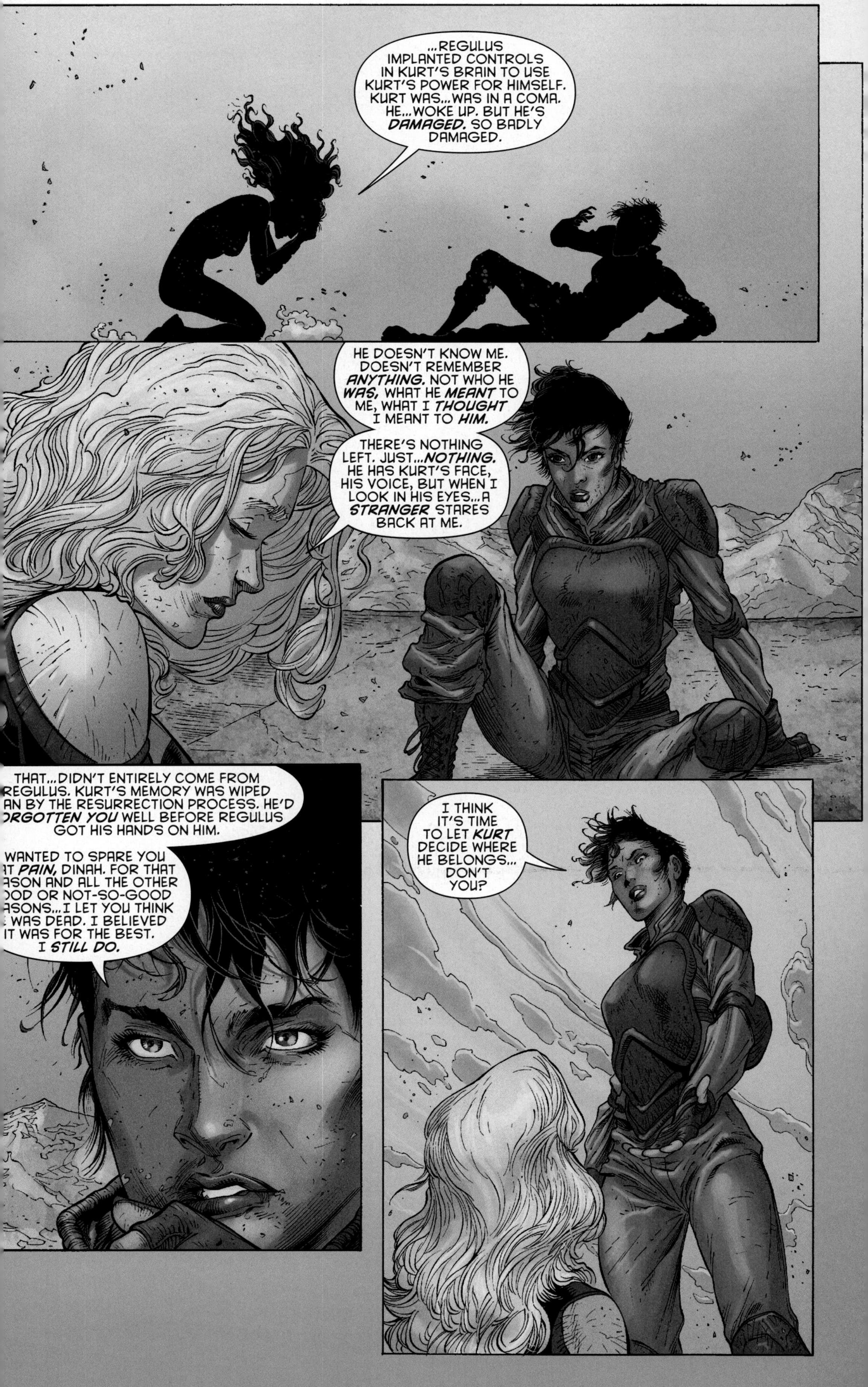
...REGULUS IMPLANTED CONTROLS IN KURT'S BRAIN TO USE KURT'S POWER FOR HIMSELF. KURT WAS...WAS IN A COMA. HE...WOKE UP. BUT HE'S DAMAGED. SO BADLY DAMAGED.
HE DOESN'T KNOW ME. DOESN'T REMEMBER ANYTHING. NOT WHO HE WAS, WHAT HE MEANT TO ME, WHAT I THOUGHT I MEANT TO HIM.
THERE'S NOTHING LEFT. JUST...NOTHING. HE HAS KURT'S FACE, HIS VOICE, BUT WHEN I LOOK IN HIS EYES...A STRANGER STARES BACK AT ME.
THAT...DIDN'T ENTIRELY COME FROM REGULUS. KURT'S MEMORY WAS WIPED AN BY THE RESURRECTION PROCESS. HE'D ORGOTTEN YOU WELL BEFORE REGULUS GOT HIS HANDS ON HIM.
WANTED TO SPARE YOU AT PAIN, DINAH. FOR THAT ASON AND ALL THE OTHER OOD OR NOT-SO-GOOD ASONS...I LET YOU THINK WAS DEAD. I BELIEVED IT WAS FOR THE BEST. I STILL DO.
I THINK IT'S TIME TO LET KURT DECIDE WHERE HE BELONGS... DON'T YOU?

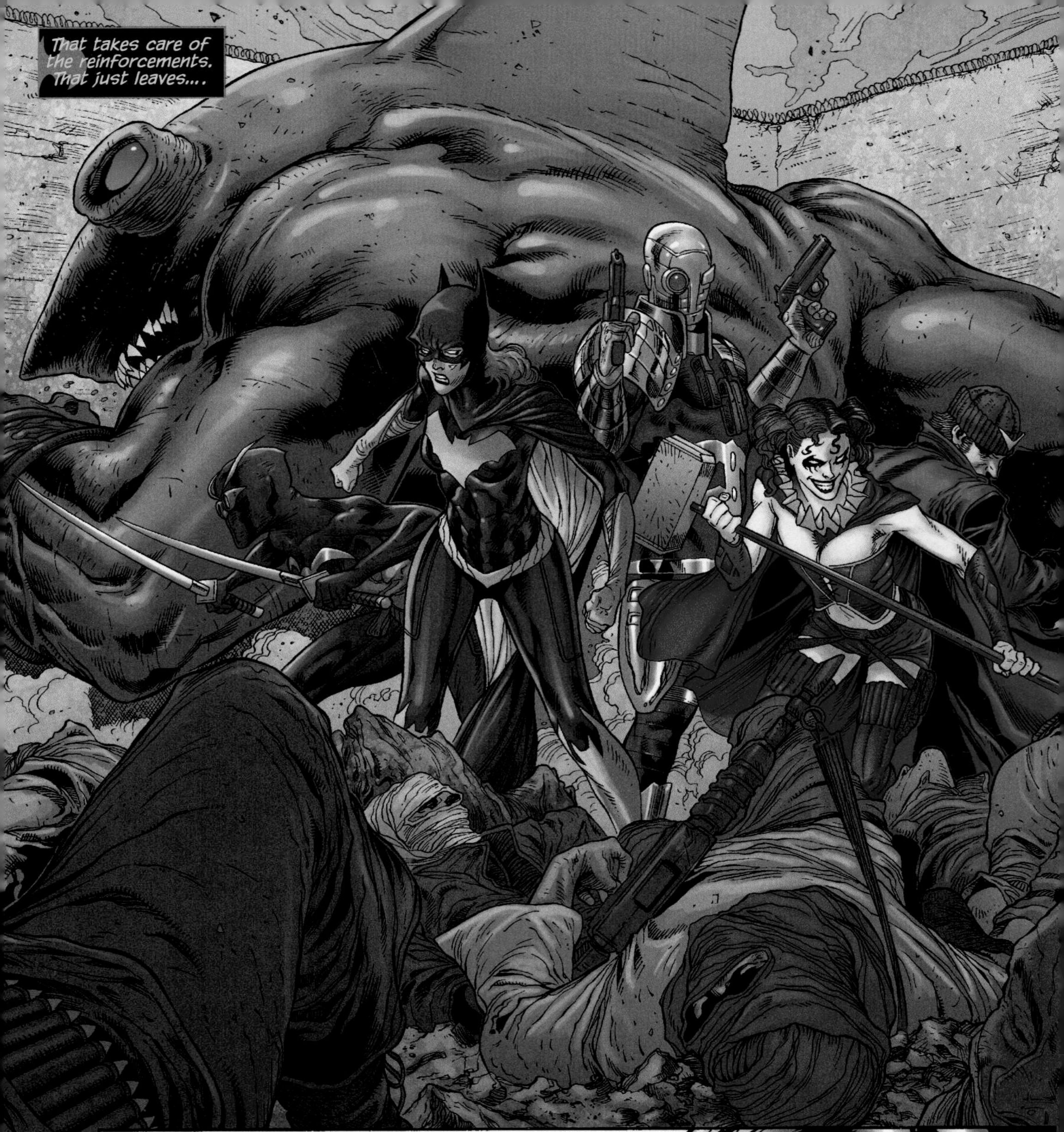
That takes care of the reinforcements. That just leaves....

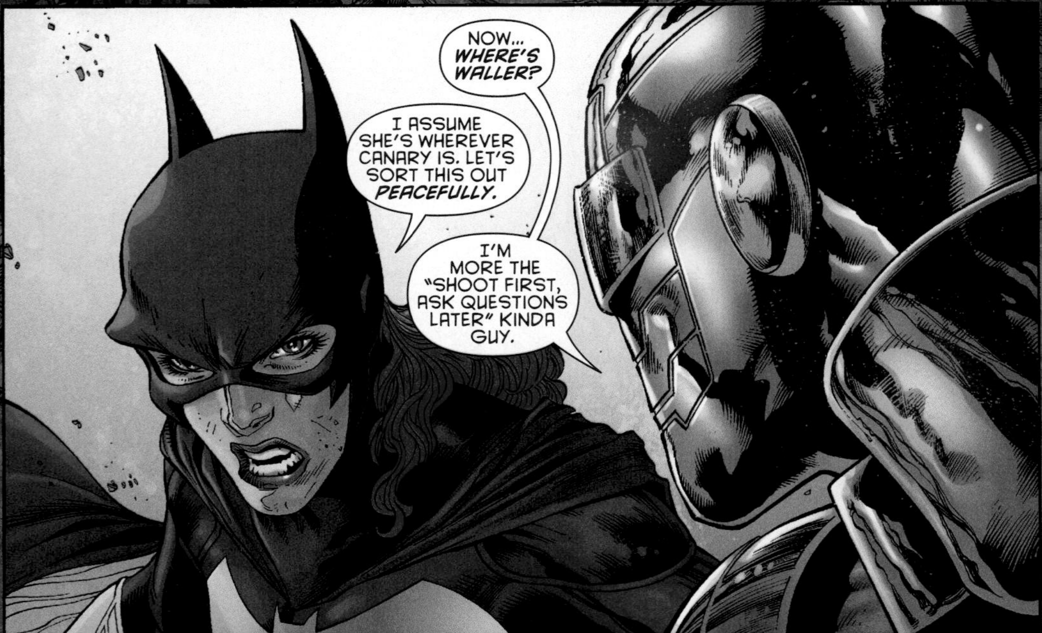
NOW... WHERE'S WALLER?
I ASSUME SHE'S WHEREVER CANARY IS. LET'S SORT THIS OUT PEACEFULLY.
I'M MORE THE "SHOOT FIRST, ASK QUESTIONS LATER" KINDA GUY.

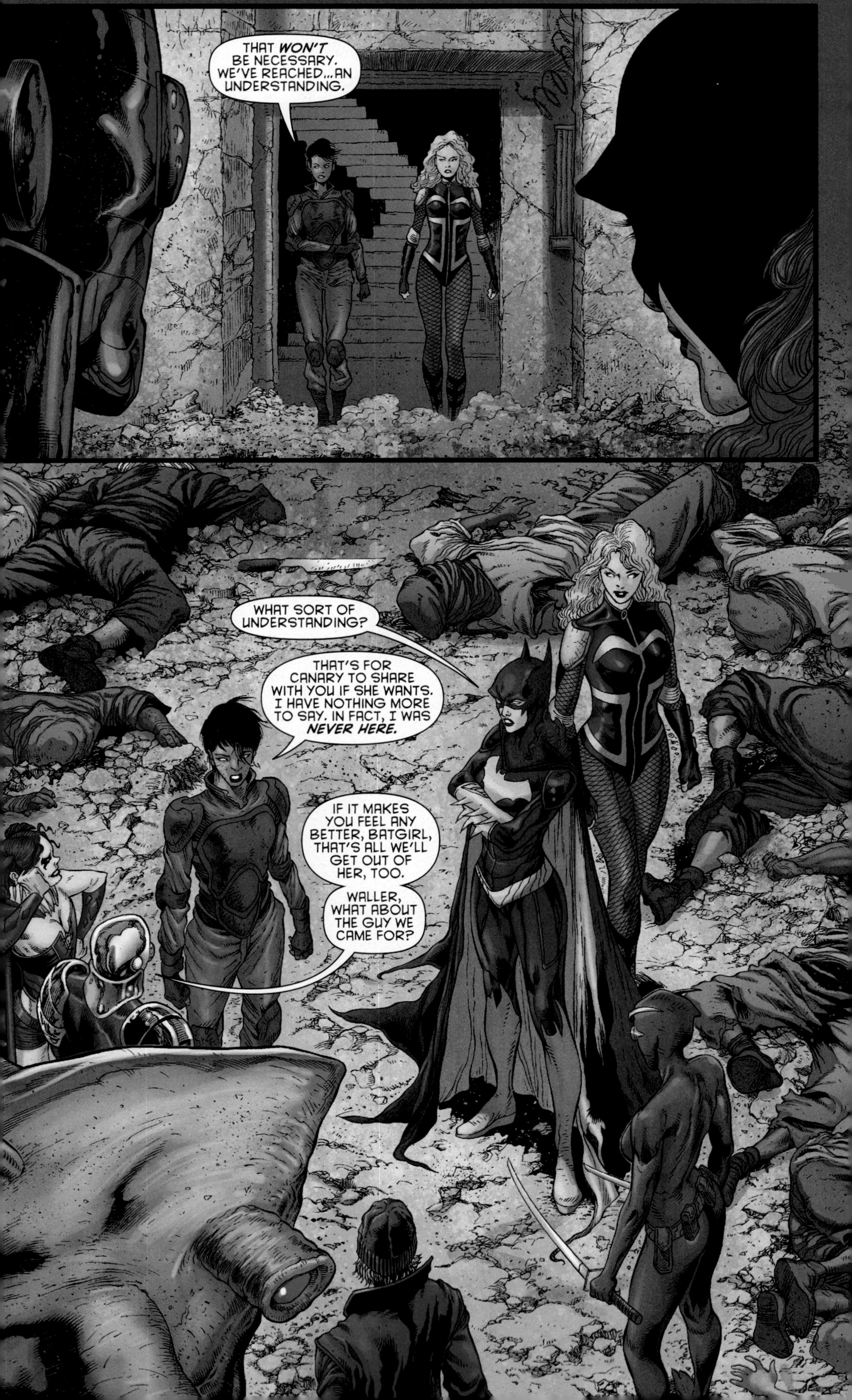
THAT WON'T BE NECESSARY. WE'VE REACHED...AN UNDERSTANDING.
WHAT SORT OF UNDERSTANDING?
THAT'S FOR CANARY TO SHARE WITH YOU IF SHE WANTS. I HAVE NOTHING MORE TO SAY. IN FACT, I WAS NEVER HERE.
IF IT MAKES YOU FEEL ANY BETTER, BATGIRL, THAT'S ALL WE'LL GET OUT OF HER, TOO.
WALLER, WHAT ABOUT THE GUY WE CAME FOR?

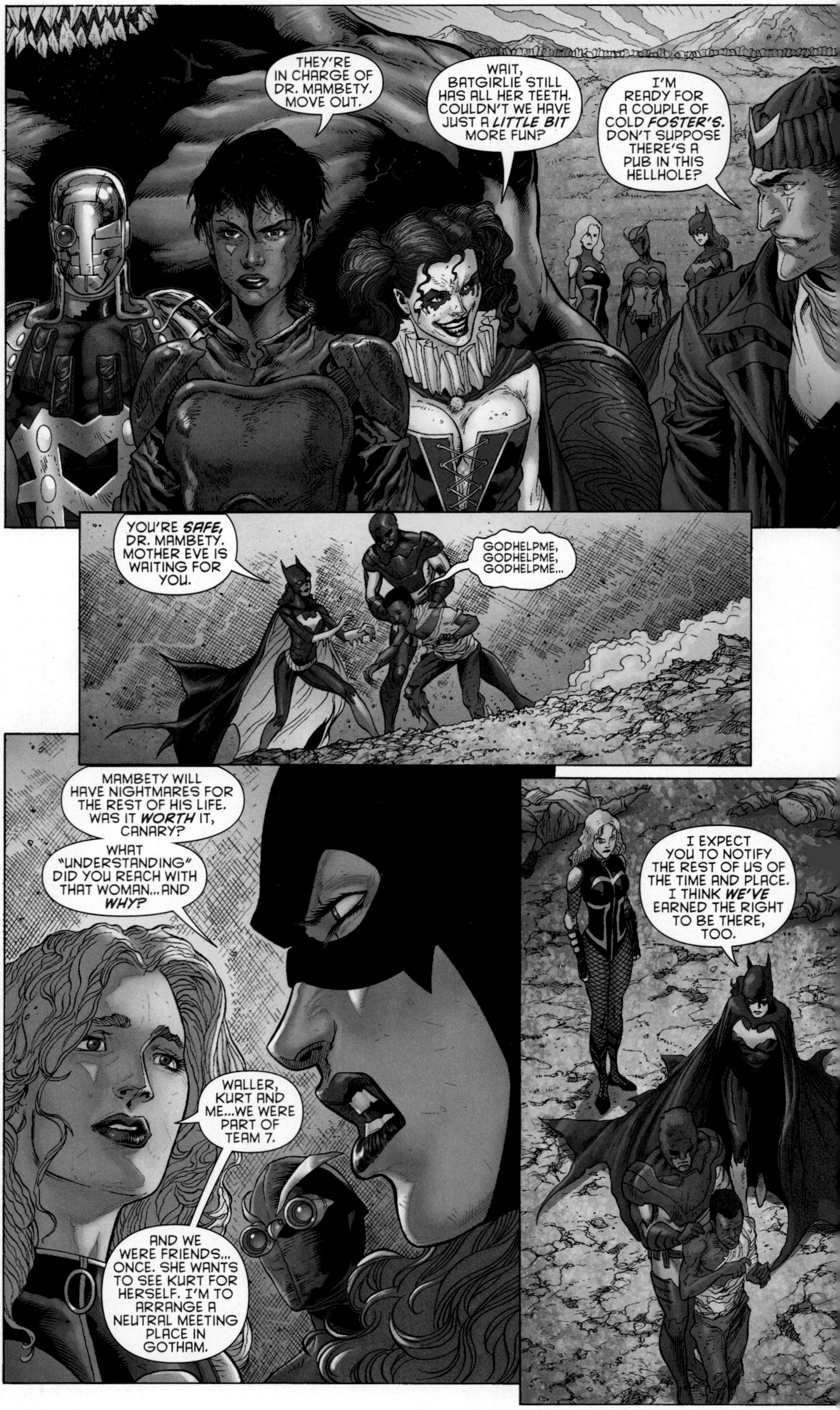
THEY'RE IN CHARGE OF DR. MAMBETY. MOVE OUT.
WAIT, BATGIRLIE STILL HAS ALL HER TEETH. COULDN'T WE HAVE JUST A LITTLE BIT MORE FUN?
I'M READY FOR A COUPLE OF COLD FOSTER'S. DON'T SUPPOSE THERE'S A PUB IN THIS HELLHOLE?
YOU'RE SAFE, DR. MAMBETY. MOTHER EVE IS WAITING FOR YOU.
GODHELPME, GODHELPME, GODHELPME...
MAMBETY WILL HAVE NIGHTMARES FOR THE REST OF HIS LIFE. WAS IT WORTH IT, CANARY?
WHAT "UNDERSTANDING" DID YOU REACH WITH THAT WOMAN...AND WHY?
WALLER, KURT AND ME...WE WERE PART OF TEAM 7.
AND WE WERE FRIENDS... ONCE. SHE WANTS TO SEE KURT FOR HERSELF. I'M TO ARRANGE A NEUTRAL MEETING PLACE IN GOTHAM.
I EXPECT YOU TO NOTIFY THE REST OF US OF THE TIME AND PLACE. I THINK WE'VE EARNED THE RIGHT TO BE THERE, TOO.

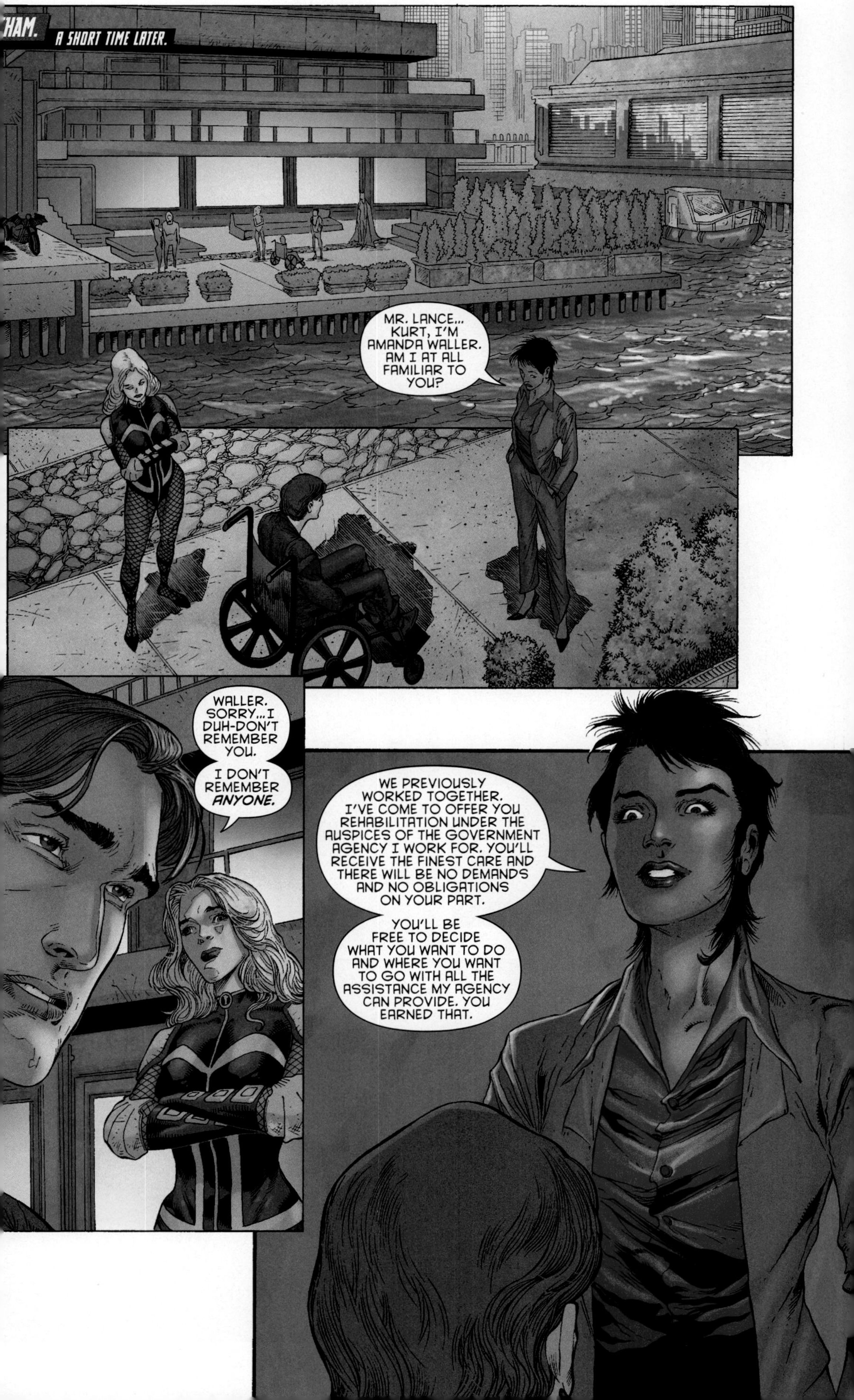

THAM.
A SHORT TIME LATER.
MR. LANCE... KURT, I'M AMANDA WALLER. AM I AT ALL FAMILIAR TO YOU?
WALLER. SORRY...I DUH-DON'T REMEMBER YOU.
I DON'T REMEMBER ANYONE.
WE PREVIOUSLY WORKED TOGETHER. I'VE COME TO OFFER YOU REHABILITATION UNDER THE AUSPICES OF THE GOVERNMENT AGENCY I WORK FOR. YOU'LL RECEIVE THE FINEST CARE AND THERE WILL BE NO DEMANDS AND NO OBLIGATIONS ON YOUR PART.
YOU'LL BE FREE TO DECIDE WHAT YOU WANT TO DO AND WHERE YOU WANT TO GO WITH ALL THE ASSISTANCE MY AGENCY CAN PROVIDE. YOU EARNED THAT.

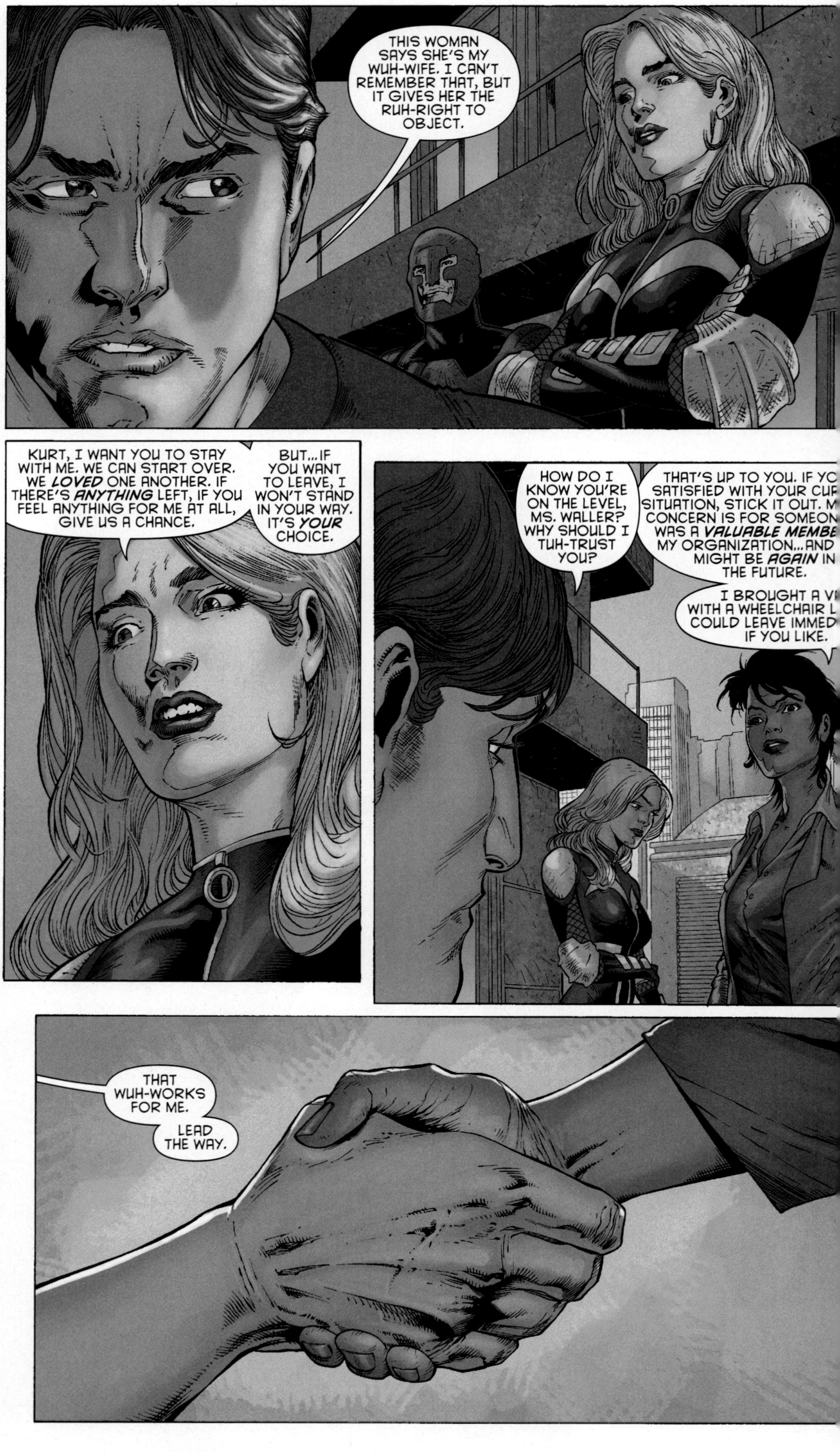
THIS WOMAN SAYS SHE'S MY WUH-WIFE. I CAN'T REMEMBER THAT, BUT IT GIVES HER THE RUH-RIGHT TO OBJECT.
KURT, I WANT YOU TO STAY WITH ME. WE CAN START OVER. WE *LOVED* ONE ANOTHER. IF THERE'S *ANYTHING* LEFT, IF YOU FEEL ANYTHING FOR ME AT ALL, GIVE US A CHANCE.
BUT... IF YOU WANT TO LEAVE, I WON'T STAND IN YOUR WAY. IT'S *YOUR* CHOICE.
HOW DO I KNOW YOU'RE ON THE LEVEL, MS. WALLER? WHY SHOULD I TUH-TRUST YOU?
THAT'S UP TO YOU. IF YO SATISFIED WITH YOUR CU SITUATION, STICK IT OUT. M CONCERN IS FOR SOMEON WAS A *VALUABLE MEMBE* MY ORGANIZATION... AND MIGHT BE *AGAIN* IN THE FUTURE.
I BROUGHT A V WITH A WHEELCHAIR L COULD LEAVE IMMED IF YOU LIKE.
THAT WUH-WORKS FOR ME.
LEAD THE WAY.

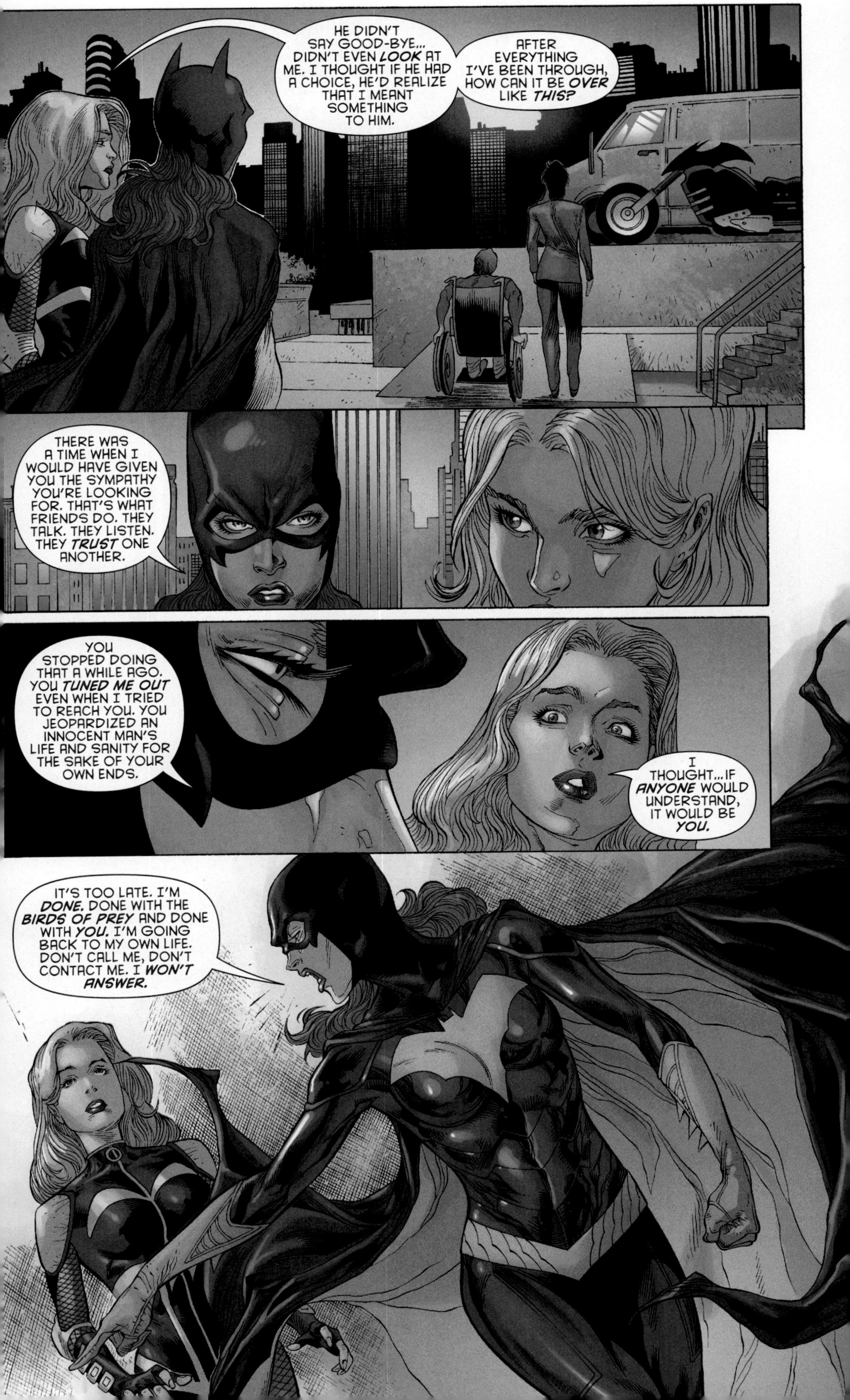
HE DIDN'T SAY GOOD-BYE... DIDN'T EVEN *LOOK* AT ME. I THOUGHT IF HE HAD A CHOICE, HE'D REALIZE THAT I MEANT SOMETHING TO HIM.
AFTER EVERYTHING I'VE BEEN THROUGH, HOW CAN IT BE *OVER* LIKE *THIS?*
THERE WAS A TIME WHEN I WOULD HAVE GIVEN YOU THE SYMPATHY YOU'RE LOOKING FOR. THAT'S WHAT FRIENDS DO. THEY TALK. THEY LISTEN. THEY *TRUST* ONE ANOTHER.
YOU STOPPED DOING THAT A WHILE AGO. YOU *TUNED ME OUT* EVEN WHEN I TRIED TO REACH YOU. YOU JEOPARDIZED AN INNOCENT MAN'S LIFE AND SANITY FOR THE SAKE OF YOUR OWN ENDS.
I THOUGHT... IF *ANYONE* WOULD UNDERSTAND, IT WOULD BE *YOU.*
IT'S TOO LATE. I'M *DONE.* DONE WITH THE *BIRDS OF PREY* AND DONE WITH *YOU.* I'M GOING BACK TO MY OWN LIFE. DON'T CALL ME, DON'T CONTACT ME. I *WON'T ANSWER.*

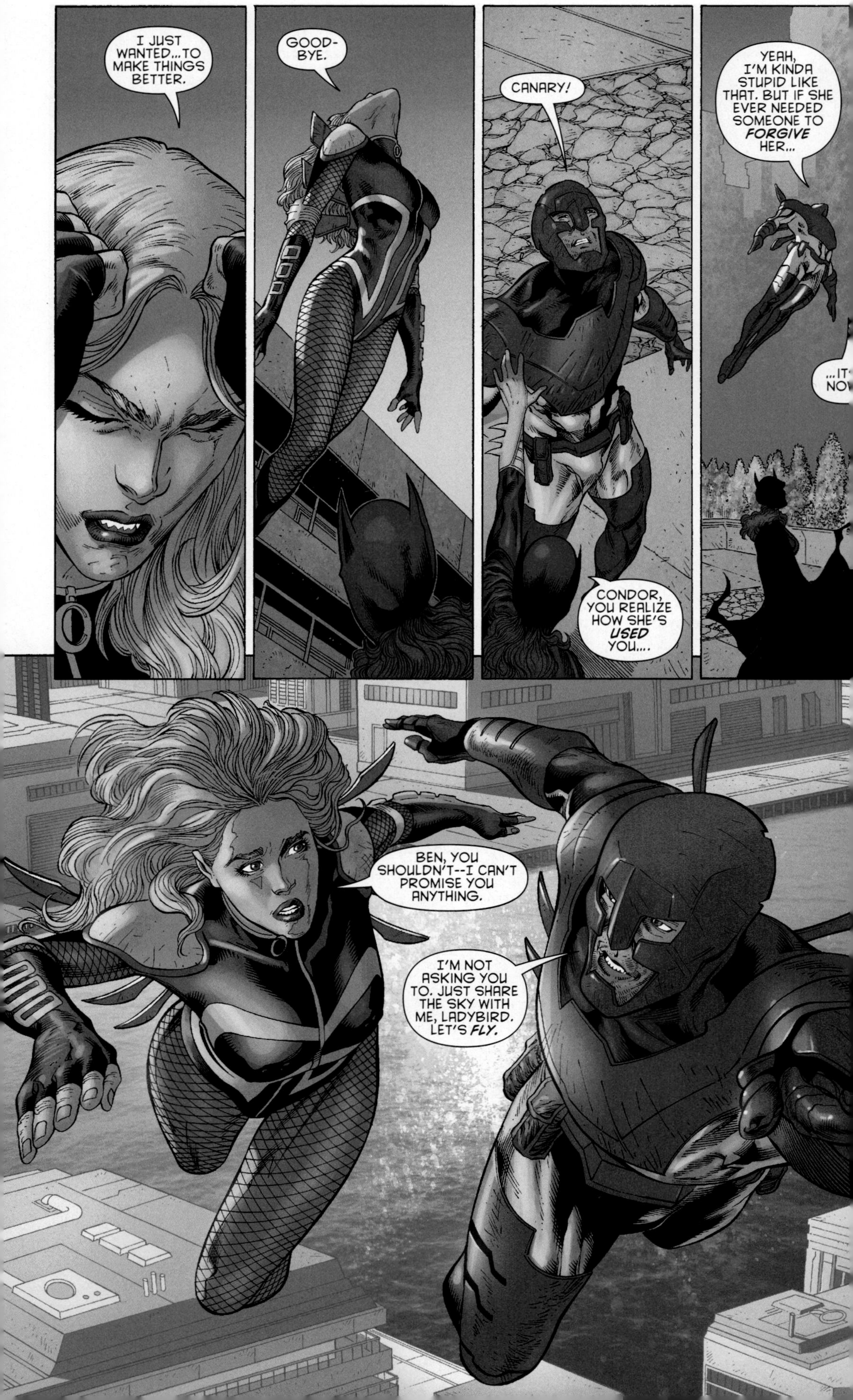
I JUST WANTED...TO MAKE THINGS BETTER.
GOOD-BYE.
CANARY!
CONDOR, YOU REALIZE HOW SHE'S USED YOU....
YEAH, I'M KINDA STUPID LIKE THAT. BUT IF SHE EVER NEEDED SOMEONE TO FORGIVE HER...
BEN, YOU SHOULDN'T--I CAN'T PROMISE YOU ANYTHING.
I'M NOT ASKING YOU TO. JUST SHARE THE SKY WITH ME, LADYBIRD. LET'S FLY.

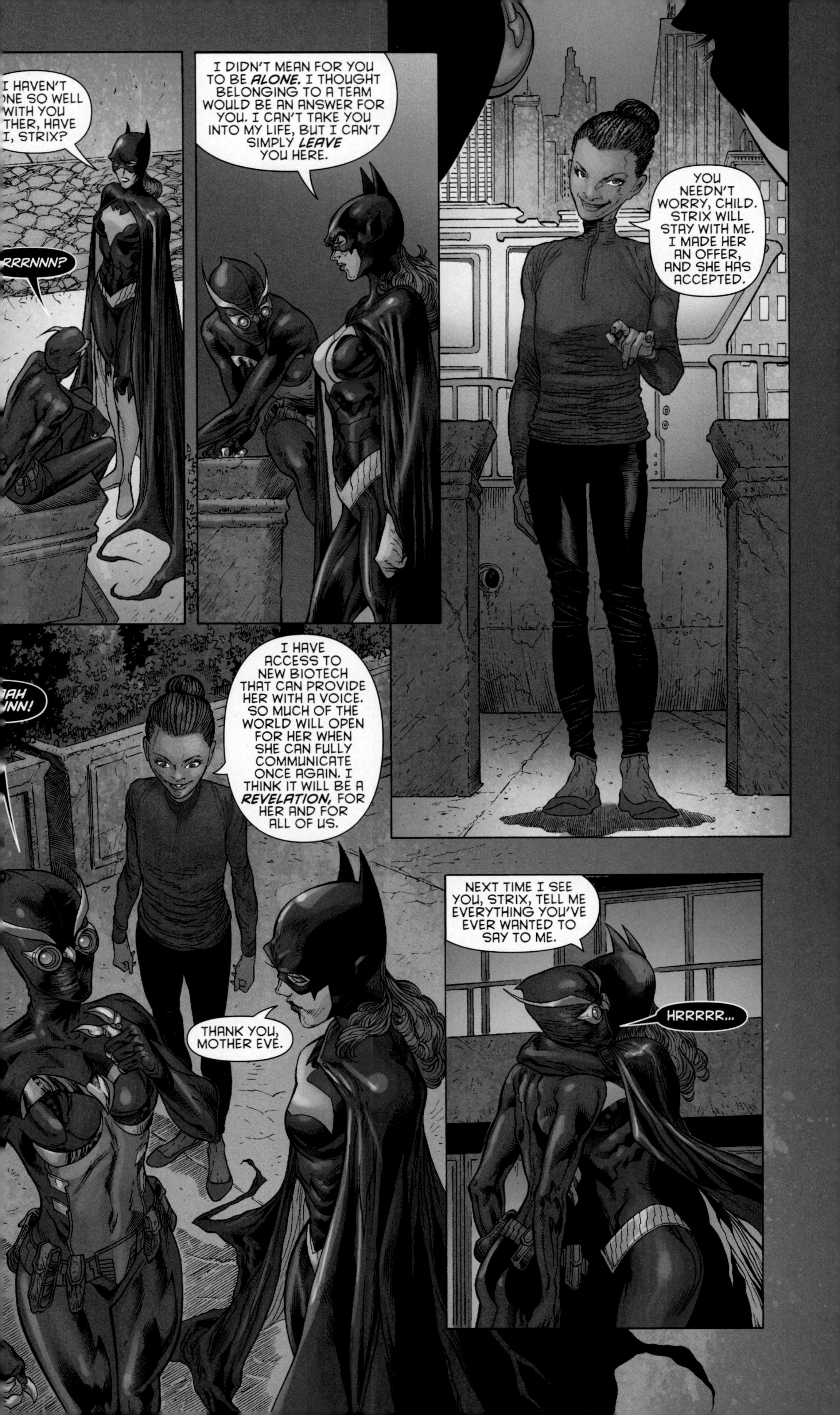
I HAVEN'T
ONE SO WELL
WITH YOU
THER, HAVE
I, STRIX?
RRRNNN?
I DIDN'T MEAN FOR YOU TO BE ALONE. I THOUGHT BELONGING TO A TEAM WOULD BE AN ANSWER FOR YOU. I CAN'T TAKE YOU INTO MY LIFE, BUT I CAN'T SIMPLY LEAVE YOU HERE.
YOU NEEDN'T WORRY, CHILD. STRIX WILL STAY WITH ME. I MADE HER AN OFFER, AND SHE HAS ACCEPTED.
AH
NN!
I HAVE ACCESS TO NEW BIOTECH THAT CAN PROVIDE HER WITH A VOICE. SO MUCH OF THE WORLD WILL OPEN FOR HER WHEN SHE CAN FULLY COMMUNICATE ONCE AGAIN. I THINK IT WILL BE A REVELATION, FOR HER AND FOR ALL OF US.
THANK YOU, MOTHER EVE.
NEXT TIME I SEE YOU, STRIX, TELL ME EVERYTHING YOU'VE EVER WANTED TO SAY TO ME.
HRRRRR...

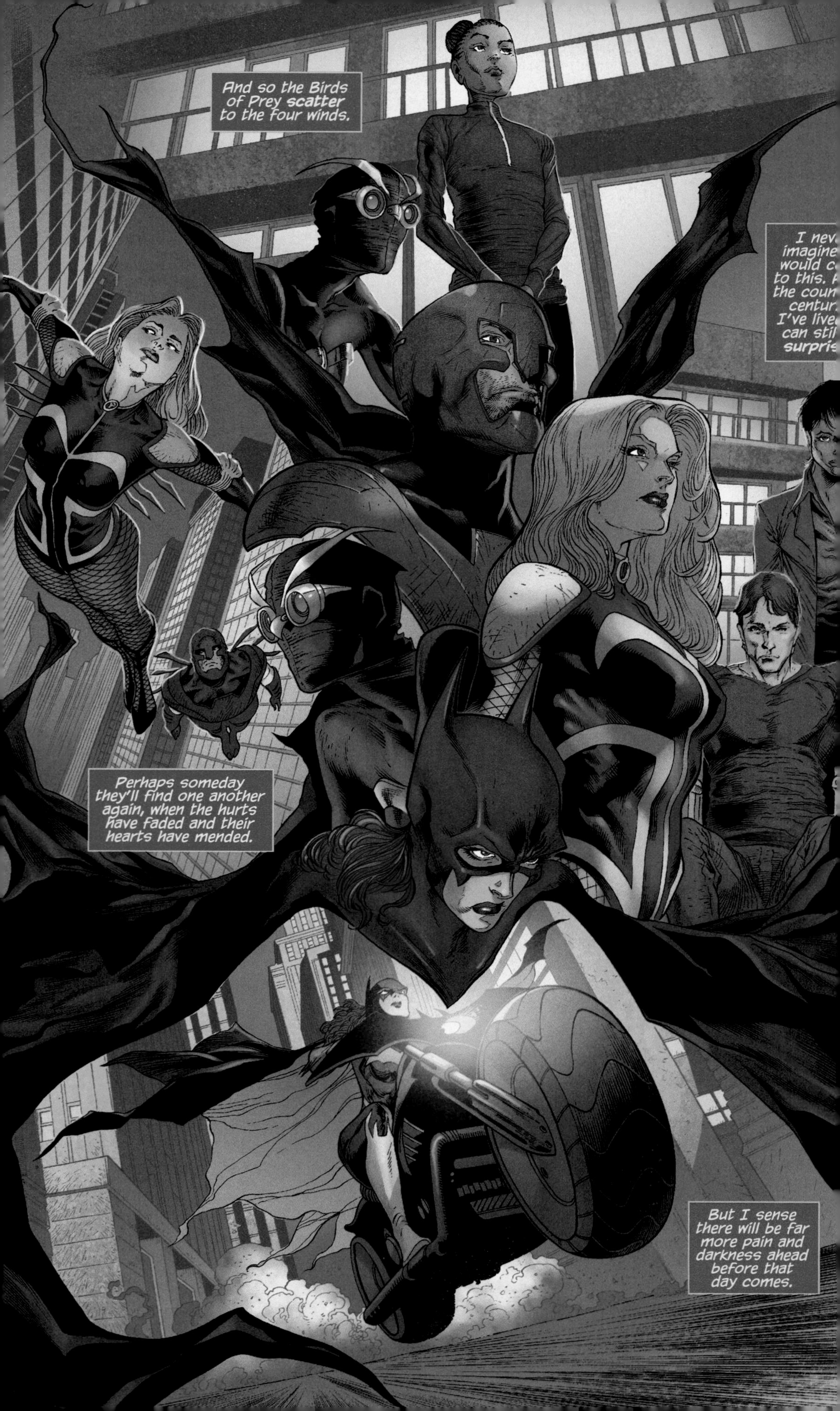
And so the Birds of Prey **scatter** to the four winds.
I nev
imagine
would c
to this.
the coun
centur
I've live
can stil
surpris
Perhaps someday they'll find one another again, when the hurts have faded and their hearts have mended.
But I sense there will be far more pain and darkness ahead before that day comes.

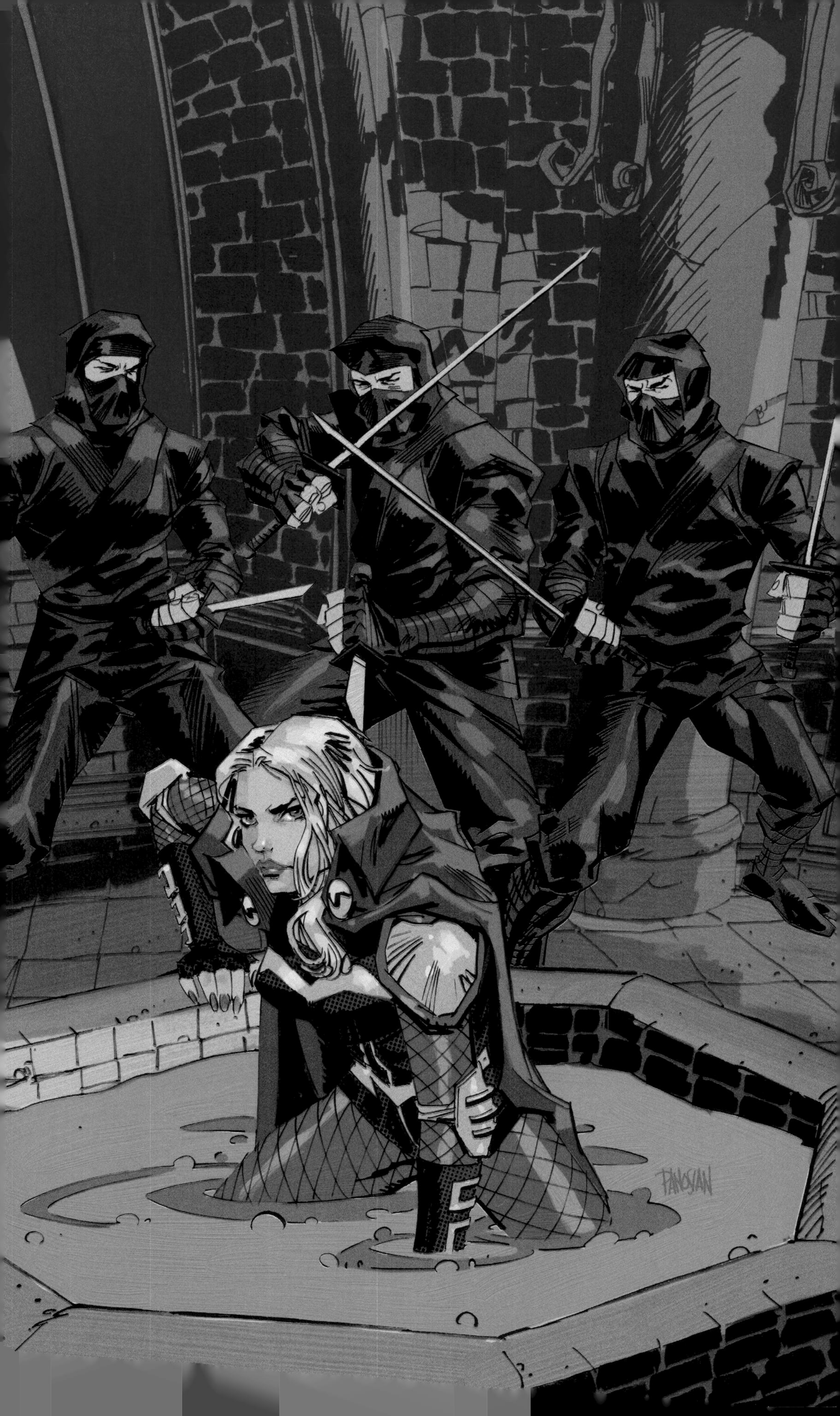
PANOSIAN

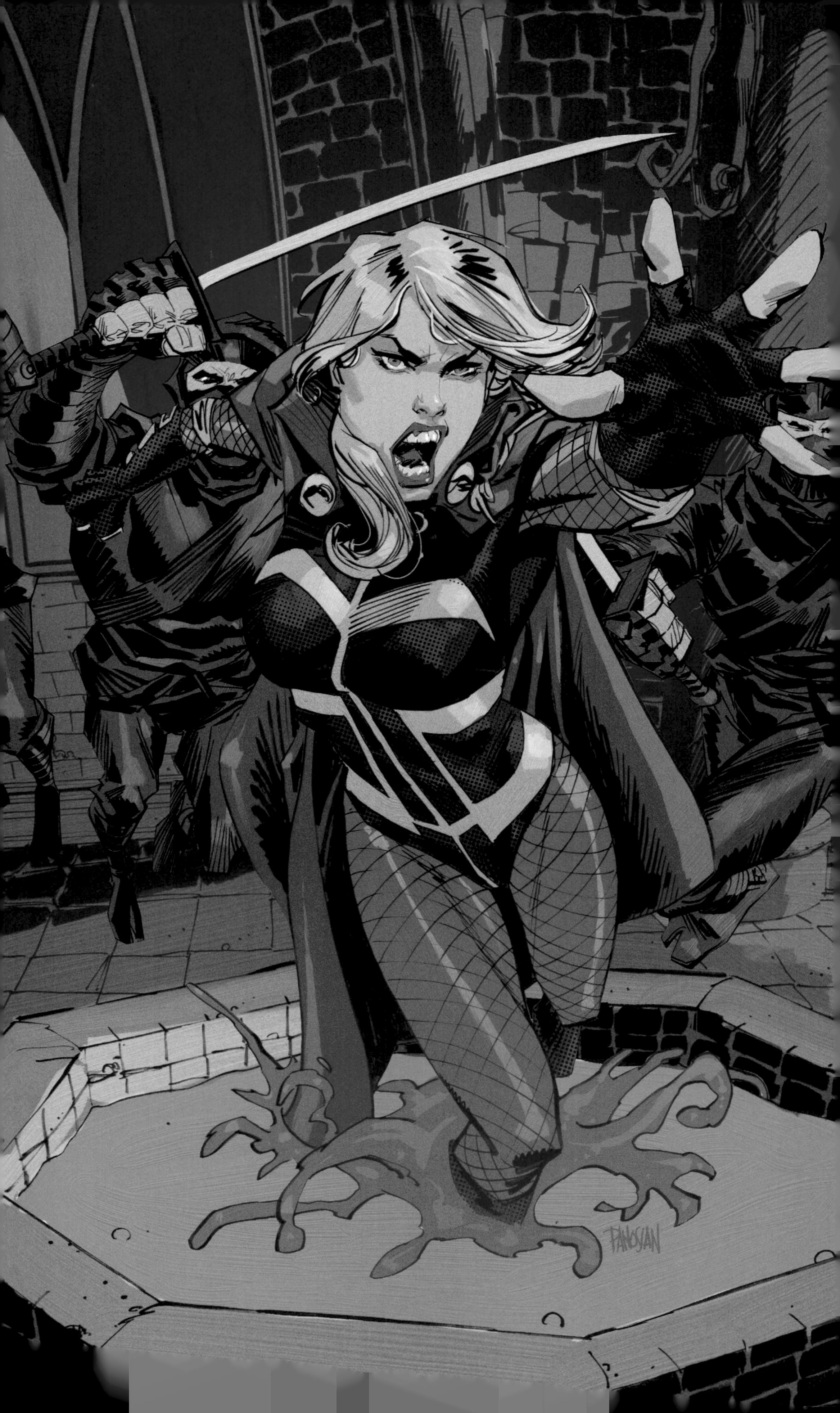
PANOSIAN

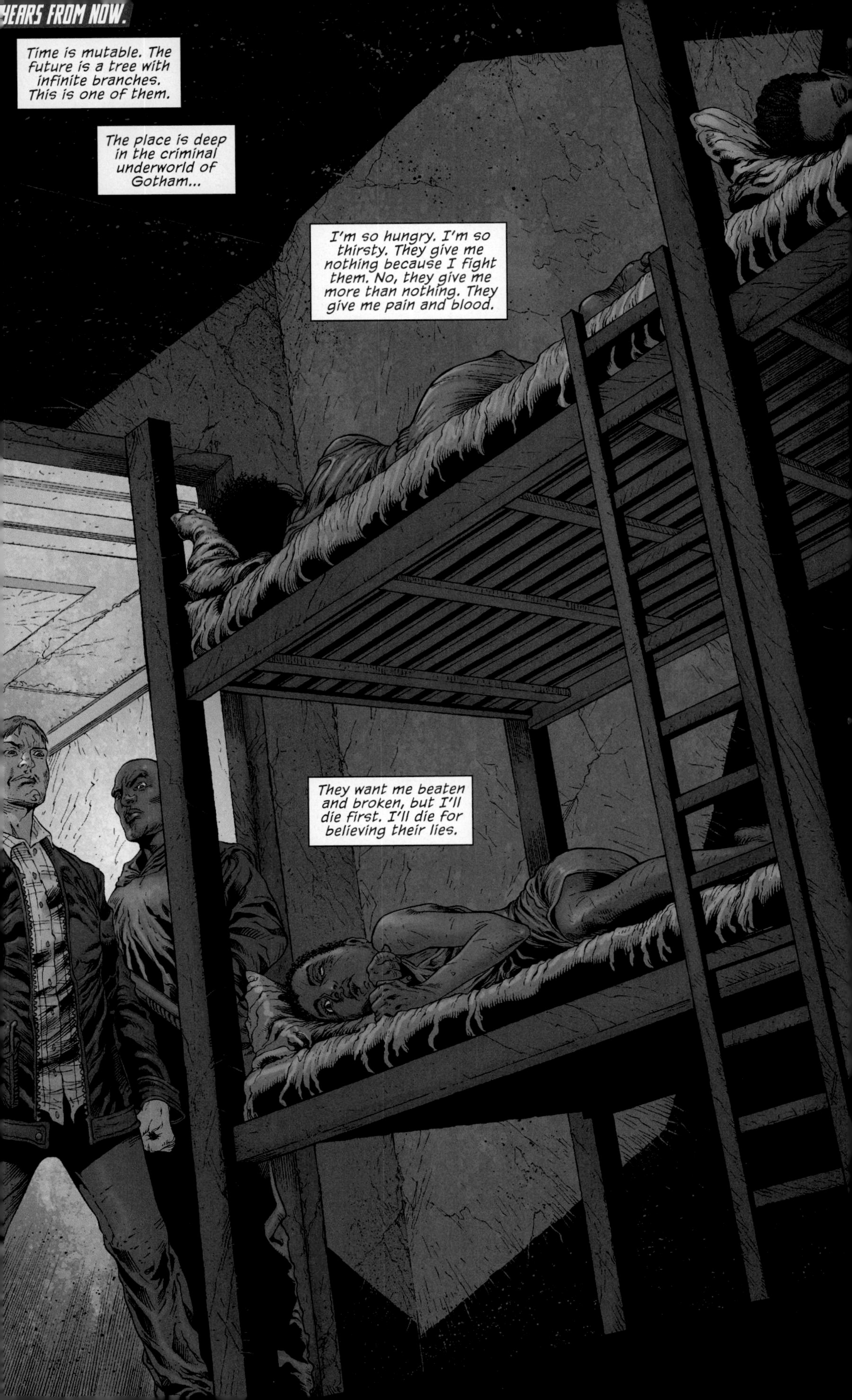
YEARS FROM NOW.
Time is mutable. The future is a tree with infinite branches. This is one of them.
The place is deep in the criminal underworld of Gotham...
I'm so hungry. I'm so thirsty. They give me nothing because I fight them. No, they give me more than nothing. They give me pain and blood.
They want me beaten and broken, but I'll die first. I'll die for believing their lies.

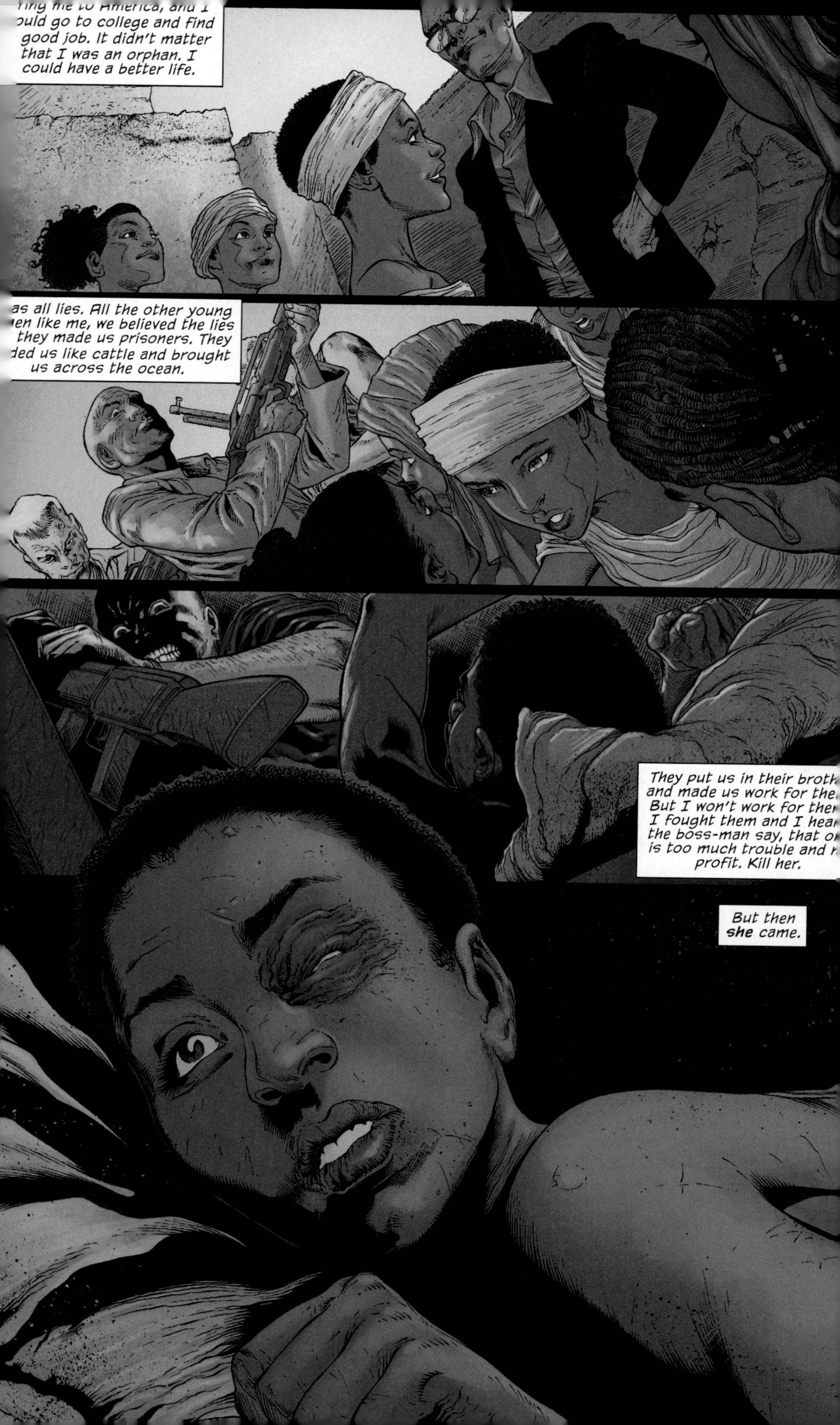
ring me to America, and I
ould go to college and find
good job. It didn't matter
that I was an orphan. I
could have a better life.
as all lies. All the other young
en like me, we believed the lies
they made us prisoners. They
ded us like cattle and brought
us across the ocean.
They put us in their broth
and made us work for the
But I won't work for the
I fought them and I hea
the boss-man say, that o
is too much trouble and n
profit. Kill her.
But then
she came.

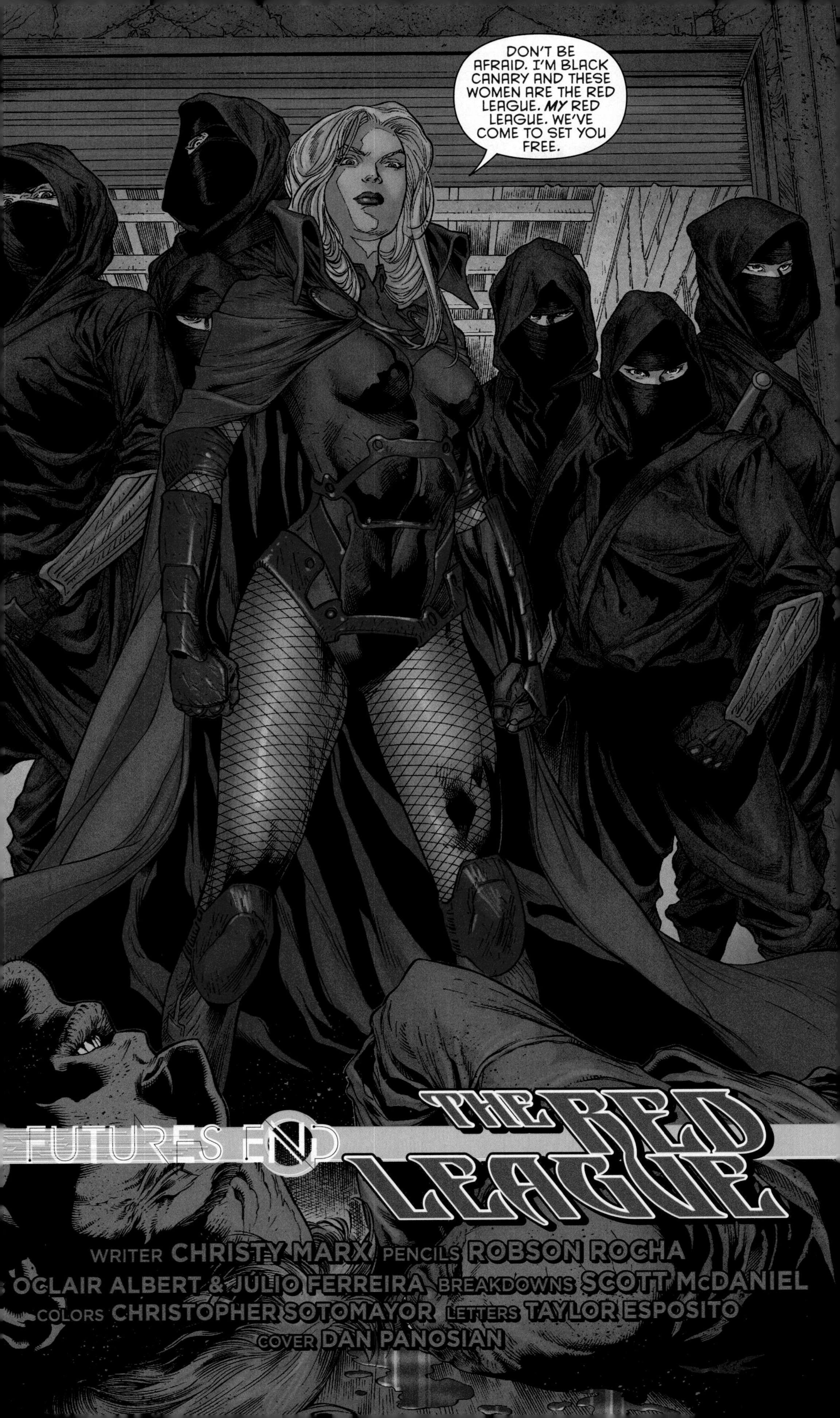
DON'T BE AFRAID. I'M BLACK CANARY AND THESE WOMEN ARE THE RED LEAGUE. *MY* RED LEAGUE. WE'VE COME TO SET YOU FREE.
FUTURES END
THE RED LEAGUE
WRITER CHRISTY MARX PENCILS ROBSON ROCHA
INKS OCLAIR ALBERT & JÚLIO FERREIRA BREAKDOWNS SCOTT McDANIEL
COLORS CHRISTOPHER SOTOMAYOR LETTERS TAYLOR ESPOSITO
COVER DAN PANOSIAN

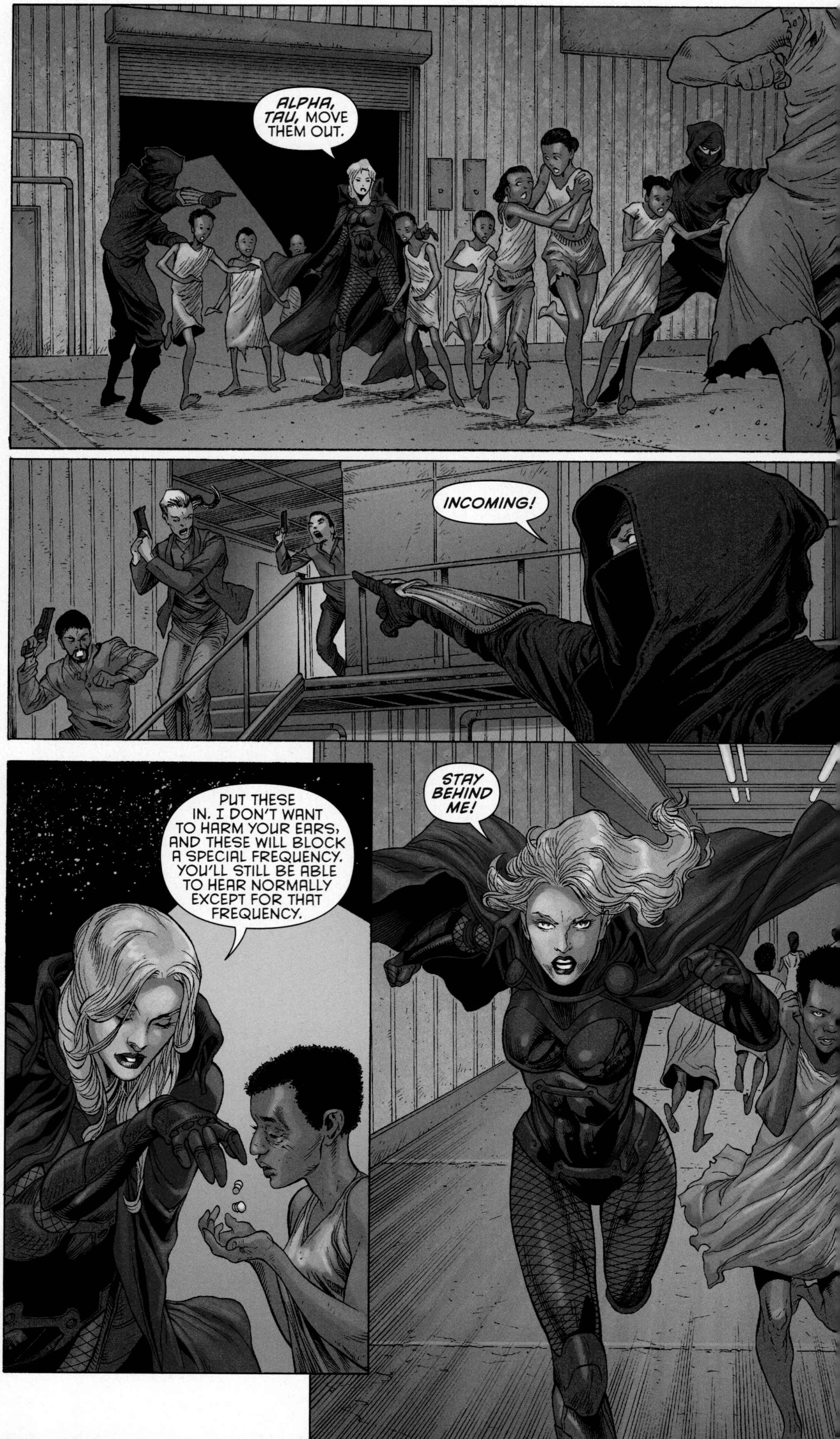
ALPHA, TAU, MOVE THEM OUT.
INCOMING!
PUT THESE IN. I DON'T WANT TO HARM YOUR EARS, AND THESE WILL BLOCK A SPECIAL FREQUENCY. YOU'LL STILL BE ABLE TO HEAR NORMALLY EXCEPT FOR THAT FREQUENCY.
STAY BEHIND ME!

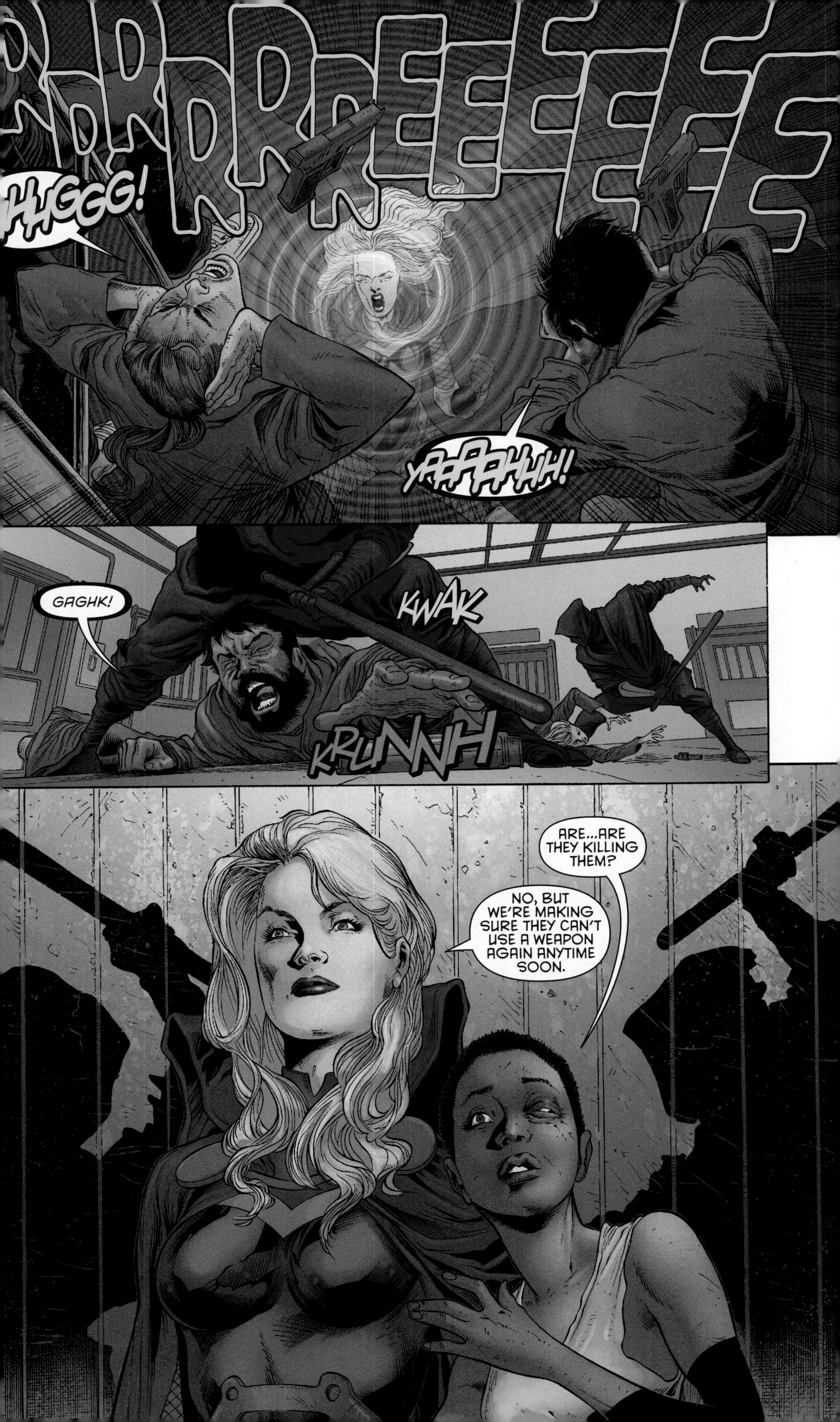

RRRREEEEEEE
HHUGGG!
YAAAAHHH!
GAGHK!
KWAK
KRUNNH
ARE...ARE THEY KILLING THEM?
NO, BUT WE'RE MAKING SURE THEY CAN'T USE A WEAPON AGAIN ANYTIME SOON.

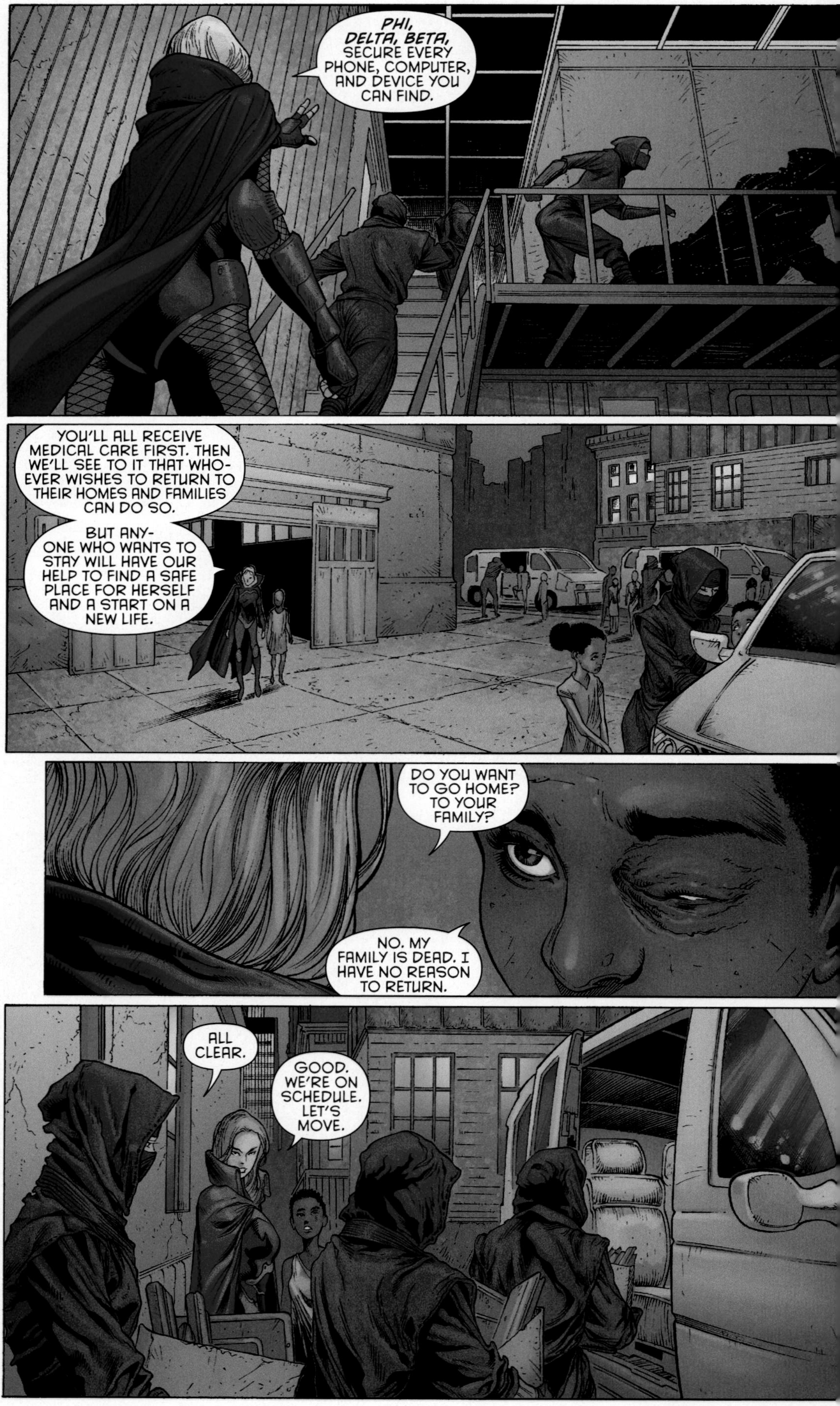
PHI, DELTA, BETA, SECURE EVERY PHONE, COMPUTER, AND DEVICE YOU CAN FIND.
YOU'LL ALL RECEIVE MEDICAL CARE FIRST. THEN WE'LL SEE TO IT THAT WHO-EVER WISHES TO RETURN TO THEIR HOMES AND FAMILIES CAN DO SO.
BUT ANY-ONE WHO WANTS TO STAY WILL HAVE OUR HELP TO FIND A SAFE PLACE FOR HERSELF AND A START ON A NEW LIFE.
DO YOU WANT TO GO HOME? TO YOUR FAMILY?
NO. MY FAMILY IS DEAD. I HAVE NO REASON TO RETURN.
ALL CLEAR.
GOOD. WE'RE ON SCHEDULE. LET'S MOVE.

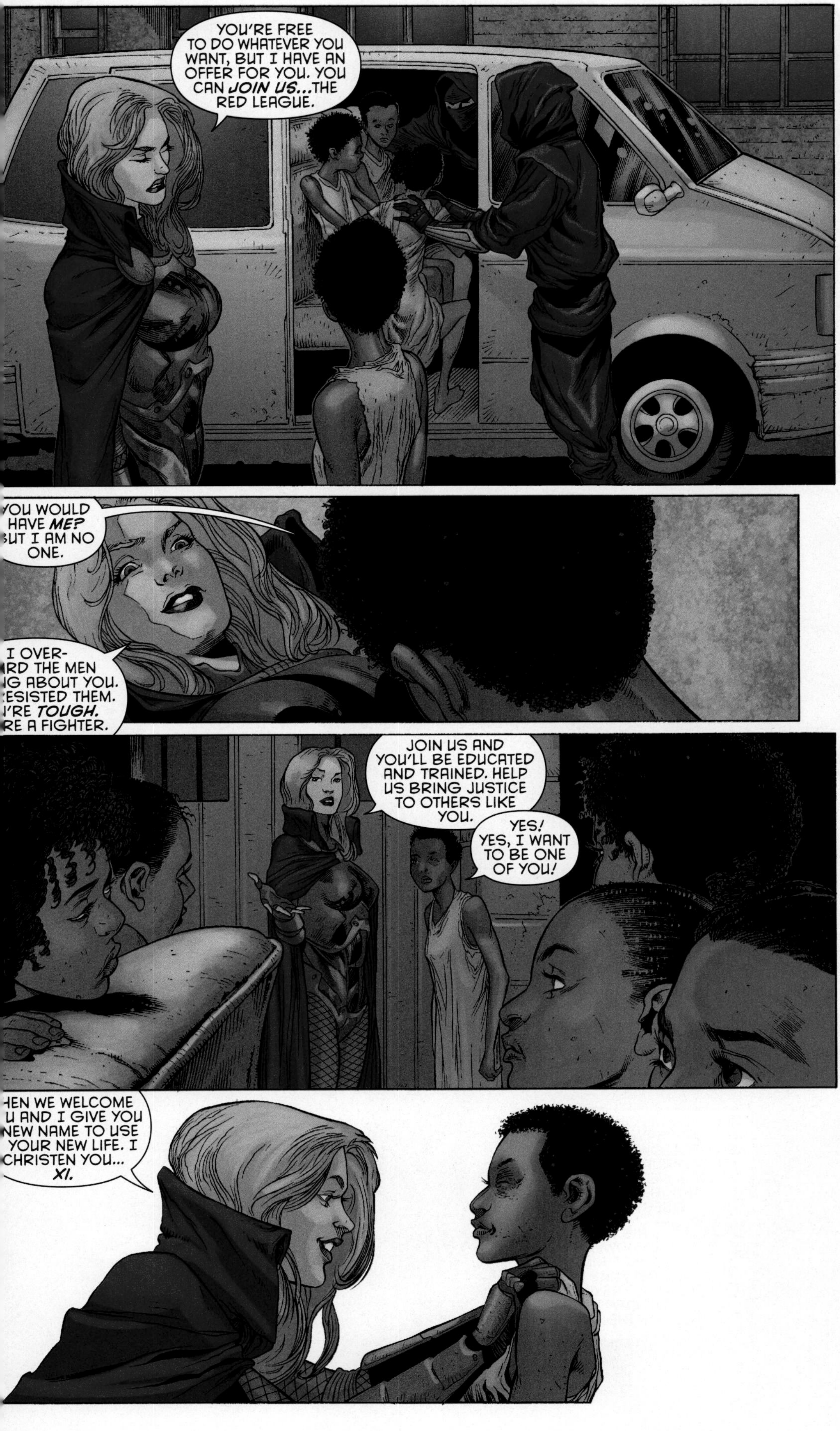
YOU'RE FREE TO DO WHATEVER YOU WANT, BUT I HAVE AN OFFER FOR YOU. YOU CAN JOIN US...THE RED LEAGUE.
YOU WOULD HAVE ME? BUT I AM NO ONE.
I OVER- RD THE MEN IG ABOUT YOU. RESISTED THEM. I'RE TOUGH. RE A FIGHTER.
JOIN US AND YOU'LL BE EDUCATED AND TRAINED. HELP US BRING JUSTICE TO OTHERS LIKE YOU.
YES! YES, I WANT TO BE ONE OF YOU!
HEN WE WELCOME U AND I GIVE YOU NEW NAME TO USE YOUR NEW LIFE. I CHRISTEN YOU... XI.

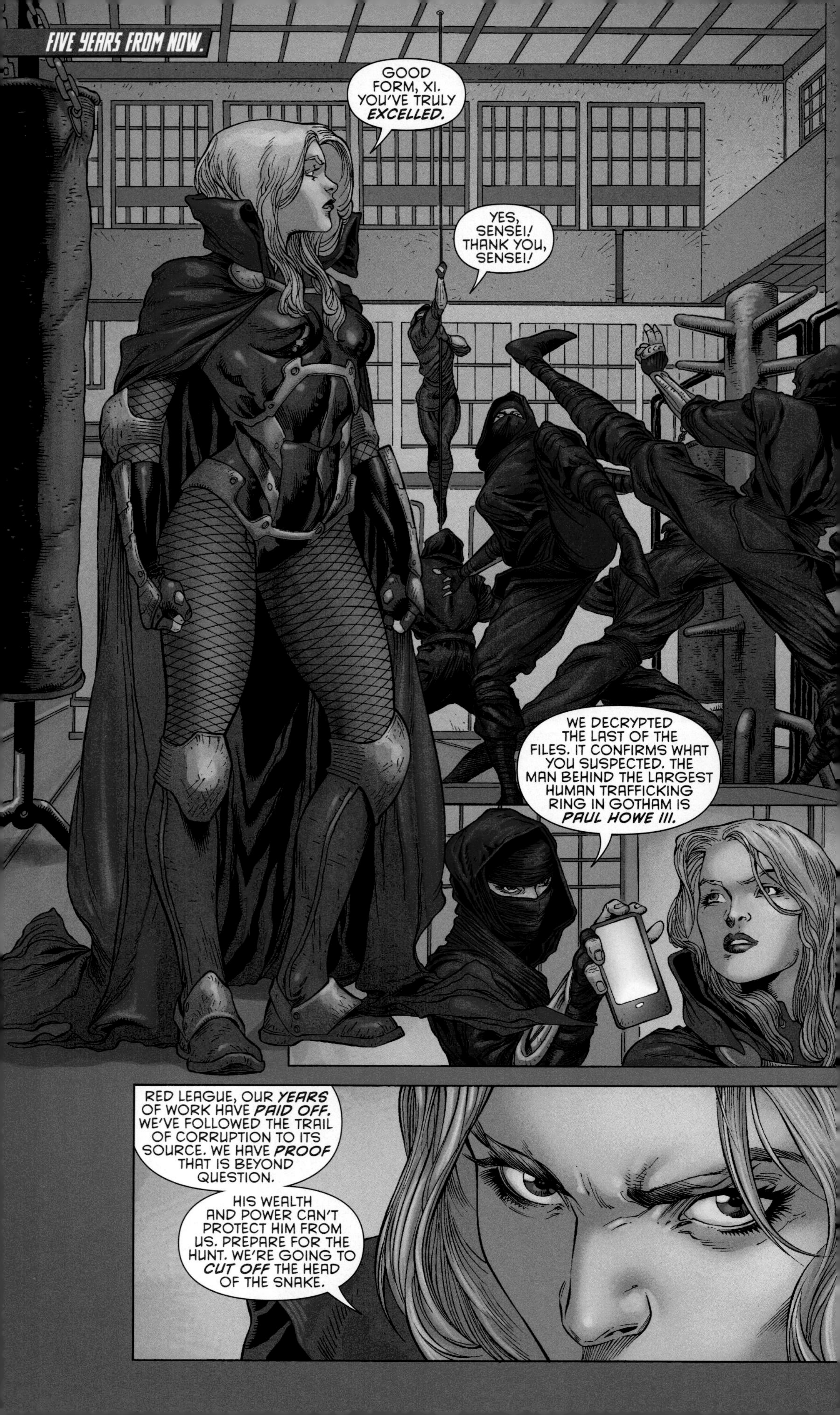

FIVE YEARS FROM NOW.
GOOD FORM, XI. YOU'VE TRULY EXCELLED.
YES, SENSEI! THANK YOU, SENSEI!
WE DECRYPTED THE LAST OF THE FILES. IT CONFIRMS WHAT YOU SUSPECTED. THE MAN BEHIND THE LARGEST HUMAN TRAFFICKING RING IN GOTHAM IS PAUL HOWE III.
RED LEAGUE, OUR YEARS OF WORK HAVE PAID OFF. WE'VE FOLLOWED THE TRAIL OF CORRUPTION TO ITS SOURCE. WE HAVE PROOF THAT IS BEYOND QUESTION.
HIS WEALTH AND POWER CAN'T PROTECT HIM FROM US. PREPARE FOR THE HUNT. WE'RE GOING TO CUT OFF THE HEAD OF THE SNAKE.

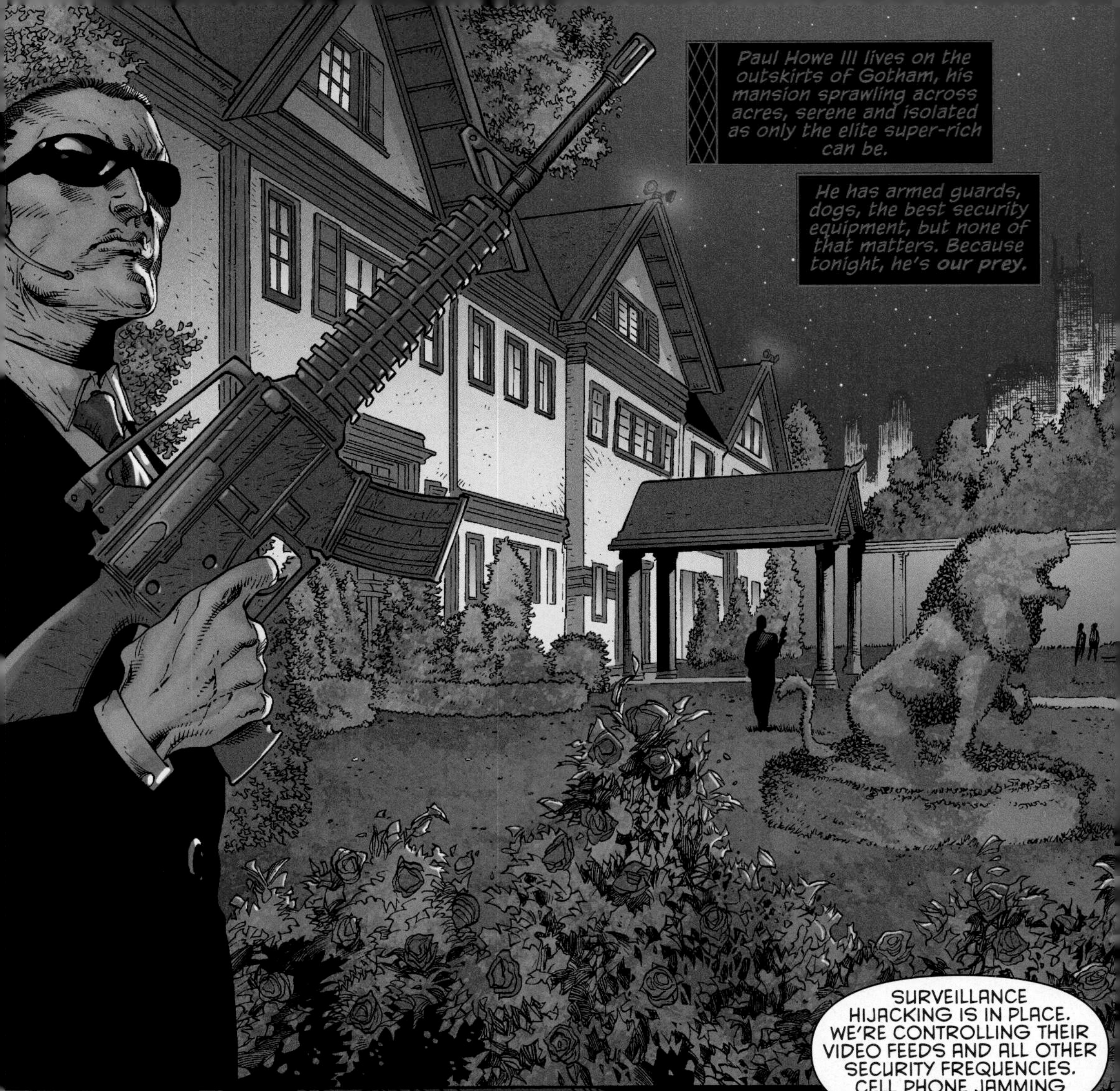
Paul Howe III lives on the outskirts of Gotham, his mansion sprawling across acres, serene and isolated as only the elite super-rich can be.
He has armed guards, dogs, the best security equipment, but none of that matters. Because tonight, he's our prey.
SURVEILLANCE HIJACKING IS IN PLACE. WE'RE CONTROLLING THEIR VIDEO FEEDS AND ALL OTHER SECURITY FREQUENCIES. CELL PHONE JAMMING IS COMPLETE.
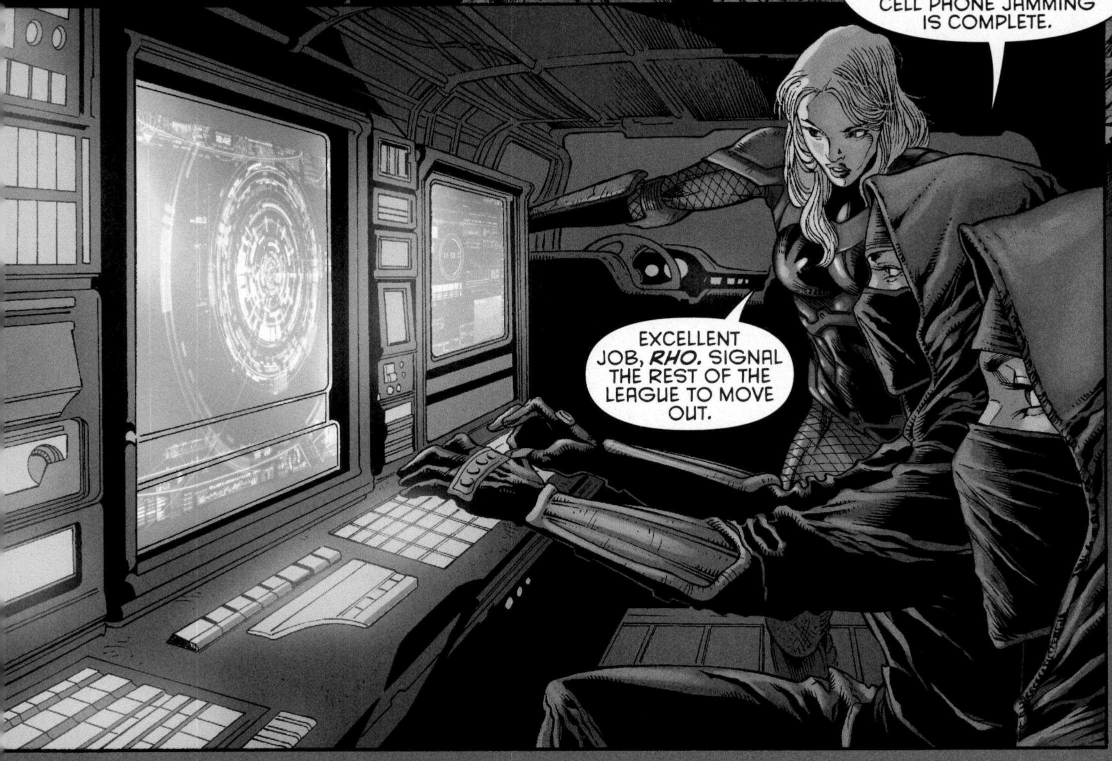
EXCELLENT JOB, RHO. SIGNAL THE REST OF THE LEAGUE TO MOVE OUT.

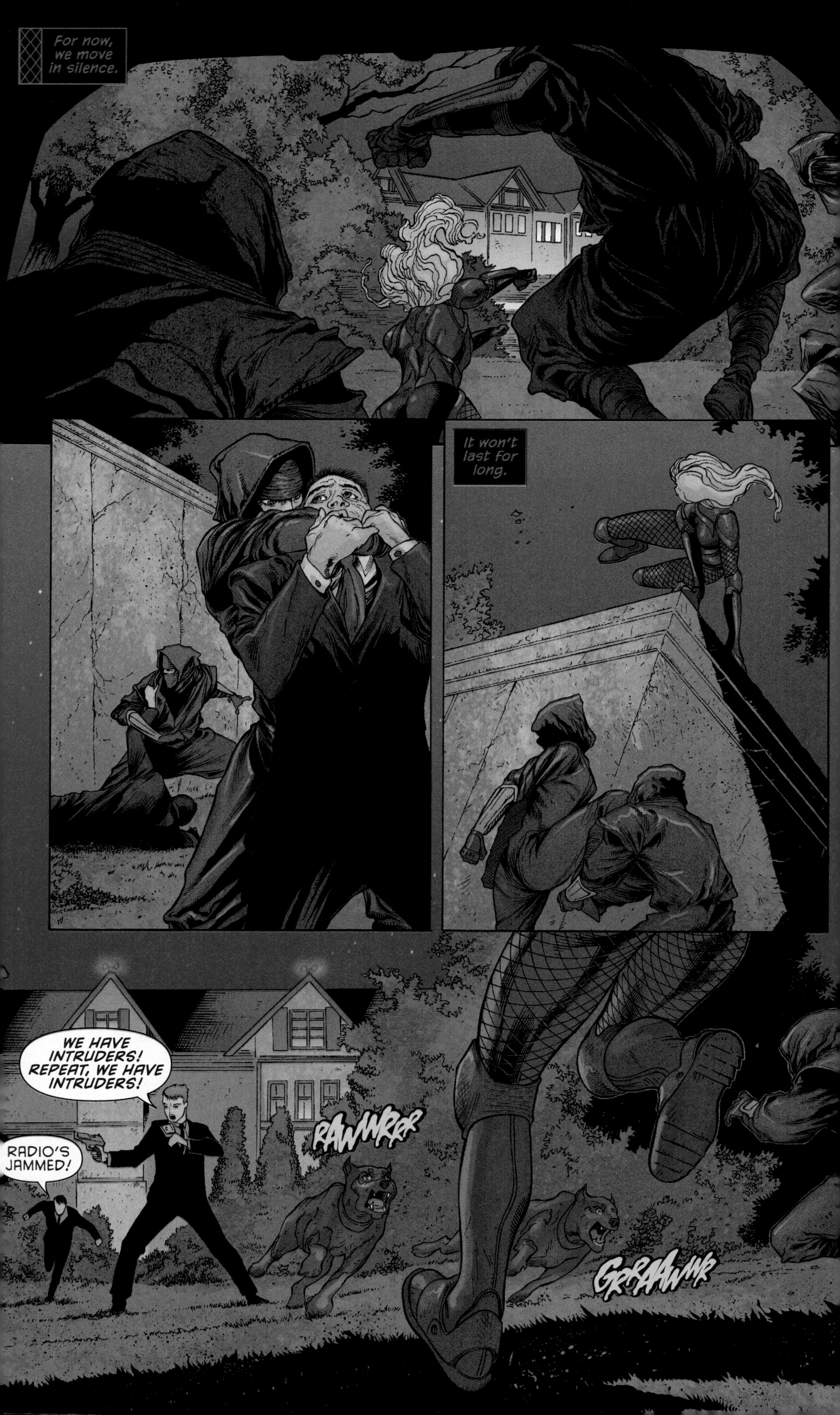
For now, we move in silence.
It won't last for long.
WE HAVE INTRUDERS! REPEAT, WE HAVE INTRUDERS!
RADIO'S JAMMED!
RAWWRRR
GRRAAWWR

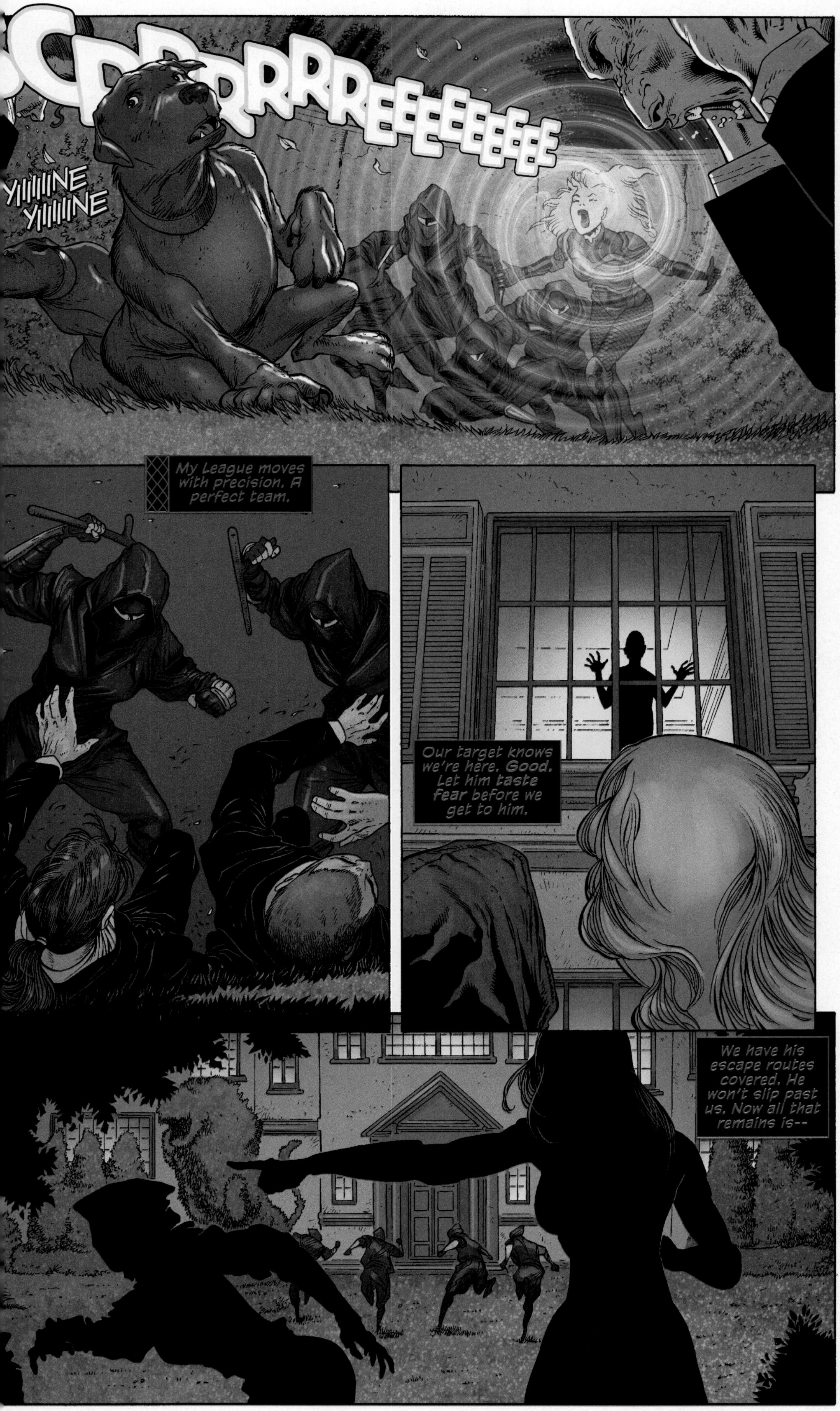
SCRRRRREEEEEEEEE
YIIIINE YIIIINE
My League moves with precision. A perfect team.
Our target knows we're here. Good. Let him taste fear before we get to him.
We have his escape routes covered. He won't slip past us. Now all that remains is--

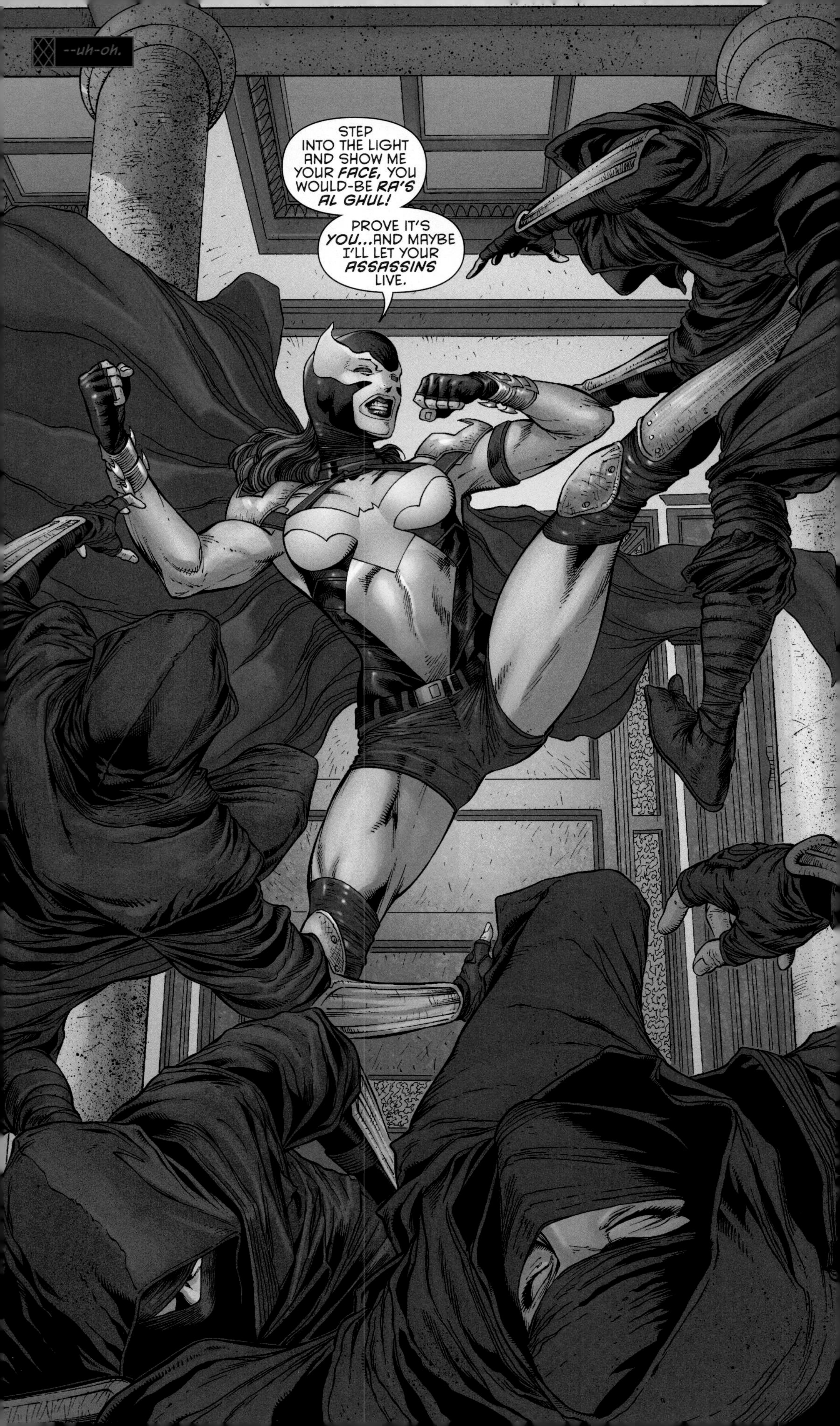
--uh-oh.
STEP INTO THE LIGHT AND SHOW ME YOUR FACE, YOU WOULD-BE RA'S AL GHUL!
PROVE IT'S YOU...AND MAYBE I'LL LET YOUR ASSASSINS LIVE.

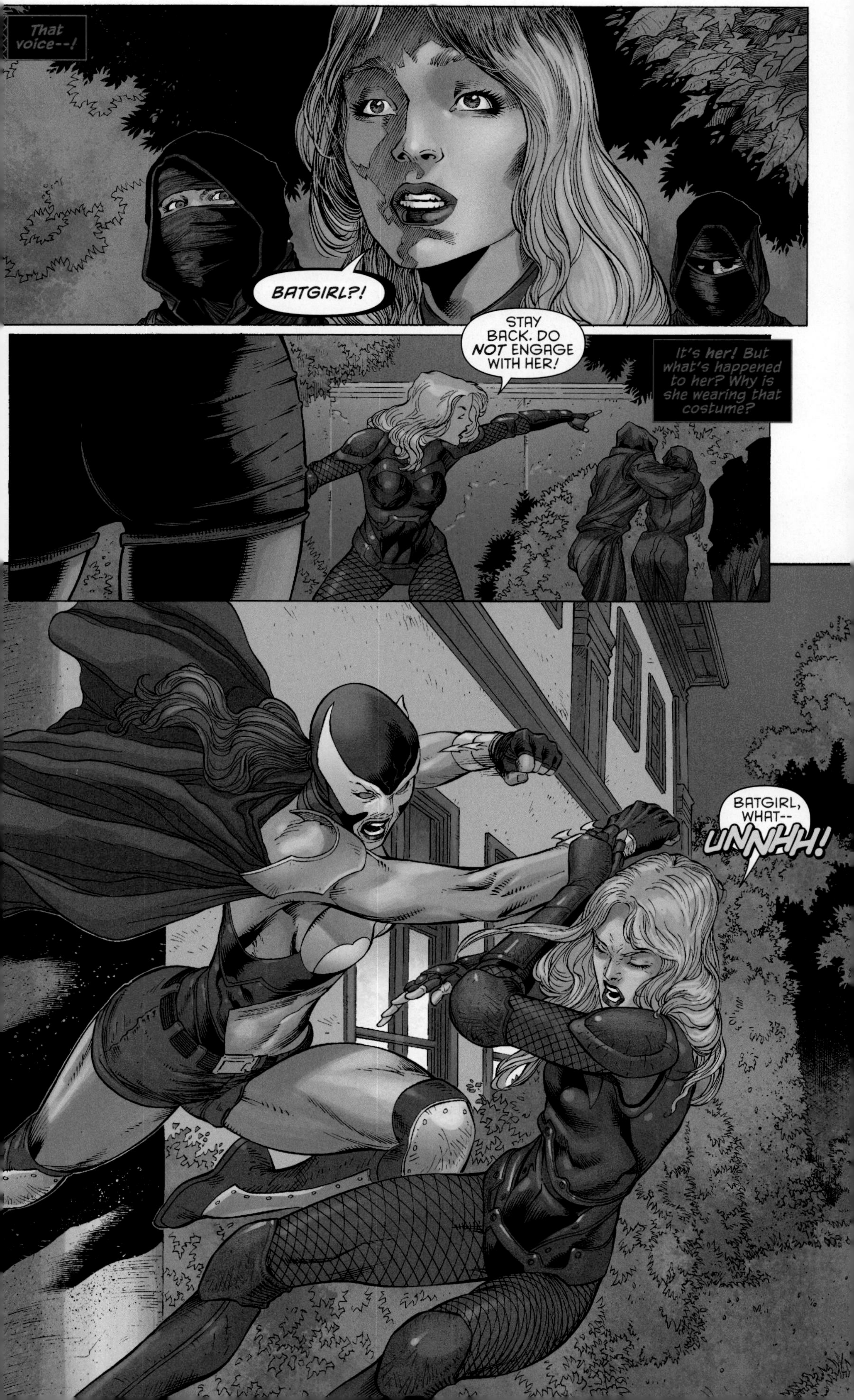
That voice--!
BATGIRL?!
STAY BACK. DO NOT ENGAGE WITH HER!
It's her! But what's happened to her? Why is she wearing that costume?
BATGIRL, WHAT--
UNNHH!

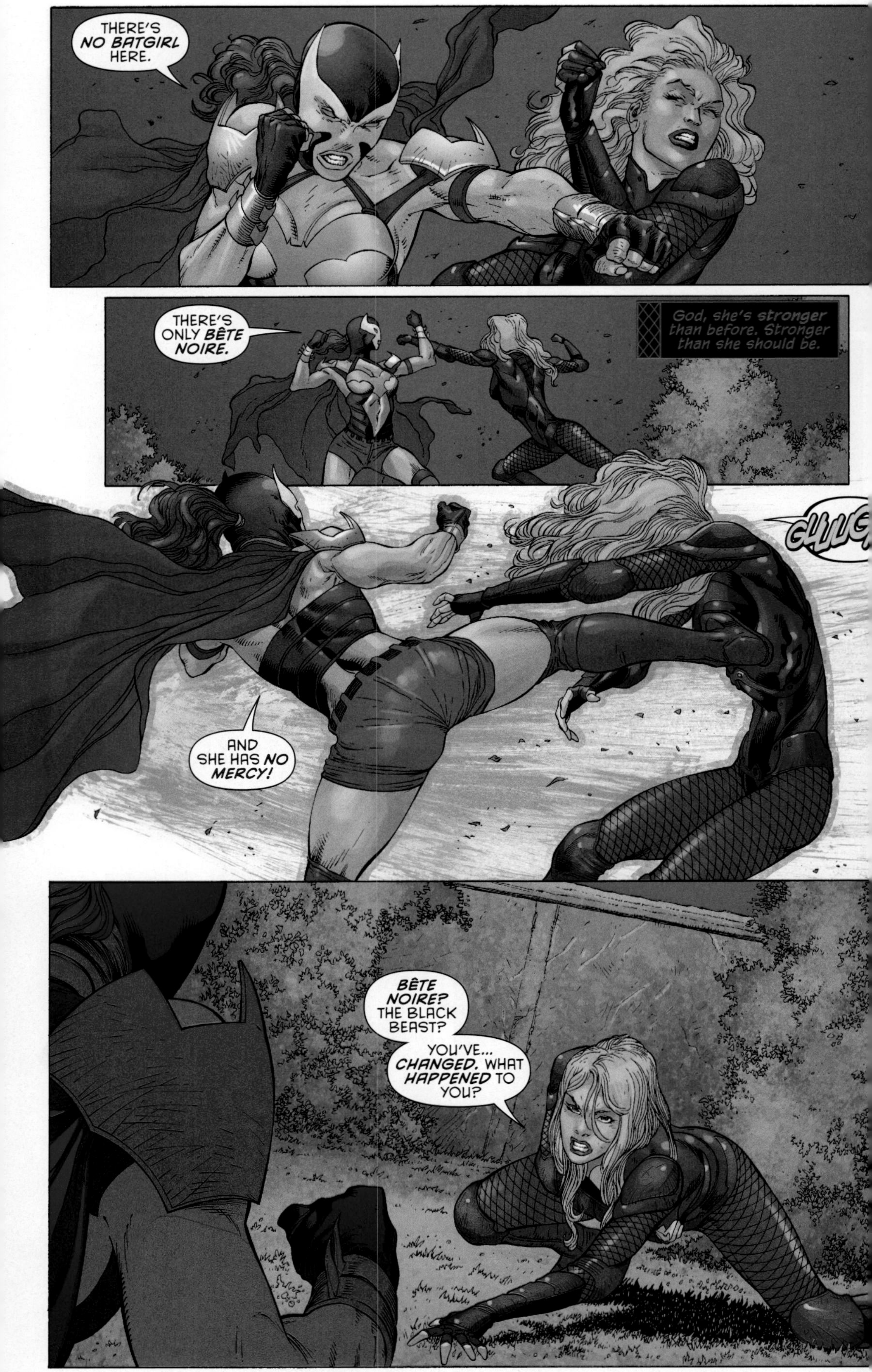
THERE'S NO BATGIRL HERE.
THERE'S ONLY BÊTE NOIRE.
God, she's stronger than before. Stronger than she should be.
AND SHE HAS NO MERCY!
BÊTE NOIRE? THE BLACK BEAST?
YOU'VE... CHANGED. WHAT HAPPENED TO YOU?

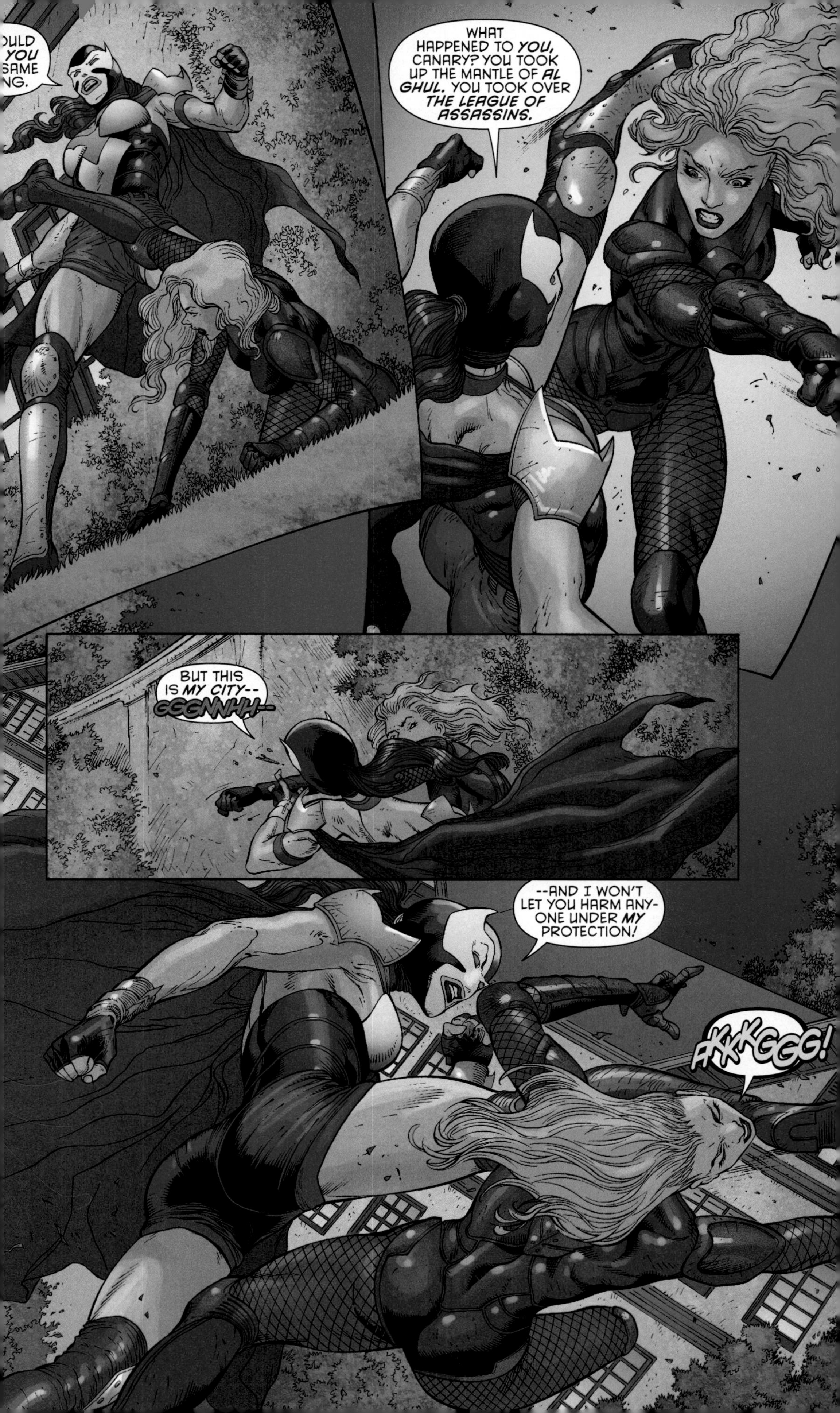
OULD
YOU
SAME
NG.
WHAT HAPPENED TO YOU, CANARY? YOU TOOK UP THE MANTLE OF AL GHUL. YOU TOOK OVER THE LEAGUE OF ASSASSINS.
BUT THIS IS MY CITY-- GGGNNHH--
--AND I WON'T LET YOU HARM ANY-ONE UNDER MY PROTECTION!
AKKGGG!

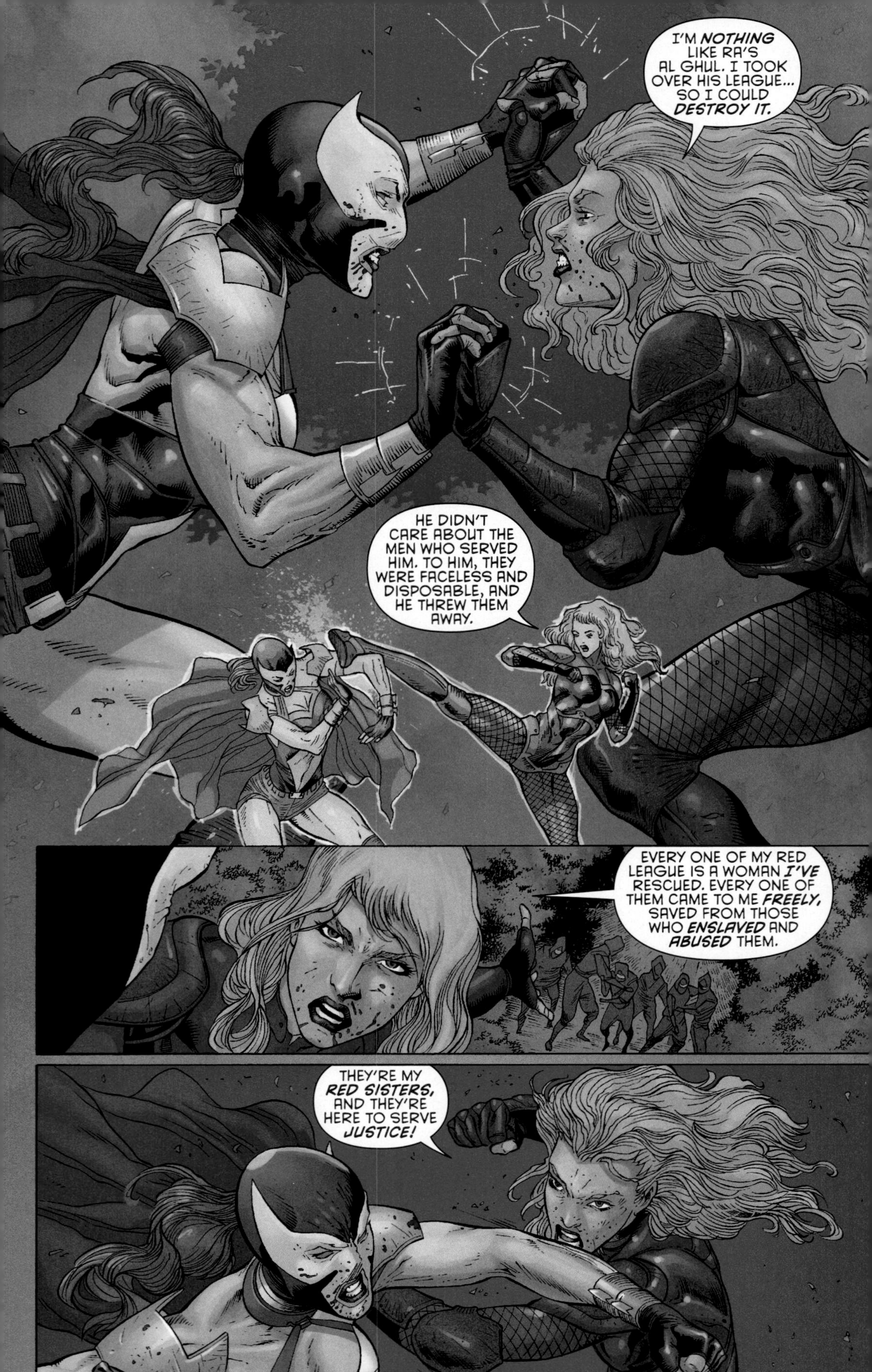
I'M NOTHING LIKE RA'S AL GHUL. I TOOK OVER HIS LEAGUE... SO I COULD DESTROY IT.
HE DIDN'T CARE ABOUT THE MEN WHO SERVED HIM. TO HIM, THEY WERE FACELESS AND DISPOSABLE, AND HE THREW THEM AWAY.
EVERY ONE OF MY RED LEAGUE IS A WOMAN I'VE RESCUED. EVERY ONE OF THEM CAME TO ME FREELY, SAVED FROM THOSE WHO ENSLAVED AND ABUSED THEM.
THEY'RE MY RED SISTERS, AND THEY'RE HERE TO SERVE JUSTICE!

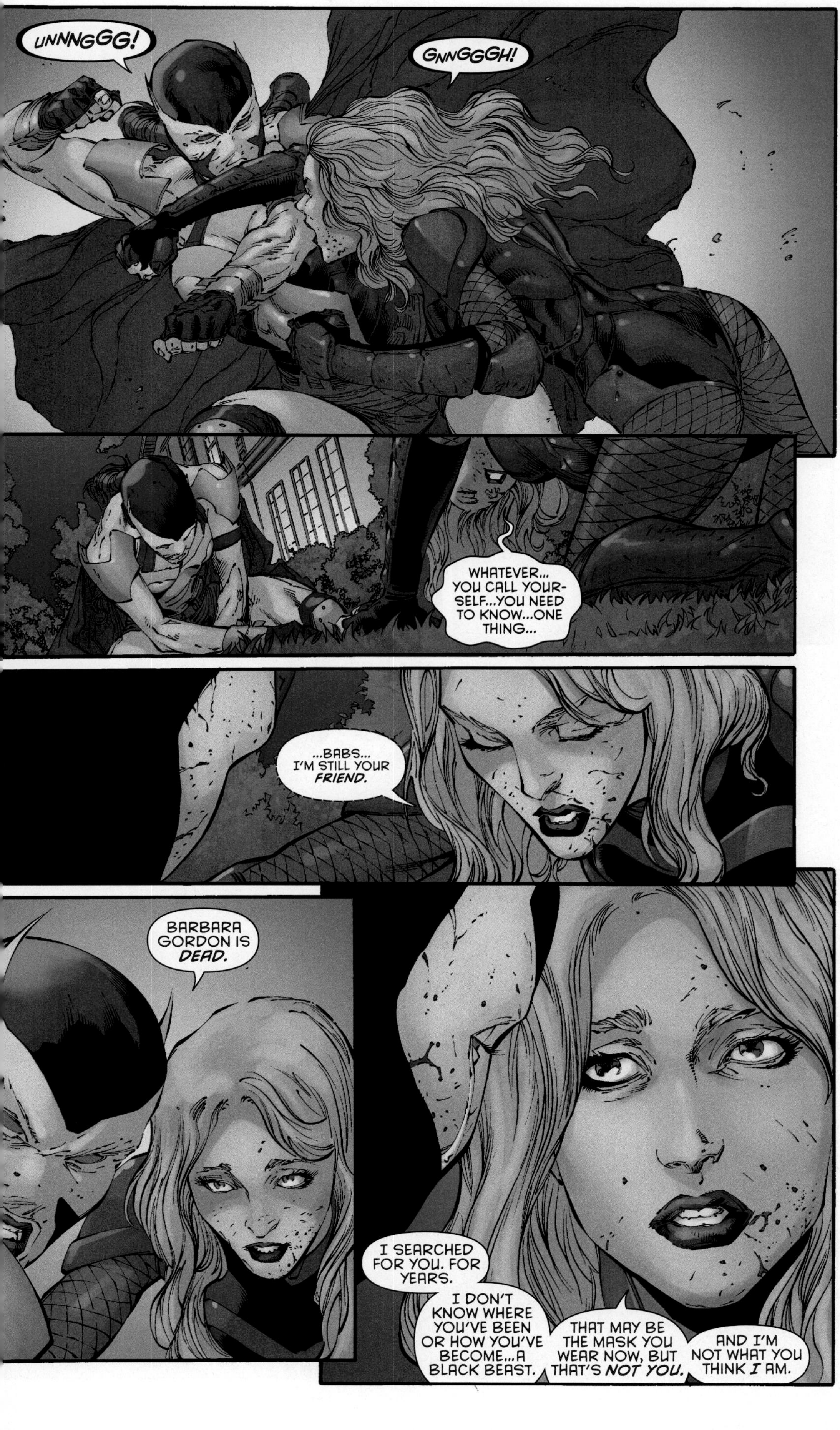
UNNNGGG!
GNNGGGH!
WHATEVER... YOU CALL YOURSELF...YOU NEED TO KNOW...ONE THING...
...BABS... I'M STILL YOUR FRIEND.
BARBARA GORDON IS DEAD.
I SEARCHED FOR YOU. FOR YEARS.
I DON'T KNOW WHERE YOU'VE BEEN OR HOW YOU'VE BECOME...A BLACK BEAST.
THAT MAY BE THE MASK YOU WEAR NOW, BUT THAT'S NOT YOU.
AND I'M NOT WHAT YOU THINK I AM.

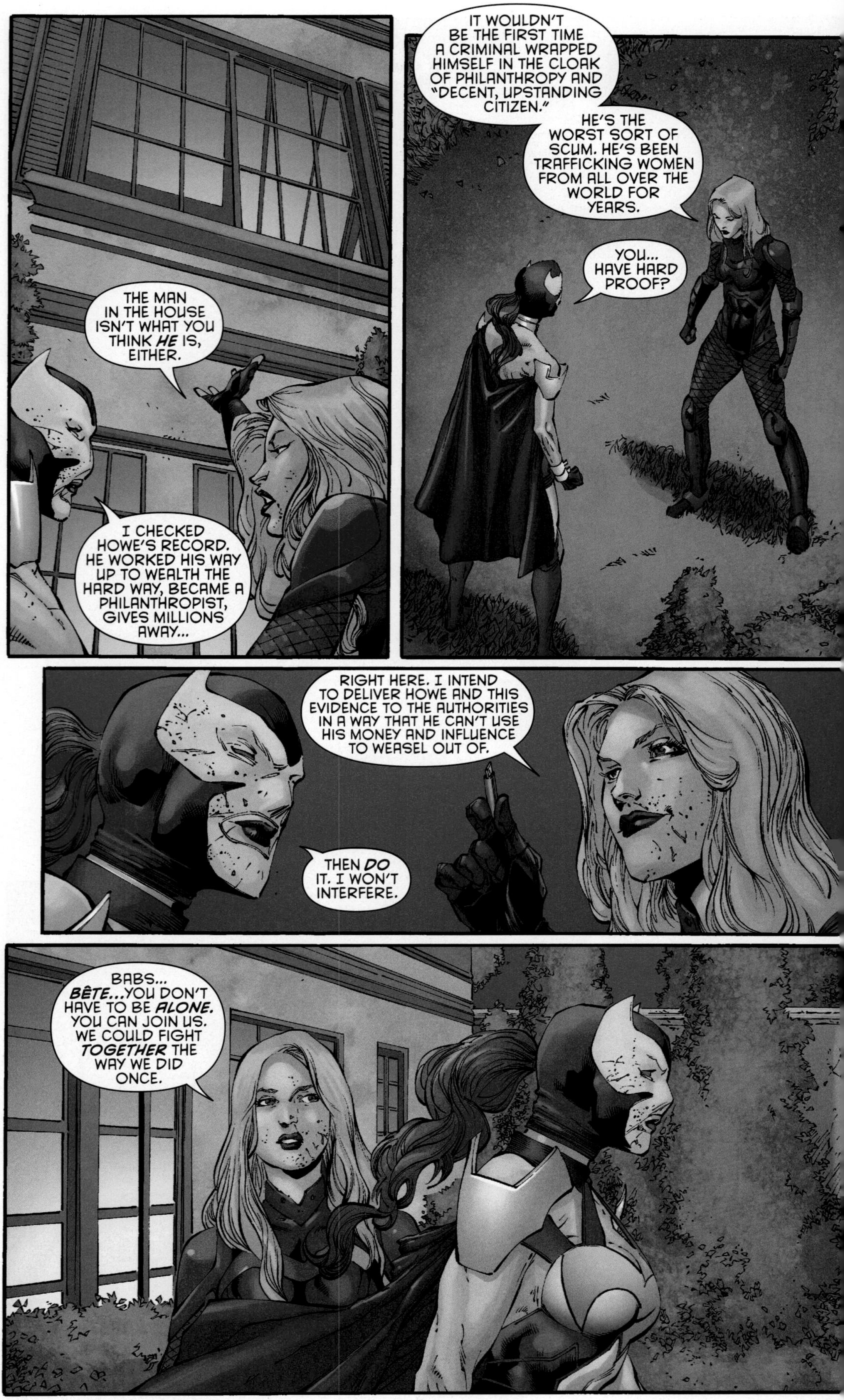
THE MAN IN THE HOUSE ISN'T WHAT YOU THINK *HE* IS, EITHER.
I CHECKED HOWE'S RECORD. HE WORKED HIS WAY UP TO WEALTH THE HARD WAY, BECAME A PHILANTHROPIST, GIVES MILLIONS AWAY...
IT WOULDN'T BE THE FIRST TIME A CRIMINAL WRAPPED HIMSELF IN THE CLOAK OF PHILANTHROPY AND "DECENT, UPSTANDING CITIZEN."
HE'S THE WORST SORT OF SCUM. HE'S BEEN TRAFFICKING WOMEN FROM ALL OVER THE WORLD FOR YEARS.
YOU... HAVE HARD PROOF?
RIGHT HERE. I INTEND TO DELIVER HOWE AND THIS EVIDENCE TO THE AUTHORITIES IN A WAY THAT HE CAN'T USE HIS MONEY AND INFLUENCE TO WEASEL OUT OF.
THEN *DO* IT. I WON'T INTERFERE.
BABS... *BÊTE*...YOU DON'T HAVE TO BE *ALONE*. YOU CAN JOIN US. WE COULD FIGHT *TOGETHER* THE WAY WE DID ONCE.

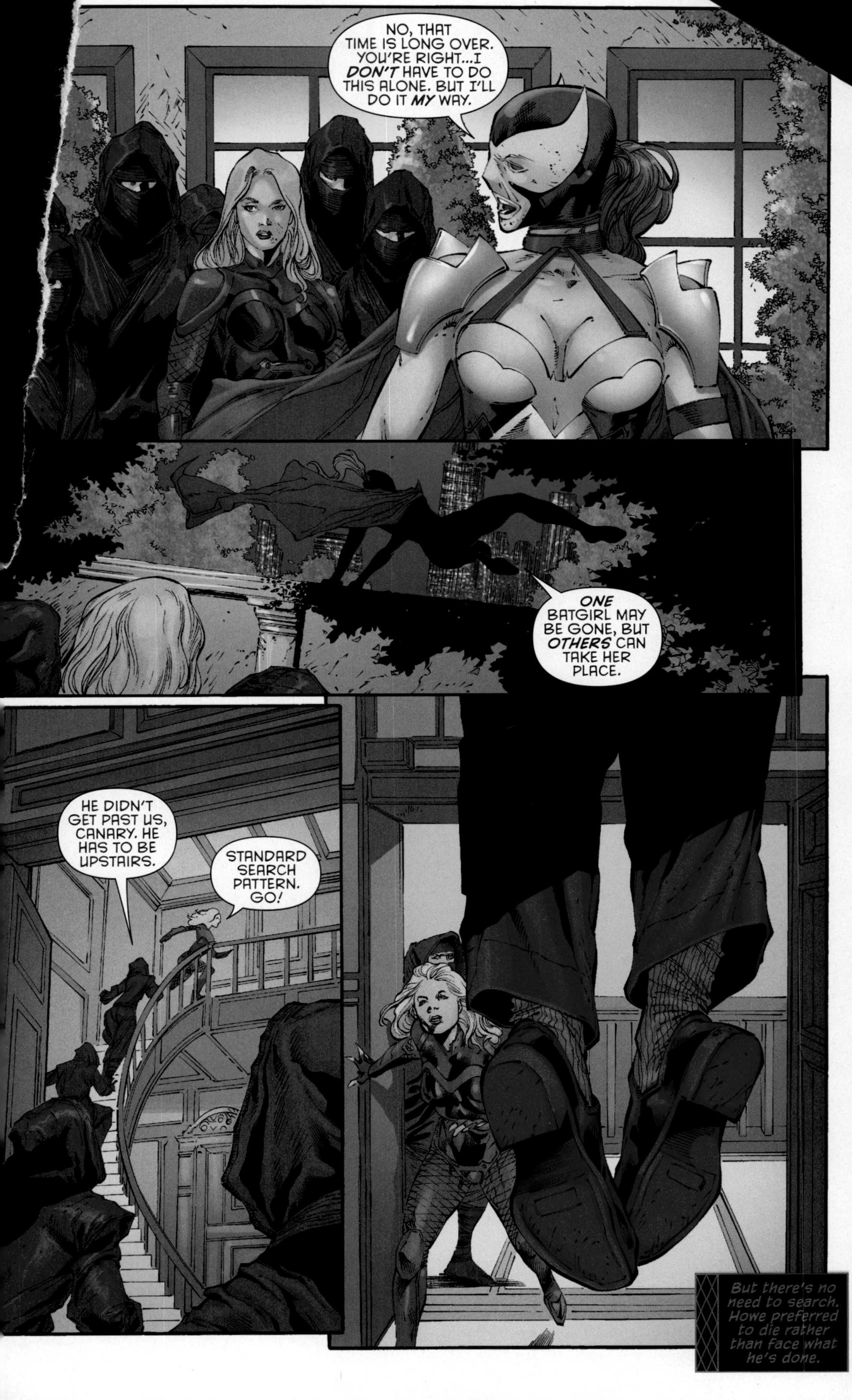
NO, THAT TIME IS LONG OVER. YOU'RE RIGHT...I DON'T HAVE TO DO THIS ALONE. BUT I'LL DO IT MY WAY.
ONE BATGIRL MAY BE GONE, BUT OTHERS CAN TAKE HER PLACE.
HE DIDN'T GET PAST US, CANARY. HE HAS TO BE UPSTAIRS.
STANDARD SEARCH PATTERN. GO!
But there's no need to search. Howe preferred to die rather than face what he's done.

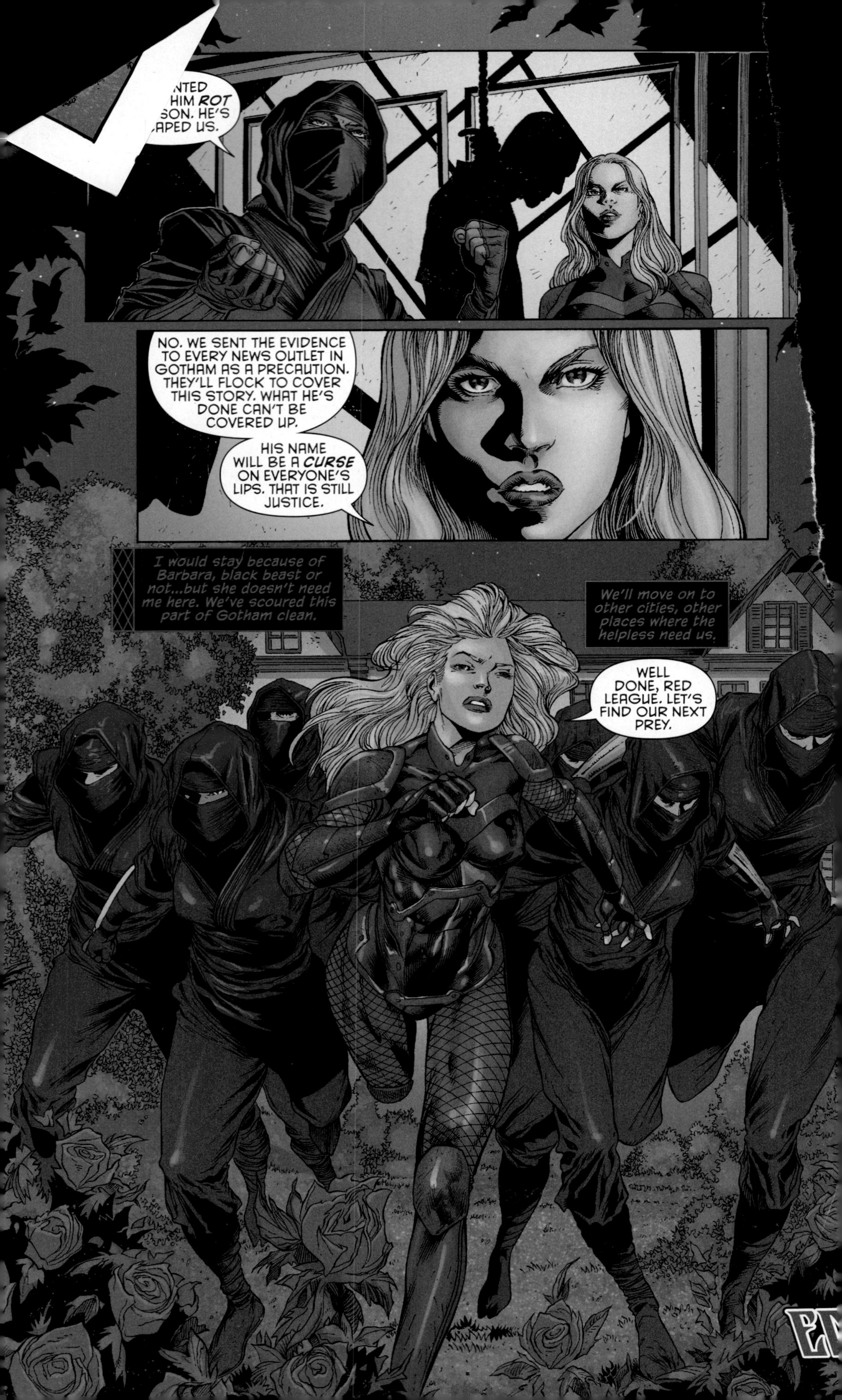
NTED HIM ROT SON. HE'S APED US.
NO. WE SENT THE EVIDENCE TO EVERY NEWS OUTLET IN GOTHAM AS A PRECAUTION. THEY'LL FLOCK TO COVER THIS STORY. WHAT HE'S DONE CAN'T BE COVERED UP.
HIS NAME WILL BE A CURSE ON EVERYONE'S LIPS. THAT IS STILL JUSTICE.
I would stay because of Barbara, black beast or not...but she doesn't need me here. We've scoured this part of Gotham clean.
We'll move on to other cities, other places where the helpless need us.
WELL DONE, RED LEAGUE. LET'S FIND OUR NEXT PREY.